W9-ATT-677

W. E. B. Du Bois

A Reader

W. E. B.
Du Bois

A Reader

EDITED BY

David Levering Lewis

A JOHN MACRAE BOOK
HENRY HOLT AND COMPANY
NEW YORK

Henry Holt and Company, Inc.
Publishers since 1866
115 West 18th Street
New York, New York 10011

Henry Holt® is a registered trademark of
Henry Holt and Company, Inc.

Published in Canada by Fitzhenry & Whiteside Ltd.,
195 Allstate Parkway, Markham, Ontario L3R 4T8.

Library of Congress Cataloging-in-Publication Data
Du Bois, W. E. B. (William Edward Burghardt), 1868–1963.
[Selections. 1995]
W. E. B. Du Bois : a reader / edited by David Levering Lewis. — 1st ed.
p.   cm.
"A John Macrae book."
Includes bibliographical references.
1. Afro-Americans.   2. Africa.   I. Lewis, David L.   II. Title.
E185.97.D73A25   1995   94-23482
973'.0496073 — dc20   CIP

ISBN 0-8050-3263-0
ISBN 0-8050-3264-9 (An Owl Book: pbk.)

Henry Holt books are available for special promotions
and premiums. For details contact:
Director, Special Markets.

First Edition — 1995

Printed in the United States of America
All first editions are printed on acid-free paper. ∞

1   3   5   7   9   10   8   6   4   2
1   3   5   7   9   10   8   6   4   2
pbk.

TO THE SOLUTIONS OF THE
21ST CENTURY

Contents

Contents

Contents

Contents

VIII. White Supremacy and National Politics

IX. The Politics and Propaganda of Arts and Letters

X. Labor in Black and White

Contents

Contents

Introduction

If, as William Edward Burghardt Du Bois's 1903 classic, *The Souls of Black Folk*, prophesies, the problem of the twentieth century is the problem of the color line, his 1940 memoir, *Dusk of Dawn*, reveals that he sees himself virtually as the incarnation of that problem. Du Bois, who knew that he had little to be modest about, expounds upon the meaning of a race concept near the end of *Dusk of Dawn*:

> I think I may say without boasting that in the period from 1910 to 1930 I was a main factor in revolutionizing the attitude of the American Negro toward caste. My stinging hammer blows made Negroes aware of themselves, confident of their possibilities and determined in self-assertion. So much so that today common slogans among the Negro people are taken bodily from the words of my mouth.

In its almost fabulous transcendence of place, time, and, ultimately, even race, Du Bois's life holds large and enduring meaning. It bears the imprint of Afro-America's dilemmas from the post-Reconstruction Era of the early 1870s to the Civil Rights revolution of the early 1960s. He was among the first of those American intellectuals who asserted that hyphenated Americans were not a cultural contradiction, as Theodore Roosevelt once said, but the embodiment of enriching diversity. And in order to give his cultural and aesthetic claims a strong foundation, Du Bois led the way, along with anthropologists Franz Boas and Melville Herskovits, in recovering the major lost civilizations of sub-Saharan Africa, notably in books such as *The Negro* and *Black Folk Then and Now*.

Du Bois was born in Massachusetts in 1868, the year of Andrew Johnson's impeachment, and died ninety-five years later, on the eve of the March on Washington, in the year of Lyndon Johnson's installation. In these ninety-five years, William Edward Burghardt Du Bois cut an astonishing swath through four continents (his birthday was once a Chinese national holiday), pioneering in sociology and history while writing with confident provocation in other fields of the social sciences and the humanities. He was the first Harvard doctorate of his race, and his 1895 dissertation, *The Suppression of the African Slave Trade to the United States of America* (1896), became the first monograph of the influential *Harvard Historical Series*. His next book, *The Philadelphia Negro*, virtually invented the field of urban sociology. The premier architect of civil rights in the United States, he was one of the founders of the NAACP as well as the architect of Pan-Africanism. Educator, editor, propagandist, novelist, playwright, and candidate for the U.S. Senate from New York, he founded an incomparable journal of opinion, *The Crisis*, when he was forty-two, the scholarly review *Phylon* at seventy-two, cofounded the socialist quarterly *Freedomways* at ninety-two, and inaugurated the prospectively influential *Encyclopedia Africana* at ninety-three.

Always a controversial figure, he espoused racial and political beliefs of such variety and seeming contradiction as to bewilder and alienate as many Americans, black and white, as he inspired or converted. Beneath the shifting complexity of alliances and denunciations, nevertheless, there was a pattern, a congealing of inclinations, experiences, and ideas, more and more inclining Du Bois to a vision of society that became, in contrast to the lives of most men and women, increasingly radical as he grew older, until the day came when the civil liberties maverick was supplanted by the full-blown Marxist. A proud, solitary man, awesome to most people, courtly with associates, Du Bois was on intimate terms probably with no more than a dozen men during his long life. With women, Du Bois was more accessible; he was in fact enormously attractive to any woman and deeply loved by several. His monumental book, *Black Reconstruction in America*, is dedicated to one inamorata—in Latin, to be sure. One of the most vociferous male feminists of the early twentieth century (his essay "The Damnation of Women" can still quicken pulses), Du Bois often fell somewhat short of his principles in his most intimate dealings with women.

The world according to Du Bois is one of facts deftly elided and masterfully molded in those almost hypnotically lyrical books he wrote about himself and his times. The more those early years in the little town of Great Barrington in the Berkshires are probed, the more they turn out to have been magnificently transformed by the seductive prose in which *The Souls of Black Folk, Dusk of Dawn, A Pageant of Seven Decades,* and the *Autobiography* are launched. A grand prose wherein the "golden river" flowing near his birthplace is in fact the highly polluted Housatonic River; the "mighty [Burghardt] clan" of his mother's people is in reality a hardscrabble band of peasant landholders clinging to postage-stamp-size holdings; the dashing cavalier father, Alfred Du Bois, is an army deserter and philanderer; and the "gentle and decent poverty" of his childhood is more often sharp and deep.

The partial truths and blatant inaccuracies to be found in much of what Du Bois writes about his formative years are fairly unimportant in themselves. But they are essential to an understanding of the picture Du Bois wants to convey—that of the special and compelling vision of the classic Outsider whose deep understanding comes from being simultaneously within and outside the dominant society. That Outsider vision came early, according to Du Bois, when a female student, a white newcomer to Great Barrington, repelled his overtures of friendship at school: "Then it dawned upon me with a certain suddenness that I was different from the others; or like, mayhap, in heart and life, and longing, but shut out from their world by a vast veil." Du Bois proceeds then to pour into *The Souls of Black Folk* these stunning words that ever since have been quoted as summing up the African predicament in America: "It is a peculiar sensation, this double-consciousness. . . . One ever feels his two-ness—an American, a Negro; two souls, two thoughts, two unreconciled strivings; two warring ideals in one dark body, whose dogged strength alone keeps it from being torn asunder."

By the time he graduated from Fisk University in 1888, Du Bois was inclined to draw no distinction between his own fate and that of his fellow African-Americans. "Through the leadership of men like myself and my fellows," Du Bois prophesied while at Fisk, "we were going to have these enslaved Israelites out of the still enduring bondage in short order." Soon after he graduated from Harvard in 1890, prophecy merged with mysticism as this midnight diary entry of our lonely hero, then a twenty-five-year-old University of Berlin graduate student, makes clear: "These are my plans: to make a name in science, to make a name in literature, and thus to raise my race. Or perhaps to raise a visible empire in Africa. . . . And if I perish—I perish." Such effusions remind us that the difference between madness and inspiration is largely a matter of persuading others to share the vision.

At the risk of some confusion, and certainly at the price of justice to this long and rich life, it is useful to focus on four developments—turning points—in Du Bois's life by way of illustrating some of the controversies, the interpretive difficulties, and the solutions. The first concerns the controversies between Du Bois and the incomparably puissant Booker T. Washington and that between Du Bois and the charismatic Marcus Garvey; the second deals with Du Bois's two explosive exits in 1934 and 1948 from the NAACP; the third concerns his quixotic quest for foundation money during the late 1930s in order to launch the *Encyclopedia of the Negro*; and, finally, the fourth focuses on the hard turn to the Left during the 1950s.

In both *Dusk of Dawn* (1940) and the 1968 posthumous *Autobiography*, Du Bois mentions his defeated candidature for the assistant superintendency of the "colored" schools of the District of Columbia merely as another passing illustration of Booker Washington's perfidiousness. It was far more significant, however. Du Bois's once brilliant prospects as a sociology professor at Atlanta University were rapidly receding by 1900. The chill of the 1895 Atlanta Compromise, symbolized by Booker Washington's famous "cast down your buckets where you are" address, was bringing a philanthropic freeze to academically oriented African-American institutions like Atlanta University. Compounding the professional difficulties were deep family crises. His infant son Burghardt had died needlessly from diphtheria the previous summer because no competent physician could be found. His wife's sanity had been affected; she now loathed Atlanta fiercely. Du Bois himself confessed many years later that he had suffered a nervous breakdown during this time. Ambitious, restive, deeply troubled, he counted on the assistant superintendency to bring deliverance from family and professional travail.

So anxious to leave Atlanta was he that, in his request to Booker Washington for a reference, Du Bois asked almost wheedlingly of his future nemesis (a man he would soon characterize as the Machiavelli of the Black Belt), "Could I not serve both your cause and the general cause of the Negro at the national capital better than that elsewhere?" Although, oddly, it appears not to have survived, Booker Washington sent Du Bois a recommendation to pass along to the District officials. Then, the promising plans for leaving Atlanta were abruptly derailed. On March 11, 1900, a curious letter arrived from Booker Washington, fresh from conferring with powerful white men in New York:

> If you have not done so, I think it not best for you to use the letter of recommendation which I have sent you. . . . Under the circumstances it would make your case stronger for you not to present the letter which I have given you for the reason that it would tend to put you in the position of seeking the position.

Du Bois understandably blamed the Tuskegeean for the lost superintendency—who could be more deserving of the position than he, after all?—and Du Bois's friends in Washington were to conduct a no-holds-barred unsuccessful campaign to capture the public school position for Du Bois until 1907. By then, Du Bois's Niagara Movement (the civil rights group comprised of militant Talented Tenth men and women) was already two years old.

The sad truth of the Garvey–Du Bois feud is that it might well have been avoided. That Du Bois was viscerally, even aesthetically, repelled by Marcus Garvey to the point of being intellectually deaf to anything the President General of Africa had to say, is well known, of course. But if the Bookerite feud was ultimately ideological, that with the Garveyites was ultimately one about power. The bottom line was not whether Garvey was a fool whose overpriced ships sank off Brooklyn piers or a lunatic whose followers wanted to repopulate Africa, or even whether he was an anti-assimilationist whose preachings contravened the upward-mobility optimism of middle-class African-Americans, memorably dubbed by Du Bois "The Talented Tenth." Garvey may not have been capable of expressing himself otherwise than in crude hyperbole, but most of his ideas could have been made compatible with Du Bois's. What was at stake was not ideas, however, but the nature of the social class and national origins of black leadership in America: whether it would be parvenu West Indians enrolled behind charismatic Garvey, or the homegrown bourgeoisie loyal to aloof Du Bois. Whether, in a word, it would be the NAACP and the National Urban League, or the Universal Negro Improvement Association (UNIA) and its affiliates raising money from and issuing marching orders to twelve million second-class American citizens. This explains, I think, the apoplexy and vicious retaliation of Du Bois and the Talented Tenth when Garvey attacked them as mulattoes and college snobs. What Garvey said contained much truth, even though it was certainly an invidious caricature.

The second turning point comes in early 1934, twenty-four stupendous years after Du Bois had departed Atlanta University for the New York headquarters of the new NAACP. By then, he and his magazine *The Crisis* were widely perceived as the very embodiment of the NAACP's struggle for racial integration. He had sustained a drumfire of editorials denouncing the segregationist policies of Woodrow Wilson; hypocrisy of white philanthropists and duplicity of white suffragists; the barbarous repression in the South and racial exclusiveness of organized labor in the North; the systematic exploitation of Africa and Asia by Europe; the need for high standards in African-American academic, religious, and public life. He had demanded full political and social equality for his people without compromise. But in January and March, *The Crisis* carried two Du Bois editorials bearing the inflammatory titles "Segregation" and "Separation and Self-Respect." Since American Negroes had to live with segregation Du Bois called on them to turn it to their advantage. "It is impossible . . . to wait for the millennium. . . . It is," he continued, "the race-conscious black man cooperating together in his own institutions and movements who will eventually emancipate the colored race." He added quickly, "This is not turning back to the older program of Booker T. Washington."

Du Bois's program was meant to be a mild form of socialism that would buy time and resources for black America until the private enterprise system was profoundly modified. He had argued vigorously at the NAACP's controversial 1933 Amenia Conference for a "planned program for using the racial segregation . . . in order that the laboring masses might be able to have built beneath them a strong foundation for self-respect and social uplift." As Du Bois fully anticipated, his editorials raised a firestorm, roiling the NAACP in an unprecedented internal dispute and stupefying that supreme organization man, Walter Francis White, the Association's integrationist executive secretary. But why did he do it? Du Bois tells us that "by 1930, I had become convinced that the basic policies and ideals of the Association must be modified and changed." As America appeared to unravel, the Association's general staff gave only perfunctory attention to the deepening economic hardship assailing the great majority of black people—electing to pursue litigation and lobbying rather than to focus on economic strategies. Furthermore, the Depression plunge in circulation figures of Du Bois's beloved *Crisis* magazine (down from a peak 100,000 a month to 15,000) necessitated emergency loans from the NAACP's general budget and loss of editorial control to the adversarial Walter White and Roy Wilkins and the NAACP board of directors. Each week brought more hectoring memos from Wilkins and the young Thurgood Marshall, then the NAACP's chief legal counsel, about office expenditures and editorial autonomy.

His savings along with his life insurance wiped out, is it credible that a disgusted Du Bois decided to manufacture a suitably controversial departure? An early 1933 letter from his good friend and president of Atlanta University, John Hope, alludes to previous discussions between them, cryptically hurrying Du Bois to make up his mind about relocating to Atlanta by the time of their next chat in New York. What Hope had in mind was for his good friend to chair the graduate program in sociology and help make Hope's newly restructured, Rockefeller-financed institution into a great university. Rockefeller largesse to American higher education in those days was funneled through the mighty General Education Board—the GEB—which could make life-and-death decisions about colleges and universities. When word of tenure negotiations with Du Bois reached the GEB, the philanthropy immediately informed President Hope of its deep misgivings. GEB trustee Trevor Arnett's diary records that he told the chairman of the Atlanta University board of trustees, "It might be well to consider an appointment for a special period, say for a year, so that it might be seen how the matter progressed before making a definite commitment." President Hope would almost surely have told Du Bois that something quite dramatic, unexpected—like the two wholly unexpected and ambiguous editorials—had to be done in order to effect a transition from the fiery *Crisis* to the stately halls of a Rockefeller benefaction. Du Bois certainly did not see his conduct as one of Jesuitical opportunism. He was simply taking the Negro race to another place, more congenial and better salaried, from which to continue the battle for civil rights.

Once the tenure question at Atlanta University was resolved, Du Bois devoted himself to graduate students, mastery of Marx, and writing *Black Reconstruction* during 1933–34. These two years inaugurated a period in his thinking that might be called Talented Tenth Marxism—a period, from 1935 to 1948, marked by political synthesis but also by significant relapses into solid middle-class optimism. As late as 1948–49, there are orthodox civil rights pieces in *Phylon, Negro Digest,* and the Sunday *New York Times Magazine* foretelling the achievement of the American Dream "if the progress in race relations and Negro advancement which has marked the last thirty years can be maintained for another generation." It was a time of terrific activity: supervising graduate students; completing the Reconstruction monograph that would gradually transform the study of the subject; and travel to Germany, Russia, China, and Japan during 1936.

Now came a third turning point in Du Bois's career—the fulfillment of a grand idea that had been with him since the turn of the century: the multi-volume *Encyclopedia of the Negro.* "Cruel" is the word best describing the roller coaster involving Du Bois and the major foundations over the funding of his ambitious project of research and education. His old faith in the power of ideas, scientifically formulated, to make the world better had welled up again after a quarter-century of activism and propaganda. The encyclopedia project generated preliminary endorsements and promises of collaboration from much of the international scholarly community. After his 1935 funding application was rejected by the Rockefeller-dominated combine of four or five private foundations comprising the General Education Board, he greatly revised and elaborated the proposal for resubmission, the Phelps Stokes Fund providing seed money. Growing national and even international support for Du Bois among the experts began to exert formidable pressures for foundation funding of the encyclopedia. Rather surprisingly, one of the General Education Board's principal officers, Jackson Davis, had become an *Encyclopedia* convert, introducing Du Bois to the right New York notables, stroking his own trustees, and lobbying the Carnegie Corporation for favorable action on the Carnegie portion of the Du Bois grant application. Melville Herskovits, a competitor for foundation funds, began to fret about Du Bois's bagging the $250,000 research budget.

He need not have worried. Clearly, an encyclopedia encompassing the full range of race and race relations in America and directed by Du Bois was to say the least troubling to the custodians of social science orthodoxy. The seven-member executive committee of the GEB—Raymond B. Fosdick presiding and John D. Rockefeller III participating—rejected the *Encyclopedia* at the beginning of May 1937. In his conference a few days later with Carnegie Corporation president Frederick Keppel, GEB's Jackson Davis paradoxically pleaded for favorable Carnegie consideration of the project. "Dr. Du Bois is the most influential Negro in the United States," Davis reminded Keppel. "This project would keep him busy for the rest of his life." Predictably, Carnegie declined. Within a remarkably short time, the study of the Negro (generously underwritten by the Carnegie Corporation) found a quite different direction under a Swedish scholar then unknown in the field of race relations, one whose understanding of American race problems was to be distinctly more psychological and less economic than was Du Bois's.

The precise moment of preemption is recorded in a remarkable September 1939 exchange between President Robert Maynard Hutchins of the University of Chicago and Director Edwin Embree of the Rosenwald Fund: "Ed, somebody tells me that Keppel has rented the forty-sixth floor of the Chrysler Building and turned it over to a Swede named Gunnar Myrdal to make an elaborate study of negro education. What's it all about?" "Bob, not Negro education, but the whole realm of the negro in American civilization [to] take the place of the proposed Negro Encyclopedia in which the Phelps Stokes Fund has been greatly interested." When the president of the Phelps Stokes Fund wrote Du Bois in 1944 at the time of the publication of *An American Dilemma* that "there has been no one who has been quite so often quoted by Myrdal than yourself," Du Bois must have savored the irony.

Increasingly a whale in the Atlanta University puddle, Du Bois caused the successor to the deceased president John Hope considerable heartburn. In November 1944 the seventy-six-year-old professor was suddenly informed of his voluntary retirement from the university. Pressured by several members of the NAACP board, Walter White invited the septuagenarian back as an ornament. "They assumed that my days of work were over," Du Bois said. The NAACP badly miscalculated. *Color and Democracy*, Du Bois's antiimperialist book, reached his publisher in January 1945. That same month, his Chicago *Defender* column, under the heading "Reason and Reality," adumbrated a new toughmindedness, the beginning of the end of Du Boisian intellectual idealism. "I had, I believed, launched a program which was destined to settle the Negro problem," Du Bois modestly reminded his readers. "It was no pat panacea. . . . In one respect alone was it vulnerable, and that was whether the world would allow it to be done." Clearly, he believed the world of the GEB, the Carnegie Corporation, and slavish Atlanta University trustees would not allow his scholarship to serve as a beacon to American race relations.

Collaborating with Paul Robeson, Max Yergan, and Alphaeus Hunton of the Council on African Affairs, he convened an April 1945 conference (attended by Ghana's future president Kwame Nkrumah) at the New York Public Library's Schomburg Collection. This Harlem meeting complemented the George Padmore — planned Pan African Congress meeting held in Manchester, England, in October, which Du Bois also attended as an active presiding officer. Appointed by President Roosevelt as a Consulting Delegate, along with Walter White and Mary McLeod Bethune, to the founding of the United Nations in May 1945, Du Bois began what would become ever sharper public attacks upon the policies of an international body whose charter was ambivalent about the rights of colonial peoples. Although the NAACP board had unanimously endorsed Du Bois's 1947 document "An Appeal to the World: A Statement on the Denial of Human Rights to Minorities in the Case of Citizens of Negro Descent in the United States of America," by June 1948, new NAACP board member and U.N. delegate Eleanor Roosevelt made it plain that international circulation of the petition and repeated attempts at U.N. General Assembly presentation "embarrassed" her and the nation. By then, Du Bois had virtually endorsed Henry Wallace's Progressive Party candidacy, denounced the Marshall Plan and NATO as capitalist aggression, and distributed an explosively detailed memorandum for restructuring NAACP national headquarters.

Already shaken in 1947 by historian Arthur Schlesinger, Jr.'s charges in *Life* magazine of Communist infiltration, the NAACP chose Mrs. Roosevelt and fired Du Bois in September 1948. From then on, it was politics in earnest for Du Bois. This was the beginning of the fourth and final turning point. He plunged into the March 1949 Cultural and Scientific Conference for World Peace, organized by Harlowe Shapley, Linus Pauling, and Lillian Hellman, chairing the writers' subcommittee with Norman Mailer and A. A. Fadayev at the Waldorf-Astoria, delivering an electric closing speech at Madison Square Garden. In April he gripped the huge audience attending the Paris World Peace Conference, flaying the Atlantic Pact, Truman, and imperialism. "Drunk with power," he exclaimed, the United States was "leading the world to hell in a new colonialism with the same old human slavery which once ruined us; and to a third world war which will ruin the world." Next stop, Moscow, for another peace conference. Then, in 1950, at eighty-two, a run for the U.S. Senate from New York, on the American Labor Party ticket. Out of 5 million voters, 205,000 liked his campaign speeches enough to vote for him.

Parallel with his Senate race, Du Bois also served as a director of the new Peace Information Center (PIC), which raised funds and provided speakers to garner 2.5 million signatures for the Stockholm Peace Petition for nuclear disarmament. On July 13, 1950, Secretary of State Dean Acheson attacked the PIC in the *New York Times*. The newspaper also carried Du Bois's hard-hitting reply: "Have we come to the tragic pass," he asked, "where, by declaration of our own Secretary of State, there is no possibility of mediating our differences with the Soviet Union? Does it not occur to you, Sir, that there are honest Americans who, regardless of their differences . . . , hate and fear war?" On February 9, 1951, five days before his marriage to novelist-dramatist-activist Shirley Graham, he, Elizabeth Moos, Abbott Simon, and two other officers of the PIC were indicted in Washington by the Justice Department as foreign agents. "If W. E. B. Du Bois goes to jail a wave of wonder will sweep around the world," Langston Hughes wrote in the Chicago *Defender*. In fact, the case was so farcical that the judge threw it out in midtrial and thus deprived students of the Cold War of what would have been Du Bois's memorable testimony.

Du Bois's published reaction, in his book *In Battle for Peace* (1952), struck a philosophical chord. But, as his friends confirm, the experience was traumatizing. What wounded him so savagely was that, with the exception of sociologist E. Franklin Frazier, poet Langston Hughes, librarian Dorothy Porter-Wesley, and perhaps a half dozen others, the Talented Tenth ran for cover, while large numbers of working-class blacks and whites attended Du Bois fundraisers across the country. It was true that one brave columnist wrote in the Pittsburgh *Courier* that "we have to take a stand here and now with Dr. Du Bois . . . else it will be dangerous for a Negro to belong to anything but a church." Nevertheless, the fact was that the Talented Tenth had waffled and cowered. The emotional impact of the trial-experience made Du Bois profoundly pessimistic about the cause that had engaged his long life. It was now that he concluded that, for the sake of underdeveloped peoples everywhere—but especially in the Third World—all tactics that contained American capitalism were fair. Dismissing civil rights advances, he concluded that socialism alone would lift Africans in America. Thus, because the enemies of his enemies were his friends in Africa and Asia, neither Marxism's doctrinal shortcomings nor the Soviet Union's 1956 rampages in Eastern Europe shook his evolving Communist commitment. His passport restored, Du Bois and his second wife, Shirley Graham, spent 1959 in red carpet travel through Eastern Europe, the Soviet Union, and China, adding to his 1959 Lenin Peace Prize honorary doctorates from ancient universities. In a private Kremlin talk with Nikita Khrushchev, he persuaded the Soviet premier to create immediately the Institute of African Studies in the Academy of Sciences.

On October 1, 1961 (the anniversary of the Russian Revolution), Du Bois petitioned the Communist Party of the United States for membership. "Today, I have reached a firm conclusion," his letter reads in language that now sounds weirdly wrong. "Capitalism cannot reform itself; it is doomed to self-destruction." Why did he do it at this time—at ninety-three, five years after

Khrushchev's revelations of Stalin-era crimes and the Soviet invasions of Hungary and Poland, three years after the court-ordered return of his own passport, and two years into the Sino-Soviet split? What was the meaning of an act that imposed self-exile in West Africa just as lunch-counter sit-ins and freedom bus rides foreshadowed the beginning of the end of the racial segregation in America that Du Bois had spent his life fighting? Du Bois's splendidly mischievous admission at the end of his life was only a partial explanation. "I would have been hailed with approval if I had died at fifty," he said. "At seventy-five my death was practically requested." His affronted ego relished controversy. He had the intellectual's towering impatience with fools. His own life he came to see as one in which his exceptional achievements served only to prove the rule of racism. The urge to thumb his nose, to make one last, Homeric gesture of defiance, proved irresistible. Finally, he concluded that if the problem of the century was the problem of the color line, its solution could be found only in a strong Third World.

In the early days, Du Bois had believed that advancement of the so-called "darker peoples" would come through wise policies based on scientific knowledge. In the sunset of his days, however, he came to believe in economic revolution and political force. Integrated lunch counters and public schools were fine in themselves, but pathetically insufficient to solve the problem of the color line in America, he believed. The appearance of Martin Luther King, Jr., therefore, was something of an enigma for Du Bois. Musing about the 1955 Montgomery Bus Boycott, an agnostic and anticlerical Du Bois admitted that he had expected to live to see many things, but never a militant Baptist preacher. Interestingly, Martin Luther King's earliest assessment of W. E. B. Du Bois's concept of leadership was just as severe when he wrote in *Stride Toward Freedom* that it was "a tactic for an aristocratic elite who would themselves be benefitted while leaving behind the 'untalented' 90 per cent." King's courage Du Bois admired, but, even as lunch counters were integrated and the first federal civil rights act since Reconstruction enacted (1957), Du Bois predicted deepening class conflict within black America and superficial economic improvement at best in the lot of the great majority of black people. "This dichotomy in the Negro group, this development of class structure, was to be expected," he wrote in *In Battle for Peace*, "and will be more manifest in the future, as discrimination against Negroes as such decreases."

As for Martin Luther King, Du Bois finally decided in late 1959 that the nonviolent pastor was not Gandhi: "Gandhi submitted, but he also followed a positive program to offset his negative refusal to use violence." King's last words about W. E. B. Du Bois were spoken in Carnegie Hall just a few weeks before his own martyrdom. One hundred years to the day after Du Bois's birth—February 23, 1968—he, James Baldwin, Ossie Davis, and others gathered courageously to pay tribute to the memory of the great, widely denounced intellectual and human rights propagandist. To thunderous applause, the head of the Southern Christian Leadership Conference declared that the old warrior "confronted the establishment as a model of militant manhood and integrity. He defied them and though they heaped venom and scorn on him, his powerful voice was never still."

Philosophically, politically, psychologically, Du Bois was ready to sign up and move on to another phase of Pan Africanism. The inflexible truth he embraced was that, just as Africans in the United States "under the corporate rule of monopolized wealth . . . will be confined to the lowest wage group," so the peoples of the developing world faced subordination in the global scheme of things capitalist. As he settled into the work of editing what had now become, through the benevolence of President Nkrumah of Ghana, the *Encyclopedia Africana*, Du Bois was greatly consoled by his fully evolved vision. He was even thankful that, wise, aged humanist that he was, his life, in a sense, had left him no alternative but to come to such a vision. Ever the wordsmith of grand meanings, he would sum up the real significance of his life in the closing thoughts of his last autobiography: "Had it not been for the race problem early thrust upon me and enveloping me, I should have probably been an unquestioning worshipper at the shrine of the established social order and of the economic development into which I was born."

To collect a portion of his voluminous and multifarious writings under fifteen headings is to expose oneself to serious reproaches of arbitrariness and inadequacy. On the other hand, it is patently obvious that there could be no ideal rationale for selection of items from the vast corpus of Du Bois's work. These fifteen headings—ranging from "Africa, Pan-Africa, and Imperialism" to "The Cold War" to "Personal Loyalties, Reflections, and Creative Pieces"—therefore simply reflect the most viable schematic the editor has been able to devise.

I

Race Concepts
and the World
of Color

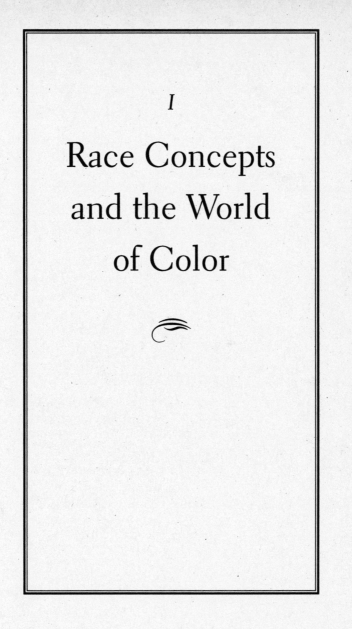

As the essay on Jefferson Davis delivered at his Harvard graduation makes clear, the early Du Bois saw the world through a lens, strongly influenced by contemporary European racism, that focussed on indelible group characteristics. In its most extreme form, Du Bois's racial romanticism sometimes verged on chauvinism. "He who ignores or seeks to override the race idea in human history ignores and overrides the central thought of all history," he thundered famously in "The Conservation of Races," his 1897 address to the American Negro Academy. In "Of Our Spiritual Strivings" and "Of the Meaning of Progress," compelling essays in *The Souls of Black Folk* (1903), Du Bois described the terrible tension at the heart of African-American identity ("two souls, two thoughts, two unreconciled strivings") and then recaptured the star-crossed efforts at self-improvement of rural black folk still living in the shadow of slavery. "The First Universal Races Congress," a strikingly sanguine account of a notable 1911 gathering of intellectuals in London; "The Black Man Brings His Gifts," a game 1925 fantasy about unique cultural contributions; and "The Negro College," a passionate 1933 text on race in the curriculum, were expressive of a Du Boisian racialism that has profoundly influenced the ideas of contemporary Afrocentrists. As time passed, his romanticism and chauvinism would be modified, becoming more complex and finally evolving into a sophisticated synthesis in which class and race functioned as mutually reinforcing constructs. Yet race pride would always remain for him a building block in group advancement; true emancipation — psychic affirmation — was impossible without it ("On Being Ashamed of Oneself" [1933]). Thus, in the articles "Japanese Colonialism"

15

and "Japan, Color, and Afro-Americans," he professed admiration for Japan notwithstanding its imperialist aggression and warlike designs. In the end, Du Bois predicted in "China and Africa" (1959), that a powerful bond of color would draw the "darker world" into solidarity against the true racial malefactors — the imperialists of Europe and America.

Jefferson Davis as a Representative of Civilization

Jefferson Davis was a typical Teutonic hero; the history of civilization during the last millennium has been the development of the idea of the Strong Man of which he was the embodiment. The Anglo-Saxon loves a soldier — Jefferson Davis was an Anglo-Saxon, Jefferson Davis was a soldier. There was not a phase in that familiarly strange life that would not have graced a mediaeval romance: from the fiery and impetuous young lieutenant who stole as his bride the daughter of a ruler-elect of the land, to the cool and ambitious politician in the Senate hall. So boldly and surely did that cadaverous figure with the thin nervous lips and flashing eye, write the first line of the new page of American history, that the historian of the future must ever see back of the War of Secession, the strong arm of one imperious man, who defied disease, trampled on precedent, would not be defeated, and never surrendered. A soldier and a lover, a statesman and a ruler; passionate, ambitious and indomitable; bold reckless guardian of a people's All — judged by the whole standard of Teutonic civilization, there is something noble in the figure of Jefferson Davis; and judged by every canon of human justice, there is something fundamentally incomplete about that standard.

I wish to consider not the man, but the type of civilization which his life represented: its foundation is the idea of the Strong Man — Individualism coupled with the rule of might — and it is this idea that has made the logic of even modern history, the cool logic of the Club. It made a naturally brave and generous man, Jefferson Davis — now advancing civilization by murdering Indians, now hero of a national disgrace called by courtesy, the Mexican War, and finally, as the crowning absurdity, the peculiar champion of a people fighting to be free in order that another people should not be free. Whenever this idea has for a moment escaped from the individual realm, it has found an

Commencement address, Harvard University, 1890.

even more secure foothold in the policy and philosophy of the State. The Strong Man and his mighty Right Arm have become the Strong Nation with its armies. Under whatever guise, however a Jefferson Davis may appear, as man, as race, or as nation, his life can only logically mean this: the advance of a part of the world at the expence of the whole: the overweening sense of the I and the consequent forgetting of the Thou. It has thus happened, that advance in civilization has always been handicapped by shortsighted national selfishness. The vital principle of division of labor has been stifled not only in industry, but also in civilization, so as to render it well nigh impossible for a new race to introduce a new idea into the world except by means of the cudgel. To say that a nation is in the way of civilization is a contradiction in terms, and a system of human culture whose principle is the rise of one race on the ruins of another is a farce and a lie. Yet this is the type of civilization which Jefferson Davis represented: it represents a field for stalwart manhood and heroic character, and at the same time for moral obtuseness and refined brutality. These striking contradictions of character always arise when a people seemingly become convinced that the object of the world is not civilization, but Teutonic civilization. Such a type is not wholly evil or fruitless: the world has needed and will need its Jefferson Davises; but such a type is incomplete and never can serve its best purpose until checked by its complementary ideas. Whence shall these come?

To the most casual observer, it must have occurred that the Rod of Empire has in these days, turned towards the South. In every Southern country, however, destined to play a future part in the world — in Southern North America, South America, Australia, and Africa — a new nation has a more or less firm foothold. This circumstance has, however, attracted but incidental notice, hitherto; for wherever the Negro people have touched civilization their rise has been singularly unromantic and unscientific. Through the glamour of history, the rise of a nation has ever been typified by the Strong Man crushing out an effete civilization. That brutality buried aught else beside Rome when it descended golden haired and drunk from the blue north has scarcely entered human imagination. Not as the muscular warrior came the Negro, but as the cringing slave. The Teutonic met civilization and crushed it — the Negro met civilization and was crushed by it. The one was the hero the world has ever worshipped, who gained unthought of triumphs and made unthought of mistakes; the other was the personification of dogged patience bending to the inevitable, and waiting. In the history of this people, we seek in vain the elements of Teutonic deification of Self, and Roman brute force, but we do find an idea of submission apart from cowardice, laziness, or stupidity, such as the world never saw before. This is the race which by its very presence must play a part in the world of tomorrow; and this is the race whose rise, I contend, has practically illustrated an idea which is at once the check and complement of the Teutonic Strong Man. It is the doctrine of the Submissive Man — given to the world by strange coincidence, by the race of whose rights, Jefferson Davis had not heard.

What then is the change made in the conception of civilization, by adding to the idea of the Strong Man, that of the Submissive Man? It is this: the submission of the strength of the Strong to the advance of all — not in mere aimless sacrifice, but recognizing the fact that, "To no one type of mind is it given to discern the totality of Truth," that civilization cannot afford to lose the contribution of the very least of nations for its full developement: that not only the assertion of the I, but also to the submission to the Thou is the highest Individualism.

The Teuton stands today as the champion of the idea of Personal Assertion: the Negro as the peculiar embodiment of the idea of Personal Submission: either, alone, tends to an abnormal development — towards Despotism on the one hand which the world has just cause to fear, and yet covertly admires, or towards slavery on the other which the world despises and which, yet is not wholly despicable. No matter how great and striking the Teutonic type of impetuous manhood may be, it must receive the cool purposeful "Ich Dien" of the African for its round and full developement. In the rise of Negro people and developement of this idea, you whose nation was founded on the loftiest ideals, and who many times forgot those ideals with a strange forgetfulness, have more than a sentimental interest, more than a sentimental duty. You owe a debt to humanity for this Ethiopia of the Out-stretched Arm, who has made her beauty, patience, and her grandeur, law.

The Conservation of Races

The American Negro has always felt an intense personal interest in discussions as to the origins and destinies of races: primarily because back of most discussions of race with which he is familiar, have lurked certain assumptions as to his natural abilities, as to his political, intellectual and moral status, which he felt were wrong. He has, consequently, been led to deprecate and minimize race distinctions, to believe intensely that out of one blood God created all nations, and to speak of human brotherhood as though it were the possibility of an already dawning to-morrow.

Nevertheless, in our calmer moments we must acknowledge that human beings are divided into races; that in this country the two most extreme types of the world's races have met, and the resulting problem as to the future relations of these types is not only of intense and living interest to us, but forms an epoch in the history of mankind.

It is necessary, therefore, in planning our movements, in guiding our future development, that at times we rise above the pressing, but smaller questions of separate schools and cars, wage-discrimination and lynch law, to survey the whole question of race in human philosophy and to lay, on a basis of broad knowledge and careful insight, those large lines of policy and higher ideals which may form our guiding lines and boundaries in the practical difficulties of every day. For it is certain that all human striving must recognize the hard limits of natural law, and that any striving, no matter how intense and earnest, which is against the constitution of the world, is vain. The question, then, which we must seriously consider is this: What is the real meaning of Race; what has, in the past, been the law of race development, and what lessons has the past history of race development to teach the rising Negro people?

American Negro Academy, *Occasional Papers*, No. 2, 1897.

When we thus come to inquire into the essential difference of races we find it hard to come at once to any definite conclusion. Many criteria of race differences have in the past been proposed, as color, hair, cranial measurements and language. And manifestly, in each of these respects, human beings differ widely. . . . All these physical characteristics are patent enough, and if they agreed with each other it would be very easy to classify mankind. Unfortunately for scientists, however, these criteria of race are most exasperatingly intermingled. Color does not agree with texture of hair, for many of the dark races have straight hair; nor does color agree with the breadth of the head, for the yellow Tartar has a broader head than the German; nor, again, has the science of language as yet succeeded in clearing up the relative authority of these various and contradictory criteria. The final word of science, so far, is that we have at least two, perhaps three, great families of human beings — the whites and Negroes, possibly the yellow race. . . .

Although the wonderful developments of human history teach that the grosser physical differences of color, hair and bone go but a short way toward explaining the different roles which groups of men have played in Human Progress, yet there are differences — subtle, delicate and elusive, though they may be — which have silently but definitely separated men into groups. While these subtle forces have generally followed the natural cleavage of common blood, descent and physical peculiarities, they have at other times swept across and ignored these. At all times, however, they have divided human beings into races, which, while they perhaps transcend scientific definition, nevertheless, are clearly defined to the eye of the Historian and Sociologist.

If this be true, then the history of the world is the history, not of individuals, but of groups, not of nations, but of races, and he who ignores or seeks to override the race idea in human history ignores and overrides the central thought of all history. What, then, is a race? It is a vast family of human beings, generally of common blood and language, always of common history, traditions and impulses, who are both voluntarily and involuntarily striving together for the accomplishment of certain more or less vividly conceived ideals of life.

Turning to real history, there can be no doubt, first, as to the widespread, nay, universal, prevalence of the race idea, the race spirit, the race ideal, and as to its efficiency as the vastest and most ingenious invention for human progress. We, who have been reared and trained under the individualistic philosophy of the Declaration of Independence and the laisser-faire philosophy of Adam Smith, are loath to see and loath to acknowledge this patent fact of human history. We see the Pharaohs, Caesars, Toussaints and Napoleons of history and forget the vast races of which they were but epitomized expressions. We are apt to think in our American impatience, that while it may have been true in the past that closed race groups made history, that here in conglomerate America *nous avons changer tout cela* — we have changed all that, and have no need of this ancient instrument of progress. This assumption of which the Negro people are especially fond, cannot be established by a careful consideration of history.

We find upon the world's stage today eight distinctly differentiated races, in the sense in which History tells us the word must be used. They are, the Slavs of eastern Europe, the Teutons of middle Europe, the English of Great Britain and America, the Romance nations of Southern and Western Europe, the Negroes of Africa and America, the Semitic people of Western Asia and Northern Africa, the Hindoos of Central Asia and the Mongolians of Eastern Asia. There are, of course, other minor race groups, as the American Indians, the Esquimaux and the South Sea Islanders; . . .

The question now is: What is the real distinction between these nations? Is it the physical differences of blood, color and cranial measurements? Certainly we must all acknowledge that physical differences play a great part, and that, with wide exceptions and qualifications, these eight great races of to-day follow the cleavage of physical race distinctions; . . . But while race differences have followed mainly physical race lines, yet no mere physical distinctions would really define or explain the deeper differences — the cohesiveness and continuity of these groups. The deeper differences are spiritual, psychical, differences — undoubtedly based on the physical, but infinitely transcending them. The forces that bind together the Teuton nations are, then, first, their race identity and common blood; secondly, and more important, a common history, common laws and religion, similar habits of thought and a conscious striving together for certain ideals of life. The whole process which has brought about these race differentiations has been a growth, and the great characteristic of this growth has been the differentiation of spiritual and mental differences between great races of mankind and the integration of physical differences.

The age of nomadic tribes of closely related individuals represents the maximum of physical differences. They were practically vast families, and there were as many groups as families. As the families came together to form cities the physical differences lessened, purity of blood was replaced by the requirement of domicile, and all who lived within the city bounds became gradually to be regarded as members of the group; i.e., there was a slight and slow breaking down of physical barriers. This, however, was accompanied by an increase of the spiritual and social differences between cities. This city became husbandmen, this, merchants, another warriors, and so on. The *ideals of life* for which the different cities struggled were different. When at last cities began to coalesce into nations there was another breaking down of barriers which separated groups of men. The larger and broader differences of color, hair and physical proportions were not by any means ignored, but myriads of minor differences disappeared, and the sociological and historical races of men began to approximate the present division of races as indicated by physical researches. At the same time the spiritual and physical differences of race groups which constituted the nations became deep and decisive. . . . striving, each in its own way, to develop for civilization its particular message, its particular ideal, which shall help to guide the world nearer and nearer that perfection of human life for which we all long, that

"one far off Divine event."

This has been the function of race differences up to the present time. What shall be its function in the future? Manifestly some of the great races of today — particularly the Negro race — have not as yet given to civilization the full spiritual message which they are capable of giving. I will not say that the Negro race has as yet given no message to the world, for it is still a mooted question among scientists as to just how far Egyptian civilization was Negro in its origin; if it was not wholly Negro, it was certainly very closely allied. Be that as it may, however, the fact still remains that the full, complete Negro message of the whole Negro race has not as yet been given to the world: that the messages and ideal of the yellow race have not been completed, and that the striving of the mighty Slavs has but begun. The question is, then: How shall this message be delivered; how shall these various ideals be realized? The answer is plain: By the development of these race groups, not as individuals, but as races. . . . We cannot reverse history; we are subject to the same natural laws as other races, and if the Negro is ever to be a factor in the world's history — if among the gaily-colored banners that deck the broad ramparts of civilization is to hang one uncompromising black, then it must be placed there by black hands, fashioned by black heads and hallowed by the travail of 200,000,000 black hearts beating in one glad song of jubilee.

For this reason, the advance guard of the Negro people — the 8,000,000 people of Negro blood in the United States of America — must soon come to realize that if they are to take their just place in the van of Pan-Negroism, then their destiny is *not* absorption by the white Americans. That if in America it is to be proven for the first time in the modern world that not only Negroes are capable of evolving individual men like Toussaint, the Saviour, but are a nation stored with wonderful possibilities of culture, then their destiny is not a servile imitation of Anglo-Saxon culture, but a stalwart originality which shall unswervingly follow Negro ideals.

It may, however, be objected here that the situation of our race in America renders this attitude impossible; that our sole hope of salvation lies in our being able to lose our race identity in the commingled blood of the nation;

and that any other course would merely increase the friction of races which we call race prejudice, and against which we have so long and so earnestly fought.

Here, then, is the dilemma, and it is a puzzling one, I admit. No Negro who has given earnest thought to the situation of his people in America has failed, at some time in life, to find himself at these cross-roads; has failed to ask himself at some time: What, after all, am I? Am I an American or am I a Negro? Can I be both? Or is it my duty to cease to be a Negro as soon as possible and be an American? If I strive as a Negro, am I not perpetuating the very cleft that threatens and separates Black and White America? Is not my only possible practical aim the subduction of all that is Negro in me to the American? Does my black blood place upon me any more obligation to assert my nationality than German, or Irish or Italian blood would?

It is such incessant self-questioning and the hesitation that arises from it, that is making the present period a time of vacillation and contradiction for the American Negro; combined race action is stifled, race responsibility is shirked, race enterprises languish, and the best blood, the best talent, the best energy of the Negro people cannot be marshalled to do the bidding of the race. They stand back to make room for every rascal and demagogue who chooses to cloak his selfish deviltry under the veil of race pride.

Is this right? Is it rational? Is it good policy? Have we in America a distinct mission as a race — a distinct sphere of action and an opportunity for race development, or is self-obliteration the highest end to which Negro blood dare aspire?

If we carefully consider what race prejudice really is, we find it, histori-cally, to be nothing but the friction between different groups of people; it is the difference in aim, in feeling, in ideals of two different races; if, now, this difference exists touching territory, laws, language, or even religion, it is manifest that these people cannot live in the same territory without fatal collision; but if, on the other hand, there is substantial agreement in laws, language and religion; if there is a satisfactory adjustment of economic life, then there is no reason why, in the same country and on the same street, two or three great national ideals might not thrive and develop, that men of different races might not strive together for their race ideals as well, perhaps even better, than in isolation. Here, it seems to me, is the reading of the riddle that puzzles so many of us. We are Americans, not only by birth and by citizenship, but by our political ideals, our language, our religion. Farther than that, our Americanism does not go. At that point, we are Negroes, members of a vast historic race that from the very dawn of creation has slept, but half awakening in the dark forests of its African fatherland. We are the first fruits of this new nation, the harbinger of that black to-morrow which is yet destined to soften the whiteness of the Teutonic to-day. We are that people whose subtle sense of song has given America its only American music, its only American fairy tales, its only touch of pathos and humor amid its mad money-getting plutocracy. As such, it is our duty to conserve our physical powers, our intellectual endowments, our spiritual ideals; as a race we must strive by race organization, by race solidarity, by race unity to the realization of that broader humanity which freely recognizes differences in men, but sternly deprecates inequality in their opportunities of development.

For the accomplishment of these ends we need race organizations: Negro colleges, Negro newspapers, Negro business organizations, a Negro school of literature and art, and an intellectual clearing house, for all these products of the Negro mind, which we may call a Negro Academy. Not only is all this necessary for positive advance, it is absolutely imperative for negative defense. Let us not deceive ourselves at our situation in this country. Weighted with a heritage of moral iniquity from our past history, hard pressed in the economic world by foreign immigrants and native prejudice, hated here, despised there and pitied everywhere; our one haven of refuge is ourselves, and but one means of advance, our own belief in our great destiny, our own implicit trust in our ability and worth. There is no power under God's high heaven that can stop the advance of eight thousand thousand honest, earnest, inspired and united people. But—and here is the rub—they *must* be honest, fearlessly criticising their own faults, zealously correcting them; they must be *earnest*. No people that laughs at itself, and ridicules itself, and wishes to God it was anything but itself ever wrote its name in history; it *must* be inspired with the Divine faith of our black mothers, that out of the blood and dust of battle will march a victorious host, a mighty nation, a peculiar people, to speak to the nations of earth a Divine truth that shall make them free. And such a people must be united; not merely united for the organized theft of political spoils, not united to disgrace religion with whoremongers and ward-heelers; not united merely to protest and pass resolutions, but united to stop the ravages of consumption among the Negro people, united to keep black boys from loafing, gambling and crime; united to guard the purity of black women and to reduce that vast army of black prostitutes that is today marching to hell; and united in serious organizations, to determine by careful conference and thoughtful interchange of opinion the broad lines of policy and action for the American Negro.

This is the reason for being which the American Negro Academy has. It aims at once to be the epitome and expression of the intellect of the black-blooded people of America, the exponent of the race ideals of one of the world's great races. As such, the Academy must, if successful, be

(*a*). Representative in character.
(*b*). Impartial in conduct.
(*c*). Firm in leadership. . . .

In the field of Sociology an appalling work lies before us. First, we must unflinchingly and bravely face the truth, not with apologies, but with solemn earnestness. The Negro Academy ought to sound a note of warning that would echo in every black cabin in the land: *Unless we conquer our present vices they will conquer us*; we are diseased, we are developing criminal tendencies, and an alarmingly large percentage of our men and women are sexually impure. The Negro Academy should stand and proclaim this over the housetops, crying with Garrison: *I will not equivocate, I will not retreat a single inch, and I will be heard*. The Academy should seek to gather about it the talented, unselfish men, the pure and noble-minded women, to fight an army of devils that disgraces our manhood and our womanhood. There does not stand today upon God's earth a race more capable in muscle, in intellect, in morals, than the American Negro, if he will bend his energies in the right direction; if he will

> Burst his birth's invidious bar
> And grasp the skirts of happy chance,
> And breast the blows of circumstance,
> And grapple with his evil star.

In science and morals, I have indicated two fields of work for the Academy. Finally, in practical policy, I wish to suggest the following *Academy Creed*:

1. We believe that the Negro people, as a race, have a contribution to make to civilization and humanity, which no other race can make.

2. We believe it the duty of the Americans of Negro descent, as a body, to maintain their race identity until this mission of the Negro people is accomplished, and the ideal of human brotherhood has become a practical possibility.

3. We believe that, unless modern civilization is a failure, it is entirely feasible and practicable for two races in such essential political, economic, and religious harmony as the white and colored people of America, to develop side by side in peace and mutual happiness, the peculiar contribution which each has to make to the culture of their common country.

4. As a means to this end we advocate, not such social equality between these races as would disregard human likes and dislikes, but such a social equilibrium as would, throughout all the complicated relations of life, give

due and just consideration to culture, ability, and moral worth, whether they be found under white or black skins.

5. We believe that the first and greatest step toward the settlement of the present friction between the races — commonly called the Negro Problem — lies in the correction of the immorality, crime and laziness among the Negroes themselves, which still remains as a heritage from slavery. We believe that only earnest and long continued efforts on our own part can cure these social ills.

6. We believe that the second great step toward a better adjustment of the relations between the races should be a more impartial selection of ability in the economic and intellectual world, and a greater respect for personal liberty and worth, regardless of race. We believe that only earnest efforts on the part of the white people of this country will bring much needed reform in these matters.

7. On the basis of the foregoing declaration, and firmly believing in our high destiny, we, as American Negroes, are resolved to strive in every honorable way for the realization of the best and highest aims, for the development of strong manhood and pure womanhood, and for the rearing of a race ideal in America and Africa, to the glory of God and the uplifting of the Negro people.

Of Our Spiritual Strivings

Between me and the other world there is ever an unasked question: unasked by some through feelings of delicacy; by others through the difficulty of rightly framing it. All, nevertheless, flutter round it. They approach me in a half-hesitant sort of way, eye me curiously or compassionately, and then, instead of saying directly, How does it feel to be a problem? they say, I know an excellent colored man in my town; or, I fought at Mechanicsville; or, Do not these Southern outrages make your blood boil? At these I smile, or am interested, or reduce the boiling to a simmer, as the occasion may require. To the real question, How does it feel to be a problem? I answer seldom a word.

And yet, being a problem is a strange experience, — peculiar even for one who has never been anything else, save perhaps in babyhood and in Europe. It is in the early days of rollicking boyhood that the revelation first bursts upon one, all in a day, as it were. I remember well when the shadow swept across me. I was a little thing, away up in the hills of New England, where the dark Housatonic winds between Hoosac and Taghkanic to the sea. In a wee wooden schoolhouse, something put it into the boys' and girls' heads to buy gorgeous visiting-cards — ten cents a package — and exchange. The exchange was merry, till one girl, a tall newcomer, refused my card, — refused it peremptorily, with a glance. Then it dawned upon me with a certain suddenness that I was different from the others; or like, mayhap, in heart and life and longing, but shut out from their world by a vast veil. I had thereafter no desire to tear down that veil, to creep through; I held all beyond it in common contempt, and lived above it in a region of blue sky and great wandering shadows. That sky was bluest when I could beat my mates at examination-time, or beat them at a foot-race, or even beat their stringy heads. Alas, with the years all this fine contempt began to fade; for the worlds I longed for, and all their dazzling opportunities, were theirs, not mine. But they should not keep these prizes, I said; some, all, I would wrest from them. Just how I would do it I could never decide: by reading law, by healing the sick, by telling the wonderful tales that swam in my head, — some way. With other black boys the strife was not so fiercely sunny: their youth shrunk into tasteless sycophancy, or into silent hatred of the pale world about them and mocking distrust of

From *The Souls of Black Folk* (1903).

everything white; or wasted itself in a bitter cry, Why did God make me an outcast and a stranger in mine own house? The shades of the prison-house closed round about us all: walls strait and stubborn to the whitest, but relentlessly narrow, tall, and unscalable to sons of night who must plod darkly on in resignation, or beat unavailing palms against the stone, or steadily, half hopelessly, watch the streak of blue above.

After the Egyptian and Indian, the Greek and Roman, the Teuton and Mongolian, the Negro is a sort of seventh son, born with a veil, and gifted with second-sight in this American world, — a world which yields him no true self-consciousness, but only lets him see himself through the revelation of the other world. It is a peculiar sensation, this double-consciousness, this sense of always looking at one's self through the eyes of others, of measuring one's soul by the tape of a world that looks on in amused contempt and pity. One ever feels his two-ness, — an American, a Negro; two souls, two thoughts, two unreconciled strivings; two warring ideals in one dark body, whose dogged strength alone keeps it from being torn asunder.

The history of the American Negro is the history of this strife, — this longing to attain self-conscious manhood, to merge his double self into a better and truer self. In this merging he wishes neither of the older selves to be lost. He would not Africanize America, for America has too much to teach the world and Africa. He would not bleach his Negro soul in a flood of white Americanism, for he knows that Negro blood has a message for the world. He simply wishes to make it possible for a man to be both a Negro and an American, without being cursed and spit upon by his fellows, without having the doors of Opportunity closed roughly in his face.

This, then, is the end of his striving: to be a co-worker in the kingdom of culture, to escape both death and isolation, to husband and use his best powers and his latent genius. These powers of body and mind have in the past been strangely wasted, dispersed, or forgotten. The shadow of a mighty Negro past flits through the tale of Ethiopia the Shadowy and of Egypt the Sphinx. Throughout history, the powers of single black men flash here and there like falling stars, and die sometimes before the world has rightly gauged their brightness. Here in America, in the few days since Emancipation, the black man's turning hither and thither in hesitant and doubtful striving has often made his very strength to lose effectiveness, to seem like absence of power, like weakness. And yet it is not weakness, — it is the contradiction of double aims. The double-aimed struggle of the black artisan — on the one hand to escape white contempt for a nation of mere hewers of wood and drawers of water, and on the other hand to plough and nail and dig for a poverty-stricken horde — could only result in making him a poor craftsman, for he had but half a heart in either cause. By the poverty and ignorance of his people, the Negro minister or doctor was tempted toward quackery and demagogy; and by the criticism of the other world, toward ideals that made him ashamed of his lowly tasks. The would-be black *savant* was confronted by the paradox that the knowledge his people needed was a twice-told tale to his white neighbors, while the knowledge which would teach the white world was Greek to his own flesh and blood. The innate love of harmony and beauty that set the ruder souls of his people a-dancing and a-singing raised but confusion and doubt in the soul of the black artist; for the beauty revealed to him was the soul-beauty of a race which his larger audience despised, and he could not articulate the message of another people. This waste of double aims, this seeking to satisfy two unreconciled ideals, has wrought sad havoc with the courage and faith and deeds of ten thousand thousand people, — has sent them often wooing false gods and invoking false means of salvation, and at times has even seemed about to make them ashamed of themselves.

Away back in the days of bondage they thought to see in one divine event the end of all doubt and disappointment; few men ever worshipped Freedom with half such unquestioning faith as did the American Negro for two centuries. To him, so far as he thought and dreamed, slavery was indeed the sum of all villainies, the cause of all sorrow, the root of all prejudice; Emancipation was the key to a promised land of sweeter beauty than ever stretched before the eyes of wearied Israelites. In song and exhortation swelled one refrain — Liberty; in his tears and curses the God he implored had Freedom in his right hand. At last it came, — suddenly, fearfully, like a dream. With one wild carnival of blood and passion came the message in his own plaintive cadences: —

> "Shout, O children!
> Shout, you're free!
> For God has bought your liberty!"

Years have passed away since then, — ten, twenty, forty; forty years of national life, forty years of renewal and development, and yet the swarthy spectre sits in its accustomed seat at the Nation's feast. In vain do we cry to this our vastest social problem: —

> "Take any shape but that, and my firm nerves
> Shall never tremble!"

The Nation has not yet found peace from its sins; the freedman has not yet found in freedom his promised land. Whatever of good may have come in these years of change, the shadow of a deep disappointment rests upon the Negro people, — a disappointment all the more bitter because the unattained ideal was unbounded save by the simple ignorance of a lowly people.

The first decade was merely a prolongation of the vain search for freedom, the boon that seemed ever barely to elude their grasp, — like a tantalizing will-o'-the-wisp, maddening and misleading the headless host. The holocaust of war, the terrors of the Ku-Klux Klan, the lies of carpet-baggers, the disorganization of industry, and the contradictory advice of friends and foes, left the bewildered serf with no new watchword beyond the old cry for freedom. As the time flew, however, he began to grasp a new idea. The ideal of liberty demanded for its attainment powerful means, and these the Fifteenth Amendment gave him. The ballot, which before he had looked upon as a visible sign of freedom, he now regarded as the chief means of gaining and perfecting the liberty with which war had partially endowed him. And why not? Had not votes made war and emancipated millions? Had not votes enfranchised the freedmen? Was anything impossible to a power that had done all this? A million black men started with renewed zeal to vote themselves into the kingdom. So the decade flew away, the revolution of 1876 came, and left the half-free serf weary, wondering, but still inspired. Slowly but steadily, in the following years, a new vision began gradually to replace the dream of political power, — a powerful movement, the rise of another ideal to guide the unguided, another pillar of fire by night after a clouded day. It was the ideal of "book-learning"; the curiosity, born of compulsory ignorance, to know and test the power of the cabalistic letters of the white man, the longing to know. Here at last seemed to have been discovered the mountain path to Canaan; longer than the highway of Emancipation and law, steep and rugged, but straight, leading to heights high enough to overlook life.

Up the new path the advance guard toiled, slowly heavily, doggedly; only those who have watched and guided the faltering feet, the misty minds, the dull understandings, of the dark pupils of these schools know how faithfully, how piteously, this people strove to learn. It was weary work. The cold statistician wrote down the inches of progress here and there, noted also where here and there a foot had slipped or some one had fallen. To the tired climbers, the horizon was ever dark, the mists were often cold, the Canaan was always dim and far away. If, however, the vistas disclosed as yet no goal, no resting-place, little but flattery and criticism, the journey at least gave leisure for reflection and self-examination; it changed the child of Emancipation to the youth with dawning self-consciousness, self-realization, self-respect. In those sombre forests of his striving his own soul rose before him, and he saw himself, — darkly as through a veil; and yet he saw in himself some faint revelation of his power, of his mission. He began to have a dim feeling that, to attain his place in the world, he must be himself, and not another. For the first time he sought to analyze the burden he bore upon his back, that dead-weight of social degradation partially masked behind a half-named Negro problem. He felt his poverty; without a cent, without a home, without land, tools, or savings, he had entered into competition with rich, landed, skilled neighbors. To be a poor man is hard, but to be a poor race in a land of dollars is the very bottom of hardships. He felt the weight of his ignorance, — not simply of letters, but of life, of business, of the humanities; the accumulated sloth and shirking and awkwardness of decades and centuries shackled his hands and feet. Nor was his burden all poverty and ignorance. The red stain of bastardy, which two centuries of systematic legal defilement of Negro women had stamped upon his race, meant not only the loss of ancient African chastity, but also the hereditary weight of a mass of corruption from white adulterers, threatening almost the obliteration of the Negro home.

A people thus handicapped ought not to be asked to race with the world, but rather allowed to give all its time and thought to its own social problems. But alas! while sociologists gleefully count his bastards and his prostitutes, the very soul of the toiling, sweating black man is darkened by the shadow of a vast despair. Men call the shadow prejudice, and learnedly explain it as the natural defence of culture against barbarism, learning against ignorance, purity against crime, the "higher" against the "lower" races. To which the Negro cries Amen! and swears that to so much of this strange prejudice as is founded on just homage to civilization, culture, righteousness, and progress, he humbly bows and meekly does obeisance. But before that nameless prejudice that leaps beyond all this he stands helpless, dismayed, and well-nigh speechless; before that personal disrespect and mockery, the ridicule and systematic humiliation, the distortion of fact and wanton license of fancy, the cynical ignoring of the better and the boisterous welcoming of the worse, the all-pervading desire to inculcate disdain for everything black, from Toussaint to the devil, — before this there rises a sickening despair that would disarm and discourage any nation save that black host to whom "discouragement" is an unwritten word.

But the facing of so vast a prejudice could not but bring the inevitable self-questioning, self-disparagement, and lowering of ideals which ever accompany repression and breed in an atmosphere of contempt and hate. Whisperings and portents came borne upon the four winds: Lo! we are diseased and dying, cried the dark hosts; we cannot write, our voting is vain; what need of education, since we must always cook and serve? And the Nation echoed and enforced this self-criticism, saying: Be content to be servants, and nothing more; what need of higher culture for half-men? Away with the black man's ballot, by force or fraud, — and behold the suicide of a race! Nevertheless, out of the evil came something of good, — the more careful adjustment of education to real life, the clearer perception of the Negroes' social responsibilities, and the sobering realization of the meaning of progress.

So dawned the time of *Sturm und Drang*: storm and stress to-day rocks our little boat on the mad waters of the world-sea; there is within and without the sound of conflict, the burning of body and rending of soul; inspiration strives with doubt, and faith with vain questionings. The bright ideals of the past, — physical freedom, political power, the training of brains and the training of hands, — all these in turn have waxed and waned, until even the last grows dim and overcast. Are they all wrong, — all false? No, not that, but each alone was over-simple and incomplete, — the dreams of a credulous race-childhood, or the fond imaginings of the other world which does not know and does not want to know our power. To be really true, all these ideals must be melted and welded into one. The training of the schools we need to-day more than ever, — the training of deft hands, quick eyes and ears, and above all the broader, deeper, higher culture of gifted minds and pure hearts. The power of the ballot we need in sheer self-defence, — else what shall save us from a second slavery? Freedom, too, the long-sought, we still seek, — the freedom of life and limb, the freedom to work and think, the freedom to love and aspire. Work, culture, liberty, — all these we need, not singly but together, not successively but together, each growing and aiding each, and all striving toward that vaster ideal that swims before the Negro people, the ideal of human brotherhood, gained through the unifying ideal of Race; the ideal of fostering and developing the traits and talents of the Negro, not in opposition to or contempt for other races, but rather in large conformity to the greater ideals of the American Republic, in order that some day on American soil two world-races may give each to each those characteristics both so sadly lack. We the darker ones come even now not altogether empty-handed: there are to-day no truer exponents of the pure human spirit of the Declaration of Independence than the American Negroes; there is no true American music but the wild sweet melodies of the Negro slave; the American fairy tales and folk-lore are Indian and African; and, all in all, we black men seem the sole oasis of simple faith and reverence in a dusty desert of dollars and smartness. Will America be poorer if she replace her brutal dyspeptic blundering with light-hearted but determined Negro humility? or her coarse and cruel wit with loving jovial good-humor? or her vulgar music with the soul of the Sorrow Songs?

Merely a concrete test of the underlying principles of the great republic is the Negro Problem, and the spiritual striving of the freedmen's sons is the travail of souls whose burden is almost beyond the measure of their strength, but who bear it in the name of an historic race, in the name of this the land of their fathers' fathers, and in the name of human opportunity.

And now what I have briefly sketched in large outline let me on coming pages tell again in many ways, with loving emphasis and deeper detail, that men may listen to the striving in the souls of black folk.

Of the Meaning of Progress

Once upon a time I taught school in the hills of Tennessee, where the broad dark vale of the Mississippi begins to roll and crumple to greet the Alleghanies. I was a Fisk student then, and all Fisk men thought that Tennessee — beyond the Veil — was theirs alone, and in vacation time they sallied forth in lusty bands to meet the county school-commissioners. Young and happy, I too went, and I shall not soon forget that summer, seventeen years ago.

First, there was a Teachers' Institute at the county-seat; and there distinguished guests of the superintendent taught the teachers fractions and spelling and other mysteries, — white teachers in the morning, Negroes at night. A picnic now and then, and a supper, and the rough world was softened by laughter and song. I remember how — But I wander.

There came a day when all the teachers left the Institute and began the hunt for schools. I learn from hearsay (for my mother was mortally afraid of fire-arms) that the hunting of ducks and bears and men is wonderfully interesting, but I am sure that the man who has never hunted a country school has something to learn of the pleasures of the chase. I see now the white, hot roads lazily rise and fall and wind before me under the burning July sun; I feel the deep weariness of heart and limb as ten, eight, six miles stretch relentlessly ahead; I feel my heart sink heavily as I hear again and again, "Got a teacher? Yes." So I walked on and on — horses were too expensive — until I had wandered beyond railways, beyond stage lines, to a land of "varmints" and rattlesnakes, where the coming of a stranger was an event, and men lived and died in the shadow of one blue hill.

Sprinkled over hill and dale lay cabins and farm-houses, shut out from the world by the forests and the rolling hills toward the east. There I found at last a little school. Josie told me of it; she was a thin, homely girl of twenty, with a dark-brown face and thick, hard hair. I had crossed the stream at Watertown, and rested under the great willows; then I had gone to the little cabin in the lot

From *The Souls of Black Folk* (1903).

where Josie was resting on her way to town. The gaunt farmer made me welcome, and Josie, hearing my errand, told me anxiously that they wanted a school over the hill; that but once since the war had a teacher been there; that she herself longed to learn, — and thus she ran on, talking fast and loud, with much earnestness and energy.

Next morning I crossed the tall round hill, lingered to look at the blue and yellow mountains stretching toward the Carolinas, then plunged into the wood, and came out at Josie's home. It was a dull frame cottage with four rooms, perched just below the brow of the hill, amid peach-trees. The father was a quiet, simple soul, calmly ignorant, with no touch of vulgarity. The mother was different, — strong, bustling, and energetic, with a quick, restless tongue, and an ambition to live "like folks." There was a crowd of children. Two boys had gone away. There remained two growing girls; a shy midget of eight; John, tall, awkward, and eighteen; Jim, younger, quicker, and better looking; and two babies of indefinite age. Then there was Josie herself. She seemed to be the centre of the family: always busy at service, or at home, or berry-picking; a little nervous and inclined to scold, like her mother, yet faithful, too, like her father. She had about her a certain fineness, the shadow of an unconscious moral heroism that would willingly give all of life to make life broader, deeper, and fuller for her and hers. I saw much of this family afterwards, and grew to love them for their honest efforts to be decent and comfortable, and for their knowledge of their own ignorance. There was with them no affectation. The mother would scold the father for being so "easy"; Josie would roundly berate the boys for carelessness; and all knew that it was a hard thing to dig a living out of a rocky side-hill.

I secured the school. I remember the day I rode horseback out to the commissioner's house with a pleasant young white fellow who wanted the white school. The road ran down the bed of a stream; the sun laughed and the water jingled, and we rode on. "Come in," said the commissioner, — "come in. Have a seat. Yes, that certificate will do. Stay to dinner. What do you want a month?" "Oh," thought I, "this is lucky"; but even then fell the awful shadow of the Veil, for they ate first, then I — alone.

The schoolhouse was a log hut, where Colonel Wheeler used to shelter his corn. It sat in a lot behind a rail fence and thorn bushes, near the sweetest of springs. There was an entrance where a door once was, and within, a massive rickety fireplace; great chinks between the logs served as windows. Furniture was scarce. A pale blackboard crouched in the corner. My desk was made of three boards, reinforced at critical points, and my chair, borrowed from the landlady, had to be returned every night. Seats for the children — these puzzled me much. I was haunted by a New England vision of neat little desks and chairs, but, alas! the reality was rough plank benches without backs, and at times without legs. They had the one virtue of making naps dangerous, — possibly fatal, for the floor was not to be trusted.

It was a hot morning late in July when the school opened. I trembled when I heard the patter of little feet down the dusty road, and saw the growing row of dark solemn faces and bright eager eyes facing me. First came Josie and her brothers and sisters. The longing to know, to be a student in the great school at Nashville, hovered like a star above this child-woman amid her work and worry, and she studied doggedly. There were the Dowells from their farm over toward Alexandria, — Fanny, with her smooth black face and wondering eyes; Martha, brown and dull; the pretty girl-wife of a brother, and the younger brood.

There were the Burkes, — two brown and yellow lads, and a tiny haughty-eyed girl. Fat Reuben's little chubby girl came, with golden face and old-gold hair, faithful and solemn. 'Thenie was on hand early, — a jolly, ugly, good-hearted girl, who slyly dipped snuff and looked after her little bow-legged brother. When her mother could spare her, 'Tildy came, — a midnight beauty, with starry eyes and tapering limbs; and her brother, correspondingly homely. And then the big boys, — the hulking Lawrences; the lazy Neills, unfathered sons of mother and daughter; Hickman, with a stoop in his shoulders; and the rest.

There they sat, nearly thirty of them, on the rough benches, their faces shading from a pale cream to a deep brown, the little feet bare and swinging, the eyes full of expectation, with here and there a twinkle of mischief, and the hands grasping Webster's blue-back spelling-book. I loved my school, and the fine faith the children had in the wisdom of their teacher was truly marvellous. We read and spelled together, wrote a little, picked flowers, sang, and listened to stories of the world beyond the hill. At times the school would dwindle away, and I would start out. I would visit Mun Eddings, who lived in two very dirty rooms, and ask why little Lugene, whose flaming face seemed ever ablaze with the dark-red hair uncombed, was absent all last week, or why I missed so often the inimitable rags of Mack and Ed. Then the father, who worked Colonel Wheeler's farm on shares, would tell me how the crops needed the boys; and the thin, slovenly mother, whose face was pretty when washed, assured me that Lugene must mind the baby. "But we'll start them again next week." When the Lawrences stopped, I knew that the doubts of the old folks about book-learning had conquered again, and so, toiling up the hill, and getting as far into the cabin as possible, I put Cicero "pro Archia Poeta" into the simplest English with local applications, and usually convinced them — for a week or so.

On Friday nights I often went home with some of the children, — sometimes to Doc Burke's farm. He was a great, loud, thin Black, ever working, and trying to buy the seventy-five acres of hill and dale where he lived; but people said that he would surely fail, and the "white folks would get it all." His wife was a magnificent Amazon, with saffron face and shining hair, uncorseted and barefooted, and the children were strong and beautiful. They lived in a one-and-a-half-room cabin in the hollow of the farm, near the spring. The front room was full of great fat white beds, scrupulously neat; and there were bad chromos on the walls, and a tired centre-table. In the tiny back kitchen I was often invited to "take out and help" myself to fried chicken and wheat biscuit, "meat" and corn pone, string-beans and berries. At first I used to be a little alarmed at the approach of bedtime in the one lone bedroom, but embarrassment was very deftly avoided. First, all the children nodded and slept, and were stowed away in one great pile of goose feathers; next, the mother and the father discreetly slipped away to the kitchen while I went to bed; then, blowing out the dim light, they retired in the dark. In the morning all were up and away before I thought of awaking. Across the road, where fat Reuben lived, they all went outdoors while the teacher retired, because they did not boast the luxury of a kitchen.

I liked to stay with the Dowells, for they had four rooms and plenty of good country fare. Uncle Bird had a small, rough farm, all woods and hills, miles from the big road; but he was full of tales, — he preached now and then, — and with his children, berries, horses, and wheat he was happy and prosperous. Often, to keep the peace, I must go where life was less lovely; for instance, 'Tildy's mother was incorrigibly dirty, Reuben's larder was limited seriously, and herds of untamed insects wandered over the Eddingses' beds. Best of all I loved to go to Josie's, and sit on the porch, eating peaches, while the mother bustled and talked: how Josie had bought the sewing-machine; how Josie worked at service in winter, but that four dollars a month was "mighty little" wages; how Josie longed to go away to school, but that it "looked like" they never could get far enough ahead to let her; how the crops failed and the well was yet unfinished; and, finally, how "mean" some of the white folks were.

For two summers I lived in this little world; it was dull and humdrum. The girls looked at the hill in wistful longing, and the boys fretted and haunted Alexandria. Alexandria was "town," — a straggling, lazy village of houses, churches, and shops, and an aristocracy of Toms, Dicks, and Captains. Cuddled on the hill to the north was the village of the colored folks, who lived in three- or four-room unpainted cottages, some neat and homelike, and some dirty. The dwellings were scattered rather aimlessly, but they centred about the twin temples of the hamlet, the Methodist, and the Hard-Shell Baptist churches. These, in turn, leaned gingerly on a sad-colored schoolhouse. Hither my little world wended its crooked way on Sunday to meet other worlds, and gossip, and wonder, and make the weekly sacrifice with frenzied priest at the altar of the "old-time religion." Then the soft melody and mighty cadences of Negro song fluttered and thundered.

I have called my tiny community a world, and so its isolation made it; and yet there was among us but a half-awakened common consciousness, sprung from common joy and grief, at burial, birth, or wedding; from a common hardship in poverty, poor land, and low wages; and, above all, from the sight of the Veil that hung between us and Opportunity. All this caused us to think some thoughts together; but these, when ripe for speech, were spoken in various languages. Those whose eyes twenty-five and more years before had seen "the glory of the coming of the Lord," saw in every present hindrance or help a dark fatalism bound to bring all things right in His own good time. The mass of those to whom slavery was a dim recollection of childhood found the world a puzzling thing: it asked little of them, and they answered with little, and yet it ridiculed their offering. Such a paradox they could not understand, and therefore sank into listless indifference, or shiftlessness, or reckless bravado. There were, however, some — such as Josie, Jim, and Ben — to whom War, Hell, and Slavery were but childhood tales, whose young appetites had been whetted to an edge by school and story and half-awakened thought. Ill could they be content, born without and beyond the World. And their weak wings beat against their barriers, — barriers of caste, of youth, of life; at last, in dangerous moments, against everything that opposed even a whim.

The ten years that follow youth, the years when first the realization comes that life is leading somewhere, — these were the years that passed after I left my little school. When they were past, I came by chance once more to the walls of Fisk University, to the halls of the chapel of melody. As I lingered there in the joy and pain of meeting old school-friends, there swept over me a sudden longing to pass again beyond the blue hill, and to see the homes and the school of other days, and to learn how life had gone with my school-children; and I went.

Josie was dead, and the gray-haired mother said simply, "We've had a heap of trouble since you've been away." I had feared for Jim. With a cultured parentage and a social caste to uphold him, he might have made a venturesome merchant or a West Point cadet. But here he was, angry with life and reckless; and when Farmer Durham charged him with stealing wheat, the old man had to ride fast to escape the stones which the furious fool hurled after him. They told Jim to run away; but he would not run, and the constable came that afternoon. It grieved Josie, and great awkward John walked nine miles every day to see his little brother through the bars of Lebanon jail. At last the two came back together in the dark night. The mother cooked supper, and Josie emptied her purse, and the boys stole away. Josie grew thin and silent, yet worked the more. The hill became steep for the quiet old father, and with the boys away there was little to do in the valley. Josie helped them to sell the old farm, and they moved nearer town. Brother Dennis, the carpenter, built a new house with six rooms; Josie toiled a year in Nashville, and brought back ninety dollars to furnish the house and change it to a home.

When the spring came, and the birds twittered, and the stream ran proud and full, little sister Lizzie, bold and thoughtless, flushed with the passion of youth, bestowed herself on the tempter, and brought home a nameless child. Josie shivered and worked on, with the vision of schooldays all fled, with a face wan and tired, — worked until, on a summer's day, some one married another; then Josie crept to her mother like a hurt child, and slept — and sleeps.

I paused to scent the breeze as I entered the valley. The Lawrences have gone, — father and son forever, — and the other son lazily digs in the earth to live. A new young widow rents out their cabin to fat Reuben. Reuben is a Baptist preacher now, but I fear as lazy as ever, though his cabin has three rooms; and little Ella has grown into a bouncing woman, and is ploughing corn on the hot hillside. There are babies a-plenty, and one half-witted girl. Across the valley is a house I did not know before, and there I found, rocking one baby and expecting another, one of my schoolgirls, a daughter of Uncle Bird Dowell. She looked somewhat worried with her new duties, but soon bristled into pride over her neat cabin and the tale of her thrifty husband, the horse and cow, and the farm they were planning to buy.

My log schoolhouse was gone. In its place stood Progress; and Progress, I understand, is necessarily ugly. The crazy foundation stones still marked the former site of my poor little cabin, and not far away, on six weary boulders, perched a jaunty board house, perhaps twenty by thirty feet, with three windows and a door that locked. Some of the window-glass was broken, and part of an old iron stove lay mournfully under the house. I peeped through the window half reverently, and found things that were more familiar. The blackboard had grown by about two feet, and the seats were still without backs. The county owns the lot now, I hear, and every year there is a session of school. As I sat by the spring and looked on the Old and the New I felt glad, very glad, and yet —

After two long drinks I started on. There was the great double log-house on the corner. I remembered the broken, blighted family that used to live there. The strong, hard face of the mother, with its wilderness of hair, rose before me. She had driven her husband away, and while I taught school a strange man lived there, big and jovial, and people talked. I felt sure that Ben and 'Tildy would come to naught from such a home. But this is an odd world; for Ben is a busy farmer in Smith County, "doing well, too," they say, and he had cared for little 'Tildy until last spring, when a lover married her. A hard life the lad had led, toiling for meat, and laughed at because he was homely and crooked. There was Sam Carlon, an impudent old skinflint, who had definite notions about "niggers," and hired Ben a summer and would not pay him. Then the hungry boy gathered his sacks together, and in broad daylight went into Carlon's corn; and when the hard-fisted farmer set upon him, the angry boy flew at him like a beast. Doc Burke saved a murder and a lynching that day.

The story reminded me again of the Burkes, and an impatience seized me to know who won in the battle, Doc or the seventy-five acres. For it is a hard thing to make a farm out of nothing, even in fifteen years. So I hurried on, thinking of the Burkes. They used to have a certain magnificent barbarism about them that I liked. They were never vulgar, never immoral, but rather rough and primitive, with an unconventionality that spent itself in loud guffaws, slaps on the back, and naps in the corner. I hurried by the cottage of the misborn Neill boys. It was empty, and they were grown into fat, lazy farm-hands. I saw the home of the Hickmans, but Albert, with his stooping shoulders, had passed from the world. Then I came to the Burkes' gate and peered through; the inclosure looked rough and untrimmed, and yet there were the same fences around the old farm save to the left, where lay twenty-five other acres. And lo! the cabin in the hollow had climbed the hill and swollen to a half-finished six-room cottage.

The Burkes held a hundred acres, but they were still in debt. Indeed, the gaunt father who toiled night and day would scarcely be happy out of debt, being so used to it. Some day he must stop, for his massive frame is showing decline. The mother wore shoes, but the lion-like physique of other days was broken. The children had grown up. Rob, the image of his father, was loud and rough with laughter. Birdie, my school baby of six, had grown to a picture of maiden beauty, tall and tawny. "Edgar is gone," said the mother, with head half bowed, — "gone to work in Nashville; he and his father couldn't agree."

Little Doc, the boy born since the time of my school, took me horseback down the creek next morning toward Farmer Dowell's. The road and the stream were battling for mastery, and the stream had the better of it. We splashed and waded, and the merry boy, perched behind me, chattered and laughed. He showed me where Simon Thompson had bought a bit of ground and a home; but his daughter Lana, a plump, brown, slow girl, was not there. She had married a man and a farm twenty miles away. We wound on down the stream till we came to a gate that I did not recognize, but the boy insisted that it was "Uncle Bird's." The farm was fat with the growing crop. In that little valley was a strange stillness as I rode up; for death and marriage had stolen youth and left age and childhood there. We sat and talked that night after the chores were done. Uncle Bird was grayer, and his eyes did not see so well, but he was still jovial. We talked of the acres bought, — one hundred and twenty-five, — of the new guest-chamber added, of Martha's marrying. Then we talked of death: Fanny and Fred were gone; a shadow hung over the other daughter, and when it lifted she was to go to Nashville to school. At last we spoke of the neighbors, and as night fell, Uncle Bird told me how, on a night like that, 'Thenie came wandering back to her home over yonder, to escape the blows of her husband. And next morning she died in the home that her little bow-legged brother, working and saving, had bought for their widowed mother.

My journey was done, and behind me lay hill and dale, and Life and Death. How shall man measure Progress there where the dark-faced Josie lies? How many heartfuls of sorrow shall balance a bushel of wheat? How hard a thing is life to the lowly, and yet how human and real! And all this life and love and strife and failure, — is it the twilight of nightfall or the flush of some faint-dawning day?

Thus sadly musing, I rode to Nashville in the Jim Crow car.

The Color Line Belts
the World

We have a way in America of wanting to be "rid" of problems. It is not so much a desire to reach the best and largest solution as it is to clean the board and start a new game. For instance, most Americans are simply tired and impatient over our most sinister social problem, the Negro. They do not want to solve it, they do not want to understand it, they want to simply be done with it and hear the last of it. Of all possible attitudes this is the most dangerous, because it fails to realize the most significant fact of the opening century, viz.: The Negro problem in America is but a local phase of a world problem. "The problem of the twentieth century is the problem of the Color Line." Many smile incredulously at such a proposition, but let us see.

The tendency of the great nations of the day is territorial, political and economic expansion, but in every case this has brought them in contact with darker peoples, so that we have to-day England, France, Holland, Belgium, Italy, Portugal, and the United States in close contact with brown and black peoples, and Russia and Austria in contact with the yellow. The older idea was that the whites would eventually displace the native races and inherit their lands, but this idea has been rudely shaken in the increase of American Negroes, the experience of the English in Africa, India and the West Indies, and the development of South America. The policy of expansion, then, simply means world problems of the Color Line. The question enters into European imperial politics and floods our continents from Alaska to Patagonia.

This is not all. Since 732, when Charles Martel beat back the Saracens at Tours, the white races have had the hegemony of civilization — so far so that "white" and "civilized" have become synonymous in every-day speech; and men have forgotten where civilization started. For the first time in a thousand

From *Collier's Weekly*, October 20, 1906, p.30.

years a great white nation has measured arms with a colored nation and been found wanting. The Russo-Japanese War has marked an epoch. The magic of the word "white" is already broken, and the Color Line in civilization has been crossed in modern times as it was in the great past. The awakening of the yellow races is certain. That the awakening of the brown and black races will follow in time, no unprejudiced student of history can doubt. Shall the awakening of these sleepy millions be in accordance with, and aided by, the great ideals of white civilization, or in spite of them and against them? This is the problem of the Color Line. Force and Fear have hitherto marked the white attitude toward darker races; shall this continue or be replaced by Freedom and Friendship?

The First Universal
Races Congress

Of the two thousand international meetings that have taken place in the last seventy-five years there have been few that have so touched the imagination as the Universal Races Congress of this summer.

Such a meeting may be viewed in many lights: as a meeting of widely separated men, as a reunion of East and West, as a glance across the color line or as a sort of World Grievance Committee. Perhaps it was in part something of each of these. There was, however, one thing that this congress could do of inestimable importance. Outside the discussion of racial problems, it could make clear the present state of scientific knowledge concerning the meaning of the term "race."

This the congress did and this was its most important work. There were practically no reports of new anthropological knowledge. There were, however, several reviews and restatements in popular terms of the present *dicta* of the science in the matter of human races, exprest with a clearness, force and authority that deserve especial mention.

The scientific men who contributed papers to the congress, and who were with few exceptions there in person to take part in the discussions, were, many of them, of the first rank: Von Luschan and Von Ranke, of Germany; Sergi, of Italy; Myers, Lyde and Hadden, of England, and Boas, of America, are all well known; among the other speakers were the Indian scholar, Seal; Lacerda, of Brazil; Fino of France, and Reinsch, of America. All those mentioned, save Boas, were present in person.

To realize the full meaning of the statements made by these men one must not forget the racial philosophy upon which America has long been nursed. The central idea of that philosophy has been that there are vast and, for all practical purposes, unbridgeable differences between the races of men, the whites representing the higher nobler stock, the blacks the lower meaner race. Between the lowest races (who are certainly undeveloped and probably

From *The Independent*, 70 (August 24, 1911): 401–403.

incapable of any considerable development) and the highest, range the brown and yellow peoples with various intermediate capacities.

The proofs of these assumptions have been repeatedly pointed out; the high civilization of the whites, the lack of culture among the blacks, the apparent incapacity for self-rule in many non-Europeans, and the stagnation of Asia. The reasons for this condition were variously stated: some assumed separate development for each race, while others spoke as tho the various races represented different stages in the same general development, with thousands of years between, the Negro remaining nearest the ape, the whites furthest from the common ancestor.

Had these assumptions remained merely academic opinions it would not be necessary to recall them, but they have become the scientific sanction for widespread and decisive political action — like the disfranchisement of American Negroes, the subjection of India and the partition of Africa. Under the aegis of this philosophy strong arguments have justified human slavery and peonage, conquest, enforced ignorance, the dishonoring of women and the exploitation of children. It was divine to enslave Negroes; Mexican peonage is the only remedy for laziness; powerful nations must rule the mass of men who are not fit and cannot be fitted to rule themselves; colored women must not be expected to be treated like white, and if commerce is arranged so as to make the dark world toil for the luxury and ease of the white, this is but the law of nature.

As I sat in the great hall of the University of London, I wondered how many of those audiences of five, six and seven hundred who daily braved the sweltering heat of a midsummer meeting realized how epoch-making many of the words quietly spoken there were, and how far they went toward undermining long and comfortably cherished beliefs.

The anthropologists were not rash in statement. They spoke with full realization of the prevalent attitude of Europeans toward other races. Some, like Von Luschan, took pains to emphasize separate racial development for the sake of the "hassenkampf," but he began with the sweeping assertion that "mankind is one":

Fair and dark races, long and short-headed, intelligent and primitive, all come from one stock. Favorable circumstances and surroundings, especially a good environment . . . caused one group to advance more quickly than another.

Moreover both he and Von Ranke, Sergi and others ridiculed the possibility of a "science" of race, or, indeed, of the possibility or desirability of drawing complete racial lines: "The question of the number of human races," said Von Luschan, "has quite lost its *raison d'être*, and has become a subject of

45

philosophical speculation, rather than of scientific research. It is of no more importance to know how many races there are than to know how many angels dance on the point of a needle!"

Especial insistence was made against regarding races as unchangeable accomplished facts; they were, in the words of Boas and Seal, "growing developing entities" and "the old idea of the absolute stability of racial types must evidently be given up; and with it the belief in the hereditary superiority of certain types over others."

This brought the discussion to the crucial point, for granted that human beings form a family thru which it is difficult to draw absolute lines, yet does not the present advancement of the various groups of men correspond on the whole with their physical characteristics? No proposition was more emphatically denied than this. In physique, said Seal, quoting Weisbach, "each race has its share of the characteristics of inferiority," and it is impossible to arrange the main groups of men in an ascending scale of physical development. Lyde, of Oxford, added that even color, which is today made the greatest of racial barriers, is with little doubt "entirely a matter of climatic control."

Nevertheless there are tremendous differences in the present condition of the various groups of men — whence do they arise and how permanent are they? Practically every anthropologist present laid the chief stress on environment in explaining these differences; not simply physical environment but the even more important social environment in which the individual is educated. Von Luschan traced dark-skinned primitive man from Southern Asia to the Negro and Negroid toward the Northwest, the Indo-European toward the North and the Mongol toward the Northeast. "We have thus the three chief varieties of mankind," he said, "all branching off the same primitive stock, diverging from each other for thousands of years, but all three forming a complete unity, intermarrying in all directions without the slightest decrease of fertility." Sir Harry Johnston emphasized this early interpenetration of primitive races and found traces of Negro blood from Asia to Ireland. Others like Reinsch showed that the differences that arose among the scattered branches of men were due at first to physical environment, and pointed out the way in which the contrasting geography of Greece and Africa, and Europe and Asia had influenced the history of their inhabitants.

Had not this long difference of environment left traces in the characters of races so ingrained as to be today practically ineradicable? Myers, of Oxford, asserted, in answer to this, that the mental characteristics of the majority of Europe were today essentially the same as those of the primitive peoples of the earth; that such differences as exist are due to present social and physical environment and that therefore "the progressive development of all primitive people must be conceded if the environment can be appropriately changed."

From the papers submitted to the congress and from his own studies, Gustav Spiller, the secretary, stated that a fair interpretation of the scientific evidence would support these propositions:

1. It is not legitimate to argue from differences in physical characteristics to difference in mental characteristics.
2. Physical and mental characteristics of races are not permanent, nor are they modifiable only thru long ages. On the contrary they are capable of being profoundly modified in a few generations by changes in education, public sentiment and environment generally.
3. The status of a race at any particular time offers no index as to its innate or inherited capacities.

As to race mixture all the anthropologists said that there were no "pure" races and that modern peoples were all more or less mixt. Nevertheless while many of these mixtures were obviously beneficial, it was not clear whether all racial mixtures would be. Certainly it was unscientific to assert that mulattoes and Eurasians were degenerate in the absence of all scientific data. Lacerda, of Brazil, showed the high proportion of mulattoes in the population of Brazil and the leading rôle they had played in emancipating the slaves, in establishing the republic and in the literary and political life of the day. Sir Charles Bruce and Sir Sidney Olivier made somewhat similar statements concerning the West Indies.

It would be too much to say that all anthropologists today would subscribe to the main conclusions of those who attended the Races Congress or that the doctrine of inevitable race superiority is dead. On the other hand there is good reason to affirm with Finot, in the *brochure* which he gave to the congress:

The conception of races as of so many watertight compartments into which human beings can be crammed as if they were so many breeds of horses or cattle, has had its day. The word race will doubtless long survive, even tho it may have lost all meaning. From time immemorial men have taken far more pains to damn their souls than would have sufficed to save them. Hence they will be certain to preserve this most scientific term which incites to hatred and unjustifiable contempt for our fellow men, instead of replacing it by some word implying the brotherhood of man.

The congress itself recorded its judgment on the matter of race differences by

Urging the vital importance at this juncture of history of discountenancing race prejudice, as tending to inflict on humanity incalculable harm, and as based on generalizations unworthy of an enlightened and progressive age.

The Negro Problems

It is impossible to separate the population of the world accurately by race, since that is no scientific criterion by which to divide races. If we divide the world, however, roughly into African Negroes and Negroids, European whites, and Asiatic and American brown and yellow peoples, we have approximately 150,000,000 Negroes, 500,000,000 whites, and 900,000,000 yellow and brown peoples. Of the 150,000,000 Negroes, 121,000,000 live in Africa, 27,000,000[1] in the new world, and 2,000,000 in Asia.

What is to be the future relation of the Negro race to the rest of the world? The visitor from Altruria might see here no peculiar problem. He would expect the Negro race to develop along the lines of other human races. In Africa his economic and political development would restore and eventually outrun the ancient glories of Egypt, Ethiopia, and Yoruba; overseas the West Indies would become a new and nobler Africa, built in the very pathway of the new highway of commerce between East and West—the real sea route to India; while in the United States a large part of its citizenship (showing for perhaps centuries their dark descent, but nevertheless equal sharers of and contributors to the civilization of the West) would be the descendants of the wretched victims of the seventeenth, eighteenth, and nineteenth century slave trade.

This natural assumption of a stranger finds, however, lodging in the minds of few present-day thinkers. On the contrary, such an outcome is usually dismissed summarily. Most persons have accepted that tacit but clear modern philosophy which assigns to the white race alone the hegemony of the world and assumes that other races, and particularly the Negro race, will either be content to serve the interests of the whites or die out before their all-conquering march. This philosophy is the child of the African slave trade and of the expansion of Europe during the nineteenth century.

The Negro slave trade was the first step in modern world commerce,

From *The Negro* (1915).

followed by the modern theory of colonial expansion. Slaves as an article of commerce were shipped as long as the traffic paid. When the Americas had enough black laborers for their immediate demand, the moral action of the eighteenth century had a chance to make its faint voice heard.

The moral repugnance was powerfully reënforced by the revolt of the slaves in the West Indies and South America, and by the fact that North America early began to regard itself as the seat of advanced ideas in politics, religion, and humanity.

Finally European capital began to find better investments than slave shipping and flew to them. These better investments were the fruit of the new industrial revolution of the nineteenth century, with its factory system; they were also in part the result of the cheapened price of gold and silver, brought about by slavery and the slave trade to the new world. Commodities other than gold, and commodities capable of manufacture and exploitation in Europe out of materials furnishable by America, became enhanced in value; the bottom fell out of the commercial slave trade and its suppression became possible.

The middle of the nineteenth century saw the beginning of the rise of the modern working class. By means of political power the laborers slowly but surely began to demand a larger share in the profiting industry. In the United States their demand bade fair to be halted by the competition of slave labor. The labor vote, therefore, first confined slavery to limits in which it could not live, and when the slave power sought to exceed these territorial limits, it was suddenly and unintentionally abolished.

As the emancipation of millions of dark workers took place in the West Indies, North and South America, and parts of Africa at this time, it was natural to assume that the uplift of this working class lay along the same paths with that of European and American whites. This was the *first* suggested solution of the Negro problem. Consequently these Negroes received partial enfranchisement, the beginnings of education, and some of the elementary rights of wage earners and property holders, while the independence of Liberia and Hayti was recognized. However, long before they were strong enough to assert the rights thus granted or to gather intelligence enough for proper group leadership, the new colonialism of the later nineteenth and twentieth centuries began to dawn. The new colonial theory transferred the reign of commercial privilege and extraordinary profit from the exploitation of the European working class to the exploitation of backward races under the political domination of Europe. For the purpose of carrying out this idea the European and white American working class was practically invited to share in this new exploitation, and particularly were flattered by popular appeals to their inherent superiority to "Dagoes," "Chinks," "Japs," and "Niggers."

This tendency was strengthened by the fact that the new colonial expansion centered in Africa. Thus in 1875 something less than one-tenth of Africa was under nominal European control, but the Franco-Prussian War and the exploration of the Congo led to new and fateful things. Germany desired economic expansion and, being shut out from America by the Monroe Doctrine, turned to Africa. France, humiliated in war, dreamed of an African empire from the Atlantic to the Red Sea. Italy became ambitious for Tripoli and Abyssinia. Great Britain began to take new interest in her African realm, but found herself largely checkmated by the jealousy of all Europe. Portugal sought to make good her ancient claim to the larger part of the whole southern peninsula. It was Leopold of Belgium who started to make the exploration and civilization of Africa an international movement. This project failed, and the Congo Free State became in time simply a Belgian colony. While the project was under discussion, the international scramble for Africa began. As a result the Berlin Conference and subsequent wars and treaties gave Great Britain control of 2,101,411 square miles of African territory, in addition to Egypt and the Egyptian Sudan with 1,600,000 square miles. This includes South Africa, Bechuanaland and Rhodesia, East Africa, Uganda and Zanzibar, Nigeria, and British West Africa. The French hold 4,106,950 square miles, including nearly all North Africa (except Tripoli) west of the Niger valley and Libyan Desert, and touching the Atlantic at four points. To this is added the Island of Madagascar. The Germans have 910,150 square miles, principally in Southeast and Southwest Africa and the Kamerun. The Portuguese retain 787,500 square miles in Southeast and Southwest Africa. The Belgians have 900,000 square miles, while Liberia (43,000 square miles) and Abyssinia (350,000 square miles) are independent. The Italians have about 600,000 square miles and the Spanish less than 100,000 square miles.

This partition of Africa brought revision of the ideas of Negro uplift. Why was it necessary, the European investors argued, to push a continent of black workers along the paths of social uplift by education, trades-unionism, property holding, and the electoral franchise when the workers desired no change, and the rate of European profit would suffer?

There quickly arose then the *second* suggestion for settling the Negro problem. It called for the virtual enslavement of natives in certain industries, as rubber and ivory collecting in the Belgian Congo, cocoa raising in Portuguese Angola, and diamond mining in South Africa. This new slavery or "forced" labor was stoutly defended as a necessary foundation for implanting modern industry in a barbarous land; but its likeness to slavery was too clear and it has been modified, but not wholly abolished.

The *third* attempted solution of the Negro sought the result of the *second* by less direct methods. Negroes in Africa, the West Indies, and America were to be forced to work by land monopoly, taxation, and little or no education. In this way a docile industrial class working for low wages, and not intelligent enough to unite in labor unions, was to be developed. The peonage systems in parts of the United States and the labor systems of many of the African colonies of Great Britain and Germany illustrate this phase of solution.[2] It is also illustrated in many of the West Indian islands where we have a predominant Negro population, and this population freed from slavery and partially enfranchised. Land and capital, however, have for the most part been so managed amd monopolized that the black peasantry have been reduced to straits to earn a living in one of the richest parts of the world. The problem is now going to be intensified when the world's commerce begins to sweep through the Panama Canal.

All these solutions and methods, however, run directly counter to modern philanthropy, and have to be carried on with a certain concealment and half-hypocrisy which is not only distasteful in itself, but always liable to be discovered and exposed by some liberal or religious movement of the masses of men and suddenly overthrown. These solutions are, therefore, gradually merging into a *fourth* solution, which is to-day very popular. This solution says: Negroes differ from whites in their inherent genius and stage of development. Their development must not, therefore, be sought along European lines, but along their own native lines. Consequently the effort is made to-day in British Nigeria, in the French Congo and Sudan, in Uganda and Rhodesia to leave so far as possible the outward structure of native life intact; the king or chief reigns, the popular assemblies meet and act, the native courts adjudicate, and native social and family life and religion prevail. All this, however, is subject to the veto and command of a European magistracy supported by a native army with European officers. The advantage of this method is that on its face it carries no clue to its real working. Indeed it can always point to certain undoubted advantages: the abolition of the slave trade, the suppression of war and feud, the encouragement of peaceful industry. On the other hand, back of practically all these experiments stands the economic motive — the determination to use the organization, the land, and the people, not for their own benefit, but for the benefit of white Europe. For this reason education is seldom encouraged, modern religious ideas are carefully limited, sound political development is sternly frowned upon, and industry is degraded and changed to the demands of European markets. The most ruthless class of white mercantile exploiters is allowed large liberty, if not a free hand, and protected by a concerted attempt to deify white men as such in the eyes of the native and in their own imagination.[3]

White missionary societies are spending perhaps as much as five million dollars a year in Africa and accomplishing much good, but at the same time white merchants are sending at least twenty million dollars' worth of European liquor into Africa each year, and the debauchery of the almost unrestricted rum traffic goes far to neutralize missionary effort.

Under this last mentioned solution of the Negro problems we may put the attempts at the segregation of Negroes and mulattoes in the United States and to some extent in the West Indies. Ostensibly this is "separation" of the races in society, civil rights, etc. In practice it is the subordination of colored people of all grades under white tutelage, and their separation as far as possible from contact with civilization in dwelling place, in education, and in public life.

On the other hand the economic significance of the Negro to-day is tremendous. Black Africa to-day exports annually nearly two hundred million dollars' worth of goods, and its economic development has scarcely begun. The black West Indies export nearly one hundred million dollars' worth of goods; to this must be added the labor value of Negroes in South Africa, Egypt, the West Indies, North, Central, and South America, where the result is blended in the common output of many races. The economic foundation of the Negro problem can easily be seen to be a matter of many hundreds of millions to-day, and ready to rise to the billions to-morrow.

Such figures and facts give some slight idea of the economic meaning of the Negro to-day as a worker and industrial factor. "Tropical Africa and its peoples are being brought more irrevocably every year into the vortex of the economic influences that sway the western world."[4]

What do Negroes themselves think of these their problems and the attitude of the world toward them? First and most significant, they are thinking. There is as yet no great single centralizing of thought or unification of opinion, but there are centers which are growing larger and larger and touching edges. The most significant centers of this new thinking are, perhaps naturally, outside Africa and in America: in the United States and in the West Indies; this is followed by South Africa and West Africa and then, more vaguely, by South America, with faint beginnings in East Central Africa, Nigeria, and the Sudan.

The Pan-African movement when it comes will not, however, be merely a narrow racial propaganda. Already the more far-seeing Negroes sense the coming unities: a unity of the working classes everywhere, a unity of the colored races, a new unity of men. The proposed economic solution of the Negro problem in Africa and America has turned the thoughts of Negroes toward a realization of the fact that the modern white laborer of Europe and America has the key to the serfdom of black folk, in his support of militarism and colonial expansion. He is beginning to say to these workingmen that, so long as black laborers are slaves, white laborers cannot be free. Already there are signs in South Africa and the United States of the beginning of understanding between the two classes.

In a conscious sense of unity among colored races there is to-day only a growing interest. There is slowly arising not only a curiously strong brotherhood of Negro blood throughout the world, but the common cause of the darker races against the intolerable assumptions and insults of Europeans has already found expression. Most men in this world are colored. A belief in humanity means a belief in colored men. The future world will, in all reasonable probability, be what colored men make it. In order for this colored world to come into its heritage, must the earth again be drenched in the blood of fighting, snarling human beasts, or will Reason and Good Will prevail? That such may be true, the character of the Negro race is the best and greatest hope; for in its normal condition it is at once the strongest and gentlest of the races of men: "Semper novi quid ex Africa!"

Notes

1. Sir Harry Johnston estimates 135,000,000 Negroes, of whom 24,591,000 live in America. See *Inter-Racial Problems*, p. 335.
2. The South African natives, in an appeal to the English Parliament, show in an astonishing way the confiscation of their land by the English. They say that in the Union of South Africa 1,250,000 whites own 264,000,000 acres of land, while the 4,500,000 natives have only 21,000,000 acres. On top of this the Union Parliament has passed a law making even the future purchase of land by Negroes illegal save in restricted areas!
3. The traveler Glave writes in the *Century Magazine* (LIII, 913): "Formerly [in the Congo Free State] an ordinary white man was merely called 'bwana' or 'Mzunga'; now the merest insect of a pale face earns the title of 'bwana Mkubwa' [big master]."
4. E. D. Morel, in the *Nineteenth Century*.

The Gift of the Spirit

How the fine sweet spirit of black folk, despite superstition and passion has breathed the soul of humility and forgiveness into the formalism and cant of American religion.

/

Above and beyond all that we have mentioned, perhaps least tangible but just as true, is the peculiar spiritual quality which the Negro has injected into American life and civilization. It is hard to define or characterize it — a certain spiritual joyousness; a sensuous, tropical love of life, in vivid contrast to the cool and cautious New England reason; a slow and dreamful conception of the universe, a drawling and slurring of speech, an intense sensitiveness to spiritual values — all these things and others like to them, tell of the imprint of Africa on Europe in America. There is no gainsaying or explaining away this tremendous influence of the contact of the north and south, of black and white, of Anglo Saxon and Negro.

One way this influence has been brought to bear is through the actual mingling of blood. But this is the smaller cause of Negro influence. Heredity is always stronger through the influence of acts and deeds and imitations than through actual blood descent; and the presence of the Negro in the United States quite apart from the mingling of blood has always strongly influenced the land. We have spoken of its influence in politics, literature and art, but we have yet to speak of that potent influence in another sphere of the world's spiritual activities: religion.

America early became a refuge for religion — a place of mighty spaces and glorious physical and mental freedom where silent men might sit and think quietly of God and his world. Hither out of the blood and dust of war-wrecked Europe with its jealousies, blows, persecutions and fear of words and thought, came Puritans, Anabaptists, Catholics, Quakers, Moravians, Methodists — all

From *The Gift of Black Folk* (1924).

sorts of men and "isms" and sects searching for God and Truth in the lonely bitter wilderness.

Hither too came the Negro. From the first he was the concrete test of that search for Truth, of the strife toward a God, of that body of belief which is the essence of true religion. His presence rent and tore and tried the souls of men. "Away with the slave!" some cried—but where away and why? Was not his body there for work and his soul—what of his soul? Bring hither the slaves of all Africa and let us convert their souls, this is God's good reason for slavery. But convert them to what? to freedom? to emancipation? to being white men? Impossible. Convert them, yes. But let them still be slaves for their own good and ours. This was quibbling and good men felt it, but at least here was a practical path, follow it.

Thus arose the great mission movements to the blacks. The Catholic Church began it and not only were there Negro proselytes but black priests and an order of black monks in Spanish America early in the 16th century. In the middle of the 17th century a Negro freedman and charcoal burner lived to see his son, Francisco Xavier de Luna Victoria, raised to head the Bishopric of Panama where he reigned eight years as the first native Catholic Bishop in America.

In Spanish America and in French America the history of Negro religion is bound up with the history of the Catholic Church. On the other hand in the present territory of the United States with the exception of Maryland and Louisiana organized religion was practically and almost exclusively Protestant and Catholics indeed were often bracketed with Negroes for persecution. They could not marry Protestants at one time in colonial South Carolina; Catholics and Negroes could not appear in court as witnesses in Virginia by the law of 1705; Negroes and Catholics were held to be the cause of the "Negro plot" in New York in 1741.

The work then of the Catholic Church among Negroes began in the United States well into the 19th century and by Negroes themselves. In Baltimore, for instance, in 1829, colored refugees from the French West Indies established a sisterhood and academy and gave an initial endowment of furniture, real estate and some $50,000 in money. In 1842 in New Orleans, four free Negro women gave their wealth to form the Sisters of the Holy Family and this work expanded and grew especially after 1893 when a mulatto, Thomy Lafon, endowed the work with over three quarters of a million dollars, his life savings. Later, in 1896, a colored man, Colonel John McKee of Philadelphia, left a million dollars in real estate to the Catholic Church for colored and white orphans.

Outside of these colored sisterhoods and colored philanthropists, the church hesitated long before it began any systematic proselyting among Negroes. This was because of the comparative weakness of the church in early days and later when the Irish migration strengthened it the new Catholics were thrown into violent economic competition with slaves and free Negroes, and their fight to escape slave competition easily resolved itself into a serious anti-Negro hatred which was back of much of the rioting in Cincinnati, Philadelphia and New York. It was not then until the 20th century that the church began active work by establishing a special mission for Negroes and engaging in it nearly two hundred white priests. This new impetus was caused by the benevolence of Katherine Drexel and the Sisters of the Blessed Sacrament. Notwithstanding all this and since the beginning of the 18th century only six Negroes have been ordained to the Catholic priesthood.

The main question of the conversion of the Negro to Christianity in the United States was therefore the task of the Protestant Church and it was, if the truth must be told, a task which it did not at all relish. The whole situation was fraught with perplexing contradictions: Could Christians be slaves? Could slaves be Christians? Was the object of slavery the Christianizing of the black man, and when the black man was Christianized was the mission of slavery done and ended? Was it possible to make modern Christians of these persons whom the new slavery began to paint as brutes? The English Episcopal Church finally began the work in 1701 through the Society for the Propagation of the Gospel. It had notable officials, the Archbishop of Canterbury being its first president; it worked in America 82 years, accomplishing something but after all not very much, on account of the persistent objection of the masters. The Moravians were more eager and sent missionaries to the Negroes, converting large numbers in the West Indies and some in the United States in the 18th century. Into the new Methodist Church which came to America in 1766, large numbers of Negroes poured from the first, and finally the Baptists in the 18th century had at least one fourth of their membership composed of Negroes; so that in 1800 there were 14,000 black Methodists and some 20,000 black Baptists.[1]

It must not be assumed that this missionary work acted on raw material. Rather it reacted and was itself influenced by a very definite and important body of thought and belief on the part of the Negroes. Religion in the United States was not simply brought to the Negro by the missionaries. To treat it in that way is to miss the essence of the Negro action and reaction upon American religion. We must think of the transplanting of the Negro as transplanting to the United States a certain spiritual entity, and an unbreakable set of world-old beliefs, manners, morals, superstitions and religious observances. The religion of Africa is the universal animism or fetishism of primitive peoples, rising to polytheism and approaching monotheism chiefly, but not wholly, as a result of Christian and Islamic missions. Of fetishism there is much misapprehension. It is not mere senseless degradation. It is a philosophy of life. Among primitive Negroes there can be, as Miss Kingsley reminds us, no such divorce of religion from practical life as is common in civilized lands. Religion is life, and fetish an expression of the practical recognition of dominant forces in which the Negro lives. To him all the world is spirit. Miss Kingsley says: "It is this power of being able logically to account for everything that is, I believe, at the back of the tremendous permanency of fetish in Africa, and the cause of many of the relapses into it by Africans converted to other religions; it is also the explanation of the fact that white men who live in the districts where death and danger are everyday affairs, under a grim pall of boredom, are liable to believe in fetish, though ashamed of so doing. For the African, whose mind has been soaked in fetish during his early and most impressionable years, the voice of fetish is almost irresistible when affliction comes to him."[2]

At first sight it would seem that slavery completely destroyed every vestige of spontaneous social movement among the Negroes; the home had deteriorated; political authority and economic initiative were in the hands of the masters; property, as a social institution, did not exist on the plantation; and, indeed, it is usually assumed by historians and sociologists that every vestige of internal development disappeared, leaving the slaves no means of expression for their common life, thought, and striving. This is not strictly true; the vast power of the priest in the African state still survived; his realm alone — the province of religion and medicine — remained largely unaffected by the plantation system in many important particulars. The Negro priest, therefore, early became an important figure on the plantation and found his function as the interpreter of the supernatural, the comforter of the sorrowing, and as the one who expressed, rudely, but picturesquely, the longing and disappointment and resentment of a stolen people. From such beginnings arose and spread with marvelous rapidity the Negro church, the first distinctively Negro American social institution. It was not at first by any means a Christian Church, but a mere adaptation of those heathen rites which we roughly designate by the term Obe Worship or "Voodooism." Association and missionary effort soon gave these rites a veneer of Christianity, and gradually, after two centuries, the Church became Christian, with a simple Calvinistic creed, but with many of the old customs still clinging to the services. It is this historic fact that the Negro Church today bases itself upon the sole surviving social institution of the African fatherland, that accounts for its extraordinary growth and vitality. We easily forget that in the United States today there is a Church organization for every sixty Negro families. This institution, therefore, naturally assumed many functions which the other harshly suppressed social organs had to surrender; the Church became the center of amusements, of what little spontaneous economic activity remained, of education, and of all social intercourse, of music and art. . . .[3]

Notes

1. Charles C. Jones, *Religious Instruction of the Negroes*, Savannah, 1842.
2. M. H. Kingsley, *West African Studies*.
3. Atlanta University Publications, *The Negro Church*, 1903.

The Black Man Brings
His Gifts

We've got a pretty fine town out here in middle Indiana. We claim fifty thousand inhabitants although the census cheats us out of nearly half. You can't depend on those guys in Washington. The new Pennsylvania station has just gone up and looks big and clean although a bit empty on account of the new anti-loafing ordinance. There is a White Way extending down through the business section which makes us quite gay at night. Of course, we have Rotary, Kiwanis, the Chamber of Commerce and the Federation of Women's Clubs. There are six churches, not counting the colored folks'.

Well, last year somebody suggested we have an America's Making pageant just like New York. You see, we need something to sort of bring us together after the war. We had a lot of Germans here and near-Germans and we had to pull them up pretty stiff. In all, we had seven or eight races or nations, not counting the colored people. We salute the flag and many of us can sing The Star Spangled Banner without books. But we really need Americanization; a sort of wholesome getting together.

So, as I have said, last year the Federation of Women's Clubs started the matter and got a committee appointed. They appointed me and Birdie; Mrs. Cadwalader Lee (who is an awfully aristocratic Southern lady); Bill Graves, who runs the biggest store; the editor of the daily paper and the Methodist preacher, who has the biggest church. They made me secretary but Birdie suggested that we needed an impartial chairman who knew something about the subject, for, says she, "What with the Germans, Poles, Scandinavians and Italians, everybody will claim so much that there'll be nothing left for the real Americans." We met and considered the idea favorably and wrote to the state university. They sent us down a professor with a funny name and any number

From *The Survey* (New York), 53 (March 1, 1925): 655–657, 710.

of degrees. It seems that he taught sociology and "applied ethics," whatever that may be.

"I'll bet he's a Jew," said Birdie as soon as she looked at him. "I've got nothing against Jews but I just don't like them. They're too pushing."

First thing off the bat, this professor, who wore a cloak and spoke exceedingly proper and too low for anybody to hear unless they were listening, asked if the colored people ought not to be represented. That took us a bit by surprise as we hadn't thought of them at all. Mrs. Cadwalader Lee said she thought it might be best to have a small auxiliary colored committee and that she would ask her cook to get one up.

"Well," says I, after we had gotten nicely settled for our first real meeting, "what is the first thing that's gone to making America and who did it?" I had my own mind on music and painting and I know that Birdie is daft on architecture; but before we either of us could speak, Bill Graves grinned and said, "hard work."

The chairman nodded and said, "Quite true, labor."

I didn't know just what to say but I whispered to Birdie that it seemed to me that we ought to stress some of the higher things. The chairman must have heard me because he said that all higher things rested on the foundation of human toil.

"But, whose labor?" asked the editor. "Since we are all descended from working people, isn't labor a sort of common contribution which, as it comes from everybody, need not be counted?"

"I should hardly consent to that statement," said Mrs. Cadwalader Lee, who is said to be descended from a governor and a lord.

"At any rate," said the chairman, "the Negroes were America's first great labor force."

"Negroes!" shrilled Birdie, "but we can't have them!"

"I should think," said Mrs. Cadwalader Lee, softly, "that we might have a very interesting darky scene. Negroes hoeing cotton and that sort of thing." We all were thankful to Mrs. Lee and immediately saw that that would be rather good; Mrs. Lee again said she would consult her cook, a very intelligent and exemplary person.

"Next," I said firmly, "comes music."

"Folk songs," said the Methodist preacher.

"Yes," I continued. "There would be Italian and German and — "

"But I thought this was to be American," said the chairman.

"Sure," I answered, "German-American and Italian-American and so forth."

"There ain't no such animal," says Birdie, but Mrs. Cadwalader Lee reminded us of Foster's work and thought we might have a chorus to sing Old Folks at Home, Old Kentucky Home and Nelly Was a Lady. Here the editor pulled out a book on American folk songs by Krehbiel or some such German name and read an extract. (I had to copy it for the minutes.) It said:

The only considerable body of songs which has come into existence in the territory now compassed by the United States, I might even say in North America, excepting the primitive songs of the Indians (which present an entirely different aspect), are the songs of the former black slaves. In Canada the songs of the people, or that portion of the people that can be said still to sing from impulse, are predominantly French, not only in language but in subject. They were for the greater part transferred to this continent with the bodily integrity which they now possess. Only a small portion show an admixture of Indian elements; but the songs of the black slaves of the South are original and native products. They contain idioms which were transplanted from Africa, but as songs they are the product of American institutions; of the social, political and geographical environment within which their creators were placed in America; of the influences to which they were subjected in America; of the joys, sorrows and experiences which fell to their lot in America.

Nowhere save on the plantations of the South could the emotional life which is essential to the development of true folksong be developed; nowhere else was there the necessary meeting of the spiritual cause and the simple agent and vehicle. The white inhabitants of the continent have never been in the state of cultural ingenuousness which prompts spontaneous emotional utterances in music.

This rather took our breath and the chairman suggested that the auxiliary colored committee might attend to this. Mrs. Cadwalader Lee was very nice about it. (She has such lovely manners and gets her dresses direct from New York.) She said that she was sure it could all be worked out satisfactorily. We would need a number of servants and helpers. Well, under the leadership of that gifted cook, we'd have a cotton-hoeing scene to represent labor and while hoeing they would sing Negro ditties; afterward they could serve the food and clean up.

That was fine, but I didn't propose to be sidetracked.

"But," I says, "we don't want to confine ourselves to folk songs. There is a lot of splendid American music like that of Victor Herbert and Irving Berlin."

The editor grinned. But the chairman was real nice and he mentioned several folks I never heard of — Paine, Buck, Chadwick and DeKoven. And, of course, I know of Nevin and McDowell. Still that editor grinned and said, "Yes, and Harry Burleigh and W. C. Handy and Nathaniel Dett."

Here the preacher spoke up. "I especially like that man, Dett. Our choir sang his Listen to the Lambs last Christmas."

"Oh, yes," said Mrs. Cadwalader Lee, "and Burleigh's Young Warrior was one of the greatest of our war songs."

"I am sure," said the Methodist preacher, "that our choir will be glad to furnish the music."

"But are they colored?" asked the chairman, who had been silent.

"Colored?" we gasped.

"Well, you see, each race was to furnish its own contribution."

"Yes," we chorused, "but this is white American music."

"Not on your life," said the editor, who is awfully slangy. "Of course you know Burleigh and Dett and Handy are all Negroes."

"I think you're mistaken," said Mrs. Cadwalader Lee, getting a bit red in the face.

But sure enough, the chairman said they were and we did not dare dispute him. He even said that Foster's melodies were based on Negro musical themes.

"Well," said the preacher, "I am sure there are no Negroes in town who could sing Listen to the Lambs," and the editor added, "And I hardly think your choir could render The Memphis Blues just as it ought to be." We looked at each other dubiously and I saw right then and there that America's Making had a small chance of being put on in our town. Somebody said that there was a choir in one of the colored churches that could sing this music, but Mrs. Cadwalader Lee reminded us that there would be insuperable difficulties if we tried to bring in obstreperous and high-brow Negroes who demanded social equality. It seems that one of these churches had hired a new social worker — a most objectionable colored person who complained when Mrs. Lee called her by her first name.

"That editor is just lugging the Negroes in," said I to Birdie.

"The Negroes seem to be lugging us in," she replied, and she launched us into architecture. From architecture we went to painting. There were Sargent and Whistler and Abbey. Birdie had seen Tanner's Raising of Lazarus in the Luxembourg and suggested a tableau.

"We might get him to help," said the editor. "He's having an exhibit in New York." We were thrilled, all except Mrs. Lee. "I understand he has Negro blood," she said coldly, "and besides, I do not think much of his work." We dropped that and hurried to inventions.

Here, of course, America is preeminent and we must pick and choose. First the preacher asked what kinds of inventions we ought to stress since America was so very inventive. Bill Graves wanted to stress those which had made big money, while the preacher wanted to emphasize those which had "made for righteousness." Birdie said she was strong for those which were really helpful and the chairman suggested the telephone, things that had helped travel, labor-saving devices, etc.

Well, we named over a number of things and especially stressed the telephone. The editor mentioned Granville Wood as one who had helped to perfect the telephone but we didn't listen. I'm sure he was a Negro. But in spite of all, the chairman spoke up again.

"Shoes," he said.

"Well," said I, "I didn't know we invented shoes. I thought they were pretty common before America was discovered."

"But American shoes are the best in the world," said the editor, and then the chairman told us of the United Shoe Machinery Company and how they made shoes.

"And," he added, "that lasting machine which is at the bottom of their success was invented by a Negro."

"I don't believe it," said Birdie flatly, looking at Mrs. Cadwalader Lee. Mrs. Lee got pale this time.

"Of course," she said, "if you are just going to drag in the Negro by the ears—"

"Still," said the editor, "we are after the truth, ain't we? And it is certainly true that Matzeliger invented the lasting machine and you wouldn't want your sister to marry Matzeliger, now would you?"

"Ain't he dead?" asked Birdie, and Mrs. Cadwalader Lee doubted if we ought to be interested in anything as common as shoes.

"I should think automobiles and locomotives would express our genius better."

"Only, we didn't invent them," said the editor. ▬▬

"But we did invent a method of oiling them while in motion," said the chairman.

"And I'll bet a colored man did that," said Birdie.

"Quite true," answered the chairman. "His name was Elijah McCoy. He is still living in Detroit and I talked with him the other day."

"Might I ask," said Mrs. Cadwalader Lee, looking the chairman full in the face, "if you yourself are of pure white blood?" We all started and we looked the chairman over. He was of dark complexion and his hair was none too straight. He had big black eyes that did not smile much; and yet there couldn't be any doubt about his being white. Wasn't he a professor in the state university and would they hire a colored man no matter how much he knew? The chairman answered.

"I do not know about the purity of my blood although I have usually been called white. Still, one never knows," and he looked solemnly at Mrs. Cadwalader Lee.

Of course, I rushed in, angels being afraid, and cried,

"Dancing — we haven't provided for dancing and we ought to have a lot of that."

"Lovely," says Birdie, "I know a Mexican girl who can do a tango and we could have folk-dancing for the Irish and Scotch."

"The Negroes invented the tango as well as the cake walk and the whole modern dance craze is theirs," said the editor.

This time the preacher saved us. "I'm afraid," said he, "that I could not countenance public dancing. I am aware that our church has changed its traditional attitude somewhat, but I am old-fashioned. If you are to have dancing — " We hastened to reassure him unanimously. We would have no dancing. We dropped it then and there.

Mrs. Lee now spoke up. "It seems to me," she said, "that the real greatness of America lies in her literature. Not only the great writers like Poe and Lanier but in our folk-lore. There are the lovely legends of the mountain whites and, of course, the Uncle Remus tales. I sometimes used to recite them and would not be unwilling to give my services to this pageant."

"Negro dialect, aren't they?" asked the editor, with vast innocence.

"Yes," said Mrs. Lee, "but I am quite familiar with the dialect."

"But oughtn't they to be given by a Negro?" persisted the editor.

"Certainly not; they were written by a white man, Joel Chandler Harris."

"Yes," added the chairman, "he set them down, but the Negroes originated them — they are thoroughly African."

Mrs. Cadwalader Lee actually sniffed. "I am sorry," she said, "but it seems to me that this matter has taken a turn quite different from our original purpose and I'm afraid I may not be able to take part." This would kill the thing, to my mind, but Birdie was not sure.

"Oh, I don't know," she whispered, "she is too high-brow anyway and this thing ought to be a matter of the common people. I don't mind having a few colored people take part so long as they don't want to sit and eat with us; but I do draw the line on Jews."

Well, we took up education next and before we got through, in popped Booker T. Washington. And then came democracy and it looked like everybody had had a hand in that, even the Germans and Italians. The chairman also said that two hundred thousand Negroes had fought for their own liberty in the Civil War and in the war to make the world safe for democracy. But that didn't impress Mrs. Lee or any of the rest of us and we concluded to leave the Negro out of democracy.

"First thing you know you'll have us eating with Negroes," said Birdie, and the chairman said that he'd eaten with Republicans and sinners. I suppose he meant to slur Democrats and Socialists but it was a funny way to do it. Somehow I couldn't just figure out that chairman. I kept watching him.

Then up pops that editor with a lot of notes and papers. "What about exploration?" he asks. Well, we had forgotten that, but naturally the Italians could stage a good stunt with Columbus.

"And the French and Spanish," said Birdie, "only there are none of them in town, thank God!"

"But there are colored folk!" said that chairman. I just gave him a withering look.

"Were they Columbus' cooks?" I asked.

"Probably," said the chairman, "but the one I have in mind discovered New Mexico and Arizona. But I'm afraid," he added slowly, "that we're getting nowhere."

"We've already got there," said Birdie. But the chairman continued: "How could we when we're talking for people and not letting them express themselves?"

"But aren't we the committee?" I asked.

"Yes, and by our own appointment."

"But we represent all the races," I insisted, "except, well — except the Negroes."

"Just so," replied the chairman, "and while I may seem to you to be unduly stressing the work of Negroes, that is simply because they are not represented here. I promise to say nothing further on the matter if you will indulge me a few minutes. In the next room, a colored woman is waiting. She is that social worker at the colored church and she is here by my invitation, I had hoped to have her invited to sit on this committee. As that does not seem possible, may she say just a word?"

He looked at me. I looked at Birdie and Birdie stared at Mrs. Cadwalader Lee. Mrs. Lee arose.

"Certainly — oh, certainly," she said sweetly. "Don't let me interfere. But, of course, you will understand that we Lees must draw the line somewhere," and out she sailed.

I knew the whole thing was dead as a door nail and I was just about to tell Birdie so when in marched that Negro before we'd had a chance to talk about her. She had on a tailor-made gown that cost fifty dollars if a cent, a smart toque and (would you believe it?) she was a graduate of the University of

Chicago! If there's anything I hate it's a college woman. And here was a black one at that. I didn't know just how to treat her so I sort of half turned my shoulder to her and looked out the window. She began with an essay. It had a lot of long words which sounded right even if they weren't. What she seemed to be driving at was this:

Who made this big country? Not the millionaires, the ministers and the "know-alls," but laborers and drudges and slaves. And she said that we had no business to forget this and pretend that we were all descended from the nobility and gentry and college graduates. She even went so far as to say that cranks and prostitutes and plain fools had a hand in making this republic, and that the real glory of America was what it proved as to the possibilities of common-place people and that the hope of the future lay right in these every-day people.

It was the truth and I knew it and so did all of us, but, of course, we didn't dare to let on to each other, much less to her. So I just kept staring out the window and she laid aside her essay and began to talk. She handed to the Negro, music, painting sculpture, drama, dancing, poetry and letters. She named a lot of people I never heard of; and others like Dunbar and Braithwaite and Chesnutt, but I had always thought they were white. She reminded us of Bert Williams and told us of some fellows named Aldridge and Gilpin.

And then she got on our nerves. She said all this writing and doing beautiful things hurt. That it was born of suffering. That sometimes the pain blurred the message, but that the blood and crying lurked beneath. And at last she took out a little thin black book and read.

She read about this country not belonging to white folks any more than it did to black folks and that the black folks got here before the pilgrims. I couldn't help stepping on Birdie's toes because she says her people came in on some boat named after a flower so long ago she's forgot their names. The black girl said that the story of the Negro could be found on every page of the story of America. This made me sick and I turned and glared right at her. But she looked right through me and went on. She said Negroes had been soldiers in all our wars, had nursed the babies, cooked the food and sung and danced besides working so hard that "working like a nigger" was about the hardest work you could picture.

And she asked us if America could have been America without Negroes.

She had me up a tree, I must admit. And I reckon the rest felt as I did — all except that editor.

The chairman looked at us with owl-like eyes; then he shoved a paper at me and read it aloud as he did:

"*Timeo Nigros et dona ferentes.*"

Nobody knows what he meant and nobody gave him the satisfaction of asking.

Well, we just sat and stared until she left. Then we went on talking but we didn't touch the real question; and that was, could we have America's Making without Mrs. Cadwalader Lee and with the Negroes?

We couldn't make up our minds and before we had courage to say so openly we went smash on religion.

We might possibly have had some sort of an America's Making pageant if we hadn't discussed religion. You see, the editor who is downright malicious and hates the Federation of Women's Clubs because they start things, got us all wrong by trying to get a definition of religion. He was strong on meekness and humility and turning the other cheek and that sort of thing and I know he didn't mean a word of it.

"I suppose," said Birdie, "that you'll be saying that the Negroes have given us all our religion because they're cowards and allowed themselves to be slaves and take insult today meekly."

"I must admit," said the preacher, "that if the meek inherit the earth, the American Negro will get a large share."

"But will the meek inherit the earth?" I asked.

"I think so," said the chairman calmly.

Birdie jumped up and reached for her cloak. "I believe you're a Jew and a pacifist," she said.

"I am both," he answered.

"And I suppose," said I, getting my hat on straight, "that when somebody slaps you over, you turn the other cheek."

"I did," said he.

"Well, you're a fool," I answered, reaching for my coat.

And Birdie yelled, "And what did they do to you after you turned the other cheek? Answer me that?"

"They crucified me," said the chairman.

The Negro College

It has been said many times that a Negro University is nothing more and nothing less than a university. Quite recently one of the great leaders of education in the United States, Abraham Flexner, said something of that sort concerning Howard. As President of the Board of Trustees, he said he was seeking to build not a Negro university, but a University. And by those words he brought again before our eyes the ideal of a great institution of learning which becomes a center of universal culture. With all good will toward them that say such words — it is the object of this paper to insist that there can be no college for Negroes which is not a Negro college and that while an American Negro university, just like a German or Swiss university may rightly aspire to a universal culture unhampered by limitations of race and culture, yet it must start on the earth where we sit and not in the skies whither we aspire. May I develop this thought.

In the first place, we have got to remember that here in America, in the year 1933, we have a situation which cannot be ignored. There was a time when it seemed as though we might best attack the Negro problem by ignoring its most unpleasant features. It was not and is not yet in good taste to speak generally about certain facts which characterize our situation in America. We are politically hamstrung. We have the greatest difficulty in getting suitable and remunerative work. Our education is more and more not only being confined to our own schools but to a segregated public school system far below the average of the nation with one-third of our children continuously out of school. And above all, and this we like least to mention, we suffer social ostracism which is so deadening and discouraging that we are compelled either to lie about it or to turn our faces to the red flag of revolution. It consists of studied and repeated and emphasized public insult of the sort which during all the long history of the world has led men to kill or be killed. And in the full face of any effort which any black man may make to escape this ostracism for

From *The Crisis*, August 1933.

himself, stands this flaming sword of racial doctrine which will distract his effort and energy if it does not lead him to spiritual suicide.

We boast and have right to boast of our accomplishment between the days that I studied here and this forty-fifth anniversary of my graduation. It is a calm appraisal of fact to say that the history of modern civilization cannot surpass if it can parallel the advance of American Negroes in every essential line of culture in these years. And yet, when we have said this we must have the common courage honestly to admit that every step we have made forward has been greeted by a step backward on the part of the American public in caste intolerance, mob law, and racial hatred.

I need but remind you that when I graduated from Fisk there was no "Jim Crow" car in Tennessee and I saw Hunter of '89 once sweep a brakeman aside at the Union Station and escort a crowd of Fisk students into the first-class seats for which they had paid. There was no legal disfranchisement and a black Fiskite sat in the Legislature; and while the Chancellor of the Vanderbilt University had annually to be reintroduced to the President of Fisk, yet no white Southern group presumed to dictate the internal social life of this institution.

Manifestly with all that can be said, pro and con, and in extenuation, and by way of excuse and hope, this is the situation and we know it. There is no human way by which these facts can be ignored. We cannot do our daily work, sing a song or write a book or carry on a university and act as though these things were not.

If this is true, then no matter how much we may dislike the statement, the American Negro problem is and must be the center of the Negro American university. It has got to be. You are teaching Negroes. There is no use pretending that you are teaching Chinese or that you are teaching white Americans or that you are teaching citizens of the world. You are teaching American Negroes in 1933, and they are the subjects of a caste system in the Republic of the United States of America and their life problem is primarily this problem of caste.

Upon these foundations, therefore, your university must start and build. Nor is the thing so entirely unusual or unheard of as it sounds. A university in Spain is not simply a university. It is a Spanish university. It is a university located in Spain. It uses the Spanish language. It starts with Spanish history and makes conditions in Spain the starting point of its teaching. Its education is for Spaniards—not for them as they may be or ought to be, but as they are with their present problems and disadvantages and opportunities.

In other words, the Spanish university is founded and grounded in Spain, just as surely as a French university is French. There are some people who have difficulty in apprehending this very clear truth. They assume, for instance, that the French university is in a singular sense universal, and is based on a comprehension and inclusion of all mankind and of their problems. But it is not so, and the assumption that it is arises simply because so much of French culture has been built into universal civilization. A French university is founded in France; it uses the French language and assumes a knowledge of French history. The present problems of the French people are its major problems and it becomes universal only so far as other peoples of the world comprehend and are at one with France in its mighty and beautiful history.

In the same way, a Negro university in the United States of America begins with Negroes. It uses that variety of the English idiom which they understand; and above all, it is founded or it should be founded on a knowledge of the history of their people in Africa and in the United States, and their present condition. Without whitewashing or translating wish into fact, it begins with that; and then it asks how shall these young men and women be trained to earn a living and live a life under the circumstances in which they find themselves or with such changing of those circumstances as time and work and determination will permit.

Is this statement of the field of a Negro university a denial of aspiration or a change from older ideals? I do not think it is, although I admit in my own mind some change of thought and modification of method. The system of learning which bases itself upon the actual condition of certain classes and groups of human beings is tempted to suppress a minor premise of fatal menace. It proposes that the knowledge given and the methods pursued in such institutions of learning shall be for the definite object of perpetuating present conditions or of leaving their amelioration in the hands of and at the initiative of other forces and other folk. This was the great criticism that those of us who fought for higher education of Negroes thirty years ago, brought against the industrial school.

The industrial school founded itself and rightly upon the actual situation of American Negroes and said: "What can be done to change this situation?" And its answer was: "A training in technique and method such as would incorporate the disadvantaged group into the industrial organization of the country," and in that organization the leaders of the Negro had perfect faith. Since that day the industrial machine has cracked and groaned. Its technique has changed faster than any school could teach; the relations of capital and labor have increased in complication and it has become so clear that Negro poverty is not primarily caused by ignorance of technical knowledge that the industrial school has almost surrendered its program.

In opposition to that, the opponents of college training in those earlier years said: "What black men need is the broader and more universal training so that they can apply the general principle of knowledge to the particular circumstances of their condition."

Here again was the indubitable truth but incomplete truth. The technical problem lay in the method of teaching this broader and more universal truth and here just as in the industrial program, we must start where we are and not where we wish to be.

As I said a few years ago at Howard University, both these positions had thus something of truth and right. Because of the peculiar economic situation in our country the program of the industrial school came to grief first and has practically been given up. Starting even though we may with the actual condition of the Negro peasant and artisan, we cannot ameliorate his condition simply by learning a trade which is the technique of a passing era. More vision and knowledge are needed than that. But on the other hand, while the Negro college of a generation ago set down a defensible and true program of applying knowledge to facts, it unfortunately could not completely carry it out, and it did not carry it out, because the one thing that the industrial philosophy gave to education, the Negro college did not take and that was that the university education of black men in the United States must be grounded in the condition and work of those black men!

On the other hand, it would be of course idiotic to say, as the former industrial philosophy almost said, that so far as most black men are concerned education must stop with this. No, starting with present conditions and using the facts and the knowledge of the present situation of American Negroes, the Negro university expands toward the possession and the conquest of all knowledge. It seeks from a beginning of the history of the Negro in America and in Africa to interpret all history; from a beginning of social development among Negro slaves and freedmen in America and Negro tribes and kingdoms in Africa, to interpret and understand the social development of all mankind in all ages. It seeks to reach modern science of matter and life from the surroundings and habits and aptitudes of American Negroes and thus lead up to understanding of life and matter in the universe.

And this is a different program than a similar function would be in a white university or in a Russian university or in an English university, because it starts from a different point. It is a matter of beginnings and integrations of one group which sweep instinctive knowledge and inheritance and current reactions into a universal world of science, sociology, and art. In no other way can the American Negro college function. It cannot begin with history and lead to Negro history. It cannot start with sociology and lead to Negro sociology.

Why was it that the Renaissance of literature which began among Negroes ten years ago has never taken real and lasting root? It was because it was a transplanted and exotic thing. It was a literature written for the benefit of white people and at the behest of white readers, and starting out privately from the white point of view. It never had a real Negro constituency and it did not grow out of the inmost heart and frank experience of Negroes; on such an artificial basis no real literature can grow.

On the other hand, if starting in a great Negro university you have knowledge, beginning with the particular, and going out to universal comprehension and unhampered expression, you are going to begin to realize for the American Negro the full life which is denied him now. And then after that comes a realization of the older object of our college — to bring this universal culture down and apply it to the individual life and individual conditions of living Negroes.

The university must become not simply a center of knowledge but a center of applied knowledge and guide of action. And this is all the more necessary now since we easily see that planned action especially in economic life, is going to be the watchword of civilization.

If the college does not thus root itself in the group life and afterward apply its knowledge and culture to actual living, other social organs must replace the college in this function. A strong, intelligent family life may adjust the student to higher culture; and, too, a social clan may receive the graduate and induct him into life. This has happened and is happening among a minority of privileged people. But it costs society a fatal price. It tends to hinder progress and hamper change; it makes education propaganda for things as they are. It leaves the mass of those without family training and without social standing misfits and rebels who despite their education are uneducated in its meaning and application. The only college which stands for the progress of all, mass as well as aristocracy, functions in root and blossom as well as in the overshadowing and heaven-filling tree. No system of learning — no university can be universal before it is German, French, Negro. Grounded in inexorable fact and condition, in Poland, Italy, or elsewhere, it may seek the universal and haply it may find it — and finding it, bring it down to earth and us.

We have imbibed from the surrounding white world a childish idea of progress. Progress means bigger and better results always and forever. But there is no such rule of life. In six thousand years of human culture, the losses and retrogressions have been enormous. We have no assurance this twentieth century civilization will survive. We do not know that American Negroes will survive. There are sinister signs about us, antecedent to and unconnected with the Great Depression. The organized might of industry North and South is relegating the Negro to the edge of survival and using him as a labor reservoir on starvation wage. No secure professional class, no science, literature, nor art can live on such a subsoil. It is an insistent, deep-throated cry for rescue, guidance, and organized advance that greets the black leader today, and the college that trains him has got to let him know at least as much about the great black miners' strike in Alabama as about the age of Pericles.

We are on the threshold of a new era. Let us not deceive ourselves with outworn ideals of wealth and servants and luxuries, reared on a foundation of ignorance, starvation, and want. Instinctively, we have absorbed these ideals from our twisted white American environment. This new economic planning is not for us unless we do it. Unless the American Negro today, led by trained university men of broad vision, sits down to work out by economics and mathematics, by physics and chemistry, by history and sociology, exactly how and where he is to earn a living and how he is to establish a reasonable Life in the United States or elsewhere — unless this is done, the university has missed its field and function and the American Negro is doomed to be a suppressed and inferior caste in the United States for incalculable time.

Here, then, is a job for the American Negro university. It cannot be successfully ignored or dodged without the growing menace of disaster. I lay the problem before you as one which you must not ignore.

To carry out this plan, two things and only two things are necessary — teachers and students. Buildings and endowments may help, but they are not indispensable. It is necessary first to have teachers who comprehend this program and know how to make it live among their students. This is calling for a good deal, because it asks that teachers teach that which they have learned in no American school and which they never will learn until we have a Negro university of the sort that I am envisioning. No teacher, black or white, who comes to a university like Fisk, filled simply with general ideas of human culture or general knowledge of disembodied science, is going to make a university of this school. Because a university is made of human beings, learning of the things they do not know from the things they do know in their own lives.

And secondly, we must have students. They must be chosen for their ability to learn. There is always the temptation to assume that the children of the privileged classes — the rich, the noble, the white — are those who can best take education. One has but to express this to realize its utter futility. But perhaps the most dangerous thing among us is for us, without thought, to imitate the white world and assume that we can choose students at Fisk because of the amount of money which their parents have happened to get hold of. That basis of selection is going to give us an extraordinary aggregation. We want, by the nicest methods possible, to seek out the talented and the gifted among our constituency, quite regardless of their wealth or position, and to fill this university and similar institutions with persons who have got brains enough to take fullest advantage of what the university offers. There is no other way. With teachers who know what they are teaching and whom they

73

are teaching, and the life that surrounds both the knowledge and the knower, and with students who have the capacity and the will to absorb this knowledge, we can build the sort of Negro university which will emancipate not simply the black folk of the United States, but those white folk who in their effort to suppress Negroes have killed their own culture.

Men in their desperate effort to replace equality with caste and to build inordinate wealth on a foundation of abject poverty have succeeded in killing democracy, art, and religion.

Only a universal system of learning rooted in the will and condition of the masses and blossoming from that manure up toward the stars is worth the name. Once built it can only grow as it brings down sunlight and starshine and impregnates the mud.

The chief obstacle in this rich land endowed with every national resource and with the abilities of a hundred different peoples — the chief and only obstacle to the coming of that kingdom of economic equality which is the only logical end of work, is the determination of the white world to keep the black world poor and make themselves rich. The disaster which this selfish and shortsighted policy has brought lies at the bottom of this present depression, and too, its cure lies beside it. Your clear vision of a world without wealth, of capital without profit, of income based on work alone, is the path out not only for you but for all men.

Is not this a program of segregation, emphasis of race, and particularism as against national unity and universal humanity? It is and it is not by choice but by force; you do not get humanity by wishing it nor do you become American citizens simply because you want to. A Negro university, from its high ground of unfaltering facing of the truth, from its unblinking stare at hard facts does not advocate segregation by race; it simply accepts the bald fact that we are segregated, apart, hammered into a separate unity by spiritual intolerance and legal sanction backed by mob law, and that this separation is growing in strength and fixation; that it is worse today than a half century ago and that no character, address, culture, or desert is going to change it in our day or for centuries to come. Recognizing this brute fact, groups of cultured, trained and devoted men gathering in great institutions of learning proceed to ask, What are we going to do about it? It is silly to ignore the gloss of truth; it is idiotic to proceed as though we were white or yellow, English or Russian. Here we stand. We are American Negroes. It is beside the point to ask whether we form a real race. Biologically we are mingled of all conceivable elements, but race is psychology, not biology; and psychologically we are a unified race with one history, one red memory, and one revolt. It is not ours to argue whether we will be segregated or whether we ought to be a caste. We are segregated; we are a caste. This is our given and at present unalterable fact.

Our problem is how far and in what way can we consciously and scientifically guide our future so as to ensure our physical survival, our spiritual freedom and our social growth? Either we do this or we die. There is no alternative. If America proposed the murder of this group, its moral descent into imbecility and crime and its utter loss of manhood, self-assertion, and courage, the sooner we realize this the better. By that great line of McKay:

"If we must die, let it not be like hogs."

But the alternative of not dying like hogs is not that of dying or killing like snarling dogs. It is rather conquering the world by thought and brain and plan; by expression and organized cultural ideals. Therefore let us not beat futile wings in impotent frenzy, but carefully plan and guide our segregated life, organize in industry and politics to protect it and expand it and above all to give it unhampered spiritual expression in art and literature. It is the counsel of fear and cowardice to say this cannot be done. What must be can be and it is only a question of science and sacrifice to bring the great consummation.

What that will be, no one knows. It may be a great physical segregation of the world along the color line; it may be an economic rebirth which ensures spiritual and group integrity amid physical diversity. It may be utter annihilation of class and race and color barriers in one ultimate mankind, differentiated by talent, susceptibility and gift—but any of these ends are matters of long centuries and not years. We live in years, swift-flying, transient years. We hold the possible future in our hands but not by wish and will, only by thought, plan, knowledge, and organization. If the college can pour into the coming age an American Negro who knows himself and his plight and how to protect himself and fight race prejudice, then the world of our dream will come and not otherwise.

On Being Ashamed of Oneself

An Essay on Race Pride

My grandfather left a passage in his diary expressing his indignation at receiving an invitation to a "Negro" picnic. Alexander Du Bois, born in the Bahamas, son of Dr. James Du Bois of the well-known Du Bois family of Poughkeepsie, N.Y., had been trained as a gentleman in the Cheshire School of Connecticut, and the implications of a Negro picnic were anathema to his fastidious soul. It meant close association with poverty, ignorance and suppressed and disadvantaged people, dirty and with bad manners.

This was in 1856. Seventy years later. Marcus Garvey discovered that a black skin was in itself a sort of patent to nobility, and that Negroes ought to be proud of themselves and their ancestors, for the same or analogous reasons that made white folk feel superior.

Thus, within the space of three-fourths of a century, the pendulum has swung between race pride and race suicide, between attempts to build up a racial ethos and attempts to escape from ourselves. In the years between emancipation and 1900, the theory of escape was dominant. We were, by birth, law and training, American citizens. We were going to escape into the mass of Americans in the same way that the Irish and Scandinavians and even the Italians were beginning to disappear. The process was going to be slower on account of the badge of color; but then, after all, it was not so much the matter of physical assimilation as of spiritual and psychic amalgamation with the American people.

For this reason, we must oppose all segregation and all racial patriotism; we must salute the American flag and sing "Our Country 'Tis of Thee" with devotion and fervor, and we must fight for our rights with a long and carefully planned campaign; uniting for this purpose with all sympathetic people, colored and white.

From *The Crisis*, September 1933.

This is still the dominant philosophy of most American Negroes and it is back of the objection to even using a special designation like "Negro" or even "Afro-American" or any such term.

But there are certain practical difficulties connected with this program which are becoming more and more clear today. First of all comes the fact that we are still ashamed of ourselves and are thus estopped from valid objection when white folks are ashamed to call us human. The reasons of course, are not as emphatic as they were in the case of my grandfather. I remember a colored man, now ex-patriate, who made this discovery in my company, some twenty-five years ago. He was a handsome burning brown, tall, straight and well-educated, and he occupied a position which he had won, across and in spite of the color line. He did not believe in Negroes, for himself or his family, and he planned elaborately to escape the trammels of race. Yet, he had responded to a call for a meeting of colored folk which touched his interests, and he came. He found men of his own caliber and training; he found men charming and companionable. He was thoroughly delighted. I know that never before, or I doubt if ever since, he had been in such congenial company. He could not help mentioning his joy continually and reiterating it.

All colored folk had gone through the same experience, for more and more largely in the last twenty-five years, colored America has discovered itself; has discovered groups of people, association with whom is a poignant joy and despite their ideal of American assimilation, in more and more cases and with more and more determined object they seek each other.

That involves, however, a drawing of class lines inside the Negro race, and it means the emergence of a certain social aristocracy, who by reasons of looks and means the emergence of a certain social aristocracy, who by reasons of looks and income, education and contact, form the sort of upper social group which the world has long known and helped to manufacture and preserve. The early basis of this Negro group was simply color and a bald imitation of the white environment. Later, it tended, more and more, to be based on wealth and still more recently on education and social position.

This leaves a mass of untrained and uncultured colored folk and even of trained but ill-mannered people and groups of impoverished workers of whom this upper class of colored Americans are ashamed. They are ashamed both directly and indirectly, just as any richer or better sustained group in a nation is ashamed of those less fortunate and withdraws its skirts from touching them. But more than that, because the upper colored group is desperately afraid of being represented before American whites by this lower group, or being mistaken for them, or being treated as though they were part of it, they are pushed to the extreme of effort to avoid contact with the poorest classes of

Negroes. This exaggerates, at once, the secret shame of being identified with such people and the anomaly of insisting that the physical characteristics of these folk which the upper class shares, are not the stigmata of degradation.

When, therefore, in offense or defense, the leading group of Negroes must make common cause with the masses of their own race, the embarrassment or hesitation becomes apparent. They are embarrassed and indignant because an educated man should be treated as a Negro, and that no Negroes receive credit for social standing. They are ashamed and embarrassed because of the compulsion of being classed with a mass of people over whom they have no real control and whose action they can influence only with difficulty and compromise and with every risk of defeat.

Especially is all natural control over this group difficult — I mean control of law and police, of economic power, of guiding standards and ideals, of news propaganda. On this comes even greater difficulty because of the incompatibility of any action which looks toward racial integrity and race action with previous ideals. What are we really aiming at? The building of a new nation or the integration of a new group into an old nation? The latter has long been our ideal. Must it be changed? Should it be changed? If we seek new group loyalty, new pride of race, new racial integrity — how, where and by what method shall these things be attained? A new plan must be built up. It cannot be the mere rhodomontade and fatuous propaganda on which Garveyism was based. It has got to be far-sighted planning. It will involve increased segregation and perhaps migration. It will be pounced upon and aided and encouraged by every "nigger-hater" in the land.

Moreover, in further comment on all this, it may be pointed out that this is not the day for the experiment of new nations or the emphasis of racial lines. This is, or at least we thought it was, the day of the Inter-nation, of Humanity, and the disappearance of "race" from our vocabulary. Are we American Negroes seeking to move against, or into the face of this fine philosophy? Here then is the real problem, the real new dilemma between rights of American citizens and racial pride, which faces American Negroes today and which is not always or often clearly faced.

The situation is this: America, in denying equality of rights, of employment and social recognition to American Negroes, has said in the past that the Negro was so far below the average nation in social position, that he could not be recognized until he had developed further. In the answer to this, the Negro has eliminated five-sixths of his illiteracy according to official figures, and greatly increased the number of colored persons who have received education of the higher sort. They still are poor with a large number of delinquents and dependents. Nevertheless, their average situation in this respect has been greatly improved and, on the other hand, the emergence and accomplishment of colored men of ability have been undoubted. Notwithstanding this, the Negro is still a group apart, with almost no social recognition, subject to insult and discrimination, with income and wage far below the average of the nation and the most deliberately exploited industrial class in America. Even trained Negroes have increasing difficulty in making a living sufficient to sustain a civilized standard of life. Particularly in the recent vast economic changes, color discrimination as it now goes on, is going to make it increasingly difficult for the Negro to remain an integral part of the industrial machine or to increase his participation in accordance with his ability.

The integration of industry is making it more and more possible for executives to exercise their judgment in choosing for key positions persons who can guide the industrial machine, and the exclusion of persons from such positions merely on the basis of race and color or even Negro descent is a widely recognized and easily defended prerogative. All that is necessary for any Christian American gentleman of high position and wide power to say in denying place and promotion to an eligible candidate is: "He is of Negro descent." The answer and excuse are final and all but universally accepted. For this reason, the Negro's opportunity in State directed industry and his opportunity in the great private organization of industry if not actually growing less, is certainly much smaller than his growth in education and ability. Either the industry of the nation in the future is to be conducted by private trusts or by government control. There seems in both to be little or no chance of advancement for the Negro worker, the educated artisan and the educated leader.

On the other hand, organized labor is giving Negroes less recognition today than ever. It has practically excluded them from all the higher lines of skilled work, on railroads, in machine-shops, in manufacture and in the basic industries. In agriculture, where the Negro has theoretically the largest opportunity, he is excluded from successful participation, not only by conditions common to all farmers, but by special conditions due to lynching, lawlessness, disfranchisement and social degradation.

Facing these indisputable facts, there is on the part of the leaders of public opinion in America no effective response to our agitation or organized propaganda. Our advance in the last quarter century has been in segregated, racially integrated institutions and efforts and not in effective entrance into American national life. In Negro churches, Negro schools, Negro colleges, Negro business and Negro art and literature our advance has been determined and inspiring; but in industry, general professional careers and national life, we have fought battle after battle and lost more often than we have won. There seems no hope that America in our day will yield in its color or race hatred any substantial ground and we have no physical nor economic power, nor any alliance with other social or economic classes that will force compliance with decent civilized ideals in Church, State, industry or art.

The next step, then, is certainly one on the part of the Negro and it involves group action. It involves the organization of intelligent and earnest people of Negro descent for their preservation and advancement in America, in the West Indies and in Africa; and no sentimental distaste for racial or national unity can be allowed to hold them back from a step which sheer necessity demands.

A new organized group action along economic lines, guided by intelligence and with the express object of making it possible for Negroes to earn a better living and, therefore, more effectively to support agencies for social uplift, is without the slightest doubt the next step. It will involve no opposition from white America because they do not believe we can accomplish it. They expect always to be able to crush, insult, ignore and exploit 12,000,000 individual Negroes without intelligent organized opposition. This organization is going to involve deliberate propaganda for race pride. That is, it is going to start out by convincing American Negroes that there is no reason for their being ashamed of themselves; that their record is one which should make them proud; that their history in Africa and the world is a history of effort, success and trial, comparable with that of any other people.

Such measured statements can, and will be exaggerated. There will be those who will want to say that the black race is the first and greatest of races, that its accomplishments are most extraordinary, that its desert is most obvious and its mistakes negligible. This is the kind of talk we hear from people with the superiority complex among the white and the yellow races.

We cannot entirely escape it, since it is just as true, and just as false as such statements among other races; but we can use intelligence in modifying and restraining it. We can refuse deliberately to lie about our history, while at the same time taking just pride in Nefertari, Askia, Moshesh, Toussaint and Frederick Douglass, and testing and encouraging belief in our own ability by organized economic and social action.

There is no other way; let us not be deceived. American Negroes will be beaten into submission and degradation if they merely wait unorganized to find some place voluntarily given them in the new reconstruction of the economic world. They must themselves force their race into the new economic set-up and bring with them the millions of West Indians and Africans by peaceful organization for normative action or else drift into greater poverty, greater crime, greater helplessness until there is no resort but the last red alternative of revolt, revenge and war.

The Present Plight of the German Jew

There has been no tragedy in modern times equal in its awful effects to the fight on the Jew in Germany. It is an attack on civilization, comparable only to such horrors as the Spanish Inquisition and the African slave trade. It has set civilization back a hundred years, and in particular has it made the settlement and understanding of race problems more difficult and more doubtful. It is widely believed by many that the Jewish problem in Germany was episodic, and is already passing. Visitors to the Olympic Games are apt to have gotten that impression. They saw no Jewish oppression. Just as Northern visitors to Mississippi see no Negro oppression.

This conclusion is largely based on a knowledge of the essential character of the German people. They are a kindly folk, good-hearted, hating oppression, widely sympathetic with suffering, and filled with longing ideals for all mankind. This is true. I know no folk in Europe of whom this characterization is truer. But one must not forget that the active German folk today is the National Socialist Party, under Adolf Hitler, his coadjutors and backers. And that they set the unquestioned and today unquestionable policy of Germany. An integral part of that policy, just as prominent now as earlier and perhaps growing in prominence, is world war on Jews. The proof of this is incontrovertible, and must comfort all those in any part of the world who depend on race hate as the salvation of men.

Adolf Hitler hardly ever makes a speech today — and his speeches reach every corner of Germany, by radio, newspaper, placard, movie and public announcement — without belittling, blaming or cursing Jews. From my window as I write I see a great red poster, seven feet high, asking the German people to contribute to winter relief of the poor, so that Germany will not sink to the level of the "Jewish-Bolshevist countries of the rest of the world." At

From the *Pittsburgh Courier*, December 19, 1936.

Nuremberg recently he accused the "foreign Jewish element" as causing the rotting of the Aryan world. His propaganda minister was more insulting, and said that the whole oppression of Germany by the world was caused by Jewish emigrants. Every misfortune of the world is in whole or in part blamed on Jews — the Spanish rebellion, the obstruction to world trade, etc. One finds cases in the papers: Jews jailed for sex relations with German women; a marriage disallowed because a Jewish justice of the peace witnessed it; Masons excluded from office in the National Socialist Party, because Jews are Masons; advertisements excluding Jews; the total disfranchisement of all Jews; deprivation of civil rights and inability to remain or become German citizens; limited rights of education, and narrowly limited right to work in trades, professions and the civil service; the threat of boycott, loss of work and even mob violence, for any German who trades with a Jew; and, above all, the continued circulation of Julius Streicher's *Stuermer*, the most shameless, lying advocate of race hate in the world, not excluding Florida. It could not sell a copy without Hitler's consent.

Japanese Colonialism

I brush aside as immaterial the question as to whether Manchoukuo is an independent state or a colony of Japan. The main question for me is: What is Japan doing for the people of Manchuria and how is she doing it? Is she building up a caste of Superiors and Inferiors? Is she reducing the mass of the people to slavery and poverty? Is she stealing the land and monopolizing the natural resources? Are the people of Manchuria happier or more miserable for the presence of this foreign power on their soil? I have been in Manchuria only a week. But in that time I have seen its borders north, west and south; its capital and their chief cities and many towns; I have walked the streets night and day; I have talked with officials, visited industries and read reports. I came prepared to compare this colonial situation with colonies in Africa and the West Indies, under white European control. I have come to the firm conclusion that in no colony that I have seen or read of is there such clear evidence of

(1) Absence of racial or color caste;
(2) Impartial law and order;
(3) Public control of private capital for the general welfare;
(4) Services for health, education, city-planning, housing, consumers' co-operation and other social ends;
(5) The incorporation of the natives into the administration of government and social readjustment.

There is undoubtedly much still to be done in all these lines, but the amount already accomplished in four years is nothing less than marvelous. The people appear happy, and there is no unemployment. There is public peace and order. A lynching in Manchoukuo would be unthinkable. There are public services to improve crops, market them and increase their

From the *Pittsburgh Courier*, February 13, 1937.

prices. Manchoukuans are in the police force and the schools and public services. I could see nothing that savored of caste: they separate schools for Manchoukuans and Japanese. But this is based largely, if not wholly, on the fact that one people speak Chinese, and there is no separation in the higher schools. The Japanese hold no absolute monopoly of the offices of the state. The new housing and new cities take account of the Chinese as well as the Japanese. There has been private investment of capital on a considerable scale; but the railroads are partially owned by the state; electricity, water, gas, telegraph and telephone are public services. The largest open cut coal mine in the world is in Manchuria: these mines send out 23,000 thousand tons of semibituminous coal in a day; they manufacture coke and sulphuric acid and 24,000 tons of gasoline; they employ 30,000 miners; they have schools, library, hospital, water, sewage and parks. Electricity for a large part of Manchuria is made here — a total of 130,000 kilowatts. Yet all this is not only half owned by the government, but the private employer is under strict government control and regulation. This does not mean that the government of Manchoukuo is controlling capital for the benefit of the workers. But neither, so far as that is concerned, is Japan. There is, however, no apparent discrimination between motherland and colony in this respect. Nowhere else in the world, to my knowledge, is this true. And why? Because Japanese and Manchoukuans are so nearly related in race that there is nor can be no race prejudice. Ergo: no nation should rule a colony whose people they cannot conceive as Equals.

Tomorrow I leave Manchoukuo after a stay marked by courtesy, sympathy and hospitality. Today for four hours I have sat in conference with citizens, explaining by means of an interpreter the intricacies of the Negro problem. I was driven to Port Arthur and entertained at lunch and later invited to dinner. Graduates of several American universities were present. Tonight the American consul called.

Shanghai

Shanghai is an epitome of the racial strife, economic struggle, the human paradox of modern life. Here is the greatest city of the largest nation on earth, with the larger part of it owned, governed and policed by foreign white nations; with Europe largely controlling its capital, commerce, mines, rivers and manufactures; with a vast welter of the hardest working class in the world paid less than an average of 25 cents a day; with a glittering modern life of skyscrapers, beautiful hotels, theaters and night clubs. In this city of nations are 19,000 Japanese, 11,000 British, 10,000 Russians, 4,000 Americans and 10,000 other foreigners, living in the midst of 3,000,000 Chinese. The city is divided openly by nations; foreign troops parade its streets; foreign warships sit calmly in her gates; foreigners tell this city what it may and may not do. And yet matters are not as bad as they once were: foreigners now acknowledge that Chinese have some rights in China. It is not common now to kick a coolie or throw a rickshaw's fare on the ground. But I saw last night a little white boy of perhaps four years order three Chinese out of his imperial way on the sidewalk of the Bund, and they meekly obeyed: it looked quite like Mississippi. And, too, I met a "missionary" from Mississippi teaching in the Baptist University of Shanghai — I mean, a white one!

From the *Pittsburgh Courier*, February 27, 1937.

Japan, Color, and Afro-Americans

Every American Negro has been unhappy over the war with Japan because it is a war between nations of different colors, between Europe and Asia. And because we cannot help but believe that the fundamental impulse back of this war was, on the one hand, the century-old determination of Europe to dominate the yellow peoples for the benefit of the white; and on the other hand, the resentment of Asiatics at being considered and treated as inferior to Europeans.

This we see as the basic pattern; but it would not by any means excuse in our minds the unwise and ill-considered attack upon the United States at Pearl Harbor. That very act gave us pause. Many Negroes, many times, and in many places, have looked on revolt and war as the necessary and sole solution of race friction. The experience of Japan has proven two things: that domination of one people by other and selfish races, bad as it is, is no whit better than domination within a race by elements whose aims and ideals are anti-social.

So far as Japan was fighting against color caste, and striving against the domination of Asia by Europeans, she was absolutely right. But so far as she tried to substitute for European, an Asiatic caste system under a "superior" Japanese race; and for the domination and exploitation of the peasants of Asia by Japanese trusts and industrialists, she was offering Asia no acceptable exchange for Western exploitation.

Uneasy, therefore, as we have been about war between the United States and Japan, and about our having as colored people to fight colored people possibly only for the benefit of white people, we have this to remember and sustain us: we are facing the beginning of the end of European domination in Asia. The ideas which Japan started and did not carry through, are not dead,

From the *Chicago Defender*, August 25, 1945.

but growing. The utter smashing of the terrible Japanese machine by the American technique is not an exhibition of race superiority of white over yellow: it is the overthrow of an economy and social tyranny which had gripped a fine and progressive people by the throat, and which deserved to be overthrown.

Now comes the question, after the overthrow of the dominant powers in Japan, what have we to offer in its place? Here again we are puzzled and discouraged. It is outrageous to have at the head of our fighting forces a man like Halsey whose bitter contempt of colored people can hardly be restrained. He is not fighting a system — he is fighting and hating a colored race. How far does he represent America? Is there an America which can find itself in this struggle and demand for an emancipated Japanese people, freedom and equality, self-government and development, without slavery and without the contempt of white folk?

The recent declaration by the Allies of the terms offered Japan are reassuring. They are complete disarmament; the deprivation of recent conquests; the installation of democratic methods in Japan's government; destruction of her war-making industry, but access to outside raw materials. Until a new order of peace and justice is established the Allies will occupy designated points in Japanese territory.

This last requirement is unfortunate and perhaps unnecessary. Whenever white troops are put in control in a colored country the results are notorious. It is to be hoped that this part of the Allied program will be sternly limited in space and time.

Negroes Have an Old Culture

An organization, called Men Of Good Will, in New York City has published a pamphlet on the problem of racial minorities, written by Alice A. Baily. It has a curious and interesting reference to the Negro: "This problem is totally different to that of the Jews. In the first case you have an exceedingly ancient people who for thousands of years have played their part in the arena of world history.

"In the case of the Negro, we are considering a people who have begun to rise in the scale of human endeavor. Two hundred years ago, they were what the European and American regarded as 'raw savages,' divided into countless tribes, living in a state of nature, primitive, warlike, totally uneducated from the modern point of view."

This is ethnologically and historically false. The civilization of black African Negroes is even more ancient than that of Asiatic Jews. It is untrue that two hundred years ago Africans were raw savages "in a state of nature, totally uneducated" and engaged in internecine wars.

Leo Africanus who visited Negro Africa, south of Sahara and north of the Gulf of Guinea in the 15th century, describes Timbuctoo as follows: "The rich king of Tombuto hath many plates and sceptres of gold, somewhere of weigh 1300 pounds; and he keeps a magnificent and well-furnished court. Here are great store of doctors, judges, priests, and other learned men, that are bountifully maintained at the king's cost and charges. And hither are brought divers manuscripts or written books out of Berbarie, which are sold for more money than any other merchandize . . ."

The Mellestine further to the west reached its greatest power between 1307 and 1332. "The Negroes possess some admirable qualities. They are seldom unjust, and have a greater abhorrence of injustice than any other people. Their sultan shows no mercy to anyone who is guilty of the least act of it. There is complete security in their country. Neither traveler nor inhabitant in

From the *People's Voice*, November 1, 1947.

it has anything to fear, from robbers or men of violence. They do not confiscate the property of any white man who dies in their country, even if it be uncounted wealth. On the contrary, they give it into the charge of some trustworthy person among the whites, until the rightful heir takes possession of it."

What was it then that happened "two hundred years ago"? It was the filth and cruelty of Europe led by England which descended upon Africa and inaugurated for a century the African slave trade which tore the people of Africa from their country to become the foundation of the work and development of America. It is to be hoped that the persons who are publishing this extraordinary misinterpretation of the civilization of Africa will try to base their future publications upon the truth and not upon fairy tales.

Gandhi and
the American Negroes

Mohandas Gandhi was born nineteen months after my birth. As a school-boy in a small town in the northeastern part of the United States, I knew little of Asia and the schools taught less. The one tenuous link which bound me to India was skin color. That was important in America and even in my town, although little was said about it. But I was conscious of being the only brown face in my school and although my dark family had lived in this valley for two hundred years or more, I was early cognizant of a status different from that of my white schoolmates.

As I grew up there seemed to be no future for me in the place of my birth, and at seventeen I went South, where formerly colored people had been slaves, so that I could be trained to work among them. There at Fisk University I first became aware of a world of colored folk and I learned not only of the condition of American Negroes but began to read of China and India; and to make Africa the special object of my study. I published my first book in 1896 while Gandhi was in South Africa, and my subject was the African slave trade. We did not at the time have much direct news from Africa in the American newspapers, but I did have several black students from South Africa and began to sense the tragedy of that awful land. It was not until after the First World War that I came to realize Gandhi's work for Africa and the world.

I was torn by the problem of peace. As a youth I was certain that freedom for the colored peoples of the earth would come only by war; by doing to white Europe and America what they had done to black Africa and colored Asia. This seemed the natural conclusion from the fairy tales called history on which I had been nourished. Then in the last decades of the 19th century, as I came to manhood, I caught the vision of world peace and signed the pledge never to take part in war.

From *Gandhi Marg* (Bombay), 1 (July 1957): 1–4.

With the First World War came my first knowledge of Gandhi. I came to know Lajpat Rai and Madame Naidu. John Haynes Holmes was one of my co-workers in the National Association for the Advancement of Colored People, and he was a friend and admirer of Gandhi. Indeed the "Colored People" referred to in our name was not originally confined to America. I remember the discussion we had on inviting Gandhi to visit America and how we were forced to conclude that this land was not civilized enough to receive a colored man as an honored guest.

In 1929, as the Depression loomed, I asked Gandhi for a message to American Negroes, which I published in the *Crisis*. He said:

Let not the 12 million Negroes be ashamed of the fact that they are the grandchildren of slaves. There is dishonor in being slave-owners. But let us not think of honor or dishonor in connection with the past. Let us realize that the future is with those who would be pure, truthful and loving. For as the old wise men have said: Truth ever is, untruth never was. Love alone binds and truth and love accrue only to the truly humble.

This was written on May Day, 1929. Through what phantasmagoria of hurt and evil the world has passed since then! We American Negroes have reeled and staggered from side to side and forward and back. In the First World War, we joined with American capital to keep Germany and Italy from sharing the spoils of colonial imperialism. In the Depression we sank beneath the burden of poverty, ignorance and disease due to discrimination, unemployment and crime. In the Second World War, we again joined Western capital against Fascism and failed to realize how the Soviet Union sacrificed her blood and savings to save the world.

But we did realize how out of war began to arise a new colored world free from the control of Europe and America. We began too to realize the role of Gandhi and to evaluate his work as a guide for the black people of the United States. As an integral part of this country, as workers, consumers and co-creators of its culture, we could not look forward to physical separation except as a change of masters. But what of Gandhi's program of peace and non-violence? Only in the last year have American Negroes begun to see the possibility of this program being applied to the Negro problems in the United States.

Personally I was long puzzled. After the World Depression, I sensed a recurring contradiction. I saw Gandhi's non-violence gain freedom for India, only to be followed by violence in all the world. I realized that the vaunted "hundred years of peace," from Waterloo to the Battle of the Marne, was not peace at all but war, of Europe and North America on Africa and Asia, with only troubled bits of peace between the colonial conquerors. I saw Britain, France, Belgium and North America trying to continue to force the world to sever them by monopoly of land, technique and machines, backed by physical force which has now culminated in the use of atomic power. Only the possession of this power by the Soviet Union prevents the restoration of colonial imperialism of the West over Asia and Africa, under the leadership of men like [John Foster] Dulles and [Anthony] Eden. Perhaps in this extraordinary impasse the teachings of Mahatma Gandhi may have a chance to prevail in the world. Recent events in the former slave territory of the United States throw a curious light on this possibility.

In Montgomery, Alabama, the former capital of the Confederate States which fought for years to make America a slave nation, the black workers last year refused any longer to use the public buses on which their seats had long been segregated from those of the white passengers, paying the same fare. In addition to separation, there was abuse and insult by the white conductors. This custom had continued for 75 years. Then last year a colored seamstress got tired of insult and refused to give her seat to a white man. The black workers led by young, educated ministers began a strike which stopped the discrimination, aroused the state and the nation and presented an unbending front of non-violence to the murderous mob which hitherto has ruled the South. The occurrence was extraordinary. It was not based on any first-hand knowledge of Gandhi and his work. Their leaders like Martin Luther King knew of non-resistance in India; many of the educated teachers, business and professional men had heard of Gandhi. But the rise and spread of this movement was due to the truth of its underlying principles and not to direct teaching or propaganda. In this aspect it is a most interesting proof of the truth of the Gandhian philosophy.

The American Negro is not yet free. He is still discriminated against, oppressed and exploited. The recent court decisions in his favor are excellent but are as yet only partially enforced. It may well be that the enforcement of these laws and real human equality and brotherhood in the United States will come only under the leadership of another Gandhi.

China and Africa

By courtesy of the government of the 680 million people of the Chinese Republic, I am permitted on my ninety-first birthday to speak to the people of China and Africa and through them to the world. Hail, then, and farewell, dwelling places of the yellow and black races. Hail human kind!

I speak with no authority: no assumption of age nor rank; I hold no position, I have no wealth. One thing alone I own and that is my own soul. Ownership of that I have even while in my own country for near a century I have been nothing but a "nigger." On this basis and this alone I dare speak, I dare advise.

China after long centuries has arisen to her feet and leapt forward. Africa arise, and stand straight, speak and think! Act! Turn from the West and your slavery and humiliation for the last 500 years and face the rising sun. Behold a people, the most populous nation on this ancient earth which has burst its shackles, not by boasting and strutting, not by lying about its history and its conquests, but by patience and long suffering, by hard, backbreaking labor and with bowed head and blind struggle, moved up and on toward the crimson sky. She aims to "make men holy; to make men free." But what men? Not simply the mandarins but including mandarins; not simply the rich, but not excluding the rich. Not simply the learned, but led by knowledge to the end that no man shall be poor, nor sick, nor ignorant; but that the humblest worker as well as the sons of emperors shall be fed and taught and healed and that there emerge on earth a single unified people, free, well and educated.

You have been told, my Africa: My Africa in Africa and all your children's children overseas; you have been told and the telling so beaten into you by rods and whips, that you believe it yourselves, that this is impossible; that mankind can only rise by walking on men; by cheating them and killing them; that only on a doormat of the despised and dying, the dead and rotten,

From *Peking Review* 2 (March 3, 1959): 11–13.

can a British aristocracy, a French cultural élite or an American millionaire be nurtured and grown. This is a lie. It is an ancient lie spread by church and state, spread by priest and historian, and believed in by fools and cowards, as well as by the down-trodden and the children of despair.

Speak, China, and tell your truth to Africa and the world. What people have been despised as you have? Who more than you have been rejected of men? Recall when lordly Britishers threw the rickshaw money on the ground to avoid touching a filthy hand. Forget not, the time when in Shanghai no Chinaman dare set foot in a park which he paid for. Tell this to Africa, for today Africa stands on new feet, with new eyesight, with new brains and asks: Where am I and why? The Western sirens answer; Britain wheedles; France cajoles; while America, my America, where my ancestors and descendants for eight generations have lived and toiled; America loudest of all, yells and promises freedom. If only Africa allows American investment. Beware Africa, America bargains for your soul. America would have you believe that they freed your grandchildren; that Afro-Americans are full American citizens, treated like equals, paid fair wages as workers, promoted for desert and free to learn and earn and travel across the world. This is not true. Some are near freedom; some approach equality with whites; some have achieved education; but the price for this has too often been slavery of mind, distortion of truth and oppression of our own people. Of 18 million Afro-Americans, 12 million are still second-class citizens of the United States, serfs in farming, low-paid laborers in industry, and repressed members of union labor. Most American Negroes do not vote. Even the rising 6 million are liable to insult and discrimination at any time.

But this, Africa, relates to your descendants, not to you. Once I thought of you Africans as children, whom we educated Afro-Americans would lead to liberty. I was wrong. We could not even lead ourselves, much less you. Today I see you rising under your own leadership, guided by your own brains.

Africa does not ask alms from China nor from the Soviet Union nor from France, Britain, nor the United States. It asks friendship and sympathy and no nation better than China can offer this to the Dark Continent. Let it be given freely and generously. Let Chinese visit Africa, send their scientists there and their artists and writers. Let Africa send its students to China and its seekers after knowledge. It will not find on earth a richer goal, a more promising mine of information. On the other hand, watch the West. The new British West Indian Federation is not a form of democratic progress but a cunning attempt to reduce these islands to the control of British and American investors. Haiti is dying under rich Haitian investors who with American money are enslaving the peasantry. Cuba is showing what the West Indies, Central and South America are suffering under American Big Business. The American worker himself does not always realize this. He has high wages and many comforts. Rather than lose these, he keeps in office by his vote the servants of industrial exploitation so long as they maintain his wage. His labor leaders represent exploitation and not the fight against the exploitation of labor by private capital. These two sets of exploiters fall out only when one demands too large a share of the loot. This China knows. This Africa must learn. This the American Negro has failed so far to learn. I am frightened by the so-called friends who are flocking to Africa. Negro Americans trying to make money from your toil, white Americans who seek by investment at high interest to bind you in serfdom to business as the New East is bound and as South America is struggling with. For this America is tempting your leaders, bribing your young scholars, and arming your soldiers. What shall you do?

First, understand! Realize that the great mass of mankind is freeing itself from wage slavery, while private capital in Britain, France, and now in America, is still trying to maintain civilization and comfort for a few on the toil, disease, and ignorance of the mass of men. Understand this, and understanding comes from direct knowledge. You know America and France and Britain to your sorrow. Now know the Soviet Union and its allied nations, but particularly know China.

II

Personal Loyalties, Reflections, and Creative Pieces

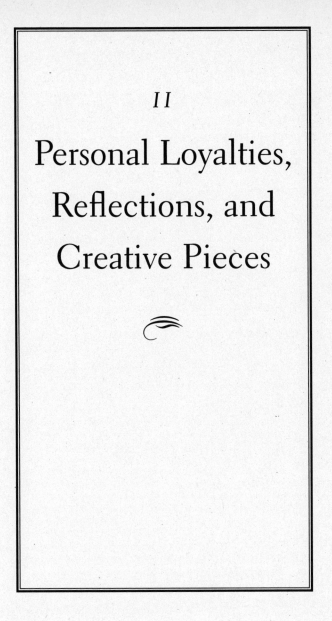

W. E. B. Du Bois was often said to be aloof, coldly arrogant. The lofty sense of self—of what his life represented in terms of intellectual and racial accomplishment—that characterizes "A Vista of Ninety Fruitful Years" (1958) and much of Du Bois's writings undoubtedly caused him to be impatient with those he saw as fools and intolerant of those who appeared to lack commitment and urgency. In his defense, Du Bois and those who knew him well insisted that what many others mistook for haughtiness was a natural shyness and an aversion to informality bred of an old-fashioned New England restraint. His Calvinist nurturing in the western Massachusetts town of Great Barrington and Victorian response to the wider world Du Bois recalls in "The Shadow of Years," a vivid chapter in *Darkwater* (1920). Certainly, as the 1904 piece "Credo" reveals, Du Bois was capable of considerable passion on paper. He cared deeply about ideas and people who lived by them, as shown by "As the Crow Flies." Furthermore, beneath Du Bois's rather austere surface beat the heart of a novelist and poet, vividly expressed in "The Song of the Smoke" and "The Case." While it is true that he did not have many intimate friends, Du Bois made up in loyalty and intensity for what he lacked in a wide circle of confiding relationships. "Charles Young" (1922) and "William Monroe Trotter" (1934) were such friends. Finally, Du Bois occasionally succumbed to a confessional mode of arresting poignancy (as in "Of the Passing of the First-Born" [1903] and "I Bury My Wife" [1950]") or buoyant celebration (as in "So the Girl Marries" [1928]) when writing about his wife and children.

Of the Passing of the
First-Born

"Unto you a child is born," sang the bit of yellow paper that fluttered into my room one brown October morning. Then the fear of fatherhood mingled wildly with the joy of creation; I wondered how it looked and how it felt, — what were its eyes, and how its hair curled and crumpled itself. And I thought in awe of her, — she who had slept with Death to tear a man-child from underneath her heart, while I was unconsciously wandering. I fled to my wife and child, repeating the while to myself half wonderingly, "Wife and child? Wife and child?" — fled fast and faster than boat and steam-car, and yet must ever impatiently await them; away from the hard-voiced city, away from the flickering sea into my own Berkshire Hills that sit all sadly guarding the gates of Massachusetts.

Up the stairs I ran to the wan mother and whimpering babe, to the sanctuary on whose altar a life at my bidding had offered itself to win a life, and won. What is this tiny formless thing, this newborn wail from an unknown world, — all head and voice? I handle it curiously, and watch perplexed its winking, breathing, and sneezing. I did not love it then; it seemed a ludicrous thing to love; but her I loved, my girl-mother, she whom now I saw unfolding like the glory of the morning — the transfigured woman.

Through her I came to love the wee thing, as it grew and waxed strong; as its little soul unfolded itself in twitter and cry and half-formed word, and as its eyes caught the gleam and flash of life. How beautiful he was, with his olive-tinted flesh and dark gold ringlets, his eyes of mingled blue and brown, his perfect little limbs, and the soft voluptuous roll which the blood of Africa had moulded into his features! I held him in my arms, after we had sped far away to our Southern home, — held him, and glanced at the hot red soil of Georgia and the breathless city of a hundred hills, and felt a vague unrest. Why was his

From *The Souls of Black Folk* (1903).

hair tinted with gold? An evil omen was golden hair in my life. Why had not the brown of his eyes crushed out and killed the blue? — for brown were his father's eyes, and his father's father's. And thus in the Land of the Color-line I . saw, as it fell across my baby, the shadow of the Veil.

Within the Veil was he born, said I; and there within shall he live, — a Negro and a Negro's son. Holding in that little head — ah, bitterly! — the unbowed pride of a hunted race, clinging with that tiny dimpled hand — ah, wearily! — to a hope not hopeless but unhopeful, and seeing with those bright wondering eyes that peer into my soul a land whose freedom is to us a mockery and whose liberty a lie. I saw the shadow of the Veil as it passed over my baby, I saw the cold city towering above the blood-red land. I held my face beside his little cheek, showed him the star-children and the twinkling lights as they began to flash, and stilled with an even-song the unvoiced terror of my life.

So sturdy and masterful he grew, so filled with bubbling life, so tremulous with the unspoken wisdom of a life but eighteen months distant from the All-life, — we were not far from worshipping this revelation of the divine, my wife and I. Her own life builded and moulded itself upon the child; he tinged her every dream and idealized her every effort. No hands but hers must touch and garnish those little limbs; no dress or frill must touch them that had not wearied her fingers; no voice but hers could coax him off to Dreamland, and she and he together spoke some soft and unknown tongue and in it held communion. I too mused above his little white bed; saw the strength of my own arm stretched onward through the ages through the newer strength of his; saw the dream of my black fathers stagger a step onward in the wild phantasm of the world; heard in his baby voice the voice of the Prophet that was to rise within the Veil.

And so we dreamed and loved and planned by fall and winter, and the full flush of the long Southern spring, till the hot winds rolled from the fetid Gulf, till the roses shivered and the still stern sun quivered its awful light over the hills of Atlanta. And then one night the little feet pattered wearily to the wee white bed, and the tiny hands trembled; and a warm flushed face tossed on the pillow, and we knew baby was sick. Ten days he lay there, — a swift week and three endless days, wasting, wasting away. Cheerily the mother nursed him the first days, and laughed into the little eyes that smiled again. Tenderly then she hovered round him, till the smile fled away and Fear crouched beside the little bed.

Then the day ended not, and night was a dreamless terror, and joy and sleep slipped away. I hear now that Voice at midnight calling me from dull and dreamless trance, — crying, "The Shadow of Death! The Shadow of Death!" Out into the starlight I crept, to rouse the gray physician, — the Shadow of Death, the Shadow of Death. The hours trembled on; the night listened; the ghastly dawn glided like a tired thing across the lamplight. Then we two alone looked upon the child as he turned toward us with great eyes, and stretched his string-like hands, — the Shadow of Death! And we spoke no word, and turned away.

He died at eventide, when the sun lay like a brooding sorrow above the western hills, veiling its face; when the winds spoke not, and the trees, the great green trees he loved, stood motionless. I saw his breath beat quicker and quicker, pause, and then his little soul leapt like a star that travels in the night and left a world of darkness in its train. The day changed not; the same tall trees peeped in at the windows, the same green grass glinted in the setting sun. Only in the chamber of death writhed the world's most piteous thing — a childless mother.

I shirk not. I long for work. I pant for a life full of striving. I am no coward, to shrink before the rugged rush of the storm, nor even quail before the awful shadow of the Veil. But hearken, O Death! Is not this my life hard enough, — is not that dull land that stretches its sneering web about me cold enough, — is not all the world beyond these four little walls pitiless enough, but that thou must needs enter here, — thou, O Death? About my head the thundering storm beat like a heartless voice, and the crazy forest pulsed with the curses of the weak; but what cared I, within my home beside my wife and baby boy? Wast thou so jealous of one little coign of happiness that thou must needs enter there, — thou, O Death?

A perfect life was his, all joy and love, with tears to make it brighter, — sweet as a summer's day beside the Housatonic. The world loved him; the women kissed his curls, the men looked gravely into his wonderful eyes, and the children hovered and fluttered about him. I can see him now, changing like the sky from sparkling laughter to darkening frowns, and then to wondering thoughtfulness as he watched the world. He knew no Color-line, poor dear, — and the Veil, though it shadowed him, had not yet darkened half his sun. He loved the white matron, he loved his black nurse; and in his little world walked souls alone, uncolored and unclothed. I — yea, all men — are larger and purer by the infinite breadth of that one little life. She who in simple clearness of vision sees beyond the stars said when he had flown, "He will be happy There; he ever loved beautiful things." And I, far more ignorant, and blind by the web of mine own weaving, sit alone winding words and muttering, "If still he be, and he be There, and there be a There, let him be happy, O Fate!"

Blithe was the morning of his burial, with bird and song and sweet-smelling flowers. The trees whispered to the grass, but the children sat with hushed faces. And yet it seemed a ghostly unreal day, — the wraith of Life. We seemed to rumble down an unknown street behind a little white bundle of posies, with the shadow of a song in our ears. The busy city dinned about us; they did not say much, those pale-faced hurrying men and women; they did not say much, — they only glanced and said, "Niggers!"

We could not lay him in the ground there in Georgia, for the earth there is strangely red; so we bore him away to the northward, with his flowers and his little folded hands. In vain, in vain! — for where, O God! beneath thy broad blue sky shall my dark baby rest in peace, — where Reverence dwells, and Goodness, and a Freedom that is free?

All that day and all that night there sat an awful gladness in my heart, — nay, blame me not if I see the world thus darkly through the Veil, — and my soul whispers ever to me, saying, "Not dead, not dead, but escaped; not bond, but free." No bitter meanness now shall sicken his baby heart till it die a living death, no taunt shall madden his happy boyhood. Fool that I was to think or wish that this little soul should grow choked and deformed within the Veil! I might have known that yonder deep unworldly look that ever and anon floated past his eyes was peering far beyond this narrow Now. In the poise of his little curl-crowned head did there not sit all that wild pride of being which his father had hardly crushed in his own heart? For what, forsooth, shall a Negro want with pride amid the studied humiliations of fifty million fellows? Well sped, my boy, before the world had dubbed your ambition insolence, had held your ideals unattainable, and taught you to cringe and bow. Better far this nameless void that stops my life than a sea of sorrow for you.

Idle words; he might have borne his burden more bravely than we, — aye, and found it lighter too, some day; for surely, surely this is not the end. Surely there shall yet dawn some mighty morning to lift the Veil and set the prisoned free. Not for me, — I shall die in my bonds, — but for fresh young souls who have not known the night and waken to the morning; a morning when men ask of the workman, not "Is he white?" but "Can he work?" When men ask artists, not "Are they black?" but "Do they know?" Some morning this may be, long, long years to come. But now there wails, on that dark shore within the Veil, the same deep voice, *Thou shalt forgo!* And all have I forgone at that command, and with small complaint, — all save that fair young form that lies so coldly wed with death in the nest I had builded.

If one must have gone, why not I? Why may I not rest me from this restlessness and sleep from this wide waking? Was not the world's alembic, Time, in his young hands, and is not my time waning? Are there so many workers in the vineyard that the fair promise of this little body could lightly be tossed away? The wretched of my race that line the alleys of the nation sit fatherless and unmothered; but Love sat beside his cradle, and in his ear Wisdom waited to speak. Perhaps now he knows the All-love, and needs not to be wise. Sleep, then, child, — sleep till I sleep and waken to a baby voice and the ceaseless patter of little feet — above the Veil.

Credo

I believe in God who made of one blood all races that dwell on earth. I believe that all men, black and brown and white, are brothers, varying through Time and Opportunity, in form and gift and feature, but differing in no essential particular, and alike in soul and in the possibility of infinite development.

Especially do I believe in the Negro Race; in the beauty of its genius, the sweetness of its soul and its strength in that meekness which shall yet inherit this turbulent earth.

I believe in pride of race and lineage and self; in pride of self so deep as to scorn injustice to other selves; in pride of lineage so great as to despise no man's father; in pride of race so chivalrous as neither to offer bastardy to the weak nor beg wedlock of the strong, knowing that men may be brothers in Christ, even they be not brothers-in-law.

I believe in Service—humble reverent service, from the blackening of boots to the whitening of souls; for Work is Heaven, Idleness Hell, and Wage is the "Well done!" of the Master who summoned all them that labor and are heavy laden, making no distinction between the black sweating cotton-hands of Georgia and the First Families of Virginia, since all distinction not based on deed is devilish and not divine.

I believe in the Devil and his angels, who wantonly work to narrow the opportunity of struggling human beings, especially if they be black; who spit in the faces of the fallen, strike them that cannot strike again, believe the worst and work to prove it, hating the image which their Maker stamped on a brother's soul.

I believe in the Prince of Peace. I believe that War is Murder. I believe that armies and navies are at bottom the tinsel and braggadocio of oppression and wrong; and I believe that the wicked conquest of weaker and darker nations by nations whiter and stronger but foreshadows the death of that strength.

From *The Independent*, 57 (October 6, 1904): 787.

I believe in Liberty for all men; the space to stretch their arms and their souls; the right to breathe and the right to vote, the freedom to choose their friends, enjoy the sunshine and ride on the railroads, uncursed by color; thinking, dreaming, working as they will in a kingdom of God and love.

I believe in the training of children, black even as white; the leading out of little souls into the green pastures and beside the still waters, not for self or peace, but for Life lit by some large vision of beauty and goodness and truth; lest we forget, and the sons of the fathers, like Esau, for more meat barter their birthright in a mighty nation.

Finally, I believe in Patience — patience with the weakness of the Weak and the strength of the Strong, the prejudice of the ignorant and the ignorance of the Blind; patience with the tardy triumph of Joy and the mad chastening of Sorrow — patience with God.

The Song of the Smoke

I am the Smoke King
I am black!
I am swinging in the sky,
I am wringing worlds awry;
I am the thought of the throbbing mills,
I am the soul of the soul-toil kills,
Wraith of the ripple of trading rills;
Up I'm curling from the sod,
I am whirling home to God;
   I am the Smoke King
   I am black.

I am the Smoke King,
I am black!
I am wreathing broken hearts,
I am sheathing love's light darts;
   Inspiration of iron times
   Wedding the toil of toiling climes,
   Shedding the blood of bloodless crimes—
Lurid lowering 'mid the blue,
Torrid towering toward the true,
   I am the Smoke King,
   I am black.

I am the Smoke King,
I am black!
I am darkening with song,

From *The Horizon*, February 1907.

I am hearkening to wrong!
  I will be black as blackness can —
  The blacker the mantle, the mightier the man!
  For blackness was ancient ere whiteness began.
I am daubing God in night,
I am swabbing Hell in white;
  I am the Smoke King
  I am black.

The Case

I had taken the morning train at Washington for New Orleans on the Southern. I was not feeling very well and it was a dull, gray day. Few other people were foolish to ride in such unpleasant weather. I yawned and stretched — tried to look at the landscape but there wasn't any worth looking at. Then I looked at the porter. He was a finely-made fellow — tall, strong, with velvet dark brown skin and pleasant, smiling eyes. If he had been white — but he wasn't. I growled: "Won't these trains ever run on time?" But he smiled and said nothing. We left the straggling Virginia station at last and wound along slowly southward. Things seemed to grow worse — bad trains, bad food, no company. I strolled to the smoking room and lit a cigar. It was also bad. "Heavens," I said, addressing the porter again, "even a wreck would be a diversion for this sort of thing." He smiled. "I guess you've never been in a wreck," he said in excellent English. "No," I replied, "have you?" "Lots of them; one only last trip," said he. "Is that so?" said I encouragingly — but he was gone. A sickly, fussy old lady in the car wanted a softer pillow. Pretty soon he came back. "You must have a good many adventures on these trains," I said. "No, not many," he said slowly — then after a pause, "you see we get stories now and then but only parts of them, just glimpses you know." "Suppose you have to guess at the rest?" "Yes," he replied. I thought he was going at least to tell me about the wreck but as he didn't start I began again to encourage him. "Anybody killed in that wreck?" "One lady," he said, and he looked thoughtfully out the window. The little bell rang again and he went out. The fussy old lady wanted a glass of water. By and by he came back. "Have a cigar?" I said. "No thank you," he said, "against the rules." "Well tell me about that wreck," I said at last determinedly. "You see 'twas this way," he replied settling down on the arm of one of the chairs. "I was starting out of the Washington depot one morning hurrying to the train with the plan of my Pullman when a man ran against me, big, ugly-looking fellow and he cursed me when 'twas

From *The Horizon*, July 1907.

really his own fault. I turned around to him as good as he sent, when a lady standing near him said in a soft voice, 'You are going to the train?' I tell you she was a stunning-looking woman, not so very tall yet with an appearance of tallness, brunette with dark hair and the most wonderful misty eyes you ever looked at. I've seen a good many pretty women on these trains and other places but I think she was about the prettiest. She had an air, too — wasn't exactly a lady — ." "What do you mean by that?" I growled. "O well, I mean she hadn't always been used to money and good society, perhaps, still she had the making of a lady in her. I don't know that I can just explain what I mean, but you perhaps understand." I did but I said nothing. He continued, " 'Yes ma'am,' " said I. 'Won't you take this bag along?' I took the bag altho it was the depot porter's work and she hurried out after me. At the gate we met a young clergyman; a tall, fresh-faced, hearty, honest-looking fellow, evidently young, and he stepped aside very courteously to let the lady have his place. It proved however that she was at the wrong gate and was not going on the Southern but on the Seaboard. I thought I noticed a little regret on the clergyman's face, she thanked me, tipped me generously and glided toward the other gate. Well it was a day something like this, cold and gray and chilly and to make it worse the train was about an hour and a half late waiting on Northern connections so that the Seaboard went and left us. The clergyman proved to be the only passenger in my car and I tell you he was lonely. He sat looking around disconsolately and in my opinion thinking of the beautiful woman he had seen at the gate. We started on down through Virginia about as fast as we are going today." "Ting-a-ling-a-ling" went the bell and off the porter went leaving me to relight my cigar. By and by he came back. I smiled, "Are women often as troublesome as this one?" "This is a mild case," he said imperturbably. "Well about dark we got to Greensboro and as I was standing outside, a veiled woman hurried toward me. 'All aboard,' the conductor shouted and the train began to quiver. I thought I recognized the figure. Sure enough it was the woman of the Washington train. How on earth could she have gotten here? Then I remembered that she could get over from Raleigh by Durham but I didn't know of any train that came at that time of night. She must have made it through some way. I seized her bag but she hesitated. 'Oh!' she said, 'have you any room in the car?' 'Plenty,' said I as I swung her up the step but she paused again. 'Are there many passengers?' 'One,' said I, 'madam.' She raised her veil and started perceptibly. 'Oh, you are the porter who carried my bag in Washington — very well,' she said and smiled as she started into the car. Of course I gave her number 7 right opposite number 6 where the clergyman was, and immediately the clergyman sat up and began to take notice. They were the only passengers in the car. He handed her a paper and then magazine, picked up her gloves and exchanged remarks about the weather, while I dusted around the seats. Pretty soon on returning from the smoking room I found them sitting together talking. Afterward they went in and had dinner together and when they came back, he was enthusiastic and she radiant. They were getting along very rapidly and I was watching them with a great deal of interest. Evidently he was much impressed and no wonder. The woman looked even more beautiful than she had in the morning. She was not only beautiful — she had a certain indefinable grace and innocence and vigor; a soft, subtle southern witchery as lovely as her accent. At the same time watching her narrowly I was not so certain about her. There was something not quite right about her and yet it struck me that she was excited, no sign of wrong in it, that she was listening for something.

Beneath all her enthusiasm and interest there were little furtive gleams almost of terror that came into her otherwise beautiful eyes, when his were turned away. Now and then a far away look of passionate pleading struggled across the very mirth of her laughter — little things, not much you know, nothing that he noticed probably but I could see — I am used to noting such things. Suddenly the train stopped, there was commotion on ahead and I went forward. When I came back the lady asked casually in tone but yet with a penetrating glance at me, 'What's the matter, porter?' 'Officers boarding the train looking for something.' She didn't say anything, yet I noticed a certain grayish whitening about her eyes, the tightening of her lips. 'Oh! go see what it is, won't you?' she said to the clergyman. He rose and hurried forward. He had scarcely reached the little passage way, when she turned suddenly to me and reaching down, took up a case; a large, leather-bound, square case. She rose stiffly and said with a sort of pleading command, 'Take this' — I supplied the rest quietly — 'hide it.' 'Yes,' she said looking me squarely in the eyes while a cruel harsh gleam came in hers. I bowed and stepping quickly back two sections, raised the cushion and put the case beneath the pillows, then as I was apparently brushing out the section the clergyman sauntered back. 'Oh it is nothing,' he said, 'they are searching for somebody. I don't know just what is the matter.' The lady bent and made some gay remark, and then pointed out the window. He followed her finger laughingly but I wasn't fooled. I saw the dull, gray pallor creeping up her cheek. I saw the tremor in the delicate tapering of the pointed finger. I saw the flash of dull, blue steel as her other hand left her bosom. I rushed forward as there was murder or suicide in the air, when a man appeared at the entrance. 'No alarm, ladies and gentlemen,' he said, 'but we are officers and are searching the passengers on this train.' 'But,' expostulated the clergyman angrily, as he saw the dead white face of the lady, 'this is outrageous. I — .' Another official-looking personage entered — a quiet man with sharp eyes looking into every corner of the car. The clergyman glanced up and a look of recognition came over him. 'Why, hello John

111

Travers,' he said. 'Why, Corrothers is that you?' cried the man shaking his hand heartily, 'how do you do? Why I never thought of meeting you here. This is a great pleasure. I am on a little official business — .' He glanced at the lady and hesitated. In a flash she had risen to the occasion. She looked at the clergyman with a deep blush and said demurely, 'I give you back your promise — you may introduce your — wife,' and she let her eyes fall full on his. The clergyman floundered a minute and then rose to the suggestion, 'My wife; Mr. Travers.' The other man started. 'Your wife? I beg your pardon, I didn't know you were married. I am delighted to meet Mrs. Carrothers [*sic*]. Why didn't you tell us, you sly dog? Well I must rush. Porter, any one else?' 'No sir,' I said. 'We won't search this car, Simmons,' he said and hurried out. I discreetly withdrew — that is into the darkness of the passage. The clergyman stood with glowing face a moment and then with a sudden gesture stretched his arms — 'My wife to be,' he cried. She shuddered backward with a little gasp of pain. 'You do not understand,' she faltered. 'It was just a joke — I hated to — I could not let them search and tumble my bags.' 'I know, I know all,' he insisted, 'but make the joke a reality, a dear reality.' But her voice and face fell in misery. 'You know — nothing,' she wailed and then suddenly drew herself up. 'No,' she said, 'no!' and her face grew cold and stern. 'I — I think much, very much of you but I am not — .' He listened no longer but bending forward crushed, almost smothered her in his arms. 'Hooked,' said I, but then I saw her face. I changed my mind again. I've never seen such a curious combination of looks on a face. Surely this was no evil woman. There lay love and bewilderment, honor and yearning, beneath it trouble and fear; not perfectly written but curiously intertwined. She stepped slowly from him and sat clasping and unclasping her hands nervously. Then she bent forward and spoke rapidly but too low for me to hear, and rising quickly, her burning eyes fixed straight on mine, came rapidly toward the ladies' toilet. I was in confusion at being caught listening but she did not notice and whispered as she rustled by — 'a telegraph blank, quick!' I gave it to her and she was gone but a moment and then as she glided back she slipped a bill in my hand and whispered, 'Get it off, quick, for God's sake!' I swung off at the little station and gave the message, 'James Magruder, Charlotte. Safe — meet me at train. Rosalyn.' The train started. I swung back on but the porter in the next car called and I went to help him. 'Charlotte,' cried the train hand. I rushed toward my car, entered, seized the hidden case and hurried to the land. She stood white and still and a great tear was wandering down her cheek. Then it happened."

"What happened?" I asked. "The wreck. Quickly, suddenly as it always happens, crashing, grinding, and twisting. I saw a great long bar of timber crash through the side window and crush her down in all her splendid young beauty and grind her between the seats while the car jolted and screamed. I turned and hid my face and the clergyman staggered limp and white into the opposite section. There was a long silence. Just then a man burst into the car. I recognized him in the minute. It was the same tall rough fellow who had run against me in the Washington depot. He saw the dead body of the lady, ran quickly towards her, looked at her, glanced around and knelt down by her side. The clergyman rose, the stranger too and they faced each other silently looking across the dead body. Then the stranger saw the case in my hand. He rushed and seized it. I did not resist—I was too puzzled. Just then the train crew came in and there was confusion and moving about. I saw the stranger passing out. 'Got a match?' he said. I handed him one and that was the last I saw of him." I waited a moment. "Well?" said I. "That's all," said the porter. "All?" I cried. "Yes." "Was the girl dead?" "Yes." "And the clergyman?" "I never saw him again." "How about that case?" "I never saw that again or heard of it." "What was in it?" "I don't know," said the porter. "You know, as I told you, we only get pieces of stories on a train, they never finish themselves."

"Ting-a-ling-a-ling," said the bell.

Howells and Black Folk

In the composite picture which William Dean Howells, as his life work, has painted of America he has not hesitated to be truthful and to include the most significant thing in the land — the black man. With lie and twistings most Americans seek to ignore the mighty and portentous shadow of ten growing millions, or, if it insists on darkening the landscape, to label it as joke or crime. But Howells, in his "Imperative Duty," faced our national foolishness and shuffling and evasion. Here was a white girl engaged to a white man who discovers herself to be "black." The problem looms before her as tremendous, awful. The world wavers. She peers beyond the Veil and shudders and then — tells her story frankly, marries her man, and goes her way as thousands of others have done and are doing.

It was Howells, too, that discovered Dunbar. We have had a score of artists and poets in black America, but few critics dared call them so. Most of them, therefore, starved; or, like Timrod, "passed" as white. Howells dared take Dunbar by the hand and say to the world, not simply here is a black artist, but here is an artist who happens to be black. Not only that, but as an artist Dunbar had studied black folk and realized the soul of this most artistic of all races. "I said," wrote Howells, "that a race which had come to this effect in any member of it had attained civilization in him, and I permitted myself the imaginative prophecy that the hostilities and the prejudices which had so long constrained his race were destined to vanish in the arts; that these were to be the final proof that God had made one blood of all nations of men."

Finally when, on the centenary of Lincoln's birth, a band of earnest men said, we must finish the work of Negro emancipation and break the spiritual bonds that still enslave this people, William Dean Howells was among the first to sign the call. From this call came the National Association for the Advancement of Colored People and *The Crisis* magazine.

From *The Crisis*, November 1913.

The Shadow of Years

I was born by a golden river and in the shadow of two great hills, five years after the Emancipation Proclamation. The house was quaint, with clapboards running up and down, neatly trimmed, and there were five rooms, a tiny porch, a rosy front yard, and unbelievably delicious strawberries in the rear. A South Carolinian, lately come to the Berkshire Hills, owned all this — tall, thin, and black, with golden earrings, and given to religious trances. We were his transient tenants for the time.

My own people were part of a great clan. Fully two hundred years before, Tom Burghardt had come through the western pass from the Hudson with his Dutch captor, "Coenraet Burghardt," sullen in his slavery and achieving his freedom by volunteering for the Revolution at a time of sudden alarm. His wife was a little, black, Bantu woman, who never became reconciled to this strange land; she clasped her knees and rocked and crooned:

> "Do bana coba — gene me, gene me!
> Ben d'nuli, ben d'le ———"

Tom died about 1787, but of him came many sons, and one, Jack, who helped in the War of 1812. Of Jack and his wife, Violet, was born a mighty family, splendidly named: Harlow and Ira, Cloë, Lucinda, Maria, and Othello! I dimly remember my grandfather, Othello, — or "Uncle Tallow," — a brown man, strong-voiced and redolent with tobacco, who sat stiffly in a great high chair because his hip was broken. He was probably a bit lazy and given to wassail. At any rate, grandmother had a shrewish tongue and often berated him. This grandmother was Sarah — "Aunt Sally" — a stern, tall, Dutch-African woman, beak-nosed, but beautiful-eyed and golden-skinned. Ten or more children were theirs, of whom the youngest was Mary, my mother.

From *Darkwater: Voices from Within the Veil* (1920).

Mother was dark shining bronze, with a tiny ripple in her black hair, black-eyed, with a heavy, kind face. She gave one the impression of infinite patience, but a curious determination was concealed in her softness. The family were small farmers on Egremont Plain, between Great Barrington and Sheffield, Massachusetts. The bits of land were too small to support the great families born on them and we were always poor. I never remember being cold or hungry, but I do remember that shoes and coal, and sometimes flour, caused mother moments of anxious thought in winter, and a new suit was an event!

At about the time of my birth economic pressure was transmuting the family generally from farmers to "hired" help. Some revolted and migrated westward, others went cityward as cooks and barbers. Mother worked for some years at house service in Great Barrington, and after a disappointed love episode with a cousin, who went to California, she met and married Alfred Du Bois and went to town to live by the golden river where I was born.

Alfred, my father, must have seemed a splendid vision in that little valley under the shelter of those mighty hills. He was small and beautiful of face and feature, just tinted with the sun, his curly hair chiefly revealing his kinship to Africa. In nature he was a dreamer, — romantic, indolent, kind, unreliable. He had in him the making of a poet, an adventurer, or a Beloved Vagabond, according to the life that closed round him; and that life gave him all too little. His father, Alexander Du Bois, cloaked under a stern, austere demeanor a passionate revolt against the world. He, too, was small, but squarish. I remember him as I saw him first, in his home in New Bedford, — white hair close-cropped; a seamed, hard face, but high in tone, with a gray eye that could twinkle or glare.

Long years before him Louis XIV drove two Huguenots, Jacques and Louis Du Bois, into wild Ulster County, New York. One of them in the third or fourth generation had a descendant, Dr. James Du Bois, a gay, rich bachelor, who made his money in the Bahamas, where he and the Gilberts had plantations. There he took a beautiful little mulatto slave as his mistress, and two sons were born: Alexander in 1803 and John, later. They were fine, straight, clear-eyed boys, white enough to "pass." He brought them to America and put Alexander in the celebrated Cheshire School, in Connecticut. Here he often visited him, but one last time, fell dead. He left no will, and his relations made short shrift of these sons. They gathered in the property, apprenticed grandfather to a shoemaker; then dropped him.

Grandfather took his bitter dose like a thoroughbred. Wild as was his inner revolt against this treatment, he uttered no word against the thieves and made no plea. He tried his fortunes here and in Haiti, where, during his short, restless sojourn, my own father was born. Eventually, grandfather became chief steward on the passenger boat between New York and New Haven; later he was a small merchant in Springfield; and finally he retired and ended his days at New Bedford. Always he held his head high, took no insults, made few friends. He was not a "Negro"; he was a man! Yet the current was too strong even for him. Then even more than now a colored man had colored friends or none at all, lived in a colored world or lived alone. A few fine, strong, black men gained the heart of this silent, bitter man in New York and New Haven. If he had scant sympathy with their social clannishness, he was with them in fighting discrimination. So, when the white Episcopalians of Trinity Parish, New Haven, showed plainly that they no longer wanted black folk as fellow Christians, he led the revolt which resulted in St. Luke's Parish, and was for years its senior warden. He lies dead in the Grove Street Cemetery, beside Jehudi Ashmun.

Beneath his sternness was a very human man. Slyly he wrote poetry, — stilted, pleading things from a soul astray. He loved women in his masterful way, marrying three beautiful wives in succession and clinging to each with a certain desperate, even if unsympathetic, affection. As a father he was, naturally, a failure, — hard, domineering, unyielding. His four children reacted characteristically: one was until past middle life a thin spinster, the mental image of her father; one died; one passed over into the white world and her children's children are now white, with no knowledge of their Negro blood; the fourth, my father, bent before grandfather, but did not break — better if he had. He yielded and flared back, asked forgiveness and forgot why, became the harshly-held favorite, who ran away and rioted and roamed and loved and married my brown mother.

So with some circumstance having finally gotten myself born, with a flood of Negro blood, a strain of French, a bit of Dutch, but, thank God! no "Anglo-Saxon," I come to the days of my childhood.

They were very happy. Early we moved back to Grandfather Burghardt's home, — I barely remember its stone fireplace, big kitchen, and delightful woodshed. Then this house passed to other branches of the clan and we moved to rented quarters in town, — to one delectable place "upstairs," with a wide yard full of shrubbery, and a brook; to another house abutting a railroad, with infinite interests and astonishing playmates; and finally back to the quiet street on which I was born, — down a long lane and in a homely, cozy cottage, with a living-room, a tiny sitting-room, a pantry, and two attic bedrooms. Here mother and I lived until she died, in 1884, for father early began his restless wanderings. I last remember urgent letters for us to come to New Milford, where he had started a barber shop. Later he became a preacher. But mother no longer trusted his dreams, and he soon faded out of our lives into silence.

From the age of five until I was sixteen I went to school on the same grounds, — down a lane, into a widened yard, with a big choke-cherry tree and two buildings, wood and brick. Here I got acquainted with my world, and soon had my criterions of judgment.

Wealth had no particular lure. On the other hand, the shadow of wealth was about us. That river of my birth was golden because of the woolen and paper waste that soiled it. The gold was theirs, not ours; but the gleam and glint was for all. To me it was all in order and I took it philosophically. I cordially despised the poor Irish and South Germans, who slaved in the mills, and annexed the rich and well-to-do as my natural companions. Of such is the kingdom of snobs!

Most of our townfolk were, naturally, the well-to-do, shading downward, but seldom reaching poverty. As playmate of the children I saw the homes of nearly every one, except a few immigrant New Yorkers, of whom none of us approved. The homes I saw impressed me, but did not overwhelm me. Many were bigger than mine, with newer and shinier things, but they did not seem to differ in kind. I think I probably surprised my hosts more than they me, for I was easily at home and perfectly happy and they looked to me just like ordinary people, while my brown face and frizzled hair must have seemed strange to them.

Yet I was very much one of them. I was a center and sometimes the leader of the town gang of boys. We were noisy, but never very bad, — and, indeed, my mother's quiet influence came in here, as I realize now. She did not try to make me perfect. To her I was already perfect. She simply warned me of a few things, especially saloons. In my town the saloon was the open door to hell. The best families had their drunkards and the worst had little else.

Very gradually, — I cannot now distinguish the steps, though here and there I remember a jump or a jolt — but very gradually I found myself assuming quite placidly that I was different from other children. At first I think I connected the difference with a manifest ability to get my lessons rather better than most and to recite with a certain happy, almost taunting, glibness, which brought frowns here and there. Then, slowly, I realized that some folks, a few, even several, actually considered my brown skin a misfortune; once or twice I became painfully aware that some human beings even thought it a crime. I was not for a moment daunted, — although, of course, there were some days of secret tears — rather I was spurred to tireless effort. If they beat me at anything, I was grimly determined to make them sweat for it! Once I remember challenging a great, hard farmer-boy to battle, when I knew he could whip me; and he did. But ever after, he was polite.

As time flew I felt not so much disowned and rejected as rather drawn up into higher spaces and made part of a mightier mission. At times I almost pitied my pale companions, who were not of the Lord's anointed and who saw in their dreams no splendid quests of golden fleeces.

Even in the matter of girls my peculiar phantasy asserted itself. Naturally, it was in our town voted bad form for boys of twelve and fourteen to show any evident weakness for girls. We tolerated them loftily, and now and then they played in our games, when I joined in quite as naturally as the rest. It was when strangers came, or summer boarders, or when the oldest girls grew up that my sharp senses noted little hesitancies in public and searchings for possible public opinion. Then I flamed! I lifted my chin and strode off to the mountains, where I viewed the world at my feet and strained my eyes across the shadow of the hills.

I was graduated from high school at sixteen, and I talked of "Wendell Phillips." This was my first sweet taste of the world's applause. There were flowers and upturned faces, music and marching, and there was my mother's smile. She was lame, then, and a bit drawn, but very happy. It was her great day and that very year she lay down with a sigh of content and has not yet awakened. I felt a certain gladness to see her, at last, at peace, for she had worried all her life. Of my own loss I had then little realization. That came only with the after-years. Now it was the choking gladness and solemn feel of wings! At last, I was going beyond the hills and into the world that beckoned steadily.

There came a little pause, — a singular pause. I was given to understand that I was almost too young for the world. Harvard was the goal of my dreams, but my white friends hesitated and my colored friends were silent. Harvard was a mighty conjure-word in that hill town, and even the mill owners' sons had aimed lower. Finally it was tactfully explained that the place for me was in the South among my people. A scholarship had been already arranged at Fisk, and my summer earnings would pay the fare. My relatives grumbled, but after a twinge I felt a strange delight! I forgot, or did not thoroughly realize, the curious irony by which I was not looked upon as a real citizen of my birth-town, with a future and a career, and instead was being sent to a far land among strangers who were regarded as (and in truth were) "mine own people."

Ah! the wonder of that journey, with its faint spice of adventure, as I entered the land of slaves; the never-to-be-forgotten marvel of that first supper at Fisk with the world "colored" and opposite two of the most beautiful beings God ever revealed to the eyes of seventeen. I promptly lost my appetite, but I was deliriously happy!

As I peer back through the shadow of my years, seeing not too clearly, but through the thickening veil of wish and after-thought, I seem to view my life divided into four distinct parts: the Age of Miracles, the Days of Disillusion, the Discipline of Work and Play, and the Second Miracle Age.

119

The Age of Miracles began with Fisk and ended with Germany. I was bursting with the joy of living. I seemed to ride in conquering might. I was captain of my soul and master of fate! I *willed* to do! It was done. I *wished!* The wish came true.

Now and then out of the void flashed the great sword of hate to remind me of the battle. I remember once, in Nashville, brushing by accident against a white woman on the street. Politely and eagerly I raised my hat to apologize. That was thirty-five years ago. From that day to this I have never knowingly raised my hat to a Southern white woman.

I suspect that beneath all of my seeming triumphs there were many failures and disappointments, but the realities loomed so large that they swept away even the memory of other dreams and wishes. Consider, for a moment, how miraculous it all was to a boy of seventeen, just escaped from a narrow valley: I willed and lo! my people came dancing about me, — riotous in color, gay in laughter, full of sympathy, need, and pleading; darkly delicious girls — "colored" girls — sat beside me and actually talked to me while I gazed in tongue-tied silence or babbled in boastful dreams. Boys with my own experiences and out of my own world, who knew and understood, wrought out with me great remedies. I studied eagerly under teachers who bent in subtle sympathy, feeling themselves some shadow of the Veil and lifting it gently that we darker souls might peer through to other worlds.

I willed and lo! I was walking beneath the elms of Harvard, — the name of allurement, the college of my youngest, wildest visions! I needed money; scholarships and prizes fell into my lap, — not all I wanted or strove for, but all I needed to keep in school. Commencement came and standing before governor, president, and grave, gowned men, I told them certain astonishing truths, waving my arms and breathing fast! They applauded with what now seems to me uncalled-for fervor, but then! I walked home on pink clouds of glory! I asked for a fellowship and got it. I announced my plan of studying in Germany, but Harvard had no more fellowships for me. A friend, however, told me of the Slater Fund and how the Board was looking for colored men worth educating. No thought of modest hesitation occurred to me. I rushed at the chance.

The trustees of the Slater Fund excused themselves politely. They acknowledged that they had in the past looked for colored boys of ability to educate, but, being unsuccessful, they had stopped searching. I went at them hammer and tongs! I plied them with testimonials and mid-year and final marks. I intimated plainly, impudently, that they were "stalling"! In vain did the chairman, Ex-President Hayes, explain and excuse. I took no excuses and brushed explanations aside. I wonder now that he did not brush me aside, too, as a conceited meddler, but instead he smiled and surrendered.

I crossed the ocean in a trance. Always I seemed to be saying, "It is not real; I must be dreaming!" I can live it again—the little, Dutch ship—the blue waters—the smell of new-mown hay—Holland and the Rhine. I saw the Wartburg and Berlin; I made the Harzreise and climbed the Brocken; I saw the Hansa towns and the cities and dorfs of South Germany; I saw the Alps at Berne, the Cathedral at Milan, Florence, Rome, Venice, Vienna, and Pesth; I looked on the boundaries of Russia; and I sat in Paris and London.

On mountain and valley, in home and school, I met men and women as I had never met them before. Slowly they became, not white folks, but folks. The unity beneath all life clutched me. I was not less fanatically a Negro, but "Negro" meant a greater, broader sense of humanity and world-fellowship. I felt myself standing, not against the world, but simply against American narrowness and color prejudice, with the greater, finer world at my back urging me on.

I builded great castles in Spain and lived therein. I dreamed and loved and wandered and sang; then, after two long years, I dropped suddenly back into "nigger"-hating America!

My Days of Disillusion were not disappointing enough to discourage me. I was still upheld by that fund of infinite faith, although dimly about me I saw the shadow of disaster. I began to realize how much of what I had called Will and Ability was sheer Luck! *Suppose* my good mother had preferred a steady income from my child labor rather than bank on the precarious dividend of my higher training? *Suppose* that pompous old village judge, whose dignity we often ruffled and whose apples we stole, had had his way and sent me while a child to a "reform" school to learn a "trade"? *Suppose* Principal Hosmer had been born with no faith in "darkies," and instead of giving me Greek and Latin had taught me carpentry and the making of tin pans? *Suppose* I had missed a Harvard scholarship? *Suppose* the Slater Board had then, as now, distinct ideas as to where the education of Negroes should stop? Suppose *and* suppose! As I sat down calmly on flat earth and looked at my life a certain great fear seized me. Was I the masterful captain or the pawn of laughing sprites? Who was I to fight a world of color prejudice? I raise my hat to myself when I remember that, even with these thoughts, I did not hesitate or waver; but just went doggedly to work, and therein lay whatever salvation I have achieved.

First came the task of earning a living. I was not nice or hard to please. I just got down on my knees and begged for work, anything and anywhere. I wrote to Hampton, Tuskegee, and a dozen other places. They politely declined, with many regrets. The trustees of a backwoods Tennessee town considered me, but were eventually afraid. Then, suddenly, Wilberforce offered to let me teach Latin and Greek at $750 a year. I was overjoyed!

I did not know anything about Latin and Greek, but I did know of Wilberforce. The breath of that great name had swept the water and dropped into southern Ohio, where Southerners had taken their cure at Tawawa Springs and where white Methodists had planted a school; then came the little bishop, Daniel Payne, who made it a school of the African Methodists. This was the school that called me, and when re-considered offers from Tuskegee and Jefferson City followed, I refused; I was so thankful for that first offer.

I went to Wilberforce with high ideals. I wanted to help to build a great university. I was willing to work night as well as day. I taught Latin, Greek, English, and German. I helped in the discipline, took part in the social life, begged to be allowed to lecture on sociology, and began to write books. But I found myself against a stone wall. Nothing stirred before my impatient pounding! Or if it stirred, it soon slept again.

Of course, I was too impatient! The snarl of years was not to be undone in days. I set at solving the problem before I knew it. Wilberforce was a colored church-school. In it were mingled the problems of poorly-prepared pupils, an inadequately-equipped plant, the natural politics of bishoprics, and the provincial reactions of a country town loaded with traditions. It was my first introduction to a Negro world, and I was at once marvelously inspired and deeply depressed. I was inspired with the children, — had I not rubbed against the children of the world and did I not find here the same eagerness, the same joy of life, the same brains as in New England, France, and Germany? But, on the other hand, the ropes and myths and knots and hindrances; the thundering waves of the white world beyond beating us back; the scalding breakers of this inner world, — its currents and back eddies — its meanness and smallness — its sorrow and tragedy — its screaming farce!

In all this I was as one bound hand and foot. Struggle, work, fight as I would, I seemed to get nowhere and accomplish nothing. I had all the wild intolerance of youth, and no experience in human tangles. For the first time in my life I realized that there were limits to my will to do. The Day of Miracles was past, and a long, gray road of dogged work lay ahead.

I had, naturally, my triumphs here and there. I defied the bishops in the matter of public extemporaneous prayer and they yielded. I bearded the poor, hunted president in his den, and yet was re-elected to my position. I was slowly winning a way, but quickly losing faith in the value of the way won. Was this the place to begin my life work? Was this the work which I was best fitted to do? What business had I, anyhow, to teach Greek when I had studied men? I grew sure that I had made a mistake. So I determined to leave Wilberforce and try elsewhere. Thus, the third period of my life began.

First, in 1896, I married — a slip of a girl, beautifully dark-eyed and thorough and good as a German housewife. Then I accepted a job to make a study of Negroes in Philadelphia for the University of Pennsylvania, — one year at six hundred dollars. How did I dare these two things? I do not know. Yet they spelled salvation. To remain at Wilberforce without doing my ideals meant spiritual death. Both my wife and I were homeless. I dared a home and a temporary job. But it was a different daring from the days of my first youth. I was ready to admit that the best of men might fail. I meant still to be captain of my soul, but I realized that even captains are not omnipotent in uncharted and angry seas.

I essayed a thorough piece of work in Philadelphia. I labored morning, noon, and night. Nobody ever reads that fat volume on "The Philadelphia Negro," but they treat it with respect, and that consoles me. The colored people of Philadelphia received me with no open arms. They had a natural dislike to being studied like a strange species. I met again and in different guise those curious cross-currents and inner social whirlings of my own people. They set me to groping. I concluded that I did not know so much as I might about my own people, and when President Bumstead invited me to Atlanta University the next year to teach sociology and study the American Negro, I accepted gladly, at a salary of twelve hundred dollars.

My real life work was done at Atlanta for thirteen years, from my twenty-ninth to my forty-second birthday. They were years of great spiritual upturn-ing, of the making and unmaking of ideals, of hard work and hard play. Here I found myself. I lost most of my mannerisms. I grew more broadly human, made my closest and most holy friendships, and studied human beings. I became widely-acquainted with the real condition of my people. I realized the terrific odds which faced them. At Wilberforce I was their captious critic. In Philadelphia I was their cold and scientific investigator, with microscope and probe. It took but a few years of Atlanta to bring me to hot and indignant defense. I saw the race-hatred of the whites as I had never dreamed of it before, — naked and unashamed! The faint discrimination of my hopes and intangible dislikes paled into nothing before this great, red monster of cruel oppression. I held back with more difficulty each day my mounting indigna-tion against injustice and misrepresentation.

With all this came the strengthening and hardening of my own character. The billows of birth, love, and death swept over me. I saw life through all its paradox and contradiction of streaming eyes and mad merriment. I emerged into full manhood, with the ruins of some ideals about me, but with others planted above the stars; scarred and a bit grim, but hugging to my soul the divine gift of laughter and withal determined, even unto stubbornness, to fight the good fight.

At last, forbear and waver as I would, I faced the great Decision. My life's last and greatest door stood ajar. What with all my dreaming, studying, and teaching was I going to *do* in this fierce fight? Despite all my youthful conceit and bumptiousness, I found developed beneath it all a reticence and new fear of forwardness, which sprang from searching criticisms of motive and high ideals of efficiency; but contrary to my dream of racial solidarity and notwithstanding my deep desire to serve and follow and think, rather than to lead and inspire and decide, I found myself suddenly the leader of a great wing of people fighting against another and greater wing.

Nor could any effort of mine keep this fight from sinking to the personal plane. Heaven knows I tried. That first meeting of a knot of enthusiasts, at Niagara Falls, had all the earnestness of self-devotion. At the second meeting, at Harpers Ferry, it arose to the solemnity of a holy crusade and yet without and to the cold, hard stare of the world it seemed merely the envy of fools against a great man, Booker Washington.

Of the movement I was willy-nilly leader. I hated the rôle. For the first time I faced criticism and *cared*. Every ideal and habit of my life was cruelly misjudged. I who had always overstriven to give credit for good work, who had never consciously stooped to envy was accused by honest colored people of every sort of small and petty jealousy, while white people said I was ashamed of my race and wanted to be white! And this of me, whose one life fanaticism had been belief in my Negro blood!

Away back in the little years of my boyhood I had sold the Springfield *Republican* and written for Mr. Fortune's *Globe*. I dreamed of being an editor myself some day. I am an editor. In the great, slashing days of college life I dreamed of a strong organization to fight the battles of the Negro race. The National Association for the Advancement of Colored People is such a body, and it grows daily. In the dark days at Wilberforce I planned a time when I could speak freely to my people and of them, interpreting between two worlds. I am speaking now. In the study at Atlanta I grew to fear lest my radical beliefs should so hurt the college that either my silence or the institution's ruin would result. Powers and principalities have not yet curbed my tongue and Atlanta still lives.

It all came — this new Age of Miracles — because a few persons in 1909 determined to celebrate Lincoln's Birthday properly by calling for the final emancipation of the American Negro. I came at their call. My salary even for a year was not assured, but it was the "Voice without reply." The result has been the National Association for the Advancement of Colored People and *The Crisis* and this book, which I am finishing on my Fiftieth Birthday.

Last year I looked death in the face and found its lineaments not unkind. But it was not my time. Yet in nature some time soon and in the fullness of days I shall die, quietly, I trust, with my face turned South and eastward; and, dreaming or dreamless, I shall, I am sure, enjoy death as I have enjoyed life.

Charles Young

The life of Charles Young was a triumph of tragedy. No one ever knew the truth about the Hell he went through at West Point. He seldom even mentioned it. The pain was too great. Few knew what faced him always in his army life. It was not enough for him to do well — he must always do better; and so much and so conspicuously better, as to disarm the scoundrels that ever trailed him. He lived in the army surrounded by insult and intrigue and yet he set his teeth and kept his soul serene and triumphed.

He was one of the few men I know who literally turned the other cheek with Jesus Christ. He was laughed at for it and his own people chided him bitterly, yet he persisted. When a white Southern pigmy at West Point protested at taking food from a dish passed first to Young, Young passed it to him first and afterward to himself. When officers of inferior rank refused to salute a "nigger," he saluted them. Seldom did he lose his temper, seldom complain.

With his own people he was always the genial, hearty, half-boyish friend. He kissed the girls, slapped the boys on the back, threw his arms about his friends, scattered his money in charity; only now and then behind the Veil did his nearest comrades see the Hurt and Pain graven on his heart; and when it appeared he promptly drowned it in his music — his beloved music, which always poured from his quick, nervous fingers, to caress and bathe his soul.

Steadily, unswervingly he did his duty. And Duty to him, as to few modern men, was spelled in capitals. It was his lodestar, his soul; and neither force nor reason swerved him from it. His second going to Africa, after a terrible attack of black water fever, was suicide. He knew it. His wife knew it. His friends knew it. He had been sent to *Africa* because the Army considered his blood pressure too high to let him go to *Europe*! They sent him there to die. They sent him there because he was one of the very best officers in the service and if he had gone to Europe he could not have been denied the stars of a General. They could not stand a black American General. Therefore they sent him to

From *The Crisis*, February 1922.

the fever coast of Africa. They ordered him to make roads back in the haunted jungle. He knew what they wanted and intended. He could have escaped it by accepting his retirement from active service, refusing his call to active duty and then he could have lounged and lived at leisure on his retirement pay. But Africa needed him. He did not yell and collect money and advertise great schemes and parade in crimson — he just went quietly, ignoring appeal and protest.

He is dead. But the heart of the Great Black Race, the Ancient of Days — the Undying and Eternal — rises and salutes his shining memory: Well done! Charles Young, Soldier and Man and unswerving Friend.

The United Nations

The sun and the stars are all ringing
With song rising strong from the earth,
The hope of humanity singing
A hymn to a new world in birth.

Chorus

United Nations on the march
With flags unfurled
Together fight for victory
A free new world

Take heart all you nations swept under,
By powers of darkness that ride,
The wrath of the people shall thunder,
Relentless as time and the tide.

Chorus

As sure as the sun meets the morning
The rivers go down to the sea,
A new day for mankind is dawning,
Our children shall live proud and free.

Chorus

From undated mimeographed sheet, circa 1944–45, in the Papers of W. E. B. Du Bois, University of Massachusetts at Amherst.

So the Girl Marries

The problem of marriage among our present American Negroes is a difficult one. On the one hand go conflicting philosophies: should we black folk breed children or commit biological suicide? On the other hand, should we seek larger sex freedom or closer conventional rules? Should we guide and mate our children like the French or leave the whole matter of sex intermingling to the chance of the street, like Americans? These are puzzling questions and all the more so because we do not often honestly face them.

I was a little startled when I became father of a girl. I scented far-off difficulties. But she became soon a round little bunch of Joy: plump and jolly, full of smiles and fun — a flash of twinkling legs and bubbling mischief. Always there on the broad campus of Atlanta University she was in scrapes and escapades — how many I never dreamed until years after: running away from her sleepy nurse; riding old Billy, the sage and dignified draft horse; climbing walls; bullying the Matron; cajoling the cooks and becoming the thoroughly spoiled and immeasurably loved Baby of the Campus. How far the spoiling had gone I became suddenly aware one summer, when we stopped a while to breathe the salt sea air at Atlantic City. This tot of four years marched beside me down the Boardwalk amid the unmoved and almost unnoticing crowd. She was puzzled. Never before in her memory had the world treated her quite so differently.

"Papa," she exclaimed at last, impatiently, "I guess they don't know I'm here!"

As the Girl grew so grew her problems: School; Multiplication Tables; Play-mates; Latin; Clothes — Boys! No sooner had we faced one than the other loomed, the last lingered — the next threatened. She went to Kindergarten with her playmates of the Campus — kids and half-grown-ups. The half-grown-ups, Normal students, did me the special courtesy of letting the Girl

From *The Crisis*, June 1928.

dawdle and play and cut up. So when she came at the age of ten to the Ethical Culture School in New York there loomed the unlearned Multiplication Table; and a time we had! For despite all proposals of "letting the Child develop as it Will!" she must learn to read and count; and the school taught her — but at a price!

Then came the days of gawky growth; the impossible children of the street; someone to play with; wild tears at going to bed; excursions, games — and far, far in the offing, the shadow of the Fear of the Color Line.

I had a Grand Idea. Before the time loomed — before the Hurt pierced and lingered and festered, off to England she should go for high school and come back armed with manners and knowledge, cap-a-pie, to fight American race hate and insult. Off the Girl went to Bedale's, just as war thundered in the world. As a professor of Economics and History, I knew the war would be short — a few months. So away went Mother and Girl. Two mighty years rolled turbulently by and back came both through the Submarine Zone. The Girl had grown. She was a reticent stranger with whom soul-revealing converse was difficult. I found myself groping for continual introductions.

Then came Latin. The English teacher talked Latin and his class at Bedale's romped with Caesar through a living Gallia. The American teacher in the Brooklyn Girl's High did not even talk English and regarded Latin as a crossword puzzle with three inches of daily solution. "Decline Stella!"; "Conjugate Amo"; "What is the subject of 'Gallia est omnis divisa — ' " "Nonsense," said the Girl (which was quite true), "I've dropped Latin!"

"But the colleges haven't," I moaned. "Why college?" countered the Girl.

Why indeed? I tried Cicero "pro Archia Poeta." The Girl was cold. Then I pleaded for my own spiritual integrity: "I have told 12 millions to go to college — what will they say if you don't go?" The Girl admitted that that was reasonable but she said she was considering marriage and really thought she knew about all that schools could teach effectively. I, too, was reasonable and most considerate, despite the fact that I was internally aghast. This baby — married — My God! — but, of course, I said aloud: Honorable state and all that; and "Go ahead, if you like — but how about a year in college as a sort of, well, introduction to life in general and for furnishing topics of conversation in the long years to come? How about it?" "Fair enough," said the Girl and she went to college.

Boys! queer animals. Hereditary enemies of Fathers-with-daughters and Mothers! Mother had chaperoned the Girl relentlessly through High School. Most Mothers didn't bother. It was a bore and one felt like the uninvited guest or the veritable Death's Head. The Girl didn't mind much, only — "Well, really Mother you don't need to go or even to sit up." But Mother stuck to her job. I've always had the feeling that the real trick was turned in those years, by a very soft-voiced and persistent Mother who was always hanging about unobtrusively. The boys liked her, the girls were good-naturedly condescending; the Girl laughed. It was so funny. Father, of course, was busy with larger matters and weightier problems, including himself.

Clothes. In the midst of high school came sudden clothes. The problem of raiment. The astonishing transformation of the hoyden and hiker and basketball expert into an amazing butterfly. We parents had expressed loftily disdain for the new colored beauty parlors — straightening and bleaching, the very idea! But they didn't straighten, they cleaned and curled; they didn't whiten, they delicately darkened. They did for colored girls' style of beauty what two sophisticated centuries had been doing for blonde frights. When the finished product stood forth all silked and embroidered, briefly skirted and long-limbed with impudent lip-stick and jaunty toque — well, Thrift hung its diminished head and Philosophy stammered. What shall we do about our daughter's extravagant dress? The beauty of colored girls has increased 100% in a decade because they give to it time and trouble. Can we stop it? Should we? Where shall we draw the line, with good silk stockings at $1.95 per pair?

"Girl! You take so long to dress! I can dress in fifteen minutes."

"Yes — Mamma and you look it!" came the frankly unfilial answer.

College. College was absence and premonition. Empty absence and occasional letters and abrupt pauses. One wondered uneasily what they were doing with the Girl: *who* rather than what was educating her. Four years of vague uneasiness with flashes of hectic and puzzling vacations. Once with startling abruptness there arose the Shadow of Death — acute appendicitis; the hospital — the cold, sharp knife; the horror of waiting and the namelessly sweet thrill of recovery. Of course, all the spoiling began again and it literally rained silk and gold.

Absence, too, resulted in the unexpected increase in Parent-valuation. Mother was enshrined and worshipped by the absent Girl: no longer was she merely convenient and at times in the way. She was desperately adored. Even Father took on unaccustomed importance and dignity and found new place in the scheme of things. We both felt quite set up.

Then graduation and a Woman appeared in the family. A sudden woman — sedate, self-contained, casual, grown: with a personality — with wants, expenses, plans. "There will be a caller tonight." — "Tomorrow night I'm going out."

It was a bit disconcerting, this transforming of a rubber ball of childish joy into a lady whose address was at your own house. I acquired the habit of discussing the world with this stranger — as impersonally and coolly as possible: teaching — travel — reading — art — marriage. I achieved quite a detached air, letting the domineering daddy burst through only at intervals, when it seemed impossible not to remark — "It's midnight, my dear," and "when is the gentleman going? You need sleep!"

My part in Mate-selection was admittedly small but I flatter myself not altogether negligible. We talked the young men over — their fathers and grandfathers; their education; their ability to earn particular sorts of living; their dispositions. All this incidentally mind you — not didactically or systematically. Once or twice I went on long letter hunts for facts; usually facts were all too clear and only deductions necessary. What was the result? I really don't know. Sometimes I half suspect that the Girl arranged it all and that I was the large and solemn fly on the wheel. At other times I flatter myself that I was astute, secret, wise and powerful. Truth doubtless lurks between. So the Girl marries.

I remember the Boy came to me somewhat breathlessly one Christmas eve with a ring in his pocket. I told him as I had told others. "Ask her — she'll settle the matter; not I." But he was a nice boy. A rather unusual boy with the promise of fine manhood. I wished him luck. But I did not dare plead his cause. I had learned — well, I had learned.

Thus the world grew and blossomed and changed and so the Girl marries. It is the end of an era — a sudden break and beginning. I rub my eyes and readjust my soul. I plan frantically. It will be a simple, quiet ceremony —

"In a church, Father!"

"Oh! in a church? Of course, in a church. Well, a church wedding would be a little larger, but — "

"With Countée's father and the Reverend Frazier Miller assisting."

"To be sure — well, that is possible and, indeed, probable."

"And there will be sixteen bridesmaids."

One has to be firm somewhere — "But my dear! who ever *heard* of sixteen bridesmaids!"

"But Papa, there are eleven Moles, and five indispensables and Margaret — "

Why argue? What has to be, must be; and this evidently had to be. I struggled faintly but succumbed. Now with sixteen bridesmaids and ten ushers must go at least as many invited guests.

You who in travail of soul have struggled with the devastating puzzle of selecting a small bridge party out of your total of twenty-five intimate friends, lend me your sympathy! For we faced the world-shattering problem of selecting for two only children, the friends of a pastor with twenty-five years' service in one church; and the friends of a man who knows good people in forty-five states and three continents. I may recover from it but I shall never look quite the same. I shall always have a furtive feeling in my soul. I know that at the next corner I shall meet my Best Friend and remember that I forgot to invite him. Never in all eternity can I explain. How can I say: "Bill, I just forgot you!" Or "My *dear* Mrs. Blubenski, I didn't remember where on earth you were or indeed if you were at all or ever!" No, one can't say such things. I shall only stare at them pleadingly, in doubt and pain, and slink wordlessly away.

Thirteen hundred were bidden to the marriage and no human being has one thousand three hundred friends! Five hundred came down to greet the bride at a jolly reception which I had originally planned for twenty-five. Of course, I was glad they were there. I expanded and wished for a thousand. Three thousand saw the marriage and a thousand waited on the streets. It was a great pageant; a heart-swelling throng; birds sang and Melville Charlton let the organ roll and swell beneath his quivering hands. A sweet young voice sang of Love; and then came the holy:

"Freudig gefuert, Zichet dahin!"

The symbolism of that procession was tremendous. It was not the mere marriage of a maiden. It was not simply the wedding of a fine young poet. It was the symbolic march of young and black America. America, because there was Harvard, Columbia, Smith, Brown, Howard, Chicago, Syracuse, Penn and Cornell. There were three Masters of Arts and fourteen Bachelors. There were poets and teachers, actors, artists and students. But it was not simply conventional America — it had a dark and shimmering beauty all its own; a calm and high restraint and sense of new power; it was a new race; a new thought; a new thing rejoicing in a ceremony as old as the world. (And after it all and before it, such a jolly, happy crowd; some of the girls even smoked cigarettes!)

Why should there have been so much of pomp and ceremony — flowers and carriages and silk hats; wedding cake and wedding music? After all marriage in its essence is and should be very simple: a clasp of friendly hands; a walking away together of Two who say: "Let us try to be One and face and fight a lonely world together!" What more? Is that not enough? Quite; and were I merely white I should have sought to make it end with this.

But it seems to me that I owe something extra to an Idea, a Tradition. We who are black and panting up hurried hills of hate and hindrance — we have got to establish new footholds on the slipping by-paths through which we come.

They must at once be footholds of the free and the eternal, the new and the enthralled. With all of our just flouting of white convention and black religion, some things remain eternally so — Birth, Death, Pain, Mating, Children, Age. Ever and anon we must point to these truths and if the pointing be beautiful with music and ceremony or bare with silence and darkness — what matter? The width or narrowness of the gesture is a matter of choice. That one will have it stripped to the essence. It is still good and true. This soul wants color with bursting cords and scores of smiling eyes in happy raiment. It must be as this soul wills. The Girl wills this. So the Girl marries.

Immortality

My thought on personal immortality is easily explained. I do not know. I do not see how any one could know. Our whole basis of knowledge is so relative and contingent that when we get to argue concerning ultimate reality and the real essence of life and the past and the future, we seem to be talking without real data and getting nowhere. I have every respect for people who believe in the future life, but I cannot accept their belief or their wish as knowledge. Equally, I am not impressed by those who deny the possibility of future life. I have no knowledge of the possibilities of this universe and I know of no one who has.

From *We Believe in Immortality*, ed. Sydney Strong (New York: Coward-McCann, 1929), p. 18.

William Monroe Trotter

Monroe Trotter was a man of heroic proportions, and probably one of the most selfless of Negro leaders during all our American history. His father was Recorder of Deeds for the District of Columbia, at the time when Recorders were paid by fees; and as a result, he retired from office with a small fortune, which he husbanded carefully. Thus, his son was born in comfortable circumstances, and with his talent for business, and his wide acquaintanceship with the best class of young Massachusetts men in his day, might easily have accumulated wealth.

But he turned aside. He had in his soul all that went to make a fanatic, a knight errant. Ready to sacrifice himself, fearing nobody and nothing, strong in body, sturdy in conviction, full of unbending belief.

I remember when I first saw him as a student at Harvard. He was several classes below me. I should liked to have known him and spoken to him, but he was curiously aloof. He was even then forming his philosophy of life. Colored students must not herd together, just because they were colored. He had his white friends and companions, and they liked him. He was no hanger-on, but a leader among them. But he did not seek other colored students as companions. I was a bit lonesome in those days, but I saw his point, and I did not seek him.

Out of this rose his life-long philosophy: Intense hatred of all racial discrimination and segregation. He was particularly incensed at the compromising philosophy of Booker T. Washington; at his industrialism, and his condoning of the deeds of the South.

In the first years of the 20th Century, with George Forbes, Monroe Trotter began the publication of *The Guardian*. Several times young men have started radical sheets among us, like *The Messenger*, and others. But nothing, I think, that for sheer biting invective and unswerving courage, ever quite equaled the *Boston Guardian* in its earlier days. Mr. Washington and his

From *The Crisis*, May 1934.

followers literally shrivelled before it, and it was, of course, often as unfair as it was inspired.

I had come to know Trotter, then, especially because I knew Deenie Pindell as a girl before they were married. We were to stop with them one summer. Mrs. Du Bois was already there when I arrived in Boston, and on the elevated platform, I learned of the Zion Church riot. It was called a riot in the newspapers, and they were full of it. As a matter of fact, Trotter and Forbes had tried to ask Booker T. Washington certain pointed questions, after a speech which he made in the colored church; and immediately he was arrested, according to the careful plans which William L. Lewis, Washington's attorney, had laid. I was incensed at Trotter. I thought that he had been needlessly violent, and had compromised me as his guest; but when I learned the exact facts, and how little cause for riot there was, and when they clapped Trotter in the Charles Street Jail, all of us more conservative, younger men rose in revolt.

Out of this incident, within a year or two, arose the Niagara movement, and Trotter was present.

But Trotter was not an organization man. He was a free lance; too intense and sturdy to loan himself to that compromise which is the basis of all real organization. Trouble arose in the Niagara movement, and afterward when the Niagara movement joined the new N.A.A.C.P., Trotter stood out in revolt, and curiously enough, did not join the new organization because of his suspicion of the white elements who were co-operating with us.

He devoted himself to *The Guardian*, and it became one of the first of the nation-wide colored weeklies. His wife worked with him in utter devotion; giving up all thought of children; giving up her pretty home in Roxbury; living and lunching with him in the *Guardian* office, and knowing hunger and cold. It was a magnificent partnership, and she died to pay for it.

The Trotter philosophy was carried out remorselessly in his paper, and his philosophy. He stood unflinchingly for fighting separation and discrimination in church and school, and in professional and business life. He would not allow a colored Y.M.C.A. in Boston, and he hated to recognize colored churches, or colored colleges. On this battle line he fought a long, exhausting fight for over a quarter of a century. What has been the result? There are fewer Negroes in Boston churches today than when Trotter began a crusade, and colored people sat in the pews under Phillips Brooks' preaching. There may be more colored teachers in the schools, but certainly they are playing no such part as Maria Baldwin did, as principal of the best Cambridge Grammar School.

When Trotter began, not a single hotel in Boston dared to refuse colored guests. Today, there are few Boston hotels where colored people are received. There is still no colored Y.M.C.A., but on the other hand, there are practically no colored members of the white "Y," and young colored men are deprived of club house and recreational facilities which they sorely need. In the professions, in general employment, and in business, there is certainly not less, and probably more discrimination than there used to be.

Does this mean that Monroe Trotter's life was a failure? Never. He lived up to his belief to the best of his ability. He fought like a man. The ultimate object of his fighting was absolutely right, but he miscalculated the opposition. He thought that Boston and America would yield to clear reason and determined agitation. They did not. On the contrary, to some extent, the very agitation carried on in these years has solidified opposition. This does not mean that agitation does not pay; but it means that you cannot necessarily cash in quickly upon it. It means that sacrifice, even to blood and tears, must be given to this great fight; and not one but a thousand lives, like that of Monroe Trotter, is necessary to victory.

More than that, inner organization is demanded. The free lance like Trotter is not strong enough. The mailed fist has got to be clenched. The united effort of twelve millions has got to be made to mean more than the individual effort of those who think aright. Yet this very inner organization involves segregation. It involves voluntary racial organization, and this racial grouping invites further effort at enforced segregation by law and custom from without. Nevertheless, there is no alternative. We have got to unite to save ourselves, and while the unbending devotion to principle, such as Monroe Trotter shows, has and must ever have, its value, with sorrow, and yet with conviction, we know that this is not enough.

I can understand his death. I can see a man of sixty, tired and disappointed, facing poverty and defeat. Standing amid indifferent friends and triumphant enemies. So he went to the window of his Dark Tower, and beckoned to Death; up from where She lay among the lilies. And Death, like a whirlwind, swept up to him. I shall think of him as lying silent, cold and still; at last at peace, dreamless and serene. Let no trump of doom disturb him from his perfect and eternal rest.

As the Crow Flies

DR. CHARLES DREW

The world has lost a great and valuable healer of men in Charles Drew. He died because of an American custom which must be discarded. He attended an official banquet for the athletes of Howard, Thursday night and made the main address. On Friday, he attended a banquet for the faculty of the Howard Medical School, and of course he worked the days between. He could not get away until 2 o'clock Saturday morning, but without sleep he started to drive from Washington to Tuskegee. At 7:30 Saturday morning he nodded at the wheel of his big car; it ran off the concrete highway onto the soft shoulder of the road; sharply he jerked it back and two tons of steel hurtled over and over, crushing his shoulders, legs, arms and chest. He died 30 minutes later.

Why? Why? Why? What was the hurry, the rush? He could have gone comfortably by Pullman to Cheehaw, he could have flown quickly by airplane to Montgomery. I know how tempting a trip by automobile is. I know what it means to feel the purr of that smooth, mighty mechanism and to be free of world and sky and even land. For 30 years I drove my car over nearly all the United States, Canada and Cuba. But I never forgot that my powerful machine was servant only as long as I was master. When I was tired I did not drive; when I drove I did not drink. When my friends jeered because it took me three days to get from New York to Atlanta, I laughed too. But I still did but 300 miles a day and slept peacefully each night. Drew had a treasure in himself for mankind. He had served humanity tremendously in a short life. His own continued work was precious beyond calculation. Why was there no one by his side to say: "You are too tired to drive. You are too valuable to risk your life!" No one spoke; no one warned a genius too weary to realize. And so the Father of the blood bank which gave life to thousands is himself dead.

From the *Chicago Globe*, April 29, 1950.

GEORGE PADMORE

George Padmore who lives in London is one of the best informed writers on economic subjects in the world. He is a West Indian who has lived in the United States, Russia and Germany, and for the last ten or fifteen years, in London. He has written six books of which the best known is, "How Britain Rules Africa." This year he has published his seventh book, "Africa — Britain's Third Empire." It is a splendid piece of work and calls for wide reading. I am going to refer to it often, but this time I am quoting three paragraphs in the Introduction: "This book originated in a request from the Pan African Congress for a brief over-all survey of the Colonial Problem in British Africa, in the light of the new Economic Imperialism, euphemistically described as Colonial Development and Welfare.

"Parliament, the press and radio — politicians, journalists and broadcasters — vie with one another in assuring the British people that what they have lost in Asia they will recover in Africa. Truly, 'The sun of Empire will not set, while Empire nuts abound,' (i.e., palm nuts and oil). Two factors are largely responsible for this post-war interest in the African El Dorado. The first is the decline of British Imperial power in the East. For centuries Asia, the largest, richest and most densely populated of the continents, was Britain's chief milch-cow. Now that India and Burma have broken the fetters of Imperialism, Ceylon has attained qualified Dominion status, and Malaya is straining at the leash, the British ruling classes have been forced to look elsewhere for new sources of profits.

"Strategically, Africa has been cast for the role of 'savior' of Western European Christian Civilization against Asiatic Communism — ex Africa semper aliquid novi."

CARTER G. WOODSON

Carter Woodson was a dynamic character, whose chief fame will rest on his initiation of Negro History Week and his "Journal of Negro History," first published in January 1916, and now in its 34th volume. Woodson represents the kind of man who concentrated his life on one object. He never faltered. He seldom hesitated. He was turned aside at times by need of earning a living, by teaching and collegiate work; but that did not tempt him long from his main work, the study of Negro history; and this, his life object, he accomplished splendidly.

On the other hand, this devotion to one ideal cost him and the world something. He was not a companionable man; he did not have a large circle of friends. He had an independence and austerity which often repelled people, even those who had for him the greatest admiration. He never married and had no family ties, his income was always meager; but his output in books and articles was large. It was an astonishing task which he accomplished in making the United States, white and black, stop once a year and remember that the American Negro had done things: had thought, and toiled and sung and contributed to the development of the nation. It would of course have been logical if he had received generous support for his work. When we think of the wealth of America; when we remember the number of foundations today which have sums that they dó not know how to use, it is no credit to the nation that they helped Woodson so little.

LONELY FIGURE

Many of them of course will declare that they were willing to help, but that Woodson was not exactly to be "trusted"; he would not come to heel when whistled to, and fawn. Their willingness to help was therefore always accompanied by a desire, unobtrusively, of course, to control or at least direct in general lines the work which Woodson was doing. This Woodson absolutely and definitely refused to allow. In this refusal he probably went to extremes; there might have been much help available, where the control would have been at a minimum and where he would have had large freedom of work; this he did not believe and therefore he went forward in his own way, a lonely, austere figure, with bitter individuality and independence but with absolute sincerity and unceasing work.

Twice I tried to see if I could not arrange for the continuation of his work after death and the lightening of his burden of self-support. Once I almost got his consent to join my department of Publications and Research, in the NAACP; but he finally decided that if he came to the NAACP, he must have a separate and independent department. This I could not guarantee him, because I knew that the organization was not disposed to set up another department. Then later, I tried to use what little influence I had so that his work would be integrated with that of Howard University. He went there in the capacity of Dean and very naturally did not like executive work. It was probably well that he did not stay; if he had, it would have been another case where a scholar was turned into doing chores. So it happened, and this in itself was an accomplishment, that his work was mainly supported by colored people; people of small income and limited erudition, who gave to the Association of Negro Life and History in order to keep the work going. This meant of course that his funds were always limited, that he had difficulty in paying for publication and that he could not hire the help and assistance and do the research which he needed to do, and which would have been of so great help to his main object. But that it was possible for a Negro scholar to support himself from the small contributions mainly from his own people and perform the miracle of making a small scientific journal on an unpopular subject, self-supporting for a generation is a tribute to Carter Woodson, and to the American Negro.

No white university ever recognized his work; no white scientific society ever honored him. Perhaps this was his greatest award.

I Bury My Wife

I have just returned from the town where I was born, Great Barrington, Massachusetts. There I laid to rest, in the sunshine and under the great and beautiful elms, the wife to whom I have been married for 55 years. With all of its sadness it was a beautiful experience, because after decades of work and years of sickness, the life of this woman was brought to a beautiful end, and the dark fear that somehow she might outlive me and that I would be unable to care for her until the end — this was gone.

We had been married over half a century. I met Nina Gomer at Wilber-force, where I first began my life work as a teacher. She was a student there. In appearance, of remarkable beauty with her great mass of coiled black hair and extraordinarily beautiful eyes. People used to stop and stare at her on the street. But she had no consciousness of her beauty and paid little personal attention to it. Indeed her looks were not her chief characteristic and I never thought so even when at the age of 27, I married her. Her great gift was her singularly honest character; her passion for cleanliness and order and her loyalty. That was her contribution to our joint life. Sometimes I felt burdened under it; our home seemed a bit too clean and too carefully kept. I wanted many times to have her forget her housework and throw away her careful plans for daily life and romp and laugh. She seldom did this, because she could not; it was not in her nature. She was always serious and yet a good companion. She held the balance true and her concept of the reality of life kept me from surging and wandering and perhaps from overturning our chariot of life.

I was not, on the whole, what one would describe as a good husband. The family and its interests were never the main center of my life. I was always striving to guide the world and certainly the Negro group, so that always I was ranging away in body or in soul and leaving the home to my wife. She must often have been lonesome and wanted more regular and personal

From the *Chicago Globe*, July 15, 1950.

companionship than I gave. And yet on the other hand, she was as avid for the things I thought I was doing and as proud of any accomplishments as I was. One never knows under such circumstances, just what might have been changed for the better. Ours was a pleasant and fruitful partnership, not completely ideal for it had ups and downs, but it was peaceful and good. In one respect it was near the ideal, and of this I was proud because according to my bringing up I was a "good provider." My wife was never in financial trouble. We always had a good home, even beautiful; we had food and clothes. We traveled, not only over large parts of the United States, but in England, France and Italy. We saw something of the Good Life; we were never "in want." In fact in all these 55 years, I do not think it once occurred to either of us as probable or possible that we should ever be separated or the family tie broken. Both of us had been brought up under the old-fashioned concept of marriage as permanent, "until death do us part."

We had two children. One, a little boy who came suddenly, unexpectedly, miraculously. Physically he was a perfect child and in the few months of his life, vivid in personality. But down in Atlanta, he caught one of those spring intestinal infections, which might easily have been avoided and even stopped had we been persons of greater experience. As it was, at the age of only a year and a half, suddenly he died. And in a sense my wife died too. Never after that was she quite the same in her attitude toward life and the world. Down below was all this great ocean dark bitterness. It seemed all so unfair. I too, felt the blow. Something was gone from my life which would not come back. But after all Life was left and the World and I could plunge back into it as she could not. Even when our little girl came two years later, she could not altogether replace the One. So it seemed fitting that at the end of her life, she should go back to the hills of Berkshire, where the boy had been born and be buried beside him, in soil where my fathers for more than two centuries lived and died. I feel that here she will lie in peace. And I am infinitely glad that I lived long enough to keep her from poverty and worry and excess of pain and to see her die in honor and love.

A Vista of Ninety Fruitful Years

This is the month of my 90th birthday. I have lived to an age which is increasingly distasteful to this nation. Unless by 60 a man has gained possession of enough to support himself without paid employment, he faces the distinct possibility of starvation. He is liable to lose his job and to refusal if he seeks another. At 70 he is frowned upon by the Church and if he is foolish enough to survive until 90, he is often regarded as a freak.

This is because in the face of human experience the United States has discovered that Youth knows more than Age. When a man of 35 becomes president of a great institution of learning or United State Senator or head of a multi-million dollar corporation, a cry of triumph rings in the land. Why? To pretend that 15 years bring of themselves more wisdom and understanding than 50 is a contradiction in terms.

Given a fool, a hundred years will not make him wise; but given an idiot, he will not be wise at 20. Youth is more courageous than age because it knows less. Age is wiser than youth because it knows more. This all mankind has affirmed from Egypt and China 5,000 years ago to Britain and Germany today.

The United States knows better. I would have been hailed with approval if I had died at 50. At 75 my death was practically requested. If living does not give value, wisdom and meaning to life, then there is no sense in living at all. If immature and inexperienced men rule the earth, then the earth deserves what it gets: the repetition of age-old mistakes, and wild welcome for what men knew a thousand years ago was disaster.

I do not apologize for living long. High on the ramparts of this blistering hell of life, I sit and see the Truth. I look it full in the face, and I will not lie about it, neither to myself nor to the world. I see my country as what Cedric Belfrage aptly characterizes as a "Frightened Giant," afraid of the Truth, afraid of Peace. I see a land which is degenerating and faces decadence, unless it has sense enough to turn about and start back.

From the *National Guardian*, February 17, 1958.

It is no sin to fail. It is the habit of man. It is disaster to go on when you know you are going wrong. I judge this land not merely by statistics or reading lies agreed upon by historians. I judge by what I have seen, heard, and lived through for near a century.

There was a day when the world rightly called Americans honest even if crude; earning their living by hard work; telling the truth no matter whom it hurt; and going to war only in what they believed a just cause after nothing else seemed possible.

Today we are lying, stealing, and killing. We call all this by finer names: Advertising, Free Enterprise, and National Defense. But names in the end deceive no one; today we use science to help us deceive our fellows; we take wealth that we never earned and we are devoting all our energies to kill, maim, and drive insane, men, women and children who dare refuse to do what we want done.

No nation threatens us. We threaten the world. Our President says that Foster Dulles is the wisest man he knows. If Dulles is wise, God help our fools—the fools who rule us.

They know why we fail—these military masters of men—we haven't taught our children mathematics and physics. No, it is because we have not taught our children to read and write or to behave like human beings and not like hoodlums. Every child on my street is whooping it up with toy guns and big boys with real pistols. When Elvis Presley goes through the motions of copulation on the public stage it takes the city police force to hold back teen-age children from hysteria.

What are we doing about it? Half the Christian churches of New York are trying to ruin the free public schools in order to replace them by religious dogma; and the other half are too interested in Venezuelan oil to assist the best center in Brooklyn in fighting youthful delinquency, or to prevent a bishop from kicking William Howard Melish into the street and closing his church. Which of the hundreds of churches sitting half empty protests about this? None. They hire Billy Graham to replace the circus in Madison Square Garden.

All this must not be mentioned even if you know it and see it. America must never be criticized even by honest and sincere men. America must always be praised, or you lose your job or are ostracized or land in jail.

Criticism is treason, and treason or the hint of treason testified to by hired liars may be punished by shameful death. I saw Ethel Rosenberg lying beautiful in her coffin beside her mate. I tried to stammer futile words above her grave. But not over graves should we shout this failure of justice, but from the housetops of the world.

Honest men may and must criticize America: describe how she has ruined her democracy, sold out her jury system, and led her seats of justice astray. The only question that may arise is whether this criticism is based on truth, not whether it may be openly expressed.

What is truth? What can it be when the President of the United States, guiding the nation, stands up in public and says: *"The world also thinks of us as a land which has never enslaved anyone."* Everyone who heard this knew it was not true. Yet here stands the successor of George Washington who bought, owned, and sold slaves; the successor of Abraham Lincoln who freed four million slaves after they had helped him win victory over the slave-holding South. And so far as I have seen, not a single periodical, not even a Negro weekly, has dared challenge or even criticize that extraordinary falsehood.

This is what I call decadence. It could not have happened 50 years ago. In the day of our fiercest controversy we have not dared thus publicly to silence opinion. I have lived through disagreement, vilification, and war and war again. But in all that time, I have never seen the right of human beings to think so challenged and denied as today.

The day after I was born, Andrew Johnson was impeached. He deserved punishment as a traitor to the poor Southern whites and poorer freedmen. Yet during his life, no one denied him the right to defend himself.

A half century ago, in 1910, I tried to state and carry into realization unpopular ideas against a powerful opposition — in the white South, in the reactionary North, and even among my own people. I found my thought being misconstrued and I planned an organ of propaganda — *The Crisis* — where I would be free to say what I believed.

This was no easy sailing. My magazine reached but a fraction of the nation. It was bitterly attacked and once the government suppressed it. But in the end I maintained a platform of radical thinking on the Negro question which influenced many minds. War and depression ended my independence of thought and forced me to return to teaching, but with the certainty that I had at least started a new line of belief and action.

As a result of my work and that of others, the Supreme Court began to restore democracy in the South and finally outlawed discrimination in public services based on color. This caused rebellion in the South which the nation is afraid to meet.

The Negro stands bewildered and attempt is made by appointments to unimportant offices and trips abroad to bribe him into silence. His art and literature cease to function. He is scared. Only the children like those at Little Rock stand and fight.

The Yale sophomore who replaced a periodical of brains by a book of pictures concealed in advertisements, proposed that America rule the world. This failed because we could not rule ourselves. But Texas to the rescue, as

Lyndon Johnson proposes that America take over outer space. Somewhere beyond the moon there must be sentient creatures rolling in inextinguishable laughter at the antics of our earth.

We tax ourselves into poverty and crime so as to make the rich richer and bring more crime and poverty. We know the cause of this: it is to permit our rich business interests to stop socialism and to prevent the ideals of communism from ever triumphing on earth. The aim is impossible.

Socialism progresses and will progress. All we can do is to silence and jail its promoters. I believe in socialism. I seek a world where the ideals of communism will triumph — to each according to his need; from each according to his ability. For this I will work as long as I live. And I still live.

III

Social Science
and Civil Rights

At its best, Du Bois's scholarship blended empirical rigor and moral indignation. Although he professed a commitment to objective social science, he was temperamentally incapable of neutrality. "The lesson" of the calamity of slavery, he lectured in his first publication, *The Suppression of the African Slave Trade to the United States of America, 1638–1870* (1896), was that "it behooves nations as well as men to do things at the very moment when they ought to be done." The series of conference reports edited and published annually by Du Bois from 1898 to 1910, informally known as the Atlanta University Studies, perfectly incorporated "objective" data painstakingly accumulated and value judgments condignly rendered. Du Bois's "The Laboratory in Sociology at Atlanta University," a cogent statement appearing in the May 1903 issue of the *Annals of the American Academy of Political and Social Science*, outlined the groundbreaking research he believed would demystify the mores and institutions of urban and rural African-Americans and provide, consequently, a rational basis for race relations policies. Declaring in *The Philadelphia Negro* (1899) that "the world was thinking wrong about race, because it did not know," Du Bois sought to put social science squarely in the service of civil rights through prolific output of essays, monographs, and reviews on such subjects covered in this section as John Brown, slavery, Reconstruction, and group intelligence. "The Propaganda of History," the fiery essay concluding *Black Reconstruction in America*, his magisterial 1935 work of historical revisionism, reveals Du Bois at his moralizing finest. After fourteen years as founding editor of *The Crisis*, he returned to the classroom and, as "The Negro Encyclopedia," the piece in *Crisis* appearing shortly before his departure from the NAACP, shows, Du Bois never abandoned his early belief in the power of scholarship to change society.

Economics

The history of slavery and the slave-trade after 1820 must be read in the light of the industrial revolution through which the civilized world passed in the first half of the nineteenth century. Between the years 1775 and 1825 occurred economic events and changes of the highest importance and widest influence. Though all branches of industry felt the impulse of this new industrial life, yet, "if we consider single industries, cotton manufacture has, during the nineteenth century, made the most magnificent and gigantic advances."[1] This fact is easily explained by the remarkable series of inventions that revolutionized this industry between 1738 and 1830, including Arkwright's, Watt's, Compton's, and Cartwright's epoch-making contrivances.[2] The effect which these inventions had on the manufacture of cotton goods is best illustrated by the fact that in England, the chief cotton market of the world, the consumption of raw cotton rose steadily from 13,000 bales in 1781, to 572,000 in 1820, to 871,000 in 1830, and to 3,366,000 in 1860.[3] Very early, therefore, came the query whence the supply of raw cotton was to come. Tentative experiments on the rich, broad fields of the Southern United States, together with the indispensable invention of Whitney's cotton-gin, soon answered this question: a new economic future was opened up to this land, and immediately the whole South began to extend its cotton culture, and more and more to throw its whole energy into this one staple.

Here it was that the fatal mistake of compromising with slavery in the beginning, and of the policy of *laissez-faire* pursued thereafter, became painfully manifest; for, instead now of a healthy, normal, economic development along proper industrial lines, we have the abnormal and fatal rise of a slave-labor large-farming system, which, before it was realized, had so intertwined itself with and braced itself upon the economic forces of an industrial age, that a vast and terrible civil war was necessary to displace it. The tendencies to a patriarchal serfdom, recognizable in the age of Washington and Jefferson,

From *The Suppression of the African Slave Trade to the United States of America, 1638–1870* (1896).

began slowly but surely to disappear; and in the second quarter of the century Southern slavery was irresistibly changing from a family institution to an industrial system.

The development of Southern slavery has heretofore been viewed so exclusively from the ethical and social standpoint that we are apt to forget its close and indissoluble connection with the world's cotton market. Beginning with 1820, a little after the close of the Napoleonic wars, when the industry of cotton manufacture had begun its modern development and the South had definitely assumed her position as chief producer of raw cotton, we find the average price of cotton per pound, 8½d. From this time until 1845 the price steadily fell, until in the latter year it reached 4d.; the only exception to this fall was in the years 1832–1839, when, among other things, a strong increase in the English demand, together with an attempt of the young slave power to "corner" the market, sent the price up as high as 11d. The demand for cotton goods soon outran a crop which McCullough had pronounced "prodigious," and after 1845 the price started on a steady rise, which, except for the checks suffered during the continental revolutions and the Crimean War, continued until 1860.[4] The steady increase in the production of cotton explains the fall in price down to 1845. In 1822 the crop was a half-million bales; in 1831, a million; in 1838, a million and a half; and in 1840–1843, two million. By this time the world's consumption of cotton goods began to increase so rapidly that, in spite of the increase in Southern crops, the price kept rising. Three million bales were gathered in 1852, three and a half million in 1856, and the remarkable crop of five million bales in 1860.[5]

Here we have data to explain largely the economic development of the South. By 1822 the large-plantation slave system had gained footing; in 1838–1839 it was able to show its power in the cotton "corner": by the end of the next decade it had not only gained a solid economic foundation, but it had built a closed oligarchy with a political policy. The changes in price during the next few years drove out of competition many survivors of the small-farming free-labor system, and put the slave *régime* in position to dictate the policy of the nation. The zenith of the system and the first inevitable signs of decay came in the years 1850–1860, when the rising price of cotton threw the whole economic energy of the South into its cultivation, leading to a terrible consumption of soil and slaves, to a great increase in the size of plantations, and to increasing power and effrontery on the part of the slave barons. Finally, when a rising moral crusade conjoined with threatened economic disaster, the oligarchy, encouraged by the state of the cotton market, risked all on a political *coup-d'état*, which failed in the war of 1861–1865.[6]

The attitude of the South toward the slave-trade changed *pari passu* with this development of the cotton trade. From 1808 to 1820 the South half wished to get rid of a troublesome and abnormal institution, and yet saw no way to do so. The fear of insurrection and of the further spread of the disagreeable system led her to consent to the partial prohibition of the trade by severe national enactments. Nevertheless, she had in the matter no settled policy: she refused to support vigorously the execution of the laws she had helped to make, and at the same time she acknowledged the theoretical necessity of these laws. After 1820, however, there came a gradual change. The South found herself supplied with a body of slave laborers, whose number had been augmented by large illicit importations, with an abundance of rich land, and with all other natural facilities for raising a crop which was in large demand and peculiarly adapted to slave labor. The increasing crop caused a new demand for slaves, and an inter-state slave-traffic arose between the Border and the Gulf States, which turned the former into slave-breeding districts, and bound them to the slave States by ties of strong economic interest.

As the cotton crop continued to increase, this source of supply became inadequate, especially as the theory of land and slave consumption broke down former ethical and prudential bounds. It was, for example, found cheaper to work a slave to death in a few years, and buy a new one, than to care for him in sickness and old age; so, too, it was easier to despoil rich, new land in a few years of intensive culture, and move on to the Southwest, than to fertilize and conserve the soil.[7] Consequently, there early came a demand for land and slaves greater than the country could supply. The demand for land showed itself in the annexation of Texas, the conquest of Mexico, and the movement toward the acquisition of Cuba. The demand for slaves was manifested in the illicit traffic that noticeably increased about 1835, and reached large proportions by 1860. It was also seen in a disposition to attack the government for stigmatizing the trade as criminal,[8] then in a disinclination to take any measures which would have rendered our repressive laws effective; and finally in such articulate declarations by prominent men as this: "Experience having settled the point, that this Trade *cannot be abolished by the use of force*, and that blockading squadrons serve only to make it more profitable and more cruel, I am surprised that the attempt is persisted in, unless as it serves as a cloak to some other purposes. It would be far better than it now is, for the African, if the trade was free from all restrictions, and left to the mitigation and decay which time and competition would surely bring about."[9]

• • •

Economic measures against the trade were those which from the beginning had the best chance of success, but which were least tried. They included tariff measures; efforts to encourage the immigration of free laborers and the emigration of the slaves; measures for changing the character of Southern industry; and, finally, plans to restore the economic balance which slavery destroyed, by raising the condition of the slave to that of complete freedom and responsibility. Like the political efforts, these rested in part on a moral basis; and, as legal enactments, they were also themselves often political measures. They differed, however, from purely moral and political efforts, in having as a main motive the economic gain which a substitution of free for slave labor promised.

The simplest form of such efforts was the revenue duty on slaves that existed in all the colonies. This developed into the prohibitive tariff, and into measures encouraging immigration or industrial improvements. The colonization movement was another form of these efforts; it was inadequately conceived, and not altogether sincere, but it had a sound, although in this case impracticable, economic basis. The one great measure which finally stopped the slave-trade forever was, naturally, the abolition of slavery, i.e., the giving to the Negro the right to sell his labor at a price consistent with his own welfare. The abolition of slavery itself, while due in part to direct moral appeal and political sagacity, was largely the result of the economic collapse of the large-farming slave system.

It may be doubted if ever before such political mistakes as the slavery compromises of the Constitutional Convention had such serious results, and yet, by a succession of unexpected accidents, still left a nation in position to work out its destiny. No American can study the connection of slavery with United States history, and not devoutly pray that his country may never have a similar social problem to solve, until it shows more capacity for such work than it has shown in the past. It is neither profitable nor in accordance with scientific truth to consider that whatever the constitutional fathers did was right, or that slavery was a plague sent from God and fated to be eliminated in due time. We must face the fact that this problem arose principally from the cupidity and carelessness of our ancestors. It was the plain duty of the colonies to crush the trade and the system in its infancy: they preferred to enrich themselves on its profits. It was the plain duty of a Revolution based upon "Liberty" to take steps toward the abolition of slavery: it preferred promises to straightforward action. It was the plain duty of the Constitutional Convention, in founding a new nation, to compromise with a threatening social evil only in case its settlement would thereby be postponed to a more favorable time: this was not the case in the slavery and the slave-trade compromises; there never was a time in the history of America when the system had a slighter economic, political, and moral justification than in 1787; and yet with this real, existent, growing evil before their eyes, a bargain largely of dollars and cents was allowed to open the highway that led straight to the Civil War. Moreover, it was due to no wisdom and foresight on the part of the fathers that fortuitous circumstances made the result of that war what it was, nor was it due to exceptional philanthropy on the part of their descendants that that result included the abolition of slavery.

With the faith of the nation broken at the very outset, the system of slavery untouched, and twenty years' respite given to the slave-trade to feed and foster it, there began, with 1787, that system of bargaining, truckling, and compromising with a moral, political, and economic monstrosity, which makes the history of our dealing with slavery in the first half of the nineteenth century so discreditable to a great people. Each generation sought to shift its load upon the next, and the burden rolled on, until a generation came which was both too weak and too strong to bear it longer. One cannot, to be sure, demand of whole nations exceptional moral foresight and heroism; but a certain hard common-sense in facing the complicated phenomena of political life must be expected in every progressive people. In some respects we as a nation seem to lack this; we have the somewhat inchoate idea that we are not destined to be harassed with great social questions, and that even if we are, and fail to answer them, the fault is with the question and not with us. Consequently we often congratulate ourselves more on getting rid of a problem than on solving it. Such an attitude is dangerous; we have and shall have, as other peoples have had, critical, momentous, and pressing questions to answer. The riddle of the Sphinx may be postponed, it may be evasively answered now; sometime it must be fully answered.

It behooves the United States, therefore, in the interest both of scientific truth and of future social reform, carefully to study such chapters of her history as that of the suppression of the slave-trade. The most obvious question which this study suggests is: How far in a State can a recognized moral wrong safely be compromised? And although this chapter of history can give us no definite answer suited to the ever-varying aspects of political life, yet it would seem to warn any nation from allowing, through carelessness and moral cowardice, any social evil to grow. No persons would have seen the Civil War with more surprise and horror than the Revolutionists of 1776; yet from the small and apparently dying institution of their day arose the walled and castled Slave-Power. From this we may conclude that it behooves nations as well as men to do things at the very moment when they ought to be done.

Notes

1. Beer, *Geschichte des Welthandels im* 19ten *Jahrhundert*, II. 67.
2. A list of these inventions most graphically illustrates this advance: —

    1738,   John Jay, fly-shuttle.
             John Wyatt, spinning by rollers.
    1748,   Lewis Paul, carding-machine.
     1760,   Robert Kay, drop-box.
    1769,   Richard Arkwright, water-frame and throstle.
             James Watt, steam-engine.
    1772,   James Lees, improvements on carding-machine.
    1775,   Richard Arkwright, series of combinations.
    1779,   Samuel Compton, mule.
    1785,   Edmund Cartwright, power-loom.
    1803–4,   Radcliffe and Johnson, dressing-machine.
    1817,   Roberts, fly-frame.
    1818,   William Eaton, self-acting frame.
    1825–30,   Roberts, improvements on mule.

    Cf. Baines, *History of the Cotton Manufacture*, pp. 116–231; *Encyclopædia Britannica*, 9th ed., article "Cotton."
3. Baines, *History of the Cotton Manufacture*, p. 215. A bale weighed from 375 lbs. to 400 lbs.
4. The prices cited are from Newmarch and Tooke, and refer to the London market. The average price in 1855–60 was about 7*d.*
5. From United States census reports.
6. Cf. United States census reports; and Olmsted, *The Cotton Kingdom*.
7. Cf. *Ibid.*
8. As early as 1836 Calhoun declared that he should ever regret that the term "piracy" had been applied to the slave-trade in our laws: Benton, *Abridgment of Debates*, XII. 718.
9. Governor J. H. Hammond of South Carolina, in *Letters to Clarkson*, No. I, p. 2.

Methodology

In the fall of 1896 a house to house visitation was made to all the Negro
families of this ward [Philadelphia's Seventh Ward]. The visitor went in
person to each residence and called for the head of the family. The housewife usually responded, the husband now and then, and sometimes an older
daughter or other member of the family. The fact that the University was
making an investigation of this character was known and discussed in the
ward, but its exact scope and character were not known. The mere announcement of the purpose secured, in all but about twelve cases,[1] immediate admission. Seated then in the parlor, kitchen, or living room, the visitor
began the questioning, using his discretion as to the order in which they
were put, and omitting or adding questions as the circumstances suggested.
Now and then the purpose of a particular query was explained, and usually
the object of the whole inquiry indicated. General discussions often arose as
to the condition of the Negroes, which were instructive. From ten minutes
to an hour was spent in each home, the average time being fifteen to twenty-
five minutes.

Usually the answers were prompt and candid, and gave no suspicion of
previous preparation. In some cases there was evident falsification or evasion.
In such cases the visitor made free use of his best judgment and either inserted
no answer at all, or one which seemed approximately true. In some cases the
families visited were not at home, and a second or third visit was paid. In other
cases, and especially in the case of the large class of lodgers, the testimony of
landlords and neighbors often had to be taken.

No one can make an inquiry of this sort and not be painfully conscious of a
large margin of error from omissions, errors of judgment and deliberate
deception. Of such errors this study has, without doubt, its full share. Only
one fact was peculiarly favorable and that is the proverbial good nature and
candor of the Negro. With a more cautious and suspicious people much less

From *The Philadelphia Negro: A Social Study* (1899).

success could have been obtained. Naturally some questions were answered better than others; the chief difficulty arising in regard to the questions of age and income. The ages given for people forty and over have a large margin of error, owing to ignorance of the real birthday. The question of income was naturally a delicate one, and often had to be gotten at indirectly. The yearly income, as a round sum, was seldom asked for; rather the daily or weekly wages taken and the time employed during the year.

On December 1, 1896, there were in the Seventh Ward of Philadelphia 9675 Negroes; 4501 males and 5174 females. This total includes all persons of Negro descent, and 33 intermarried whites.[2] It does not include residents of the ward then in prisons or in almshouses. There were a considerable number of omissions among the loafers and criminals without homes, the class of lodgers and the club-house habitués. These were mostly males, and their inclusion would somewhat affect the division by sexes, although probably not to a great extent.[3] The increase of the Negro population in this ward for six and a half years is 814, or at the rate of 14.13 per cent per decade. This is perhaps somewhat smaller than that for the population of the city at large, for the Seventh Ward is crowded and overflowing into other wards. Possibly the present Negro population of the city is between 43,000 and 45,000. At all events it is probable that the crest of the tide of immigration is passed, and that the increase for the decade 1890–1900 will not be nearly as large as the 24 per cent of the decade 1880–1890.

NEGRO POPULATION OF SEVENTH WARD.

Age.	Male.	Female.
Under 10	570	641
10 to 19	483	675
20 to 29	1,276	1,444
30 to 39	1,046	1,084
40 to 49	553	632
50 to 59	298	331
60 to 69	114	155
70 and over	41	96
Age unknown	120	116
Total	4,501	5,174
Grand total		9,675

The division by sex indicates still a very large, and it would seem, growing excess of women. The return shows 1150 females to every 1000 males. Possibly through the omission of men and the unavoidable duplication of some servants lodging away from their place of service, the disproportion of the sexes is exaggerated. At any rate it is great, and if growing, may be an indication of increased restriction in the employments open to Negro men since 1880 or even since 1890. . . .

Notes

1. The majority of these were brothels. A few, however, were homes of respectable people who resented the investigation as unwarranted and unnecessary.
2. Twenty-nine women and four men. . . .
3. There may have been some duplication in the counting of servant girls who do not lodge where they work. Special pains was taken to count them only where they lodge, but there must have been some errors. Again, the Seventh Ward has a very large number of lodgers; some of these form a sort of floating population, and here were omissions; some were forgotten by landladies and others purposely omitted.

The Meaning of All This

Two sorts of answers are usually returned to the bewildered American who asks seriously: What is the Negro problem? The one is straightforward and clear: it is simply this, or simply that, and one simple remedy long enough applied will in time cause it to disappear. The other answer is apt to be hopelessly involved and complex — to indicate no simple panacea, and to end in a somewhat hopeless — There it is; what can we do? Both of these sorts of answers have something of truth in them: the Negro problem looked at in one way is but the old world questions of ignorance, poverty, crime, and the dislike of the stranger. On the other hand it is a mistake to think that attacking each of these questions single-handed without reference to the others will settle the matter: a combination of social problems is far more than a matter of mere addition, — the combination itself is a problem. Nevertheless the Negro problems are not more hopelessly complex than many others have been. Their elements despite their bewildering complication can be kept clearly in view: they are after all the same difficulties over which the world has grown gray: the question as to how far human intelligence can be trusted and trained; as to whether we must always have the poor with us; as to whether it is possible for the mass of men to attain righteousness on earth; and then to this is added that question of questions: After all who are Men? Is every featherless biped to be counted a man and brother? Are all races and types to be joint heirs of the new earth that men have striven to raise in thirty centuries and more? Shall we not swamp civilization in barbarism and drown genius in indulgence if we seek a mythical Humanity which shall shadow all men? The answer of the early centuries to this puzzle was clear: those of any nation who can be called Men and endowed with rights are few: they are the privileged classes — the well-born and the accidents of low-birth called up by the King. The rest, the mass of the nation, the *pöbel*, the mob, are fit to follow, to obey, to dig and delve, but not to think or rule or play the gentleman. We who were born to another

From *The Philadelphia Negro: A Social Study* (1899).

162

philosophy hardly realize how deep-seated and plausible this view of human capabilities and powers once was; how utterly incomprehensible this republic would have been to Charlemagne or Charles V or Charles I. We rather hasten to forget that once the courtiers of English kings looked upon the ancestors of most Americans with far greater contempt than these Americans look upon Negroes — and perhaps, indeed, had more cause. We forget that once French peasants were the "Niggers" of France, and that German princelings once discussed with doubt the brains and humanity of the *bauer*.

Much of this — or at least some of it — has passed and the world has glided by blood and iron into a wider humanity, a wider respect for simple manhood unadorned by ancestors or privilege. Not that we have discovered, as some hoped and some feared, that all men were created free and equal, but rather that the differences in men are not so vast as we had assumed. We still yield the well-born the advantages of birth, we still see that each nation has its dangerous flock of fools and rascals; but we also find most men have brains to be cultivated and souls to be saved.

And still this widening of the idea of common Humanity is of slow growth and to-day but dimly realized. We grant full citizenship in the World-Commonwealth to the "Anglo-Saxon" (whatever that may mean), the Teuton and the Latin; then with just a shade of reluctance we extend it to the Celt and Slav. We half deny it to the yellow races of Asia, admit the brown Indians to an ante-room only on the strength of an undeniable past; but with the Negroes of Africa we come to a full stop, and in its heart the civilized world with one accord denies that these come within the pale of nineteenth century Humanity. This feeling, widespread and deep-seated, is, in America, the vastest of the Negro problems; we have, to be sure, a threatening problem of ignorance but the ancestors of most Americans were far more ignorant than the freedmen's sons; these ex-slaves are poor but not as poor as the Irish peasants used to be; crime is rampant but not more so, if as much, as in Italy; but the difference is that the ancestors of the English and the Irish and the Italians were felt to be worth educating, helping and guiding because they were men and brothers, while in America a census which gives a slight indication of the utter disappearance of the American Negro from the earth is greeted with ill-concealed delight.

Other centuries looking back upon the culture of the nineteenth would have a right to suppose that if, in a land of freemen, eight millions of human beings were found to be dying of disease, the nation would cry with one voice, "Heal them!" If they were staggering on in ignorance, it would cry, "Train them!" If they were harming themselves and others by crime, it would cry, "Guide them!" And such cries are heard and have been heard in the land; but it was not one voice and its volume has been ever broken by counter-cries and echoes, "Let them die!" "Train them like slaves!" "Let them stagger downward!"

This is the spirit that enters in and complicates all Negro social problems and this is a problem which only civilization and humanity can successfully solve. Meantime we have the other problems before us — we have the problems arising from the uniting of so many social questions about one centre. In such a situation we need only to avoid underestimating the difficulties on the one hand and overestimating them on the other. The problems are difficult, extremely difficult, but they are such as the world has conquered before and can conquer again. Moreover the battle involves more than a mere altruistic interest in an alien people. It is a battle for humanity and human culture. If in the hey-dey of the greatest of the world's civilizations, it is possible for one people ruthlessly to steal another, drag them helpless across the water, enslave them, debauch them, and then slowly murder them by economic and social exclusion until they disappear from the face of the earth — if the consummation of such a crime be possible in the twentieth century, then our civilization is vain and the republic is a mockery and a farce.

But this will not be; first, even with the terribly adverse circumstances under which Negroes live, there is not the slightest likelihood of their dying out; a nation that has endured the slave-trade, slavery, reconstruction, and present prejudice three hundred years, and under it increased in numbers and efficiency, is not in any immediate danger of extinction. Nor is the thought of voluntary or involuntary emigration more than a dream of men who forget that there are half as many Negroes in the United States as Spaniards in Spain. If this be so then a few plain propositions may be laid down as axiomatic:

1. The Negro is here to stay.

2. It is to the advantage of all, both black and white, that every Negro should make the best of himself.

3. It is the duty of the Negro to raise himself by every effort to the standards of modern civilization and not to lower those standards in any degree.

4. It is the duty of the white people to guard their civilization against debauchment by themselves or others; but in order to do this it is not necessary to hinder and retard the efforts of an earnest people to rise, simply because they lack faith in the ability of that people.

5. With these duties in mind and with a spirit of self-help, mutual aid and co-operation, the two races should strive side by side to realize the ideals of the republic and make this truly a land of equal opportunity for all men. . . .

The Laboratory in Sociology
at Atlanta University

There is some ground for suspicion when a small institution of learning offers courses in sociology. Very often such work means simply prolonged discussions of society and social units, which degenerate into bad metaphysics and false psychology, or it may take a statistical turn and the student become so immersed in mere figures as to forget, or be entirely unacquainted with, the concrete facts standing back of the counting.

On the other hand every one feels how necessary social study is, — how widespread in modern times is our ignorance of social facts and processes. In such matters we still linger in a Middle Age of credulity and superstition. We print in the opening chapters of our children's histories theories of the origin and destiny of races over which the gravest of us must smile; we assume, for instance, elaborate theories of an "Aryan" type of political institution, and then discover in the pits of the South African Basutos as perfect an agora or tungemot as ever existed among Greeks or Germans. At the same time all of us feel the rhythm in human action; we are sure that the element of chance is at least not supreme, and no generation has taken to the study of social phenomena more energetically or successfully than ours. Have we, however, accomplished enough or settled the matter of scope and method sufficiently to introduce the subject of sociology successfully into the small college or the high school?

I am not sure that our experience at Atlanta University contributes much toward answering this question, for our position is somewhat exceptional, and yet I think it throws light on it. Atlanta University is situated within a few miles of the geographical centre of the Negro population of the nation, and is, therefore, near the centre of that congeries of human problems which cluster

From the *Annals of the American Academy of Political and Social Science*, 21 (May 1903): 160–163.

round the black American. This institution, which forms in itself a "Negro problem," and which prepares students whose lives must of necessity be further factors in this same problem, cannot logically escape the study and teaching of some things connected with that mass of social questions. Nor can these things all be reduced to history and ethics — the mass of them fall logically under sociology.

We have arranged, therefore, what amounts to about two years of sociological work for the junior and senior college students, and we carry on in our conferences postgraduate work in original research. The undergraduate courses in sociology are simply an attempt to study systematically conditions of living right around the university and to compare these conditions with conditions elsewhere about which we are able to learn. For this purpose one of the two years is taken up principally with a course in economics. Here the methods of study are largely inductive, going from field work and personal knowledge to the establishment of the main principles. There is no text-book, but a class-room reference library with from five to ten duplicate copies of well-known works.

In the next year the study comes nearer what is understood by sociology. Here again after much experiment, we have discarded the text-book, not because a book of a certain sort would not be valuable in the hands of students, but rather because available text-books are distinctly and glaringly unsuitable. The book most constantly referred to is Mayo-Smith's "Statistics and Sociology" [Richmond Mayo-Smith, *Science of Statistics*, (New York: Macmillan, 1899)], and after that the United States censuses. Our main object in this year of work is to find out what characteristics of human life can be known, classified and compared. Students are expected to know what the average death-rate of American Negroes is, how it varies, and what it means when compared with the death-rates of other peoples and classes. When they learn by search in the census and their own mathematical calculations that 30 per cent of the Negroes of New York City are twenty to thirty years of age, they immediately set to work to explain this anomaly, and so on. A large part of their work consists of special reports, in which the results of first-hand study of some locality or some characteristic of Negro life are compared with general conditions in the United States and Europe. Thus in a way we measure the Negro problem.

Sometimes these studies are of real scientific value: the class of '99 furnished local studies, which, after some rearrangement, were published in No. 22 of the Bulletin of the United States Department of Labor; the work of another class was used in a series of articles on the housing of the Negro in the *Southern Workman*, and a great deal of the work of other classes has been used in the reports of the Atlanta Conferences. Our main object in the undergraduate work, however, is human training and not the collection of material, and in this we have been fairly successful. The classes are enthusiastic and of average intelligence, and the knowledge of life and of the meaning of life in the modern world is certainly much greater among these students than it would be without such a course of study.

Our postgraduate work in sociology was inaugurated with the thought that a university is primarily a seat of learning, and that Atlanta University, being in the midst of the Negro problems, ought to become a centre of such a systematic and thoroughgoing study of those problems as would gradually raise many of the questions above the realm of opinion and guess into that of scientific knowledge. It goes without saying that our ideals in this respect are far from being realized. Although our researches have cost less than $500 a year, yet we find it difficult and sometimes impossible to raise that meagre sum. We lack proper appliances for statistical work and proper clerical aid; notwithstanding this, something has been done. The plan of work is this: a subject is chosen; it is always a definite, limited subject covering some phase of the general Negro problem; schedules are then prepared, and these with letters are sent to the voluntary correspondents, mostly graduates of this and other Negro institutions of higher training. They, by means of local inquiry, fill out and return the schedules; then other sources of information, depending on the question under discussion, are tried, until after six or eight months' work a body of material is gathered. Then a local meeting is held, at which speakers, who are specially acquainted with the subject studied, discuss it. Finally, about a year after the beginning of the study, a printed report is issued, with full results of the study, digested and tabulated and enlarged by the addition of historical and other material. In this way the following reports have been issued:

No. 1.—Mortality among Negroes in Cities. 51 pp. 1896. (Out of print.)

No. 2.—Social and Physical Conditions of Negroes in Cities. 86 pp. 1897. 50 cents.

No. 3.—Some Efforts of Negroes for Social Betterment. 66 pp. 1898. 50 cents.

No. 4.—The Negro in Business. 78 pp. 1899. 50 cents.

No. 5.—The College-Bred Negro. 115 pp. 1900. (Out of print.) The College-Bred Negro. Second edition, abridged. 32 pp. 25 cents.

No. 6.—The Negro Common School. 118 pp. 1901. 25 cents.

No. 7.—The Negro Artisan. 200 pp. 1902. 50 cents.

No. 8.—The Negro Church. (To be published in 1903.)

Of the effect of this sociological work it is difficult for us who are largely responsible for it to judge. Certain it is that there is a call for scientific study of the American Negro, and it is also clear that no agency is doing anything in this line except Atlanta University, the United States Census Bureau and the United States Department of Labor. In general our reports have been well received, both in this country and in England, and their material has been widely used. In fact they have not received as much criticism as they deserved, which is perhaps one discouraging feature.

Upon the school, the community and the Negro race, the emphasis put on this sort of study has undoubtedly exerted a wholesome influence. It has directed thought and discussion into definite and many times unnoticed channels; it has led to various efforts at social betterment, such as the formation of the National Negro Business League, and it has stimulated healthy self-criticism based on accurate knowledge.

The Call of Kansas

... The North, on the other hand, angry enough at even the necessity of disputing slavery north of the long established line, nevertheless began in good faith to prepare to vote slavery out of Kansas by pouring in free settlers.

Thereupon ensued one of the strangest duels of modern times — a political battle between two economic systems: On the one side were all the machinery of government, close proximity to the battle-field and a deep-seated social ideal which did not propose to abide by the rules of the game; on the other hand were strong moral conviction, pressing economic necessity and capacity for organization. It took four years to fight the battle — from the middle of 1854, when the Kansas-Nebraska Bill was passed and the Indians were hustled out of their rights, until 1858, when the pro-slavery constitution was definitely buried under free state votes.

In the beginning, the fall of 1854, the fatal misunderstanding of the two sections was clear: The New England Emigrant Aid Society assumed that the contest was simply a matter of votes, and that if they hurried settlers to Kansas from the North a majority for freedom was reasonably certain. Missouri and the South, on the other hand, assumed that Kansas was already of right a slave state and resented as an impertinence the attempt to make it free by any means. Thus at Lawrence, on August 1st, the bewildered and unarmed Northern settlers and their immediate successors, such as John Brown's sons, were literally pounced upon by the furious Missourians, who crossed the border like an invading army. "To those who have qualms of conscience as to violating laws, state or national, the time has come when such impositions must be disregarded, as your rights and property are in danger," cried Stringfellow of Missouri. Thereupon 5,000 Missourians proceeded to elect a pro-slavery legislature and Congressional delegate; and led by what Sumner called "hirelings, picked from the drunken spew and vomit of an uneasy civilization," flourished their pistols and bowie-knives, driving some of the free

From *John Brown* (1909).

169

state immigrants back home and the rest into apprehensive inaction and silence.

Snatching thus the whip-hand, with pro-slavery governor, judges, marshal and legislature, they then proceeded in 1855 to deliver blow upon blow to the free state cause until it seemed inevitable that Kansas should become a slave state, with a code of laws which made even an assertion against the right of slaveholding a felony punishable with imprisonment.

The free state settlers hesitatingly began to take serious counsel. They found themselves in three parties: a few who hated slavery, more who hated Negroes, and many who hated slaves. Easily the political *finesse*, afterward unsuccessfully attempted, might now have pitted the parties against one another in such irreconcilable difference as would slip even slavery through. But unblushing force and fraud united them to an appeal for justice at Big Springs in the fall of 1855 — where John Brown's sons were present and active — and a declaration of passive, with a threat of active, resistance to the "bogus" legislature. A peace program was laid down: they would ignore the patent fraud, organize a state and appeal to Congress and the nation. This they did in October and November, 1855, making Topeka their nominal and Lawrence their real capital.

The pro-slavery party, however, was quick to see the weakness of this program and they took the first opportunity to force the free state men into collision with the authorities. A characteristic occasion soon arose: a peaceful free state settler was brutally killed and instead of arresting the murderer, the pro-slavery sheriff arrested the chief witness against him. A few of the bolder free state neighbors released the prisoner and took him to Lawrence. Immediately the sheriff gathered an army of 1,500 deputies from Missouri, and surrounded 500 free state men in Lawrence just after John Brown arrived in Kansas. Things looked serious enough even to the drunken governor, and with the aid of some artifice, liquor and stormy weather, the threatened clash was temporarily averted. The wild and ice-bound winter that fell on Kansas gave a moment's pause, but with the opening spring the pro-slavery forces gathered themselves for a last crushing blow. Armed bands came out of the South with flying banners, the Missouri River was blockaded to Northern immigrants, and the border ruffians rode unhindered over the Missouri line. The free state men, alarmed, appealed to the East and immigrants were hurried forward; but slavery "with the chief justice, the tamed and domesticated chief justice who waited on him like a familiar spirit," declared the passive resistance movement "constructive treason" and the pro-slavery marshal arrested the free state leaders from the governor down, and clapped them into prison. Two thousand Missourians then surrounded Lawrence and while the hesitating free state men were striving to keep the peace, sacked and half burned the town on the day before Brooks broke Sumner's head in the Senate chamber, for telling the truth about Kansas.

The deed was done. Kansas was a slave territory. The free state program had been repudiated by the United States government and had broken like a reed before the assaults of the pro-slavery party. There were mutterings in the East but the cause of freedom was at its lowest ebb. Then suddenly there came the flash of an awful stroke — a deed of retaliation from the free state side so bloody, relentless and cruel that it sent a shudder through all Kansas and Missouri, and aroused the nation. In one black night, John Brown, four of his sons, a son-in-law and two others, the chosen executors of the boldest free state leaders, seized and killed five of the worst of the border ruffians who were harrying the free state settlers, and practically swept out of existence the "Dutch Henry" pro-slavery settlement in the Swamp of the Swan. The rank and file of the free state men themselves recoiled at first in consternation and loudly, then faintly, disclaimed the deed. Suddenly they saw and laid the lie aside, and seized their Sharps rifles. There was war in Kansas — a quick sweeping change from the passive appeal to law and justice which did not respond, to the appeal to force and blood. The deed did not make Kansas free — no one, least of all John Brown, dreamed that it would. But it brought to the fore in free state councils the men who were determined to fight for freedom, and it meant the end of passive resistance. The carnival of crime and rapine that ensued was a disgrace to civilization but it was the cost of freedom, and it was less than the price of repression. There were pitched battles, the building and besieging of forts, the burning of homes, stealing of property, raping of women and murder of men, until the scared governor signed a truce, exchanged prisoners and fled for his life. The wildest pro-slavery elements, now loosed from all restraint, planned a last desperate blow. Nearly 3,000 men were mustered in Missouri. The new governor, whose *cortège* barely escaped highway robbery, found "desolation and ruin" on every hand; "homes and firesides were deserted; the smoke of burning dwellings darkened the atmosphere; women and children, driven from their habitations, wandered over the prairies and among the woodlands, or sought refuge and protection even among the Indian tribes; the highways were infested with numerous predatory bands, and the towns were fortified and garrisoned by armies of conflicting partisans, each excited almost to frenzy, and determined upon mutual extermination." Not only that, but the territorial "treasury was bankrupt, there were no pecuniary resources within herself to meet the exigencies of the time; the Congressional appropriations intended to defray the expenses of a year, were insufficient to meet the demands of a fortnight; the laws were null, the courts virtually suspended and the civil arm of the government almost entirely powerless."*

Governor Geary came in the nick of time and he came with peremptory orders from the frightened government at Washington, who saw that they must either check the whirlwind they had raised, or lose the presidential election of 1856. For not only was there "hell in Kansas" but the North was aflame — the very thing which John Brown and Lane and their fellows designed. A great convention met at Buffalo and mass-meetings were held everywhere. Clothes, money, arms, and men began to pour out of the North. It was no longer a program of peaceful voting; it was fight. The Southern party was certain to be swamped by an army of men, who, though most of them had few convictions as to slavery, did not propose to settle among slaves. The wilder pro-slavery men did not heed. When Shannon ran away and before Geary came, they planned to strike their blow at the free state forces. An army of nearly 3,000 was collected; one wing sacked Osawatomie and the main body was to capture and destroy Lawrence. No sooner was this done than the force of the United States army was to be called in to keep the conquered down. The success of the plan at this juncture might have precipitated Civil War in 1856 instead of 1861, and Geary hurried breathlessly to ward off the mad blow. He succeeded, and by strenuous exertions he was able with some truth to report in Washington before election time: "Peace now reigns in Kansas."

The news, though it helped to elect Buchanan, was received but coldly in Washington, for the Southerners knew how high a price Geary had paid. So evidently was the governor out of favor that before the spring of 1857, the third governor fled in mad haste from his post because of the enmity of his own supporters. It was clear to Washington that Geary's recognition of the free state cause, with the heavy immigration, had already destroyed the possibility of making Kansas a slave state. There were still, however, certain possibilities for *finesse* and political maneuvering. Slaves were already in Kansas and the Dred Scott Decision on March 6, 1857, legalized them there. Moreover, southeast Kansas, thanks to one of the most brutal raids in its history, in the fall of 1856, was still strongly pro-slavery. The constitutional convention was also in that party's hands. By gracefully yielding the legislature therefore to the patent free state majority, it seemed possible that political manipulation might legalize the slaves already in the state. Once this was conceded, there was still a chance to make Kansas a slave state. The pro-slavery men, however, trained in

---

* Farewell address of Governor Geary, *Transactions* of the Kansas State Historical Society, Vol. IV, p. 739.

the upheaval of 1856, were poor material to follow and support the astute Governor Walker. They itched for the law of the club, and made but bungling work of the Lecompton constitution. Then too the more determined spirits in the Territory, together with many naturally lawless elements, saw the pro-slavery danger in southeast Kansas, and proceeded to wage guerrilla warfare against the squatters on claims whence free state men had been driven. It was a cruel relentless battle on both sides with murder and rapine — the last expiring flame of the four years' war dying down to sullen peace in the fall of 1858, after the English bill with its bribe of land for slaves had been killed in the spring.

So Kansas was free. In vain did the sullen Senate in Washington fume and threaten and keep the young state knocking for admission; the game had been played and lost and Kansas was free. Free because the slave barons played for an imperial stake in defiance of modern humanity and economic development. Free because strong men had suffered and fought not against slavery but against slaves in Kansas. Above all, free because one man hated slavery and on a terrible night rode down with his sons among the shadows of the Swamp of the Swan — that long, low-winding and sombre stream "fringed everywhere with woods" and dark with bloody memory. Forty-eight hours they lingered there, and then of a pale May morning rode up to the world again. Behind them lay five twisted, red and mangled corpses. Behind them rose the stifled wailing of widows and little children. Behind them the fearful driver gazed and shuddered. But before them rode a man, tall, dark, grim-faced and awful. His hands were red and his name was John Brown. Such was the cost of freedom.

But behind it was greater cost: a million Indians lived in North America when the white man came, with a world of cultures behind them and many beginnings of civilization. But again and again catastrophe struck and the last was the discovery of America by Columbus. They received the white Europeans with curiosity and kindness. They gave them food and gold. In turn the white man stole and killed and tried to enslave, and their last theft was land. They stole the land of America from the Indians, used its wealth of fruit and gave it over to the rape of aristocrat, Puritan, slave and immigrant. Kansas was the last chapter of this great theft.

Reconstruction and
Its Benefits

There is danger to-day that between the intense feeling of the South and the conciliatory spirit of the North grave injustice will be done the Negro American in the history of Reconstruction. Those who see in Negro suffrage the cause of the main evils of Reconstruction must remember that if there had not been a single freedman left in the South after the war the problems of Reconstruction would still have been grave. Property in slaves to the extent of perhaps two thousand million dollars had suddenly disappeared. One thousand five hundred more millions, representing the Confederate war debt, had largely disappeared. Large amounts of real estate and other property had been destroyed, industry had been disorganized, 250,000 men had been killed and many more maimed. With this went the moral effect of an unsuccessful war with all its letting down of social standards and quickening of hatred and discouragement — a situation which would make it difficult under any circumstances to reconstruct a new government and a new civilization. Add to all this the presence of four million freedmen and the situation is further complicated. But this complication is very largely a matter of well-known historical causes. Any human being "doomed in his own person, and his posterity, to live without knowledge, and without the capacity to make anything his own, and to toil that another may reap the fruits,"[1] is bound, on sudden emancipation, to loom like a great dread on the horizon.

How to train and treat these ex-slaves easily became a central problem of Reconstruction, although by no means the only problem. Three agencies undertook the solution of this problem at first and their influence is apt to be forgotten. Without them the problems of Reconstruction would have been far graver than they were. These agencies were: (a) the Negro church, (b) the Negro school, and (c) the Freedmen's Bureau. After the war the white churches of the South got rid of their Negro members and the Negro church organizations of the North invaded the South. The 20,000 members of the African Methodist Episcopal Church in 1856 leaped to 75,000 in 1866 and

From the *American Historical Review*, 15 (July 1910); 781–799. Paper read at the annual meeting of the American Historical Association in New York, December 1909.

200,000 in 1876, while their property increased sevenfold. The Negro Baptists with 150,000 members in 1850 had fully a half million in 1870. There were, before the end of Reconstruction, perhaps 10,000 local bodies touching the majority of the freed population, centering almost the whole of their social life, and teaching them organization and autonomy. They were primitive, ill-governed, at times fantastic groups of human beings, and yet it is difficult to exaggerate the influence of this new responsibility — the first social institution fully controlled by black men in America, with traditions that rooted back to Africa and with possibilities which make the 35,000 Negro American churches to-day, with their three and one-half million members, the most powerful Negro institutions in the world.

With the Negro church, but separate from it, arose the school as the first expression of the missionary activity of Northern religious bodies. Seldom in the history of the world has an almost totally illiterate population been given the means of self-education in so short a time. The movement started with the Negroes themselves and they continued to form the dynamic force behind it. "This great multitude rose up simultaneously and asked for intelligence."[2] The education of this mass had to begin at the top with the training of teachers, and within a few years a dozen colleges and normal schools started; by 1877, 571,506 Negro children were in school. There can be no doubt that these schools were a great conservative steadying force to which the South owes much. It must not be forgotten that among the agents of the Freedmen's Bureau were not only soldiers and politicians but school-teachers and educational leaders like Edmund Ware and Erastus Cravath.

Granted that the situation was in any case bad and that Negro churches and schools stood as conservative educative forces, how far did Negro suffrage hinder progress, and was it expedient? The difficulties that stared Reconstruction politicians in the face were these: (a) They must act quickly. (b) Emancipation had increased the political power of the South by one-sixth: could this increased political power be put in the hands of those who, in defense of slavery, had disrupted the Union? (c) How was the abolition of slavery to be made effective? (d) What was to be the political position of the freedmen?

Andrew Johnson said in 1864, in regard to calling a convention to restore the state of Tennessee,

who shall restore and re-establish it? Shall the man who gave his influence and his means to destroy the Government? Is he to participate in the great work of re-organization? Shall he who brought this misery upon the State be permitted to control its destinies? If this be so, then all this precious blood of our brave soldiers and officers so freely poured out will have been wantonly spilled.[3]

To settle these and other difficulties, three ways were suggested: (1) the Freedmen's Bureau, (2) partial Negro suffrage, and (3) full manhood suffrage for Negroes.

The Freedmen's Bureau was an attempt to establish a government guardianship over the Negroes and insure their economic and civil rights. Its establishment was a herculean task both physically and socially, and it not only met the solid opposition of the white South, but even the North looked at the new thing as socialistic and over-paternal. It accomplished a great task but it was repudiated. Carl Schurz in 1865 felt warranted in saying

> that not half of the labor that has been done in the south this year, or will be done there next year, would have been or would be done but for the exertions of the Freedmen's Bureau. . . . No other agency, except one placed there by the national government, could have wielded that moral power whose interposition was so necessary to prevent the southern society from falling at once into the chaos of a general collision between its different elements.[4]

Notwithstanding this the Bureau was temporary, was regarded as a makeshift and soon abandoned.

Meantime, partial Negro suffrage seemed not only just but almost inevitable. Lincoln in 1864 "cautiously suggested" to Louisiana's private consideration, "whether some of the colored people may not be let in, as, for instance, the very intelligent, and especially those who fought gallantly in our ranks. They would probably help, in some trying to come, to keep the jewel of liberty in the family of freedom."[5] Indeed, the "family of freedom" in Louisiana being somewhat small just then, who else was to be intrusted with the "jewel"? Later and for different reasons, Johnson in 1865 wrote to Mississippi:

> If you could extend the elective franchise to all persons of color who can read the Constitution of the United States in English and write their names, and to all persons of color who own real estate valued at not less that two hundred and fifty dollars, and pay taxes thereon, you would completely disarm the adversary and set an example the other States will follow. This you can do with perfect safety, and you thus place the southern States, in reference to free persons of color, upon the same basis with the free States. I hope and trust your convention will do this.[6]

Meantime the Negroes themselves began to ask for the suffrage — the Georgia Convention in Augusta, 1866, advocating "a proposition to give those who could write and read well, and possessed a certain property qualification, the right of suffrage." The reply of the South to these suggestions was decisive. In Tennessee alone was any action attempted that even suggested possible Negro suffrage in the future, and that failed. In all other states the "Black Codes" adopted were certainly not reassuring to friends of freedom. To be sure it was not a time to look for calm, cool, thoughtful action on the part of the white South. Their economic condition was pitiable, their fear of Negro freedom genuine; yet it was reasonable to expect from them something less than repression and utter reaction toward slavery. To some extent this expectation was fulfilled: the abolition of slavery was recognized and the civil rights of owning property and appearing as a witness in cases in which he was a party were generally granted the Negro; yet with these went in many cases harsh and unbearable regulations which largely neutralized the concessions and certainly gave ground for the assumption that once free the South would virtually re-enslave the Negro. The colored people themselves naturally feared this and protested as in Mississippi "against the reactionary policy prevailing, and expressing the fear that the Legislature will pass such proscriptive laws as will drive the freedmen from the State, or practically re-enslave them."[7]

The Codes spoke for themselves. They have often been reprinted and quoted. No open-minded student can read them without being convinced that they meant nothing more nor less than slavery in daily toil. Not only this but as Professor Burgess (whom no one accuses of being Negrophile) says:[8]

> Almost every act, word or gesture of the Negro, not consonant with good taste and good manners as well as good morals, was made a crime or misdemeanor, for which he could first be fined by the magistrates and then be consigned to a condition of almost slavery for an indefinite time, if he could not pay the bill.

These laws might have been interpreted and applied liberally, but the picture painted by Carl Schurz does not lead one to anticipate this:

> Some planters held back their former slaves on their plantations by brute force. Armed bands of white men patrolled the country roads to drive back the negroes wandering about. Dead bodies of murdered negroes were found on and near the highways and by-paths. Gruesome reports came from the hospitals — reports of colored men and women whose ears had been cut off, whose skulls had been broken by blows, whose bodies had been slashed by knives or lacerated with scourges. A number of such cases I had occasion to examine myself. A veritable reign of terror prevailed in many parts of the South. The negro found scant justice in the local courts against the white man. He could look for protection only to the military forces of the United States still garrisoning the "States lately in rebellion" and to the Freedmen's Bureau.

All things considered, it seems probable that if the South had been permitted to have its way in 1865 the harshness of Negro slavery would have been mitigated so as to make slave-trading difficult, and to make it possible for a Negro to hold property and appear in some cases in court; but that in most other respects the blacks would have remained in slavery.

What could prevent this? A Freedmen's Bureau, established for ten, twenty or forty years with a careful distribution of land and capital and a system of education for the children, might have prevented such an extension of slavery. But the country would not listen to such a comprehensive plan. A restricted grant of the suffrage voluntarily made by the states would have been reassuring proof of a desire to treat the freedmen fairly, and would have balanced, in part at least, the increased political power of the South. There was no such disposition evident. On the other hand, there was ground for the conclusion in the Reconstruction report of June 18, 1866, that so far as slavery was concerned "the language of all the provisions and ordinances of these States on the subject amounts to nothing more than an unwilling admission of an unwelcome truth." This was of course natural, but was it unnatural that the North should feel that better guarantees were needed to abolish slavery? Carl Schurz wrote:

> I deem it proper, however, to offer a few remarks on the assertion frequently put forth, that the franchise is likely to be extended to the colored man by the voluntary action of the Southern whites themselves. My observation leads me to a contrary opinion. Aside from a very few enlightened men, I found but one class of people in favor of the enfranchisement of the blacks: it was the class of Unionists who found themselves politically ostracised and looked upon the enfranchisement of the loyal Negroes as the salvation of the whole loyal element. . . . The masses are strongly opposed to colored suffrage; anybody that dares to advocate it is stigmatized as a dangerous fanatic.
>
> The only manner in which, in my opinion, the southern people can be induced to grant the freedman some measure of self-protecting power in the form of suffrage, is to make it a condition precedent to "readmission."[9]

Even in Louisiana, under the proposed reconstruction

> not one negro was allowed to vote, though at that very time the wealthy intelligent free colored people of the state paid taxes on property assessed at $15,000,000 and many of them were well known for their patriotic zeal and love for the Union. Thousands of colored men whose homes were in Louisiana, served bravely in the national army and navy, and many of the so-called negroes in New Orleans could not be distinguished by the most intelligent strangers from the best class of white gentlemen, either by color or manner, dress or language, still, as it was known by tradition and common fame that they were not of pure Caucasian descent, they could not vote.[10]

The United States government might now have taken any one of three courses:

1. Allowed the whites to reorganize the states and take no measures to enfranchise the freedmen.
2. Allowed the whites to reorganize the states but provided that after the lapse of a reasonable length of time there should be no discrimination in the right of suffrage on account of "race, color or previous condition of servitude."
3. Admitted all men, black and white, to take part in reorganizing the states and then provided that future restrictions on the suffrage should be made on any basis except "race, color and previous condition of servitude."

The first course was clearly inadmissible since it meant virtually giving up the great principle on which the war was largely fought and won, *i.e.*, human freedom; a giving of freedom which contented itself with an edict, and then turned the "freed" slaves over to the tender mercies of their impoverished and angry ex-masters was no gift at all. The second course was theoretically attractive but practically impossible. It meant at least a prolongation of slavery and instead of attempts to raise the freedmen, it gave the white community strong incentives for keeping the blacks down so that as few as possible would ever qualify for the suffrage. Negro schools would have been discouraged and economic fetters would have held the black man as a serf for an indefinite time. On the other hand, the arguments for universal Negro suffrage from the start were strong and are still strong, and no one would question their strength were it not for the assumption that the experiment failed. Frederick Douglass said to President Johnson: "Your noble and humane predecessor placed in our hands the sword to assist in saving the nation, and we do hope that you, his able successor, will favorably regard the placing in our hands the ballot with which to save ourselves."[11] And when Johnson demurred on account of the hostility between blacks and poor whites, a committee of prominent colored men replied:

> Even if it were true, as you allege, that the hostility of the blacks toward the poor whites must necessarily project itself into a state of freedom, and that this enmity between the two races is even more intense in a state of freedom than in a state of slavery, in the name of Heaven, we reverently ask, how can you, in view of your professed desire to promote the welfare of the black man, deprive him of all means of defence, and clothe him whom you regard as his enemy in the panoply of political power?[12]

Carl Schurz expressed this argument most emphatically:

The emancipation of the slaves is submitted to only in so far as chattel slavery in the old form could not be kept up. But although the freedman is no longer considered the property of the individual master, he is considered the slave of society, and all independent State legislation will share the tendency to make him such.

The solution of the problem would be very much facilitated by enabling all the loyal and free-labor elements in the south to exercise a healthy influence upon legislation. It will hardly be possible to secure the freedman against oppressive class legislation and private persecution, unless he be endowed with a certain measure of political power.[13]

To the argument of ignorance Schurz replied:

The effect of the extension of the franchise to the colored people upon the development of free labor and upon the security of human rights in the south being the principal object in view, the objections raised on the ground of the ignorance of the freedmen become unimportant. Practical liberty is a good school. . . . It is idle to say that it will be time to speak of negro suffrage when the whole colored race will be educated, for the ballot may be necessary to him to secure his education.[14]

The granting of full Negro suffrage meant one of two alternatives to the South: (a) the uplift of the Negro for sheer self-preservation; this is what Schurz and the saner North expected; as one Southern superintendent said: "the elevation of this class is a matter of prime importance since a ballot in the hands of a black citizen is quite as potent as in the hands of a white one." Or (b) a determined concentration of Southern effort by actual force to deprive the Negro of the ballot or nullify its use. This is what happened, but even in this case so much energy was taken in keeping the Negro from voting that the plan for keeping him in virtual slavery and denying him education failed. It took ten years to nullify Negro suffrage in part and twenty years to escape the fear of federal intervention. In these twenty years a vast number of Negroes had risen so far as to escape slavery forever. Debt peonage could be fastened on part of the rural South, and was, but even here the new Negro landholder appeared. Thus despite everything the Fifteenth Amendment and that alone struck the death knell of slavery.

The steps that ended in the Fifteenth Amendment were not, however, taken suddenly. The Negroes were given the right by universal suffrage to join in reconstructing the state governments and the reasons for it were cogently set forth in the report of the Joint Committee on Reconstruction in 1866, which began as follows:

A large proportion of the population had become, instead of mere chattels, free men and citizens. Through all the past struggle these had remained true and loyal, and had, in large numbers, fought on the side of the Union. It was impossible to abandon them without securing them their rights as free men and citizens. The whole civilized world would have cried out against such base ingratitude, and the bare idea is offensive to all right-thinking men. Hence it became important to inquire what could be done to secure their rights, civil and political.[15]

The report then proceeded to emphasize the increased political power of the South and recommended the Fourteenth Amendment, since

It appeared to your committee that the rights of these persons by whom the basis of representation had been thus increased should be recognized by the General Government. While slaves, they were not considered as having any rights, civil or political. It did not seem just or proper that all the political advantages derived from their becoming free should be confined to their former masters, who had fought against the Union, and withheld from themselves, who had always been loyal.[16]

It was soon seen that this expedient of the Fourteenth Amendment was going to prove abortive and that determined and organized effort would be used to deprive the freedmen of the ballot. Thereupon the United States said the final word of simple justice, namely: the states may still regulate the suffrage as they please but they may not deprive a man of the right to vote simply because he is a Negro.

For such reasons the Negro was enfranchised. What was the result? No language has been spared to describe these results as the worst imaginable. Nor is it necessary to dispute for a moment that there were bad results, and bad results arising from Negro suffrage; but it may be questioned if the results were as bad as painted or if Negro suffrage was the prime cause.

Let us not forget that the white South believed it to be of vital interest to its welfare that the experiment of Negro suffrage should fail ignominiously, and that almost to a man the whites were willing to insure this failure either by active force or passive acquiescence; that beside this there were, as might be expected, men, black and white, Northern and Southern, only too eager to take advantage of such a situation for feathering their own nests. The results in such case had to be evil but to charge the evil to Negro suffrage is unfair. It may be charged to anger, poverty, venality, and ignorance; but the anger and poverty were the almost inevitable aftermath of war; the venality was much greater among whites than Negroes, and while ignorance was the curse of the Negroes, the fault was not theirs, and they took the initiative to correct it.

The chief charges against the Negro governments are extravagance, theft,

and incompetency of officials. There is no serious charge that these governments threatened civilization or the foundations of social order. The charge is
that they threatened property, and that they were inefficient. These charges
are in part undoubtedly true, but they are often exaggerated. When a man has,
in his opinion, been robbed and maltreated he is sensitive about money
matters. The South had been terribly impoverished and saddled with new
social burdens. In other words, a state with smaller resources was asked not
only to do a work of restoration but a larger social work. The property-holders
were aghast. They not only demurred, but, predicting ruin and revolution,
they appealed to secret societies, to intimidation, force, and murder. They
refused to believe that these novices in government and their friends were
aught but scamps and fools. Under the circumstances occurring directly after
the war, the wisest statesman would have been compelled to resort to increased taxation and would in turn have been execrated as extravagant and
even dishonest. When now, in addition to this, the new legislators, white and
black, were undoubtedly in a large number of cases extravagant, dishonest,
and incompetent, it is easy to see what flaming and incredible stories of
Reconstruction governments could gain wide currency and belief. In fact, the
extravagance, although great, was not universal, and much of it was due to the
extravagant spirit pervading the whole country in a day of inflated currency
and speculation. The ignorance was deplorable but a deliberate legacy from
the past, and some of the extravagance and much of the effort were to remedy
this ignorance. The incompetency was in part real and in part emphasized by
the attitude of the whites of the better class.

When incompetency gains political power in an extravagant age the result
is widespread dishonesty. The dishonesty in the reconstruction of the South
was helped on by four circumstances:

1. The former dishonesty in the political South.
2. The presence of many dishonest Northern politicians.
3. The temptation to Southern politicians at once to profit by dishonesty and to discredit Negro government.
4. The poverty of the Negro.

(1) Dishonesty in public life has no monopoly of time or place in America.
To take one state: In 1839 it was reported in Mississippi that ninety per cent. of
the fines collected by sheriffs and clerks were unaccounted for. In 1841 the
state treasurer acknowledges himself "at a loss to determine the precise
liabilities of the state and her means of paying the same." And in 1839 the
auditor's books had not been posted for eighteen months, no entries made for
a year, and no vouchers examined for three years. Congress gave Jefferson

College, Natchez, more than 46,000 acres of land; before the war this whole property had "disappeared" and the college was closed. Congress gave to Mississippi among other states the "16th section" of the public lands for schools. In thirty years the proceeds of this land in Mississippi were embezzled to the amount of at least one and a half millions of dollars. In Columbus, Mississippi, a receiver of public money stole $100,000 and resigned. His successor stole $55,000, and a treasury agent wrote: "Another receiver would probably follow in the footsteps of the two. You will not be surprised if I recommend his being retained in preference to another appointment." From 1830 to 1860 Southern men in federal offices alone embezzled more than a million dollars — a far larger sum then than now. There might have been less stealing in the South during Reconstruction without Negro suffrage but it is certainly highly instructive to remember that the mark of the thief which dragged its slime across nearly every great Northern state and almost up to the presidential chair could not certainly in those cases be charged against the vote of black men. This was the day when a national secretary of war was caught stealing, a vice-president presumably took bribes, a private secretary of the president, a chief clerk of the Treasury, and eighty-six government officials stole millions in the whiskey frauds, while the Credit Mobilier filched fifty millions and bribed the government to an extent never fully revealed; not to mention less distinguished thieves like Tweed.

Is it surprising that in such an atmosphere a new race learning the a-b-c of government should have become the tools of thieves? And when they did was the stealing their fault or was it justly chargeable to their enfranchisement?

Undoubtedly there were many ridiculous things connected with Reconstruction governments: the placing of ignorant field-hands who could neither read nor write in the legislature, the gold spittoons of South Carolina, the enormous public printing bill of Mississippi — all these were extravagant and funny, and yet somehow, to one who sees beneath all that is bizarre, the real human tragedy of the upward striving of down-trodden men, the groping for light among people born in darkness, there is less tendency to laugh and gibe than among shallower minds and easier consciences. All that is funny is not bad.

Then too a careful examination of the alleged stealing in the South reveals much. First, there is repeated exaggeration. For instance it is said that the taxation in Mississippi was *fourteen* times as great in 1874 as in 1869. This sounds staggering until we learn that the state taxation in 1869 was only ten cents on one hundred dollars, and that the expenses of government in 1874 were only twice as great as in 1860, and that too with a depreciated currency. It could certainly be argued that the state government in Mississippi was doing enough additional work in 1874 to warrant greatly increased cost. A Southern white historian acknowledges that the work of restoration which the government was obliged to undertake, made increased expenses necessary. During the period of the war, and for several years thereafter, public buildings and state institutions were permitted to fall into decay. The state house and grounds, the executive mansion, the penitentiary, the insane asylum, and the buildings for the blind, deaf, and dumb were in a dilapidated condition, and had to be extended and repaired. A new building for the blind was purchased and fitted up. The reconstructionists established a public school system and spent money to maintain and support it, perhaps too freely, in view of the impoverishment of the people. When they took hold, warrants were worth but sixty or seventy cents on the dollar, a fact which made the price of building materials used in the work of construction correspondingly higher. So far as the conduct of state officials who were intrusted with the custody of public funds is concerned, it may be said that there were no great embezzlements or other cases of misappropriation during the period of Republican rule.[17]

The state debt of Mississippi was said to have been increased from a half million to twenty million when in fact it had not been increased at all.

The character of the real thieving shows that white men must have been the chief beneficiaries and that as a former South Carolina slaveholder said:

> The legislature, ignorant as it is, could not have been bribed without money, that must have been furnished from some source that it is our duty to discover. A legislature composed chiefly of our former slaves has been bribed. One prominent feature of this transaction is the part which native Carolinians have played in it, some of our own household men whom the state, in the past, has delighted to honor, appealing to their cupidity and avarice make them the instruments to effect the robbery of their impoverished white brethren. Our former slaves have been bribed by these men to give them the privilege by law of plundering the property-holders of the state.[18]

The character of much of the stealing shows who were the thieves. The frauds through the manipulation of state and railway bonds and of bank-notes must have inured chiefly to the benefit of experienced white men, and this must have been largely the case in the furnishing and printing frauds. It was chiefly in the extravagance for "sundries and incidentals" and direct money payments for votes that the Negroes received their share.

That the Negroes led by astute thieves became tools and received a small share of the spoils is true. But two considerations must be added: much of the legislation which resulted in fraud was represented to the Negroes as good legislation, and thus their votes were secured by deliberate misrepresentation. Take for instance the land frauds of South Carolina. A wise Negro leader of that state, advocating the state purchase of lands, said:

One of the greatest of slavery bulwarks was the infernal plantation system, one man owning his thousand, another his twenty, another fifty thousand acres of land. This is the only way by which we will break up that system, and I maintain that our freedom will be of no effect if we allow it to continue. What is the main cause of the prosperity of the North? It is because every man has his own farm and is free and independent. Let the lands of the South be similarly divided.

From such arguments the Negroes were induced to aid a scheme to buy land and distribute it; yet a large part of $800,000 appropriated was wasted and went to the white landholder's pockets. The railroad schemes were in most cases feasible and eventually carried out; it was not the object but the method that was wrong.

Granted then that the Negroes were to some extent venal but to a much larger extent ignorant and deceived, the question is: did they show any signs of a disposition to learn better things? The theory of democratic government is not that the will of the people is always right, but rather that normal human beings of average intelligence will, if given a chance, learn the right and best course by bitter experience. This is precisely what the Negro voters showed indubitable signs of doing. First, they strove for schools to abolish ignorance, and, second, a large and growing number of them revolted against the carnival of extravagance and stealing that marred the beginning of Reconstruction, and joined with the best elements to institute reform; and the greatest stigma on the white South is not that it opposed Negro suffrage and resented theft and incompetence, but that when it saw the reform movement growing and even in some cases triumphing, and a larger and larger number of black voters learning to vote for honesty and ability, it still preferred a Reign of Terror to a campaign of education, and disfranchised Negroes instead of punishing rascals.

No one has expressed this more convincingly than a Negro who was himself a member of the Reconstruction legislature of South Carolina and who spoke at the convention which disfranchised him, against one of the onslaughts of Tillman:

> The gentleman from Edgefield [Mr. Tillman] speaks of the piling up of the State debt; of jobbery and peculation during the period between 1869 and 1873 in South Carolina, but he has not found voice eloquent enough, nor pen exact enough to mention those imperishable gifts bestowed upon South Carolina between 1873 and 1876 by Negro legislators — the laws relative to finance, the building of penal and charitable institutions, and, greatest of all, the establishment of the public school system. Starting as infants in legislation in 1869, many wise measures were not thought of, many injudicious acts were passed. But in the administration of affairs for

the next four years, having learned by experience the result of bad acts, we immediately passed reformatory laws touching every department of state, county, municipal and town governments. These enactments are today upon the statute books of South Carolina. They stand as living witnesses of the Negro's fitness to vote and legislate upon the rights of mankind.

When we came into power town governments could lend the credit of their respective towns to secure funds at any rate of interest that the council saw fit to pay. Some of the towns paid as high as twenty per cent. We passed an act prohibiting town governments from pledging the credit of their hamlets for money bearing a greater rate of interest than five per cent.

Up to 1874, inclusive, the State Treasurer had the power to pay out State funds as he pleased. He could elect whether he would pay out the funds on appropriations that would place the money in the hands of the speculators, or would apply them to appropriations that were honest and necessary. We saw the evil of this and passed an act of making specific levies and collections of taxes for specific appropriations.

Another source of profligacy in the expenditure of funds was the law that provided for and empowered the levying and collecting of special taxes by school districts, in the name of the schools. We saw its evil and by a constitutional amendment provided that there should only be levied and collected annually a tax of two mills for school purposes, and took away from the school districts the power to levy and to collect taxes of any kind. By this act we cured the evils that had been inflicted upon us in the name of the schools, settled the public school question for all time to come, and established the system upon an honest, financial basis.

Next, we learned during the period from 1869 to 1874, inclusive, that what was denominated the floating indebtedness, covering the printing schemes and other indefinite expenditures, amounted to nearly $2,000,000. A conference was called of the leading Negro representatives in the two houses together with the State Treasurer, also a Negro. After this conference we passed an act for the purpose of ascertaining the bona fide floating debt and found that it did not amount to more than $250,000 for the four years; we created a commission to sift that indebtedness and to scale it. Hence when the Democratic party came into power they found the floating debt covering the legislative and all other expenditures, fixed at the certain sum of $250,000. This same class of Negro legislators led by the State Treasurer, Mr. F. L. Cardozo, knowing that there were millions of fraudulent bonds charged against the credit of the State, passed another act to ascertain the true bonded indebtedness, and to provide for its settlement. Under this law, at one sweep, those entrusted with the power to do so, through Negro legislators, stamped six millions of bonds, denominated as conversion bonds, "fraudulent." The commission did not finish its work before 1876. In that year, when the [Wade] Hampton government came into power, there were still to be examined into and settled under the terms of the act passed by us providing for the legitimate bonded indebtedness of the state, a little over two and a half million dollars worth of bonds and coupons which had not been passed upon.

Governor Hampton, General Hagood, Judge Simonton, Judge Wallace and in fact, all of the conservative thinking Democrats aligned themselves under the provision enacted by us for the certain and final settlement of the bonded indebtedness and appealed to their Democratic legislators to stand by the Republican legislation on the subject and to confirm it. A faction in the Democratic party obtained a majority of the Democrats in the legislature against settling the question and they endeavored to open up anew the whole subject of the state debt. We had a little over thirty members in the house and enough Republican senators to sustain the Hampton conservative faction and to stand up for honest finance, or by our votes place the debt question of the old state into the hands of the plunderers and peculators. We were appealed to by General Hagood, through me, and my answer to him was in these words: "General, our people have learned the difference between profligate and honest legislation. We have passed acts of financial reform, and with the assistance of God when the vote shall have been taken, you will be able to record for the thirty odd Negroes, slandered though they have been through the press, that they voted solidly with you all for honest legislation and the preservation of the credit of the State." The thirty odd Negroes in the legislature and their senators, by their votes did settle the debt question and saved the state $13,000,000. We were eight years in power. We had built school houses, established charitable institutions, built and maintained the penitentiary system, provided for the education of the deaf and dumb, rebuilt the jails and court houses, rebuilt the bridges and re-established the ferries. In short, we had reconstructed the State and placed it upon the road to prosperity and, at the same time, by our acts of financial reform transmitted to the Hampton Government an indebtedness not greater by more than $2,500,000 than was the bonded debt of the State in 1868, before the Republican Negroes and their white allies came into power.[19]

So, too, in Louisiana in 1872 and in Mississippi later the better element of the Republicans triumphed at the polls and joining with the Democrats instituted reforms, repudiated the worst extravagance, and started toward better things. But unfortunately there was one thing that the white South feared more than Negro dishonesty, ignorance, and incompetency, and that was Negro honesty, knowledge, and efficiency.

In the midst of all these difficulties the Negro governments in the South accomplished much of positive good. We may recognize three things which Negro rule gave to the South:

1. Democratic government.
2. Free public schools.
3. New social legislation.

Two states will illustrate conditions of government in the South before and after Negro rule. In South Carolina there was before the war a property qualification for office-holders, and, in part, for voters. The Constitution of 1868, on the other hand, was a modern democratic document starting (in marked contrast to the old constitutions) with a declaration that "We, the People," framed it, and preceded by a broad Declaration of Rights which did away with property qualifications and based representation directly upon population instead of property. It especially took up new subjects of social legislation, declaring navigable rivers free public highways, instituting homestead exemptions, establishing boards of county commissioners, providing for a new penal code of laws, establishing universal manhood suffrage "without distinction of race or color," devoting six sections to charitable and penal institutions and six to corporations, providing separate property for married women, etc. Above all, eleven sections of the Tenth Article were devoted to the establishment of a complete public-school system.

So satisfactory was the constitution thus adopted by Negro suffrage and by a convention composed of a majority of blacks that the state lived twenty-seven years under it without essential change and when the constitution was revised in 1895, the revision was practically nothing more than an amplification of the Constitution of 1868. No essential advance step of the former document was changed except the suffrage article.

In Mississippi the Constitution of 1868 was, as compared with that before the war, more democratic. It not only forbade distinctions on account of color but abolished all property qualifications for jury service, and property and educational qualifications for office; it prohibited the lending of the credit of the state for private corporations — an abuse dating back as far as 1830. It increased the powers of the governor, raised the low state salaries, and increased the number of state officials. New ideas like the public-school system and the immigration bureau were introduced and in general the activity of the state greatly and necessarily enlarged. Finally, that was the only constitution ever submitted in popular approval at the polls. This constitution remained in force twenty-two years.

In general the words of Judge Albion W. Tourgee, a "carpetbagger," are true when he says of the Negro governments:

They obeyed the Constitution of the United States, and annulled the bonds of states, counties, and cities which had been issued to carry on the war of rebellion and maintain armies in the field against the Union. They instituted a public school system in a realm where public schools had been unknown. They opened the ballot box and jury box to thousands of white men who had been debarred from them by a lack of earthly possessions. They introduced home rule to the South. They abolished the whipping post, the branding iron, the stocks and other barbarous forms of punishment which had up to that time prevailed. They reduced capital felonies from about twenty to two or three. In an age of extravagance they were extravagant in the sums appropriated for public works. In all of that time no man's rights of person were invaded under the forms of law. Every Democrat's life, home, fireside and business were safe. No man obstructed any white man's way to the ballot box, interfered with his freedom of speech, or boycotted him on account of his political faith.[20]

A thorough study of the legislation accompanying these constitutions and its changes since would of course be necessary before a full picture of the situation could be given. This has not been done, but so far as my studies have gone I have been surprised at the comparatively small amount of change in law and government which the overthrow of Negro rule brought about. There were sharp and often hurtful economies introduced marking the return of property to power, there was a sweeping change of officials, but the main body of Reconstruction legislation stood.

This democracy brought forward new leaders and men and definitely overthrew the old Southern aristocracy. Among these new men were Negroes of worth and ability. John R. Lynch when speaker of the Mississippi house of representatives was given a public testimonial by Republicans and Democrats and the leading Democratic paper said:

> His bearing in office had been so proper, and his rulings in such marked contrast to the partisan conduct of the ignoble whites of his party who have aspired to be leaders of the blacks, that the conservatives cheerfully joined the testimonial.[21]

Of the colored treasurer of South Carolina, Governor [D. H.] Chamberlain said:

> I have never heard one word or seen one act of Mr. Cardozo's which did not confirm my confidence in his personal integrity and his political honor and zeal for the honest administration of the State Government. On every occasion, and under all circumstances, he has been against fraud and jobbery, and in favor of good measures and good men.[22]

Jonathan C. Gibbs, a colored man and the first state superintendent of instruction in Florida, was a graduate of Dartmouth. He established the system and brought it to success, dying in harness in 1874. Such men — and there were others — ought not to be forgotten or confounded with other types of colored and white Reconstruction leaders.

There is no doubt but that the thirst of the black man for knowledge — a thirst which has been too persistent and durable to be mere curiosity or whim — gave birth to the public free-school system of the South. It was the question upon which black voters and legislators insisted more than anything else and while it is possible to find some vestiges of free schools in some of the Southern States before the war yet a universal, well-established system dates from the day that the black man got political power. Common-school instruction in the South, in the modern sense of the term, was begun for Negroes by the Freedmen's Bureau and missionary societies, and the state public-school systems for all children were formed mainly by Negro Reconstruction governments. The earlier state constitutions of Mississippi "from 1817 to 1865 contained a declaration that 'Religion, morality and knowledge being necessary to good government, the preservation of liberty and the happiness of mankind, schools and the means of education shall forever be encouraged.' It was not, however, until 1868 that encouragement was given to any general system of public schools meant to embrace the whole youthful population." The Constitution of 1868 makes it the duty of the legislature to establish "a uniform system of free public schools, by taxation or otherwise, for all children between the ages of five and twenty-one years." In Alabama the Reconstruction Constitution of 1868 provided that "It shall be the duty of the Board of Education to establish throughout the State, in each township or other school district which it may have created, one or more schools at which all the children of the State between the ages of five and twenty-one years may attend free of charge." Arkansas in 1868, Florida in 1869, Louisiana in 1868, North Carolina in 1869, South Carolina in 1868, and Virginia in 1870, established school systems. The Constitution of 1868 in Louisiana required the general assembly to establish "at least one free public school in every parish," and that these schools should make no "distinction of race, color or previous condition." Georgia's system was not fully established until 1873.

We are apt to forget that in all human probability the granting of Negro manhood suffrage and the passage of the Fifteenth Amendment were decisive in rendering permanent the foundation of the Negro common school. Even after the overthrow of the Negro governments, if the Negroes had been left a servile caste, personally free, but politically powerless, it is not reasonable to think that a system of common schools would have been provided for them by the Southern States. Serfdom and education have ever proven contradictory terms. But when Congress, backed by the nation, determined to make the Negroes full-fledged voting citizens, the South had a hard dilemma before her: either to keep the Negroes under as an ignorant proletariat and stand the chance of being ruled eventually from the slums and jails, or to join in helping to raise these wards of the nation to a position of intelligence and thrift by means of a public-school system. The "carpet-bag" governments hastened the decision of the South, and although there was a period of hesitation and retrogression after the overthrow of Negro rule in the early seventies, yet the South saw that to abolish Negro schools in addition to nullifying the Negro vote would invite Northern interference; and thus eventually every Southern state confirmed the work of the Negro legislators and maintained the Negro public schools along with the white.

Finally, in legislation covering property, the wider functions of the state, the punishment of crime and the like, it is sufficient to say that the laws on these points established by Reconstruction legislatures were not only different from and even revolutionary to the laws in the older South, but they were so wise and so well suited to the needs of the new South that in spite of a retrogressive movement following the overthrow of the Negro governments the mass of this legislation, with elaboration and development, still stands on the statute books of the South.

Reconstruction constitutions, practically unaltered, were kept in

> Florida, 1868–1885 . . . . 17 years.
> Virginia, 1870–1902 . . . . 32 years.
> South Carolina, 1868–1895 . . . 27 years.
> Mississippi, 1868–1890 . . . . 22 years.

Even in the case of states like Alabama, Georgia, North Carolina, and Louisiana, which adopted new constitutions to signify the overthrow of Negro rule, the new constitutions are nearer the model of the Reconstruction document than they are to the previous constitutions. They differ from the Negro constitutions in minor details but very little in general conception.

Besides this there stands on the statute books of the South to-day law after law passed between 1868 and 1876, and which has been found wise, effective, and worthy of preservation.

Paint the "carpet-bag" governments and Negro rule as black as may be, the fact remains that the essence of the revolution which the overturning of the Negro governments made was to put these black men and their friends out of power. Outside the curtailing of expenses and stopping of extravagance, not only did their successors make few changes in the work which these legislatures and conventions had done, but they largely carried out their plans, followed their suggestions, and strengthened their institutions. Practically the whole new growth of the South has been accomplished under laws which black men helped to frame thirty years ago. I know of no greater compliment to Negro suffrage.

Notes

1. State *v.* Mann, *North Carolina Reports,* 2 Devereaux 263.
2. First General Report of the Inspector of Schools, Freedmen's Bureau.
3. McPherson. *Reconstruction,* p. 46.
4. Schurz. Report to the President, 1865. *Senate Ex. Doc. No.* 2, 39 Cong., 1 sess., p. 40.
5. Letter to Hahn, March 13. McPherson, p. 20.
6. Johnson to Sharkey, August 15. McPherson, p. 19.
7. October 7, 1865.
8. John W. Burgess, *Reconstruction and the Constitution, 1866–1876* (New York: Charles Scribner's Sons, 1902), p. 53.
9. Report to the President, 1865. *Senate Ex. Doc. No.* 2, 39 Cong., 1 sess., p. 44.
10. Brewster, *Sketches of Southern Mystery, Treason, and Murder,* p. 116.
11. Frederick Douglass to Johnson, February 7, 1866. McPherson, p. 52.
12. McPherson, p. 56.
13. Report to the President, 1865. *Senate Ex. Doc. No.* 2, 39 Cong., 1 sess., p. 45.
14. Report to the President, p. 43.
15. *House Reports, No.* 30, 39 Cong., 1 sess., p. xiii.
16. *House Reports, No.* 30, p. xiii.
17. Garner, *Reconstruction in Mississippi,* p. 322.
18. Hon. F. F. Warley in Brewster's *Sketches,* p. 150.
19. Speech of Thomas E. Miller, one of the six Negro members of the South Carolina Constitutional Convention of 1895. The speech was not published in the *Journal* but may be found in the *Occasional Papers* of the American Negro Academy, no. 6, pp. 11–13.
20. *Occasional Papers* of the American Negro Academy, no. 6, p. 10; Chicago *Weekly Inter Ocean,* December 26, 1890.
21. Jackson (Mississippi) *Clarion,* April 24, 1873.
22. Allen, *Governor Chamberlain's Administration in South Carolina,* p. 82.

American Negro Slavery:
A Survey of the Supply,
Employment and Control of
Negro Labor as Determined
by the Plantation Regime

by Ulrich Bonnell Phillips

Mr. Phillips' work is not a history of American slavery but an economic study of American slaveholders and their land and crops. As such it gives evidence of wide reading and knowledge of the facts. Two hundred of its five hundred pages are mainly historical, treating of Africa and the slave trade and West Indian and American conditions. Two hundred other pages contain a series of essays on aspects of slavery—the cotton crop, plantation economy, etc. The other chapters are devoted to freedom and crime among slaves and slave codes.

Mr. Phillips was born and lived in earlier life on a Southern plantation (p. 313, note), and bases some of his information on this experience. To this he had added a knowledge of the standard authorities like Helps, Hakluyt, Nieboer, Kingsley, and Ellis, and the less well-known Saco and Scelle. He has made wide use of Southern newspapers and pamphlets and some manuscript materials, but has done little with any Negro sources most of which he regards as "of dubious value" (p. 455, note).

The result is a readable book but one curiously incomplete and unfortunately biased. The Negro as a responsible human being has no place in the book. To be sure individual Negroes are treated here and there but mainly as

Book review from *American Political Science Review*, November 1918; 12:722–26.

exceptional or as illustrative facts for purposes outside themselves. Nowhere is there any adequate conception of "darkies," "niggers," and "negroes" (words liberally used throughout the book) as making a living mass of humanity with all the usual human reactions.

This intrigues the reader, for a history of slavery would ordinarily deal largely with slaves and their point of view, while this book deals chiefly with the economics of slaveholders and is without exception from their point of view. Its thesis is that slavery was an ordinary human labor problem not unlike that of modern factory labor. It had little to do with humanity, and even its sufferings were not different from the ordinary hardships of laboring people (pp. 52, 181, 182, 307).

This thesis, however, encounters the difficulty that most writers, even of the ultra-economic sort, have regarded slavery as a peculiar sort of labor problem because of its degradation of the laborer and the reflex action of this on the master class. Mr. Phillips sees this difficulty and notes the horrors of the Roman *latifundia* and Cato's code (p. 341); but he surmounts the difficulty by two premises, nowhere clearly stated, but always implicit in his narrative. The unstated major premise is that Negroes were not ordinary slaves nor indeed ordinary human beings. "The heartlessness of the Roman *latifundiarii* was the product partly of their absenteeism . . . . and partly of the lack of difference between masters and slaves in racial traits. In the ante-bellum South all these conditions were reversed."

Mr. Phillips recurs again and again to this inborn character of Negroes: they are "submissive," "light-hearted" and "ingratiating" (p. 342), very "fond of display" (pp. 1, 291), with a "proneness to superstition" and "acceptance of subordination" (p. 291); "chaffing, and chattering" (p. 292) with "humble nonchalance and a freedom from carking care" (p. 416). From the four-teenth to the twentieth century Mr. Phillips sees no essential change in these predominant characteristics of the mass of Negroes; and while he is finishing his book in a Y.M.C.A. army hut in the South all he sees in the Negro soldier is the "same easy-going amiable serio-comic obedience," and all he hears is the throwing of dice (pp. viii, ix). This Negro nature is, to Mr. Phillips, fixed and unchangeable. A generation of freedom has brought little change (p. ix). Even the few exceptional Negroes whom he mentions are of interest mainly because of their unexpected "ambition" and not for any especial accomplishment (p. 432). The fighting black maroons were overcome by "fright" (p. 466), and the Negroes' part in the public movements like the Revolution was "barely appreciable" (p. 116); in-deed his main picture is of "inert Negroes, the majority of whom are as yet perhaps less efficient in freedom than their forebears were as slaves" (p. 396)!

Having now rather by innuendo and assumption than by dogmatic statement established these subhuman slaves Mr. Phillips, by a similar method, evokes the slaveholding superman.

Slavery, we are told (p. 401), was "less a business than a life; it made fewer fortunes than it made men." Life among Negro slaves "promoted, and well-nigh necessitated the blending of foresight and firmness with kindliness and patience" (p. 287). In fact the slave system was "analogous in kind and in consequence to the domestication of the beasts of the field" (p. 344). With such masters, Mr. Phillips finds the treatment of slaves on the whole excellent. He notes the "interest of the master in the future of his workers" (p. 357). The surviving vestiges of slave quarters prove how comfortably they were housed (p. 298). Planters had to "guard their slaves' health and life as among the most vital of their own interests" (p. 301), and the tradition of the mistreatment of slaves in the Southern South was simply spread by border state masters "in the amiable purpose of keeping their own slaves content" (p. 305).

"There was clearly no general prevalence of severity and strain in the régime" (p. 307). "The generality of the Negroes insisted upon possessing and being possessed in a cordial but respectful intimacy" (p. 307). White and black children were playmates; returning masters had their hands and feet kissed; and the result of the whole system was no fatigue or overwork, as the "sturdy sleekness as well as the joviality" of most of the slaves proved (p. 384). Slaves were rarely sold by a master (p. 397), and if hired out their masters were most solicitous for their "moral and physical welfare" (p. 410). Among town slaves there was "much comfort and even luxury" (p. 424).

The author quotes some cases where this idyllic picture seems a bit beside the truth, but he immediately marshals overwhelming witnesses to the contrary. As for instance, on page 251, he gives two inches to Fannie Kemble's picture of a wretched plantation, and follows it with three pages of contradicting testimony. The various severe indictments of certain aspects of slavery Mr. Phillips touches lightly but surely. The breaking up of families by sale is dismissed by the statement that slave owners "deplored" it (p. 202). Breeding for the domestic slave trade is dismissed as "extremely doubtful" (p. 362). Concubinage and illicit intercourse between master and servant receive but passing mention. Fugitive slaves are camouflaged as "truants." As for overwork, "anyone who has had experience with Negro labor may reasonably be skeptical when told that healthy, well-fed Negroes, whether slave or free, can by any routine insistence of the employer be driven beyond the point at which fatigue begins to be injurious" (p. 384).

After having painted this picture of the slave régime, Mr. Phillips is too logical a thinker not to see that he has overshot his mark for the ugly fact remains that this institution of born slaves, kindly masters, and favorable conditions in crops was a tragic economic failure. Why was this? It was not, Mr. Phillips assures us, because of any especial moral delinquency of the South and he uses the *Tu quoque* argument against New England abolitionists and English philanthropists with inspiring if not convincing keenness, even to the extent of making Oglethorpe "the manager" of the Royal African Company. He finds Cairnes' stinging indictment of the slave barons full of "grotesqueries" (p. 356). He attacks Loria's socialistic explanation of the overvaluation of slaves as a "fallacy;" and finally he, himself, explains the economic failure of slavery as chiefly due to the fact that "the routine efficiency of slave labor itself caused the South to spoil the market for its distinctive crops by producing greater quantities than the world would buy at remunerative prices. To this the solicitude of the masters for the health of their slaves contributed" (p. 398)!

Mr. Phillips elaborates this thesis and also offers other and apparently contradicting explanations; on the whole this is by far the weakest part of the book and leaves the reader much befogged.

The last chapters come as more or less illogical addenda to the main thesis. Under "Town Slaves," the servant problem of the whites is mainly treated. Under "Free Negroes," we are told of some slaves who won deserved freedom and of others who tasting freedom returned to the beloved plantation. Slave crime includes the stories of such "criminals" as Denmark, Vesey and Toussaint L'Overture; and the treatment of slave codes shows, according to Mr. Phillips, that "the government of slaves was, for the ninety and nine, by men, and only for the hundredth by laws. There were injustice, oppression, brutality and heartburning in the regime — but where in the struggling world are these absent? There were also gentleness, kind-hearted friendship and mutual loyalty to a degree hard for him to believe who regards the system with a theorist's eye and a partisan squint" (p. 514).

On the whole this book, despite its undoubted evidence of labor and research, its wealth of illustrative material and its moderate tone, is deeply disappointing. It is a defense of American slavery — a defense of an institution which was at best a mistake and at worst a crime — made in a day when we need sharp and implacable judgment against collective wrongdoing by cultured and courteous men. The case against American slavery is too strong to be moved by this kind of special pleading. The mere fact that it left to the world today a heritage of ignorance, crime, lynching, lawlessness and economic injustice, to be struggled with by this and succeeding generations, is a condemnation unanswered by Mr. Phillips and unanswerable.

Race Intelligence

For a century or more it has been the dream of those who do not believe
Negroes are human that their wish should find some scientific basis. For years
they depended on the weight of the human brain, trusting that the alleged
underweight of less than a thousand Negro brains, measured without reference to age, stature, nutrition or cause of death, would convince the world
that black men simply could not be educated. Today scientists acknowledge
that there is no warrant for such a conclusion and that in any case the absolute
weight of the brain is no criterion of racial ability.

Measurements of the bony skeleton followed and great hopes of the scientific demonstration of race inferiority were held for a while. But they had to be
surrendered when Zulus and Englishmen were found in the same dol-
ichocephalic class.

Then came psychology: the children of the public schools were studied
and it was discovered that some colored children ranked lower than white
children. This gave wide satisfaction even though it was pointed out that the
average included most of both races and that considering the educational
opportunities and social environment of the races the differences were measurements simply of the ignorance and poverty of the black child's surroundings.

Today, however, all is settled. "A workably accurate scientific classification
of brain power" has been discovered and by none other than our astute army
officers. The tests were in two sets for literates and illiterates and were
simplicity itself. For instance, among other things the literates were asked in
three minutes "to look at each row of numbers below and on the two dotted
lines write the two numbers that should come next."

From *The Crisis*, July 1920.

3	4	5	6	7	8	...	...
8	7	6	5	4	3	...	...
10	15	20	25	30	35	...	...
81	27	9	3	1	⅓	...	...
1	4	9	16	25	36	...	...
16	17	15	18	14	19	...	...
3	6	8	16	18	36	...	...

Illiterates were asked, for example, to complete pictures where the net was missing in a tennis court or a ball in a bowling alley!

For these tests were chosen 4730 Negroes *from Louisiana and Mississippi* and 28,052 white recruits *from Illinois*. The result? Do you need to ask? M. R. Trabue, Director, Bureau of Educational Service, Columbia University, assures us that the intelligence of the average southern Negro is equal to that of a 9-year-old white boy and that we should arrange our educational program to make "waiters, porters, scavengers and the like" of most Negroes!

Is it conceivable that a great university should employ a man whose "science" consists of such utter rot?

The Negro Encyclopedia

At the invitation of the trustees of the Phelps Stokes Fund there was held in November 7, 1931, a conference at Washington, D.C., "to consider the possibility and advisability of publishing, with the help of the Phelps Stokes Fund and other foundations, groups and individuals who may be interested, an Encyclopedia of the Negro." There were present at that conference twenty persons, of whom ten were white and ten colored. Among the colored persons present were Professor Benjamin Brawley and President Mordecai Johnson of Howard University, Dr. George Haynes of New York, James Weldon Johnson and Charles S. Johnson of Fisk, Eugene Kinkle Jones of New York, Professor Kelly Miller of Howard University, Walter F. White of New York, Monroe Work of Tuskegee and President John Hope of Atlanta. At that meeting it was unanimously recommended among other things that there should be added to the list of the conferees, Dr. Carter G. Woodson of Washington, D.C., Dr. Alain Locke of Howard University and Dr. W.E.B. Du Bois of New York.

At a second conference, January 9, 1932, there were twenty-one persons present, of whom thirteen were colored. Dr. Locke and Dr. Du Bois were present but Dr. Woodson was not. At this conference, the proposed encyclopedia was further discussed, and a Board of Directors was nominated by a committee consisting of Anson Phelps Stokes, Mordecai Johnson and W.E.B. Du Bois, and including these three. This Board of Directors consisted of seventeen members, of whom nine were colored. The colored members were Professor Brawley, Dr. Otelia D. Cromwell, Dr. Du Bois, Dr. John Hope, Dr. Charles S. Johnson, Mr. James Weldon Johnson, Dr. R. R. Moton, Mr. Monroe N. Work, Mr. Eugene Kinkle Jones and President Mordecai Johnson. A special invitation was issued to Dr. Carter G. Woodson to join this Board of Directors but he declined.

The white members of the Board are W. W. Alexander of Atlanta, Dr. James H. Dillard, formerly of the Jeanes and Slater Funds, Dr. C. T. Loram of

From *The Crisis*, August 1932.

Yale University, President Read of Spelman College, Dr. Anson Phelps Stokes, President of the Stokes Fund, Dr. J. E. Spingarn, of the National Association for the Advancement of Colored People, Dr. Waldo G. Leland, Secretary of the Council of Learned Societies, Dr. Radcliffe Brown of the University of Chicago and W. A. Aery of Hampton.

An Executive Committee was appointed, consisting of Dr. Stokes, Dr. Brawley, Dr. Moton, Dr. Dillard, Dr. Du Bois, President M. W. Johnson and Dr. Loram. Four of these are colored.

Finally, a third meeting was held on March 12, and it was voted to incorporate the Directors and to take tentative steps toward the selection of an editorial board. Here the matter rests. Its further progress depends upon the possibility of raising sufficient funds to meet the necessarily large expenses of such an undertaking. It is hoped that the sum may be raised and the work begun in 1933.

The Propaganda of History

How the facts of American history have in the last half
century been falsified because the nation was ashamed. The
South was ashamed because it fought to perpetuate human
slavery. The North was ashamed because it had to call in the
black men to save the Union, abolish slavery and establish
democracy

What are American children taught today about Reconstruction? Helen
Boardman has made a study of current textbooks and notes these three
dominant theses:

1. *All Negroes were ignorant.*

"All were ignorant of public business." (Woodburn and Moran, "Elementary American History and Government," p. 397.)

"Although the Negroes were now free, they were also ignorant and unfit to
govern themselves." (Everett Barnes, "American History for Grammar
Grades," p. 334.)

"The Negroes got control of these states. They had been slaves all their
lives, and were so ignorant they did not even know the letters of the alphabet.
Yet they now sat in the state legislatures and made the laws." (D. H. Montgomery, "The Leading Facts of American History," p. 332.)

"In the South, the Negroes who had so suddenly gained their freedom did
not know what to do with it." (Hubert Cornish and Thomas Hughes, "History
of the United States for Schools," p. 345.)

"In the legislatures, the Negroes were so ignorant that they could only
watch their white leaders — carpetbaggers, and vote aye or no as they were
told." (S. E. Forman, "Advanced American History," Revised Edition, p. 452.)

From *Black Reconstruction in America* (1935).

"Some legislatures were made up of a few dishonest white men and several Negroes, many too ignorant to know anything about law-making." (Hubert Cornish and Thomas Hughes, "History of the United States for Schools," p. 349.)

2. *All Negroes were lazy, dishonest and extravagant.*

"These men knew not only nothing about the government, but also cared for nothing except what they could gain for themselves." (Helen F. Giles, "How the United States Became a World Power," p. 7.)

"Legislatures were often at the mercy of Negroes, childishly ignorant, who sold their votes openly, and whose 'loyalty' was gained by allowing them to eat, drink and clothe themselves at the state's expense." (William J. Long, "America—A History of Our Country," p. 392.)

"Some Negroes spent their money foolishly, and were worse off than they had been before." (Carl Russell Fish, "History of America," p. 385.)

"This assistance led many freed men to believe that they need no longer work. They also ignorantly believed that the lands of their former masters were to be turned over by Congress to them, and that every Negro was to have as his allotment 'forty acres and a mule.'" (W. F. Gordy, "History of the United States," Part II, p. 336.)

"Thinking that slavery meant toil and that freedom meant only idleness, the slave after he was set free was disposed to try out his freedom by refusing to work." (S. E. Forman, "Advanced American History," Revised Edition.)

"They began to wander about, stealing and plundering. In one week, in a Georgia town, 150 Negroes were arrested for thieving." (Helen F. Giles, "How the United States Became a World Power," p. 6.)

3. *Negroes were responsible for bad government during Reconstruction:*

"Foolish laws were passed by the black law-makers, the public money was wasted terribly and thousands of dollars were stolen straight. Self-respecting Southerners chafed under the horrible régime." (Emerson David Fite, "These United States," p. 37.)

"In the exhausted states already amply 'punished' by the desolation of war, the rule of the Negro and his unscrupulous carpetbagger and scalawag patrons, was an orgy of extravagance, fraud and disgusting incompetency." (David Saville Muzzey, "History of the American People," p. 408.)

"The picture of Reconstruction which the average pupil in these sixteen States receives is limited to the South. The South found it necessary to pass Black-Codes for the control of the shiftless and sometimes vicious freedmen. The Freedmen's Bureau caused the Negroes to look to the North rather than to the South for support and by giving them a false sense of equality did more harm than good. With the scalawags, the ignorant and non-propertyholding Negroes under the leadership of the carpetbaggers, engaged in a wild orgy of spending in the legislatures. The humiliation and distress of the Southern whites was in part relieved by the Ku Klux Klan, a secret organization which frightened the superstitious blacks."[1]

Grounded in such elementary and high school teaching, an American youth attending college today would learn from current textbooks of history that the Constitution recognized slavery; that the chance of getting rid of slavery by peaceful methods was ruined by the Abolitionists; that after the period of Andrew Jackson, the two sections of the United States "had become fully conscious of their conflicting interests. Two irreconcilable forms of civilization . . . in the North, the democratic . . . in the South, a more stationary and aristocratic civilization." He would read that Harriet Beecher Stowe brought on the Civil War; that the assault on Charles Sumner was due to his "coarse invective" against a South Carolina Senator; and that Negroes were the only people to achieve emancipation with no effort on their part. That Reconstruction was a disgraceful attempt to subject white people to ignorant Negro rule; and that, according to a Harvard professor of history (the italics are ours), "Legislative expenses were grotesquely extravagant; the *colored members in some states engaging in a saturnalia of corrupt expenditure*" (*Encyclopaedia Britannica*, 14th Edition, Volume 22, p. 815, by Frederick Jackson Turner).

In other words, he would in all probability complete his education without any idea of the part which the black race has played in America; of the tremendous moral problem of abolition; of the cause and meaning of the Civil War and the relation which Reconstruction had to democratic government and the labor movement today.

Herein lies more than mere omission and difference of emphasis. The treatment of the period of Reconstruction reflects small credit upon American historians as scientists. We have too often a deliberate attempt so to change the facts of history that the story will make pleasant reading for Americans. The editors of the fourteenth edition of the *Encyclopaedia Britannica* asked me for an article on the history of the American Negro. From my manuscript they cut out all my references to Reconstruction. I insisted on including the following statement:

"White historians have ascribed the faults and failures of Reconstruction to Negro ignorance and corruption. But the Negro insists that it was Negro loyalty and the Negro vote alone that restored the South to the Union; established the new democracy, both for white and black, and instituted the public schools."

This the editor refused to print, although he said that the article otherwise was "in my judgment, and in the judgment of others in the office, an excellent one, and one with which it seems to me we may all be well satisfied." I was not satisfied and refused to allow the article to appear.

War and especially civil strife leave terrible wounds. It is the duty of humanity to heal them. It was therefore soon conceived as neither wise not patriotic to speak of all the causes of strife and the terrible results to which sectional differences in the United States had led. And so, first of all, we minimized the slavery controversy which convulsed the nation from the Missouri Compromise down to the Civil War. On top of that, we passed by Reconstruction with a phrase of regret or disgust.

But are these reasons of courtesy and philanthropy sufficient for denying Truth? If history is going to be scientific, if the record of human action is going to be set down with that accuracy and faithfulness of detail which will allow its use as a measuring rod and guidepost for the future of nations, there must be set some standards of ethics in research and interpretation.

If, on the other hand, we are going to use history for our pleasure and amusement, for inflating our national ego, and giving us a false but pleasurable sense of accomplishment, then we must give up the idea of history either as a science or as an art using the results of science, and admit frankly that we are using a version of historic fact in order to influence and educate the new generation along the way we wish.

It is propaganda like this that has led men in the past to insist that history is "lies agreed upon"; and to point out the danger in such misinformation. It is indeed extremely doubtful if any permanent benefit comes to the world through such action. Nations reel and stagger on their way; they make hideous mistakes; they commit frightful wrongs; they do great and beautiful things. And shall we not best guide humanity by telling the truth about all this, so far as the truth is ascertainable?

Here in the United States we have a clear example. It was morally wrong and economically retrogressive to build human slavery in the United States in the eighteenth century. We know that now, perfectly well; and there were many Americans, North and South, who knew this and said it in the eighteenth century. Today, in the face of new slavery established elsewhere in the world under other names and guises, we ought to emphasize this lesson of the past. Moreover, it is not well to be reticent in describing that past. Our histories tend to discuss American slavery so impartially, that in the end nobody seems to have done wrong and everybody was right. Slavery appears to have been thrust upon unwilling helpless America, while the South was blameless in becoming its center. The difference of development, North and South, is explained as a sort of working out of cosmic social and economic law. . . .

Yet in this sweeping mechanistic interpretation, there is no room for the real plot of the story, for the clear mistake and guilt of rebuilding a new slavery of the working class in the midst of a fateful experiment in democracy; for the triumph of sheer moral courage and sacrifice in the abolition crusade; and for the hurt and struggle of degraded black millions in their fight for freedom and their attempt to enter democracy. Can all this be omitted or half suppressed in a treatise that calls itself scientific?

Or, to come nearer the center and climax of this fascinating history: What was slavery in the United States? Just what did it mean to the owner and the owned? Shall we accept the conventional story of the old slave plantation and its owner's fine, aristocratic life of cultured leisure? Or shall we note slave biographies, like those of Charles Ball, Sojourner Truth, Harriet Tubman and Frederick Douglass; the careful observations of Olmsted and the indictment of Hinton Helper?

No one can read that first thin autobiography of Frederick Douglass and have left many illusions about slavery. And if truth is our object, no amount of flowery romance and the personal reminiscences of its protected beneficiaries can keep the world from knowing that slavery was a cruel, dirty, costly and inexcusable anachronism, which nearly ruined the world's greatest experiment in democracy. No serious and unbiased student can be deceived by the fairy tale of a beautiful Southern slave civilization. If those who really had opportunity to know the South before the war wrote the truth, it was a center of widespread ignorance, undeveloped resources, suppressed humanity and unrestrained passions, with whatever veneer of manners and culture that could lie above these depths.

Coming now to the Civil War, how for a moment can anyone who reads the *Congressional Globe* from 1850 to 1860, the lives of contemporary statesmen and public characters, North and South, the discourses in the newspapers and accounts of meetings and speeches, doubt that Negro slavery was the cause of the Civil War? What do we gain by evading this clear fact, and talking in vague ways about "Union" and "State Rights" and differences in civilization as the cause of that catastrophe?

Of all historic facts there can be none clearer than that for four long and fearful years the South fought to perpetuate human slavery; and that the nation which "rose so bright and fair and died so pure of stain" was one that had a perfect right to be ashamed of its birth and glad of its death. Yet one monument in North Carolina achieves the impossible by recording of Confederate soldiers: "They died fighting for liberty!"

On the other hand, consider the North and the Civil War. Why should we be deliberately false, like Woodward, in "Meet General Grant," and represent the North as magnanimously freeing the slave without any effort on his part?

"The American Negroes are the only people in the history of the world, so far as I know, that ever became free without any effort of their own. . . .

"They had not started the war nor ended it. They twanged banjos around the railroad stations, sang melodious spirituals, and believed that some Yankee would soon come along and give each of them forty acres of land and a mule."[2]

The North went to war without the slightest idea of freeing the slave. The great majority of Northerners from Lincoln down pledged themselves to protect slavery, and they hated and harried Abolitionists. But on the other hand, the thesis which Beale tends to support that the whole North during and after the war was chiefly interested in making money, is only half true; it was abolition and belief in democracy that gained for a time the upper hand after the war and led the North in Reconstruction; business followed abolition in order to maintain the tariff, pay the bonds and defend the banks. To call this business program "the program of the North" and ignore abolition is un-historical. In growing ascendancy for a calculable time was a great moral movement which turned the North from its economic defense of slavery and led it to Emancipation. Abolitionists attacked slavery because it was wrong and their moral battle cannot be truthfully minimized or forgotten. Nor does this fact deny that the majority of Northerners before the war were not abolitionists, that they attacked slavery only in order to win the war and enfranchised the Negro to secure this result.

One has but to read the debates in Congress and state papers from Abraham Lincoln down to know that the decisive action which ended the Civil War was the emancipation and arming of the black slave; that, as Lincoln said: "Without the military help of black freedmen, the war against the South could not have been won." The freedmen, far from being the inert recipients of freedom at the hands of philanthropists, furnished 200,000 soldiers in the Civil War who took part in nearly 200 battles and skirmishes, and in addition perhaps 300,000 others as effective laborers and helpers. In proportion to population, more Negroes than whites fought in the Civil War. These people, withdrawn from the support of the Confederacy, with threat of the withdrawal of millions more, made the opposition of the slaveholder useless, unless they themselves freed and armed their own slaves. This was exactly what they started to do; they were only restrained by realizing that such action removed the very cause for which they began fighting. Yet one would search current American histories almost in vain to find a clear statement or even faint recognition of these perfectly well-authenticated facts.

All this is but preliminary to the kernel of the historic problem with which this book deals, and that is Reconstruction. The chorus of agreement concerning the attempt to reconstruct and organize the South after the Civil War and

Emancipation is overwhelming. There is scarce a child in the street that cannot tell you that the whole effort was a hideous mistake and an unfortunate incident, based on ignorance, revenge and the perverse determination to attempt the impossible; that the history of the United States from 1866 to 1876 is something of which the nation ought to be ashamed and which did more to retard and set back the American Negro than anything that has happened to him; while at the same time it grievously and wantonly wounded again a part of the nation already hurt to death.

True it is that the Northern historians writing just after the war had scant sympathy for the South, and wrote ruthlessly of "rebels" and "slave-drivers." They had at least the excuse of a war psychosis. . . .

First of all, we have James Ford Rhodes' history of the United States. Rhodes was trained not as an historian but as an Ohio business man. He had no broad formal education. When he had accumulated a fortune, he surrounded himself with a retinue of clerks and proceeded to manufacture a history of the United States by mass production. His method was simple. He gathered a vast number of authorities; he selected from these authorities those whose testimony supported his thesis, and he discarded the others. . . .

Above all, he begins his inquiry convinced, without admitting any necessity of investigation, that Negroes are an inferior race:

"No large policy in our country has ever been so conspicuous a failure as that of forcing universal Negro suffrage upon the South. The Negroes who simply acted out their nature, were not to blame. How indeed could they acquire political honesty? What idea could barbarism thrust into slavery obtain of the rights of property? . . .

"From the Republican policy came no real good to the Negroes. Most of them developed no political capacity, and the few who raised themselves above the mass, did not reach a high order of intelligence."[3]

Rhodes was primarily the historian of property; of economic history and the labor movement, he knew nothing; of democratic government, he was contemptuous. He was trained to make profits. He used his profits to write history. He speaks again and again of the rulership of "intelligence and property" and he makes a plea that intelligent use of the ballot for the benefit of property is the only real foundation of democracy.

The real frontal attack on Reconstruction, as interpreted by the leaders of national thought in 1870 and for some time thereafter, came from the universities and particularly from Columbia and Johns Hopkins.

The movement began with Columbia University and with the advent of John W. Burgess of Tennessee and William A. Dunning of New Jersey as professors of political science and history.

Burgess was an ex-Confederate soldier who started a little Southern college with a box of books, a box of tallow candles and a Negro boy; and his attitude toward the Negro race in after years was subtly colored by this early conception of Negroes as essentially property like books and candles. Dunning was a kindly and impressive professor who was deeply influenced by a growing group of young Southern students and began with them to re-write the history of the nation from 1860 to 1880, in more or less conscious opposition to the classic interpretations of New England.

Burgess was frank and determined in his anti-Negro thought. He expounded his theory of Nordic supremacy which colored all his political theories:

"The claim that there is nothing in the color of the skin from the point of view of political ethics is a great sophism. A black skin means membership in a race of men which has never of itself succeeded in subjecting passion to reason, has never, therefore, created any civilization of any kind. To put such a race of men in possession of a 'state' government in a system of federal government is to trust them with the development of political and legal civilization upon the most important subjects of human life, and to do this in communities with a large white population is simply to establish barbarism in power over civilization."

Burgess is a Tory and open apostle of reaction. He tells us that the nation now believes "that it is the white man's mission, his duty and his right, to hold the reins of political power in his own hands for the civilization of the world and the welfare of mankind."[4]

For this reason America is following "the European idea of the duty of civilized races to impose their political sovereignty upon civilized, or half civilized, or not fully civilized, races anywhere and everywhere in the world."[5]

He complacently believes that "There is something natural in the subordination of an inferior race to a superior race, even to the point of the enslavement of the inferior race, but there is nothing natural in the opposite."[6] He therefore denominates Reconstruction as the rule "of the uncivilized Negroes over the whites of the South."[7] This has been the teaching of one of our greatest universities for nearly fifty years.

Dunning was less dogmatic as a writer, and his own statements are often judicious. But even Dunning can declare that "all the forces [in the South] that made for civilization were dominated by a mass of barbarous freedmen"; and that "the antithesis and antipathy of race and color were crucial and ineradicable. . . ."[8]

The Columbia school of historians and social investigators have issued between 1895 and the present time sixteen studies of Reconstruction in the Southern States, all based on the same thesis and all done according to the same method: first, endless sympathy with the white South; second, ridicule, contempt or silence for the Negro; third, a judicial attitude towards the North, which concludes that the North under great misapprehension did a grievous wrong, but eventually saw its mistake and retreated.

These studies vary, of course, in their methods. Dunning's own work is usually silent so far as the Negro is concerned. Burgess is more than fair in law but reactionary in matters of race and property, regarding the treatment of a Negro as a man as nothing less than a crime, and admitting that "the mainstay of property is the courts."

In the books on Reconstruction written by graduates of these universities and others, the studies of Texas, North Carolina, Florida, Virginia, and Louisiana are thoroughly bad, giving no complete picture of what happened during Reconstruction, written for the most part by men and women without broad historical or social background, and all designed not to seek the truth but to prove a thesis. Hamilton reaches the climax of this school when he characterizes the black codes, which even Burgess condemned, as "not only . . . on the whole reasonable, temperate and kindly, but, in the main, necessary."[9]

Thompson's "Georgia" is another case in point. It seeks to be fair, but silly stories about Negroes indicating utter lack of even common sense are included, and every noble sentiment from white people. When two Negro workers, William and Jim, put a straightforward advertisement in a local paper, the author says that it was "evidently written by a white friend." There is not the slightest historical evidence to prove this, and there were plenty of educated Negroes in Augusta at the time who might have written this. Lonn's "Louisiana" puts Sheridan's words in Sherman's mouth to prove a petty point.

There are certain of these studies which, though influenced by the same general attitude, nevertheless have more of scientific poise and cultural background. Garner's "Reconstruction in Mississippi" conceives the Negro as an integral part of the scene and treats him as a human being. With this should be bracketed the recent study of "Reconstruction in South Carolina" by Simkins and Woody. This is not as fair as Garner's, but in the midst of conventional judgment and conclusion, and reproductions of all available caricatures of Negroes, it does not hesitate to give a fair account of the Negroes and of some of their work. It gives the impression of combining in one book two antagonistic points of view, but in the clash much truth emerges.

Ficklen's "Louisiana" and the works of Fleming are anti-Negro in spirit, but, nevertheless, they have a certain fairness and sense of historic honesty. Fleming's "Documentary History of Reconstruction" is done by a man who has a thesis to support, and his selection of documents supports the thesis. His study of Alabama is pure propaganda.

Next come a number of books which are openly and blatantly propaganda, like Herbert's "Solid South," and the books by Pike and Reynolds on South Carolina, the works by Pollard and Carpenter, and especially those by Ulrich Phillips. One of the latest and most popular of this series is "The Tragic Era" by Claude Bowers, which is an excellent and readable piece of current newspaper reporting, absolutely devoid of historical judgment or sociological knowledge. It is a classic example of historical propaganda of the cheaper sort.

We have books like Milton's "Age of Hate" and Winston's "Andrew Johnson" which attempt to re-write the character of Andrew Johnson. They certainly add to our knowledge of the man and our sympathy for his weakness. But they cannot, for students, change the calm testimony of unshaken historical facts. Fuess' "Carl Schurz" paints the picture of this fine liberal, and yet goes out of its way to show that he was quite wrong in what he said he saw in the South.

The chief witness in Reconstruction, the emancipated slave himself, has been almost barred from court. His written Reconstruction record has been largely destroyed and nearly always neglected. Only three or four states have preserved the debates in the Reconstruction conventions; there are few biographies of black leaders. The Negro is refused a hearing because he was poor and ignorant. It is therefore assumed that all Negroes in Reconstruction were ignorant and silly and that therefore a history of Reconstruction in any state can quite ignore him. The result is that most unfair caricatures of Negroes have been carefully preserved; but serious speeches, successful administration and upright character are almost universally ignored and forgotten. Wherever a black head rises to historic view, it is promptly slain by an adjective — "shrewd," "notorious," "cunning" — or pilloried by a sneer; or put out of view by some quite unproven charge of bad moral character. In other words, every effort has been made to treat the Negro's part in Reconstruction with silence and contempt.

When recently a student tried to write on education in Florida, he found that the official records of the excellent administration of the colored Superintendent of Education, Gibbs, who virtually established the Florida public school, had been destroyed. Alabama has tried to obliterate all printed records of Reconstruction.

Especially noticeable is the fact that little attempt has been made to trace carefully the rise and economic development of the poor whites and their relation to the planters and to Negro labor after the war. . . .

The whole development of Reconstruction was primarily an economic development, but no economic history or proper material for it has been written. It has been regarded as a purely political matter, and of politics most naturally divorced from industry.[10]

All this is reflected in the textbooks of the day and in the encyclopedias, until we have got to the place where we cannot use our experiences during and after the Civil War for the uplift and enlightenment of mankind. We have spoiled and misconceived the position of the historian. If we are going, in the future, not simply with regard to this one question, but with regard to all social problems, to be able to use human experience for the guidance of mankind, we have got clearly to distinguish between fact and desire.

In the first place, somebody in each era must make clear the facts with utter disregard to his own wish and desire and belief. What we have got to know, so far as possible, are the things that actually happened in the world. Then with that much clear and open to every reader, the philosopher and prophet has a chance to interpret these facts; but the historian has no right, posing as scientist, to conceal or distort facts; and until we distinguish between these two functions of the chronicler of human action, we are going to render it easy for a muddled world out of sheer ignorance to make the same mistake ten times over.

One is astonished in the study of history at the recurrence of the idea that evil must be forgotten, distorted, skimmed over. . . . The difficulty, of course, with this philosophy is that history loses its value as an incentive and example; it paints perfect men and noble nations, but it does not tell the truth. . . .

Not a single great leader of the nation during the Civil War and Reconstruction has escaped attack and libel. The magnificent figures of Charles Sumner and Thaddeus Stevens have been besmirched almost beyond recognition. We have been cajoling and flattering the South and slurring the North, because the South is determined to re-write the history of slavery and the North is not interested in history but in wealth.

This, then, is the book basis upon which today we judge Reconstruction. In order to paint the South as a martyr to inescapable fate, to make the North the magnanimous emancipator, and to ridicule the Negro as the impossible joke in the whole development, we have in fifty years, by libel, innuendo, and silence, so completely misstated and obliterated the history of the Negro in America and his relation to its work and government that today it is almost unknown. This may be fine romance, but it is not science. It may be inspiring, but it is certainly not the truth. And beyond this it is dangerous. It is not only part foundation of our present lawlessness and loss of democratic ideals; it has, more than that, led the world to embrace and worship the color bar as social salvation and it is helping to range mankind in ranks of mutual hatred and contempt, at the summons of a cheap and false myth.

Nearly all recent books on Reconstruction agree with each other in discarding the government reports and substituting selected diaries, letters, and gossip. Yet it happens that the government records are an historic source of wide and unrivaled authenticity. . . .

Certain monographs deserve all praise, like those of Kendrick and Pierce. The work of Flack is prejudiced but built on study. The defense of the carpetbag régime by Tourgée and Allen, Powell Clayton, Holden, and Warmoth are worthy antidotes to the certain writers. . . .

It will be noted that for my authority in this work I have depended very largely upon secondary material; upon state histories of Reconstruction, written in the main by those who were convinced before they began to write that the Negro was incapable of government, or of becoming a constituent part of a civilized state. The fairest of these histories have not tried to conceal facts; in other cases, the black man has been largely ignored; while in still others, he has been traduced and ridiculed. If I had had time and money and opportunity to go back to the original sources in all cases, there can be no doubt that the weight of this work would have been vastly strengthened, and as I firmly believe, the case of the Negro more convincingly set forth.

Various volumes of papers in the great libraries like the Johnson papers in the Library of Congress, the Sumner manuscripts at Harvard, the Schurz correspondence, the Wells papers, the Chase papers, the Fessenden and Greeley collections, the McCulloch, McPherson, Sherman, Stevens, and Trumbull papers, all must have much of great interest to the historians of the American Negro. I have not had time nor opportunity to examine these, and most of those who have examined them had little interest in black folk.

Negroes have done some excellent work on their own history and defense. It suffers of course from natural partisanship and a desire to prove a case in the face of a chorus of unfair attacks. Its best work also suffers from the fact that Negroes with difficulty reach an audience. But this is also true of such white writers as Skaggs and Bancroft who could not get first-class publishers because they were saying something that the nation did not like.

The Negro historians began with autobiographies and reminiscences. The older historians were George W. Williams and Joseph T. Wilson; the new school of historians is led by Carter G. Woodson; and I have been greatly helped by the unpublished theses of four of the youngest Negro students. It is most unfortunate that while many young white Southerners can get funds to attack and ridicule the Negro and his friends, it is almost impossible for first-class Negro students to get a chance for research or to get finished work in print.

I write then in a field devastated by passion and belief. Naturally, as a Negro, I cannot do this writing without believing in the essential humanity of Negroes, in their ability to be educated, to do the work of the modern world, to take their place as equal citizens with others. I cannot for a moment subscribe to that bizarre doctrine of race that makes most men inferior to the few. But, too, as a student of science, I want to be fair, objective, and judicial; to let no searing of the memory by intolerable insult and cruelty make me fail to sympathize with human frailties and contradiction, in the eternal paradox of good and evil. But armed and warned by all this, and fortified by long study of the facts, I stand at the end of this writing, literally aghast at what American historians have done to this field.

What is the object of writing the history of Reconstruction? Is it to wipe out the disgrace of a people which fought to make slaves of Negroes? Is it to show that the North had higher motives than freeing black men? Is it to prove that Negroes were black angels? No, it is simply to establish the Truth, on which Right in the future may be built. We shall never have a science of history until we have in our colleges men who regard the truth as more important than the defense of the white race, and who will not deliberately encourage students to gather thesis material in order to support a prejudice or buttress a lie.

Three-fourths of the testimony against the Negro in Reconstruction is on the unsupported evidence of men who hated and despised Negroes and regarded it as loyalty to blood, patriotism to country, and filial tribute to the fathers to lie, steal, or kill in order to discredit these black folk. This may be a natural result when a people have been humbled and impoverished and degraded in their own life; but what is inconceivable is that another generation and another group should regard this testimony as scientific truth, when it is contradicted by logic and by fact. This chapter, therefore, which in logic should be a survey of books and sources, becomes of sheer necessity an arraignment of American historians and an indictment of their ideals. With a determination unparalleled in science, the mass of American writers have started out so to distort the facts of the greatest critical period of American history as to prove right wrong and wrong right. I am not familiar enough with the vast field of human history to pronounce on the relative guilt of these and historians of other times and fields; but I do say that if the history of the past has been written in the same fashion, it is useless as science and misleading as ethics. It simply shows that with sufficient general agreement and determination among the dominant classes, the truth of history may be utterly distorted and contradicted and changed to any convenient fairy tale that the masters of men wish.

I cannot believe that any unbiased mind, with an ideal of truth and of scientific judgment, can read the plain, authentic facts of our history, during 1860–1880, and come to conclusions essentially different from mine; and yet I stand virtually alone in this interpretation. So much so that the very cogency of my facts would make me hesitate, did I not seem to see plain reasons. Subtract from Burgess his belief that only white people can rule, and he is in essential agreement with me. Remember that Rhodes was an uneducated money-maker who hired clerks to find the facts which he needed to support his thesis, and one is convinced that the same labor and expense could easily produce quite opposite results.

One fact and one alone explains the attitude of most recent writers toward Reconstruction; they cannot conceive Negroes as men; in their minds the word "Negro" connotes "inferiority" and "stupidity" lightened only by unreasoning gayety and humor. . . .

Assuming, therefore, as axiomatic the endless inferiority of the Negro race, these newer historians, mostly Southerners, some Northerners who deeply sympathized with the South, misinterpreted, distorted, even deliberately ignored any fact that challenged or contradicted this assumption. If the Negro was admittedly sub-human, what need to waste time delving into his Reconstruction history? Consequently historians of Reconstruction with a few exceptions ignore the Negro as completely as possible, leaving the reader wondering why an element apparently so insignificant filled the whole Southern picture at the time. The only real excuse for this attitude is loyalty to a lost cause, reverence for brave fathers and suffering mothers and sisters, and fidelity to the ideals of a clan and class. But in propaganda against the Negro since emancipation in this land, we face one of the most stupendous efforts the world ever saw to discredit human beings, an effort involving universities, history, science, social life, and religion. . . .

Notes

1. "Racial Attitudes in American History Textbooks," *Journal of Negro History*, XIX, p. 257.
2. W. E. Woodward, *Meet General Grant*, p. 372.
3. Rhodes, *History of the United States*, VII, pp. 232–233.
4. Burgess, *Reconstruction and the Constitution*, pp. viii, ix.
5. Ibid., p. 218.
6. Ibid., pp. 244–245.
7. Ibid., p. 218.
8. Dunning, *Reconstruction, Political and Economic*, pp. 212, 213.
9. Hamilton, "Southern Legislation in Respect to Freedmen," in *Studies in Southern History and Politics*, p. 156.
10. *The Economic History of the South* by E. Q. Hawk is merely a compilation of census reports and conventionalities.

Apology

There are today so many periodicals, and some of such excellence, that persons proposing a new venture ought clearly to indicate its object and the need of such enterprise. This quarterly review proposes to study and survey the field of race and culture, and of racial and cultural relations. It uses both designations more or less interchangeably; because it would emphasize that view of race which regards it as cultural and historical in essence, rather than primarily biological and psychological.

Because of the reality back of it, we continue the use of the older concept of the word "race," referring to the greater groups of human kind which by outer pressure and inner cohesiveness, still form and have long formed a stronger or weaker unity of thought and action. Among these groups appear both biological and psychological likenesses, although we believe that these aspects have in the past been overemphasized in the face of many contradictory facts. While, therefore, we continue to study and measure all human differences we seem to see the basis of real and practical racial unity in culture. We use then the old word in new containers. A culture consists of the ideas, habits and values, the technical processes and goods which any group becomes possessed of either by inheritance or adoption.

Looking over the world today we see as incentive to economic gain, as cause of war, and as infinite source of cultural inspiration nothing so important as race and group contact. Here if anywhere the leadership of science is demanded not to obliterate all race and group distinctions, but to know and study them, to see and appreciate them at their true values, to emphasize the use and place of human differences as tool and method of progress; to make straight the path to a common world humanity through the development of cultural gifts to their highest possibilities.

Studying then group and human culture, we wish to establish ourselves as a place of Re-Views: — that is, as an organ for considering again and after the

From *Phylon: The Atlanta University Review of Race and Culture* 1, First Quarter (1940): 3–5.

event, the happenings and opinions which have to do with the cultural advance and inter-cultural relations of men, in order to reach more final and definite judgments. We shall not attempt to present happenings as news but rather to submit both recent and past occurrences and opinions to more careful scrutiny and interpretation.

This effort of ours is, in a sense, a revival of the old Atlanta University Publications issued between 1897 and 1914. Those publications formed the first scientific basis for factual study of the condition and relations of one racial group in the United States, and was the beginning in America of applied Sociology and Anthropology to group problems. This pioneer work has been supplemented widely since 1914 by institutions like Fisk University and the University of North Carolina, and by individual students in such investigations as Frazier's *Negro Family in the United States*, Johnson's *Negro College Graduate*, Caroline Bond Day's *Negro-White Families*, Abram Harris' *The Negro as Capitalist*, Cayton and Mitchell's *Black Workers and the New Unions*, Reid's studies of Pittsburgh and New Jersey, Bond's *Negro Education in Alabama*; not to mention an increasing volume of government reports.

We seem to see today a new orientation and duty which will call not simply for the internal study of race groups as such, but for a general view of that progress of human beings which takes place through the instrumentality and activity of group culture; so that we hope to view not simply the one race in which this institution, by long and honorable tradition, is interested; nor even to confine our investigations to those darker races, whose advance is least known or appreciated; but rather to look at all groups of men. Naturally we shall usually proceed from the point of view and the experience of the black folk where we live and work, to the wider world.

We do not mean to duplicate work in history, education, and opinion now being done. We recognize the space now being given to racial questions in the leading magazines of the land; and especially in the case of the Negro we know the great accomplishment and field of the *Journal of Negro History*; the new and exhaustive activity of the *Journal of Negro Education*; the tumultuous news gathering of the Negro weekly press.

But we feel decidedly that a new view of the social sciences is necessary, as comprehending the actions of men and reducing them to systematic study and understanding. In this way we foresee a re-interpretation of history, education, and sociology; a re-writing of history from the ideological and economic point of view; a re-establishment of education, not as a science but as the applied art of training men by means of approved psychological method, into ability to know and use the main results of knowledge as accumulated and clarified by physics, chemistry, biology, and anthropology; and especially in sociology, a broad historical, political, and psychological

216

grasp of the actions of men — their rhythms and probabilities, and a frank facing of the mystery of purposeful will on social reform. We shall strive to abolish the present economic illiteracy and paralysis; and openly hold up to frank criticism that widespread assumption that the industrial organization of the nineteenth century was something permanent and sacred and furnished a final word which estops the twentieth century from facing the problem of abolishing poverty as a first step toward real freedom, democracy, and art among men, through the use of industrial technique and planned economy.

This we admit is a wide and steep path. We approach it humbly by means of original research both direct and indirect, by essays on analogous but widely separated subjects, by a careful chronicle of events and an intelligent review of opinion; and at the same time by recognizing the scientific value of the creative impulse in prose, poetry, and illustration.

Our title "Phylon" — race — we transliterate from the Greek, not in pedantry of learning, but to fix and adapt a thought-provoking designation which may easily be remembered. Our full program of publication can only achieve and develop itself in time and with reasonable provision of financial resources. The first year, therefore, will be more or less a year of experiment but we ask patient public support during that time; and to encourage this we set a preliminary subscription price of a dollar, well within the reach of every one; not because our enterprise is going to be cheap and merely popular, but because we do not want to let any reasonable obstacle stand between us and a wide and intelligent audience.

Collaborating directly in the conduct of this magazine are eight members of the faculty of Atlanta University. The editor-in-chief is W. E. B. Du Bois, editor of the former Atlanta University Publications, for 23 years editor of the *Crisis*, author of eleven books and now head of the Department of Sociology of the University. Collaborating with him are: Ira De A. Reid, managing editor, author of *The Negro Immigrant, Urban Negro Worker in the United States, Adult Education Among Negroes*; William Stanley Braithwaite, for years editor of the Anthology of Magazine Verse; W. Mercer Cook, who has spent much time in France and written *Le Noir* and *Portraits Americains*; Rushton Coulborn, a former Vice-Principal of Sussex House, London; William H. Dean, Jr., sometime fellow of Harvard University, and author of a monograph in economics now used at Harvard; and Oran W. Eagleson, who has contributed to the *Journal of Psychology* and the *Journal of Applied Psychology*. The president of the University is also actively associated with us. We have the cooperation of a small board of contributing editors.

For this, our venture in social science, we ask the sympathy and support of all open minds and sincere souls.

The Negro Family in the United States

by E. Franklin Frazier

THE SOCIAL DEVELOPMENT
OF THE AMERICAN NEGRO

This book is not only a great and significant contribution to the science of sociology; it is also a piece of English literature which one can take joy in reading. It is more than a statistical study of the family. It is the study of the development of a human group from the point of view of that social unit which is for biological and social reasons the most persistent and characteristic center of growth and change. It has already been called by great authority "the most valuable contribution to the literature on the family" for twenty years. The study is based on wide documentation and long and intensive study in various parts of the United States and is valuable for insight into human conditions everywhere and not simply for a study of a single race.

It is particularly interesting for me to realize how those pioneer attempts to study the American Negro which were begun in Atlanta University in 1896 and carried on for eighteen years were not altogether sterile weeds. Out of these studies have come Caroline Bond Day's *Negro-White Families in the United States* done at Harvard; Charles Johnson's *Negro College Graduate* done at Fisk; Abram Harris' *The Negro as Capitalist*; Horace M. Bond's *Negro Education in Alabama*; and Cayton and Mitchell's *Black Workers and the New Unions*. As a climax to all this comes Mr. Frazier's study of the family. Leading up to this work have been many preliminary essays on the part of the author. He has written on the Negro Community, on Negro Harlem, on The Family Life of the Negro in the Small Town, Occupational Classes Among Negroes in Cities, the Changing Status of the Negro Family, the Negro Family in

Book review from the *Journal of Negro Education*, April 1940; 9:212–13.

Chicago, Conflict in the Negro Family, the Free Negro Family and numbers of other works besides statistical studies all of which are brought together to furnish the basis for the twenty-two chapters of this work.

The work is divided into five parts: four chapters form Part I "The House of the Master," which is a study of the social development of the American slave and the emergence of the mother as the head of the one group which bore the burden of social survival. Part II "In the House of the Mother" studies in four chapters the development of the matriarchate, showing how the broken family led by the mother and the grandmother established a new social basis for the American Negro. Part III "In the House of the Father," shows how emancipation gave the black father a chance to found and guide a new family unity and how this was accomplished not only among the mass of freedmen but in racial islands of various sorts of mixed folk.

Part IV "In the City of Destruction" contains six chapters which show how the weak Negro family staggering out of slavery and plunged into the modern city fought and died, differentiated and survived in old and new patterns, developing from roving men and homeless women to broken and deserted families and outlawed mothers through criminal youth and divorce into new and encouraging patterns. Part V "In the City of Rebirth" has three revealing chapters which show the new class development among American Negroes which is organizing a middle class of professional people and white collar workers and a black proletariat; a middle class whose leadership of the workers is to some extent disputed and interfered with by the development of the labor movement which is sweeping the Negro along in its current.

The concluding chapter points out that the book has traced less than a century and a half of history. "Yet, during that comparatively brief period, from the standpoint of human history, the Negro, stripped of the relatively simple preliterate culture in which he was nurtured, has created a folk culture and has gradually taken over the more sophisticated American culture. Although only three-quarters of a century has elapsed since the arrival of the last representative of preliterate African races, the type of culture from which he came was as unlike the culture of the civilized American Negro today as the culture of the Germans of Tacitus' day was unlike the culture of German-Americans."

It is an astonishing and revealing study and no one, much less an American Negro, can henceforth talk intelligently concerning present and future conditions without knowing the contents of this book. A large reference apparatus is appended; seventy-five pages of family-history documents; seventy-one pages of supplementary statistical tables covering all aspects of family life, while a classified and complete bibliography fills twenty-eight pages.

The World and Africa

The story of the outpouring of Asia into Africa from A.D. 500
to 1500, and the effect which the interaction of these two
continents had on the world.

The connection between Asia and Africa has always been close. There was
probably actual land connection in prehistoric times, and the black race
appears in both continents in the earliest records, making it doubtful which
continent is the point of origin. Certainly the Negroid people of Asia have
played a leading part in her history. The blacks of Melanesia have scoured the
seas, and Charles Taüber makes them inventors of one of the world's first
written languages: thus "this greatest of all human inventions was made by
aborigines whose descendants today rank among the lowest, the proto-
Australians. . . ."

The Mohammedans organized for proselyting the world, overthrew Persia,
and took Syria and eventually Egypt and North Africa from the Eastern
Roman Empire. They went east as far as India and west to Spain, and
eventually the Golden Horde, as the Russian Mongols had come to be called,
became followers of Islam and thus religious brothers of the Mohammedan
Arabs.

The Arabs brought the new religion of Mohammed into North Africa.
During the seventh century they did not migrate in great numbers. Spain was
conquered not by Arabs, but by armies of Berbers and Negroids led by Arabs.
Later, in the eleventh century, another wave of Arabs came, but the number
was never large and their prestige came from their religion and their language,
which became a *lingua franca* for the peoples north and south of the Sahara.
The total substitution of Arabian for Berber or Negro blood was small.

From *The World and Africa: An Inquiry into the Part Which Africa Has Played in World History* (1947).

Anyone who has traveled in the Sudan knows that most of the "Arabs" he has met are dark-skinned, sometimes practically black, often have Negroid features, and hair that may be almost Negro in quality. It is then obvious that in Africa the term "Arab" is applied to any people professing Islam, however much race mixture has occurred, so that while the term has a cultural value it is of little ethnic significance and is often misleading.

The Arabs were too nearly akin to Negroes to draw an absolute color line. Antar, one of the great pre-Islamic poets of Arabia, was the son of a black woman; and one of the great poets at the court of Harun-al-Rashid was black. In the twelfth century a learned Negro poet resided at Seville.

The Mohammedans crossed the Pyrenees in A.D. 719 and met Charles Martel at Poitiers; repulsed, the invaders turned back and settled in Spain. The conflict for the control of the Mohammedan world eventually left Spain in anarchy. A prince of the Omayyads arrived in 758. This Abdurahman, after thirty years of fighting, founded an independent government which became the Caliphate of Cordova. His power was based on his army of Negro and white Christian slaves. He established a magnificent court and restored order, and his son gave protection to writers and thinkers.

Eventually rule passed into the hands of a mulatto, Almanzor, who kept order with his army of Berbers and Negroes, making fifty invasions into Christian territory. He died in 1002, and in a few years the Caliphate declined and the Christians began to reconquer the country. The Mohammedans looked to Africa for refuge.

In the eleventh century there was quite a large Arab immigration. The Berbers and some Negroes by that time had adopted the Arab tongue and the Mohammedan religion, and Mohammedanism had spread slowly southward across the Sahara.[1]

The invasions of the eleventh century were launched in 1048 by the Vizier of Egypt under the colored Caliph Mustansir. Each man was provided with a camel and given a gold piece, the only condition being that he must settle in the west. In two years they pillaged Cyrenaica and Tripoli and captured Kairwan. The invaders for the most part settled in Tripoli and Tunis, while their companions pressed on westward into Morocco. This exemplifies the process of arabization in North Africa, and it was to a large extent a reflex from the invasion that had most to do with the arabization of the Nile valley. It is thus responsible for much of the present-day distribution of the "Arab" tribes of the Sudan.

The Arabs invaded African Egypt, taking it from the Eastern Roman Emperors and securing as allies the native Negroid Egyptians, now called Copts, and using Sudanese blacks, Persians, and Turks in their armies. They came in 639 under Amr-ibn-el-Asr, partly as friends of Egyptians against the

221

tyranny of the Eastern Roman Empire, partly even as defenders of the hereti-
cal Coptic Church. It must be remembered that they were related by blood
and history to the Negroid peoples. One of Mohammed's concubines was a
dark curly-haired Coptic woman, May; and Nubians from the Sudan took
frequent part in these wars. Alexandria surrendered in 642, and ten years later
the Arabs invaded Nubia and attacked Dongola crying, "Ye people of Nubia,
Ye shall dwell in safety!"[2]

For two centuries from 651 there were ninety-eight Mohammedan governors of Egypt under Caliphs of Medina, Damascus, and Bagdad. The Copts,
representing the majority of the Egyptians, for the most part submitted to this
rulership, but the black Nubians continued to be unruly and even came to the
defense of the Copts. In 722 King Cyriacus of Nubia marched into Egypt with
one hundred thousand soldiers and secured release of the imprisoned Coptic
patriarch. There is an intriguing story of a black virgin whom the Mohammedans had seized and who promised them an unguent to make them
invulnerable. To prove it she put it on her own neck, and when the Arab
soldier swept his sword down upon her, her head fell off as she had intended.[3]

The change from the Omayyad to the Abasid Caliphs took place in Egypt
peacefully in the middle of the eighth century. By 832 Egypt had become
almost entirely Mohammedan, by conversion of the Copts through economic
and social pressure. In 852 the last Arab governor ruled in Egypt, and in 856
the Turks began to replace the Arabs and to favor the Copts. There was much
misrule, and from 868 to 884 Ahmad-ibn-Tulun, a Turkish slave, ruled. The
Berga people of the Sudan refused further tribute of four hundred slaves
annually and revolted in 854; the army of Ali Baba, "King of the Sudan," led
the revolt, but spears and shields strove against mail armor and Arab ships, and
failed.

We know that in 850 four hundred black East Africans had been enrolled
in the army of Abu'l Abbas, ruler of Bagdad, and that they rose in revolt with a
Negro, called "Lord of the Blacks," at their head. In 869 the Persian adventurer, Al Kabith, summoned the black slaves to revolt, and they flocked to his
side in tens of thousands. In 871 they captured Basra and for fourteen years
dominated the Euphrates delta. When Masudi visited this country fourteen
years later, he was told that this conquest by famine and sword had killed at
least a million people.

Syria was annexed to Egypt in 872, and from that time until the eleventh
century Egypt, Syria, Palestine, and Mesopotamia form one realm, more or
less closely united. When Syria was first annexed, Egypt ruled from the
Euphrates to Barka and Aswan, and the famous black cavalry of ten thousand
or more took part in the conquest. In 883 the Zeng Negroes of East Africa

revolted, and some settled in Mesopotamia. The Tulun dynasty finally ended in 905, and there were thirty years of unsettled rule in Egypt under the suzerainty of weak caliphs. From 935 to 946 Ikshid was governor of Egypt.

He was succeeded by a black Abyssinian eunuch, Abu-l-Misk Kafur, "Musky Camphor," for whom Ikshid named a celebrated garden in Cairo. Kafur was a clever man of deep black color with smooth shiny skin, who had been guardian of the sons of Ikshid. He read history and listened to music and was lavish with his vast wealth. Daily at his table there were served two hundred sheep and lamb, seven hundred and fifty fowls, and a thousand birds and one hundred jars of sweetmeats. He attracted men of learning and letters and began an era of art and literature which placed Egypt as a cultural center next to Bagdad, Damascus, and Cordova.[4] The poet Muttanabi praised him as "The Moon of Darkness."

Kafur ruled Egypt for twenty-two years, from 946 to 968; he was regent for nineteen years, but the two sons of Ikshid who were nominally on the throne were playboys without power. Kafur ruled three years alone, from 965 to 968. He conquered Damascus and Aleppo and incorporated Syria under Egyptian rule. Trouble arose from time to time in Syria, while in Egypt there were earthquakes, bad Nile seasons, and a Nubian revolt. Nevertheless, in general good order was maintained. He died in 968 and was succeeded by a child, then by the Caliph Hoseyn, and finally by Moizz.

The Shiites or Fatimids from Morocco, under the man who called himself the Mahdi, now began to war on Egypt and conquered it. They sent an embassy to George, King of Nubia; reconquered Syria and became rich with gold and jewelry, ivory and silk. By the middle of the twelfth century the Mohammedan empire included North Africa, Syria, Sicily, and Hejaz; Turkish slaves and Sudanese troops held the empire.

Moizz was helped by Killis, a Jew who had been Kafur's righthand man; and had a bodyguard of four thousand young men, white and black. By the help of Negro troops another Syrian revolt was quelled. Then came the reign of mad Hakim and finally Zahir.

Zahir ruled Egypt from 1021 to 1026. His wife was a black Sudanese woman, and after the death of her husband largely influenced the rule of her son, who came to the throne in 1036 and ruled until 1094, the longest reign in the dynasty. This son, M'add, took the name of Mustansir and is regarded as the best and ablest of the rulers of his time. He loved and encouraged learning and had a library of a hundred and twenty thousand volumes. The Black Dowager, who had great influence over him, sailed the Nile in her silver barge and imported additional Negro troops from the south, until Mustansir had in his escort fifty thousand black soldiers and swordsmen, twenty thousand Berbers, ten thousand Turks, and thirty thousand white slaves. For years all Upper Egypt was held by black regiments.

Mustansir had enormous wealth, including his celebrated golden mattress. Makrizi described his jewels, gold plate, and ivory. Cairo consisted at this time of twenty thousand brick houses; there was art in pottery and glass work, and a beautiful "Lake of the Abyssinians." Mustansir had difficulties with Syria and nearly lost his power in 1068; his library was destroyed and the Black Dowager had to flee to Bagdad for sanctuary. Through the aid of Bedar, his prime minister, he regained power and restored Syria to Egyptian rule.

Then the Seljukian Turks appeared. They subdued Persia, captured Bagdad, and attacked Syria. Jerusalem was captured in 1071, and this became the excuse for the European Crusades which began in 1096, two years after Mustansir died. The Europeans took Jerusalem in 1099 and later seized most of Syria, but Egypt, with the aid of the black veterans of Mustansir's former army, eventually defeated Baldwin in 1102. From 1169 to 1193 Saladin, the Kurd, ruled Egypt and the East.

After Saladin's accession, black Nubian troops attacked Egypt, and the rebellion continued for many years. Gradually Saladin asserted his power in Nubia, and peace was made with the African Zeng in Mesopotamia. Mesopotamia had been ruined by the Mongols, and Cairo now became the greatest cultural center in the Orient, and indeed in the world, from 1196 to 1250. Saint Francis of Assisi preached there in 1219, and world trade centered in Alexandria.

Artists flocked to Egypt from Asia Minor. Men of culture lived at court, poets and writers. The Thousand and One Nights stories were collected. Indian stories and European romances were combined with Egyptian materials. A companion collection of poems made at this time were those of Antarbin-Shaddad. He was born about A.D. 498, the son of a black slave girl, Zebbeda, and of Shaddad, a nobleman of the tribe of Abs. Antar is famous. One of his works is found as the sixth poem of the Mo'allaqat—the "golden verses"—which are considered in Arabia the greatest poems ever written. The story is that they were hung on the Ka'bah at the Holy Temple at Mecca so that all the pilgrims who came there might know them and do obeisance to them. The Mo'allaqat belongs to the first school of Arabian poetry—to the "Gahilieh"—"time of ignorance." The Antar poem belongs to the time of the war of Dahis, and, like the five poems which preceded it in the epic, it lauds the victors of the battlefield, describes the beauties of nature, and praises the camel of the desert. The main theme, however, is love.

Rimski-Korsakov's Symphony *Antar*, with its wealth of barbaric color and oriental fire has been deservedly popular. The libretto is drawn from the voluminous work known as *The Romance of Antar*, which was published in

Cairo in thirty-two volumes and has been translated in sections from the Arabic by various scholars. There are two editions of the work — one known as the *Syrian Antar*, the other as the *Arabian Antar*. The abridged work was first introduced to European readers in 1802; a translation was made and issued in four books by Terrick Hamilton in 1819. The *Romance* is a companion piece to the *Arabian Nights* and is a standard Arabian work. The seemingly number-less tales that are incorporated in *The Romance of Antar* are traditional tales of the desert that were retold and preserved by Asmai during the reign of Harun-al-Rashid.

As autocratic power grew among the Mohammedans, a number of reli-gious and political malcontents migrated down the eastern coast of Africa. They filtered through for a number of centuries, not as conquerors, and they were permitted to live and trade in limited areas and mingled and intermar-ried with the black Bantu. An Arab settlement was made about A.D. 684 under a son-in-law of Mohammed. Then came another migration in 908, and many of the Arabs wandered inland. Cities were established and soon were trading with the gold-mining peoples of Sofala. Masudi, an Arab geographer, visited this part of Africa in the tenth century and described the gold trade and the kingdom of the Waklimi. Marco Polo, writing in 1298, described the islands of Madagascar and Zanzibar as peopled with blacks.

There are indications of trade between Nupe in West Africa and Sofala on the East Coast, and certainly trade between Asia and East Africa dates back earlier than the beginning of the Christian era. Asiatic traders settled on the East Coast, and by means of mulatto and Negro merchants brought Central Africa into contact with Arabia, India, China, and Malaysia.

Zaide, great-grandson of Ali, nephew and son-in-law of Mohammed, was banished from Arabia. He passed over to Africa and formed settlements. His people mingled with the blacks, and the resulting mulatto traders, known as the Emoxaidi, seem to have wandered as far south as the equator. Other Arabian families came over on account of oppression and founded the towns of Magadosho and Brava, both not far north of the equator. The Emoxaidi, whom the later immigrants regarded as heretics, were driven inland and became the interpreting traders between the coast and the Bantu. Some wanderers from Magadosho came into the port of Sofala and there learned that gold could be obtained. This led to a small Arab settlement at that place.

Seventy years later, and about 150 years before the Norman conquest of England, certain Persians settled at Kilwa in East Africa, led by Hasan-ibn-Ali, who was the son of a black Abyssinian slave mother, and accompanied by his own six sons.

Ibn Batuta, who was acquainted with Arab life on the Mediterranean coast and at Mecca in the fourteenth century, was surprised by the wealth and civilization of East Africa. Kilwa he describes as "one of the most beautiful and best built towns." Mombasa is a "large" and Magadosho an "exceedingly large city."

Duarte Barbosa, visiting the coast ten years later, described Kilwa as "a Moorish town with many fair houses of stone and mortar, with many windows after our fashion, very well laid out in streets, with many flat roofs. The doors are of wood, well carved, with excellent joinery. Around it are streams and orchards and fruit-gardens with many channels of sweet water. . . . And in this town was great plenty of gold, as no ships passed to or from Sofala without coming to this island." Of the Moors, he continued: "There are some fair and some black: they are finely clad in many rich garments of gold and silver in chains and bracelets . . . and many jewelled ear-rings in their ears." Mombasa, again, is "a very fair place, with lofty stone and mortar houses, well lined in streets. . . . Their women go very bravely attired."[5]

It is probable that Chinese ships traded directly with Africa from the eighth to the twelfth centuries. When the Portuguese came they found the Arabs intermarried and integrated with the Bantu and in control of the trade.

Notes

1. See Du Bois, Black Folk, pp. 41–53.
2. E. Stanley Lane-Poole, History of Egypt in Medieval Times, edited by W. M. Flinders Petrie (London: Methuen & Co., 1914), Vol. VI, pp. 22, 28, 89.
3. Cf., ibid., p. 28.
4. Cf., ibid., p. 89.
5. The Book of Duarte Barbosa, tr. from the Portuguese by M. L. Davis (London: Hakluyt Society, 1918), Vol. I, pp. 11–13, 18–20.

IV

Institutions

Family, Church,
College, Business

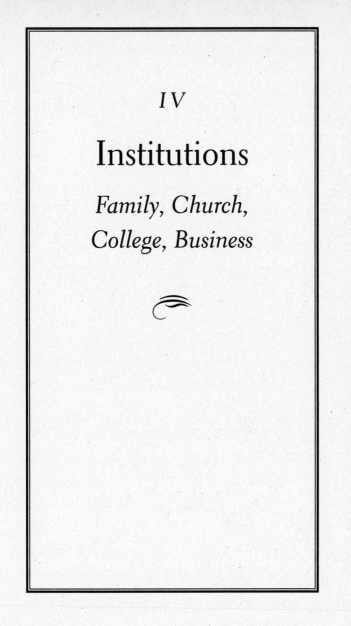

The 1898 study commissioned by the U.S. Department of Labor "The Negroes of Farmville, Virginia" was a model social science investigation. Based on census data, newspapers, and extensive written and oral interviews during a summer spent in the town, Du Bois formulated significant conceptions about class structure, consequences of urbanization, and the broad economic and social evolution of African-Americans. He carried the preliminary observations and astute projections of the Farmville research experience over into what are among the first studies of the black church ("The Negro Church" [1912]) and business community ("The Upbuilding of Black Durham" [1912]). Du Bois's eloquent insistence on the paramount role of higher education in the preparation of the African-American leadership class was in striking contrast to the growing emphasis upon vocational and technical education promoted by exponents of Hampton and Tuskegee institutes. The 1905 essay "Atlanta University" exemplifies Du Bois's high hopes and resolute defense of liberal arts as the avenue to full citizenship rights for his race. As the biting 1918 critique "Negro Education" and sardonic piece "Gifts and Education," written twenty years later, show, nothing evoked his ire more than when Du Bois saw the race-specific policies of the great northern foundations being ratified by supposedly objective studies and implemented through the restriction of funds to institutions willing to deemphasize literature, history, philosophy, sociology, and the physical sciences. The memoir "A Negro Student at Harvard at the End of the Nineteenth Century" is engrossing as a personal document and for what it reveals about the formation of the citizenship values undergirding Du Bois's appreciation of family, church, college, and business enterprise.

The Negroes of Farmville, Virginia

The Negroes of Farmville, Israel Hill, and the neighboring county districts form a closed and in many respects an independent group life. They live largely in neighborhoods with one another, they have their own churches and organizations and their own social life, they read their own books and papers, and their group life touches that of the white people only in economic matters. Even here the strong influence of group attraction is being felt, and Negroes are beginning to patronize either business enterprises conducted by themselves or those conducted in a manner to attract their trade. Thus, instead of the complete economic dependence of blacks upon whites, we see growing a nicely adjusted economic interdependence of the two races, which promises much in the way of mutual forbearance and understanding.

The most highly developed and characteristic expression of Negro group life in this town, as throughout the Union, is the Negro church. The church is, among American Negroes, the primitive social group of the slaves on American soil, replacing the tribal life roughly disorganized by the slave ship, and in many respects antedating the establishment of the Negro monogamic home. The church is much more than a religious organization; it is the chief organ of social and intellectual intercourse. As such it naturally finds the free democratic organizations of the Baptists and Methodists better suited to its purpose than the stricter bonds of the Presbyterians or the more aristocratic and ceremonious Episcopalians. Of the 262 families of Farmville, only 1 is Episcopalian and 3 are Presbyterian; of the rest, 26 are Methodist and 218 Baptist. In the town of Farmville there are 3 colored church edifices, and in the surrounding country there are 3 or 4 others.

The chief and overshadowing organization is the First Baptist Church of

From "The Negroes of Farmville, Virginia: A Social Study." U.S. Department of Labor, *Bulletin*, no. 14 (January 1898).

Farmville. It owns a large brick edifice on Main street. The auditorium, which seats about 500 people, is tastefully finished in lightwood with carpet, small organ, and stained glass windows. Beneath this is a large assembly room with benches. This building is really the central clubhouse of the community, and in greater degree than is true of the country church in New England or the West. Various organizations meet here, entertainments and lectures take place here, the church collects and distributes considerable sums of money, and the whole social life of the town centers here. The unifying and directing force is, however, religious exercises of some sort. The result of this is not so much that recreation and social life have become stiff and austere, but rather that religious exercises have acquired a free and easy expression and in some respects serve as amusement-giving agencies. For instance, the camp meeting is simply a picnic, with incidental sermon and singing; the rally of country churches, called the "big meeting," is the occasion of the pleasantest social intercourse, with a free barbecue; the Sunday-school convention and the various preachers' conventions are occasions of reunions and festivities. Even the weekly Sunday service serves as a pleasant meeting and greeting place for working people who find little time for visiting during the week.

From such facts, however, one must not hastily form the conclusion that the religion of such churches is hollow or their spiritual influence bad. While under present circumstances the Negro church can not be simply a spiritual agency, but must also be a social, intellectual, and economic center, it nevertheless is a spiritual center of wide influence; and in Farmville its influence carries nothing immoral or baneful. The sermons are apt to be fervent repetitions of an orthodox Calvinism, in which, however, hell has lost something of its terrors through endless repetition; and joined to this is advice directed against the grosser excesses of drunkenness, gambling, and other forms disguised under the general term "pleasure" and against the anti-social peccadillos of gossip, "meanness," and undue pride of position. Very often a distinctly selfish tone inculcating something very like sordid greed and covetousness is, perhaps unconsciously, used; on the other hand, kindliness, charity, and sacrifice are often taught. In the midst of all, the most determined, energetic, and searching means are taken to keep up and increase the membership of the church, and "revivals," long-continued and loud, although looked upon by most of the community as necessary evils, are annually instituted in the August vacation time. Revivals in Farmville have few of the wild scenes of excitement which used to be the rule; some excitement and screaming, however, are encouraged, and as a result nearly all the youth are "converted" before they are of age. Certainly such crude conversions and the joining of the church are far better than no efforts to curb and guide the young.

The Methodist church, with a small membership, is the second social center of Farmville, and there is also a second Baptist church, of a little lower grade, with more habitual noise and shouting.

Next to the churches in importance come the secret and beneficial organizations, which are of considerable influence. Their real function is to provide a fund for relief in cases of sickness and for funeral expenses. The burden which would otherwise fall on one person or family is, by small, regular contributions, made to fall on the group. This business feature is then made attractive by a ritual, ceremonies, officers, often a regalia, and various social features. On the whole, the societies have been peculiarly successful when we remember that they are conducted wholly by people whose greatest weakness is lack of training in business methods.

The oldest society is one composed of 40 or 50 women — the Benevolent Society — which has been in existence in Farmville for over twenty years. There is a local lodge of Odd Fellows with about 35 members, which owns a hall. The Randolph Lodge of Masons has 25 members, and holds its sessions in a hired hall, together with the Good Samaritans, a semireligious secret order, with 25 local members. One of the most remarkable orders is that of the True Reformers, which has headquarters in Richmond, conducts a bank there, and has real estate all over Virginia. There are two "fountains" of this order in Farmville, with perhaps 50 members in all.

There have lately been some interesting attempts at cooperative industrial enterprises, and some capital was collected. Nothing tangible has, however, as yet resulted.

There is a genial and pleasant social life maintained among the Farmville Negroes, clustering chiefly about the churches. Three pretty distinctly differentiated social classes appear. The highest class is composed of farmers, teachers, grocers, and artisans, who own their homes, and do not usually go out to domestic service; the majority of them can read and write, and many of the younger ones have been away to school. The investigator met this class in several of their social gatherings; once at a supper given by one of the grocers. The host was a young man in the thirties, with good common school training. There were eight in his family — a mother-in law, wife, five children, and himself. The house, a neat two-story frame, with six or eight rooms, was on Main street, and was recently purchased of white people at a cost of about $1,500. There was a flower and vegetable garden, cow and pigs, etc. The party consisted of a mail clerk and his wife; a barber's wife, the widowed daughter of the wood merchant; a young man, an employee in a tobacco factory, and his wife, who had been in service in Connecticut; a middle aged woman, graduate of Hampton, and others. After a preliminary chat, the company assembled in a back dining room. The host and hostess did not seat themselves, but served the company with chicken, ham, potatoes, corn, bread and butter, cake, and ice cream. Afterwards the company went to the parlor and talked, and sang—mostly hymns—by the aid of a little organ, which the widow played. At another time there was a country picnic on a farm 20 miles from town. The company started early and arrived at 10 o'clock on a fine old Virginia plantation, with manor house, trees, and lawn. The time was passed in playing croquet, tossing the bean bag, dancing, and lunching.

Again, a considerable company was invited to a farm house about a mile from town, near Israel Hill, where an evening was passed in eating and dancing.* Often the brickmaker opened his hospitable door and entertained with loaded tables and games of various sorts.

Among this class of people the investigator failed to notice a single instance of any action not indicating a thoroughly good moral tone. There was no drinking, no lewdness, no questionable conversation, nor was there any one in any of the assemblies against whose character there was any well-founded accusation. The circle was, to be sure, rather small, and there was a scarcity of young men. It was particularly noticeable that three families in the town, who, by reason of their incomes and education would have naturally moved in the best circle, were rigidly excluded. In two of these there were illegitimate children, and in the third a wayward wife. Of the Farmville families about 40—possibly fewer—belonged to this highest class.

Leaving the middle class for a moment, let us turn to the Farmville slums. There are three pretty well-defined slum districts—one near the railroad, one on South street, and one near the race track. In all, there would appear to be about 45 or 50 families of Negroes who are below the line of ordinary respectability, living in loose sexual relationship, responsible for most of the illegitimate children, chief supporters of the two liquor shops, and furnishing a half-dozen street walkers and numerous gamblers and rowdies. It is the emigration of this class of people to the larger cities that has recently brought to notice the large number of Negro criminals and the development of a distinct criminal class among them. Probably no people suffer more from the depredations of this class than the mass of colored people themselves, and none are less protected against them, because the careless observer overlooks patent social differences and attributes to the race excesses indulged in by a distinctly differentiated class. These slum elements are not particularly vicious and quarrelsome, but rather shiftless and debauched. Laziness and promiscuous sexual intercourse are their besetting sins. Considerable whisky and cider are consumed, but there is not much open

---

* Dancing, although indulged in somewhat, is frowned upon by the churches and is not a general amusement with the better classes.

drunkenness. Undoubtedly this class severely taxes the patience of the public authorities of the town.

The remaining 170 or more families, the great mass of the population, belong to a class between the two already described, with tendencies distinctly toward the better class rather than toward the worse. This class is composed of working people, domestic servants, factory hands, porters, and the like; they are a happy minded, sympathetic people, teachable and faithful; at the same time they are not generally very energetic or resourceful, and, as a natural result of long repression, lack "push." They have but recently become used to responsibility, and their moral standards have not yet acquired that fixed character and superhuman sanction necessary in a new people. Here and there their daughters have fallen before temptation, or their sons contracted slothful or vicious habits. However, the effort to maintain and raise the moral standard is sincere and continuous. No black woman can to-day, in the town of Farmville, be concubine to a white man without losing all social position — a vast revolution in twenty years; no black girl of the town can have an illegitimate child without being shut off from the best class of people and looked at askance by ordinary folks. Usually such girls find it pleasanter to go North and work at service, leaving their children with their mothers.

Finally, it remains to be noted that the whole group life of Farmville Negroes is pervaded by a peculiar hopefulness on the part of the people themselves. No one of them doubts in the least but that one day black people will have all rights they are now striving for, and that the Negro will be recognized among the earth's great peoples. Perhaps this simple faith is, of all products of emancipation, the one of the greatest social and economic value.

CONCLUSION

A study of a community like Farmville brings to light facts favorable and unfavorable, and conditions good, bad, and indifferent. Just how the whole should be interpreted is perhaps doubtful. One thing, however, is clear, and that is the growing differentiation of classes among Negroes, even in small communities. This most natural and encouraging result of thirty years' development has not yet been sufficiently impressed upon general students of the subject, and leads to endless contradiction and confusion. For instance, a visitor might tell us that the Negroes of Farmville are idle, unreliable, careless with their earnings, and lewd; another visitor, a month later, might say that Farmville Negroes are industrious, owners of property, and slowly but steadily advancing in education and morals. These apparently contradictory statements made continually of Negro groups all over the land are both true to a degree, and become mischievous and misleading only when stated without reservation as true of a whole community, when they are in reality true only of certain classes in the community. The question then becomes, not whether the Negro is lazy and criminal, or industrious and ambitious, but rather what, in a given community, is the proportion of lazy to industrious Negroes, of paupers to property holders, and what is the tendency of development in these classes. Bearing this in mind, it seems fair to conclude, after an impartial study of Farmville conditions, that the industrious and property accumulating class of the Negro citizens best represents, on the whole, the general tendencies of the group. At the same time, the mass of sloth and immorality is still large and threatening.

How far Farmville conditions are true elsewhere in Virginia the present investigator has no means of determining. He sought by inquiry and general study to choose a town which should in large degree typify the condition of the Virginia Negro to-day. How far Farmville fulfills this wish can only be determined by further study.

Atlanta University

Most men in this world are colored. A faith in humanity, therefore, a belief in the gradual growth and perfectability of men must, if honest, be primarily a belief in colored men. Atlanta University was founded as an expression of the same faith in humanity within, as in humanity without the color line. That faith in men meant a firm belief that the great mass of human beings of all races and nations, withal their differences and peculiarities, were capable of essentially similar development and that the method of bringing about that development was by the education of youth. The founders of Atlanta University did not wait until this thesis was absolutely proven beyond peradventure — they held it to be a perfectly valid assumption to make, and to work on, immediately, and therefore they established Atlanta University, two years after Lee surrendered.

They did not establish simply a primary school, or a grammar school, or a high school. On the contrary they established all these schools and in addition to this a college, and made the college the centre and norm of all their work. They did this, first for the development of individual Negro talent, — second, for inspiration and leadership of Negro communities, and third, for the supplying of teachers. Their primary idea was stated in perfectly plain language; they proposed to train men; they believed that a black boy with the capacity to learn, was worth teaching and that the only limitations to the development of an individual human soul were that soul's capacity and its obligations to its fellow men — its duty to society. In the case of the emancipated and enfranchised Negro this duty to his fellow men revealed itself most pressingly and imperatively as a call for enlightenment and inspiration for the mass from leaders. Much as the Negro race needed to know in agriculture, they needed to know still more as to life. They were poor carpenters, but they

In *From Servitude to Service: Being the Old South Lectures on the History and Work of Southern Institutions for the Education of the Negro* (Boston: American Unitarian Association, 1905), pp. 155–97.

were still poorer fathers and mothers; they did not understand the methods of modern industry, but they knew even less of the aims of that civilization which industry serves. Sad it was that the slave was an undeveloped hand, it was far sadder that he was an undeveloped man. This, then, was the second problem to which the founders of Atlanta University addressed themselves, and it was no small one. There are many ways of developing manhood and inspiring men. All ways this institution did not try, but it did try one which the experience of four thousand years of civilized life on this earth has proven of foremost value — and that is the sending of missionaries of culture among the masses. This is not the only teaching a mass of untaught people need — they need teaching in the technique of industry, in methods of business, in the science of agriculture. But they need especially in their halting, hesitating beginnings the guidance of men who know what civilization means — who stand before them as guides not simply to teach them how to walk, but to teach them whither to go, and while logically we may argue that learning to walk ought to precede preparations for a great journey, yet as a matter of fact and history, it is the inspiration of some goal to be reached that has ever led men to learn how to get there.

The third object of Atlanta University was to train teachers. Everybody, both in Reconstruction days and now, agrees that some amount of elementary training is necessary for the Freedmen's sons. Missionaries, government agents and army officers all agreed from the first that schools were needed. But schools call for teachers and, therefore Normal schools were needed. Nor was this all. A Normal school in Massachusetts trains an educated person in the art of teaching. In the South, among Negroes after the war, there was no such educated class to train. A Normal school then in the South must be primarily a high school and college; it must first educate its teachers and then train them to teach.

And, moreover, in case it cannot do both these things well, surely it is far better to send out among the masses educated persons who lack technical training in methods of teaching rather than to send persons who have technique without education. So that in these three ways Atlanta University was demanded: to train talented Negro youth, to disseminate civilization among the untaught masses, and to educate teachers.

It is, however, one thing to conceive a great human need and quite another thing to realize this in deeds and sacrifices, in bricks and stone. And when in the world's history struggling human beings have in doubt and travail, in weariness and anxiety, established a great engine of human betterment, it behooves us who sit and see and hope in God's good time to help — to ask what they did and how they did it and who were the men that did these things. These questions it is my task to answer and to show how there to the

238

southward, where the great Blue Ridge first bows and crumbles before the far-off sea, twelve men in 1867 founded an institution of learning which has meant so much to the higher aspirations and untrammelled development of two hundred million black men on this earth. These men created on the barren red mud of North Georgia a little cluster of brick buildings, now six in number, which have mothered five thousand sons and daughters in thirty-five years and which first, last and ever have stood for one unwavering ideal. They created this institution out of poverty and distrust in the midst of enmity and danger, in the face of ignorance and crime. Dying, they left their legacy to us — their legacy and their burden.

What sort of men established and carried on the work of Atlanta University? They were not all visionaries and dreamers, and yet among them were men who saw the vision and dreamed the dream. Two of the original founders represented the American Missionary Association, that great movement born at the slaveship that wandered into Connecticut and coming to the fullness of manhood just as the nation needed it in the reconstruction crisis. One was a tall and dark-haired man, who afterward carried the idea of equal opportunity for black men to Nashville and founded Fisk University there; three were northern business men, resident in Atlanta; two were Negroes, new clothed with authority, and one was Edmund Ware. These men are nearly all dead to-day, but around the work of their hands have clustered many and diverse helpers. A bishop like Atticus G. Haygood, Southern bred, but emancipated and honest; a justice of the Georgia Supreme Court like McKay; a president of one of Atlanta's greatest banks; and men like Charles Cuthbert Hall, of New York, and Samuel M. Crothers, of Cambridge. To-day Atlanta University is directed by four of its own graduates and by members of the governing boards or faculties of Harvard and Yale Universities, Williams and Dartmouth Colleges, Union Theological Seminary, and Tuskegee Institute.

But, after all, the founder of Atlanta University was Edmund Ware, and Edmund Ware was a man of faith. We are not dealing in faith these days. We are discounting it, and sometimes half sneering at it. Because in the past a certain type of simple-hearted enthusiast has believed so piteously in things absurd, impossible and false, we have come to discount the whole proceeding, striving to know even where knowledge is yet impossible, and pitying loftily that old-fashioned goodness that believed in men, that glorified in sacrifice, and had an unwavering faith that somewhere beyond the mists was a good God, and that the world was as good as the God that made it. Edmund Asa Ware was born in North Wrentham, now Norfolk, Mass., a few miles from Boston, in 1837. He fitted for college at the Norwich Free Academy, Connecticut, and was graduated from Yale University in 1863. After his graduation, he taught for a time in the school in which he had fitted for college, and then was principal of a public school in Nashville, Tenn. Soon the way opened for him to enter a field of labor of which he had dreamed and planned in his schoolboy days, and he began the life work for which he believed he had a divine commission and from which he could not be diverted by his alluring offers of money, comfort and position. His friend has written of him:

"He was conscientious. His mother had no recollection of his ever being untruthful. His village teachers all commended him for his unvarying conformity to the right in school. It is said that when fifteen years old, he had never been absent a day, nor had a mark for tardiness. One morning as the bell stopped, writes one, his seat was observed to be vacant. Those near the windows, looking out, saw him running at full speed, trying to gain his seat before his name should be called. The teacher was seen to cast an eye to the window and then to linger a moment before he called the roll. Thus he was seated to respond when the W's were reached."

What sort of a man did such a boy make? Certainly not a good business man in the modern sense; not a leader in literature or polite society; not a member of Congress; nor even a promising pillar of the State Legislature. And yet, after this man had lived less than fifty years and lay white, thin and dead in the darkened halls of Atlanta University, there came a stream of men who had known him, black and white, student and teacher, Northerner and Southerner, and this is the picture they painted:

The Superintendent of the Freedmen's Bureau for Georgia, said: "It was he who counselled and advised with the colored and other members of the constitution convention and secured the wise provision in the constitution for the establishment of a public school system, and afterwards, with members of the first Legislature, by which it was established and put into operation. He was in thorough sympathy with the religious work carried on at the same time by the Christian teachers and church organizations, but found oftentimes his greatest difficulties in overcoming the sectarian differences which interfered with the harmonious operation of the school work. This he had always in view, and, by his gentleness and forbearance and generous catholic spirit, he removed many ignorant prejudices that stood in the way."

A student said: "His manner of speech was terse, laconic, forceful, animated, in perfect harmony with the fervency of soul, with that restless activity which was so peculiarly manifest in all his doings. On leaving him I felt that I had been talking with a man who was living a higher life, living above the ordinary aims and petty ambitions of this world, a man who, though toiling in a field obscure and unpopular, nevertheless was entirely devoted to the cause he had espoused, and showed in every look and word a faith which rose sublimely above the mists and shadows of the present.". . . "This spirit of work which so completely possessed Mr. Ware, he naturally endeavored to transfuse into his pupils. I shall never forget those talks he used to give to the students every year just before the closing of school for the summer vacation. With what emphasis he used to say to the young men: 'Now, if you can get schools to teach, it is well. Teach them. Do all the good you can. But if you can't get schools to teach, don't hesitate a minute to work with your hands. Go into the field. Dig, hoe, pick cotton. Labor is honorable.' "

Another graduate said: "After that interview with him alone, after feeling his tender caresses as he sat near me, and after listening to the mild tones of his voice, and seeing, face to face, those eyes, not now indignantly flashing, but full of sweetness and tenderness, after this, there never was any terror in that face or those eyes for me during all the following years that I knew him. During the last eighteen or nineteen years I have seen many a student quail before that steady, withering gaze, which Mr. Ware knew so well how to use. But for me there ever remained that same soft expression, first seen during our first interview, in the little library upstairs at Storrs' School in 1867. That look has, in a great measure, influenced my course of life; has often kept me in the right path, when temptation was strong to go otherwise."

A friend added: "I think I never knew a man so strong of will who was so free from the lower self. If ordinary ambition entered into his calculations, it strengthened by the reaction it aroused, the very virtue it assailed. It was preëminently as moral teacher and quickener that he excelled. True as steel himself, he felt a lie as men feel a personal insult. He did not like even an insincere or merely conventional tone."

And finally Bishop Atticus G. Haygood, of the Methodist Episcopal Church, South, and author of the "Brother in Black," and who was at one time a trustee of the University, in speaking of the "Man who can wait," said: "Only those who began with Mr. Ware nearly twenty years ago this new and difficult work of trying to educate in a rational and Christian manner the enfranchised people of this country, and so to help in introducing into the family of Christian and civilized nations a new race, can understand how much Edmund Ware, when he first began work in this city, needed to be a man who could do his work and wait. The conditions under which this work is carried on are different now; very small encouragement do workers in this field get from us of the white race in the Southern States, although next to the Negro race, we are, of all men on earth, most concerned in the success of your work and most concerned because we have most at stake in this work. The social environments are not inspiring now; but let me assure you 1885 is very far from 1865. To have gone on as President Ware did during those early years there must have been in his heart deathless love and pity for men who needed what he could give them, — a faith in the gospel and eternal righteousness that never wavered, and a love for God that made work easy and suffering joy."

I have dwelt upon the character of this man because, in some places, it is the fashion of the day to represent those who went south after the war to help the freedmen as officious busy-bodies, goody-goody sort of folk, with heads very nearly as soft as their hearts. And yet that wonderful call which sounded in the ears of the sons and daughters of the North in the later sixties was a call to far greater heroism and self-sacrifice than that which called them earlier through the smoke of Sumter. They could not, like the soldiers, expect monuments, the notice of historians, or even (shall I write it?) pensions, but they could expect work, danger, contempt, and forgetfulness, and those who dared this, at least deserve the respect and reverence of thinking men!

I said that Edmund Ware was a man of faith. As early as 1867 he was writing North in his capacity as state superintendent of education; he said:

"The Education Association will meet in Macon on the 9th of October, and then will come the demand for teachers. Please let me know before the time, how many teachers (board paid by colored people) you can give me, besides those at the points you already hold. Make a rough estimate, only make it large enough. You must do something on faith. I know the people of the North will do much more than they have yet done, if the matter is only presented in the right way to them. Get young ladies in each town to agree to carry round a paper, and get all the people to subscribe from ten cents to ten dollars per month, and then go round and collect it monthly. All that is wanted is a few workers in each city and town and it will all be done."

After he became president of an institution on paper, then this wonderful unwavering faith, slowly, surely became transmuted. The first building came from the American Missionary Association; the second from the State of Georgia, with its growing number of black legislators. The Recitation hall and the Manual Training building came from two Massachusetts women, the Housekeeping Cottage from circles of the King's Daughters and Rev. Dr. D. L. Furber, the Training School from the General Educational Board and other friends, and now a Library from Andrew Carnegie. This has been the material growth. But that which Western colleges call the "plant" of Atlanta University, is the least of its real being. Our buildings are simple and small, not unpleasing in appearance, neat and substantial, but nothing calculated especially to impress the beholder. The peculiar spiritual growth which this institution typifies is on the other hand the object of our especial pride. Not even the heavy loss caused by President Ware's premature death checked for a moment this inner growth, for a leader and successor stood ready trained in heart and mind for the work.

Atlanta University is fortunate in having but two presidents in her thirty-five years of existence. The successor of President Ware was the son of a man who, at one time, furnished many of the text-books which were used in the schools of Boston, and a nephew of Nathaniel P. Willis.

President Bumstead was born in Boston in 1841, was graduated at the Boston Latin School, and in 1863 at Yale. He was major of the Forty-third United States Colored troops in the civil war and afterward graduated at Andover and entered the ministry. He joined Atlanta University as teacher of Science in 1875, and since that time as teacher and president has given to that institution the best years of a singularly devoted life. His name will go down in history as that of the Apostle of the Higher Education of the American Negro.

Many men and women of energy and devotion have built their lives into this work. Every stone on that broad campus has meant the pulse of some man's life blood and the sacrifice of some woman's heart. There sits to-night within those Southern walls a woman bent and bowed, old with years, and yet ever young in the hearts of a thousand black men to whom, for thirty years, she was more than mother; there sounds within those halls to-day the voice of a white-haired man who, thirty-five years ago, sacrificed a government position and a good salary and brought his young wife down to live with black people. Not all the money that you and yours could give for a hundred years would do half as much to convince dark and outcast millions of the South that they have some friends in this world, as the sacrifice of such lives as these to the cause.

I have said that the founder of this institution planned a college — even a university. How far has that plan honestly been carried out? There are in name to-day numerous universities in the South for colored men, and this is often brought as an argument against Negro colleges — their absurdly overwhelming number. This is, in reality, untrue. There are very few institutions in the United States really doing college work for Negroes. Many institutions called colleges represent an ambition or an ideal, while as a matter of present fact such schools are higher institutions simply in name; in reality they are great primary and grammar schools with a score of high school students and a few or none of college grade. They represent, in many cases, high hopes and laudable ambition, but in some cases they have no present prospect or design of developing into real colleges, and in some other cases they have been tempted to be content with calling a high school a college, possibly after the venerable example of Harvard in its early days. This practice, however, has led to the suspicion that all Negro colleges are of low rank and parading more or less under false pretenses.

There are in the United States to-day about five institutions which, by reason of the number of students and grade of work done, deserve to rank as Negro colleges. How far, now, is the work done at an institution like Atlanta University deserving of the respect due to liberal training?

If there is one thing at Atlanta University upon which we pride ourselves it is that we have never succumbed to the temptation of mere numbers. We have to-day seventy-five students of a rank above the high school — fifty in the regular college course, and twenty-five in the teacher's college. It is fair to say that we might, by a general lowering of standard, easily have a college of one hundred to one hundred and fifty. This we have steadily refused to do. On the contrary, we have sought unceasingly, year by year, to raise and fix a fair standard, and I think it is perfectly just to say that so far as our work goes in Atlanta University, the standard equals that of any New England school. We have a high school of two hundred and twenty-five pupils, divided into two parallel courses of three years, an English and classical. This gives one year less than the New England high schools with their four-year courses. Above the high school there are two courses of study offered: a regular college course of four years, leading to the bachelor's degree and a teacher's training course of two years, leading to a normal diploma. Our college rank is thus one year behind the smaller New England colleges, and this rank has been proven in case of several of our graduates, who have afterward taken the A.B. degree in leading Northern colleges after one year's study.

In maintaining this standard we have, of course, our peculiar troubles. In New England there is difficulty in articulating the high school and college courses. In the South the almost total absence of high schools for Negroes makes a preparatory department necessary to a college like ours. All other Negro colleges in the South have grammar grades in addition, but we have simply the high school and the college, and consequently find our great difficulty in fitting our Junior high school year to the eighth grade of the public schools. The varying quality of work done in the public schools makes it necessary that our first year should be one of sifting and examination. About one-half of our public school candidates do the work of this class in a year; a fourth more do the work in something over a year, and are given electives so as to start even with the regular second year class. The other fourth, from poor preparation or lack of ability and other reasons, drop out.

For admission to the high school we require eight grades of common school work. If the pupil proposes to take the full college course, he has before him about 2,800 recitation periods of forty-five minutes each, or, in laboratory work, of twice that length. Three-tenths of these are given to ancient languages, three-tenths evenly divided between science and mathematics, two-tenths to English and modern languages at the rate of English seven and German two, and two-tenths to history, sociology, philosophy and pedagogy at the rate of history and sociology nine and other studies two. In addition to this there are 384 hours of manual training. By electives the proportion of modern languages can be increased.

The length of the entire normal course is five years, and the total number of recitation periods, of forty-five minutes each, is 2,028. Three-tenths of these are given to pedagogy, three-tenths to mathematics and science, two and a half tenths to English, one-tenth to philosophy and history, etc.

How far is the charge true that old-fashioned studies and out-of-date methods are being used in Negro colleges to fit black boys for a world which prides itself on being rather ahead of time than even up with it? We willingly plead guilty to a persistent clinging to many of the older forms of discipline. We still count the teacher as of considerably more importance than the thing taught. This explains considerable amount of Latin in our curriculum. We have one of the most successful Latin teachers in the South, a man not only learned in method, but of great and peculiar personal influence. We are willing and anxious for our college men to have four or five years' contact with this man, and we seriously doubt if a greater course in engineering under a lesser man would be a real gain for the development of manhood among us. On the other hand, our teachers and instructors have been drawn from Yale, Harvard, Dartmouth, Wellesley, Boston University, Worcester Polytechnic, Fisk, and our own institution. Our dean ranked his class at Dartmouth; a former dean was the DeForest medal man at Yale; the head of our normal department is from Bridgewater, and for sixteen years has done some of the most successful normal work in the South; two classmates of President Ware at Yale joined him in his work, and now his two children, from Yale and Columbia, are taking up their father's mantle.

There are five full professors and ten instructors. The library has 11,500 volumes, classified by the Dewey system and well selected. There is a physical laboratory 50 × 22 feet, in which all class work is carried on by individual experiments and measurements. Adjoining this is a science lecture room with considerable apparatus. The chemical laboratory is 50 × 25 feet, with individual desks and chemicals. There are small geological and mineralogical cabinets, and the beginning of a zoological cabinet in the lower orders. The astronomy class has a small telescope, and in the mathematical department there are surveying and engineering instruments. The department of Sociology and History has sets of modern and ancient maps and a class room library with reference works, duplicate text-books and statistical treatises. The recitation rooms are large and light, and nearly all furnished with the tablet chairs.

Manual training is an integral part of our work, and is carried on in two buildings, one for the girls and one for the boys. Manual training is required of all high school students. The boys' building has a floor devoted to wood working, with power saws, planers, etc., a lumber storage room and a paint room. Another floor is occupied by the turning lathes, twenty individual benches with tools, and a drawing room with eighteen sets of instruments. In the basement, iron-working is carried on with forges and lathes. The printing office has a full equipment, including a power press.

Manual training for girls is carried on at the Housekeeping Cottage, and consists in cooking, sewing, dressmaking, drawing and general housekeeping.

When we enumerate these facilities for manual training, people are usually surprised, and say, "Why, you have, then, an industrial school after all!" This we disclaim. We do not have an industrial department for the important work of teaching trades. Our equipment, almost without exception, is an integral part of our educational work, and is designed for its educational effect alone. Just as the boy works with his own hands in the chemical laboratory or the laboratory in sociology, so he works in the manual training shop, and the object in all three cases is the same, viz.: to develop the boy to the full capacity of his powers, mental and physical. With the education thus gained, the boy might use his chemistry in the study of medicine, or his sociology in the ministry, or his manual dexterity at a trade school, but we do not pretend to train either physicians, clergymen or carpenters. I speak of this because there is so much confusion of ideas on the point, especially so far as Southern schools are concerned. Schools of higher training in the South are often supposed to be places without manual training, despising and ridiculing it, and knowing nothing of its great educative power, while an industrial school is supposed to be necessarily and always a centre of education.

If you should visit Atlanta University you would see little evidence of student manual work in finished products of wood, or iron, or stone. Our furniture is from the factory, our buildings erected by hired labor, and our important repairs largely done by outside workmen. Nevertheless, the influence of our manual training of the students is easily traceable in their after life. When the Conference for Southern Education, popularly associated with the Ogden parties, met in Athens, Ga., they especially admired the industrial exhibit of the Negro schools. "That is the sort of work that is needed," they said repeatedly, "where was the Principal trained?" And then they found out that he and all his teachers came from Atlanta University. They had never learned basket making or clay modelling there, but they had received a far more fundamental training in human power. With this as a basis, it took them but a short time to master the technique.

The work of teacher training is also carried on by the laboratory method — that is it is centred in the model school containing a kindergarten and four grades (to be extended to eight grades eventually) with all the equipment of a modern school. Here, under instructors, the normal students teach, observe and experiment.

I have indicated the formal curriculum of Atlanta University and the facilities for carrying it out. But this is not all of our educational work with our students. A centre of education with us is our school Home; among the earliest ideals entertained by the University is one that may be designated as home-building. In its first days, officers and teachers kept before the minds of students and their parents the desirability of securing land and homes, and many a cottage in Atlanta owes its existence to the personal counsel and pecuniary assistance of some teacher in the University; and when, at the beginning of a summer vacation, some three or four hundred were sent out to teach school in the smaller towns and rural districts, among other injunctions it was impressed upon them to encourage and assist the people among whom they were to labor, to buy land and make themselves homes, and specific items of information with reference to accomplishing this were given them. And when these student teachers returned from their summer's work they were asked to report what they had done in this line and also to give facts they had gathered as to the amount of land the people owned or were buying.

The effect of this policy is shown in the statistics of Negro property in Georgia. Of course it would not be fair to claim that Atlanta University is solely responsible for this record, but certainly the influence of this institution has been a potent factor in the increase of property from nearly nothing in 1860 to a real value of nearly thirty-five millions in 1905.

Atlanta University is more than a school, it is a home. The dormitories are not simply a collection of rooms where students may study and lodge and care for themselves, but each of them is under the supervision of a competent woman, who takes the place of a mother and sees that the students are regular in their habits, tidy in dress, neat in the care of rooms, attentive to study, polite in manners, careful in regard to health, and made comfortable in illness. The dining room, too, where teachers and students assemble for meals, is not merely a commons, where simply a sufficient quantity of food is furnished, but is a place where teachers and students eat together, talk and learn to know each other; where the etiquette of family life is carefully observed — indeed this is one of the few places in America where black and white people meet as simple, friendly human souls, unveiled from light and unguarded from feared contagion; bound in human sympathy and help.

And so, in these ways, is carried out the intention expressed in the first catalogue of 1868–70, and in the latest 1903–04, in these words: "It is designed to make the school as far as possible a home for those who attend," and it may be added that in thus making it a home it becomes a home builder.

With the home life go the home chores and duties — the care of the rooms, the sweeping of the halls, the washing of the dishes, and the little errands here and there. The comparatively small number of our students makes the home life peculiarly cheerful and cozy. Teachers and students know each other intimately, and in a way impossible in large institutions, and always the graduate looks back upon the home life as the greatest and best gift of the Alma Mater.

Not only is Atlanta University a school and a home; it is in the larger sense of the word, a church. I do not mean by that anything narrow or sectarian, but I do mean that we whose work it is to train youth in the South have to face some patent facts: first, the religious conditions among both whites and blacks are such that the differences between Methodists and Baptists sometimes overshadow the differences between heaven and hell; that particularly among young educated Negroes this is a day of rapid religious evolution which might easily end anywhere or nowhere; consequently it will not do in the South to leave moral training to individual homes, since their homes are just recovering from the debauchery of slavery, and only in a minority of instances are they capable of the necessary teaching. As the larger home, then, of its sons and daughters, Atlanta University is, and always has been, a teacher of religion and morality. Our chaplain, the son of the late president, and a graduate of Union Theological Seminary, is a young man of clear-hearted devotion, and both his work and example are of great influence. A part of our religious exercises are voluntary and all of them are maintained at a level of high earnestness with a minimum of cant and empty form.

Such is our course of training. The great question, however, which men of right may ask of Atlanta University is, "What has this training resulted in? How far has this institution justified its existence? How far has it trained men of talent, civilized communities, and given real teachers to the black South?"

It is in the answer to this question that Atlanta University makes its greatest claim to public attention; and yet it is a very difficult thing to exhibit a process of education to the eye.

The experience in this line with which every teacher is so familiar is exaggerated in our case, for we and the whole Negro race are often judged for time and eternity by a fifteen-minute visitor.

On the other hand, when in the towns and country districts of the South the work of the graduates and former students of this institution is carefully studied, the verdict is always unanimous; that there is not in the country an institution which, in thirty-five years of work, has sent into the world a set of men and women stronger in character and attainment, and more useful in their fields of labor. The General Educational Board, after investigation, came to its endorsement on this ground particularly. Southern born men who still oppose Negro colleges have repeatedly acknowledged the remarkable character of our graduates. The School Board of Atlanta has put the Negro public schools of the city under the almost complete control of teachers whom we have trained; the state of Georgia, while it gave us aid repeatedly, bore testimony through its committees of the high quality of work done, and when afterwards that aid was taken from us and given to a new institution at Savannah, the institution was largely manned with our graduates, from its president down.

Atlanta University has taught some five thousand students. Of these 677 have finished a full high school course, and 487 of them have received a degree or normal diploma:

Occupations of Graduates	College	Normal	Total
Total	124	367	*489
Male	101	15	116
Female..........................	23	352	*373
Living	108	311	*417
Dead	16	41	57
Teachers	62	178	240
Ministers	13	...	13
Physicians	4	...	4
Lawyers	2	...	2
Dentists..........................	1	...	1
U. S. Service	12	2	14
Business..........................	7	8	15
Students..........................	4	3	7
Wives..........................	1	†110	111
Others	2	10	12

* Two graduated in two departments.
† 44 other wives are classed as teachers.

In its work of training teachers, Atlanta University has rendered its greatest service to the country. Sixty per cent of our graduates teach; they teach in city and county, in public and private schools, in primary, secondary and higher schools, and the schools of all religious denominations; five are presidents of colleges and normal schools, fourteen are principals of high and secondary schools, twenty are connected with industrial schools. I presume it is no exaggeration to say that our graduates and former students are reaching 20,000 black boys and girls each year, and handing on the light which they have received.

The work done by these men as students has been honest and fair. Our graduates have made good records at Harvard, Dartmouth, and the University of Chicago, University of Michigan, and Northern professional schools like Andover and Hartford theological seminaries, and the University of Pennsylvania Medical School. Research work done at our institution has been, in several cases, published by the United States government, and even recognized abroad. We have not, so far as we know, graduated any men of very exceptional genius, but we have sent out a score of men of unusual ability, measured by any standard, and we have trained a few who, by ability and forceful personality, are above the average of the trained men of any race.

Our great work, however, has been the sending of missionaries of culture throughout the South, and in this work Atlanta University has had conspicuous success. Of course such an influence is difficult to measure.

Considering the intimate connection of Atlanta University with the State of Georgia, we may, perhaps, best measure its influence by studying that state; in a sense Atlanta University founded the public school system of the state, since its first president was the first state superintendent of education. Of the thirteen leading Negro institutions in the state outside of Atlanta University, seven have presidents trained at this school, and two or three others have some of our graduates as teachers; and all of them have students trained by our graduates. The public schools of all the leading cities, Atlanta, Savannah, Athens, Columbus, and Macon, are very largely manned by our former students, and in all walks of life the influence of our graduates and former students is felt.

A recent study of Georgia* shows that Negro population, property and literacy in Georgia are increasing, while serious crime has begun to decrease.

This record is not due to any one single cause, but certainly the influence of Atlanta University has been a most potent factor. In the work of Negro uplift throughout the land our graduates are not alone nor altogether singular — graduates of a score of other worthy institutions are working with them, but the long, thorough courses of study in our work, the unbending mental discipline as a foundation for all work, whether manual or intellectual, has left its enduring mark on the Atlanta University man. The work of these college trained men from this and other institutions is not to be judged simply by what they have done, but still more from what they have prevented. I am persuaded that Americans do not dwell enough on this side of the case. You complain of crime and vagrancy among Negroes, and both are large and threatening, as it is perfectly natural they should be, but consider what they might have been if this race had been left without leaders — not leaders who could simply read and write and hoe, but real thinkers, men of vision, men who realized the

* Some Notes on Negro Crime. Atlanta University Publication, No. 9.

250

tremendous import of this vast social movement and could stand ever ready within the veil to calm passion and direct energy and say to the turbulent waters, "Peace be still."

The peculiar character of work, however, makes Atlanta University more than a simple college—it is a social settlement where, for six or seven years, the best we can find of the growing generation of Negroes is brought into contact with the standards of modern culture in school and home and campus. Nor do we wish to stop here—the Social Settlement aims to do more than teach the slums; it seeks also by studying slums to teach the world what slums mean. And Atlanta University seeks to become a centre for the careful, earnest and minute study of the Negro problems, through the experience and active cooperation of other graduates scattered all over the South. For this purpose we have established a department of social inquiry and an Annual Conference to study the Negro problem; we have been careful not to let the size of the field or the intricacy and delicacy of the subject tempt us into superficial or hasty work. Each year some definite phase of the problem is taken, the inquiry is limited in extent, and every effort is made to get thorough unbiased returns. To establish such a work with few funds, and untrained investigators was difficult, but to-day, after nine years of work, we feel as though the department was permanently organized for efficient work, and that interesting and instructive results will follow its further prosecution. The nine investigations already accomplished make a fairly well rounded study of human life as lived by the American Negro.

They consist of the following studies:

1. Mortality among Negroes in Cities, 1896.
2. Social and Physical Condition of Negroes in Cities, 1897.
3. Some Efforts of Negroes for Social Betterment, 1898.
4. The Negro in Business, 1899.
5. The College-bred Negro, 1900.
6. The Negro Common School, 1901.
7. The Negro Artisan, 1902.
8. The Negro Church, 1903.
9. Crime Among Negroes, 1904.
10. Methods and Results of Ten Years' Study, 1905.

Our present plan is to begin a second cycle of studies similar to these beginning with a study of Negro Mortality in 1906.

The results of these studies have been widely used; they are in the chief libraries of the world and have been commended by the *London Times, The*

Spectator, The Manchester Guardian, The Outlook, The Nation, The Dial, The Independent, and leading daily papers.

While we believe that social inquiry of this sort is fully justified if it seeks merely to know and publish that knowledge, we have also sought in addition to this to inspire our graduates in various communities to use the information we collect as a basis of concrete efforts in social betterment, and we can already point to some results of this policy. . . .

The Upbuilding of
Black Durham

Durham, N.C., is a place which the world instinctively associates with tobacco. It has, however, other claims to notice, not only as the scene of
Johnston's surrender at the end of the Civil War but particularly to-day as the
seat of Trinity College, a notable institution.

It is, however, because of another aspect of its life that this article is written:
namely, its solution of the race problem. There is in this small city a group of
five thousand or more colored people, whose social and economic development is perhaps more striking than that of any similar group in the nation.

The Negroes of Durham County pay taxes on about a half million dollars'
worth of property or an average of nearly $500 a family, and this property has
more than doubled in value in the last ten years.

A cursory glance at the colored people of Durham would discover little to
differentiate them from their fellows in dozens of similar Southern towns.
They work as laborers and servants, washerwomen and janitors. A second
glance might show that they were well represented in the building trades and
it would arouse interest to see 500 colored girls at work as spinners in one of
the big hosiery mills.

The chief interest of any visitor who stayed long enough to notice, would,
however, center in the unusual inner organization of this group of men,
women, and children. It is a new "group economy" that characterizes the rise
of the Negro American — the closed circle of social intercourse, teaching and
preaching, buying and selling, employing and hiring, and even manufacturing, which, because it is confined chiefly to Negroes, escapes the notice of the
white world.

In all colored groups one may notice something of this coöperation in
church, school, and grocery store. But in Durham, the development has

From *The World's Work*, 13 (January 1912): 334–338.

surpassed most other groups and become of economic importance to the whole town.

There are, for instance, among the colored people of the town fifteen grocery stores, eight barber shops, seven meat and fish dealers, two drug stores, a shoe store, a haberdashery, and an undertaking establishment. These stores carry stocks averaging (save in the case of the smaller groceries) from $2,000 to $8,000 in value.

This differs only in degree from a number of towns; but black Durham has in addition to this developed five manufacturing establishments which turn out mattresses, hosiery, brick, iron articles, and dressed lumber. These enterprises represent an investment of more than $50,000. Beyond this the colored people have a number of financial enterprises among which are a building and loan association, a real estate company, a bank, and three industrial insurance companies.

The coöperative bonds of the group are completed in social lines by a couple of dozen professional men, twenty school teachers, and twenty churches.

All this shows an unusual economic development and leads to four questions: (1) How far are these enterprises effective working businesses? (2) How did they originate? (3) What has been the attitude of the whites? (4) What does this development mean?

The first thing I saw in black Durham was its new training school — four neat white buildings suddenly set on the sides of a ravine, where a summer Chautauqua for colored teachers was being held. The whole thing had been built in four months by colored contractors after plans made by a colored architect, out of lumber from the colored planing mill and ironwork largely from the colored foundry. Those of its two hundred and fifty students who boarded at the school, slept on mattresses from the colored factory and listened to colored instructors from New York, Florida, Georgia, Virginia, Pennsylvania, New Jersey, and North Carolina. All this was the partially realized dream of one colored man, James E. Shepard. He formerly worked as secretary for a great Christian organization, but dissatisfied at a peculiarly un-Christian drawing of the color line, he determined to erect at Durham a kind of training school for ministers and social workers which would be "different."

One morning there came out to the school a sharp-eyed brown man of thirty, C. C. Spaulding, who manages the largest Negro industrial insurance company in the world. At his own expense he took the whole school to town in carriages to "show them what colored people were doing in Durham."

Naturally he took them first to the home of his company — "The North Carolina Mutual and Provident Association," an institution which is now twelve years old. One has a right to view industrial insurance with some suspicion and the Insurance Commissioner of South Carolina made last year a fifteen days' thorough examination of this enterprise. Then he wrote: "I can not but feel that if all other companies are put on the same basis as yours, that it will mean a great deal to industrial insurance in North and South Carolina, and especially a great benefit to the Negro race."

The company's business has increased from less than a thousand dollars in 1899 to an income of a quarter of a million in 1910. It has 200,000 members, has paid a half million dollars in benefits, and owns its office buildings in three cities.

Not only is the society thus prosperous at present but it is making a careful effort to avoid the rocks upon which the great colored order of "True Reformers" split, by placing its business on an approved scientific basis. It is installing a new card bookkeeping system, it is beginning to construct morbidity and mortality records, and its manager is a moving spirit of the Federated Insurance League for colored societies which meets annually at Hampton, Va.

The Durham office building of this company is neat and light. Down stairs in the rented portion we visited the men's furnishing store which seemed a businesslike establishment and carried a considerable stock of goods. The shoe store was newer and looked more experimental; the drug store was small and pretty.

From here we went to the hosiery mill and the planing mill. The hosiery mill was to me of singular interest. Three years ago I met the manager, C. C. Amey. He was then teaching school, but he had much unsatisfied mechanical genius. The white hosiery mills in Durham were succeeding and one of them employed colored hands. Amey asked for permission here to learn to manage the intricate machines, but was refused. Finally, however, the manufacturers of the machines told him that they would teach him if he came to Philadelphia. He went and learned. A company was formed and thirteen knitting and ribbing machines at seventy dollars apiece were installed, with a capacity of sixty dozen men's socks a day. At present the sales are rapid and satisfactory, and already machines are ordered to double the present output; a dyeing department and factory building are planned for the near future.

The brick yard and planing mill are part of the general economic organization of the town. R. B. Fitzgerald, a Northern-born Negro, has long furnished brick for a large portion of the state and can turn out 30,000 bricks a day.

To finance these Negro businesses, which are said to handle a million and a half dollars a year, a small banking institution has been started. The "Mechanics' and Farmers' Bank" looks small and experimental and owes its existence to rather lenient banking laws. It has a paid-in capital of $11,000 and it has $17,000 deposited by 500 different persons.

A careful examination of the origin of this Durham development shows that in a peculiar way it is due to a combination of training, business capacity, and character. The men who built 200 enterprises are unusual, not because the enterprises in themselves are so remarkable, but because their establishment met peculiar difficulties. To-day the white man who would go into insurance or haberdashery or hosiery making gathers his capital from rich men and hires expert managers who know these businesses. The Negro gathers capital by pennies from people unused to investing; he has no experts whom he may hire and small chance to train experts; and he must literally grope for success through repeated failure.

Three men began the economic building of black Durham: a minister with college training, a physician with professional training, and a barber who saved his money. These three called to their aid a bright hustling young graduate of the public schools, and with these four, representing vision, knowledge, thrift, and efficiency, the development began. The college man planned the insurance society, but it took the young hustler to put it through. The barber put his savings into the young business man's hands, the physician gave his time and general intelligence. Others were drawn in — the brickmaker, several teachers, a few college-bred men, and a number of mechanics. As the group began to make money, it expanded and reached out. None of the men are rich — the richest has an income of about $25,000 a year from business investments and eighty tenements; the others of the inner group are making from $5,000 to $15,000 — a very modest reward as such rewards go in America.

Quite a number of the colored people have built themselves pretty and well-equipped homes — perhaps fourteen of these homes cost from $2,500 to $10,000 — they are rebuilding their churches on a scale almost luxurious, and they are deeply interested in their new training school. There is no evidence of luxury — a horse and carriage, and the sending of children off to school is almost the only sign of more than ordinary expenditure.

If, now, we were considering a single group, geographically isolated, this story might end here. But never forget that Durham is in the South and that around these five thousand Negroes are twice as many whites who own most of the property, dominate the political life exclusively, and form the main current of social life. What now has been the attitude of these people toward the Negroes? In the case of a notable few it has been sincerely sympathetic and helpful, and in the case of a majority of the whites it has not been hostile. Of the two attitudes, great as has undoubtedly been the value of the active friendship of the Duke family, General Julian S. Carr, and others, I consider the greatest factor in Durham's development to have been the disposition of the mass of ordinary white citizens of Durham to say: "Hands off — give them a chance — don't interfere." As the editor of the local daily put it in a well deserved rebuke to former Governor Glenn of North Carolina: "If the Negro is going down, for God's sake let it be because of his own fault, and not because we are pushing him."

Active benevolence can, of course, do much in a community, and in Durham it has given the Negroes a hospital. The late Mr. Washington Duke conceived the idea of building a monument to ex-slaves on the Trinity College campus. This the colored people succeeded in transmuting to the founding of a hospital. The Duke family gave nearly $20,000 for building and equipping the building and the Negroes give largely to its support. Beside this, some white men have helped the Negroes by advice, as, for instance, in the intricacies of banking; and they have contributed to the new training school. Not only have Southern philanthropists thus helped, but they have allowed the Negroes to administer these gifts themselves. The hospital, for instance, is not simply *for* Negroes, but it is conducted *by* them; and the training school is under a colored corps of teachers.

But all this aid is as nothing beside that more general spirit which allows a black contractor to bid on equal terms with a white, which affords fair police protection and reasonable justice in court, which grants substantial courtesy and consideration on the street and in the press, and which in general says: "Hands off, don't hinder, let them grow." It is precisely the opposite spirit in places like Atlanta, which makes the way of the black man there so hard, despite individual friends.

A Southern community is thus seen to have it in its power to choose its Negro inhabitants. If it is afraid of ambition and enterprise on the part of black folk, if it believes that "education spoils a nigger," then it will get the shiftless happy-go-lucky semi-criminal black man and the ambitious and enterprising one will either sink or migrate. On the other hand, many honest Southerners fear to encourage the pushing, enterprising Negro Durham has not feared. It has distinctly encouraged the best type of black man by active aid and passive tolerance.

What accounts for this? I may be over-emphasizing facts, but I think not when I answer in a word: Trinity College. The influence of a Southern institution of learning of high ideals; with a president and professors who have dared to speak out for justice toward black men; with a quarterly journal, the learning and catholicism of which is well known — this has made white Durham willing to see black Durham rise without organizing mobs or secret societies to "keep the niggers down."

To be sure, the future still has its problems, for the significance of the rise of a group of black people to the Durham height and higher, means not a disappearance but, in some respects, an accentuation of the race problem.

But let the future lay its own ghosts; to-day there is a singular group in Durham where a black man may get up in the morning from a mattress made by black men, in a house which a black man built out of lumber which black men cut and planed; he may put on a suit which he bought at a colored haberdashery and socks knit at a colored mill; he may cook victuals from a colored grocery and stove which black men fashioned; he may earn his living working for colored men, be sick in a colored hospital and buried from a colored church; and the Negro insurance society will pay his widow enough to keep his children in a colored school. This is surely progress.

The Negro Church

It happens that during this month, in the North, West, and South, there are meeting the ruling Methodist ecclesiastical bodies representing a membership of 1,175,000 colored Americans. Later, in midsummer, the Baptist conventions, which represent 2,300,000 members, will meet. These three and a half million people represent the great middle class of colored Americans. The lowest class of outcasts have never been reached; the highest class of the educated and thoughtful are being gradually lost. The great middle mass remains, and in 35,000 churches holding $57,000,000 worth of property they form a peculiar organized government of men. Under some 50 powerful leaders and 30,000 salaried local preachers they raise and expend over 7,000,000 dollars a year.

Before such an organization one must bow with respect. It has accomplished much. It has instilled and conserved morals, it has helped family life, it has taught and developed ability and given the colored man his best business training. It has planted in every city and town in the Union, with few exceptions, meeting places for colored folk which vary from shelters to luxurious and beautiful edifices.

Notwithstanding this, all is not well with the colored church. First, its fifty leaders are in too many cases not the men they should be. This is not peculiar to the Negro church, but it is true to a larger degree than is healthful. We can point to pure-minded, efficient, unselfish prelates like the late Bishop Paine, the present Bishop Lee and J. W. White. We have men of scholarship and standing like Bishop J. Albert Johnson, and we have efficient men of affairs like John F. Hurst, M. C. B. Mason and R. H. Boyd.

The trouble is, however, this: there are too few such men. The paths and the higher places are choked with pretentious, ill-trained men and in far too many cases with men dishonest and otherwise immoral. Such men make the way of upright and businesslike candidates for power extremely difficult. They put an undue premium upon finesse and personal influence.

From *The Crisis*, May 1912.

Having thus a partially tainted leadership, small wonder that the 30,000 colored ministers fall as a mass far below expectations. There are among them hustling businessmen, eloquent talkers, suave companions and hale fellows, but only here and there does one meet men like Henry L. Phillips of Philadelphia — burning spiritual guides of a troubled, panting people, utterly self-forgetful, utterly devoted to a great ideal of righteousness.

Yet this is precisely the type for which the church — the white church as well as the black church — is crying. This is the only type which will hold thoughtful, reasonable men to membership with this organization. Today the tendencies are not this way. Today the church is still inveighing against dancing and theatregoing, still blaming educated people for objecting to silly and empty sermons, boasting and noise, still building churches when people need homes and schools, and persisting in crucifying critics rather than realizing the handwriting on the wall.

Let us trust that these great churches in conference, remembering the leaders of the past and conscious of all that the church has done well, will set their faces to these deeds:

1. Electing as bishops and leaders only men of honesty, probity, and efficiency and rejecting the noisy and unclean leaders of the thoughtless mob.

2. Weeding out the ministry so as to increase the clean apostles of service and sacrifice.

3. Initiating positive programs of education and social uplift and discouraging extravagant building and mere ostentation.

4. Bending every effort to make the Negro church a place where colored men and women of education and energy can work for the best things regardless of their belief or disbelief in unimportant dogmas and ancient and outworn creeds.

Negro Education

The casual reader has greeted this study of Negro education with pleasure. It is the first attempt to cover the field of secondary and higher education among colored Americans with anything like completeness. It is published with the sanction and prestige of the United States government and has many excellent points as, for instance, full statistics on such matters as the public expenditure for Negro school systems, the amount of philanthropy given private schools, Negro property, etc.; there is excellent and continued insistence upon the poor support which the colored public schools are receiving today. The need of continued philanthropic aid to private schools is emphasized and there are several good maps. Despite, then, some evidently careless proofreading (pages 59, 129, 157), the ordinary reader unacquainted with the tremendous ramifications of the Negro problem will hail this report with unstinted praise.

Thinking Negroes, however, and other persons who know the problem of educating the American Negro will regard the Jones* report, despite its many praiseworthy features, as a dangerous and in many respects unfortunate publication.

THE THESIS OF THE REPORT

This report again and again insists by direct statements, by inference, and by continued repetition on three principles of a thesis which we may state as follows: *First*, that the present tendency toward academic and higher

---

* Negro Education, a Study of the Private and Higher Schools for Colored People in the United States; prepared in co-operation with the Phelps Stokes Fund, under the direction of Thomas Jesse Jones, specialist in education of racial groups. Bureau of Education. Two volumes, 8 vo., 424, 724 pages. Washington, 1917.

From *The Crisis*, February 1918.

education among Negroes should be restricted and replaced by a larger insistence on manual training, industrial education, and agricultural training; *secondly*, the private schools in the South must "cooperate" with the Southern whites; and, *third*, that there should be more thoroughgoing unity of purpose among education boards and foundations working among Negroes.

THE NEGRO COLLEGE

The whole trend of Mr. Jones' study and of his general recommendations is to make the higher training of Negroes practically difficult, if not impossible, despite the fact that his statistics show (in 1914–15) only 1643 colored students studying college subjects in all the private Negro schools out of 12,726 pupils. He shows that there are (in proportion to population) ten times as many whites in the public high schools as there are colored pupils and only sixty-four public high schools for Negroes in the whole South! He shows that even at present there are few Negro colleges and that they have no easy chance for survival. What he is criticizing, then, is not the fact that Negroes are tumbling into college in enormous numbers, but their wish to go to college and their endeavor to support and maintain even poor college departments.

What, in fact, is back of this wish? Is it merely a silly desire to study "Greek," as Mr. Jones several times intimates, or is it not rather a desire on the part of American Negroes to develop a class of thoroughly educated men according to modern standards? If such a class is to be developed these Negro colleges must be planned as far as possible according to the standards of white colleges, otherwise colored students would be shut out of the best colleges of the country.

The curriculum offered at the colored southern colleges, however, brings the author's caustic criticism. Why, for instance, should "Greek and Latin" be maintained to the exclusion of economics, sociology, and "a strong course in biology"?

The reason for the maintenance of these older courses of study in the colored colleges is not at all, as the author assumes, that Negroes have a childish love for "classics." It is very easily and simply explicable. Take, for instance, Fisk University. Fisk University maintained Greek longer than most northern colleges, for the reason that it had in Adam K. Spence not simply a finished Greek scholar, pupil of the great D'Ooge, but a man of singularly strong personality and fine soul. It did not make much difference whether the students were studying Greek or biology — the great thing was that they were studying under Spence. So, in a large number of cases the curriculum of the southern Negro college has been determined by the personnel of the available men. These men were beyond price and working for their devotion to the

cause. The college was unable to call men representing the newer sciences —
young sociologists and biologists. They were unable to equip laboratories, but
they did with infinite pains and often heartbreaking endeavor keep within
touch of the standard set by the higher northern schools and the proof that
they did well came from the men they turned out and not simply from the
courses they studied.

This, Mr. Jones either forgets or does not know and is thus led into
exceedingly unfortunate statements as when, for instance, he says that the
underlying principle of the industrial school "is the adaptation of educational
activities whether industrial or literary to the needs of the pupils and the
community," which is, of course, the object of any educational institution and
it is grossly unfair to speak of it as being the object of only a part of the great
Negro schools of the South. Any school that does not have this for its object is
not a school but a fraud.

THE PUBLIC SCHOOLS

Not only does this report continually decry the Negro college and its curriculum but, on the other hand, it seeks to put in its place schools and courses of
study which make it absolutely impossible for Negro students to be thoroughly trained according to modern standards. To illustrate: Mr. Jones shows
(page 90) that in Butte, Mont., manual training has been put into the elementary schools at the rate of *half a day a week* during the first six years and *two
half days a week* in the seventh and eighth grades. When, however, it comes to
the smaller elementary industrial schools of the South Mr. Jones recommends *one-half day* classroom work and *one-half* practice in the field and
shops *every day.*

What, now, is the real difference between these two schemes of education?
The difference is that in the Butte schools for white pupils, a chance is held
open for the pupil to go through high school and college and to advance at the
rate which the modern curriculum demands; that in the colored schools, on
the other hand, a program is being made out that will land the boy at the time
he becomes self-conscious and aware of his own possibilities in an educational
impasse. He cannot go on in the public schools even if he should move to a
place where there are good public schools because he is too old. Even if he
has done the elementary work in twice the time that a student is supposed to,
it has been work of a kind that will not admit him to a northern high school.
No matter, then, how gifted the boy may be, he is absolutely estopped from a
higher education. This is not only unfair to the boy but it is grossly unfair to
the Negro race.

The argument, then, against the kind of school that is being foisted upon Negroes in the name of industrial education is not any dislike on the part of the Negroes for having their children trained in vocations, or in having manual training used as a means of education; it is rather in having a series of schools established which deliberately shut the door of opportunity in the face of bright Negro students.

INDUSTRIAL TRAINING

With the drive that has been made to industrialize elementary schools before the children have learned to read and write and to turn the high schools to vocational teaching without giving any of the pupils a chance to train for college, it is, of course, beside the mark to criticize the colored colleges because the children that come to them are poorly trained.

Much of the criticism of colored teachers is also unfair. Even well-trained teachers are having curious pressure put upon them. . . .

With its insistent criticizing of Negro colleges this report touches with curious hesitation and diffidence upon the shortcomings of industrial schools. Their failure to distinguish between general education and technical trade training has resulted in sending out numbers of so-called teachers from educational schools who cannot read and write the English language and who are yet put in public and other schools as teachers. They may show children how to make tin pans and cobble shoes, but they are not the right persons to train youth, mentally or morally. In the second place, most of the trades taught by these trade schools are, because of hostile public opinion and poverty, decadent trades: carpentry, which is rapidly falling below the level of skilled trades; the patching of shoes; blacksmithing, in the sense of repair work, etc. The important trades of the world that are today assembled in factories and call for skilled technique and costly machinery are not taught in the vast majority of Negro industrial schools. Moreover, the higher industrial training calls for more education than the industrial schools give. . . .

That the course of study in the southern schools as well as in the schools of the nation has got to be changed and adapted is absolutely true, but the object of a school system is to carry the child as far as possible in its knowledge of the accumulated wisdom of the world and then when economic or physical reasons demand that this education must stop, vocational training to prepare for life work should follow. That some of this vocational training may be made educational in object is true; that normal training may use manual training and even to some extent vocational training is true, but it is not true that the industrializing of any curriculum necessarily makes it better or that you can at one and the same time educate the race in modern civilization and train it simply to be servants and laborers. Anyone who suggests by sneering at books and "literary courses" that the great heritage of human thought ought to be displaced simply for the reason of teaching the technique of modern industry is pitifully wrong and, if the comparison must be made, more wrong than the man who would sacrifice modern technique to the heritage of ancient thought.

COOPERATION

The second part of Mr. Jones' thesis lies in an insistence that the private schools of the Negro should "cooperate" with the South. He stresses the adaptation of education to the needs of the "community" (page 18), evidently meaning the *white* community. He quotes on page 25 the resolution of the white Southern Educational Association which deplores that the Negro schools are isolated from the "community," meaning again the *white* community. He instances Willcox County, Ala., where there are almost no public schools and recommends that the private schools established there be put under "community" authorities (page 149). Now what is this "community" with which the colored people are to cooperate?

In the first place, Mr. Jones admits (pages 4 and 5), that it is only the progressive few in the white South that care anything at all about Negro schools. He might go even further and acknowledge that if a plebescite were taken tomorrow in the South the popular vote of white people would shut every single Negro school by a large majority. The hostile majority is kept from such radical action by the more progressive minority and by fear of northern interference, but the condition in which they have today left the colored schools is shown by this report to be truly lamentable.

Mr. Jones quotes from southern white men who speak of Negro school houses as "miserable beyond all description," of teachers as "absolutely untrained" and paid "the princely fortune of $80.92 for the whole term." He goes on with fact after fact to show the absolute inadequacy in the provision for colored children in the public schools of the South. On the other hand, he shows the increase in Negro property, the larger and larger amounts which Negroes are contributing to the school funds; and with all this he practically asks that the domination of the Negro private schools, which are now bearing the burden of nearly all the secondary and higher education of the Negro and much of the elementary education — that the domination of these schools be put into the hands of the same people who are doing so little for the public schools!

There is not in the whole report a single word about *taxation without representation*. There is not a single protest against a public school system in which the public which it serves has absolutely no voice, vote, or influence. There is no defense of those colored people of vision who see the public schools being used as training schools for cheap labor and menial servants instead of for education and who are protesting against this by submitting to double taxation in the support of private schools; who cannot see that these schools should be turned over to people who by their actions prove themselves to be enemies of the Negro race and its advancement.

Until the southern Negro has a vote and representation on school boards public control of his education will mean his spiritual and economic death and that despite the good intentions of the small white minority in the South who believe in justice for the Negro. It is, therefore, contradictory for this report to insist, on the one hand, on the continuation of northern philanthropy for these schools and, on the other, to commend various southern schools in proportion as they have gained the approval of the white community.

Compare, for instance, Fisk University and Atlanta University. Both Cravath of Fisk and Ware of Atlanta were men radical in their belief in Negro possibility and in their determination to establish well equipped Negro colleges. Cravath, however, lived in a more enlightened community which was earlier converted to his ideals. He did not yield his opinion any more than Ware, but Ware lived in a community that to this day will not furnish even a high school for its colored pupils. To say that Fisk should receive on this account more support than Atlanta is rank injustice; if anything Atlanta deserves the greater credit.

Cooperation with the white South means in many cases the surrender of the very foundations of self-respect. Mr. Jones inserts in his report one picture of a colored principal and his assistant waiting on table while the white trustees of his school eat. The colored people of the South do not care a rap whether white folks eat with them or not, but if white officials are coming into their schools as persons in control or advisors, then to ask that in those schools and in their homes the colored people shall voluntarily treat themselves as inferiors is to ask more than any self-respecting man is going to do.

The white community, undoubtedly, wants to keep the Negro in the country as a peasant under working conditions least removed from slavery. The colored man wishes to escape from those conditions. Mr. Jones seeks to persuade him to stay there by asserting that the advance of the Negro in the rural South has been greatest (pages 97 and 123), and he refers to the "delusion" of city life even among white people. This may be all good enough propaganda but, in fact, it is untrue. Civilization has always depended upon the cities. The advance of the cities has been greatest for all people, white and colored, and for any colored man to take his family to the country districts of South Georgia in order to grow and develop and secure education and uplift would be idiotic.

Mr. Jones touches the State schools very lightly. Here are cases where the whites have control and stories of graft and misappropriation of funds and poor organization are well known to everybody with the slightest knowledge of southern conditions. Teachers there and in the public schools are often selected not from the best available, but from the worst or most complacent. In small towns and country districts white trustees may maintain their mistresses as teachers and the protest of the colored people has fallen upon deaf ears. Until, then, colored people have a voice in the community, surrender to the domination of the white South is unthinkable.

NORTHERN PHILANTHROPY

This brings us to the third part of Mr. Jones' thesis, namely, that the boards working for southern education should unite as far as possible with one policy. This is an unfortunate and dangerous proposal for the simple reason that the great dominating philanthropic agency, the General Education Board, long ago surrendered to the white South by practically saying that the educational needs of the white South must be attended to before any attention should be paid to the education of Negroes; that the Negro must be trained according to the will of the white South and not as the Negro desires to be trained. It is this board that is spending more money today in helping Negroes learn how to can vegetables than in helping them to go through college. It is this board that by a system of interlocking directorates bids fair to dominate philanthropy toward the Negro in the United States. Indeed, the moving thought back of the present report is the idea of a single authority who is to say which Negro school is right or is wrong, which system is right and which is wrong, etc.

No one doubts the efficiency of concentration and unity in certain lines of work but always, even in work that can be unified, the question is *whose* influence is going to dominate; it may well be that diversity and even a certain chaos would be better than unity under a wrong idea. This is even more true in educational than in economic matters. Of course, the economic foundation of all recent educational philanthropy, particularly toward the Negro, is evident. Mr. Jones rather naively speaks of the fact that at certain times of the year "it is exceedingly difficult to prevail upon children to attend school" in the colored South which is, of course, another way of saying that bread and butter in the cotton fields is of more importance than trained intelligence.

Undoubtedly, there has already been a strong public opinion manufactured in the country which looks upon the training of Negroes in the South as cheap, contented labor to be used in emergency and for keeping white union labor from extravagant demands as a feasible and workable program. It is, in fact, one of the most dangerous programs ever thought out and is responsible for much of the lynching, unrest, and unhappiness in the South. Its genesis came easily with the idea of working *for* the Negro rather than working *with* him, a thing which Mr. Jones condemns, but hardly lives up to his condemnation.

In this very report the Negro was practically unrepresented. Instead of choosing a strong, experienced colored man to represent the Negro race (like W. T. B. Williams, or President Young of Tallahassee, or President Hope of Morehouse) an inexperienced young man was taken, of excellent character but absolutely without weight or influence. Of course, back of all this is the great difficulty of ordinary social intercourse. The reason that boards of trustees like those that control the Phelps Stokes Fund find it so much easier to work *for* the Negro than *with* him; the reason that forgetting the investigations by Negroes at Atlanta University they turned to white institutions to encourage investigation and neglected established and worthy work is because if they are going to cooperate with the dominant white South and even with certain classes of Northerners they cannot meet Negroes as men. The propaganda that is so largely carried on and the influence that is so often formed through social intercourse must always, at present, be offered with the Negro unrepresented and unheard.

There follows easily the habit of having no patience with the man who does not agree with the decisions of such boards. The Negro who comes with his hat in his hand and flatters and cajoles the philanthropist — that Negro gets money. If these foundations raise, as they do in this report, the cry of fraud they have themselves to thank. They more than any other agency have encouraged that kind of person. On the other hand, the Negro who shows the slightest independence of thought or character is apt to be read out of all possible influence not only by the white South but by the philanthropic North.

If philanthropic agencies could unite for certain obvious great movements how splendid it would be! Take, for instance, the duplication of higher educational schools which Mr. Jones repeatedly denounces and which, undoubtedly, is a source of weakness. The General Education Board could settle the matter with the greatest ease. Let it offer in Atlanta an endowment of $500,000 for a single Negro college, provided that there be but one college there for Negroes. The boards of the different schools immediately would have something to act upon. As it is, nothing that they can do individually would really better the situation. A new college formed by a federation of colored colleges in Atlanta, Marshall, Texas, and elsewhere, would be easily possible if an endowment was in sight.

S U M M A R Y

Here, then, is the weakness and sinister danger of Mr. Jones' report. It calls for a union of philanthropic effort with no attempt to make sure of the proper and just lines along which this united effort should work. It calls for cooperation with the white South without insisting on the Negro being represented by voice and vote in such "cooperation," and it calls for a recasting of the educational program for Negroes without insisting on leaving the door of opportunity open for the development of a thoroughly trained class of leaders at the bottom, in the very beginnings of education, as well as at the top.

Gifts and Education

The recent gifts of Duke and Eastman to Negro education, together with the former benefactions of Rockefeller, Carnegie, Peabody and others, must call for gratitude from black folk. Under present conditions, the only hope for Negro education lies in the gifts of the rich and without these ignorance and caste will be the continued lot of American Negroes.

Nevertheless, it is a shame that present conditions make this necessary. It is a shame that the white laborers of the South will not allow the states to support decent common schools and high schools for Negroes, and compel the race to go begging up and down the land, hat in hand, crawling to the door steps of the rich and powerful for the dole of knowledge. And then these same laborers, backed by organized labor in the North, sneer and yell and curse at black labor because it is not intelligent and underbids them.

It is a shame that the rotten boroughs of the South, voting without intelligence or conscience, wielding from two to seven times the political power of the East and Middle West, can send to Congress big-mouthed demagogues who oppose appropriations to Howard, our only university supported by national taxation, and starve it and hamper it and curtail its growth.

It is a shame that our dependence on the rich for donations to absolutely necessary causes makes intelligent, free and self-respecting manhood and frank, open and honest criticism increasingly difficult among us. If someone starts to tell the truth or disclose incompetency or rebel at injustice, a chorus of "Sh!" arises from the whole black race. "Sh!" You're opposing the General Education Board! "Hush!" You're making enemies in the Rockefeller Foundation! "Keep still!" or the Phelps Stokes Fund will get you. "Stop!" or the rich Mr. This and the affluent Mrs. That will dam the flow of funds to Fisk or Talladega, to hospital or home.

Whether the fear be true or not—whether these organizations or persons would be influenced or not by honest criticism, the *fear* of the thing is sapping the manhood of the race. It is breeding cowards and sycophants. It is lifting fools and flatterers to place and power and crucifying honest men. We thank the givers for priceless gifts but we eternally damn the system that makes education depend upon charity.

From *The Crisis*, February 1925.

A Negro Student at Harvard at the End of the Nineteenth Century

Harvard University in 1888 was a great institution of learning. It was 238 years old and on its governing board were Alexander Agassiz, Phillips Brooks, Henry Cabot Lodge and Charles Francis Adams; and a John Quincy Adams, but not the ex-President. Charles William Eliot, a gentleman by training and a scholar by broad study and travel, was president. Among its teachers emeriti were Oliver Wendell Holmes and James Russell Lowell. Among the active teachers were Francis Child, Charles Eliot Norton, Justin Winsor and John Trowbridge; Frank Taussig, Nathaniel Shaler, George Palmer, William James, Francis Peabody, Josiah Royce, Barrett Wendell, Edward Channing and Albert Bushnell Hart. In 1890 arrived a young instructor, George Santayana. Seldom, if ever, has any American university had such a galaxy of great men and fine teachers as Harvard in the decade between 1885 and 1895.

To make my own attitude toward the Harvard of that day clear, it must be remembered that I went to Harvard as a Negro, not simply by birth, but recognizing myself as a member of a segregated caste whose situation I accepted. But I was determined to work from within that caste to find my way out.

The Harvard of which most white students conceived I knew little. I had not even heard of Phi Beta Kappa, and of such important social organizations as the Hasty Pudding Club, I knew nothing. I was in Harvard for education and not for high marks, except as marks would insure my staying. I did not pick out "snap" courses. I was there to enlarge my grasp of the meaning of the universe. We had had, for instance, no chemical laboratory at Fisk; our mathematics courses were limited. Above all I wanted to study philosophy! I wanted to get hold of the bases of knowledge, and explore foundations and

From *Massachusetts Review*, 1 (Spring 1960): 439–458.

beginnings. I chose, therefore, Palmer's course in ethics, but since Palmer was on sabbatical that year, William James replaced him, and I became a devoted follower of James at the time he was developing his pragmatic philosophy.

Fortunately I did not fall into the mistake of regarding Harvard as the beginning rather than the continuing of my college training. I did not find better teachers at Harvard, but teachers better known, who had had wider facilities for gaining knowledge and lived in a broader atmosphere for approaching truth.

I hoped to pursue philosophy as my life career, with teaching for support. With this program I studied at Harvard from the fall of 1888 to 1890, as undergraduate. I took a varied course in chemistry, geology, social science and philosophy. My salvation here was the type of teacher I met rather than the content of the courses. William James guided me out of the sterilities of scholastic philosophy to realist pragmatism; from Peabody's social reform with a religious tinge I turned to Albert Bushnell Hart to study history with documentary research; and from Taussig, with his reactionary British economics of the Ricardo school, I approached what was later to become sociology. Meantime Karl Marx was mentioned, but only incidentally and as one whose doubtful theories had long since been refuted. Socialism was dismissed as unimportant, as a dream of philanthropy or as a will-o-wisp of hotheads.

When I arrived at Harvard, the question of board and lodging was of first importance. Naturally, I could not afford a room in the college Yard in the old and venerable buildings which housed most of the well-to-do students under the magnificent elms. Neither did I think of looking for lodgings among white families, where numbers of the ordinary students lived. I tried to find a colored home, and finally at 20 Flagg Street I came upon the neat home of a colored woman from Nova Scotia, a descendant of those black Jamaican Maroons whom Britain had deported after solemnly promising them peace if they would surrender. For a very reasonable sum I rented the second story front room and for four years this was my home. I wrote of this abode at the time:

> My room is, for a college man's abode, very ordinary indeed. It is quite pleasantly situated — second floor, front, with a bay window and one other window. . . . As you enter you will perceive the bed in the opposite corner, small and decorated with floral designs calculated to puzzle a botanist. . . . On the left hand is a bureau with a mirror of doubtful accuracy. In front of the bay window is a stand with three shelves of books, and on the left of the bureau is an improvised bookcase made of unpainted boards and uprights, containing most of my library of which I am growing quite proud. Over the heat register, near the door, is a mantel with a plaster of Paris pug-dog and a calendar, and the usual array of odds and ends. . . . On the wall are a few quite ordinary pictures. In this commonplace den I am quite content.

Following the attitudes which I had adopted in the South, I sought no friendships among my white fellow students, nor even acquaintanceships. Of course I wanted friends, but I could not seek them. My class was large — some three hundred students. I doubt if I knew a dozen of them. I did not seek them, and naturally they did not seek me. I made no attempt to contribute to the college periodicals since the editors were not interested in my major interests. But I did have a good singing voice and loved music, so I entered the competition for the Glee Club. I ought to have known that Harvard could not afford to have a Negro on its Glee Club travelling about the country. Quite naturally I was rejected.

I was happy at Harvard, but for unusual reasons. One of these was my acceptance of racial segregation. Had I gone from Great Barrington high school directly to Harvard, I would have sought companionship with my white fellows and been disappointed and embittered by a discovery of social limitations to which I had not been used. But I came by way of Fisk and the South and there I had accepted color caste and embraced eagerly the companionship of those of my own color. This was of course no final solution. Eventually, in mass assault, led by culture, we Negroes were going to break down the boundaries of race; but at present we were banded together in a great crusade, and happily so. Indeed, I suspect that the prospect of ultimate full human intercourse, without reservations and annoying distinctions, made me all too willing to consort with my own and to disdain and forget as far as was possible that outer, whiter world.

In general, I asked nothing of Harvard but the tutelage of teachers and the freedom of the laboratory and library. I was quite voluntarily and willingly outside its social life. I sought only such contacts with white teachers as lay directly in the line of my work. I joined certain clubs, like the Philosophical Club; I was a member of the Foxcroft dining club because it was cheap. James and one or two other teachers had me at their homes at meal and reception. I escorted colored girls to various gatherings, and as pretty ones as I could find to the vesper exercises, and later to the class day and commencement social functions. Naturally we attracted attention and the *Crimson* noted my girl friends. Sometimes the shadow of insult fell, as when at one reception a white woman seemed determined to mistake me for a waiter.

In general, I was encased in a completely colored world, self-sufficient and provincial, and ignoring just as far as possible the white world which conditioned it. This was self-protective coloration, with perhaps an inferiority complex, but with belief in the ability and future of black folk.

My friends and companions were drawn mainly from the colored students of Harvard and neighboring institutions, and the colored folk of Boston and surrounding towns. With them I led a happy and inspiring life. There were among them many educated and well-to-do folk, many young people studying or planning to study, many charming young women. We met and ate, danced and argued, and planned a new world.

Towards whites I was not arrogant; I was simply not obsequious, and to a white Harvard student of my day a Negro student who did not seek recognition was trying to be more than a Negro. The same Harvard man had much the same attitude toward Jews and Irishmen.

I was, however, exceptional among Negroes at Harvard in my ideas on voluntary race segregation. They for the most part saw salvation only in integration at the earliest moment and on almost any terms in white culture; I was firm in my criticism of white folk and in my dream of a self-sufficient Negro culture even in America.

This cutting of myself off from my white fellows, or being cut off, did not mean unhappiness or resentment. I was in my early manhood, unusually full of high spirits and humor. I thoroughly enjoyed life. I was conscious of understanding and power, and conceited enough still to imagine, as in high school, that they who did not know me were the losers, not I. On the other hand, I do not think that my white classmates found me personally objectionable. I was clean, not well-dressed but decently clothed. Manners I regarded as more or less superfluous and deliberately cultivated a certain brusquerie. Personal adornment I regarded as pleasant but not important. I was in Harvard, but not of it, and realized all the irony of my singing "Fair Harvard." I sang it because I liked the music, and not from any pride in the pilgrims.

With my colored friends I carried on lively social intercourse, but necessarily one which involved little expenditure of money. I called at their homes and ate at their tables. We danced at private parties. We went on excursions down the Bay. Once, with a group of colored students gathered from surrounding institutions, we gave Aristophanes' *The Birds* in a Boston colored church. The rendition was good, but not outstanding, not quite appreciated by the colored audience, but well worth doing. Even though it worked me near to death, I was proud of it.

Thus the group of professional men, students, white collar workers and upper servants, whose common bond was color of skin in themselves or in their fathers, together with a common history and current experience of discrimination, formed a unit that like many tens of thousands of like units across the nation had or were getting to have a common culture pattern which made them an interlocking mass, so that increasingly a colored person in Boston was more neighbor to a colored person in Chicago than to a white person across the street.

Mrs. [Josephine St. Pierre] Ruffin of Charles Street, Boston, and her daughter Birdie were often hostesses to this colored group. She was widow of the first colored judge appointed in Massachusetts, an aristocratic lady, with olive skin and high piled masses of white hair. Once a Boston white lady said to Mrs. Ruffin ingratiatingly: "I have always been interested in your race." Mrs. Ruffin flared: "Which race?" She began a national organization of colored women and published the *Courant*, a type of small colored weekly paper which was then spreading over the nation. In this I published many of my Harvard daily themes.

Naturally in this close group there grew up among the young people friendships ending in marriages. I myself, outgrowing the youthful attractions of Fisk, began serious dreams of love and marriage. There were, however, still my study plans to hold me back and there were curious other reasons. For instance, it happened that two of the girls whom I particularly liked had what was to me then the insuperable handicap of looking like whites, while they had enough black ancestry to make them "Negroes" in America. I could not let the world even imagine that I had married a white wife. Yet these girls were intelligent and companionable. One went to Vassar College, which then refused entrance to Negroes. Years later when I went there to lecture I remember disagreeing violently with a teacher who thought the girl ought not to have "deceived" the college by graduating before it knew of her Negro descent! Another favorite of mine was Deenie Pindell. She was a fine forth-right woman, blonde, blue-eyed and fragile. In the end I had no chance to choose her, for she married Monroe Trotter.

Trotter was the son of a well-to-do colored father and entered Harvard in my first year in the Graduate School. He was thick-set, yellow, with close-cut dark hair. He was stubborn and strait-laced and an influential member of his class. He organized the first Total Abstinence Club in the Yard. I came to know him and joined the company when he and other colored students took in a trip to Amherst to see our friends [George] Forbes and [William H.] Lewis graduate in the class with Calvin Coolidge.

Lewis afterward entered the Harvard Law School and became the cele-brated center rush of the Harvard football team. He married the beautiful Bessie Baker, who had been with us on that Amherst trip. Forbes, a brilliant, cynical dark man, later joined with Trotter in publishing the *Guardian*, the first Negro paper to attack Booker T. Washington openly. Washington's friends retorted by sending Trotter to jail when he dared to heckle Washington in a public Boston meeting on his political views. I was not present nor privy to this occurrence, but the unfairness of the jail sentence led me eventually to form the Niagara movement, which later became the NAACP.

Thus I lived near to life, love and tragedy; and when I met Maud Cuney, I became doubly interested. She was a tall, imperious brunette with gold-bronze skin, brilliant eyes and coils of black hair, daughter of the Collector of

Customs at Galveston, Texas. She had come to study music and was a skilled performer. When the New England Conservatory of Music tried to "Jim Crow" her in the dormitory, we students rushed to her defense and we won. I fell deeply in love with her, and we were engaged.

Thus it is clear how in the general social intercourse on the campus I consciously missed nothing. Some white students made themselves known to me and a few, a very few, became lifelong friends. Most of my classmates I knew neither by sight nor name. Among them many made their mark in life: Norman Hapgood, Robert Herrick, Herbert Croly, George Dorsey, Homer Folks, Augustus Hand, James Brown Scott, and others. I knew none of these intimately. For the most part I do not doubt that I was voted a somewhat selfish and self-centered "grind" with a chip on my shoulder and a sharp tongue.

Only once or twice did I come to the surface of college life. First I found by careful calculation that I needed the cash of one of the Boylston prizes in oratory to piece out my year's expenses. I got it through winning a second oratorical prize. The occasion was noteworthy by the fact that another black student, Clement Morgan, got first prize at the same contest.

With the increase at Harvard of students who had grown up outside New England, there arose at this time a certain resentment at the way New England students were dominating and conducting college affairs. The class marshal on commencement day was always a Saltonstall, a Cabot, a Lowell, or from some such New England family. The crew and most of the heads of other athletic teams were selected from similarly limited social groups. The class poet, class orator, and other commencement officials invariably were selected because of family and not for merit. It so happened that when the officials of the class of 1890 were being selected in early spring, a plot ripened. Personally, I knew nothing of it and was not greatly interested. But in Boston and in the Harvard Yard the result of the elections was of tremendous significance, for this conspiratorial clique selected Clement Morgan as class orator. New England and indeed the whole country reverberated.

Morgan was a black man. He had been working in a barber shop in St. Louis at the time when he ought to have been in school. With the encouragement and help of a colored teacher, whom he later married, he came to Boston and entered the Latin School. This meant that when he finally entered Harvard, he entered as freshman in the orthodox way and was well acquainted with his classmates. He was fairly well received, considering his color. He was a pleasant unassuming person and one of the best speakers of clearly enunciated English on the campus. In his junior year he had earned the first Boylston prize for oratory in the same contest where I won second prize. It was, then, logical for him to become class orator, and yet this was against all the traditions of America. There were editorials in the leading newspapers, and the South especially raged and sneered at the audience of "black washerwomen" who would replace Boston society at the next Harvard commencement.

Morgan's success was contagious, and that year and the next in several leading Northern colleges colored students became the class orators. Ex-President Hayes, as I shall relate later, sneered at this fact. While, as I have said, I had nothing to do with the plot, and was not even present at the election which chose Morgan, I was greatly pleased at this breaking of the color line. Morgan and I became fast friends and spent a summer giving readings along the North Shore to defray our college costs.

Harvard of this day was a great opportunity for a young man and a young American Negro and I realized it. I formed habits of work rather different from those of most of the other students. I burned no midnight oil. I did my studying in the daytime and had my day parceled out almost to the minute. I spent a great deal of time in the library and did my assignments with thoroughness and with prevision of the kind of work I wanted to do later. From the beginning my relations with most of the teachers at Harvard were pleasant. They were on the whole glad to receive a serious student, to whom extracurricular activities were not of paramount importance, and one who in a general way knew what he wanted.

Harvard had in the social sciences no such leadership of thought and breadth of learning as in philosophy, literature and physical science. She was then groping and is still groping toward a scientific treatment of human action. She was facing at the end of the century a tremendous economic era. In the United States, finance was succeeding in monopolizing transportation and raw materials like sugar, coal and oil. The power of the trust and combine was so great that the Sherman Act was passed in 1890. On the other hand, the tariff, at the demand of manufacturers, continued to rise in height from the McKinley to the indefensible Wilson tariff, making that domination easier. The understanding between the Industrial North and the New South was being perfected and, beginning in 1890, a series of disfranchising laws was enacted by the Southern states that was destined in the next sixteen years to make voting by Southern Negroes practically impossible. A financial crisis shook the land in 1893 and popular discontent showed itself in the Populist movement and Coxey's Army. The whole question of the burden of taxation began to be discussed.

These things we discussed with some clearness and factual understanding at Harvard. The tendency was toward English free trade and against the American tariff policy. We reverenced [David] Ricardo and wasted long hours on the "Wages-fund." I remember [Frank] Taussig's course supporting dying Ricardean economics. Wages came from what employers had left for labor

277

after they had subtracted their own reward. Suppose that this profit was too small to attract the employer, what would the poor worker do but starve! The trusts and monopolies were viewed frankly as dangerous enemies of democracies, but at the same time as inevitable methods of industry. We were strong for the gold standard and fearful of silver. On the other hand, the attitude of Harvard toward labor was on the whole contemptuous and condemnatory. Strikes like that of the anarchists in Chicago and the railway strikes of 1886, the terrible Homestead strike of 1892 and Coxey's Army of 1894 were pictured as ignorant lawlessness, lurching against conditions largely inevitable.

Karl Marx was mentioned only to point out how thoroughly his theses had been disproven; of the theory itself almost nothing was said. Henry George was given but tolerant notice. The anarchists of Spain, the Nihilists of Russia, the British miners — all these were viewed not as part of political and economic development but as sporadic evil. This was natural. Harvard was the child of its era. The intellectual freedom and flowering of the late eighteenth and early nineteenth centuries were yielding to the deadening economic pressure which would make Harvard rich but reactionary. This defender of wealth and capital, already half ashamed of Sumner and Phillips, was willing finally to replace an Eliot with a manufacturer and a nervous warmonger. The social community that mobbed Garrison easily electrocuted Sacco and Vanzetti.

It was not until I was long out of college and had finished my first studies of economics and politics that I realized the fundamental influence man's efforts to earn a living had upon all his other efforts. The politics which we studied in college were conventional, especially when it came to describing and elucidating the current scene in Europe. The Queen's Jubilee in June, 1887, while I was still at Fisk, set the pattern of our thinking. The little old woman at Windsor became a magnificent symbol of Empire. Here was England with her flag draped around the world, ruling more black folk than white and leading the colored peoples of the earth to Christian baptism, and, as we assumed, to civilization and eventual self-rule. In 1885, [Henry] Stanley, the traveling American reporter, became a hero and symbol of white world leadership in Africa. The wild, fierce fight of the Mahdi and the driving of the English out of the Sudan for thirteen years did not reveal their inner truth to me. I heard only of the martyrdom of the drunken Bible-reader and free-booter, Chinese Gordon.

After the Congo Free State was established, the Berlin Conference of 1885 was reported to be an act of civilization against the slave trade and liquor. French, English and Germans pushed on in Africa, but I did not question the interpretation which pictured this as the advance of civilization and the benevolent tutelage of barbarians. I read of the confirmation of the Triple Alliance in 1891. Later I saw the celebration of the renewed Triple Alliance on the Tempelhofer Feld, with the new young Emperor Wilhelm II, who, fresh from his dismissal of Bismarck, led the splendid pageantry; and, finally, the year I left Germany, Nicholas II became Czar of all the Russias. In all this I had not yet linked the political development of Europe with the race problem in America.

I was repeatedly a guest in the home of William James; he was my friend and guide to clear thinking; as a member of the Philosophical Club I talked with Royce and Palmer; I remember vividly once standing beside Mrs. Royce at a small reception. We ceased conversation for a moment and both glanced across the room. Professor Royce was opposite talking excitedly. He was an extraordinary sight: a little body, indifferently clothed; a big red-thatched head and blazing blue eyes. Mrs. Royce put my thoughts into words: "Funny-looking man, isn't he?" I nearly fainted! Yet I knew how she worshipped him.

I sat in an upper room and read Kant's *Critique* with Santayana; Shaler invited a Southerner, who objected to sitting beside me, to leave his class; he said he wasn't doing very well, anyway. I became one of Hart's favorite pupils and was afterwards guided by him through my graduate course and started on my work in Germany. Most of my courses of study went well. It was in English that I came nearest my Waterloo at Harvard. I had unwittingly arrived at Harvard in the midst of a violent controversy about poor English among students. A number of fastidious scholars like Barrett Wendell, the great pundit of Harvard English, had come to the campus about this time; moreover, New England itself was getting sensitive over Western slang and Southern drawls and general ignorance of grammar. Freshmen at this time could elect nearly all their courses except English; that was compulsory, with daily themes, theses, and tough examinations. But I was at the point in my intellectual development when the content rather than the form of my writing was to me of prime importance. Words and ideas surged in my mind and spilled out with disregard of exact accuracy in grammar, taste in word or restraint in style. I knew the Negro problem and this was more important to me than literary form. I knew grammar fairly well, and I had a pretty wide vocabulary; but I was bitter, angry and intemperate in my first thesis. Naturally my English instructors had no idea of nor interest in the way in which Southern attacks on the Negro were scratching me on the raw flesh. Tillman was raging like a beast in the Senate, and literary clubs, especially those of rich and well-dressed women, engaged his services eagerly and listened avidly. Senator Morgan of Alabama had just published a scathing attack on "niggers" in a leading magazine, when my first Harvard thesis was due. I let go at him with no holds barred. My long and blazing effort came back marked "E" — not passed!

It was the first time in my scholastic career that I had encountered such a failure. I was aghast, but I was not a fool. I did not doubt but that my instructors were fair in judging my English technically even if they did not understand the Negro problem. I went to work at my English and by the end of that term had raised it to a "C". I realized that while style is subordinate to content, and that no real literature can be composed simply of meticulous and fastidious phrases, nevertheless solid content with literary style carries a message further than poor grammar and muddled syntax. I elected the best course on the campus for English composition — English 12.

I have before me a theme which I submitted on October 3, 1890, to Barrett Wendell. I wrote:

> Spurred by my circumstances, I have always been given to systematically planning my future, not indeed without many mistakes and frequent alterations, but always with what I now conceive to have been a strangely early and deep appreciation of the fact that to live is a serious thing. I determined while in high school to go to college — partly because other men did, partly because I foresaw that such discipline would best fit me for life. . . . I believe, foolishly perhaps, but sincerely, that I have something to say to the world, and I have taken English 12 in order to say it well.

Barrett Wendell liked that last sentence. Out of fifty essays, he picked this out to read to the class.

Commencement was approaching, when, one day, I found myself at midnight on one of the swaggering streetcars that used to roll out from Boston on its way to Cambridge. It was in the spring of 1890, and quite accidentally I was sitting by a classmate who would graduate with me in June. As I dimly remember, he was a nice-looking young man; well-dressed, almost dapper, charming in manner. Probably he was rich or at least well-to-do, and doubtless belonged to an exclusive fraternity, although that did not interest me. Indeed I have even forgotten his name. But one thing I shall never forget and that was his rather regretful admission (which slipped out as we gossiped) that he had no idea as to what his life work would be, because, as he added, "There's nothing in which I am particularly interested!"

I was more than astonished — I was almost outraged to meet any human being of the mature age of twenty-one who did not have his life all planned before him, at least in general outline, and who was not supremely, if not desperately, interested in what he planned to do.

In June 1890, I received my bachelor's degree from Harvard *cum laude* in philosophy. I was one of the five graduating students selected to speak at commencement. My subject was "Jefferson Davis." I chose it with the deliberate intent of facing Harvard and the nation with a discussion of slavery as illustrated in the person of the president of the Confederate States of America. Naturally, my effort made a sensation. I said, among other things:

I wish to consider not the man, but the type of civilization which his life represented: its foundation is the idea of the strong man — Individualism coupled with the rule of might — and it is this idea that has made the logic of even modern history, the cool logic of the Club. It made of a naturally brave and generous man, Jefferson Davis, one who advanced civilization by murdering Indians; then a hero of a national disgrace, called by courtesy the Mexican War; and finally, as the crowning absurdity, the peculiar champion of a people fighting to be free in order that another people should not be free. Whenever this idea has for a moment escaped from the individual realm, it has found an even more secure foothold in the policy and philosophy of the State. The strong man and his mighty Right Arm has become the Strong Nation with its armies. However, under whatever guise a Jefferson Davis may appear as man, as race, or as a nation, his life can only logically mean this: the advance of a part of the world at the expense of the whole; the overwhelming sense of the I, and the consequent forgetting of the Thou. It has thus happened that advance in civilization has always been handicapped by shortsighted national selfishness. The vital principle of division of labor has been stifled not only in industry, but also in civilization; so as to render it well-nigh impossible for a new race to introduce a new idea into the world except by means of the cudgel. To say that a nation is in the way of civilization is a contradiction in terms, and a system of human culture whose principle is the rise of one race on the ruins of another is a farce and a lie. Yet this is the type of civilization which Jefferson Davis represented: it represents a field for stalwart manhood and heroic character, and at the same time for moral obtuseness and refined brutality. These striking contradictions of character always arise when a people seemingly become convinced that the object of the world is not civilization, but Teutonic civilization.

A Harvard professor wrote to *Kate Field's Washington*, then a leading periodical:

Du Bois, the colored orator of the commencement stage, made a ten-strike. It is agreed upon by all the people I have seen that he was the star of the occasion. His paper was on "Jefferson Davis," and you would have been surprised to hear a colored man deal with him so generously. Such phrases as a "great man," a "keen thinker," a "strong leader," and others akin occurred in the address. One of the trustees of the University told me yesterday that the paper was considered masterly in every way. Du Bois is from Great Barrington, Massachusetts, and doubtless has some white blood in his veins. He, too, has been in my classes the past year. If he did not head the class, he came pretty near the head, for he is an excellent scholar in every way, and altogether the best black man that has come to Cambridge.

Bishop Potter of New York wrote in the *Boston Herald*:

When at the last commencement of Harvard University, I saw a young colored man appear. . . . and heard his brilliant and eloquent address, I said to myself: "Here is what an historic race can do if they have a clear field, a high purpose, and a resolute will."

Already I had now received more education than most young white men, having been almost continuously in school from the age of six to twenty-two. But I did not yet feel prepared. I felt that to cope with the new and extraordinary situations then developing in the United States and the world I needed to go further and that as a matter of fact I had just well begun my training in knowledge of social conditions.

I revelled in the keen analysis of William James, Josiah Royce and young George Santayana. But it was James with his pragmatism and Albert Bushnell Hart with his research method who turned me back from the lovely but sterile land of philosophic speculation to the social sciences as the field for gathering and interpreting that body of fact which would apply to my program for the Negro. As undergraduate, I had talked frankly with William James about teaching philosophy, my major subject. He discouraged me, but not by any means because of my record in his classes. He used to give me "A's" and even "A-plus," but as he said candidly, there is "not much chance of anyone earning a living as a philosopher." He was repeating just what Chase of Fisk had said a few years previously.

I knew by this time that practically my sole chance of earning a living combined with study was to teach, and after my work with Hart in United States history I conceived the idea of applying philosophy to an historical interpretation of race relations. In other words, I was trying to take my first steps toward sociology as the science of human action. It goes without saying that no such field of study was then recognized at Harvard or came to be recognized for twenty years after. But I began with some research in Negro history and finally at the suggestion of Hart, I chose the suppression of the African slave trade to America as my doctor's thesis. Then came the question as to whether I could continue study in the graduate school. I had no resources in wealth or friends. I applied for a fellowship in the graduate school of Harvard, was appointed Henry Bromfield Rogers fellow for a year and later the appointment was renewed; so that from 1890 to 1892 I was a fellow in Harvard University, studying history and political science and what would have been sociology if Harvard had yet recognized such a field.

I finished the first draft of my thesis and delivered an outline of it at the seminars of American history and political economy December 7, 1891. I received my master's degree in the spring. I was thereupon elected to the American Historical Society and asked to speak in Washington at their meeting in December, 1891. The *New York Independent* noted this among the "three best papers presented," and continued:

> The article upon the "enforcement of the Slave Laws" was written and read by a black man. It was thrilling when one could, for a moment turn his thoughts from listening to think that scarcely thirty years have elapsed since the war that freed his race, and here was an audience of white men listening to a black man—listening, moreover, to a careful, cool, philosophical history of the laws which had not prevented the enslavement of his race. The voice, the diction, the manner of the speaker were faultless. As one looked at him, one could not help saying, "Let us not worry about the future of our country in the matter of race distinctions."

I had begun with a bibliography of Nat Turner and ended with a history of the suppression of the African slave trade to America; neither would need to be done again, at least in my day. Thus in my quest for basic knowledge with which to help guide the American Negro, I came to the study of sociology, by way of philosophy and history rather than by physics and biology. After hesitating between history and economics, I chose history. On the other hand, psychology, hovering then on the threshold of experiment under [Hugo] Muensterberg, soon took a new orientation which I could understand from the beginning.

Already I had made up my mind that what I needed was further training in Europe. The German universities were at the top of their reputation. Any American scholar who wanted preferment went to Germany for study. The faculties of Johns Hopkins and the new University of Chicago were beginning to be filled with German Ph.D.'s, and even Harvard, where Kuno Frank had long taught, had imported Muensterberg. British universities did not recognize American degrees and French universities made no special effort to encourage American graduates. I wanted then to study in Germany. I was determined that any failure on my part to become a recognized American scholar must not be based on lack of modern training.

I was confident. So far I had met no failure. I willed and lo! I was walking beneath the elms of Harvard—the name of allurement, the college of my youngest, wildest visions! I needed money; scholarships and prizes fell into my lap—not all I wanted or strove for, but all I needed to keep me in school. Commencement came, and standing before governor, president, and grave gowned men, I told them certain truths, waving my arms and breathing fast! They applauded with what may have seemed to many as uncalled-for fervor, but I walked home on pink clouds of glory! I asked for a fellowship and got it. I announced my plan of studying in Germany, but Harvard had no more fellowships for me. A friend, however, told me of the Slater Fund and that the board was looking for colored men worth educating.

No thought of modest hesitation occurred to me. I rush at the chance. It was one of those tricks of fortune which always seem partly due to chance. In 1882, the Slater Fund for the education of Negroes had been established and the board in 1890 was headed by ex-President R. B. Hayes. Ex-President Hayes went down to Johns Hopkins University, which admitted no Negro students, and told a "darkey" joke in a frank talk about the plans of the fund. The *Boston Herald* of November 2, 1890 quoted him as saying: "If there is any young colored man in the South whom we find to have a talent for art or literature or any special aptitude for study, we are willing to give him money from the educational funds to send him to Europe or give him advanced education." He added that so far they had been able to find only "orators." This seemed to me a nasty fling at my black classmate, Morgan, who had been Harvard class orator a few months earlier.

The Hayes statement was brought to my attention at a card party one evening; it not only made me good and angry but inspired me to write ex-President Hayes and ask for a scholarship. I received a pleasant reply saying that the newspaper quotation was incorrect; that his board had some such program in the past but had no present plans for such scholarships. I responded referring him to my teachers and to others who knew me, and intimating that his change of plan did not seem to me fair nor honest. He wrote again in apologetic mood and said that he was sorry the plan had been given up, that he recognized that I was a candidate who might otherwise have been given attention. I then sat down and wrote Mr. Hayes this letter:

May 25, 1891

Your favor of the 2nd, is at hand. I thank you for your kind wishes. You will pardon me if I add a few words of explanation as to my application. The outcome of the matter is as I expected it would be. The announcement that any agency of the American people was willing to give a Negro a thoroughly liberal education and that it had been looking in vain for men to educate was to say the least rather startling. When the newspaper clipping was handed me in a company of friends, my first impulse was to make in some public way a categorical statement denying that such an offer had ever been made known to colored students. I saw this would be injudicious and fruitless, and I therefore determined on the plan of applying myself. I did so and have been refused along with a "number of cases" beside mine.

As to my case, I personally care little. I am perfectly capable of fighting alone for an education if the trustees do not see fit to help me. On the other hand the injury you have — unwittingly I trust — done the race I represent, and are not ashamed of, is almost irreparable. You went before a number of keenly observant men who looked upon you as an authority in the matter, and told them in substance that the Negroes of the United States either couldn't or wouldn't embrace a most liberal opportunity for advancement. That statement went all over the country. When now finally you receive three or four applications for the fulfillment of that offer, the offer is suddenly withdrawn, while the impression still remains.

If the offer was an experiment, you ought to have had at least one case before withdrawing it; if you have given aid before (and I mean here toward liberal education — not toward training plowmen) then your statement at Johns Hopkins was partial. From the above facts I think you owe an apology to the Negro people. We are ready to furnish competent men for every European scholarship furnished us off paper. But we can't educate ourselves on nothing and we can't have the moral courage to try, if in the midst of our work our friends turn public sentiment against us by making statements which injure us and which they cannot stand by.

That you have been looking for men to liberally educate in the past may be so but it is certainly strange so few have heard it. It was never mentioned during my three years stay at Fisk University. President Price of Livingstone [then a leading Negro spokesman] has told me that he never heard of it, and students from various other Southern schools have expressed great surprise at the offer. The fact is that when I was wanting to come to Harvard, while yet in the South, I wrote to Dr. Haygood [Atticus G. Haygood, a leader of Southern white liberals], for a loan merely, and he never even answered my letter. I find men willing to help me thro' cheap theological schools. I find men willing to help me use my hands before I have got my brains in working order. I have an abundance of good wishes on hand, but I never found a man willing to help me get a Harvard Ph.D.

Hayes was stirred. He promised to take up the matter the next year with the board. Thereupon, the next year I proceeded to write the board: "At the close of the last academic year at Harvard, I received the degree of Master of Arts, and was reappointed to my fellowship for the year 1891–92. I have spent most of the year in the preparation of my doctor's thesis on the Suppression of the Slave Trade in America. I prepared a preliminary paper on this subject and read it before the American Historical Association at its annual meeting at Washington during the Christmas holidays. . . . Properly to finish my education, careful training in a European university for at least a year is, in my mind and the minds of my professors, absolutely indispensable." I thereupon asked respectfully "aid to study at least a year abroad under the direction of the graduate department of Harvard or other reputable auspices" and if this was not practicable, "that the board loan me a sufficient sum for this purpose." I did not of course believe that this would get me an appointment, but I did think that possibly through the influence of people who thus came to know about my work, I might somehow borrow or beg enough to get to Europe.

I rained recommendations upon Mr. Hayes. The Slater Fund Board surrendered, and I was given a fellowship of $750 to study a year abroad, with the promise that it might possibly be renewed for a second year. To salve their souls, however, this grant was made half as gift and half as repayable loan with 5% interest. I remember rushing down to New York and talking with ex-President Hayes in the old Astor House, and emerging walking on air. I saw an especially delectable shirt in a shop window. I went in and asked about it. It cost three dollars, which was about four times as much as I had ever paid for a shirt in my life; but I bought it.

V

Women's Rights

Du Bois reserved some of his most passionate writing for women's rights, dismissing patriarchal arguments of such black antisuffragists as Kelly Miller ("Woman Suffrage" [1915]) as mindless ("sheer rot") and blasting mobs of white mysogynists ("Hail Columbia!" [1913]) with acid irony ("the place for woman is in the home, even if she hasn't got a home"). Although his deepest feelings about his own mother were both complex and ambivalent, Du Bois acknowledged in numerous essays his great debt to her for his success. Hardworking and uncomplaining, though poor and physically handicapped, a lover of learning and a nurturer of ambition, though poorly educated, Du Bois's mother served as model for the abused, resilient black women and mothers he celebrated in "The Black Mother" (1912), "The Burden of Black Women" (1907), and other pieces of often stunning poignancy. Du Bois was one of the most militant male feminists of the early twentieth century. His was a feminism that went well beyond advocacy of voting rights to demand, in effect, equal pay for equal work, as in the strikingly modern "The Damnation of Women" (1920).

The Burden of Black Women

Dark daughter of the lotus leaves that watch
    the Southern sea.
Wan spirit of a prisoned soul a-panting to be
    free
The muttered music of thy streams, the
    whispers of the deep
Have kissed each other in thy name and kissed
    a world to sleep.

———

The will of the world is a mighty wind sweeping
    a cloud-cast sky,
And not from the east and not from the west
    knelled its soul-searing cry;
But out of the past of the Past's grey past, it
    yelled from the top of the sky;
Crying: Awake, O ancient race! Wailing: O
    woman arise!
And crying and sighing and crying again as a
    voice in the midnight cries;
But the Burden of white men bore her back,
    and the white world stifled her sighs

———

The White World's vermin and filth:
    All the dirt of London,
    All the scum of New York;
    Valiant spoilers of women

From *The Horizon*, 2 (November 1907): 3–5.

And conquerors of unarmed men;
Shameless breeders of bastards
Drunk with the greed of gold.
Baiting their blood-stained hooks
With cant for the souls of the simple,
Bearing the White Man's Burden
Of Liquor and Lust and Lies!

————

Unthankful we wince in the East
Unthankful we wail from the westward,
Unthankfully thankful we sing.
In the un-won wastes of the wild:
I hate them, Oh!
I hate them well,
I hate them, Christ!
As I hate Hell,
If I were God
I'd sound their knell
This day!

————

Who raised the fools to their glory
But black men of Egypt and Ind?
Ethiopia's sons of the evening,
Chaldeans and Yellow Chinese?
The Hebrew children of Morning
And mongrels of Rome and Greece?
    Ah, well!
And they that raised the boasters:
Shall drag them down again:
Down with the thefts of their thieving
And murder and mocking of men,
Down with their barter of women
And laying and lying of creeds,

Down with their cheating of childhood,
And drunken orgies of war —
    down
      down
        deep down,
Till the Devil's strength be shorn,

Till some dim, darker Davad a hoeing of his
    corn,
And married maiden, Mother of God,
Bid the Black Christ be born!

Then shall the burden of manhood.
Be it yellow or black or white,
And Poverty, Justice and Sorrow—
The Humble and Simple and Strong
Shall sing with the Sons of Morning
And Daughters of Evensong.

Black mother of the iron hills that guard the
    blazing sea,
Wild spirit of a storm-swept soul a-struggling
    to be free,
Where 'neath the bloody finger marks, thy
    river bosom quakes,
Thicken the thunders of God's voice, and lo!
    a world awakes!

The Black Mother

The people of America, and especially the people of the Southern States, have felt so keen an appreciation of the qualities of motherhood in the Negro that they have proposed erecting a statue in the National Capital to the black mammy. The black nurse of slavery days may receive the tribute of enduring bronze from the master class.

But this appreciation of the black mammy is always of the foster mammy, not of the mother in her home, attending to her own babies. And as the colored mother has retreated to her own home, the master class has cried out against her. "She is thriftless and stupid," the white mother says, "when she refuses to nurse my baby and stays with her own. She is bringing her daughter up beyond her station when she trains her to be a teacher instead of sending her into my home to act as nursemaid to my little boy and girl. I will never enter her street, heaven forbid. A colored street is taboo, and she no longer deserves my approval when she refuses to leave her home and enter mine."

Let us hope that the black mammy, for whom so many sentimental tears have been shed, has disappeared from American life. She existed under a false social system that deprived her of husband and child. Thomas Nelson Page, after — with wet eyelids — recounting the virtues of his mammy, declares petulantly that she did not care for her own children. Doubtless this was true. How could it have been otherwise? But just so far as it was true it was a perversion of motherhood.

Let the present-day mammies suckle their own children. Let them walk in the sunshine with their own toddling boys and girls and put their own sleepy little brothers and sisters to bed. As their girls grow to womanhood, let them see to it that, if possible, they do not enter domestic service in those homes where they are unprotected, and where their womanhood is not treated with respect. In the midst of immense difficulties, surrounded by caste, and hemmed in by restricted economic opportunity, let the colored mother of today build her own statue, and let it be the four walls of her own unsullied home.

From *The Crisis*, December 1912.

Hail Columbia!

Hail Columbia, Happy Land! Again the glorious traditions of Anglo-Saxon manhood have been upheld! Again the chivalry of American white men has been magnificently vindicated. Down on your knees, black men, and hear the tale with awestruck faces. Learn from the Superior Race. We do not trust our own faltering pen and purblind sight to describe the reception of the suffragists at the capital of the land. We quote from the Southern reporters of the Northern press:

"Five thousand women, marching in the woman-suffrage pageant yesterday, practically fought their way foot by foot up Pennsylvania Avenue, through a surging mass of humanity that completely defied the Washington police, swamped the marchers, and broke their procession into little companies. The women, trudging stoutly along under great difficulties, were able to complete their march only when troops of cavalry from Fort Myer were rushed into Washington to take charge of Pennsylvania Avenue. No inauguration has ever produced such scenes, which in many instances amounted to little less than riots.

"More than 100 persons, young and old, of both sexes, were crushed and trampled in the uncontrollable crowd in Pennsylvania Avenue yesterday, while two ambulances of the Emergency Hospital came and went constantly for six hours, always impeded and at times actually opposed, so that doctor and driver literally had to fight their way to give succor to the injured."

"Hoodlums, many of them in uniform, leaned forward till their cigarettes almost touched the women's faces while blowing smoke in their eyes, and the police said not a word, not even when every kind of insult was hurled.

"To the white-haired women the men shouted continuously: 'Granny! granny! We came to see chickens, not hens! Go home and sit in the corner!' To the younger women they yelled: 'Say, what you going to do to-night? Can't we make a date?' and the police only smiled. The rowdies jumped on the

From *The Crisis*, April 1913.

running boards of the automobiles and snatched the flags from the elderly women, and they attempted to pull the girls from the floats."

Wasn't it glorious? Does it not make you burn with shame to be a mere black man when such mighty deeds are done by the Leaders of Civilization? Does it not make you "ashamed of your race?" Does it not make you "want to be white?"

And do you know (we are almost ashamed to say it) the Negro again lost a brilliant opportunity to rise in his "imitative" way. Ida Husted Harper says:

"We made the closest observation along the entire line and not in one instance did we hear a colored man make a remark, although there were thousands of them."

Another white woman writes:

"I wish to speak a word in favor of the colored people during the suffrage parade. Not one of them was boisterous or rude as with great difficulty we passed along the unprotected avenue. The difference between them and those insolent, bold white men was remarkable. They were quiet and respectable and earnest, and seemed sorry for the indignities which were incessantly heaped upon us. There were few policemen to protect us as we made our first parade in Washington, and the dignified silence of the colored people and the sympathy in their faces was a great contrast to those who should have known better. I thank them in the name of all the women for their kindness."

Now look at that! Good Lord! has the Negro *no* sense? Can he grasp no opportunity?

But let him not think to gain by any such tactics. The South sees his game and is busy promoting bills to prevent his marrying any wild-eyed suffragette who may be attracted by his pusillanimous decency. Already the Ohio legislature has been flooded by forged petitions from a "Negro advancement society of New York" to push the intermarriage bill!

No, sir! White men are on the firing line, and if they don't want white women for wives they will at least keep them for prostitutes. Beat them back, keep them down; flatter them, call them "visions of loveliness" and tell them that the place for woman is in the home, even if she hasn't got a home. If she is homely or poor or made the mistake of being born with brains, and begins to protest at the doll's house or the bawdy house, kick her and beat her and insult her until in terror she slinks back to her kennel or walks the midnight streets. Don't give in; don't give her power; don't give her a vote whatever you do. Keep the price of women down; make them weak and cheap.

Shall the time ever dawn in this Land of the Brave when a free white American citizen may not buy as many women as his purse permits? Perish the thought and Hail Columbia, Happy Land!

Woman Suffrage

This month 200,000 Negro voters will be called upon to vote on the question of giving the right of suffrage to women. *The Crisis* sincerely trusts that everyone of them will vote *Yes*. But *The Crisis* would not have them go to the polls without having considered every side of the question. Intelligence in voting is the only real support of democracy. For this reason we publish with pleasure Dean Kelly Miller's article against woman suffrage. We trust that our readers will give it careful attention and that they will compare it with that marvelous symposium which we had the pleasure to publish in our August number. Meantime, Dean Miller will pardon us for a word in answer to his argument.

Briefly put, Mr. Miller believes that the bearing and rearing of the young is a function which makes it practically impossible for women to take any large part in general, industrial and public affairs; that women are weaker than men; that women are adequately protected under man's suffrage; that no adequate results have appeared from woman suffrage and that office-holding by women is "risky."

All these arguments sound today ancient. If we turn to easily available statistics we find that instead of the women of this country or of any other country being confined chiefly to child-bearing they are as a matter of fact engaged and engaged successfully in practically every pursuit in which men are engaged. The actual work of the world today depends more largely upon women than upon men. Consequently this man-ruled world faces an astonishing dilemma: either Woman the Worker is doing the world's work successfully or not. If she is not doing it well why do we not take from her the necessity of working? If she is doing it well why not treat her as a worker with a voice in the direction of work?

The statement that woman is weaker than man is sheer rot: It is the same sort of thing that we hear about "darker races" and "lower classes." Difference, either physical or spiritual, does not argue weakness or inferiority. That the

From *The Crisis*, November 1915.

average woman is spiritually different from the average man is undoubtedly just as true as the fact that the average white man differs from the average Negro; but this is no reason for disfranchising the Negro or lynching him. It is inconceivable that any person looking upon the accomplishments of women today in every field of endeavor, realizing their humiliating handicap and the astonishing prejudices which they face and yet seeing despite this that in government, in the professions, in sciences, art and literature and the industries they are leading and dominating forces and growing in power as their emancipation grows, — it is inconceivable that any fair-minded person could for a moment talk about a "weaker" sex. The sex of Judith, Candace, Queen Elizabeth, Sojourner Truth and Jane Addams was the merest incident of human function and not a mark of weakness and inferiority.

To say that men protect women with their votes is to overlook the flat testimony of the facts. In the first place there are millions of women who have no natural men protectors: the unmarried, the widowed, the deserted and those who have married failures. To put this whole army incontinently out of court and leave them unprotected and without voice in political life is more than unjust, it is a crime.

There was a day in the world when it was considered that by marriage a woman lost all her individuality as a human soul and simply became a machine for making men. We have outgrown that idea. A woman is just as much a thinking, feeling, acting person after marriage as before. She has opinions and she has a right to have them and she has a right to express them. It is conceivable, of course, for a country to decide that its unit of representation should be the family and that one person in that family should express its will. But by what possible process of rational thought can it be decided that the person to express that will should always be the male, whether he be genius or drunkard, imbecile or captain of industry? The meaning of the twentieth century is the freeing of the individual soul; the soul longest in slavery and still in the most disgusting and indefensible slavery is the soul of womanhood. God give her increased freedom this November! . . .

The Damnation of Women

I remember four women of my boyhood: my mother, cousin Inez, Emma, and Ide Fuller. They represented the problem of the widow, the wife, the maiden, and the outcast. They were, in color, brown and light-brown, yellow with brown freckles, and white. They existed not for themselves, but for men; they were named after the men to whom they were related and not after the fashion of their own souls.

They were not beings, they were relations and these relations were enfilmed with mystery and secrecy. We did not know the truth or believe it when we heard it. Motherhood! What was it? We did not know or greatly care. My mother and I were good chums. I liked her. After she was dead I loved her with a fierce sense of personal loss.

Inez was a pretty, brown cousin who married. What was marriage? We did not know, neither did she, poor thing! It came to mean for her a litter of children, poverty, a drunken, cruel companion, sickness, and death. Why?

There was no sweeter sight than Emma—slim, straight, and dainty, darkly flushed with the passion of youth; but her life was a wild, awful struggle to crush her natural, fierce joy of love. She crushed it and became a cold, calculating mockery.

Last there was that awful outcast of the town, the white woman, Ide Fuller. What she was, we did not know. She stood to us as embodied filth and wrong—but whose filth, whose wrong?

Grown up I see the problem of these women transfused; I hear all about me the unanswered call of youthful love, none the less glorious because of its clean, honest, physical passion. Why unanswered? Because the youth are too poor to marry or if they marry, too poor to have children. They turn aside, then, in three directions: to marry for support, to what men call shame, or to that which is more evil than nothing. It is an unendurable paradox; it must be changed or the bases of culture will totter and fall.

From *Darkwater: Voices from Within the Veil* (1920).

The world wants healthy babies and intelligent workers. Today we refuse to allow the combination and force thousands of intelligent workers to go childless at a horrible expenditure of moral force, or we damn them if they break our idiotic conventions. Only at the sacrifice of intelligence and the chance to do their best work can the majority of modern women bear children. This is the damnation of women.

All womanhood is hampered today because the world on which it is emerging is a world that tries to worship both virgins and mothers and in the end despises motherhood and despoils virgins.

The future woman must have a life work and economic independence. She must have knowledge. She must have the right of motherhood at her own discretion. The present mincing horror at free womanhood must pass if we are ever to be rid of the bestiality of free manhood; not by guarding the weak in weakness do we gain strength, but by making weakness free and strong.

The world must choose the free woman or the white wraith of the prostitute. Today it wavers between the prostitute and the nun. Civilization must show two things: the glory and beauty of creating life and the need and duty of power and intelligence. This and this only will make the perfect marriage of love and work.

> God is Love,
> Love is God;
> There is no God but Love
> And Work is His Prophet!

All this of woman — but what of black women?

The world that wills to worship womankind studiously forgets its darker sisters. They seem in a sense to typify that veiled Melancholy:

> Whose saintly visage is too bright
> To hit the sense of human sight,
> And, therefore, to our weaker view
> O'er-laid with black.

Yet the world must heed these daughters of sorrow, from the primal black All-Mother of men down through the ghostly throng of mighty womanhood, who walked in the mysterious dawn of Asia and Africa; from Neith, the primal mother of all, whose feet rest on hell, and whose almighty hands uphold the heavens; all religion, from beauty to beast, lies on her eager breasts; her body bears the stars, while her shoulders are necklaced by the dragon; from black Neith down to

That starr'd Ethiop queen who strove
To set her beauty's praise above
The sea-nymphs

through dusky Cleopatras, dark Candaces, and darker, fiercer Zinghas, to our own day and our own land — in gentle Phillis; Harriet, the crude Moses; the sibyl, Sojourner Truth; and the martyr, Louise De Mortie.

The father and his worship is Asia; Europe is the precocious, self-centered, forward-striving child; but the land of the mother is and was Africa. In subtle and mysterious way, despite her curious history, her slavery, polygamy, and toil, the spell of the African mother pervades her land. Isis, the mother, is still titular goddess, in thought if not in name, of the dark continent. Nor does this all seem to be solely a survival of the historic matriarchate through which all nations pass — it appears to be more than this — as if the great black race in passing up the steps of human culture gave the world, not only the Iron Age, the cultivation of the soil, and the domestication of animals, but also, in peculiar emphasis, the mother-idea.

"No mother can love more tenderly and none is more tenderly loved than the Negro mother," writes Schneider. Robin tells of the slave who bought his mother's freedom instead of his own. Mungo Park writes: "Everywhere in Africa, I have noticed that no greater affront can be offered a Negro than insulting his mother. 'Strike me,' cries a Mandingo to his enemy, 'but revile not my mother!' " And the Krus and Fantis say the same. The peoples on the Zambezi and the great lakes cry in sudden fear or joy: "O, my mother!" And the Herero swear (endless oath) "By my mother's tears!" "As the mist in the swamps," cries the Angola Negro, "so lives the love of father and mother."

A student of the present Gold Coast life describes the work of the village headman, and adds: "It is a difficult task that he is set to, but in this matter he has all-powerful helpers in the female members of the family, who will be either the aunts or the sisters or the cousins or the nieces of the headman, and as their interests are identical with his in every particular, the good women spontaneously train up their children to implicit obedience to the headman, whose rule in the family thus becomes a simple and an easy matter. 'The hand that rocks the cradle rules the world.' What a power for good in the native state system would the mothers of the Gold Coast and Ashanti become by judicious training upon native lines!"

Schweinfurth declares of one tribe: "A bond between mother and child which lasts for life is the measure of affection shown among the Dyoor" and Ratzel adds:

"Agreeable to the natural relation the mother stands first among the chief influences affecting the children. From the Zulus to the Waganda, we find the mother the most influential counsellor at the court of ferocious sovereigns, like Chaka or Mtesa; sometimes sisters take her place. Thus even with chiefs who possess wives by hundreds the bonds of blood are the strongest and that the woman, though often heavily burdened, is in herself held in no small esteem among the Negroes is clear from the numerous Negro queens, from the medicine women, from the participation in public meetings permitted to women by many Negro peoples."

As I remember through memories of others, backward among my own family, it is the mother I ever recall — the little, far-off mother of my grandmothers, who sobbed her life away in song, longing for her lost palm-trees and scented waters; the tall and bronzen grandmother, with beaked nose and shrewish eyes, who loved and scolded her black and laughing husband as he smoked lazily in his high oak chair; above all, my own mother, with all her soft brownness — the brown velvet of her skin, the sorrowful black-brown of her eyes, and the tiny brown-capped waves of her midnight hair as it lay new parted on her forehead. All the way back in these dim distances it is mothers and mothers of mothers who seem to count, while fathers are shadowy memories.

Upon this African mother-idea, the westward slave trade and American slavery struck like doom. In the cruel exigencies of the traffic in men and in the sudden, unprepared emancipation the great pendulum of social equilibrium swung from a time, in 1800 — when America had but eight or less black women to every ten black men — all too swiftly to a day, in 1870 — when there were nearly eleven women to ten men in our Negro population. This was but the outward numerical fact of social dislocation; within lay polygamy, polyandry, concubinage, and moral degradation. They fought against all this desperately, did these black slaves in the West Indies, especially among the half-free artisans; they set up their ancient household gods, and when Toussaint and Cristophe founded their kingdom in Haiti, it was based on old African tribal ties and beneath it was the mother-idea.

The crushing weight of slavery fell on black women. Under it there was no legal marriage, no legal family, no legal control over children. To be sure, custom and religion replaced here and there what the law denied, yet one has but to read advertisements like the following to see the hell beneath the system:

One hundred dollars reward will be given for my two fellows, Abram and Frank. Abram has a wife at Colonel Stewart's, in Liberty County, and a mother at Thunderbolt, and a sister in Savannah.

"WILLIAM ROBERTS."

Fifty dollars reward — Ran away from the subscriber a Negro girl named Maria. She is of a copper color, between thirteen and fourteen years of age — bare-headed and barefooted. She is small for her age — very sprightly and very likely. She stated she was going to see her mother at Maysville.

"SANFORD THOMSON."

Fifty dollars reward — Ran away from the subscriber his Negro man Paula-dore, commonly called Paul. I understand General R. Y. Hayne has pur-chased his wife and children from H. L. Pinckney, Esq., and has them now on his plantation at Goose Creek, where, no doubt, the fellow is frequently lurking.

"T. DAVIS."

The Presbyterian synod of Kentucky said to the churches under its care in 1835: "Brothers and sisters, parents and children, husbands and wives, are torn asunder and permitted to see each other no more. These acts are daily occurring in the midst of us. The shrieks and agony often witnessed on such occasions proclaim, with a trumpet tongue, the iniquity of our system. There is not a neighborhood where these heart-rending scenes are not displayed. There is not a village or road that does not behold the sad procession of manacled outcasts whose mournful countenances tell that they are exiled by force from all that their hearts hold dear."

A sister of a president of the United States declared: "We Southern ladies are complimented with the names of wives, but we are only the mistresses of seraglios."

Out of this, what sort of black women could be born into the world of today? There are those who hasten to answer this query in scathing terms and who say lightly and repeatedly that out of black slavery came nothing decent in womanhood; that adultery and uncleanness were their heritage and are their continued portion.

Fortunately so exaggerated a charge is humanly impossible of truth. The half-million women of Negro descent who lived at the beginning of the 19th century had become the mothers of two and one-fourth million daughters at the time of the Civil War and five million granddaughters in 1910. Can all these women be vile and the hunted race continue to grow in wealth and character? Impossible. Yet to save from the past the shreds and vestiges of self-respect has been a terrible task. I most sincerely doubt if any other race of women could have brought its fineness up through so devilish a fire.

Alexander Crummell once said of his sister in the blood: "In her girlhood all the delicate tenderness of her sex has been rudely outraged. In the field, in the rude cabin, in the press-room, in the factory she was thrown into the companionship of coarse and ignorant men. No chance was given her for delicate reserve or tender modesty. From her childhood she was the doomed victim of the grossest passion. All the virtues of her sex were utterly ignored. If the instinct of chastity asserted itself, then she had to fight like a tiger for the ownership and possession of her own person and ofttimes had to suffer pain and lacerations for her virtuous self-assertion. When she reached maturity, all the tender instincts of her womanhood were ruthlessly violated. At the age of marriage — always prematurely anticipated under slavery — she was mated as the stock of the plantation were mated, not to be the companion of a loved and chosen husband, but to be the breeder of human cattle for the field or the auction block."

Down in such mire has the black motherhood of this race struggled — starving its own wailing offspring to nurse to the world their swaggering masters; welding for its children chains which affronted even the moral sense of an unmoral world. Many a man and woman in the South has lived in wedlock as holy as Adam and Eve and brought forth their brown and golden children, but because the darker woman was helpless, her chivalrous and whiter mate could cast her off at his pleasure and publicly sneer at the body he had privately blasphemed.

I shall forgive the white South much in its final judgment day: I shall forgive its slavery, for slavery is a world-old habit; I shall forgive its fighting for a well-lost cause, and for remembering that struggle with tender tears; I shall forgive its so-called "pride of race," the passion of its hot blood, and even its dear, old, laughable strutting and posing; but one thing I shall never forgive, neither in this world nor the world to come: its wanton and continued and persistent insulting of the black womanhood which it sought and seeks to prostitute to its lust. I cannot forget that it is such Southern gentlemen into whose hands smug Northern hypocrites of today are seeking to place our women's eternal destiny — men who insist upon withholding from my mother and wife and daughter those signs and appellations of courtesy and respect which elsewhere he withholds only from bawds and courtesans.

The result of this history of insult and degradation has been both fearful and glorious. It has birthed the haunting prostitute, the brawler, and the beast of burden; but it has also given the world an efficient womanhood, whose strength lies in its freedom and whose chastity was won in the teeth of temptation and not in prison and swaddling clothes.

To no modern race does its women mean so much as to the Negro nor come so near to the fulfillment of its meaning. As one of our women writes: "Only the black woman can say 'when and where I enter, in the quiet, undisputed dignity of my womanhood, without violence and without suing or special patronage, then and there the whole Negro race enters with me.'"

They came first, in earlier days, like foam flashing on dark, silent waters — bits of stern, dark womanhood here and there tossed almost carelessly aloft to the world's notice. First and naturally they assumed the panoply of the ancient African mother of men, strong and black, whose very nature beat back the wilderness of oppression and contempt. Such a one was that cousin of my grandmother, whom western Massachusetts remembers as "Mum Bett." Scarred for life by a blow received in defense of a sister, she ran away to Great Barrington and was the first slave, or one of the first, to be declared free under the Bill of Rights of 1780. The son of the judge who freed her, writes:

> Even in her humble station, she had, when occasion required it, an air of command which conferred a degree of dignity and gave her an ascendancy over those of her rank, which is very unusual in persons of any rank or color. Her determined and resolute character, which enabled her to limit the ravages of Shays' mob, was manifested in her conduct and deportment during her whole life. She claimed no distinction, but it was yielded to her from her superior experience, energy, skill, and sagacity. Having known this woman as familiarly as I knew either of my parents, I cannot believe in the moral or physical inferiority of the race to which she belonged. The degradation of the African must have been otherwise caused than by natural inferiority.

It was such strong women that laid the foundations of the great Negro church of today, with its five million members and ninety millions of dollars in property. One of the early mothers of the church, Mary Still, writes thus quaintly, in the forties:

> When we were as castouts and spurned from the large churches, driven from our knees, pointed at by the proud, neglected by the careless, without a place of worship, Allen, faithful to the heavenly calling, came forward and laid the foundation of this connection. The women, like the women at the sepulcher, were early to aid in laying the foundation of the temple and in helping to carry up the noble structure and in the name of their God set up their banner; most of our aged mothers are gone from this to a better state of things. Yet some linger still on their staves, watching with intense interest the ark as it moves over the tempestuous waves of opposition and ignorance. . . .
>
> But the labors of these women stopped not here, for they knew well that they were subject to affliction and death. For the purpose of mutual aid, they banded themselves together in society capacity, that they might be

better able to administer to each others' sufferings and to soften their own pillows. So we find the females in the early history of the church abounding in good works and in acts of true benevolence.

From such spiritual ancestry came two striking figures of war-time — Harriet Tubman and Sojourner Truth.

For eight or ten years previous to the breaking out of the Civil War, Harriet Tubman was a constant attendant at anti-slavery conventions, lectures, and other meetings; she was a black woman of medium size, smiling countenance, with her upper front teeth gone, attired in coarse but neat clothes, and carrying always an old-fashioned reticule at her side. Usually as soon as she sat down she would drop off in sound sleep.

She was born a slave in Maryland, in 1820, bore the marks of the lash on her flesh; and had been made partially deaf, and perhaps to some degree mentally unbalanced by a blow on the head in childhood. Yet she was one of the most important agents of the Underground Railroad and a leader of fugitive slaves. She ran away in 1849 and went to Boston in 1854, where she was welcomed into the homes of the leading abolitionists and where every one listened with tense interest to her strange stories. She was absolutely illiterate, with no knowledge of geography, and yet year after year she penetrated the slave states and personally led North over three hundred fugitives without losing a single one. A standing reward of $10,000 was offered for her, but as she said: "The whites cannot catch us, for I was born with the charm, and the Lord has given me the power." She was one of John Brown's closest advisers and only severe sickness prevented her presence at Harpers Ferry.

When the war cloud broke, she hastened to the front, flitting down along her own mysterious paths, haunting the armies in the field, and serving as guide and nurse and spy. She followed Sherman in his great march to the sea and was with Grant at Petersburg, and always in the camps the Union officers silently saluted her.

The other woman belonged to a different type—a tall, gaunt, black, unsmiling sybil, weighted with the woe of the world. She ran away from slavery and giving up her own name took the name of Sojourner Truth. She says: "I can remember when I was a little, young girl, how my old mammy would sit out of doors in the evenings and look up at the stars and groan, and I would say, 'Mammy, what makes you groan so?' And she would say, 'I am groaning to think of my poor children; they do not know where I be and I don't know where they be. I look up at the stars and they look up at the stars!'"

Her determination was founded on unwavering faith in ultimate good. Wendell Phillips says that he was once in Faneuil Hall, when Frederick Douglass was one of the chief speakers. Douglass had been describing the wrongs of the Negro race and as he proceeded he grew more and more excited and finally ended by saying that they had no hope of justice from the whites, no possible hope except in their own right arms. It must come to blood! They must fight for themselves. Sojourner Truth was sitting, tall and dark, on the very front seat facing the platform, and in the hush of feeling when Douglass sat down she spoke out in her deep, peculiar voice, heard all over the hall: "Frederick, is God dead?"

Such strong, primitive types of Negro womanhood in America seem to some to exhaust its capabilities. They know less of a not more worthy, but a finer type of black woman wherein trembles all of that delicate sense of beauty and striving for self-realization, which is as characteristic of the Negro soul as is its quaint strength and sweet laughter. George Washington wrote in grave and gentle courtesy to a Negro woman, in 1776, that he would "be happy to see" at his headquarters at any time, a person "to whom nature has been so liberal and beneficial in her dispensations." This child, Phillis Wheatley, sang her trite and halting strain to a world that wondered and could not produce her like. Measured today her muse was slight and yet, feeling her striving spirit, we call to her still in her own words:

"Through thickest glooms look back, immortal shade."

Perhaps even higher than strength and art loom human sympathy and sacrifice as characteristic of Negro womanhood. Long years ago, before the Declaration of Independence, Kate Ferguson was born in New York. Freed, widowed, and bereaved of her children before she was twenty, she took the children of the streets of New York, white and black, to her empty arms, taught them, found them homes, and with Dr. Mason of Murray Street Church established the first modern Sunday School in Manhattan.

Sixty years later came Mary Shadd up out of Delaware. She was tall and slim, of that ravishing dream-born beauty — that twilight of the races which we call mulatto. Well-educated, vivacious, with determination shining from her sharp eyes, she threw herself singlehanded into the great Canadian pilgrimage when thousands of hunted black men hurried northward and crept beneath the protection of the lion's paw. She became teacher, editor, and lecturer; tramping afoot through winter snows, pushing without blot or blemish through crowd and turmoil to conventions and meetings, and finally becoming recruiting agent for the United States government in gathering Negro soldiers in the West.

After the war the sacrifice of Negro women for freedom and uplift is one of the finest chapters in their history. Let one life typify all: Louise De Mortie, a free-born Virginia girl, had lived most of her life in Boston. Her high forehead, swelling lips, and dark eyes marked her for a woman of feeling and intellect. She began a successful career as a public reader. Then came the War and the Call. She went to the orphaned colored children of New Orleans — out of freedom into insult and oppression and into the teeth of the yellow fever. She toiled and dreamed. In 1887 she had raised money and built an orphan home and that same year, in the thirty-fourth of her young life, she died, saying simply: "I belong to God."

As I look about me today in this veiled world of mine, despite the noisier and more spectacular advance of my brothers, I instinctively feel and know that it is the five million women of my race who really count. Black women (and women whose grandmothers were black) are today furnishing our teachers; they are the main pillars of those social settlements which we call churches; and they have with small doubt raised three-fourths of our church property. If we have today, as seems likely, over a billion dollars of accumulated goods, who shall say how much of it has been wrung from the hearts of servant girls and washerwomen and women toilers in the fields? As makers of two million homes these women are today seeking in marvelous ways to show forth our strength and beauty and our conception of the truth.

In the United States in 1910 there were 4,931,882 women of Negro descent; over twelve hundred thousand of these were children, another million were girls and young women under twenty, and two and a half-million were adults. As a mass these women were unlettered — a fourth of those from fifteen to twenty-five years of age were unable to write. These women are passing through, not only a moral, but an economic revolution. Their grandmothers married at twelve and fifteen, but twenty-seven per cent of these women today who have passed fifteen are still single.

Yet these black women toil and toil hard. There were in 1910 two and a half million Negro homes in the United States. Out of these homes walked daily to work two million women and girls over ten years of age — over half of the colored female population as against a fifth in the case of white women. These, then, are a group of workers, fighting for their daily bread like men; independent and approaching economic freedom! They furnished a million farm laborers, 80,000 farmers, 22,000 teachers, 600,000 servants and washerwomen, and 50,000 in trades and merchandizing.

The family group, however, which is the ideal of the culture with which these folk have been born, is not based on the idea of an economically independent working mother. Rather its ideal harks back to the sheltered harem with the mother emerging at first as nurse and homemaker, while the man remains the sole breadwinner. What is the inevitable result of the clash of such ideals and such facts in the colored group? Broken families.

Among native white women one in ten is separated from her husband by death, divorce, or desertion. Among Negroes the ratio is one in seven. Is the cause racial? No, it is economic, because there is the same high ratio among the white foreign-born. The breaking up of the present family is the result of modern working and sex conditions and it hits the laborers with terrible force. The Negroes are put in a peculiarly difficult position, because the wage of the male breadwinner is below the standard, while the openings for colored women in certain lines of domestic work, and now in industries, are many. Thus while toil holds the father and brother in country and town at low wages, the sisters and mothers are called to the city. As a result the Negro women outnumber the men nine or ten to eight in many cities, making what Charlotte Gilman bluntly calls "cheap women."

What shall we say to this new economic equality in a great laboring class? Some people within and without the race deplore it. "Back to the homes with the women," they cry, "and higher wage for the men." But how impossible this is has been shown by war conditions. Cessation of foreign migration has raised Negro men's wages, to be sure — but it has not only raised Negro women's wages, it has opened to them a score of new avenues of earning a living. Indeed, here, in microcosm and with differences emphasizing sex equality, is the industrial history of labor in the 19th and 20th centuries. We cannot abolish the new economic freedom of women. We cannot imprison women again in a home or require them all on pain of death to be nurses and housekeepers.

What is today the message of these black women to America and to the world? The uplift of women is, next to the problem of the color line and the peace movement, our greatest modern cause. When, now, two of these movements — woman and color — combine in one, the combination has deep meaning.

In other years women's way was clear: to be beautiful, to be petted, to bear children. Such has been their theoretic destiny and if perchance they have been ugly, hurt, and barren, that has been forgotten with studied silence. In partial compensation for this narrowed destiny the white world has lavished its politeness on its womankind — its chivalry and bows, its uncoverings and courtesies — all the accumulated homage disused for courts and kings and craving exercise. The revolt of white women against this preordained destiny has in these latter days reached splendid proportions, but it is the revolt of an aristocracy of brains and ability — the middle class and rank and file still plod on in the appointed path, paid by the homage, the almost mocking homage, of men.

From black women of America, however, (and from some others, too, but chiefly from black women and their daughters' daughters) this gauze has been withheld and without semblance of such apology they have been frankly trodden under the feet of men. They are and have been objected to, apparently for reasons peculiarly exasperating to reasoning human beings. When in this world a man comes forward with a thought, a deed, a vision, we ask not, how does he look—but what is his message? It is of but passing interest whether or not the messenger is beautiful or ugly—the *message* is the thing. This, which is axiomatic among men, has been in past ages but partially true if the messenger was a woman. The world still wants to ask that a woman primarily be pretty and if she is not, the mob pouts and asks querulously, "What else are women for?" Beauty "is its own excuse for being," but there are other excuses, as most men know, and when the white world objects to black women because it does not consider them beautiful, the black world of right asks two questions: "What is beauty?" and, "Suppose you think them ugly, what then? If ugliness and unconventionality and eccentricity of face and deed do not hinder men from doing the world's work and reaping the world's reward, why should it hinder women?"

Other things being equal, all of us, black and white, would prefer to be beautiful in face and form and suitably clothed; but most of us are not so, and one of the mightiest revolts of the century is against the devilish decree that no woman is a woman who is not by present standards a beautiful woman. This decree the black women of America have in large measure escaped from the first. Not being expected to be merely ornamental, they have girded themselves for work, instead of adorning their bodies only for play. Their sturdier minds have concluded that if a woman be clean, healthy, and educated, she is as pleasing as God wills and far more useful than most of her sisters. If in addition to this she is pink and white and straight-haired, and some of her fellow-men prefer this, well and good; but if she is black or brown and crowned in curled mists (and this to us is the most beautiful thing on earth), this is surely the flimsiest excuse for spiritual incarceration or banishment.

The very attempt to do this in the case of Negro Americans has strangely over-reached itself. By so much as the defective eyesight of the white world rejects black women as beauties, by so much the more it needs them as human beings—an enviable alternative, as many a white woman knows. Consequently, for black women alone, as a group, "handsome is that handsome does" and they are asked to be no more beautiful than God made them, but they are asked to be efficient, to be strong, fertile, muscled, and able to work. If they marry, they must as independent workers be able to help support their children, for their men are paid on a scale which makes sole support of the family often impossible.

On the whole, colored working women are paid as well as white working women for similar work, save in some higher grades, while colored men get from one-fourth to three-fourths less than white men. The result is curious and three-fold: the economic independence of black women is increased, the breaking up of Negro families must be more frequent, and the number of illegitimate children is decreased more slowly among them than other evidences of culture are increased, just as was once true in Scotland and Bavaria.

What does this mean? It forecasts a mighty dilemma which the whole world of civilization, despite its will, must one time frankly face: the unhusbanded mother or the childless wife. God send us a world with woman's freedom and married motherhood inextricably wed, but until He sends it, I see more of future promise in the betrayed girl-mothers of the black belt than in the childless wives of the white North, and I have more respect for the colored servant who yields to her frank longing for motherhood than for her white sister who offers up children for clothes. Out of a sex freedom that today makes us shudder will come in time a day when we will no longer pay men for work they do not do, for the sake of their harem; we will pay women what they earn and insist on their working and earning it; we will allow those persons to vote who know enough to vote, whether they be black or female, white or male; and we will ward [off] race suicide, not by further burdening the over-burdened, but by honoring motherhood, even when the sneaking father shirks his duty.

"Wait till the lady passes," said a Nashville white boy.

"She's no lady; she's a nigger," answered another.

So some few women are born free, and some amid insult and scarlet letters achieve freedom; but our women in black had freedom thrust contemptuously upon them. With that freedom they are buying an untrammeled independence and dear as is the price they pay for it, it will in the end be worth every taunt and groan. Today the dreams of the mothers are coming true. We have still our poverty and degradation, our lewdness and our cruel toil; but we have, too, a vast group of women of Negro blood who for strength of character, cleanness of soul, and unselfish devotion of purpose, is today easily the peer of any group of women in the civilized world. And more than that, in the great rank and file of our five million women we have the up-working of new revolutionary ideals, which must in time have vast influence on the thought and action of this land.

For this, their promise, and for their hard past, I honor the women of my race. Their beauty—their dark and mysterious beauty of midnight eyes, crumpled hair, and soft, full-featured faces—is perhaps more to me than to you, because I was born to its warm and subtle spell; but their worth is yours as well as mine. No other women on earth could have emerged from the hell of force and temptation which once engulfed and still surrounds black women in America with half the modesty and womanliness that they retain. I have always felt like bowing myself before them in all abasement, searching to bring some tribute to these long-suffering victims, these burdened sisters of mine, whom the world, the wise, white world, loves to affront and ridicule and wantonly to insult. I have known the women of many lands and nations — I have known and seen and lived beside them, but none have I known more sweetly feminine, more unswervingly loyal, more desperately earnest, and more instinctively pure in body and in soul than the daughters of my black mothers. This, then — a little thing — to their memory and inspiration.

Sex and Racism

As Mr. Mailer says, sex jealousy between races and classes is to blame for much of their friction. But I am inclined to place the chief blame for race friction in the South on the respectable white Southerners of impeccable morals, education and high social position, who for a hundred years have been silent or tacitly consenting to beliefs and measures which they knew were wrong and destructive.

There were Southerners of light and learning before the Civil War who knew that slavery was wrong and wasteful and yet were silent or blamed Abolitionists.

When for four awful years this nation murdered 500,000 human beings because the South was determined to preserve human slavery, the best brain and morality of the white South has for ninety years taught their children, told the world to set down in art and history, that slavery was not the cause of the war and that the Confederacy was a holy crusade for Freedom.

When for two generations, white mobs mobbed and lynched thousands of black victims convicted of no crime, it was well-nigh impossible to find a Southerner of high social standing who protested this barbarism; on the contrary most of them declared that lynching was necessary for the protection of white womanhood and that the preservation of the white family depended on the degradation and insult of black women; and that unless black girls could be seduced without penalty, white civilization was in danger.

The educated and decent leaders of the white South knew this was a lie; but thousands of ignorant and untrained Southerners took this as the word of God.

While the world was beginning to realize that in all essentials, black folk were equal to white, in our South, the leaders of public opinion, supinely or openly in sermon and lecture, in book and paper, in home and school let two generations of young whites grow up to believe that white people were so

From *The Independent*, March 1957, p. 6.

inherently and eternally superior to blacks, that to eat, sit, live or learn beside them was absolute degradation.

When in the last few years that which the Declaration of Independence proclaimed in 1776, could no longer be dodged and denied by the courts without confessing our sham democracy to the whole world; when the Supreme Court got the guts to say what every rational American knew, that segregation by race was unconstitutional, then the white South and much of the nation pretend to be vastly astonished because hoodlums and backwoodsmen, cheap politicians and grafters continue to follow the long leading of their ministers, lawyers, writers and social elite and refuse to obey the Supreme Court, the United Nations or the voice of humanity if they dare assert that Southern civilization does not require the Negro as a doormat for its dirty feet as it rises to world leadership.

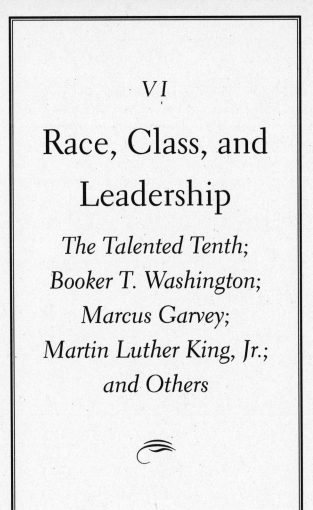

VI

Race, Class, and Leadership

The Talented Tenth;
Booker T. Washington;
Marcus Garvey;
Martin Luther King, Jr.;
and Others

With the 1903 publication of "Of Mr. Booker T. Washington and Others" in *The Souls of Black Folk* and the even more uncompromising "The Parting of the Ways" the next year, Du Bois became the recognized spokesperson for those African-Americans disillusioned with the leadership monopoly of the principal of Tuskegee Institute. Those who opposed the so-called Tuskegee Machine quickly became known as members of the "Talented Tenth," the group of mostly Northern and well-educated African-American professional men and women first identified by Du Bois in a 1900 essay. Although Booker T. Washington's demise (1915) and the nationwide consolidation by the end of the First World War of the new National Association for the Advancement of Colored People (NAACP) secured the helm of racial leadership for Du Bois and the Talented Tenth, their position was soon to be aggressively contested by Marcus Mosiah Garvey and his dynamic Universal Negro Improvement Association (UNIA). This contest for the hearts, minds, and purses of millions of working-class African-Americans resulted in several vitriolic editorials and essays, of which Du Bois's "Back to Africa" (1923) and "A Lunatic or a Traitor" (1924) are examples. The 1943 op-ed "Leadership Is Vital" commended the principled though different modes of civil rights protest embodied in the labor leadership of A. Philip Randolph and the federal service of William H. Hastie. With the end of the Second World War, Du Bois's disappointment with the *embourgeoisement* of the black middle class caused him to embrace ever more radical conceptions of leadership ("The Talented Tenth: Memorial Address" [1948] and "The Present Leadership of American Negroes" [1957]). By the end of the 1950s, he concluded that Martin Luther King, Jr.'s nonviolent passive resistance was a fraudulent copy of Gandhi's resistance to British imperialism ("Crusader Without Violence" [1959]).

317

Of Mr. Booker T. Washington
and Others

Easily the most striking thing in the history of the American Negro since 1876 is the ascendancy of Mr. Booker T. Washington. It began at the time when war memories and ideals were rapidly passing; a day of astonishing commercial development was dawning; a sense of doubt and hesitation overtook the freedmen's sons — then it was that his leading began. Mr. Washington came, with a simple definite programme, at the psychological moment when the nation was a little ashamed of having bestowed so much sentiment on Negroes, and was concentrating its energies on Dollars. His programme of industrial education, conciliation of the South, and submission and silence as to civil and political rights, was not wholly original; the Free Negroes from 1830 up to war-time had striven to build industrial schools, and the American Missionary Association had from the first taught various trades; and Price and others had sought a way of honorable alliance with the best of the Southerners. But Mr. Washington first indissolubly linked these things; he put enthusiasm, unlimited energy, and perfect faith into this programme, and changed it from a by-path into a veritable Way of Life. And the tale of the methods by which he did this is a fascinating study of human life.

It startled the nation to hear a Negro advocating such a programme after many decades of bitter complaint; it startled and won the applause of the South, it interested and won the admiration of the North; and after a confused murmur of protest, it silenced if it did not convert the Negroes themselves.

To gain the sympathy and coöperation of the various elements comprising the white South was Mr. Washington's first task; and this, at the time Tuskegee was founded, seemed, for a black man, well-nigh impossible. And yet ten years later it was done in the word spoken at Atlanta: "In all things purely social we can be as separate as the five fingers, and yet one as the hand in all things

From *The Souls of Black Folk* (1903).

essential to mutual progress." This "Atlanta Compromise" is by all odds the most notable thing in Mr. Washington's career. The South interpreted it in different ways: the radicals received it as a complete surrender of the demand for civil and political equality; the conservatives, as a generously conceived working basis for mutual understanding. So both approved it, and to-day its author is certainly the most distinguished Southerner since Jefferson Davis, and the one with the largest personal following.

Next to this achievement comes Mr. Washington's work in gaining place and consideration in the North. Others less shrewd and tactful had formerly essayed to sit on these two stools and had fallen between them; but as Mr. Washington knew the heart of the South from birth and training, so by singular insight he intuitively grasped the spirit of the age which was dominating the North. . . .

And yet this very singleness of vision and thorough oneness with his age are a mark of the successful man. It is as though Nature must needs make men narrow in order to give them force. So Mr. Washington's cult has gained unquestioning followers, his work has wonderfully prospered, his friends are legion, and his enemies are confounded. To-day he stands as the one recognized spokesman of his ten million fellows, and one of the most notable figures in a nation of seventy millions. One hesitates, therefore, to criticise a life which, beginning with so little, has done so much. And yet the time is come when one may speak in all sincerity and utter courtesy of the mistakes and shortcomings of Mr. Washington's career, as well as of his triumphs, without being thought captious or envious, and without forgetting that it is easier to do ill than well in the world.

The criticism that has hitherto met Mr. Washington has not always been of this broad character. In the South especially has he had to walk warily to avoid the harshest judgments — and naturally so, for he is dealing with the one subject of deepest sensitiveness to that section. Twice — once when at the Chicago celebration of the Spanish-American War he alluded to the color-prejudice that is "eating away the vitals of the South," and once when he dined with President Roosevelt — has the resulting Southern criticism been violent enough to threaten seriously his popularity. In the North the feeling has several times forced itself into words, that Mr. Washington's counsels of submission overlooked certain elements of true manhood, and that his educational programme was unnecessarily narrow. Usually, however, such criticism has not found open expression, although, too, the spiritual sons of the Abolitionists have not been prepared to acknowledge that the schools founded before Tuskegee, by men of broad ideals and self-sacrificing spirit, were wholly failures or worthy of ridicule. While, then, criticism has not failed to follow Mr. Washington, yet the prevailing public opinion of the land has been but too willing to deliver the solution of a wearisome problem into his hands, and say, "If that is all you and your race ask, take it."

Among his own people, however, Mr. Washington has encountered the strongest and most lasting opposition, amounting at times to bitterness, and even to-day continuing strong and insistent even though largely silenced in outward expression by the public opinion of the nation. . . .

But the hushing of the criticism of honest opponents is a dangerous thing. It leads some of the best of the critics to unfortunate silence and paralysis of effort, and others to burst into speech so passionately and intemperately as to lose listeners. . . .

Now in the past the American Negro has had instructive experience in the choosing of group leaders, founding thus a peculiar dynasty which in the light of present conditions is worth while studying. When sticks and stones and beasts form the sole environment of a people, their attitude is largely one of determined opposition to and conquest of natural forces. But when to earth and brute is added an environment of men and ideas, then the attitude of the imprisoned group may take three main forms—a feeling of revolt and revenge; an attempt to adjust all thought and action to the will of the greater group; or, finally, a determined effort at self-realization and self-development despite environing opinion. The influence of all of these attitudes at various times can be traced in the history of the American Negro, and in the evolution of his successive leaders.

Before 1750, while the fire of African freedom still burned in the veins of the slaves, there was in all leadership or attempted leadership but the one motive of revolt and revenge—typified in the terrible Maroons, the Danish blacks, and Cato of Stono, and veiling all the Americas in fear of insurrection. The liberalizing tendencies of the latter half of the eighteenth century brought, along with kindlier relations between black and white, thoughts of ultimate adjustment and assimilation. Such aspiration was especially voiced in the earnest songs of Phyllis, in the martyrdom of Attucks, the fighting of Salem and Poor, the intellectual accomplishments of Banneker and Derham, and the political demands of the Cuffes.

Stern financial and social stress after the war cooled much of the previous humanitarian ardor. The disappointment and impatience of the Negroes at the persistence of slavery and serfdom voiced itself in two movements. The slaves in the South, aroused undoubtedly by vague rumors of the Haytian revolt, made three fierce attempts at insurrection—in 1800 under Gabriel in Virginia, in 1822 under Vesey in Carolina, and in 1831 again in Virginia under the terrible Nat Turner. In the Free States, on the other hand, a new and curious attempt at self-development was made. In Philadelphia and New York color-prescription led to a withdrawal of Negro communicants from white churches and the formation of a peculiar socio-religious institution among the Negroes known as the African Church — an organization still living and controlling in its various branches over a million of men.

Walker's wild appeal against the trend of the times showed how the world was changing after the coming of the cotton-gin. By 1830 slavery seemed hopelessly fastened on the South, and the slaves thoroughly cowed into submission. The free Negroes of the North, inspired by the mulatto immigrants from the West Indies, began to change the basis of their demands; they recognized the slavery of slaves, but insisted that they themselves were freemen, and sought assimilation and amalgamation with the nation on the same terms with other men. Thus, Forten and Purvis of Philadelphia, Shad of Wilmington, Du Bois of New Haven, Barbadoes of Boston, and others, strove singly and together as men, they said, not as slaves; as "people of color," not as "Negroes." The trend of the times, however, refused them recognition save in individual and exceptional cases, considered them as one with all the despised blacks, and they soon found themselves striving to keep even the rights they formerly had of voting and working and moving as freemen. Schemes of migration and colonization arose among them; but these they refused to entertain, and they eventually turned to the Abolition movement as a final refuge.

Here, led by Remond, Nell, Wells-Brown, and Douglass, a new period of self-assertion and self-development dawned. To be sure, ultimate freedom and assimilation were the ideal before the leaders, but the assertion of the manhood rights of the Negro by himself was the main reliance, and John Brown's raid was the extreme of its logic. After the war and emancipation, the great form of Frederick Douglass, the greatest of American Negro leaders, still led the host. Self-assertion, especially in political lines, was the main programme, and behind Douglass came Elliot, Bruce, and Langston, and the Reconstruction politicians, and, less conspicuous but of greater social significance Alexander Crummell and Bishop Daniel Payne.

Then came the Revolution of 1876, the suppression of the Negro votes, the changing and shifting of ideals, and the seeking of new lights in the great night. Douglass, in his old age, still bravely stood for the ideals of his early manhood — ultimate assimilation *through* self-assertion, and on no other terms. For a time Price arose as a new leader, destined, it seemed, not to give up, but to re-state the old ideals in a form less repugnant to the white South. But he passed away in his prime. Then came the new leader. Nearly all the former ones had become leaders by the silent suffrage of their fellows, had sought to lead their own people alone, and were usually, save Douglass, little known outside their race. But Booker T. Washington arose as essentially the leader not of one race but of two — a compromiser between the South, the

North, and the Negro. Naturally the Negroes resented, at first bitterly, signs of compromise which surrendered their civil and political rights, even though this was to be exchanged for larger chances of economic development. The rich and dominating North, however, was not only weary of the race problem, but was investing largely in Southern enterprises, and welcomed any method of peaceful coöperation. Thus, by national opinion, the Negroes began to recognize Mr. Washington's leadership; and the voice of criticism was hushed.

Mr. Washington represents in Negro thought the old attitude of adjustment and submission; but adjustment at such a peculiar time as to make his programme unique. This is an age of unusual economic development, and Mr. Washington's programme naturally takes an economic cast, becoming a gospel of Work and Money to such an extent as apparently almost completely to overshadow the higher aims of life. Moreover, this is an age when the more advanced races are coming in closer contact with the less developed races, and the race-feeling is therefore intensified; and Mr. Washington's programme practically accepts the alleged inferiority of the Negro races. Again, in our own land, the reaction from the sentiment of war-time has given impetus to race-prejudice against Negroes, and Mr. Washington withdraws many of the high demands of Negroes as men and American citizens. In other periods of intensified prejudice all the Negro's tendency to self-assertion has been called forth; at this period a policy of submission is advocated. In the history of nearly all other races and peoples the doctrine preached at such crises has been that manly self-respect is worth more than lands and houses, and that a people who voluntarily surrender such respect, or cease striving for it, are not worth civilizing.

In answer to this, it has been claimed that the Negro can survive only through submission. Mr. Washington distinctly asks that black people give up, at least for the present, three things —

First, political power,

Second, insistence on civil rights,

Third, higher education of Negro youth —

and concentrate all their energies on industrial education, the accumulation of wealth, and the conciliation of the South. This policy has been courageously and insistently advocated for over fifteen years, and has been triumphant for perhaps ten years. As a result of this tender of the palm-branch, what has been the return? In these years there have occurred:

1. The disfranchisement of the Negro.
2. The legal creation of a distinct status of civil inferiority for the Negro.

3. The steady withdrawal of aid from institutions for the higher training of the Negro.

These movements are not, to be sure, direct results of Mr. Washington's teachings; but his propaganda has, without a shadow of doubt, helped their speedier accomplishment. The question then comes: Is it possible, and probable, that nine millions of men can make effective progress in economic lines if they are deprived of political rights, made a servile caste, and allowed only the most meagre chance for developing their exceptional men? If history and reason give any distinct answer to these questions, it is an emphatic No. And Mr. Washington thus faces the triple paradox of his career:

1. He is striving nobly to make Negro artisans business men and property-owners; but it is utterly impossible, under modern competitive methods, for workingmen and property-owners to defend their rights and exist without the right of suffrage.

2. He insists on thrift and self-respect, but at the same time counsels a silent submission to civic inferiority such as is bound to sap the manhood of any race in the long run.

3. He advocates common-school and industrial training, and depreciates institutions of higher learning; but neither the Negro common-schools, nor Tuskegee itself, could remain open a day were it not for teachers trained in Negro colleges, or trained by their graduates.

This triple paradox in Mr. Washington's position is the object of criticism by two classes of colored Americans. One class is spiritually descended from Toussaint the Savior, through Gabriel, Vesey, and Turner, and they represent the attitude of revolt and revenge; they hate the white South blindly and distrust the white race generally, and so far as they agree on definite action, think that the Negro's only hope lies in emigration beyond the borders of the United States. . . .

The other class of Negroes who cannot agree with Mr. Washington has hitherto said little aloud. . . . Such men feel in conscience bound to ask of this nation three things:

1. The right to vote.
2. Civic equality.
3. The education of youth according to ability.

They acknowledge Mr. Washington's invaluable service in counselling patience and courtesy in such demands; they do not ask that ignorant black men vote when ignorant whites are debarred, or that any reasonable restrictions in the suffrage should not be applied; they know that the low social level of the mass of the race is responsible for much discrimination against it, but they also know, and the nation knows, that relentless color-prejudice is more often a cause than a result of the Negro's degradation, they seek the abatement of this relic of barbarism, and not its systematic encouragement and pampering by all agencies of social power from the Associated Press to the Church of Christ. They advocate, with Mr. Washington, a broad system of Negro common-schools supplemented by thorough industrial training; but they are surprised that a man of Mr. Washington's insight cannot see that no such educational system ever has rested or can rest on any other basis than that of the well-equipped college and university, and they insist that there is a demand for a few such institutions throughout the South to train the best of the Negro youth as teachers, professional men, and leaders.

This group of men honor Mr. Washington for his attitude of conciliation toward the white South; they accept the "Atlanta Compromise" in its broadest interpretation; they recognize, with him, many signs of promise, many men of high purpose and fair judgment, in this section; they know that no easy task has been laid upon a region already tottering under heavy burdens. But, nevertheless, they insist that the way to truth and right lies in straightforward honesty, not in indiscriminate flattery; in praising those of the South who do well and criticising uncompromisingly those who do ill; in taking advantage of the opportunities at hand and urging their fellows to do the same, but at the same time in remembering that only a firm adherence to their higher ideals and aspirations will ever keep those ideals within the realm of possibility. They do not expect that the free right to vote, to enjoy civic rights, and to be educated, will come in a moment; they do not expect to see the bias and prejudices of years disappear at the blast of a trumpet; but they are absolutely certain that the way for a people to gain their reasonable rights is not by voluntarily throwing them away and insisting that they do not want them; that the way for a people to gain respect is not by continually belittling and ridiculing themselves; that, on the contrary, Negroes must insist continually, in season and out of season, that voting is necessary to modern manhood, that color discrimination is barbarism, and that black boys need education as well as white boys.

In failing thus to state plainly and unequivocally the legitimate demands of their people, even at the cost of opposing an honored leader, the thinking classes of American Negroes would shirk a heavy responsibility — a respon-sibility to themselves, a responsibility to the struggling masses, a responsibility to the darker races of men whose future depends so largely on this American experiment, but especially a responsibility to this nation — this common

Fatherland. It is wrong to encourage a man or a people in evil-doing; it is wrong to aid and abet a national crime simply because it is unpopular not to do so. The growing spirit of kindliness and reconciliation between the North and South after the frightful differences of a generation ago ought to be a source of deep congratulation to all, and especially to those whose mistreatment caused the war; but if that reconciliation is to be marked by the industrial slavery and civic death of those same black men, with permanent legislation into a position of inferiority, then those black men, if they are really men, are called upon by every consideration of patriotism and loyalty to oppose such a course by all civilized methods, even though such opposition involves disagreement with Mr. Booker T. Washington. We have no right to sit silently by while the inevitable seeds are sown for a harvest of disaster to our children, black and white.

First, it is the duty of black men to judge the South discriminatingly. The present generation of Southerners are not responsible for the past, and they should not be blindly hated or blamed for it. Furthermore, to no class is the indiscriminate endorsement of the recent course of the South toward Negroes more nauseating than to the best thought of the South. The South is not "solid"; it is a land in the ferment of social change, wherein forces of all kinds are fighting for supremacy; and to praise the ill the South is to-day perpetrating is just as wrong as to condemn the good. Discriminating and broadminded criticism is what the South needs — needs it for the sake of her own white sons and daughters, and for the insurance of robust, healthy mental and moral development.

To-day even the attitude of the Southern whites toward the blacks is not, as so many assume, in all cases the same; the ignorant Southerner hates the Negro, the workingmen fear his competition, the money-makers wish to use him as a laborer, some of the educated see a menace in his upward development, while others — usually the sons of the masters — wish to help him to rise. National opinion has enabled this last class to maintain the Negro common-schools, and to protect the Negro partially in property, life, and limb. Through the pressure of the money-makers, the Negro is in danger of being reduced to semi-slavery, especially in the country districts; the workingmen, and those of the educated who fear the Negro, have united to disfranchise him, and some have urged his deportation; while the passions of the ignorant are easily aroused to lynch and abuse any black man. To praise this intricate whirl of thought and prejudice is nonsense; to inveigh indiscriminately against "the South" is unjust; but to use the same breath in praising Governor Aycock, exposing Senator Morgan, arguing with Mr. Thomas Nelson Page, and denouncing Senator Ben Tillman, is not only sane, but the imperative duty of thinking black men.

It would be unjust to Mr. Washington not to acknowledge that in several instances he has opposed movements in the South which were unjust to the Negro; he sent memorials to the Louisiana and Alabama constitutional conventions, he has spoken against lynching, and in other ways has openly or silently set his influence against sinister schemes and unfortunate happenings. Notwithstanding this, it is equally true to assert that on the whole the distinct impression left by Mr. Washington's propaganda is, first, that the South is justified in its present attitude toward the Negro because of the Negro's degradation; secondly, that the prime cause of the Negro's failure to rise more quickly is his wrong education in the past; and, thirdly, that his future rise depends primarily on his own efforts. Each of these propositions is a dangerous half-truth. The supplementary truths must never be lost sight of: first, slavery and race-prejudice are potent if not sufficient causes of the Negro's position; second, industrial and common-school training were necessarily slow in planting because they had to await the black teachers trained by higher institutions — it being extremely doubtful if any essentially different development was possible, and certainly a Tuskegee was unthinkable before 1880; and, third, while it is a great truth to say that the Negro must strive and strive mightily to help himself, it is equally true that unless his striving be not simply seconded, but rather aroused and encouraged, by the initiative of the richer and wiser environing group, he cannot hope for great success.

In his failure to realize and impress this last point, Mr. Washington is especially to be criticised. His doctrine has tended to make the whites, North and South, shift the burden of the Negro problem to the Negro's shoulders and stand aside as critical and rather pessimistic spectators; when in fact the burden belongs to the nation, and the hands of none of us are clean if we bend not our energies to righting these great wrongs.

The South ought to be led, by candid and honest criticism, to assert her better self and do her full duty to the race she has cruelly wronged and is still wronging. The North — her co-partner in guilt — cannot salve her conscience by plastering it with gold. We cannot settle this problem by diplomacy and suaveness, by "policy" alone. If worse come to worst, can the moral fibre of this country survive the slow throttling and murder of nine millions of men?

The black men of America have a duty to perform, a duty stern and delicate — a forward movement to oppose a part of the work of their greatest leader. So far as Mr. Washington preaches Thrift, Patience, and Industrial Training for the masses, we must hold up his hands and strive with him, rejoicing in his honors and glorying in the strength of this Joshua called of God and of man to lead the headless host. But so far as Mr. Washington apologizes for injustice, North or South, does not rightly value the privilege and duty of voting, belittles the emasculating effects of caste distinctions, and opposes the higher training and ambition of our brighter minds — so far as he, the South, or the Nation, does this — we must unceasingly and firmly oppose them. By every civilized and peaceful method we must strive for the rights which the world accords to men, clinging unwaveringly to those great words which the sons of the Fathers would fain forget: "We hold these truths to be self-evident: That all men are created equal; that they are endowed by their Creator with certain unalienable rights; that among these are life, liberty, and the pursuit of happiness."

The Parting of the Ways

The points upon which American Negroes differ as to their course of action are the following: First, the scope of education; second, the necessity of the right of suffrage; third, the importance of civil rights; fourth, the conciliation of the South; fifth, the future of the race in this country.

The older opinion as built up under the leadership of our great dead, Payne, Crummell, Forten and Douglass, was that the broadest field of education should be opened to black children; that no free citizen of a republic could exist in peace and prosperity without the ballot; that self-respect and proper development of character can only take place under a system of equal civil rights; that every effort should be made to live in peace and harmony with all men, but that even for this great boon no people must willingly or passively surrender their essential rights of manhood; that in future the Negro is destined to become an American citizen with full political and civil rights, and that he must never rest contented until he has achieved this.

Since the death of the leaders of the past there have come mighty changes in the nation. The gospel of money has risen triumphant in church and state and university. The great question which Americans ask to-day is, "What is he worth?" or "What is it worth?" The ideals of human rights are obscured, and the nation has begun to swagger about the world in its useless battleships looking for helpless peoples whom it can force to buy its goods at high prices. This wave of materialism is temporary; it will pass and leave us all ashamed and surprised; but while it is here it strangely maddens and blinds us. Religious periodicals are found in the van yelling for war; peaceful ministers of Christ are leading lynchers; great universities are stuffing their pockets with greenbacks and kicking the little souls of students to make them "move faster" through the courses of study, the end of which is ever *"Etwas schaffen"* and seldom *"Etwas sein."* Yet there are signs of change. Souls long cramped and starved are stretching toward the light. Men are beginning to murmur against

From *World Today* (also known as *Hearst's Magazine*), 6 (April 1904), 521-523.

the lower tendencies and the sound of the Zeitgeist strikes sensitive ears with that harrowing discord which prefigures richer harmony to come.

Meantime an awakening race, seeing American civilization as it is, is strongly moved and naturally misled. They whisper: What is the greatness of the country? Is it not money? Well then, the one end of our education and striving should be moneymaking. The trimmings of life, smatterings of Latin and music and such stuff—let that wait till we are rich. Then as to voting, what is the good of it after all? Politics does not pay as well as the grocery business, and breeds trouble. Therefore get out of politics and let the ballot go. When we are rich we can dabble in politics along with the president of Yale. Then, again the thought arises: What is personal humiliation and the denial of ordinary civil rights compared with a chance to earn a living? Why quarrel with your bread and butter simply because of filthy Jim Crow cars? Earn a living: get rich, and all these things shall be added unto you. Moreover, conciliate your neighbors, because they are more powerful and wealthier, and the price you must pay to earn a living in America is that of humiliation and inferiority.

No one, of course, has voiced this argument quite so flatly and bluntly as I have indicated. It has been expressed rather by the emphasis given industrial and trade teaching, the decrying of suffrage as a manhood right or even necessity, the insistence on great advance among Negroes before there is any recognition of their aspirations, and a tendency to minimize the shortcomings of the South and to emphasize the mistakes and failures of black men. Now, in this there has been just that degree of truth and right which serves to make men forget its untruths. That the shiftless and poor need thrift and skill, that ignorance can not vote intelligently, that duties and rights go hand in hand, and that sympathy and understanding among neighbors is prerequisite to peace and concord, all this is true. Who has ever denied it, or ever will? But from all this does it follow that Negro colleges are not needed, that the right of suffrage is not essential for black men, that equality of civil rights is not the first of rights and that no self-respecting man can agree with the person who insists that he is a dog? Certainly not, all answer.

Yet the plain result of the attitude of mind of those who, in their advocacy of industrial schools, the unimportance of suffrage and civil rights and conciliation, have been significantly silent or evasive as to higher training and the great principle of free self-respecting manhood for black folk—the plain result of this propaganda has been to help the cutting down of educational opportunity for Negro children, the legal disfranchisement of nearly 5,000,000 of Negroes and a state of public opinion which apologizes for lynching, listens complacently to any insult or detraction directed against an eighth of the population of the land, and silently allows a new slavery to rise and clutch the South and paralyze the moral sense of a great nation.

What do Negroes say to this? I speak advisedly when I say that the overwhelming majority of them declare that the tendencies to-day are wrong and that the propaganda that encouraged them was wrong. They say that industrial and trade teaching is needed among Negroes, sadly needed; but they unhesitatingly affirm that it is not needed as much as thorough common school training and the careful education of the gifted in higher institutions; that only in this way can a people rise by intelligence and social leadership to a plane of permanent efficiency and morality. To be sure, there are shorter and quicker methods of making paying workingmen out of a people. Slavery under another name may increase the output of the Transvaal mines, and a caste system coupled with manual training may relieve the South from the domination of labor unions. But has the nation counted the cost of this? Has the Negro agreed to the price, and ought he to agree? Economic efficiency is a means and not an end; this every nation that cares for its salvation must remember.

Moreover, notwithstanding speeches and the editorials of a subsidized Negro press, black men in this land know that when they lose the ballot they lose all. They are no fools. They know it is impossible for free workingmen without a ballot to compete with free workingmen who have the ballot; they know there is no set of people so good and true as to be worth trusting with the political destiny of their fellows, and they know that it is just as true to-day as it was a century and a quarter ago that "Taxation without representation is tyranny."

Finally, the Negro knows perfectly what freedom and equality mean — opportunity to make the best of oneself, unhandicapped by wanton restraint and unreasoning prejudice. For this the most of us propose to strive. We will not, by word or deed, for a moment admit the right of any man to discriminate against us simply on account of race or color. Whenever we submit to humiliation and oppression it is because of superior brute force; and even when bending to the inevitable we bend with unabated protest and declare flatly and unswervingly that any man or section or nation who wantonly shuts the doors of opportunity and self-defense in the faces of the weak is a coward and knave. We refuse to kiss the hands that smite us, but rather insist on striving by all civilized methods to keep wide educational opportunity, to keep the right to vote, to insist on equal civil rights and to gain every right and privilege open to a free American citizen.

But, answer some, you can not accomplish this. America will never spell opportunity for black men; it spelled slavery for them in 1619 and it will spell the same thing in other letters in 1919. To this I answer simply: I do not believe it. I believe that black men will become free American citizens if they have the courage and persistence to demand the rights and treatment of men, and cease to toady and apologize and belittle themselves. The rights of humanity are worth fighting for. Those that deserve them in the long run get them. The way for black men to-day to make these rights the heritage of their children is to struggle for them unceasingly, and if they fail, die trying.

Back to Africa

It was upon the tenth of August, in High Harlem of Manhattan Island, where a hundred thousand Negroes live. There was a long, low, unfinished church basement, roofed over. A little, fat black man, ugly, but with intelligent eyes and big head, was seated on a plank platform beside a "throne," dressed in a military uniform of the gayest mid-Victorian type, heavy with gold lace, epaulets, plume, and sword. Beside him were "potentates," and before him knelt a succession of several colored gentlemen. These in the presence of a thousand or more applauding dark spectators were duly "knighted" and raised to the "peerage" as knight-commanders and dukes of Uganda and the Niger. Among the lucky recipients of titles was the former private secretary of Booker T. Washington!

What did it all mean? A casual observer might have mistaken it for the dress-rehearsal of a new comic opera, and looked instinctively for Bert Williams and Miller and Lyle. But it was not; it was a serious occasion, done on the whole soberly and solemnly. Another might have found it simply silly. All ceremonies are more or less silly. Some Negroes would have said that this ceremony had something symbolic, like the coronation, because it was part of a great "back-to-Africa" movement and represented self-determination for the Negro race and a relieving of America of her most difficult race problem by a voluntary operation.

On the other hand, many American Negroes and some others were scandalized by something which they could but regard as simply child's play. It seemed to them sinister, this enthroning of a demagogue, a blatant boaster, who with monkey-shines was deluding the people and taking their hard-earned dollars; and in High Harlem there rose an insistent cry, "Garvey must go!"

Knowledge of all this seeped through to the greater world because it was sensational and made good copy for the reporters. The great world now and

From *Century Magazine*, 105 (February 1923): 539–548.

then becomes aware of certain currents within itself—tragedies and comedies, movements of mind, gossip, personalities—in some inner whirlpool of which it had been scarcely aware before. Usually these things are of little interest or influence for the main current of events; and yet is not this same main current made up of the impinging of these smaller swirlings of little groups? No matter how segregated and silent the smaller whirlpool is, if it is American, at some time it strikes and influences the American world. What, then, is the latest news from this area of Negrodom spiritually so foreign to most of white America?

2

The sensation that Garvey created was due not so much to his program as to his processes of reasoning, his proposed methods of work, and the width of the stage upon which he essayed to play his part.

His reasoning was at first new and inexplicable to Americans because he brought to the United States a new Negro problem. We think of our problem here as *the* Negro problem, but we know more or less clearly that the problem of the American Negro is very different from the problem of the South African Negro or the problem of the Nigerian Negro or the problem of the South American Negro. We have not hitherto been so clear as to the way in which the problem of the Negro in the United States differs from the problem of the Negro in the West Indies. For a long time we have been told, and we have believed, that the race problem in the West Indies, and particularly in Jamaica, has virtually been settled.

Let us note the facts. Marcus Garvey was born on the northern coast of Jamaica in 1887. He was a poor black boy, his father dying later in the almshouse. He received a little training in the Church of England grammar-school, and then learned the trade of printing, working for years as foreman of a printing plant. Then he went to Europe, and wandered about England and France, working and observing until he finally returned to Jamaica. He found himself facing a stone wall. He was poor, he was black, he had no chance for a university education, he had no likely chance for preferment in any line, but could work as an artisan at small wage for the rest of his life.

Moreover, he knew that the so-called settlement of the race problem in Jamaica was not complete; that as a matter of fact throughout the West Indies the development has been like this: most white masters had cohabited with Negro women, and some had actually married them; their children were free by law in most cases, but were not the recognized equals of the whites either socially, politically, or economically. Because of the numbers of the free

Negroes as compared with the masters, and because of their continued growth in wealth and intelligence, they began to get political power, and they finally either expelled the whites by uniting with the blacks, as in Haiti, or forced the whites to receive the mulattoes, or at least the lighter-hued ones, as equals.

This is the West Indian solution of the Negro problem. The mulattoes are virtually regarded and treated as whites, with the assumption that they will, by continued white intermarriage, bleach out their color as soon as possible. There survive, therefore, few white colonials, save new-comers, who are not of Negro descent in some more or less remote ancestor. Mulattoes intermarry, then, largely with the whites, and the so-called disappearance of the color-line is the disappearance of the line between the whites and mulattoes, and not between the whites and the blacks or even between the mulattoes and the blacks.

Thus the privileged and exploiting group in the West Indies is composed of whites and mulattoes, while the poorly paid and ignorant proletariats are the blacks, forming a peasantry vastly in the majority, but socially, politically, and economically helpless and nearly voiceless. This peasantry, moreover, has been systematically deprived of its natural leadership because the black boy who showed initiative or who accidentally gained wealth and education soon gained the recognition of the white-mulatto group and might be incorporated with them, particularly if he married one of them. Thus his interests and efforts were identified with the mulatto-white group.

There must naturally arise a more or less insistent demand among the black peasants for self-expression and for an exposition of their grievances by one of their own group. Such leaders have indeed arisen from time to time, and Marcus Garvey was one. His notoriety comes not from his ability and accomplishment, but from the Great War. Not that he was without ability. He was a facile speaker, able to express himself in grammatical and forceful English; he had spent enough time in world cities like London to get an idea of world movements, and he honestly believed that the backwardness of the blacks was simply the result of oppression and lack of opportunity.

On the other hand, Garvey had no thorough education and a very hazy idea of the technic of civilization. He fell easily into the common error of assuming that because oppression has retarded a group, the mere removal of the injustice will at a bound restore the group to full power. Then, too, he personally had his drawbacks: he was inordinately vain and egotistic, jealous of his power, impatient of details, a poor judge of human nature, and he had the common weakness of untrained devotees that no dependence could be put upon his statements of fact. Not that he was a conscious liar, but dream, fact, fancy, wish, were all so blurred in his thinking that neither he himself nor his hearers could clearly or easily extricate them.

Then came the new economic demand for Negro peasant labor on the Panama Canal, and finally the Great War. Black West Indians began to make something like decent wages, they began to travel, and they began to talk and think. Garvey talked and thought with them. In conjunction with white and colored sympathizers he planned a small Jamaican Tuskegee. This failed, and he conceived the idea of a purely Negro organization to establish independent Negro states and link them with commerce and industry. His "Universal Negro Improvement Association," launched August 1, 1914, in Jamaica, was soon in financial difficulties. The war was beginning to change the world, and as white American laborers began to be drawn into war work there was an opening in many lines not only for Southern American Negroes as laborers and mechanics, but also for West Indians as servants and laborers. They began to migrate in larger numbers. With this new migration came Marcus Garvey.

He established a little group of his own Jamaica countrymen in Harlem and launched his program. He took no account of the American Negro problem; he knew nothing about it. What he was trying to do was to settle the Jamaican problem in the United States. On the other hand, American Negroes knew nothing about the Jamaican problem, and they were excited and indignant at being brought face to face with a man who was full of wild talk about Africa and the West Indies and steamship lines and "race pride," but who said nothing and apparently knew nothing about the right to vote, the horrors of lynching and mob law, and the problem of racial equality.

Moreover, they were especially incensed at the new West Indian conception of the color-line. Color-lines had naturally often appeared in colored America, but the development had early taken a far different direction from that in the West Indies. Migration by whites had numerically overwhelmed both masters and mulattoes, and compelled most American masters to sell their own children into slavery. Freedom, therefore, rather than color, became the first line of social distinction in the American Negro world despite the near-white aristocracies of cities like Charleston and New Orleans, and despite the fact that the proportion of mulattoes who were free and who gained some wealth and education was greater than that of blacks because of the favor of their white parents.

After emancipation, color caste tended to arise again, but the darker group was quickly welded into one despite color by caste legislation, which applied to a white man with one Negro great-grandfather as well as to a full-blooded Bantu. There were still obvious advantages to the Negro American of lighter hue in passing for white or posing as Spanish or Portuguese, but the pressing demand for ability and efficiency and honesty within this fighting, advancing group continually drove the color-line back before reason and necessity, and it came to be generally regarded as the poorest possible taste for a Negro even to refer to differences of color. Colored folk as white as the whitest came to describe themselves as Negroes. Imagine, then, the surprise and disgust of these Americans when Garvey launched his Jamaican color scheme.

He did this, of course, ignorantly and with no idea of his mistake and no wit to read the signs. He meant well. He saw what seemed to him the same color-lines which he hated in Jamaica, and he sought here as there to oppose white supremacy and the white ideal by a crude and equally brutal black supremacy and black ideal. His mistake did not lie in the utter impossibility of this program — greater upheavals in ideal have shaken the world before — but rather in its spiritual bankruptcy and futility; for what shall this poor world gain if it exchange one race supremacy for another?

Garvey soon sensed that somewhere he was making a mistake, and he began to protest that he was not excluding mulattoes from his organization. Indeed, he has men of all colors and bloods in his organization, but his propaganda still remains "all-black," because this brings cash from the Jamaica peasants. Once he was actually haled to court and made to apologize for calling a disgruntled former colleague "white"! His tirades and twistings have landed him in strange contradictions. Thus with one voice he denounced Booker T. Washington and Frederick Douglass as bastards, and with the next named his boarding-house and first steamship after these same men!

3

Aside from his color-lines, Garvey soon developed in America a definite and in many respects original and alluring program. He proposed to establish the "Black Star Line" of steamships, under Negro ownership and with Negro money, to trade between the United States, the West Indies, and Africa. He proposed to establish a factories corporation which was going to build factories and manufacture goods both for local consumption of Negroes and for export. He was going eventually to take possession of Africa and establish independent Negro governments there.

The statement of this program, with tremendous head-lines, wild eloquence, and great insistence and repetition, caught the attention of all America, white and black. When Mr. Garvey brought his cohorts to Madison Square Garden, clad in fancy costumes and with new songs and ceremonies, and when, ducking his dark head at the audience, he yelled, "We are going to Africa to tell England, France, and Belgium to get out of there," America sat up, listened, laughed, and said here at least is something new.

Negroes, especially West Indians, flocked to his movement and poured money into it. About three years ago he had some 80,000 members in his organization, and perhaps 20,000 or 30,000 were paying regularly thirty-five cents a month into his chest. These numbers grew in his imagination until he was claiming 4,500,000 followers, and speaking for "Four hundred million Negroes"! He did not, however, stop with dreams and promises. If he had been simply a calculating scoundrel, he would carefully have skirted the narrow line between promise and performance and avoided as long as possible the inevitable catastrophe. But he believed in his program and he had a childish ignorance of the stern facts of the world into whose face he was flying. Being an islander, and born in a little realm where half a day's journey takes one from ocean to ocean, the world always seemed small to him, and it was perhaps excusable for this black peasant of Jamaica to think of Africa as a similar, but slightly larger, island which could easily be taken possession of.

His first practical step toward this was to establish the Black Star Line, and here he literally left his critics and opponents breathless by suddenly announcing in 1919 that the *Frederick Douglass*, a steamship, had been bought by his line, was on exhibition at a wharf in New York, and was about to sail to the West Indies with freight and passengers. The announcement was electrical even for those who did not believe in Garvey. With a splendid, audacious faith, this poor black leader, with his storming tongue, compelled a word of admiration from all. But the seeds of failure were in his very first efforts. This first boat, the *Yarmouth* (never renamed the Frederick Douglass probably because of financial difficulties), was built in the year Garvey was born, and was an old sea-scarred hulk. He was cheated in buying it, and paid $140,000 for it—at least twice as much as the boat was worth. She made three trips to the West Indies in three years, and then was docked for repairs, attached for debt, and finally, in December, 1921, sold at auction for $1625!

The second boat that Garvey bought was a steam yacht originally built for a Standard Oil magnate. It, too, was old and of doubtful value, but Garvey paid $60,000 for it, and sent it down to do a small carrying trade between the West Indies Islands. The boat broke down, and it cost $70,000 or $80,000 more to repair it than Garvey paid for it. Finally it was wrecked or seized in Cuba, and the crew was transported to the United States at government expense.

The third boat was a Hudson River ferry-boat that Garvey bought for $35,000. With this he carried excursionists up and down the Hudson during one summer and used it as a vivid advertisement to collect more money. The boat, however, ran only that summer, and then had to be abandoned as beyond repair.

Finally, Garvey tried to buy of the United States Shipping Board the steamship *Orion* for $250,000. This boat was to be renamed the *Phyllis Wheatley*, and its sailings were advertised in Garvey's weekly paper for several months, and some passages were sold; but the boat never was delivered because sufficient payments were not made.

Thus the Black Star Line arose and disappeared, and with it went some $800,000 of the savings of West Indians and a few American Negroes. With this enterprise the initial step and greatest test of Mr. Garvey's movement failed utterly. His factories corporation never really got started. In its place he has established a number of local grocery stores in Harlem and one or two shops, including a laundry and a printing-press, which may or may not survive.

His African program was made impossible by his own pig-headedness. He proposed to make a start in Liberia with industrial enterprises. From this center he would penetrate all Africa and gradually subdue it. Instead of keeping this plan hidden and working cautiously and intelligently toward it, he yelled and shouted and telegraphed it all over the world. Without consulting the Liberians, he apparently was ready to assume partial charge of their state. He appointed officials with high-sounding titles, and announced that the headquarters of his organization was to be removed to Liberia in January, 1922. Such announcements, together with his talk about conquest and "driving Europe out," aroused European governments to inquire about Garvey and his backing. Diplomatic representations were made to Liberia, asking it how far it intended to coöperate in this program. Liberia was naturally compelled to repudiate Garveyism, root and branch. The officials told Garvey that he or any one else was welcome to migrate to Liberia and develop industry within legal lines, but that they could recognize only one authority in Liberia and that was the authority of the Liberian Government, and that Liberia could not be the seat of any intrigue against her peaceful neighbors. They made it impossible for Garvey to establish any headquarters in Africa unless it was done by the consent of the very nations whom he was threatening to drive out of Africa!

This ended his African program and reduced him to the curious alternative of sending a delegate to the third assembly of the League of Nations to ask them to hand over as a gift to his organization a German colony in order that he might begin his work. . . .

A Lunatic or a Traitor

In its endeavor to avoid any injustice toward Marcus Garvey and his followers, *The Crisis* has almost leaned backward. Notwithstanding his wanton squandering of hundreds of thousands of dollars we have refused to assume that he was a common thief. In spite of his monumental and persistent lying we have discussed only the larger and truer aspects of his propaganda. We have refrained from all comment on his trial and conviction for fraud. We have done this too in spite of his personal vituperation of the editor of *The Crisis* and persistent and unremitting repetition of falsehood after falsehood as to the editor's beliefs and acts and as to the program of the N.A.A.C.P.

In the face, however, of the unbelievable depths of debasement and humiliation to which this demagog has descended in order to keep himself out of jail, it is our duty to say openly and clearly:

Marcus Garvey is, without doubt, the most dangerous enemy of the Negro race in America and in the world. He is either a lunatic or a traitor. He is sending all over this country tons of letters and pamphlets appealing to Congressmen, business men, philanthropists and educators to join him on a platform whose half concealed planks may be interpreted as follows:

That no person of Negro descent can ever hope to become an American citizen.

That forcible separation of the races and the banishment of Negroes to Africa is the only solution of the Negro problem.

That race war is sure to follow any attempt to realize the program of the N.A.A.C.P.

We would have refused to believe that any man of Negro descent could have fathered such a propaganda if the evidence did not lie before us in black and white signed by this man. Here is a letter and part of a symposium sent to one of the most prominent business men of America and turned over to us; we select but a few phrases; the italics are ours:

From *The Crisis*, May 1924.

340

Do you believe the Negro to be a *human being*?

Do you believe the Negro *entitled to all the rights of humanity*?

Do you believe that the Negro should be taught *not to aspire to the highest political positions in Governments of the white race*, but to such positions among his own race in a Government of his own?

Would you help morally *or otherwise* to bring about such a possibility? Do you believe that the Negro should be *encouraged to aspire* to the highest industrial and commercial positions in the countries of the white man in competition with him and to his exclusion?

Do you believe that the Negro should be encouraged to regard and *respect the rights of all other races* in the same manner as other races would respect the rights of the Negro?

The pamphlets include one of the worst articles recently written *by a Southern white man* advocating the deportation of American Negroes to Liberia and several articles by Garvey and his friends. From one of Garvey's articles we abstract one phrase:

"THE WHITE RACE CAN BEST HELP THE NEGRO BY TELLING HIM THE TRUTH, AND NOT BY FLATTERING HIM INTO BELIEVING THAT HE IS AS GOOD AS ANY WHITE MAN."

Not even Tom Dixon or Ben Tillman or the hatefulest enemies of the Negro have ever stooped to a more vicious campaign than Marcus Garvey, sane or insane, is carrying on. He is not attacking white prejudice, he is grovelling before it and applauding it; his only attack is on men of his own race who are striving for freedom; his only contempt is for Negroes; his only threats are for black blood. And this leads us to a few plain words:

1. No Negro in America ever had a fairer and more patient trial than Marcus Garvey. He convicted himself by his own admissions, his swaggering monkey-shines in the court room with monocle and long tailed coat and his insults to the judge and prosecuting attorney.

2. Marcus Garvey was long refused bail, not because of his color, but because of the repeated threats and cold blooded assaults charged against his organization. He himself openly threatened to "get" the District Attorney. His followers had repeatedly to be warned from intimidating witnesses and one was sent to jail therefor. One of his former trusted officials after being put out of the Garvey organization brought the long concealed cash account of the organization to this office and we published it. Within two weeks the man was shot in the back in New Orleans and killed. We know nothing of Garvey's personal connection with these cases but we do know that today his former representative lies in jail in Liberia sentenced to death for murder. The District Attorney believed that Garvey's "army" had arms and ammunition and was prepared to "shoot up" colored Harlem if he was released. For these

and no other reasons Garvey was held in the Tombs so long without bail and until he had made abject promises, apologizing to the judge and withdrawing his threats against the District Attorney. Since his release he has not dared to print a single word against white folk. All his vituperation has been heaped on his own race.

Everybody, including the writer, who has dared to make the slightest criticism of Garvey has been intimidated by threats and threatened with libel suits. Over fifty court cases have been brought by Garvey in ten years. After my first and favorable article on Garvey, I was not only threatened with death by men declaring themselves his followers, but received letters of such unbelievable filth that they were absolutely unprintable. When I landed in this country from my trip to Africa I learned with disgust that my friends stirred by Garvey's threats had actually felt compelled to have secret police protection for me on the dock!

Friends have even begged me not to publish this editorial lest I be assassinated. To such depths have we dropped in free black America! I have been exposing white traitors for a quarter century. If the day has come when I cannot tell the truth about black traitors it is high time that I died.

The American Negroes have endured this wretch all too long with fine restraint and every effort at cooperation and understanding. But the end has come. Every man who apologizes for or defends Marcus Garvey from this day forth writes himself down as unworthy of the countenance of decent Americans. As for Garvey himself, this open ally of the Ku Klux Klan should be locked up or sent home.

Marcus Garvey and
the NAACP

Many persons are under the impression that the NAACP has been the persistent enemy of Marcus Garvey. This is due to repeated accusations published in the *Negro World* without the slightest basis of fact. For the sake of the truth, it may be well to recall certain matters of clear record.

The Crisis has published five articles on Marcus Garvey. The first two articles, March 1920 and January 1921, ended with this summary:

"To sum up: Garvey is a sincere, hard-working idealist; he is also a stubborn, domineering leader of the mass; he has worthy industrial and commercial schemes but he is an inexperienced business man. His dreams of Negro industry, commerce and the ultimate freedom of Africa are feasible; but his methods are bombastic, wasteful, illogical and ineffective and almost illegal. If he learns by experience, attracts strong and capable friends and helpers instead of making needless enemies; if he gives up secrecy and suspicion and substitutes open and frank reports as to his income and expenses, and above all if he is willing to be a co-worker and not a czar, he may yet in time succeed in at least starting some of his schemes toward accomplishment. But unless he does these things and does them quickly he cannot escape failure."

No more prophetic word was ever written about Marcus Garvey!

The third and fourth articles dealt with the Black Star Line and the Universal Negro Improvement Association and were based on published documents with little comment.

It was not until September 1922 that *The Crisis* had a sharp word of criticism. This was based on Garvey's threats against his critics, his connection with the Ku Klux Klan and his distribution of pamphlet propaganda against American Negroes. We quoted, among other things, this:

From *The Crisis*, February 1928.

"The white race can best help the Negro by telling him the truth, and not by flattering him into believing that he is as good as any white man."

Concerning this we said:

"Not even Tom Dixon or Ben Tillman or the hatefullest enemies of the Negro have ever stooped to a more vicious campaign than Marcus Garvey, sane or insane, is carrying on. He is not attacking white prejudice, he is grovelling before it and applauding it; his only attack is on men of his own race who are striving for freedom; his only contempt is for Negroes; his only threats are for black blood."

On the other hand Garvey's attacks on the NAACP have been continuous, preposterous and false. He has claimed:

1. That we kept his representative from activity in Paris in 1919.
2. That Moorfield Storey came from Boston to secure his conviction in 1924.
3. That the collapse of the Black Star Line came about "because men were paid to make this trouble by certain organizations calling themselves Negro Advancement Associations. They paid men to dismantle our machinery and otherwise damage it so as to bring about the downfall of the movement."
4. That the NAACP was responsible for his incarceration and deportation.

Every single statement in these and dozens of similar charges are absolutely false and without any basis of fact whatsoever. As *The Crisis* said in May 1924:

"No Negro in America ever had a fairer and more patient trial than Marcus Garvey. He convicted himself by his own admissions, his swaggering monkeyshines in the court room with monocle and long tailed coat and his insults to the judge and prosecuting attorney.

"Marcus Garvey was long refused bail, not because of his color, but because of the repeated threats and cold blooded assaults charged against his organization. He himself openly threatened to 'get' the District Attorney. His followers had repeatedly to be warned from intimidating witnesses and one was sent to jail therefor. One of his former trusted officials after being put out of the Garvey organization brought the long concealed cash account of the organization to this office and we published it. Within two weeks the man was shot in the back in New Orleans and killed.

"Everybody, including the writer, who has dared to make the slightest criticism of Garvey has been intimidated by threats and threatened with libel suits. Over fifty court cases have been brought by Garvey in ten years."

We are reminding our readers of all this not to revive forgotten rancor but for the sake of historical accuracy. When Garvey was sent to Atlanta, no word or action of ours accomplished the result. His release and deportation were a matter of law which no deed or wish of ours influenced in the slightest degree. We have today, no enmity against Marcus Garvey. He has a great and worthy dream. We wish him well. He is free; he has a following; he still has a chance to carry on his work in his own home and among his own people and to accomplish some of his ideals. Let him do it. We will be the first to applaud any success that he may have.

Leadership Is Vital

... But what we did say then and what thinking Negroes are still saying: without efficient leadership in fields opened by the higher training it would be impossible for us to hold our place in America and especially difficult in time of change and dislocation. Not only that, but the younger leaders trained by the colleges have not proved in the main selfish exploiters of their people. We have unselfish and really brave men. It was no ordinary deed for Judge Hastie to jeopardize his whole career by resigning from an office of unusual importance and then daring to criticize the United States Army in plain terms. Less publicized but equally brave was the resignation of Theodore Berry from the Office of Facts and Figures.

In other instances where there has not been resignation or spectacular action, there has been equally strong outstanding pressure and determination to defend American Negro rights. Perhaps most astonishing in our later leadership has been Randolph's action which compelled the issue of Presidential Order 8802 and the extraordinary storm of well-documented answers which followed the attempt of the *Reader's Digest* to smear the Negro press. All this proves to my mind the essential rightness today as yesterday of the position that long training of men and women of exceptional talent is the key to our success in the modern world. The phrase has been bandied about, but it was originally mine; "the object of education is not to make men carpenters but to make carpenters men!"

From the *Amsterdam News*, April 3, 1943.

The Talented Tenth:
Memorial Address

THE PAST

Some years ago I used the phrase "The Talented Tenth," meaning leadership of the Negro race in America by a trained few. Since then this idea has been criticized. It has been said that I had in mind the building of an aristocracy with neglect of the masses. This criticism has seemed even more valid because of emphasis on the meaning and power of the mass of people to which Karl Marx gave voice in the middle of the nineteenth century, and which has been growing in influence ever since. There have come other changes in these days, which a great many of us do not realize as Revolution through which we are passing. Because of this, it is necessary to examine the world about us and our thoughts and attitudes toward it. I want then to re-examine and restate the thesis of the Talented Tenth which I laid down many years ago.

In a day when culture is comparatively static, a man once grounded in the fundamentals of knowledge, received through current education, can depend on the more or less routine absorption of knowledge for keeping up with the world. This was true for decades during the nineteenth century, and usually has been true in the slow drift of many other centuries. But today, the tide runs swiftly, and almost every fundamental concept which most of us learned in college has undergone radical change; so that a man who was broadly educated in 1900 may be widely ignorant in 1948, unless he has made conscious, continuous, and determined effort to keep abreast with the development of knowledge and of thought in the last half century.

For instance, since 1900 physics and chemistry have been revolutionized in many of their basic concepts. Astronomy is today almost a new science as

From *Boulé Journal*, 15 (October 1948) 3–13.

compared with the time of Copernicus. Psychology has risen from guess-work and introspection to an exact science. Biology and Anthropology have changed and expanded widely; History and Sociology have begun in the middle of the twentieth century, first, to take on the shape of real sciences rather than being largely theory and opinion.

If, now, a college man of 1900, or even of 1925, has spent his time since graduation mainly in making a living, he is in fair way not to be able to understand the world of 1950. It is necessary then for men of education continually to readjust their knowledge, and this is doubly necessary in this day of swift revolution in ideas, in ideals, in industrial techniques, in rapid travel, and in varieties and kinds of human contacts.

Turn now to that complex of social problems, which surrounds and conditions our life, and which we call more or less vaguely, The Negro Problem. It is clear that in 1900, American Negroes were an inferior caste, were frequently lynched and mobbed, widely disfranchised, and usually segregated in the main areas of life. As student and worker at that time, I looked upon them and saw salvation through intelligent leadership; as I said, through a "Talented Tenth." And for this intelligence, I argued, we needed college-trained men. Therefore, I stressed college and higher training. For these men with their college training, there would be needed thorough understanding of the mass of Negroes and their problems; and, therefore, I emphasized scientific study. Willingness to work and make personal sacrifice for solving these problems was of course, the first prerequisite and *sine qua non*. I did not stress this, I assumed it.

SACRIFICE

I assumed that with knowledge, sacrifice would automatically follow. In my youth and idealism, I did not realize that selfishness is even more natural than sacrifice. I made the assumption of its wide availability because of the spirit of sacrifice learned in my mission school training.

I went South to Fisk University at the age of 17, when I was peculiarly impressionable, from a region which had opened my mind but had not filled the void. At Fisk I met a group of teachers who would be unusual in any time or place. They were not only men of learning and experience, but men and women of character and almost fanatic devotion. It was a great experience to sit under their voice and influence. It was from that experience that I assumed easily that educated people, in most cases were going out into life to see how far they could better the world. Of course, as I looked about me, I might have understood, that all students of Fisk University were not persons of this sort.

There was no lack of small and selfish souls; there were among the student body, careless and lazy fellows; and there were especially sharp young persons, who received the education given very cheaply at Fisk University, with the distinct and single-minded idea, of seeing how much they could make out of it for themselves, and nobody else.

When I came out of college into the world of work, I realized that it was quite possible that my plan of training a talented tenth might put in control and power, a group of selfish, self-indulgent, well-to-do men, whose basic interest in solving the Negro problem was personal; personal freedom and unhampered enjoyment and use of the world, without any real care, or certainly no arousing care, as to what became of the mass of American Negroes, or of the mass of any people. My Talented Tenth, I could see, might result in a sort of interracial free-for-all, with the devil taking the hindmost and the foremost taking anything they could lay hands on.

ARISTOCRACY

This, historically, has always been the danger of aristocracy. It was for a long time regarded as almost inevitable because of the scarcity of ability among men and because, naturally the aristocrat came to regard himself and his whims as necessarily the end and only end of civilization and culture. As long as the masses supported this doctrine, aristocracy and mass misery lived amiably together.

Into this situation came the revolutionary thought, first voiced in former ages by great moral leaders, which asked charity for the poor and sympathy for the ignorant and sick. And even intimated eventual justice in Heaven. But in the suddenly expanding economy and marvelous technique of the eighteenth and nineteenth centuries, there came prophets and reformers, but especially the voice of Karl Marx, to say that the poor need not always be with us, and that all men could and should be free from poverty.

Karl Marx stressed the fact that not merely the upper class but the mass of men were the real people of the world. He insisted that the masses were poor, ignorant, and sick, not by sin or by nature but by oppression. He preached that planned production of goods and just distribution of income would abolish poverty, ignorance and disease, and make the so-called upper-class, not the exception, but the rule among mankind. He declared that the world was not for the few, but for the many; that out of the masses of men could come overwhelming floods of ability and genius, if we freed men by plan and not by rare chance. Civilization not only could be shared by the vast majority of men, but such civilization founded on a wide human base would be better and more enduring than anything that the world has seen. The world would thus escape the enduring danger of being run by a selfish few for their own advantage.

Very gradually as the philosophy of Karl Marx and many of his successors seeped into my understanding, I tried to apply this doctrine with regard to Negroes. My Talented Tenth must be more than talented, and work not simply as individuals. Its passport to leadership was not alone learning but expert knowledge of modern economics as it affected American Negroes; and in addition to this and fundamental, would be its willingness to sacrifice and plan for such economic revolution in industry and just distribution of wealth, as would make the rise of our group possible. . . .

CHARACTER

In this reorientation of my ideas, my pointing out the new knowledge necessary for leadership, and new ideas of race and culture, there still remains that fundamental and basic requirement of character for any successful leadership toward great ideals. Even if the ideals are clearly perceived, honesty of character and purity of motive are needed without which no effort succeeds or deserves to succeed. We used to talk much of character — perhaps too much. At Fisk, we had it dinned into our ears. At Harvard we never mentioned it. We thought of it: but it was not good taste to talk of it: At Berlin we quite forgot it. But that was reaction. We cannot have perfection. We have few saints. But we must have honest men or we die. We must have unselfish, far-seeing leadership or we fail.

What can Sigma Pi Phi do to see that we get it for the American Negro? So far as the group before me is concerned little can be done, for the simple reason that most of our present membership will soon be dead. Unless we begin to recruit this fraternity membership with young men and large numbers of them, our biennial conclaves will be increasingly devoted to obituaries. We should have a large increase of membership, drawn from men who have received their college education since the First World War. This new membership must not simply be successful in the American sense of being rich; they must not all be physicians and lawyers. The technicians, business men, teachers and social workers admitted must be those who realize the economic revolution now sweeping the world, and do not think that private profit is the measure of public welfare. And too: we must deliberately seek honest men.

This screened young membership must be far greater in number than it is now. Baltimore for instance has more than 166,000 Negroes and only 23 in its

Boulé, representing less than 100 persons. Surely there must be at least 23 other persons in Baltimore worthy of fellowship. It is inconceivable that we should even for a moment dream that with a membership of 440 we have scratched even the tip of the top of the surface of a group representative of potential Negro leadership in America. Nothing but congenital laziness should keep us from a membership of 3,000 by the next biennium without any lowering of quality; and a membership of 30,000 by 1960. This would be an actual numerical one hundredth of our race: a body large enough really to represent all. Yet small enough to insure exceptional quality; if screened for intelligent and disinterested planning.

A PLANNED PROGRAM

Having gotten a group of predominantly active virile men of middle age and settled opinions, who have finished their education and begun their life work, what can they do? They must first of all recognize the fact that their own place in life is primarily a matter of opportunity, rather than simple desert or ability. That if such opportunity were extended and broadened, a thousand times as many Negroes could join the ranks of the educated and able, instead of sinking into poverty, disease and crime; that the primary duty of this organization would be to find desert, ability, and character among young Negroes and get for them education and opportunity; that the major opportunity should be seen as work according to gift and training with pay sufficient to furnish a decent standard of living.

A national organization of this sort must be prepared to use propaganda, make investigation, plan procedures and even finance projects. This will call for an initial body of belief which even now can be forecast in outline.

We would want to impress on the emerging generations of Negroes in America, the ideal of plain living and high thinking, in defiance of American noise, waste and display; the rehabilitation of the indispensable family group, by deliberate planning of marriages, with mates selected for heredity, physique, health and brains, with less insistence on color, comeliness or romantic sex lure, miscalled love; youth should marry young and have a limited number of healthy children; the home must be a place of education, rather than cleaning and cooking, with books, discussion and entertainment.

The schools where these children are sent must not be chosen for the color of their teachers or students, but for their efficiency in educating a particular child. In home and out children should learn not to neglect our art heritage: music is not designed solely for night clubs; drama is not aimed at Broadway;

dancing is not the handmaid of prostitution; and writing is not mainly for income.

Our religion with all of its dogma, demagoguery and showmanship, can be a center to teach character, right conduct and sacrifice. There lies here a career for a Negro Gandhi and a host of earnest followers.

The dark hosts of Liberia and Ethiopia and other parts of Africa together with Asia, the Pacific lands, South and Central America, and the Caribbean area, have need for that broad knowledge of the world and special training in technique which we might learn and take to them. They do not need us for exploitation and get-rich-quick schemes. There is no reason why the sort of thought and teaching which two thousand years ago made the groves of Athens the center of the world's salvation, could not live again in ten thousand Negro homes in America today.

Occupation should not, and need not, be left to chance or confined to what whites are doing, or are willing to let us do. It must involve innovation and experiment. It must be a carefully planned, thoroughly thought-out with wide study of human wants, technical power, trained effort and consecrated devotion with the use of every scientific procedure in physics, chemistry, biology, psychology, sociology and history.

For this central object of planned work, this organization should assemble the best knowledge and experience. It should encourage pioneering and adventure; attacking desert places with modern technique; producing new goods by new processes; avoiding the factory system and mass production as the last word in work, and returning to the ideal of personal consumption, personal taste and human desire; thinking of consumption and the consumers as coming before production, and not of production as the end of industry and profit as its motive.

The new generation must learn that the object of the world is not profit but service and happiness. They must therefore be directed away from careers which are anti-social and dishonest, but immensely profitable. Insurance can be a social help but much of it today is organized theft. We must have drug stores, but the patent nostrums in which so many of them deal deserve the penitentiary. Gambling not only as poker-playing but as a profitable career, is seeping through all kinds of American business from the stock market, factory and wholesale store, to the numbers racket, horse racing, and radio gifts. Every effort should be made to warn the next generation away from this dry rot of death and crime.

An organization adapted to such a program of propaganda and work of guidance, and able to search for and select ability and character and finance efforts to give it opportunity, will need large funds at its disposal. The sacrifice necessary to provide such funds should be regarded not as sentimental charity or mushy religious fervor but as foresight and investment in the future of the Negro in America, and canny insurance against loss by wholesale neglect of invaluable human resources. We may reach the high ideal when again the tithe, the tenth of our income will go to the perfectly feasible effort of so civilizing the American Negro that he will be able to lead the world and will want to do so.

THE GUIDING HUNDREDTH

This, then is my re-examined and restated theory of the "Talented Tenth," which has thus become the doctrine of the "Guiding Hundredth."

Naturally, I do not dream, that a word of mine will transform, to any essential degree, the form and trends of this fraternity; but I am certain the idea called for expression and that the seed must be dropped whether in this or other soil, today or tomorrow.

The Present Leadership of
American Negroes

E. Franklin Frazier, head of the Dept. of Social Sciences at Howard University
and past president of the American Sociological Assn., has just issued in
English a book which first appeared in France. *The Black Bourgeoisie* [by
E. Franklin Frazier, Glencoe, Ill.: The Free Press, 1957] is a study of the "rise
of a new Middle Class in the United States of America." It is a stern and
biting protest at the way in which American Negroes have turned from their
earlier intellectual leadership and gone in leash to a blatant group of conspicuous spenders, whose widely-advertised economic basis is so flimsy as to
bring them face to face with a blank wall of negation.

The first significance of this work lies in directing attention to the rise of
class stratification among the grandchildren of the black slaves. Most social
students continue to regard American Negroes as essentially an undifferentiated group. A glance at the increasing differences of income among them and
the growing diversity of occupation quickly dispels this assumption.

THE "TALENTED TENTH"

Even prominent Negro leaders long thought that a Negro intelligentsia
would be able to lift the Negro mass upward as a largely self-contained social
unit, with a minimum of labor exploitation and a maximum of uplifting
progress. This was the doctrine of Negro social leadership by a "Talented
Tenth," which had its kernel of truth. But some Negro leaders early pointed
out that with the tremendous growth of Big Industry in America, no self-

From the *National Guardian*, May 20, 1957.

directed Negro economy could succeed; that neither Negro consumers'
cooperation nor Negro business as such would be allowed to develop.
However, none of these thinkers followed this thought to the logical conclusion, that only under socialism could a minority group economy rise and
survive.

Frazier touches on this failure of Negro leadership, but emphasizes the
history of the way in which a Negro Middle Class arose, and the trends of its
present leadership. He notes the cultural impact of the slave plantation and
Western civilization; and the gradual rise after emancipation of a "nation
within a nation" with bounding lines of color caste and poverty.

IT DIDN'T SUCCEED

The first chapter of the book records how the ill-starred Freedman's Savings
Bank instilled the idea of rise by thrift and saving. Even the unforgivable
failure of this venture of white philanthropy left among Negroes the urge to
protect their savings and mutual aid funds by starting their own banks. Many
Negro banks were organized; some flourished and a few survive, but most
failed, just as most smaller banks among whites have failed, and largely for the
same reasons. Frantic and continued efforts at Negro business enterprises
followed. These, as Frazier points out, never succeeded as Booker Washington and other Negro leaders expected. The reason was not inefficiency (which
certainly played its part), but a fact which Frazier perhaps does not sufficiently
stress. The fact is that a handicapped group tried to get to its economic feet in
the midst of the era of tremendous development of the modern monopolistic
capitalist system.

While Negro business made no great success then, and succeeded best in
areas where race prejudice left an unoccupied gap, nevertheless the migration
of Negroes out of the South and the gradual breaking of the Color Line in
employment integrated Negroes increasingly into the national economy and
gave rise to a Negro Middle Class. In 1900, nine-tenths of the Negroes lived in
the former slave states under color caste which perpetuated many aspects of
slavery. Fifty years later a third of the 15,000,000 Negroes lived in the North,
where color discrimination was less and economic opportunity better. Also,
while, in 1900, 77% of the Negroes lived in the country and depended mainly
on decadent agriculture, in 1950 two-thirds lived in cities. This spelled social
revolution and, as Frazier estimates, it means that from a fifth to a sixth of
American Negroes now belong to a new Middle Class of professional men,
including preachers and teachers, entertainers, social workers and nurses;

artisans with skills; managers and officials, and a rapidly increasing number of clerical workers.

ROOT OF THE EVIL

Measuring this class differentiation by income is not easy, since all capitalist nations regard private income a secret to be guarded against public knowledge. Our best income statistics are therefore guesses. The median income of Negro families is reported as a little over half that of whites. Among Negroes 16% have $3,000 or more a year, while 55% among whites are in this bracket. Over half of all Negro families receive less than $1,000 a year, while one-half of one per cent receive $5,000 or more. In the North this latter class rises to one per cent and, in cities like New York and Chicago, to 10%. Here is the basis for volumes on the economic plight of Negroes.

Frazier shows how Big Business took over the education of Negroes from the hands of post-Civil War philanthropy. This turned training for social leadership and ethical ideals into training for income. The educated Negro was left small chance for thinking independently of the national thought. Despite the role of the Negro Church and the fraternal organizations, most of his racial ties were severed and he sought a new social orientation. Black nationalism of the Garvey type was stopped before birth by colonial imperialism. The literary and artistic renaissance of the '20s and '30s was promising but was stopped by lack of economic foundation.

Negro businessmen exploited Negro labor directly in their enterprises, and the rest of the Negro Middle Class became links in the white exploitation of all labor. Meantime the Negro money-makers began to displace the black intelligentsia as leaders of the race, even though their income was less than their conspicuous spending implied. In this respect Frazier might have noted that white middle class folk are falling for the same temptation, as installment buying demonstrates.

THERE WERE MODELS

This then is the world of "make believe" into which many leaders of the Black Bourgeoisie are guiding the American Negro. This, Franklin Frazier insists, is moving toward nothing and he lashes Negro society with bitter and sarcastic invective. I strongly sympathize with the author in his main thesis. I share his dislike for periodicals like *Ebony* and join in criticism of the social expenditures of Negro college fraternities. But I would add that *Ebony* is a symptom, not a cause — and that *Life* and *Vogue* are its forerunners in sin. Also it is the all-powerful white American that tempts Negroes to follow its own lunatic fringe.

We should remember that human beings must have human intercourse. They must meet one another, talk and mingle; their adolescent children must be guided; they must travel, go on vacations and seek recreation. Yet, in quest of these things, Negroes meet at every turn frustrations, repressions, criticism and insult bordering on violence.

When, some years back, my granddaughter was invited to a "coming out" party tendered by professional Negroes of Baltimore, my first reaction was like Frazier's at this "aping of white folk." But the party was lovely. It brought together a group of young folks who needed to know one another. Their colored skins and gay costumes made a strangely beautiful sight and gave these young folks just what they needed for knowing and seeing one another, choosing mates and facing a hostile world with faith and joy. Such Negroes need not, as Frazier fears, become ashamed of their race and past. On the contrary, they may for the first time see themselves as they should be.

SILENT LEADERSHIP

Frazier also here fails to point out the voluntary abdication of the Negro intelligentsia from holding and reasserting that leadership which is theirs by right. In the face of the current anti-socialist hysteria most of these leaders have been as silent as our white leaders. Negro colleges teach no socialism and malign Russia and China. Yet they must know that without the overthrow of capitalist monopoly the Negro cannot survive in the United States as a self-respecting cultural unit, integrating gradually into the nation, but not on terms which imply self-destruction or loss of his possible gifts to America.

Here then is a book of keen analysis and fearless reasoning. Frazier braves the criticism of his racial fellows, as well as the "I told-you-sos" of all the Byrds and Eastlands, for the sake of his right to say what he believes, and not simply what is popular.

Will the Great Gandhi
Live Again?

The greatest philosopher of our era pointed out the inherent contradictions in many of our universal beliefs; and he sought eventual reconciliation of these paradoxes. We realize this today. Our newly inaugurated President asks the largest expenditure for war in human history made by a nation, and proclaims this as a step toward peace! We have larger endowments devoted to peace activity than any other nation on earth, and less activity for abolishing war.

As I look back on my own attitude toward war during the last 70 years, I see repeated contradiction. In my youth, nourished as I was on fairy tales, including some called History, I quite naturally regarded war as a necessary step toward progress. I believed that if my people ever gained freedom and equality, it would be by killing white people.

Then, as a young man in the great afflatus of the late nineteenth century, I came to believe in peace. No more war. I signed the current pledge never to take part in war. Yet during the First World War, "the war to stop war," I was swept into the national maelstrom.

After the depression I sensed recurring contradictions. I saw Gandhi's nonviolence gain freedom for India, only to be followed by violence in all the world; I realized that the hundred years of peace from Waterloo to 1914 was not peace at all, but war of Europe on Africa and Asia, with troubled peace only between the colonial conquerors. I saw Britain, France, and America trying to continue to force the world to serve them by using their monopoly of land, technique, and machinery, backed by gunpowder, and then threatening atomic power.

Then Montgomery in Alabama tried to show the world the synthesis of this antithesis. And not the white Montgomery of the Slave Power; not even the

From the *National Guardian*, February 11, 1957.

black Montgomery of the Negro professional men, merchants, and teachers; but the black workers; the scrubbers and cleaners; the porters and seamstresses. They turned to a struggle not for great principles and noble truths, but just asked to be let alone after a tiring day's work; to be free of petty insult after hard and humble toil. These folk, led by a man who had read Hegel, knew of Karl Marx, and had followed Mohandas Karamchand Gandhi, preached: "Not by Might, nor by Power, but by My Spirit," saith the Lord. Did this doctrine and practice of non-violence bring solution of the race problem in Alabama? It did not. Black workers, many if not all, are still walking to work, and it is possible any day that their leader will be killed by hoodlums perfectly well known to the white police and the city administration, egged on by white councils of war, while most white people of the city say nothing and do nothing.

All over the lower South this situation prevails. Despite law, in the face of drooling religion and unctuous prayer, while the nation dances and yells and prepares to fight for peace and freedom, there is race war, jails full of the innocent, and ten times more money spent for mass murder than for education of children. Where are we, then, and whither are we going? What is the synthesis of this paradox of eternal and world-wide war and the coming of the Prince of Peace?

It lies, I think, not in the method but in the people concerned. Among normal human beings, with the education customary today in most civilized nations, nonviolence is the answer to the temptation to force. When threat is met by fist; when blow follows blow, violence becomes customary. But no normal human being of trained intelligence is going to fight the man who will not fight back. In such cases, peace begins and grows just because it is. But suppose they are wild beasts or wild men? To yield to the rush of the tiger is death, nothing less. The wildness of beasts is nature; but the wildness of men is neglect and, often, our personal neglect. This is the reason beneath our present paradox of peace and war.

For now near a century this nation has trained the South in lies, hate, and murder. We are emphasizing today that when Robert E. Lee swore to serve the nation and then broke his word to serve his clan, his social class, and his private property — that this made him a hero; that although he did not believe in human slavery, he fought four long years, with consummate skill, over thousands of dead bodies, to make it legal for the South to continue to hold four million black folk as chattel bondsmen — that this makes him a great American and candidate for the Hall of Fame.

We have for 80 years as a nation widely refused to regard the killing of a Negro in the South as murder, or the violation of a black girl as rape. We have let white folk steal millions of black folks' hard-earned wages, and openly defended this as natural for a "superior" race. As a result of this, we have today in the South millions of persons who are pathological cases. They cannot be reasoned with in matters of race. They are not normal and cannot be treated as normal. They are ignorant and their schools are poor because they cannot afford a double school system and would rather themselves remain ignorant than let Negroes learn.

Remedy for this abnormal situation would be education for all children and education all together, so as to let them grow up knowing each other as human. Precisely this path these abnormal regions refuse to follow. Here, then, is no possible synthesis. So long as a people insults, murders, and hates by hereditary teaching, non-violence can bring no peace. It will bring migration until that fails, and then attempts at bloody revenge. It will spread war and murder. Can we then by effort make the average white person in states like South Carolina, Georgia, Alabama, Mississippi, and Louisiana normal, intelligent human beings?

If we can, we solve our antithesis; great Gandhi lives again. If we cannot civilize the South, or will not even try, we continue in contradiction and riddle.

Crusader Without Violence

The merit of this biography [*Crusader Without Violence*, Lawrence Reddick (New York: Harper & Row, 1959)] is that it rests upon personal acquaintance and first-hand knowledge of its subject and not merely on documents. The author was for nine years curator of the Schomburg collection of Negro Literature in the New York Public Library. He then went South to become a librarian at Atlanta University and during the last few years has been chairman of the Dept. of History at Alabama State College in Montgomery, Alabama.

He therefore saw personally and was a close observer of what went on during the celebrated strike of Negroes against the bus lines. He became personally connected with the leader of the strike, Martin Luther King, and writes a sympathetic and intelligent story of the man. He gives a detailed account of his family, his education and his personality.

The resulting picture is interesting and appealing but also a little disturbing. Here is a young colored man of good family and careful up-bringing under the tutelage of a successful Negro minister. He receives his training at a Southern Negro college, in a New Jersey Theological school, and Boston University. His doctor's thesis is on a vague theological problem about the power of God as pictured by two of his theological teachers. But he broadens his theological training by wide contact with human beings black and white, and evolves a personal philosophy which gradually follows the ideal of Gandhi, non-violence.

His application of this philosophy in the Montgomery strike is well-known and deserves wide praise, but leaves me a little in doubt. I was sorry to see King lauded for his opposition to the young colored man in North Carolina who declared that in order to stop lynching and mob violence, Negroes must fight back.

There is no question but that King in Montgomery suffered and stood firm

From the *National Guardian*, November 9, 1959.

without surrender but it is a very grave question as to whether or not the slavery and degradation of Negroes in America has not been unnecessarily prolonged by the submission to evil.

Gandhi submitted, but he also followed a positive program to offset his negative refusal to use violence. He organized Negro opposition in South Africa; he helped in the first World War and he had an economic program to oppose the exploitation of Indian labor.

In Montgomery hundreds of Negroes have suffered and lost their jobs because of the strike. What program have King and his followers to offset this? Perhaps he is thinking along these lines, but this picture by Reddick does not make any such plan clear. It is however a book to be enjoyed together with King's own story of Montgomery.

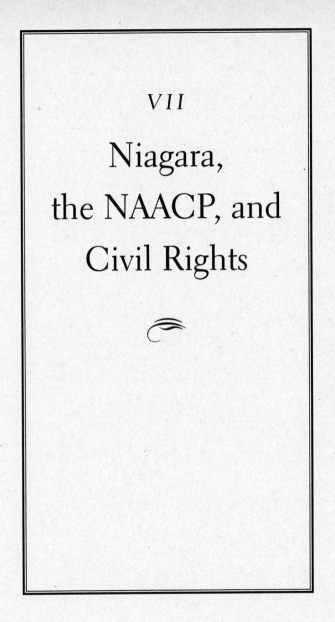

VII

Niagara,
the NAACP, and
Civil Rights

We will not be satisfied to take one jot or tittle less than our full manhood rights," Du Bois proclaimed in "Address to the Country," a 1906 statement issued at Harpers Ferry, West Virginia, by the Niagara Movement at its second annual meeting. Although the exclusively African-American organization folded three years later due to powerful enemies (black as well as white) and to internal tensions, Du Bois carried its uncompromising, confrontational civil rights *elan* into the new interracial NAACP, as the December 1910 *Crisis* editorial "NAACP" makes clear. The 1916 Amenia Conference would have been inconceivable had not Booker T. Washington died eight months earlier, but, as Du Bois's account reveals, the conference marked the acceptance by a broad array of prominent African-Americans of a more aggressive civil rights agenda. Du Bois lashed out against or lampooned mercilessly in *Crisis* magazine not only the flagrantly unconstitutional forms of racial segregation ("The Tuskegee Hospital" [1923]) but the encrusted taboos of informal practices and stickier ones of sexual relations ("On Being Crazy" [1923] and "Social Equality and Racial Intermarriage" [1922]).

"Propaganda and World War," a chapter in *Dusk of Dawn* (1940) tracking his career from Atlanta University through the first decade of the NAACP to his profound skepticism about American racial democracy after the First World War, is one of Du Bois's most seminal writings. As he moved to the left and away from belief in racial progress under the private enterprise system after the Second World War, Du Bois still experienced bouts of optimism over ameliorating economic and political trends making for racial justice, as in "Doubts Gandhi Plan" (1943) and "The Negro Since 1900" (1948). But by the late 1950s, occasional relapses into optimism about civil rights were behind him. Dismissing "all deliberate speed" as a travesty, he called for an end to capitalism as the sine qua non to the liberation of people of color ("A Program of Reason, Right and Justice for Today" [1960]). Finally, he praised China as the model for the developing world, proclaiming in the *Autobiography* (1968), "Many leading nations I have visited repeatedly. But I have never seen a nation which so amazed and touched me as China in 1959."

The Niagara Movement

Address to the Country

The men of the Niagara Movement coming from the toil of the year's hard work and pausing a moment from the earning of their daily bread turn toward the nation and again ask in the name of ten million the privilege of a hearing. In the past year the work of the Negro hater has flourished in the land. Step by step the defenders of the rights of American citizens have retreated. The work of stealing the black man's ballot has progressed and the fifty and more representatives of stolen votes still sit in the nation's capital. Discrimination in travel and public accommodation has so spread that some of our weaker brethren are actually afraid to thunder against color discrimination as such and are simply whispering for ordinary decencies.

Against this the Niagara Movement eternally protests. We will not be satisfied to take one jot or tittle less than our full manhood rights. We claim for ourselves every single right that belongs to a freeborn American, political, civil and social; and until we get these rights we will never cease to protest and assail the ears of America. The battle we wage is not for ourselves alone but for all true Americans. It is a fight for ideals, lest this, our common fatherland, false to its founding, become in truth the land of the thief and the home of the Slave — a by-word and a hissing among the nations for its sounding pretentions and pitiful accomplishment.

Never before in the modern age has a great and civilized folk threatened to adopt so cowardly a creed in the treatment of its fellow-citizens born and bred on its soil. Stripped of verbiage and subterfuge and in its naked nastiness the new American creed says: Fear to let black men even try to rise lest they become the equals of the white. And this is the land that professes to follow Jesus Christ. The blasphemy of such a course is only matched by its cowardice.

A two-page leaflet (1906).

367

In detail our demands are clear and unequivocal. First, we would vote; with the right to vote goes everything: Freedom, manhood, the honor of your wives, the chastity of your daughters, the right to work, and the chance to rise, and let no man listen to those who deny this.

We want full manhood suffrage, and we want it now, henceforth and forever.

Second. We want discrimination in public accommodation to cease. Separation in railway and street cars, based simply on race and color, is un-American, un-democratic, and silly. We protest against all such discrimination.

Third. We claim the right of freemen to walk, talk, and be with them that wish to be with us. No man has a right to choose another man's friends, and to attempt to do so is an impudent interference with the most fundamental human privilege.

Fourth. We want the laws enforced against rich as well as poor; against Capitalist as well as Laborer; against white as well as black. We are not more lawless than the white race, we are more often arrested, convicted, and mobbed. We want justice even for criminals and outlaws. We want the Constitution of the country enforced. We want Congress to take charge of Congressional elections. We want the Fourteenth amendment carried out to the letter and every State disfranchised in Congress which attempts to disfranchise its rightful voters. We want the Fifteenth amendment enforced and No State allowed to base its franchise simply on color.

The failure of the Republican Party in Congress at the session just closed to redeem its pledge of 1904 with reference to suffrage conditions at the South seems a plain, deliberate, and premeditated breach of promise, and stamps that party as guilty of obtaining votes under false pretense.

Fifth. We want our children educated. The school system in the country districts of the South is a disgrace and in few towns and cities are the Negro schools what they ought to be. We want the national government to step in and wipe out illiteracy in the South. Either the United States will destroy ignorance or ignorance will destroy the United States.

And when we call for education we mean real education. We believe in work. We ourselves are workers, but work is not necessarily education. Education is the development of power and ideal. We want our children trained as intelligent human beings should be, and we will fight for all time against any proposal to educate black boys and girls simply as servants and underlings, or simply for the use of other people. They have a right to know, to think, to aspire.

These are some of the chief things which we want. How shall we get them?

By voting where we may vote, by persistent, unceasing agitation; by hammering at the truth, by sacrifice and work.

We do not believe in violence, neither in the despised violence of the raid nor the lauded violence of the soldier, nor the barbarous violence of the mob, but we do believe in John Brown, in that incarnate spirit of justice, that hatred of a lie, that willingness to sacrifice money, reputation, and life itself on the altar of right. And here on the scene of John Brown's martyrdom we reconsecrate ourselves, our honor, our property to the final emancipation of the race which John Brown died to make free.

Our enemies, triumphant for the present, are fighting the stars in their courses. Justice and humanity must prevail. We live to tell these dark brothers of ours — scattered in counsel, wavering and weak — that no bribe of money or notoriety, no promise of wealth or fame, is worth the surrender of a people's manhood or the loss of a man's self-respect. We refuse to surrender the leadership of this race to cowards and trucklers. We are men; we will be treated as men. On this rock we have planted our banners. We will never give up, though the trump of doom find us still fighting.

And we shall win. The past promised it, the present foretells it. Thank God for John Brown! Thank God for Garrison and Douglass! Sumner and Phillips, Nat Turner and Robert Gould Shaw, and all the hallowed dead who died for freedom! Thank God for all those to-day, few though their voices be, who have not forgotten the divine brotherhood of all men white and black, rich and poor, fortunate and unfortunate.

We appeal to the young men and women of this nation, to those whose nostrils are not yet befouled by greed and snobbery and racial narrowness: Stand up for the right, prove yourselves worthy of your heritage and whether born north or south dare to treat men as men. Cannot the nation that has absorbed ten million foreigners into its political life without catastrophe absorb ten million Negro Americans into that same political life at less cost than their unjust and illegal exclusion will involve?

Courage brothers! The battle for humanity is not lost or losing. All across the skies sit signs of promise. The Slav is raising in his might, the yellow millions are tasting liberty, the black Africans are writhing toward the light, and everywhere the laborer, with ballot in his hand, is voting open the gates of Opportunity and Peace. The morning breaks over blood-stained hills. We must not falter, we may not shrink. Above are the everlasting stars.

NAACP

What is the National Association for the Advancement of Colored People? It is a union of those who believe that earnest, active opposition is the only effective way of meeting the forces of evil. They believe that the growth of race prejudice in the United States is evil. It is not always consciously evil. Much of it is born of ignorance and misapprehension, honest mistake and misguided zeal. However caused, it is none the less evil, wrong, dangerous, fertile of harm. For this reason it must be combatted. It is neither safe nor sane to sit down dumbly before such human error or to seek to combat it with smiles and hushed whispers. Fight the wrong with every human weapon in every civilized way.

The National Association for the Advancement of Colored People is organized to fight the wrong of race prejudice:

(a) By doing away with the excuses for prejudice.
(b) By showing the unreasonableness of prejudice.
(c) By exposing the evils of race prejudice.

This is a large program of reform? It is, and this is because the evil is large. There is not today in human affairs a more subtle and awful enemy of human progress, of peace and sympathy than the reaction war and hatred that lurks in the indefinite thing which we call race prejudice. Does it not call for opposition — determined, persistent opposition? Are rational beings justified in sitting silently, willingly dumb and blind to the growth of this crime? We believe not. We are organized, then to say to the world and our country:

Negroes are men with the foibles and virtues of men.

From *The Crisis*, December 1910.

To treat evil as though it were good and good as though it were evil is not only wrong but dangerous, since in the end it encourages evil and discourages good.

To treat all Negroes alike is treating evil as good and good as evil.

To draw a crass and dogged undeviating color line in human affairs is dangerous — as dangerous to those who draw it as to those against whom it is drawn. . . .

Social Equality and
Racial Intermarriage

There is no doubt but that at the bottom of the race problem in the United States is the question of "Social Equality": and the kernel of the "Social Equality" question is the question of intermarriage.

These questions moreover are made almost impossible of rational discussion because of the intense bitterness and hatred which their mere mention gives rise to: one party hotly begins the discussion by intimating in plain terms that blacks are degenerates and prostitutes, commerce with whom on any plane is monstrous. The other party retorts with a record of millions of mulattoes and mixed bloods, the deliberate degradation of black womanhood and the criminal lust of the white race the world over. With such beginnings there is no rational end of discussion, no reasonable enlightenment.

Let us here, however, seek to forget a moment the hateful and hurtful and set down in cold phrase the main elements of the problem.

1. The sexual intermingling of race groups and more particularly of the lightest and darkest races is regarded by many folk as physically monstrous.

As a scientific dictum this is false. From earliest records racial mixture has been the rule and not the exception and there are today no pure races and no scientific line can be drawn between races. There is no scientific proof that the intermingling of any and all of the branches of the present human family does not produce normal human beings.

From World Tomorrow, 5 (March 1922): 83-84.

2. It is, however, believed by many that while race mixture is not physically monstrous, nevertheless certain strains of blood are superior to
others; that the darker races have a larger number of inferior strains and
that the preservation of the best human culture calls for the survival of
the white race in as pure a state as possible.

There is undoubtedly vast difference in heredity, strains of blood leading to
the rise of individuals of great ability here and others of criminal and degenera-
tive tendencies there. It is also undoubtedly a great human duty to improve the
human stock by rational breeding and by eliminating the unfit and dangerous.
But our knowledge of human heredity is at present extremely vague and
inexact and it is a monstrous perversion of our proven scientific knowledge to
assume that the white race is the physical, mental and moral superior of other
races, and that it has a right to secure its own survival and the death of the
majority of men by any and all methods. It is quite possible that science will
eventually show just as many superior strains in black and yellow as in white
peoples, and just as much innate degeneracy in Europe as in Asia and Africa.

3. Racial intermingling, while neither monstrous nor necessarily delete-
rious, is regarded by many as at present inadvisable:
   (a) because of widespread and deep seated racial antagonisms and
   hatreds.
   (b) because of the necessity of group solidarity as a means of trans-
   mitting human culture.
   (c) because of the value of the group in initiating human culture.
   (d) because of differences of taste as to human types of efficiency
   and beauty.

Here we come to a much more reasonable basis for agreement. Humanity
always has worked in groups and while these groups have gradually increased
in size from the patriarchal family to the nation and even to the "empire" and
the race, there is little likelihood that in the next millennium race lines will
wholly disappear and we shall emerge as one undifferentiated humanity.
Undoubtedly groups and races can and will do much to initiate culture and to
transmit tradition. Moreover racial repulsions and antagonisms, within
bounds, have their uses and incentives. No one can envisage a dead level of
sameness in human types. There are the blue and blonde beauty of the
Nordic race; the golden glory of the yellow world; the soft and sensuous allure
of the brown people and the starry midnight beauty of the blacks; outside of
the mere physical appeal there is every shade of method and conception and

thought in differing groups of human hearts and minds, and the preservation and development of this interesting and stimulating variety in mankind is a great human duty.

But how are racial variety and human differentiation to be encouraged?

1. Some think that races can be kept from mingling only by force; that force should take the form of law even if this involves the prostitution of women of the darker races.

This cost is too great. If the only method of keeping races from intermingling is to force them into degradation and inferiority then it is far better to let them intermingle indiscriminately.

2. Some folk would depend on slander and gossip to discourage intermarriage. They would spread the rumor that dark races are diseased and abnormal, make impossible mates and so should be avoided.

This is simply a campaign of lies and again is socially too costly to maintain.

3. Most people depend on social exclusion — the denial of social equality to those with whom intermarriage is for any reason undesirable.

On Being Crazy

It was one o'clock and I was hungry. I walked into a restaurant, seated myself and reached for the bill-of-fare. My table companion rose.

"Sir," said he, "do you wish to force your company on those who do not want you?"

No, said I, I wish to eat.

"Are you aware, Sir, that this is social equality?"

Nothing of the sort, Sir, it is hunger — and I ate.

The day's work done, I sought the theatre. As I sank into my seat, the lady shrank and squirmed.

I beg pardon, I said.

"Do you enjoy being where you are not wanted?" she asked coldly.

Oh no, I said.

"Well you are not wanted here."

I was surprised. I fear you are mistaken, I said. I certainly want the music and I like to think the music wants me to listen to it.

"Usher," said the lady, "this is social equality."

No, madame, said the usher, it is the second movement of Beethoven's Fifth Symphony.

After the theatre, I sought the hotel where I had sent my baggage. The clerk scowled.

"What do you want?" he asked.

Rest, I said.

"This is a white hotel," he said.

I looked around. Such a color scheme requires a great deal of cleaning, I said, but I don't know that I object.

"We object," said he.

Then why — I began, but he interrupted.

"We don't keep 'niggers'," he said, "we don't want social equality."

From *The Crisis*, June 1923.

Neither do I. I replied gently, I want a bed.

I walked thoughtfully to the train. I'll take a sleeper through Texas. I'm a bit dissatisfied with this town.

"Can't sell you one."

I only want to hire it, said I, for a couple of nights.

"Can't sell you a sleeper in Texas," he maintained. "They consider that social equality."

I consider it barbarism, I said, and I think I'll walk.

Walking, I met a wayfarer who immediately walked to the other side of the road where it was muddy. I asked his reasons.

" 'Niggers' is dirty," he said.

So is mud, said I. Moreover I added, I am not as dirty as you—at least, not yet.

"But you're a 'nigger', ain't you?" he asked.

My grandfather was so-called.

"Well then!" he answered triumphantly.

Do you live in the South? I persisted, pleasantly.

"Sure," he growled, "and starve there."

I should think you and the Negroes might get together and vote out starvation.

"We don't let them vote."

We? Why not? I said in surprise.

" 'Niggers' is too ignorant to vote."

But, I said, I am not so ignorant as you.

"But you're a 'nigger'."

Yes, I'm certainly what you mean by that.

"Well then!" he returned, with that curiously inconsequential note of triumph. "Moreover," he said, "I don't want my sister to marry a nigger."

I had not seen his sister, so I merely murmured, let her say, no.

"By God you shan't marry her, even if she said yes."

But—but I don't want to marry her, I answered a little perturbed at the personal turn.

"Why not!" he yelled, angrier than ever.

Because I'm already married and I rather like my wife.

"Is she a 'nigger'?" he asked suspiciously.

Well, I said again, her grandmother—was called that.

"*Well then!*" he shouted in that oddly illogical way.

I gave up. Go on, I said, either you are crazy or I am.

"We both are," he said as he trotted along in the mud.

The Tuskegee Hospital

We have strong reasons for believing that the following are the actual facts concerning the Tuskegee Hospital:

1. The Harding administration, without consultation with Negro leaders, made Dr. R. R. Moton a sort of referee for 12 million Negroes as to the personnel of the hospital and the Veterans' Bureau promised him categorically that he would be consulted before anybody was appointed superintendent of the hospital.

2. Colonel Robert H. Stanley, a white man, was made superintendent of the hospital and arrived at Tuskegee two days before Dr. Moton was notified.

3. Plans were made to open the hospital April first with a full white staff of white doctors and *white nurses* with *colored nurse-maids* for each white nurse, in order to save them from contact with colored patients!

4. On February 14 Dr. Moton wrote President Harding and told him that if Negro physicians and nurses were debarred from service in the hospital without at least being given a chance to qualify under the Civil Service rules it would bring justifiable criticism upon him and upon the Harding administration.

5. Dr. Moton wrote to the Superintendent of the hospital asking that the opening of the hospital be delayed. The Superintendent replied that there could be no mixture of races in the staff.

6. Strong pressure was put upon Dr. Moton to make him change his position and the Governor of Alabama, together with General R. E. Steiner, telegraphed the President protesting against a mixed staff and demanding a full white staff. Steiner is the head of the American Legion in Alabama and he is the one who in New Orleans fought to keep Negro ex-service men from membership in the Legion; consequently no Negro ex-service men in Alabama can have any affiliation whatsoever with the American Legion. Mean-

From *The Crisis*, July 1923.

time Dr. Moton was threatened by the Ku Klux Klan and others and Tuskegee school had to place armed guards at his home.

7. On February 23 President Harding called Dr. Moton into conference after which the President issued an executive order calling for a special examination for Negro applicants for places on the hospital staff.

8. The only interest of white people in Alabama in this hospital is economic and racial. They want to draw the government salaries and they do not want any Negro officials in Alabama whom the state cannot dominate. To illustrate this: the contract for burying soldiers was given to a white undertaker from Greenville, South Carolina, before the bids of local colored undertakers had a chance even to be submitted.

9. The Civil Service Commission is delaying unnecessarily and unreasonably in arranging for examinations and qualifying colored physicians and without doubt are going to cheat in every possible way.

In commenting on all this we can simply gasp. Is it not inconceivable? Human hatred, meanness and cupidity gone stark mad! Separating races in hospitals and graveyards and fighting to put white men over a Negro hospital! Giving nurses black *maids* to do the work while the white "ladies" eat with the internes, dance at the balls and flirt with the doctors and black men die! Lying, postponing, deceiving, threatening to keep out black doctors and nurses. What will be the result? What *can* be the result? What decent Negro physician or devoted black nurse will dare go to this nest of barbarism?

We honor Moton for his present stand and sympathize with him in his undoubted danger and humiliation. But this leads us to condemn him all the more sharply and unsparingly for the last part which he has played in interracial politics.

Here was a great government duty to take care of black soldiers wounded in soul and body by their awful experience in the Great War. They ought to have been cared for without discrimination in the same hospitals and under the same circumstances as white soldiers. But even if this were impossible because of race hatred, certainly the last place on God's green earth to put a segregated Negro hospital was in the lynching belt of mob-ridden Alabama, Georgia, Mississippi and their ilk.

It occurred to some of our bright Northern white philanthropists and politicians that the shunting of this institution to Tuskegee was exactly the thing; and the tool they found ready to their hand to carry this out was Dr. R. R. Moton.

"Chickens come home to roost." Tuskegee is no place for such a hospital. It is not and cannot be an integral part of the school, which the public opinion of the world of the memory of Booker T. Washington partially protects from Alabama mobs. Outside of such schools as Tuskegee and the larger cities, there is no protection in central Alabama for a decent Negro pig-pen, much less for an institution to restore the life and health of those very black servants of the nation, whom Alabama, led by the cowardly Steiner, has kicked out of the American Legion.

Any Negro in such a hospital, under Southern white men and women of the type who are now fighting like beasts to control it, would be a subject of torture and murder rather than of restoration of health. The only decent method would have been to have placed the institution in the law-abiding North where it belongs; and even now, despite the fact that these millions of dollars of brick and equipment have been sunk into the morass of the black belt, the best way out of the mess would be to tear the hospital down and rebuild it within the confines of civilization.

The Amenia Conference

It was in August, 1916, and the place was Troutbeck, near Amenia [New York]. I had no sooner seen the place than I knew it was mine. It was just a long southerly extension of my own Berkshire Hills. There was the same slow, rocky uplift of land, the nestle of lake and the sturdy murmur of brooks and brown rivers. Afar off were blue and mysterious mountains, and there was a road that rose and dipped and wound and wandered and went on and on past farm and town to the great hard world beyond.

There was the village, small, important, complete, with shadows of old homes; with its broad street that was at once thoroughfare, entrance, and exit. There were the people who had always lived there and their fathers before them, and the people merely passing.

Out from the town lay the farm. I saw its great trees bending over the running brook with a sense of utter friendship and intimate memory, though in truth I had never seen it before. And then one could trudge from the more formal home and lawn, by lane and fence with rise and fall of land, until one came to the lake. The lake, dark and still, lay in the palm of a great, calm hand. The shores rose slowly on either side and had a certain sense of loneliness and calm beauty.

It was in 1916. There was war in Europe but a war far, far away. I had discussed it from time to time with a calm detachment. I had said: "A New Year, Comrades! Come, let us sit here high in the Hills of Life and take counsel one with another. How goes the battle there below, down where dark waters foam, and dun dust fills the nostrils, and the hurry and sweat of human kind is everywhere? Evil, evil, yes, I know. Yonder is murder: so thick is the air with blood and groans that our pulses no longer quicken, our eyes and ears are full. Here, to homewards, is breathless gain and gambling and the steady, unchecked, almost unnoticed growth of human hate."

A sixteen-page pamphlet (1925).

Our own battle in America, that war of colors which we who are black always sense as the principal thing in life, was forming in certain definite lines. Booker Washington is dead. He had died but the year before, 1915. I remember the morning that I heard of it. I knew that it ended an era and I wrote: "The death of Mr. Washington marks an epoch in the history of America. He was the greatest Negro leader since Frederick Douglass, and the most distinguished man, white or black, who has come out of the South since the Civil War. His fame was international and his influence far-reaching. Of the good that he accomplished there can be no doubt: he directed the attention of the Negro race in America to the pressing necessity of economic development; he emphasized technical education, and he did much to pave the way for an understanding between the white and darker races. On the other hand there can be no doubt of Mr. Washington's mistakes and shortcomings; he never adequately grasped the growing bond of politics and industry; he did not understand the deeper foundations of human training, and his basis of better understanding between white and black was founded on caste.

"We may then generously and with deep earnestness lay on the grave of Booker T. Washington testimony of our thankfulness for his undoubted help in the accumulation of Negro land and property, his establishment of Tuskegee and spreading of industrial education, and his compelling of the white South to think at least of the Negro as a possible man. On the other hand, in stern justice, we must lay on the soul of this man a heavy responsibility for the consummation of Negro disfranchisement, the decline of the Negro college and public school, and the firmer establishment of color caste in this land.

"What is done is done. This is no fit time for recrimination or complaint. Gravely and with bowed head let us receive what this great figure gave of good, silently rejecting all else. Firmly and unfalteringly let the Negro race in America, in bleeding Hayti, and throughout the world, close ranks and march steadily on, determined as never before to work and save and endure, but never to swerve from their great goal: the right to vote, the right to know, and the right to stand as men among men throughout the world."

Already we had formed the National Association for the Advancement of Colored People, a precarious thing without money, with some influential members, but we were never quite sure whether their influence would stay with us if we "fought" for Negro rights. We started in tiny offices at 20 Vesey Street and then took larger ones at 26. Finally on the eve of the undreamed-of World War we had moved to 70 Fifth Avenue.

There have been many versions as to how this organization was born, all of them true and yet not the full truth. In a sense William English Walling founded it a hundred years after Lincoln's birth, because of his indignation at a lynching in Lincoln's birthplace [*sic*]. But in reality the thing was born long years before when, under the roar of Niagara Falls, there was formed the Niagara Movement by twenty-nine colored men. How they screamed at us and threatened! The *Outlook*, then at the zenith of its power, declared that we were ashamed of our race and jealous of Mr. Washington. The colored press unanimously condemned us and listed our failures. We were told that we were fighting the stars in their courses. Yet from that beginning of the Niagara Movement in 1905 down to the formation of the National Association for the Advancement of Colored People in 1909, we were welding the weapons, breasting the blows, stating the ideals, and preparing the membership for the larger, stronger organization. Seven of the twenty-nine went on the first Board of Directors of the N.A.A.C.P., and the rest became leading members.

There came six years of work. It is, perhaps, hard to say definitely just what we accomplished in these six years. It was perhaps a matter of spirit and getting ready, and yet we established the *Crisis* magazine and had it by 1916 almost self-supporting. We had branches of our organization throughout the country. We had begun to move upon the courts with test cases. We had held mass meetings through the country. We had stirred up Congress and we had attacked lynching.

We said in the Sixth Annual Report: "The National Association for the Advancement of Colored People was first called into being on the one hundredth anniversary of the birth of Abraham Lincoln. It conceives its mission to be the completion of the work which the great emancipator began. It proposes to make a group of 10,000,000 Americans free from the lingering shackles of past slavery: physically free from peonage, mentally free from ignorance, politically free from disfranchisement, and socially free from insult.

"We are impelled to recognize the pressing necessity of such a movement when we consider these facts:

"The lynching of 2,812 prisoners without trial in the last thirty years.

"The thousands of unaccused black folk who have in these years been done to death.

"The widespread use of crime and alleged crime as a source of public revenue.

"The defenseless position of colored women, continually threatened by laws to make their bodies indefensible and their children illegitimate.

"The total disfranchisement of three-fourths of the black voters.

"The new attack on property rights.

"The widespread and growing discrimination in the simplest matters of public decency and accommodation.

"All these things indicate not simply the suffering of a people, but greater than that, they show the impotence of American democracy. And so the National Association for the Advancement of Colored People appeals to the nation to accept the clear and simple settlement of the Negro problem, which consists in treating colored men as you would like to be treated if you were colored."

Our six years of organized work did not by any means satisfy us. We wanted a bigger, stronger organization, and especially we wanted to get rid of the all too true statement that we were asking for things that colored people did not want or at least did not want with any unity. The wall between the Washington camp and those who had opposed his policies was still there; and it occurred to J. E. Spingarn and his friends that up in the peace and quiet of Amenia and around this beautiful lake, colored men and women of all shades of opinion might sit down and rest and talk and agree on many things if not on all.

The conference as Mr. Spingarn conceived it, was to be "under the auspices of the N.A.A.C.P." but wholly independent of it, and the invitations definitely said this. They were issued by Mr. Spingarn personally, and the guests were assured that they would not be bound by any program of the N.A.A.C.P. Thus the conference was intended primarily to bring about as large a degree as possible of unity of purpose among Negro leaders and to do this regardless of its effect upon any organization, although, of course, many of us hoped that some central organization and preferably the N.A.A.C.P. would eventually represent this new united purpose.

One can hardly realize today how difficult and intricate a matter it was to arrange such a conference, to say who should come and who should not, to gloss over hurts and enmities. I remember Mr. Spingarn's asking me with a speculative eye and tentative intonation if the editor of a certain paper ought not to be invited. Now that paper had had an exceedingly good time at my expense, and had said things about me and my beliefs with which I not only did not agree but which gave rise in my hot mind to convictions of deliberate misrepresentation. But after all the editor must come. He was important, and Mr. Spingarn was pleased to see that I agreed with him in this.

About two hundred invitations to white and colored people were actually issued, and in making up this list the advice of friends of Mr. Washington, like Major Moton and Mr. Emmett Scott and Mr. Fred Moore, was sought. There were messages of good will from many who could not attend: from Taft, Roosevelt, Hughes, Woodrow Wilson, and others. But all this selection of persons was the easier part of the thing. The guests had, of course, to be induced to come; fortunately it was possible to accomplish this, and sixty or more persons expressed their willingness to attend. We were going to make for ourselves a little village of tents, and there we had to be fed and amused, while a discreet program was carried out and careful hospitality extended. At this Joel and Amy and Arthur Spingarn and their friends worked long and assiduously, and the result was beautiful and satisfying.

I remember the morning when we arrived. It was misty with a northern chill in the air and a dampness all about. One felt cold and a bit lonely in those high grey uplands. There were only a few there at first, but they filtered in slowly, and with each came more of good cheer. At last we began to have a rollicking jolly time. Now and then, of course, there was just a little sense of stiffness and care in conversation when people met who for ten years had been saying hard things about each other; but not a false word was spoken. The hospitality of our hosts was perfect and the good will of all was evident.

There was a varied company. From the South came Lucy Lane, John Hope, Henry A. Hunt, and R. R. Wright of Georgia; Emmett J. Scott of Alabama, former Secretary of Booker Washington; J. C. Napier of Tennessee. From the West came Francis H. Warren of Detroit, Charles E. Bentley and George W. Ellis of Chicago, Mary B. Talbert of Buffalo, Charles W. Chesnutt of Cleveland, and B. S. Brown of Minnesota. Washington was represented by Mary Church Terrell, James A. Cobb, George W. Cook, Kelly Miller, L. M. Hershaw, Montgomery Gregory, Neval H. Thomas, and J. R. Hawkins. From Pennsylvania came Leslie Hill, L. J. Coppin, R. R. Wright, Jr., and W. Justin Carter. New York sent Fred Moore, Hutchins Bishop, James W. and J. Rosamond Johnson, Addie Hunton, W. L. Bulkley, William Pickens, and Roy Nash, then secretary of the N.A.A.C.P. Baltimore gave us Mason Hawkins and Ashbie Hawkins and Bishop [John] Hurst. New England sent William H. Lewis, George W. Crawford, and Garnet Waller.

I doubt if ever before so small a conference of American Negroes had so many colored men of distinction who represented at the same time so complete a picture of all phases of Negro thought. Its very completeness in this respect was its salvation. If it had represented one party or clique it would have been less harmonious and unanimous, because someone would surely have essayed in sheer fairness to state the opinions of men who were not there and would have stated them necessarily without compromise and without consideration. As it was, we all learned what the majority of us knew. None of us held uncompromising and unchangeable views. It was after all a matter of emphasis. We all believed in thrift, we all wanted the Negro to vote, we all wanted the laws enforced, we all wanted assertion of our essential manhood; but how to get these things, — there of course was infinite divergence of opinion.

But everybody had a chance to express his opinion, and at the same time the conference was not made up of sonorous oratory. The thing was too intimate and small. We were too near each other. We were talking to each other face to face, we knew each other pretty intimately, and there was present a pervading and saving sense of humor that laughed the poseur straight off the rostrum and that made for joke and repartee in the midst of serious argument. Of course and in fact let us confess here and now that one thing helped everything else: We were gloriously fed. There was a great tent with tables and chairs which became at will now dining-room, now auditorium. Promptly at meal time food appeared, miraculously steaming and perfectly cooked, out of the nothingness of the wide landscape. We ate hilariously in the open air with such views of the good green earth and the waving waters and the pale blue sky as all men ought often to see, yet few men do. And then filled and complacent we talked awhile of the thing which all of us called "The Problem", and after that and just as regularly we broke up and played good and hard. We swam and rowed and hiked and lingered in the forests and sat upon the hillsides and picked flowers and sang.

Our guests dropped by, the governor of the state, a member of Congress, a university president, an army officer, a distinguished grandson of William Lloyd Garrison, a Harlem real estate man, business men, and politicians. We had the women there to complete the real conference, Mrs. Terrell, Mary B. Talbert, Mrs. Hunton, Lucy Laney, Dr. Morton Jones of Brooklyn; Inez Milholland, in the glory of her young womanhood dropped by, in this which was destined to be almost the last year of her magnificent life. Mrs. Spingarn strolled over now and then and looked at us quietly and thoughtfully.

The Amenia Conference in reality marked the end of an era and the beginning. As we said in our resolutions: "The Amenia Conference believes that its members have arrived at a virtual unanimity of opinion in regard to certain principles and that a more or less definite result may be expected from its deliberations. These principles and this practical result may be summarized as follows:

"(1) The conference believes that all forms of education are desirable for the Negro and that every form of education should be encouraged and advanced.

"(2) It believes that the Negro, in common with all other races, cannot achieve its highest development without complete political freedom.

"(3) It believes that this development and this freedom cannot be furthered without organization and without a practical working understanding among the leaders of the colored race.

"(4) It believes that antiquated subjects of controversy, ancient suspicions and factional alignments must be eliminated and forgotten if this organization of the race and this practical working understanding of its leaders are to be achieved.

"(5) It realizes the peculiar difficulties which surround this problem in the South and the special need of understanding between leaders of the race who live in the South and those who live in the North. It has learned to understand and respect the good faith, methods and ideals of those who are working for the solution of this problem in various sections of the country.

"(6) The conference pledges itself to the inviolable privacy of all its deliberations. These conclusions, however, and the amicable results of all the deliberations of the conference are fair subjects for discussion in the colored press and elsewhere.

"(7) The conference feels that mutual understanding would be encouraged if the leaders of the race could meet annually for private and informal discussion under conditions similar to those which have prevailed at this conference."

It is a little difficult today to realize why it was necessary to say all this. There had been bitterness and real cause for bitterness in those years after the formation of the Niagara Movement and before the N.A.A.C.P. had come to the front. Men were angry and hurt. Booker Washington had been mobbed by Negroes in Boston, Monroe Trotter had been thrown in jail; the lowest motives that one can conceive had been attributed to antagonists on either side — jealousy, envy, greed, cowardice, intolerance, and the like. Newspapers and magazine articles had seethed with threat, charge, and innuendo.

Then there had been numberless attempts at understanding which had failed. There was, for instance, that conference in Carnegie Hall [in 1904] when Andrew Carnegie through Booker T. Washington financed a general meeting of Negro leaders. It was a much larger conference than that at Amenia but its spirit was different. It was a conference carefully manipulated. There was no confidence there and no complete revelation. It savored more of armed truce than of understanding. Those of us who represented the opposition were conscious of being forced and influenced against our will. Lyman Abbott of the *Outlook* came and talked with us benevolently. Andrew Carnegie himself came. Numbers of rich and powerful whites looked in upon us and admonished us to be good, and then the opposition between the wings flamed in bitter speech and charge. Men spoke with double tongues saying one thing and meaning another. And finally there came compromise and an attempt at constructive effort which somehow no one felt was real. I had proposed a Committee of Twelve to guide the Negro race, but when the committee was finally constituted I found that it predominately represented only one wing of the controversy and that it was financed indirectly by Andrew Carnegie, and so I indignantly withdrew and the Committee of Twelve never functioned but died leaving only a few pamphlets which Hugh Brown edited. There were other efforts, but it needed time and understanding, and when the Amenia Conference came the time was ripe.

We talked of many matters at Amenia — of education, politics, organization, and the situation in the South. First of all we spoke of the former subjects of controversy; then we made the deliberations private, and to this day there is no record of what various persons said; and finally we declared for annual meetings of the conference, and then we got to the main subjects of controversy.

If the world had not gone crazy directly after the Amenia Conference and indeed at the very time of its meeting had not been much more widely insane than most of us realized, it is probable that the aftermath of this conference would have been even greater than we can now see. It happened because of the War that there was but the one conference held at Amenia. While we were there the world was fighting and had fought two long years. In another year America was destined to join the war and the Negro race was to be torn and shaken in its very heart by new and tremendous problems. The old order was going and a new race situation was to be developed.

Of all this the Amenia Conference was a symbol. It not only marked the end of the old things and the old thoughts and the old ways of attacking the race problem, but in addition to this it was the beginning of the new things. Probably on account of our meeting the Negro race was more united and more ready to meet the problems of the world than it could possibly have been without these beautiful days of understanding. It was a "Close ranks!" before the great struggle that issued in the new world. How appropriate that so tremendous a thing should have taken place in the midst of so much quiet and beauty there at Troutbeck, which John Burroughs knew and loved throughout his life, a place of poets and fishermen, of dreamers and farmers, a place far apart and away from the bustle of the world and the centers of activity. It was all peculiarly appropriate, and those who in the future write the history of the way in which the American Negro became a man must not forget this event and landmark in 1916.

Propaganda and World War

My discussions of the concept of race, and of the white and colored worlds, are not to be regarded as digressions from the history of my life; rather my autobiography is a digressive illustration and exemplification of what race has meant in the world in the nineteenth and twentieth centuries. It is for this reason that I have named and tried to make this book an autobiography of race rather than merely a personal reminiscence, with the idea that peculiar racial situation and problems could best be explained in the life history of one who has lived them. My living gains its importance from the problems and not the problems from me.

Nothing illustrates this more than my experiences from the time I left Atlanta until the period of reconstruction after the first World War. These days were the climacteric of my pilgrimage. I had come to the place where I was convinced that science, the careful social study of the Negro problems, was not sufficient to settle them; that they were not basically, as I had assumed, difficulties due to ignorance but rather difficulties due to the determination of certain people to suppress and mistreat the darker races. I believed that this evil group formed a minority and a small minority of the nation and of all civilized peoples, and that once the majority of well-meaning folk realized their evil machinations, we would be able to secure justice.

A still further step I was not yet prepared to realize must be taken: not simply knowledge, not simply direct repression of evil, will reform the world. In long, indirect pressure and action of various and intricate sorts, the actions of men which are not due to lack of knowledge nor to evil intent, must be changed by influencing folkways, habits, customs and subconscious deeds. Here perhaps is a realm of physical and cosmic law which science does not yet control. But of all this in 1910 I had no clear concept. It took twenty more

From *Dusk of Dawn: An Essay Toward an Autobiography of a Race Concept* (1940).

388

years of living and striving to bring this revolution to my thought. Stepping, therefore, in 1910, out of my ivory tower of statistics and investigation, I sought with bare hands to lift the earth and put it in the path in which I conceived it ought to go. Little did I realize in August, 1910, that the earth was about to be shaken with earthquake, deluged with blood, whipped and starved into disaster, and that race hate and wholesale color and group subordination, not only were a prime cause of this disaster, but emphasized and sharpened its course and hindered consequent recovery.

These were the years between the Roosevelts, including the administration of Taft, the two reigns of Wilson, the interlude of Harding and Coolidge and the disaster of Hoover. The United States was living not to itself, but as part of the strain and stress of the world. I knew something of Europe in these days. I went to the Paris Exposition in 1900 with the stipend that I had received for an exhibit on Negro development prepared in my office. By grace of an English friend, Frances Hoggan, I roamed through England, Scotland and a bit of France in 1906 on a bicycle and saw the Island of Skye and Edinburgh, the Lake and Shakespeare countries and London. I saw a Europe of past beauty and present culture, fit as I fondly dreamed to realize a democracy in which I and my people could find a welcome place.

I came home rested and ready to follow the steps that led from the Niagara Movement meeting of 1906 to the Negro conference of 1909. These steps were not only the indirect ones illustrated by the difficulty of raising money for the Atlanta work, but also the series of events which led to the New York conference. Lynching continued in the United States but raised curiously enough little protest. Three hundred twenty-seven victims were publicly murdered by the mob during the years 1910 to 1914, and in 1915 the number leaped incredibly to one hundred in one year. The pulpit, the social reformers, the statesmen continued in silence before the greatest affront to civilization which the modern world has known. In 1909 William English Walling and his wife Anna Strunsky went out to investigate a lynching and anti-Negro riot in Springfield, Illinois, the birthplace [sic] of Abraham Lincoln. The upheaval took place on the one hundredth anniversary of his birth. Eventually one hundred seventeen indictments were brought in against the rioters but there was almost no actual punishment.

Walling protested in the press. He asked America if the time had not come when the work of the Great Emancipator must be finished and the Negro race not simply in law and theory, but in fact, set free. Working with Mary White Ovington, Charles Edward Russell and Oswald Garrison Villard, after meetings and correspondence, he and others called a conference in New York City. The timeliness of such a conference and such action was manifest by the formation of the Niagara Movement in 1905 and its great meeting at Harpers Ferry in 1906. Heartened and at the same time warned by the Niagara Movement, the conference of 1909 invited the members of that body to participate. They were heartened by the fact that young radical opinion among Negroes saw the necessity of immediate organized intelligent effort to complete the emancipation of the Negro; but they were also warned that this radical movement had been initiated in direct opposition to the policy and action of the greatest Negro leader since the Civil War. To a degree never before accomplished, this Negro had united liberal opinion North and South in friendliness for the Negro and it was doubtful if any organization could make headway on an anti-Washington platform. The Niagara Movement itself had made little progress, beyond its inspirational fervor, toward a united and constructive program of work.

It was therefore not without misgiving that the members of the Niagara Movement were invited into the new conference, but all save Trotter and Ida Wells Barnett came to form the backbone of the new organization. In 1910 this was incorporated as the National Association for the Advancement of Colored People. It was inevitable that I should be offered an executive position in this organization; but there again many felt that I must not be allowed to direct its policy too openly against Mr. Washington and that the work which I did should as far as possible be a continuation of what I had done in studying the American Negro and making his accomplishment known.

This was in direct accord with my own desires and plans. I did not wish to attack Booker Washington; I wished to give him credit for much good, but to oppose certain of his words and policies which could be interpreted against our best interests; I wanted to do this through propaganda of the truth and for this reason I wished to continue in New York so far as possible my studies in Atlanta, and to add to this a periodical of fact and agitation which I should edit.

I tried to accomplish this with help of the Slater Fund and actually edited the four last studies of the Atlanta series from New York with the collaboration of Augustus Dill who succeeded me in Atlanta. But President Ware was strongly advised to cut the University off from the National Association for the Advancement of Colored People entirely, and did so in 1915. The studies ceased in 1917.

I arrived in New York to find a bare office; the treasurer, Mr. Villard, said frankly: "I don't know who is going to pay your salary; I have no money." The secretary then in charge was alarmed about her own job and suspicious of my designs; and a generally critical, if not hostile, public expected the National Association to launch a bitter attack upon Booker T. Washington and Tuskegee. I placated the secretary by disclaiming any design or desire for executive work; and I heartened the treasurer, a newspaper man, by my plan to publish a periodical which should be the organ of the Association. There was, however, opposition to this. First of all, magazines of this sort were costly and the organization had no money. Secondly, organs are usually of doubtful efficiency. My good friend, Albert E. Pillsbury, then Attorney-General of Massachusetts, wrote feelingly: "If you have not decided upon a periodical, for heaven's sake don't. They are as numerous as flies." And he meant, to conclude, about as useful.

My first job was to get the *Crisis* going; and arriving on August 1, 1910, I finally got the first copy off the press in November. Later I had the collaboration and advice of a young English woman, Mary McLean, then staff writer for the Sunday edition of the New York *Times*. I owe her more than I can say. The *Crisis* came at the psychological moment and its success was phenomenal. From the one thousand which I ventured to publish first, it went up a thousand a month until by 1918 (due, of course, to special circumstances) we published and sold over a hundred thousand.

In November, 1913, and at my earnest solicitation, Augustus G. Dill, who had succeeded me at Atlanta University, left his academic work and came to be business manager of the *Crisis* magazine. From then until early in 1928 he gave to the work his utmost devotion and to him was due much of its phenomenal business success. In five years the *Crisis* became self-supporting, January 1, 1916, with an annual income increasing from $6,500 in 1911 to $24,000 in 1915. Its total income during these years was over $84,000, and it circulated nearly a million and a half copies, net paid circulation. It reached every state in the Union, beside Europe, Africa, and the South Seas.

With this organ of propaganda and defense and with its legal bureau, lecturers and writers, the National Association for the Advancement of Colored People was able to organize one of the most effective assaults of liberalism upon prejudice, and reaction that the modern world has seen. We secured extraordinary helpers: great lawyers like Moorfield Storey and Louis Marshall; earnest liberals like Milholland, John Haynes Holmes, and Jane Addams; sympathetic friends from the whole land.

Naturally the real and effective work of the organization was done by the group which centered in the office first at 20 Vesey Street, and then at 70 Fifth Avenue, where we stayed until Ginn and Company's Southern patrons forced us to move to 69. These persons were assiduous in their attendance, unfailing in their interest, and gave a large amount of their time to the work. As a result the organization was not a secretary-dominated center, with the power in the hands of one man. It was an intelligent group of considerable size which was willing and eager to learn and help.

There was one initial difficulty common to all interracial effort in the United States. Ordinarily the white members of a committee formed of Negroes and whites become dominant. Either by superior training or their influence or their wealth they take charge of the committee, guide it, and use the colored membership as their helpers and executive workers in certain directions. Usually if the opposite policy is attempted, if the Negroes attempt to dominate and conduct the committee, the whites become dissatisfied and gradually withdraw. In the NAACP it was our primary effort to achieve an equality of racial influence without stressing race and without allowing undue predominance to either group. I think we accomplished this for a time to an unusual degree.

The members studied the situations. They were expert in various lines of inquiry and effort, once we had settled down to effective work. The outstanding members of this inner group were Oswald Garrison Villard, Mary Ovington, William English Walling, Paul Kennaday, Joel Spingarn, and Charles Edward Russell. Villard became chairman of the board but in 1913 was not wholly in agreement with me and was replaced by a young man [Joel Spingarn] to whom I have dedicated this book and who stands out vividly in my mind as a scholar and a knight.

With the combined aid of these workers and many others, we could, through the *Crisis* and our officers, our secretaries and friends, place consistently and continuously before the country a clear-cut statement of the legitimate aims of the American Negro and the facts concerning his condition. We began to organize his political power and make it influential and we started a campaign against lynching and mob law which was the most effective ever organized and eventually brought the end of the evil in sight. Especially we gained a series of court victories before the highest courts of the land which perhaps never have been equaled; beginning with the overthrow of the vicious "Grandfather Clauses" in 1916 and the breaking of the backbone of residential segregation in 1917.

One of the first difficulties that the National Association met was bound to be the matter of its attitude toward Mr. Washington. I carefully tried to avoid any exaggeration of differences of thought; but to discuss the Negro question in 1910 was to discuss Booker T. Washington and almost before we were conscious of the inevitable trends, we were challenged from Europe. Mr. Washington was in Europe in 1910 and made some speeches in England on his usual conciliatory lines. John Milholland, who had been so dominant in the organization of the National Association, immediately wrote me and said that American Negroes must combat the idea that they were satisfied with conditions. I, therefore, wrote an appeal to England and Europe, under the signature of a group of colored friends so as not to involve the NAACP officially:

"If Mr. Booker T. Washington, or any other person, is giving the impression abroad that the Negro problem in America is in process of satisfactory solution, he is giving an impression which is not true. We say this without personal bitterness toward Mr. Washington. He is a distinguished American and has a perfect right to his opinion. But we are compelled to point out that Mr. Washington's large financial responsibilities have made him dependent on the rich charitable public and that, for this reason, he has for years been compelled to tell, not the whole truth, but that part of it which certain powerful interests in America wish to appear as the truth. In flat contradiction, however, to the pleasant pictures thus pointed out, let us not forget that the consensus of opinion among eminent European scholars who know the race problem in America, from De Tocqueville to Von Halle, De Laveleys, Archer, and Johnston, is that it forms the gravest of American problems. We black men who live and suffer under present conditions, and who have no reason, and refuse to accept reasons for silence, can substantiate this nearly unanimous testimony."

In further emphasis of this statement and in anticipation of the meeting of the proposed Races Congress, Mr. Milholland arranged that I should go early to London and make some addresses. The plan simmered down to an address before the Lyceum Club, the leading woman's club of London. There it encountered opposition. An American woman member wrote: "I think there is serious objection to entertaining Dr. Du Bois at the Lyceum." The result was an acrimonious controversy from which I tried to withdraw gently but was unable. Finally led by Her Highness, the then Ranee of Sarawak and Dr. Etta Sayre, a luncheon was held at the Lyceum Club with a bishop and two countesses; several knights and ladies, and men like Maurice Hewlett and Sir Harry Johnston; I was the chief speaker.

The Races Congress, held in July, 1911, in London, would have marked an epoch in the cultural history of the world, if it had not been followed so quickly by the World War. As it was, it turned out to be a great and inspiring occasion, bringing together representatives of numerous ethnic and cultural groups, and new and frank conceptions of the scientific bases of racial and social relations of people.

The Congress was planned with meticulous care and thoroughness by the clear-sighted Gustav Spiller, the organizer, working under the auspices of the English Ethical Culture movement. The papers of the Congress were printed and put into the hands of the delegates before the meeting and yet kept from general publication. An extraordinary number of distinguished persons took part and, together with Felix Adler, I was named as co-secretary to represent the United States. To be sure the Congress encountered a certain air of questioning and lack of high official sanction. There were even those in England who professed to think that it had something to do with horse-racing; but even papers like the *Times* had to notice its impressive meetings and the caliber of the participants. There were dramatic incidents like the arraignment of Christianity by the delegate from Ceylon, "where every prospect pleases and only man is vile."

I had not only my regular assigned part, but due to the sudden illness of Sir Harry Johnston from his chronic tropical fever, represented him at one of the chief sessions and made a speech which gained wide reading. Thus I had a chance twice to address the Congress and I wrote one of the two poems which greeted the assembly:

> Save us, World-Spirit, from our lesser selves,
> Grant us that war and hatred cease,
> Reveal our souls in every race and hue;
> Help us, O Human God, in this Thy Truce,
> To make Humanity divine.

Even while the Races Congress was meeting came the forewarning of coming doom: in a characteristic way a German war vessel sailed into an African port, notifying the world that Germany was determined to have larger ownership and control of cheap black labor; a demand camouflaged as the need of "a place in the sun." I fancied at the time that I knew my Europe pretty well, but familiarity with the dangers of the European scene had bred contempt of disaster. I thought with other philosophers that a general European war was impossible. The economic and cultural strands among the nations had grown too strong to be snapped by war. World peace, world organization, conference and conciliation, the gradual breaking down of trade barriers, the spread of civilization to backward peoples, the emancipation of suppressed groups like the American Negro — seem to me the natural, the inevitable path of world progress. I did not assess at the right value the envy and jealousy of those imperial powers which did not share profit in colored labor, nor did I realize that the intertwining threads of culture bound colored folk in slavery to, and not in mutual co-operation with, the whites.

Indeed it was not easily possible for the student of international affairs trained in white institutions and by European ideology to follow the partially concealed and hidden action of international intrigue, which was turning colonial empire into the threat of armed competition for markets, cheap materials, and cheap labor. Colonies still meant religious and social uplift in current propaganda. There were indications of strain in the determination of Germany to increase her sea power and to rival England in the technique of her manufactures. It was evident that the understanding between England and France both in Africa and in Asia was relegating Germany to a second place in colonial imperialism. It was evident too that the defeat of Russia by Japan had given rise to a fear of colored revolt against white exploitation.

The general outlines of this I had followed, but like most of the world I was thrown into consternation when later with sudden and unawaited violence, world war burst in 1914. I had come to New York and the editorship of the *Crisis* during the administration of Taft. William Taft, fat, genial, and mediocre, had no grasp of world affairs nor international trends. Despite his Philippine experience, he began his reactionary administration by promising the South that he would appoint no Federal official to whom the Southern people were opposed; and thus blandly announced that eight million black Southerners were not people. Not only this but his handling of the revolt of irritated and goaded black soldiers at Brownsville, Texas, and his general cynical attitude toward the race problem led me to one of my first efforts to make political solution of the race problem.

Returning to New York after the Races Congress, I was faced by the political campaign of 1912. Disappointed at the attitude of Taft, I turned eagerly toward Roosevelt and the "Bull Moose" movement, thinking that I saw there a splendid chance for a third party movement, on a broad platform of votes for Negroes and the democratization of industry. Sitting in the office of the *Crisis*, I wrote out a proposed plank for the Progressives to adopt at their Chicago meeting in 1912: "The Progressive Party recognizes that distinctions of race or class in political life have no place in a democracy. Especially does the party realize that a group of 10,000,000 people who have in a generation changed from a slave to a free labor system, re-established family life, accumulated $1,000,000,000 of real property, including 20,000,000 acres of land, and reduced their illiteracy from 80 to 30 per cent, deserves and must have justice, opportunity and a voice in their own government. The party, therefore, demands for the Americans of Negro descent the repeal of unfair discriminatory laws and the right to vote on the same terms on which other citizens vote."

This was taken to Chicago by my friend and fellow official of the NAACP, Joel Spingarn, and supported by two other directors of the Association, Dr. Henry Moskowitz and Jane Addams. They worked in vain for its adoption. Theodore Roosevelt would have none of it. He told Mr. Spingarn frankly that he should be careful of "that man Du Bois," who was in his opinion a "dangerous" person. The "Bull Moose" convention not only refused to adopt a plank anything like this, but refused to seat most of the colored delegates. They elected a Southern "lily-white" to run on the ticket with Mr. Roosevelt, and finally succeeded in splitting the Republican Party and giving Woodrow Wilson an opportunity of becoming President of the United States.

Immediately Bishop Walters of the African Zion Church, who had joined the Democratic Party in 1909, approached me with the idea that Mr. Wilson might be influenced in the Negro's behalf. I proposed, if he could, to throw the weight of the *Crisis* against Roosevelt and Taft, and for Wilson. Bishop Walters went to see Wilson. He secured from him in October, 1912, a categorical expression over his signature "of his earnest wish to see justice done the colored people in every matter; and not mere grudging justice, but justice executed with liberality and cordial good feeling. . . . I want to assure them that should I become President of the United States they may count upon me for absolute fair dealing, for everything by which I could assist in advancing the interests of their race in the United States."

I espoused the cause of Woodrow Wilson, fully aware of the political risk involved and yet impelled to this path by the reaction of Taft and disappointment at Roosevelt. I resigned from New York Local No. 1 of the Socialist Party which I had joined, to escape discipline for not voting the Socialist ticket. I could not let Negroes throw away votes. I wrote in the *Crisis* just before the election: "We sincerely believe that even in the face of promises disconcertingly vague, and in the face of the solid caste-ridden South, it is better to elect Woodrow Wilson President of the United States and prove once for all if the Democratic Party dares to be democratic when it comes to black men. It has proven that it can be in many Northern states and cities. Can it be in the nation? We hope so, and we are willing to risk a trial."

We estimated that in the North a hundred thousand black voters had supported Woodrow Wilson in 1912, and had been so distributed in strategic places as to do much to help his election. This was an unusually successful effort to divide the Negro vote; but as many Negroes had feared it brought disappointment and encouraged unexpected reaction. Among minor indications of this reaction was Wilson's odd demand of Bishop Walters. The Bishop had been called to the White House for consultation concerning the colored people in 1915. "By the way," said the President, "what about that letter that I wrote you during the campaign. I do not seem to remember it." "I have it right here," said the Bishop eagerly, and handed it to him. The President forgot to return it.

With the accession of Woodrow Wilson to the presidency in 1913 there opened for the American Negro a period, lasting through and long after the World War and culminating in 1919, which was an extraordinary test for their courage and a time of cruelty, discrimination, and wholesale murder. For this there were several causes: the return to power for the first time since the Civil War of the Southern Democracy; secondly, the apprehension and resentment aroused in the South by the campaign of the NAACP; but above and beyond that, the rising economic rivalry between colored and white workers in the United States and back of this the whole economic stress of the modern world with its industrial imperialism.

The Southern white workers had for years been lashed into enmity against the Negro by Tillman, Vardaman, Blease, and Jeff Davis of Arkansas. Representatives of these Southern workers, now seated in Congress, proceeded to demand stricter legal and economic caste; and at the meeting of Wilson's first Congress there came the greatest flood of bills proposing discriminatory legislation against Negroes that has ever been introduced into an American Congress. There were no less than twenty bills advocating "Jim Crow" cars in the District of Columbia, race segregation of Federal employees, excluding Negroes from commissions in the army and navy, forbidding the intermarriage of Negroes and whites, and excluding all immigrants of Negro descent.

Quite suddenly the program for the NAACP, which up to this time had been more or less indefinite, was made clear and intensive. Every ounce of effort was made not only against lynching and segregation, but against this new proposed discriminatory legislation in Congress and in a dozen different states, where with evident collusion similar legislation had been proposed. Most of this legislation was eventually killed; in only one state was such a measure — an anti-intermarriage bill — passed; but in Washington one proposal was put through by executive order: Wilson proceeded to segregate nearly all of the colored Federal employees, of whom there were a considerable number, herding them so far as possible in separate rooms with separate eating and toilet facilities. This was a serious reversal of Federal usage and despite repeated assaults, much of this segregation still remains in the departments of the national capital. When the militant Monroe Trotter headed a delegation to protest to the President this segregation of colored officeholders, Wilson angrily dismissed him, declaring his language "insulting."

We found that our political efforts were abortive for a reason which, while possible, did not seem to us probable. We had calculated that increased independence in the Negro vote would bring a bid for the Negro vote from opposing parties; but it did not until many years later. Indeed, it was not until the re-election of the second Roosevelt in 1936 that the Negro vote in the North came to be eagerly contended for by the two major parties. In 1914 we tried to make congressional candidates declare themselves as to our demands, but were only partially successful. The Sixty-fourth Congress saw eleven bills introduced advocating color caste and the state legislatures continued to be bombarded by similar legislation. Thus, in 1916, we found ourselves politically helpless. We had no choice. We could vote for Wilson who had segregated us or for Hughes who, despite all our requests, remained doggedly dumb on our problems.

The spread of disaster throughout the world shown by the Chinese Revolution of 1912 and the Balkan War of 1913, and the World War of 1914, was illustrated in the United States by the meeting of the National Conference of Charities and Correction in Memphis in May, 1914. Not only were there no accommodations for colored delegates, but the conference refused even to put in the agenda anything touching the race problem. As a result, Joel Spingarn, William Pickens, and myself went down to Memphis and advertised during the conference a public meeting "for all persons who love the truth and dare to hear it." A large crowd of persons black and white, including many delegates to the conference, were present.

For some time after the opening of the World War, its possible influence upon the Negro race in America was not clear. However, this world convulsion found America spiritually ill-prepared to cope with it, so far as race difficulties were concerned. In 1912 there arose the agitation for residential race segregation. It grew out of the fact that Negroes, as they increased in intelligence and property holding, were dissatisfied with the living quarters, where by long custom they had been confined in the chief cities of the land. In Baltimore came one of their first efforts to buy their way out of the back alleys and the slums into the better-paved, better-lighted main streets. This movement was encouraged by the wish of many of the owners of this property to move to newly developed suburban districts. A fierce conflict developed and Baltimore, by city ordinance, proceeded to segregate Negroes by law. This agitation throughout the North was increased by the emigration of Southern Negroes. Cheap foreign labor had been cut off by the war and Northern manufacturers began to encourage migration from the South. The stream began as soon as the European war opened. It caused not only increasing congestion in the colored districts of the North; it also began to deplete the supply of agricultural labor and common city labor in the South, and to encourage racial friction according to current social patterns.

Beginning in Baltimore this agitation with a series of ordinances and laws spread West, North and South. For a period of ten years it called for every resource and ingenuity on the part of the National Association for the Advancement of Colored People to fight the legislation in courts, to repel mob violence on home-buyers, and to seek a supporting white public opinion.

But all this was but a prelude to deeper and more serious race oppression. The United States seized Haiti in 1915. It was not alone the intrinsic importance of the country, but Haiti stood with Liberia as a continuing symbol of Negro revolt against slavery and oppression, and capacity for self-rule; and the sudden extinction of its independence by a President whom we had helped to elect, followed by exploitation at the hands of New York City banks and plundering speculators, and the killing of at least three thousand Haitians by American soldiers, was a bitter pre-war pill.

That same year occurred another, and in the end, much more insidious and hurtful attack: the new technique of the moving picture had come to America and the world. But this method of popular entertainment suddenly became great when David Griffith made the film "The Birth of a Nation." He set the pace for a new art and method: the thundering horses, the masked riders, the suspense of plot and the defense of innocent womanhood; all this was thrilling even if melodramatic and overdrawn. This would have been a great step in the development of a motion-picture art, if it had not happened that the director deliberately used as the vehicle of his picture one of the least defensible attacks upon the Negro race, made by Thomas Dixon in his books beginning with the "Leopard's Spots," and in his play "The Clansman." There was fed to the youth of the nation and to the unthinking masses as well as to the world a story which twisted the emancipation and enfranchisement of the slave in a great effort toward universal democracy, into an orgy of theft and degradation and wide rape of white women.

In combating this film, our Association was placed in a miserable dilemma. We had to ask liberals to oppose freedom of art and expression, and it was senseless for them to reply: "Use this art in your own defense." The cost of picture making and the scarcity of appropriate artistic talent made any such immediate answer beyond question. Without doubt the increase of lynching in 1915 and later was directly encouraged by this film. We did what we could to stop its showing and thereby probably succeeded in advertising it even beyond its admittedly notable merits. The combined result of these various events caused a sudden increase of lynching. The number of mob murders so increased that nearly one hundred Negroes were lynched during 1915 and a score of whites, a larger number than had occurred for more than a decade.

The year 1916 brought one decided note of hope. The Supreme Court of the United States, after having dodged the plain issue for a decade, finally at our insistence and with the help of our corps of lawyers headed by Moorfield Storey, handed down a decision which outlawed the infamous "Grandfather Clauses" of the disfranchising constitutions of the South. These clauses had given an hereditary right to vote to white illiterates while excluding colored illiterates. To overbalance this sign of hope there came, however, continued prevalence of lynching in unusually serious form. Five Negroes in Lee County, Georgia were lynched en masse and there came the horrible public burning of Jesse Washington in Waco, Texas, before a mob of thousands of men, women and children. "While a fire was being prepared of boxes, the naked boy was stabbed and the chain put over the tree. He tried to get away, but could not. He reached up to grab the chain and they cut off his fingers. The big man struck the boy on the back of the neck with a knife just as they were pulling him up on the tree. Mr. — — thought that was practically the death blow. He was lowered into the fire several times by means of the chain around his neck. Someone said they would estimate the boy had about twenty-five stab wounds, each one of them death-dealing."

In October, Anthony Crawford, well-to-do colored farmer of South Carolina, worth $20,000, and the owner of four hundred acres of land, was set upon and whipped for "impudence" in refusing to agree to a price for his cotton seed; he was then jailed, mobbed, mutilated and killed, and his family driven out of the county.

The death of Booker Washington in 1915 coincided with a change in Negro attitudes. The political defeat of Roosevelt and Taft had deprived Mr. Washington of his political influence. The Tuskegee Machine gradually ceased to function, and Tuskegee came to realize its natural place as a center of education rather than of propaganda. For some time Mr. Washington's general influence among American Negroes, especially in the face of the rising importance of the NAACP and the *Crisis*, had waned. Once he had said a word seeming to condone residential segregation which raised a storm; but on the whole the Washington controversy began to subside. The morning that I heard of Mr. Washington's death I knew that an era in the history of the American Negro had ended, and I wrote:

"The death of Mr. Washington marks an epoch in the history of America. He was the greatest Negro leader since Frederick Douglass, and the most distinguished man, white or black, who has come out of the South since the Civil War. His fame was international and his influence far-reaching. Of the good that he accomplished there can be no doubt: he directed the attention of the Negro race in America to the pressing necessity of economic development; he emphasized technical education, and he did much to pave the way for an understanding between the white and the darker races.

"On the other hand, there can be no doubt of Mr. Washington's mistakes and shortcomings: he never adequately grasped the growing bond of politics and industry; he did not understand the deeper foundations of human training, and his basis of better understanding between white and black was founded on caste.

"We may then generously and with deep earnestness lay on the grave of Booker T. Washington, testimony of our thankfulness for his undoubted help in the accumulation of Negro land and property, his establishment of Tuskegee and spreading of industrial education, and his compelling of the white South to think at least of the Negro as a possible man. On the other hand, in stern justice, we must lay on the soul of this man a heavy responsibility for the consummation of Negro disfranchisement, the decline of the Negro college and public school, and the firmer establishment of color caste in this land."

By the middle of the year 1916, it was evident to thinking people that the American Negroes were achieving a unity in thought and action, partly caused by the removal of Mr. Washington's powerful personality and partly because of pressure of outward circumstances. This realization was not entirely voluntary on our part; it was forced upon us by the concentration of effort and unity of thought which rising race segregation, discrimination and mob murder were compelling us to follow. We had to stand together; we were already in 1916 standing together to an extent unparalleled since Reconstruction. Joel Spingarn was among the first to realize this and he proposed to call in August a conference of persons interested in the race problem at his beautiful home Troutbeck, in the peace and quiet of Amenia, where once John Burroughs dreamed and wrote. Here colored and white men of all shades of opinion might sit down, and rest and talk, and find agreement so far as possible with regard to the Negro problems.

The Amenia Conference, as Spingarn conceived it, was to be "under the auspices of the NAACP," but wholly independent of it, and the invitations definitely said this. They were issued by Mr. Spingarn personally, and the guests were assured that they would not be bound by any program of the NAACP. Thus the Conference was intended primarily to bring about as large a degree as possible of unity of purpose among Negro leaders and to do this regardless of its effect upon any organization, although, of course, most of us hoped that some central organization and preferably the NAACP would eventually represent this new united purpose.

One can hardly realize today how difficult and intricate a matter it was to arrange such a conference, to say who should come and who should not, to gloss over old hurts and enmities. About two hundred invitations to white and colored people were actually issued, and sixty or more persons expressed their willingness to attend, including not only many founders of the Niagara Movement, but close personal friends of Booker Washington. There were messages of good will from many who could not attend: from Taft, Roosevelt, Hughes, Woodrow Wilson, and others.

I doubt if ever before so small a conference of American Negroes had so many colored men of distinction who represented at the same time so complete a picture of all phases of Negro thought. Its very completeness in this respect was its salvation. If it had represented one party or clique it would have been less harmonious. As it was, we all learned what the majority of us knew. None of us in the present pressure of race hate could afford to hold uncompromising and unchangeable views. It was, after all, a matter of emphasis. We all believed in thrift, we all wanted the Negro to vote, we all wanted the laws enforced, we all wanted to abolish lynching, we all wanted assertion of our essential manhood; but how to get these things — there, of course, must be wide divergence of opinion.

The Conference marked the beginning of the new era. As we said in our resolutions: "The Amenia Conference believes that its members have arrived at a virtual unanimity of opinion in regard to certain principles and that a more or less definite result may be expected from its deliberations."

Probably on account of our meeting the Negro race was more united and more ready to meet the problems of the world than it could possibly have been without these beautiful days of understanding. How appropriate that so fateful a thing should have taken place in the midst of so much quiet and beauty, in a place of poets and fishermen, of dreamers and farmers, a place far apart and away from the bustle of the world and the centers of activity.

As if in anticipation of the whirl of circumstances and stress of soul through which the next few years were to thrust me, at the very beginning of the year 1917, I went down into the valley of the shadow of death. Save for typhoid fever at the age of seventeen, I had never been sick, but now a serious operation was indicated and a second one seemed advisable following fast upon the first. I came to know what hospitals and the magic of modern surgery were. I lay for two or three weeks shrouded by the curtains of pain and then arose apparently as strong as ever, if not stronger, for the fight ahead. I needed my strength for the fight came with a surge.

Finally and in a sense inevitably, the World War actually touched America. With our participation and in anticipation of it came an extraordinary exacerbation of race hate and turmoil. Beginning with increased lynchings in 1915, there came in 1916 lynching, burning, and murder. In 1917 came the draft with its discrimination and mob rule; in 1918, the turmoil and discrimination of actual war; and finally in 1919 the worst experience of mob law and race hate that the United States had seen since Reconstruction.

The war was preceded by a spy scare — a national psychosis of fear that German intrigue would accomplish among Negroes that disloyalty and urge toward sabotage and revenge which their situation and treatment would certainly justify. It was not so much that this fear had any real support in fact; it was rather that it had every justification in reason. It was succeeded by witch-hunting — feverish endeavor to find out who dared to think differently from the increasingly major thought of the nation. Not only did Germans suffer and other foreigners, but Negroes were especially suspected. Suspicious state and Federal agents invaded even the offices of the *Crisis* and the National Association for the Advancement of Colored People and asked searching questions: "Just what, after all, were our objects and activities?" I took great satisfaction in being able to sit back in my chair and answer blandly, "We are seeking to have the Constitution of the United States thoroughly and completely enforced." It took some ingenuity, even for Southerners, to make treason out of that.

Then came the refusal to allow colored soldiers to volunteer into the army; but we consoled ourselves there by saying, "Why should we want to fight for America or America's friends; and how sure could we be that America's enemies were our enemies too?" With the actual declaration of war in April, 1917, and the forced draft May 18, the pattern of racial segregation which our organization had been fighting from the beginning was written into law and custom. The races by law must be mustered and trained separately. Eighty-three thousand Negro draftees, raised at the first call, had to go into separate units, and so far as possible, separate encampments. Hundreds of colored unfortunates found themselves called with no place prepared where they could be legally received. Colored militia units already enrolled in the North were sent South to be insulted and kicked in Southern cantonments, while thousands of draftees were engulfed in a hell of prejudice and discrimination. Not only that, but hundreds of Negroes were drafted regardless of their home duties and physical health. The government had to dismiss the Draft Board of Atlanta in a body for flagrant and open race discrimination. When sent to camp, a concerted effort was made to train Negro draftees as laborers and not as soldiers. There have been few periods in the history of the American Negro when he has been more discouraged and exasperated.

The National Association fought with its back to the wall and with all its energies, failing in some cases, and in some cases having conspicuous and unexpected success. From the beginning of the war, however, the efforts of the Association involved, in a sense, a retreat from the high ideal toward which it aimed and yet a retreat absolutely necessary and pointing the way to future deployment of its forces in the offensive against race hate. The situation arose in our attempt to secure decent treatment in encampments for colored draftees; to see that a reasonable proportion of them went to the front as soldiers bearing arms, and not merely as laborers; and to assure, above all, that some Negroes should act as commissioned officers in the army.

The opposition to Negro officers was intense and bitter; but on the other hand, the administration was alarmed. After all, this nation, with its diverse ethnic elements, with a large number of Germans and Slavs who at best could not be enthusiastic supporters of the Allies, did not dare further to complicate the situation by driving ten million Negroes into justifiable protest and opposition.

In May a conference of Negro organizations called in Washington adopted resolutions which I wrote: "We trace the real cause of this World War to the despising of the darker races by the dominant groups of men, and the consequent fierce rivalry among European nations in their effort to use darker and backward people for purposes of selfish gain regardless of the ultimate good of the oppressed. We see permanent peace only in the extension of the principle of government by the consent of the governed, not simply among the smaller nations of Europe, but among the natives of Asia and Africa, the Western Indies and the Negroes of the United States."

Efforts at last were made to placate the Negroes. First they were given a representative in Washington in the person of Emmett Scott, formerly private secretary to Booker T. Washington; Mr. Scott was without actual power, but he had access to the Secretary of War so as to be able to lay before him directly complaints voiced by the Negroes. Negroes were promised enrollment not merely as stevedores, but as actual soldiers, and also two full divisions of Negro soldiers, the Ninety-second and Ninety-third, were planned. Immediately this brought up the question of Negro officers.

In the so-called Ninety-third Division, a number of Negro units from the organized state militia who had been drafted into the war, already had Negro officers. Two regiments of draftees with white officers were added, and these units were early hurried to France and incorporated with French troops. The complete organization of this Ninety-third Division was never actually accomplished and most of the higher Negro officers were gradually dismissed on various excuses.

On the other hand, the Ninety-second Division of Negro draftees was actually organized and immediately a demand arose for Negro officers over these troops. The official answer was a decided negative: there were no trained Negro officers — or at most, only two or three; there were no camps where new Negro officers could be trained and it was illegal under the draft law to train them in camps with white officers.

Our Association itself here hesitated. It had fought segregation and discrimination in the army valiantly, but lost. Then when, as the only alternative, we must accept a separate officers' training camp or no Negro officers, many members demurred at openly advocating segregation. Had it not been for Joel Spingarn, chairman of our Board, no Negro officers would have been trained or appointed. But Spingarn started a country-wide crusade, aided whole-heartedly by the *Crisis*. First of all, he got the Negro students interested. He spoke at Howard and corresponded with students at Fisk, Atlanta, and elsewhere. They arose en masse to demand a Negro officers' camp and the campus of Howard was even offered as a place for it.

The War Department squirmed. We had to fight even to be segregated. We fell out among ourselves. A large and important section of the Negro press led by the *Afro-American* and the *Chicago Defender* firmly opposed a Negro officers' camp on any terms. We struggled from March until May, and then suddenly a camp was opened for the training of Negro officers at Des Moines, Iowa.

The man eminently fitted and almost selected by fate for the heading of this camp was a black man, Charles Young, then lieutenant-colonel in the regular United States Army. He had an unblemished army record and a splendid character. He had recently accompanied Pershing in the Mexican foray and received distinguished commendation from the future commander-in-chief of the American Expeditionary Force. He was strong, fit, and only 49 years of age, and in the accelerated promotion of war-time would have been a general in the army by 1918. This, of course, the army did not propose to have, and although the Des Moines camp was established in May, the medical board of the army in June, when Young came up for examination for his colonelcy, hastened to retire him for "high blood pressure." It was a miserable ruse. An entire corps of white officers was appointed to train the colored cadets. Only colored captains and lieutenants were to be trained; the high officers were to be white.

Even then our difficulties were not finished; there was segregation against the cadets within and without their camp. General Ballou tried to lay down certain general rules as to what Negroes should strive for. A three-months period of training ensued. At the end of that time, after hesitation, it was decided to add another month. There was widespread suspicion that the War Department did not intend actually to commission these officers. I went down to Washington and talked with the Secretary of War, Newton Baker. He said coldly, "We are not trying by this war to settle the Negro problem." "True," I retorted, "but you are trying to settle as much of it as interferes with winning the war."

Finally, October 14, 1917, 639 Negro officers were commissioned: 106 captains, 329 first lieutenants and 204 second lieutenants. It was as Champ Clark, Speaker of the House, said, a "new day" for the Negro and despite all we had been through, we felt tremendously uplifted.

In the very hour of our exaltation, the whirlwind struck us again; or perhaps I might better say, throughout this period the succession of uplift and downfall was continuous and bewildering. The very month that the Des Moines camp was authorized, a Negro was publicly burned alive in Tennessee under circumstances unusually atrocious. The mobbing and burning were publicly advertised in the press beforehand. Three thousand automobiles brought the audience, including mothers carrying children. Ten gallons of gasoline were poured over the wretch and he was burned alive, while hundreds fought for bits of his body, clothing, and the rope.

The migration of Negro workers out of the South had increased steadily. It was opposed by illegal and legal methods throughout the South, but by 1917 it had expanded to a stream and from my own travel and observation, I calculated that during the year at least a quarter of a million workers had migrated from South to North. In July came the first Northern repercussion in the East St. Louis riot, when 125 Negroes were killed by their white fellow laborers; their homes looted and destroyed; and hundreds of others maimed. It was a riot notable for its passion, cruelty, and obvious economic motive.

In helpless exasperation we turned to symbolism and staged in New York City, and on Fifth Avenue, a silent parade to protest against mobs and lynching. Many hesitated to join us, but thousands fell in line, men, women, and children, headed by the officials of the National Association and other prominent Negroes.

In September of 1917 came another terrible occurrence arising out of the war. The Twenty-fourth colored Infantry of the regular army had been quartered at Houston, Texas. It was treated by the white population with discrimination and insult, and then kept from retaliating by being disarmed. Contrary to all army regulations, a soldier in Federal uniform could be insulted with impunity. At last some of these soldiers, goaded into desperation, broke into rioting, seized arms, and killed seventeen whites. As a result thirteen Negro soldiers were hanged, forty-one imprisoned for life, and forty others held for trial.

In my effort to reconstruct in memory my thought and the fight of the National Association for the Advancement of Colored People during the World War, I have difficulty in thinking clearly. In the midst of arms, not only laws but ideas are silent. I was, in principle, opposed to war. Everyone is. I pointed out in the *Atlantic Monthly* in 1915 how the partition of Africa was a cause of the conflict. Through my knowledge of Germany, I wished to see her militarism defeated and for that reason when America entered the war I believed we would in reality fight for democracy including colored folk and not merely for war investments.

But my main attention and interest were distracted from the facts of the war in Europe to the struggle of Color Caste in America and its repercussions on the conflict. Our partial triumph in this conflict often heartened me. I felt for a moment during the war that I could be without reservation a patriotic American. The government was making sincere efforts to meet our demands. They had commissioned over seven hundred Negro officers; we had been given representation in the Departments of War and Labor; the segregation ordinances had been mostly suppressed and even the Red Cross had reluctantly promised to use Negro nurses, although it later broke its word; Newton Baker, Secretary of War, tried to be fair and just; Wilson, overcoming long reluctance at last, spoke out against lynching. At other times I was bowed down and sickened by the public burnings, the treatment of colored troops, and the widespread mob law.

At one of my periods of exaltation in July, 1918, after Negro officers had been commissioned, after news of achievement by our soldiers already in France began to come over the cables, and just as President Wilson was breaking his long silence on lynching, I wrote the editorial "Close Ranks." — "That which the German power represents today spells death to the aspirations of Negroes and all darker races for equality, freedom and democracy. Let us not hesitate. Let us, while this war lasts, forget our special grievances and close our ranks shoulder to shoulder with our own white fellow citizens and the allied nations that are fighting for democracy. We make no ordinary sacrifice, but we make it gladly and willingly with our eyes lifted to the hills."

The words were hardly out of my mouth when strong criticism was rained upon it. Who was I to talk of forgetting grievances, when my life had been given to protest against them? I replied in August, "First, This is Our Country: we have worked for it, we have suffered for it, we have fought for it; we have made its music, we have tinged its ideals, its poetry, its religion, its dreams; we have reached in this land our highest modern development and nothing, humanly speaking, can prevent us from eventually reaching here the full stature of our manhood. Our country is at war. The war is critical, dangerous and world-wide. If this is *our* country, then this is *our* war. We must fight it with every ounce of blood and treasure. . . .But what of our wrongs, cry a million voices with strained faces and bitter eyes. Our wrongs are still wrong. War does not excuse disfranchisement, 'Jim Crow' cars and social injustices, but it does make our first duty clear. It does say deep to the heart of every Negro American: — We will not bargain with our loyalty. We will not profiteer with our country's blood. We will not hesitate the fraction of a second when the God of Battles summons his dusky warriors to stand before the armposts of His Throne. Let them who call for sacrifice in this awful hour of Pain fight for the rights that should be ours; let them who make the laws writhe beneath each enactment that oppresses us, — but we? Our duty lies inexorable and splendid before us, and we shall not shirk."

I am less sure now than then of the soundness of this war attitude. I did not realize the full horror of war and its wide impotence as a method of social reform. Perhaps, despite words, I was thinking narrowly of the interest of my group and was willing to let the world go to hell, if the black man went free.

Today I do not know; and I doubt if the triumph of Germany in 1918 could have had worse results than the triumph of the Allies. Possibly passive resistance of my twelve millions to any war activity might have saved the world for black and white. Almost certainly such a proposal on my part would have fallen flat and perhaps slaughtered the American Negro body and soul. I do not know. I am puzzled. . . .

Doubts Gandhi Plan

A proposal has been made that American Negroes consider launching a broad national program based on non-violent, civil disobedience and no-cooperation, modeled along the lines of Gandhi.

I seriously doubt if this is a wise proposal. First, insofar as this partakes of the nature of a general strike, we must remember that while the Indians form practically the whole working class of India, without whose cooperation all industry would collapse, American Negroes are but a fifteenth or at most a tenth and can be and indeed often are, replaced and barred from work. A planned strike under these conditions would be playing into the hands of our enemies.

Mass breaking of law or deeply ensconced custom is a serious thing to be entered upon only in great extremity and after careful thought and will to sacrifice. Our case in America is not happy, but also it is far from desperate. Compared with the laboring masses of the world our progress in the last seventy-five years has been rapid and our outlook is hopeful.

But beyond all this, we must in a proposal of this sort, carefully examine the psychological implications. Fasting, prayer, sacrifice, and self-torture have been bred into the very bone of India for more than three thousand years. This is the reason why the fasting of a little brown man in India today is world news, and despite every effort to counteract it, is setting four hundred millions of men aquiver and may yet rock the world. A similar occurrence in England or America should be regarded as a joke or a bit of insanity. Our culture patterns in East and West differ so vastly, that what is sense in one world may be nonsense in the other. We cannot then blindly copy methods without thought and consideration.

Certain basic facts can be taken for granted among American Negroes: Resentment at the Color Bar; increasing willingness to contribute time and

From the *Amsterdam News*, March 13, 1943.

money for agitation and publicity; refusal on a wider and wider scale to submit to arbitrary and illegal discrimination. But beyond this we not only are not ready for systematic lawbreaking, but are far from convinced that this is good policy or likely to gain our ends.

My own feeling is distinctly that Agitation and Publicity are still our trump cards, and that their possibilities within bounds of law and order are by no means exhausted, especially Publicity. Why not publish Hastie's explanation of his resignation as a full-page advertisement in the *New York Times*?

The Negro Since 1900:
A Progress Report

Forty years ago Julius Rosenwald, a native and resident of Springfield, Ill., where Abraham Lincoln lies buried, was shocked by an anti-Negro riot and lynching in the town. The event started him on a long and devoted career of safeguarding rights and gaining wider privileges for all suppressed peoples, in particular Negroes. Along with many other philanthropies in this field he established in 1917 the Rosenwald Fund with an endowment which was not to be maintained in perpetuity but was to be spent — both interest and principal — within twenty-five years after his death. He said: "We may be certain that . . . the acute social need of tomorrow will be different from that of today and will doubtless call for a new kind of agency to meet it."

This year the last of the Rosenwald Fund was spent: by far the greater part of it had been devoted to the welfare of the Negro. What did the fund and the many other efforts in this field accomplish? What progress have Negroes made and what has contributed to that progress?

Between 1900 and 1940 the Negro population of the United States increased from 9,000,000 to 13,000,000, but the increase in the South was but 25 per cent, while in the North and West it was 200 percent. Since 1940 this increase North and West has been further accentuated. The rural Negro population has remained stationary since 1900, while the city population has increased more than 350 per cent. A million Negroes have left the plantations of the South, where labor is in virtual peonage, to enter domestic and personal service, industry and transport in cities North and South. Large numbers in industry have risen from unskilled to skilled labor. This is shown by the increase of Negro membership in trade unions from about 30,000 in 1900 to 100,000 in 1930, and to an estimated total of 1,000,000 at the height of the war industry.

From the *New York Times*, Sunday magazine section, November 21, 1948.

411

The Negro is entering business, first as cooperative self-service among his own people, then gradually into general small business, insurance, real estate and banking. A steady increase in white-collar occupations and in the arts and professions has attracted a third of all Negro workers.

Meantime, general conditions have improved. In 1900, a Negro boy baby at birth had a life expectation of thirty-two years; in 1947, this had increased to fifty-seven years. In 1870, nine-tenths of the Negroes were illiterate. The census of 1940 reported the illiterates at 10 per cent, probably an inaccurate figure due to our methods of collecting statistics of reading and writing. Today, certainly the Negro illiterates are below 20 per cent. In 1910 there were in school 1,644,000 or 45 per cent of all Negroes 5 to 20 years of age; in 1940, 64 per cent of such Negro children were in school, or 4,188,000. In 1900, Charles Dudley Warner, speaking for American intellectuals, said that Negroes could not assimilate and use college training. In 1910, not more than 5,000 Negroes were in college. In 1948 more than 88,000 Negroes were enrolled in college.

The year after the Rosenwald Fund went into operation, 324 Negroes received the Bachelor's degree; in 1948 some 5,635 received this degree. There are today more than 1,500 Negro students enrolled in Northern colleges and universities while from these institutions 279 have received the doctorate in philosophy. In the first edition of "Who's Who in America" there was not, so far as I can ascertain, the name of a single American of Negro descent. The fiftieth edition in 1948, contains the names of ninety-one Negroes, and in "American Men of Science" seventy-seven Negroes are listed. There are today on the faculties of the leading universities of the North seventy Negro instructors, ranging from a full professor at the University of Chicago to associate professors and instructors in other institutions.

Advancement has been made in political activity. From 1900 to the first World War the mass of American Negroes, except in Northern cities, had almost stopped voting. In the South, whether voluntarily or because of legal and economic pressure, most Negroes did not try to vote. Today not only do more than 2,500,000 Negroes in the North and West vote, but in 1947 more than 6,000,000 Negroes were registered voters in twelve Southern states. Desperate and continued effort in South Carolina, Georgia and Mississippi has not stopped this growth.

In 1947 there were six Negro members of City Councils in the country, and thirty-three members of State Legislatures, including two Senators. More than a dozen Negro judges and magistrates are presiding over courts, and there are two Negro Congressmen. In 1948, for the first time in United States history, all three major parties in their conventions pledged themselves specifically to the upholding of the political and civil rights of American Negroes.

While there is much that is positive in the above record, the continuing struggle requires a full comprehension of all the many negative factors. Even among these negations, however, we can first note some improvement. For one thing, there has been an abatement in mob violence. For another, the fallacy that the Negro is congenitally unable to assimilate American culture has virtually been abandoned.

The most barbarous expression of race hate, lynching, has notably decreased. In 1900 an average of two Negroes each week were lynched by mobs without trial. In 1947 only one lynching was reported for the entire year.

In 1900 and up to World War I it was a common argument that the Negro problem in the United States was insolubte because Negroes were an inferior race and so far below the culture of the nation that they could never expect to live in this land as equal citizens.

Since 1917 this attitude has changed gradually. First, the dogma of "race" has been widely challenged, and the existence of "inferior" races of mankind denied. Many of the old cliches can be changed and most prejudices are neither inborn nor ineradicable. Law can help and hasten human change, and the intermarriage of persons of different races depends on the individuals involved and not on their "racial" characteristics. In science, history, literature and art, in athletics, physique and courage, Negroes have repeatedly proved themselves the equal and often the superior of average Americans. There is today scarcely a single field of American culture in which some Negro is not outstanding.

Let no one assume from this record of accomplishment that the American Negro has secured or is about to secure his full rights as an American citizen. Least of all are Negroes themselves satisfied or over-optimistic. The record of progress is impressive not so much because of absolute advance as by comparison with the semi-slavery that marked the condition of Negroes in 1900. If, instead of considering absolute Negro progress, we compare Negro advancement with the condition of the mass of Americans in health, education and political power, it will be clear that the lag is ominous.

Nevertheless there is a long record of effort on the part of white Americans to help black folk. The successors of the Abolitionists were the teachers and missionaries who went to the South after the Civil War and started the education of the freed men. Large numbers of Northerners and some Southerners supported Negro social uplift and education from 1870 to 1900. In 1902 the General Education Board was endowed by John D. Rockefeller. It succeeded the Capon Springs Conferences and the Southern Education

Board and at first approached the Negro problem from the point of view of the white South.

No schools were helped or projects encouraged which were not approved by the liberal South. Industrial education was emphasized and Hampton and Tuskegee were helped, but higher education for Negroes was discouraged. By 1919, however, a more liberal element of young Southerners became members of the board and it openly began to help endow Negro colleges so that at last a broad system of higher education for Negroes was given a large endowment. Andrew Carnegie gave many libraries to Negro colleges and communities.

In 1919 many efforts at interracial cooperation which followed the Atlanta riot of 1906 coalesced into the Commission on Interracial Cooperation under the leadership of Will Alexander. This organization did outstanding work against lynching, especially by getting Southern white women from all over the South to deny the excuse of rape as a justifiable cause of mob violence.

The Commission on Race Relations of the Federal Council of Churches of Christ in America was organized in 1921 and instituted "Race Relations Sunday." The Southern Conference on Human Welfare was started in 1939 and took a strong stand for civil and political rights for Negroes. Other organizations like the Carnegie Foundation, the American Civil Liberties Union, the Workers Defense League and the Congress of Industrial Organizations Committee to Abolish Racial Discrimination helped in the same field. The combined race relation program of the Rosenwald Fund and the American Missionary Association has done much recently to study and ease racial tensions.

Philanthropy of itself, however, can never free a people. Money and goodwill can help; they can at critical times give the indispensable push, the encouragement and the confidence. But a careful consideration of the facts prove that the chief force behind the progress of the Negro since 1917 came from the Negro himself; his purposive and organized effort, from 1900 until today, and particularly since 1917, has formed the mainspring of Negro progress.

First of all, we must note among American Negroes certain persistent culture patterns: the determination to educate their children; the persistent effort at organization for uplift and progress in church and fraternity; the refusal, despite overwhelming temptation, to adopt entirely white American standards as to the good, the beautiful and the true.

But this individual push upward had to be organized. Organizations came early in religion, for social purpose, for specific objects; but the first clear-cut demand for full citizenship rights in the twentieth century came with the meeting of seventeen Negroes in 1905 to form the Niagara Movement. Four years later, in 1909, a small committee of white persons met in New York because of the Springfield riots, and in 1910 these two movements united and formed the National Association for the Advancement of Colored People.

For thirty-eight years this organization has spearheaded the pressure for Negro rights, until it has become a mass movement, built deeply into the consciousness of the American Negro. Suggested by white liberals, guided by black radicals, officered increasingly by a black staff and supported by an overwhelming mass of Negroes with a few whites, it began at the height of the Booker T. Washington appeasement campaign and declared its purpose to make American Negroes "physically free from peonage, politically free from disfranchisement, and socially free from insult." During its existence this organization has raised and spent over $4,000,000 of which 90 per cent came from poor colored workers. It has today a paid membership approximating 300,000 members.

The National Association for the Advancement of Colored People began with a crusade against lynching, starting in 1910 and culminating in 1919, when its address to the nation was signed by a former President of the United States, the Attorney General, seven Governors and heads of chief universities. Its next task was to establish the legal foundation of the Negro's political rights. From 1915 to 1948 the NAACP has brought twenty-seven cases involving the rights of Negroes before the United States Supreme Court and has won twenty-four of them. Included in these was the overthrow of the "Grandfather Clause" in several Southern states, giving certain whites the hereditary right to vote. Next came attacks on the "White Primary," which excluded all Negroes and allowed all whites of any party to vote. Four cases on the white primary had to be brought before the Supreme Court until, in 1944, a clearcut decision against this form of disfranchisement was obtained. Between 1913 and 1948 six cases legalizing Negro ghettoes, first by law and then by private contract, were fought in the Supreme Court. As late as 1947 ten square miles of Chicago residential districts were by covenant restricted to white people. In 1948 the NAACP obtained a decision denying the legal right to enforce these contracts.

In 1939–40 nine Southern states spent an average of $58 a year on each white elementary school pupil and $18 on each colored pupil; and the South spent public money on colleges and professional schools which Negroes could not enter. The attack of the NAACP on this discrimination began in 1936 and continues. Thirty-two cases were brought to stop discrimination in teachers' salaries on account of race. Of these, 23 were won, 6 by decision and 17 by consent decrees; 4 were lost, 1 dropped and 4 are pending.

Next, the NAACP began to fight for admission of Negroes to professional schools supported by public funds in the South. Cases have been won in

Missouri, Oklahoma and Texas ordering the admission of Negroes or the furnishing of equal facilities. In Maryland, Delaware and Arkansas, also by private effort, Negroes have been admitted to state-supported professional schools.

Other decisions have been obtained in three cases outlawing the exclusion of Negroes from jury duty, and a series of cases have been brought and demonstrations staged to stop mob violence and denial of due process of law. In 1923, after the riots at Elaine, Ark., twelve Negroes were sentenced to death and sixty-seven to prison terms. These cases were carried to the Supreme Court, and all seventy-nine Negroes were finally released.

Recently, in Columbia, Tenn., a clerk in a store slapped a colored woman customer for complaining of his service. Her son, a Navy veteran, knocked him through a window. A race riot ensued, and twenty-six Negroes were arrested. The NAACP defended them and obtained the release of all except one. The "third degree" to obtain confessions from Negroes was condemned by the Supreme Court in four cases.

Naturally, the work of the NAACP was not done alone. Not only have white people helped as members of the organization and as advisers in legal cases, but without the help of other Negro organizations the work could not have been done. The Negro churches, with 35,000 congregations, owning $175,000,000 in real estate and spending $28,000,000 a year, helped publicize and support the association. The Negro press, with nearly 150 weekly papers, read by every literate Negro in the nation, has achieved a news coverage which makes Negroes independent of the distortions and suppressions of the white press and lets Negroes know the facts and what is being done about them.

Other Negro organizations, like the National Urban League, have supplemented the work of the NAACP in areas which it did not reach directly. The league was founded the same year as the NAACP, and they early delimited their fields of operation — the NAACP to fight race discrimination, the Urban League to seek to open opportunities for Negro employment. Its work among employers on the one hand, and among labor leaders on the other, has placed tens of thousands of Negroes in jobs where Negroes had never been hired before. Phillip Randolph's "March on Washington" led Franklin Roosevelt to initiate the FEPC.

The discouraging note in Negro progress is the continued attitude of the white South. The reaction of the poor and ignorant and their demagogic leaders is understandable. But with notable exceptions, the liberal and educated South has not taken any leading role in Negro progress. It has increased Southern State contributions to Negro education; but the South still gives the Negro child only one-third as much as the white child. Negroes vote in larger numbers, but most Negroes do not vote and are not advised to. Lynching has decreased, but no lyncher has ever been adequately punished.

And in all these cases, it was not so much moral leadership as fear of Federal intervention which was the decisive motive. In general, the liberal white South makes no protest against the fact that in the lower South there is not a single Negro member of the Legislature, no Negro magistrate, no city or county officials and very few Negro members of juries. Meantime the better class of Negro artisans and workers is leaving the South for freer regions.

Why is this? The sudden and dramatic emergence of the Dixiecrats furnishes the explanation: Franklin Roosevelt, with the cooperation of the South, organized a progressive Democratic party. This party, with all other parties, declared for civil rights for all citizens, regardless of race and religion, in accord with the public opinion of the nation and the world. Immediately, a considerable section of the South rebelled, and not only the [Eugene] Talmadges and [John] Rankins, but known liberals of education and character.

The real reason for this revolt was that the progressive white South is not yet ready to attack race discrimination as such in the South. They still stand for Negro discrimination as such in the South. They still stand for Negro disfranchisement, discrimination in education and restriction of Negroes in work and pay. It is not simply because they know that the unlettered crowd opposes this democracy: they themselves, as modern, educated men, oppose such a program. But they are not prepared to proclaim this reactionary belief and prefer to base their opposition to civil rights on the right of states, rather than of the Federal Government, to handle these problems.

Unfortunately for their logic, the nation has decided that most of these matters are already under Federal jurisdiction; the right to vote for Federal officials is a Federal right. A state has no legal right to deny it. If it does and, as in the case of the South, uses the political power of the disfranchised Negro vote to increase the power of the white South in the councils of the nation, this infringes the rights of citizens of New York and Michigan.

Education is a state function; but if the Federal Government helps as it should the schools of poorer states, it has both the right and duty to insist that these funds be distributed without race discrimination. Interstate travel is certainly under Federal control; and the nation's need for intelligent workers makes race discrimination in work and pay of national import (even if it is not under national interdiction). When the nation is pilloried as a nation of lynch law it must have the right to stop jungle law, especially in those states where state's rights have been so surrendered to backward local communities that the state is helpless in its own weal.

The present situation therefore is the direct result of the continued refusal of the liberal South to make a front forward fight on at least the more outrageous aspects of race discrimination. The Dixiecrats, instead of coura-geously facing a problem that must be faced, sought to disfranchise the South in the Democratic Party, in order to retain the right to disfranchise the Negro in the South.

To what future can the Negro look forward? First of all, he faces a changed public opinion. The nation is no longer pessimistic on this problem. Far from believing that black and white cannot live together in peace and progress in our nation, it has awakened to the fact that peoples of all colors and races must live together in one world or perish. This gradual realization of a great revolution following two world wars has made our own problem of races a burning political question.

We begin to see that the Negro is fighting a slow, determined battle and is not going to give up. There is no indication that he will sink into lethargic acceptance of present conditions as inevitable or present progress as satisfac-tory. He proposes to reach complete equality as an American citizen. And by equality he means abolition of separate schools, the disappearance of "Jim Crow" travel, no segregation in public accommodations, the right to vote, the right to think and the right to speak, the right to work and to live in a decent home, and the right to marry any person who wishes to marry him. The Negro does not expect to reach these goals in a minute or in ten years. He is long-suffering and patient. But whether it takes thirty years or a thousand, equality is the goal and he will never stop until he reaches it.

The Negro, therefore, is not satisfied but encouraged. He firmly believes that if the progress in race relations and Negro advancement which has marked the last thirty years can be maintained for another generation the goal of democracy in America will be in sight, and the transplantation of a nation from Africa to the Western World will have proved a blessing to mankind.

What Is the Meaning of "All Deliberate Speed"?

From 1619 to 1957, the Negro in the United States has been the central thread of American history. In three periods in particular this thread has so entangled itself with the web of our history that the knots have threatened our very existence. They are:

The African Slave Trade, 1774–1808
Negro Slavery, 1850–1863
Negro Citizenship, 1876–1957

These crises — which involved (1) uniting 13 colonies into one nation; (2) Civil War over the powers of the Federal government and slavery, and (3) the status of Negro citizens — we have tried to solve "with deliberate speed," arguing repeatedly that "morals" could not be advanced by legislation. Our "speed" twice became so "deliberate" that we made little or no progress and left to our children an aggravated burden of social reform. Thus our failure to abolish slavery when we tried to stop the slave trade, left the slavery problem to be settled by Civil War. When war freed the slaves, we neglected to make the freedmen citizens and this task now faces us in the midst of a rising colored world. It is difficult to conceive what the result will be if we do not face and settle today the accumulated problems of the last 338 years.

These facts are not clear to most Americans; the story has been distorted by historians to boost our national pride; it has been kept out of textbooks so that children may not learn how evil their fathers sometimes have been.

May I then briefly retell the story of the Negro in America? The war called the "Spanish Succession" should have been designated the war to give England the monopoly of the African slave trade to America. In the

From the *National Guardian*, November 4, 1957.

18th century 15,000 Negroes a year were stolen in Africa and dumped on America; many colonies protested, but Georgia, peopled by luckless vaga-bonds, said: "Negroes are as essentially necessary to the cultivation of Georgia as axes, hoes, or any other utensil of agriculture." They got their Negroes, and today Gov. Griffin and Sen. Talmadge propose to keep them as near slavery as possible.

Other colonies wanted and got Negro slaves, but the mass of Americans regarded this new land as a land of freedom, not slavery, and proposed to unite the colonies, when they escaped British control, into a great democracy. They made a Declaration of Independence in 1776 which said:

WE HOLD THESE TRUTHS TO BE SELF-EVIDENT, THAT ALL MEN ARE CREATED EQUAL, THAT THEY ARE ENDOWED BY THEIR CRE-ATOR WITH CERTAIN UNALIENABLE RIGHTS, THAT AMONG THESE ARE LIFE, LIBERTY AND THE PURSUIT OF HAPPINESS.

This sounded magnificent, but it did not describe the new nation. That nation proceeded with such deliberate speed to legislate morals that the 500,000 slaves of 1776, whom the signers of this Declaration looked straight in the eye, had by 1860 become 4,000,000, with "no rights that the white man was bound to respect." More than this: these black workers on the free, rich land of the lower South were raising 5,000,000 bales of cotton a year. This had become the basis of a kingdom which was making Southern planters, North-ern merchants and British factory owners rich.

Southern leaders now got ideas; they had despoiled Mexico of land and slaves; they had tried repeatedly to seize the West Indies, and they had their eyes now on the Middle West. By counting their slaves as basis of representa-tion in Congress and disfranchising the poor whites, they dominated the nation. But the farmers of the North and workers, native and foreign, also eyed the rich West as the national frontier receded. They demanded "free soil." Not "free men," but free soil. They were quite willing that Negroes should remain slaves in the South, but not on the rich soil of the West.

A small group of Americans, led by William Lloyd Garrison and the free Negro Frederick Douglass, wanted to free the slaves, but the church and business bitterly opposed these fanatics, who were often mobbed and some-times killed. One of them, John Brown, went West and helped drive slave-holders out of Kansas. Then he tried to free the slaves in Virginia and was promptly hanged.

The South now demanded the right not only to expand slavery anywhere in the nation but also such guarantees as would allow the slave states to control land, labor and commerce in its territory forever: otherwise the South threatened to secede from the Union. The Republican Party reiterated its promise to protect slavery where it was but refused to recognize the right of secession. Thereupon the nation proceeded to settle this dispute by fighting. They killed 500,000 of their young men, destroyed billions in property, and raised a generation of people filled with hate for each other and especially for Negroes.

In the midst of this Civil War, Lincoln repeatedly offered to protect slavery in the South if the South would remain in the Union. The South refused. The war reached a stalemate; then Lincoln was reminded that in the South were 4,000,000 slaves working to support Southern soldiers and protect their homes. If these should help the North instead of the South, the war could be won. By promise of freedom to slaves, Lincoln armed 180,000 black soldiers and used, in addition, over 200,000 black laborers in army camps. Lincoln said that, without this help, "we would be compelled to abandon the war in three weeks." So when, with Negro help, the war was won, Lincoln declared the slaves "henceforward and forever free."

Then the nation sat down heavily and licked its wounds. It asked what was meant by "free"? Lincoln suggested privately in 1864 that a few Negroes, "the very intelligent and especially those who have fought gallantly in our ranks," might be given the right to vote. But Lincoln was killed a year later, and a Southern poor white, drunk even while taking the oath of office as Vice President, became President of the United States. He was soon taken into camp by the Southern planters and began to readmit to the Union the seceded states, with "Black Codes" which reestablished slavery in all but name.

Thus the South reappeared at the doors of Congress with 28 more votes than before the war, based on disfranchised freedmen. It proposed not only virtually to restore slavery, but to make the Federal government pay the Southern war debt; lower the tariff on which post-war industry had fattened, and overthrow the Gold Standard by which the North had made millions. This touched the pocket nerve and the North called a halt.

Two men proposed remedies: Charles Sumner proposed to make the freedmen voters with full civil rights, free elementary education, hospitalization and special protection in the courts. Thaddeus Stevens went a step further and proposed giving each Negro family 40 acres and the sum of $50 to provide a minimum of capital for an impoverished group. The nation, with the *Communist Manifesto* ringing in its ears, called this program socialism and refused to enact it. It determined to force the South to modify its plans by enfranchising the Negroes forthwith. Few Northerners expected this to work as a permanent system of government, but after the failure and confusion which they expected to ensure, the South would be prepared to compromise on suitable terms.

Negroes, migrant Northerners, and Southern poor whites thereupon established governments. They restored law and order. They began to subdivide the plantations; they enfranchised the poor whites as well as the blacks; they built roads and railroads; they established public schools and undertook new social legislation. They ran into difficulties; the rich whites refused to pay taxes; Northern and Southern adventurers manipulated public debts and stole railroads, and many poverty-stricken ex-slaves were easily bribed. But the result of eight years of black rule was such that the South began to fear not that the Negro would fail as a voter, but that he would succeed. Thereupon the mob took hold. As the predecessor of Byrnes of South Carolina testified in open Senate:

"Yes, we have stuffed ballot-boxes, and will stuff them again; we have cheated 'niggers' in elections and will cheat them again; we have disfranchised 'niggers,' and will disfranchise all we want to; we have killed and lynched 'niggers' and will kill and lynch others; we have burned 'niggers' at the stake and will burn others; a 'nigger' has no right to live anyhow, unless a white man wants him to live. If you don't like it you can lump it!"

So North and South came to a "gentleman's agreement": the Negro was to be disfranchised and a status of legal caste set up. Strong political, economic and social pressure was put on the Federal courts to go along and they did for 75 years. A nation-wide propaganda to expose the inherent and ineradicable inferiority of the Negro race was spread in college, church, science and literature over the nation. Laws disfranchising the Negro were passed in all Southern states, and inferior schools and civil disability and segregation were forced upon him.

Then in 1905 the Negroes organized and began to fight back. Slowly they beat upon public opinion and then entered the courts. The courts dodged and evaded with every subterfuge, but they faced inevitably clear decisions unless the principle of democratic government was to be completely surrendered in the presence of world war in which we claimed to lead democracy.

Several decisions had raised serious questions as to judicial honesty in this nation. The critical decision came in 1954 when the Supreme Court declared unanimously that race separation in public schools was unconstitutional.

Immediately the South appealed to the mob, and several states declared they would not obey the law. The old slogans reappeared: "States' Rights," which would make civil rights for Negroes a matter of local or even individual option; "Legislating Morality," which was the favorite escape of cowards. Finally even the Supreme Court took a step backward and said the enforcement of the law need not be immediate but could be achieved with "deliberate speed."

And here we are right back to 1776. Seven states where 6,000,000 Negroes live have taken no step toward integration of schools and the governor of one state has used the National Guard to stop integration. Nation and state face each other.

But that is not all: China, India, Burma, Malaya and Africa; the West Indies, Central and South America; in fact the whole colored world, together with the world of socialism and communism, stand asking whether the United States is a democracy or the last center of "white supremacy" and colonial imperialism.

A Program of Reason,
Right and Justice for Today

Daily lately as I read the morning news, I find myself asking if age is driving me a bit crazy or if I'm living in a crazy nation. I have lived through much history and read far more, but I can remember no situation which parallels the present. Governments and rulers have always lied. But never with the quick, bland, easy assurance such as our transformation of a spying trip which failed into a weather exploration — and then blaming the Soviet Union for "propaganda." We have only to scan our magazines to see how the United States is being transformed from an unsophisticated people of original Tinkers and Thinkers to a nation of Liars and Buyers.

President Eisenhower continues to astonish me. Yesterday this Delphic oracle came from the golf links: "We never enslaved anyone." Today we learn that Turkey is not our spy base but a "bastion of Freedom," where the NATO of the "Free World" dares not stay long enough to hear the President's welcome, because Prime Minister Menderes is trying to outrun angry students threatening his life.

Right here I draw a breath of relief. Students at last to the rescue, even in the West. I had lost faith in them as during the McCarthy nightmare I spoke at a few institutions and looked into their blank faces. But today young seekers after knowledge live again despite a woeful lack of teachers. Not only in Turkey, which we have purchased, but in Japan where they defy Prime Minister Kishi's plan to tie Nippon to the Pentagon; and in South Korea where they have driven a demagogue out of power.

Of course I am especially uplifted by the revolt of Negro students in America. With neither leadership nor encouragement from their own people (despite all the declarations of the johnnie-come-latelies frantically scrambling aboard the bandwagon), alone and unaided they put their finger

From the *National Guardian*, May 23, 1960.

on a vital spot and acted. Our Negro Problem is not simply disfranchisement, lynching, mob-law, court injustice and widespread serfdom with poverty and disease: it is a daily, unending series of petty, senseless insults carried out almost everywhere, and always by civilized people of religion and culture, for no earthly reason except senseless meanness and neglect.

In the South a Negro goes downtown to buy a few necessities, and can't buy a bite to eat; he can't get a drink; he can't go to a movie; sometimes he can't sit in a park; and of course he can't bathe in the ocean, as in Biloxi, in the most ignorant state of the Union, where there are 26 miles of beach. Black students — not agitators, not even radicals, since little economics or social science is taught in Southern schools — just honest, clear-headed youth who one day say: "We buy our school books and paper at Woolworth's; why not buy a sandwich?"

Then the proud, cultured South goes berserk. Boys and girls are arrested, clubbed and jailed. Churches sing, pray and send Billy Graham to Africa. Still students "sit down." Then Big Business moves in. It threatens colored college presidents. Some, like Wright of Fisk, refuse to yield. Some, like Trenholm of Alabama, crawl. Then Big Business squeezes parents and some parents, to save their jobs, plead with their children; but at least at one colored college 4,000 students withdraw while their president skulks. They threaten to put a white president in at Lincoln who will teach Negroes their place. They may try this at Howard. They may starve Fisk. What will result? Will the students fall back into line? I think not. Some white students feel the glorious possibilities of this day; but the nation is silent and dumb.

Are we happy at all this? No, America is scared to death. Asia has arisen. Africa arises. The Soviet Union marches on. East Europe is triumphant. Cuba is free. Panama and Latin America follow. But the United States is stubborn.

We lie about China and support a man on her borders to attack her whom we ourselves have called a scoundrel. We invest six hundred million dollars in slave labor and stolen gold, diamonds and uranium in South Africa where our Boer allies have 18,000 Negroes in jail and ten million more fated to be hammered into slavery. We woo Adenauer to preserve a Germany which our army, with the help of the leader of the AFL-CIO, fashioned as a threat for a Third World War to conquer the Soviets. We bribe Franco, cajole Italy and, as long as possible, we will hang on to Trujillo. We are intriguing in Viet-Nam and Laos and praying for war between India and China, which fails to occur.

Signs of disaster gather about our heads. We are unable to sell enough abroad to pay for what we buy and have been compelled to spend four billions in the last two years out of our hoard of gold to pay the deficit. Our cost of living rises continuously and unemployment spreads, despite our ingenious efforts to deceive the public. The gamblers of the stock market are sweating in vain to unload on the suckers the inflated values of our monopolized industry. We are soaking the sick with high-priced medicines and hospital fees beyond the reach of the poor. We are bribing our skilled labor with high wages paid out of the hides of exploited Negro and Mexican labor and from the poverty and disease of poor whites.

Our justice is showered with injustice. Our jails seethe with the revolts of the wretched and the innocent and of thousands whose only crime is being black. We murder Chessman for no crime we can prove; we jail Uphaus and Sobell, torture Winston and drive Heikkila to death. Why? The bomb-proof shelters of the editorial offices of the New York *Times* hear a rumor that our judges often actually pay two years' salary for nomination.

We are deliberately distorting history — not simply United States history so as to excuse Negro slavery and deify slave owners, to praise the traitors who solemnly swore to support their country and then fought desperately to betray it and preserve Negro slavery; but especially to twist and distort the world wars and the triumph of socialism.

We started with propaganda which out-Hitlered Hitler. Big Business monopolized news-gathering, newspapers, periodicals and publishing. The nation was led to believe that communism was a conspiracy and crime, and socialism its handmaid. We were told that the communist states were failures, their citizens serfs and prisoners, seething with revolt; their women prostitutes and their education only "brainwashing" propaganda. Many wanted to use our atom bomb immediately on Moscow, but when we found the Soviets already had it we accused them of stealing it from us, as they were certainly too dumb to have invented it.

We planned for war. Our State Department and national leaders cooperated with *Collier's* magazine in 1951. The nation was primed to conquer the Soviet Union in 1960. This is 1960. This was to be the year of conquest, *Collier's* (of blessed memory) foretold the event in 130 pages, written by Allan Nevins, our "leading" historian; Stuart Chase, our "leading" economist; Edward R. Murrow, our "great" news interpreter; Margaret Chase Smith, our woman Senator; Robert Sherwood and J. B. Priestly. Our Senator wrote of "Russia Reborn" under American soldiers, presumably armed with flaming napalm and disease germs. This victory had to be postponed, but our propaganda continued.

We continued to sneer at education and progress in the Soviet Union. I once heard Conant of Harvard, formerly High Commissioner of Germany, tell the Harvard Club of New York that Soviet leaders repeatedly refused to tell him what examinations were given high school students for entrance into college. He finally learned (here in America) that "the Communist Party would not allow any examinations!" This proved Soviet education a farce. A few years later came Sputnik and the photographing of the back of the moon. We had to acknowledge the superiority of Soviet education, the progress of her science and the fact that her industrial development might soon equal or even outstrip ours.

Khrushchev dared to visit us and, while Congress went into hiding, he made the finest speech for world peace which has been heard here since Lincoln at Gettysburg. We then photographed Russian fortifications and lied about it. Why? Because Allen Dulles and our military rulers are still determined to smash the Summit conference and plunge the world into war.

Meantime we want to help the world. We remember how American charity has often fed the hungry and healed the sick. Taking every advantage of this memory, Big Business has used it to the hilt. The Marshall Plan was to help war-torn Europe. In reality it helped American business to buy into European industry, beat back socialist labor, bribe skilled labor and pay soldiers. In fact with most of the funds we are arming all foreigners we can bribe or scare to help us fight Communists, and with what's left we are using our public tax funds to give rich American investors private capital, or to bribe native quislings in India and Africa to betray their countries to American industry. Already in New York alone we have four "African" organizations, financed by Big Business, and officered by Negroes supposed to give "information" on Africa. Pious churchmen are furnishing the requisite religious background. For all of this Eisenhower is now demanding four billions of our dollars which ought to be used for social medicine, education and housing.

However, my friends note, an election is coming up. So what? There is, to be sure, a President soon to be chosen. The expenditure of all candidates for the office in 1956 was said to have been $100,000,000. This year it may be $500,000,000. Only Big Business, well-heeled stock gamblers and the China Lobby can bid. Whether a Democrat or Republican wins, it will be the same gang. You will have no chance to vote for a meaningful third party. You will have no chance to vote for peace or war; for social medicine, housing or decent education. Why?

We know the reason. It is because the United States is no longer a democracy. Most citizens know this well and do not waste time going to the polls. If it were true that we have what we want in this nation, we could sit still and wait on reason. But it is not true. We are ruled by a minority armed with wealth and power. This usurpation we must fight. We must first demand the right to have a third party on the ballot. This the politicians prevent and these politicians must go.

Here is a program for those who have not lost hope and who yet believe in America. Forget the Presidency. It will make not a jot of difference whether

Nixon and Chiang Kai-shek, or Kennedy and Cardinal Spellman, win the office. Concentrate on Senators and Congressmen, legislators and city councilmen and ward heelers.

Insist on a chance to vote for peace, for the total abolition of the color line; for no family income above $25,000 or below $5,000; for free education from kindergarten through college; for housing on a nation-wide scale; for training of all for the work they can do in so far as such work is needed for the best interests of all. Insist on discipline for this work. Allow no laborer to be paid less than his product is worth; and let no employer take what he does not make. Curb corporations by putting most of them under government ownership.

Heal the sick as a privilege, not as a charity. Make private ownership of natural resources a crime. Stop interference with private and personal belief by religious hypocrites. Preserve the utmost freedom for dream of beauty, creative art and joy of living. Call this socialism, communism, reformed capitalism or holy rolling. Call it anything—but get it done!

Perhaps this is insane, but to me it is Reason, Right and Justice. As Bert Williams once said: "I may be crazy, but I ain't no Fool!"

China

I saw China first in 1936, on my trip from the Soviet Union to Japan. I was struck by its myriads of people. This amorphous mass of men, with age-old monuments of human power, beauty and glory; with its helpless, undefended welter of misery and toil, has an organization of life and impenetrable will to survive that neither imperial tyranny, nor industrial exploitation, nor famine, starvation and pestilence can kill — it is eternal life, facing disaster and triumphing imperturbably.

There passed a glory from the earth when Imperial China fell. Built as it was on skulls, it was bravely built and the remains are magnificent. In all essential respects they surpass the Stones of Europe. Where Europe counts its years in hundreds, Asia counts its in thousands. There is absent that all too apparent European effort to dramatize and exaggerate the past; to emphasize war and personal glory. China shows a finer effort to let the past stand silent, frank and unadorned; to tell the truth simply about men and fully; and to record the triumphs of education, family life and literature far more than murder.

I write this now as things were in 1936. I am standing on the Great Wall of China, with 23 centuries beneath my feet. The purple crags of Manchuria lie beyond the valley, while behind are the yellow and brown mountains of China. For 70 cents I have been carried up on the shoulders of four men and down again. And here I stand on what has been called the only work of man visible from Mars. It is no mud fence or pile of cobbles. It surpasses that mighty bastion of Constantinople, which for so many centuries saved Mediterranean civilization from German barbarism. This is a wall of carefully cut stone, fitted and laid with perfect matching and eternal mortar, from 20 to 50 feet high and 2,500 miles long; built by a million men, castellated with perfect

From *The Autobiography of W. E. B. Du Bois: A Soliloquy on Viewing My Life from the Last Decade of Its First Century* (Moscow, 1962; U.S.A., 1968).

brick, and standing mute and immutable for more than 2,000 years. Such is China.

Shanghai was an epitome of the racial strife, the economic struggle, the human paradox of modern life. Here was the greatest city of the most populous nation on earth, with the large part of it owned, governed and policed by foreign nations. With Europe largely controlling its capital, commerce, mines, rivers and manufactures; with a vast welter of the greatest working class in the world, paid less than an average of 25 cents a day; with a glittering modern life of skyscrapers, majestic hotels, theatres and night clubs. In this city of nations were 19,000 Japanese, 11,000 British, 10,000 Russians, 4,000 Americans, and 10,000 foreigners of other nationalities living in the midst of 3,000,000 Chinese. The city was divided openly by nations; black-bearded Sikhs under British orders policed its streets, foreign warships sat calmly at her wharfs; foreigners told this city what it may and may not do.

Even at that, matters were not as bad as they once had been. In 1936, foreigners acknowledged that Chinese had some rights in China. Chinese who could afford it might even visit the city race track from which they and dogs were long excluded. It was no longer common to kick a coolie or throw a rickshaw's driver on the ground. Yet, the afternoon before I saw a little English boy of perhaps four years order three Chinese children out of his imperial way on the sidewalk of the Bund; and they meekly obeyed and walked in the gutter. It looked quite like Mississippi. And, too, I met a "missionary" from Mississippi, teaching in the Baptist University of Shanghai!

I went by invitation to the American-supported University of Shanghai and I said to the president that I should like to talk to a group of Chinese and discuss frankly racial and social matters. He arranged a luncheon at the Chinese Banker's Club. There were present one of the editors of the China press, the secretary-general of the Bank of China, the general manager of the China Publishing Company, the director of the Chinese Schools for Shanghai, and the executive secretary of the China Institute of International Relations.

We talked nearly three hours. I plunged in recklessly. I told them of my slave ancestors, of my education and travels; of the Negro problem. Then I turned on them and said, "How far do you think Europe can continue to dominate the world, or how far do you envisage a world whose spiritual center is Asia and the colored races? You have escaped from the domination of Europe politically since the World War — at least in part; but how do you propose to escape from the domination of European capital? How are your working classes progressing? Why is it that you hate Japan more than Europe when you have suffered more from England, France and Germany than from Japan?"

There ensued a considerable silence, in which I joined. Then we talked. They said, "Asia is still under the spell of Europe, although not as completely as a while back. It is not our ideal simply to ape Europe. We know little of India or Africa, or Africa in America. We see the danger of European capital and are slowly extricating ourselves, by seeking to establish control of capital by the political power of taxation and regulation. We have stabilized our currency—no longer do English Hong Kong notes form our chief circulating medium. Our wages are too low but slowly rising; labor legislation is appearing; we have 16 million children in school with short terms and inadequate equipment, but a beginning of the fight against our 90 per cent illiteracy."

We talked three hours but it was nearly a quarter of a century before I realized how much we did not say. The Soviet Union was scarcely mentioned, although I knew how the Soviet Union was teaching the Chinese. Nothing was said of the Long March which had just ended its 6,000 miles from Kiangsi to Yenan, led by Mao Tse-tung and Chu Teh. We mentioned America only for its benefactions and scarcely for its exploitation. Of the Kuomintang and Chiang Kai-shek, almost nothing was said, but hatred of Japan for its betrayal of Asia was amply pointed out.

In 1959 I came again to China. I wanted to re-visit China because it is a land of colored people; and again because in 1956 China had officially invited me to visit and lecture, but the United States had refused to permit me. My passport stated that it was "not good for travel to China." It was a fair conclusion that if I did not use this passport to secure entrance to China and made no claim on the United States for protection, the State Department had no legal right to forbid me to visit China. Certainly the United States could give me no less protection in China than it could in Mississippi. On the other hand by legal fiction, the United States was still "at war" with China, since the Korean War had never been legally finished. It was possible then if I went to China, to jail me for "trading with the enemy." This risk I thought it my duty to take, since my invitation to visit had been renewed by the cultural minister, Kuo Mo-jo and by Madame Soong Ching-ling.

I left Moscow February 9 and returned April 6. It was the most fascinating eight weeks of travel and sight-seeing I have ever experienced. We remember Peking; a city of six million; its hard workers, its building and re-building; that great avenue which passes the former forbidden city, and is as wide as Central Park; the bicycles and pedicycles, the carts and barrows. There was the university where I lectured on Africa, and a college of the 50 or more races of

China. We looked out from our hotel window at the workers. They all wore raincoats beneath the drizzle. We saw the planning of a nation and a system of work rising over the entrails of dead empire.

I have traveled widely on this earth since my first trip to Europe 67 years ago. Save South America and India, I have seen most of the civilized world and much of its backward regions. Many leading nations I have visited repeatedly. But I have never seen a nation which so amazed and touched me as China in 1959.

I traveled 5,000 miles, by railway, boat, plane and auto. I saw all the great cities: Peking, Shanghai, Hankow and its sisters; Canton, Chungking, Chengtu, Junming and Nanking. I rode its vast rivers, passed through its villages and sat in its communes. I visited its schools and colleges, lectured and broadcast to the world. I visited its minority groups. I spent four hours with Mao Tse-tung and dined twice with Chou En-lai, the tireless Prime Minister of this nation of 680 million souls.

We come to Chengtu. We ride about this farthest Western stopping place, close to the crowds and the workers and the homes, old and new. We visit a commune of 60,000 members. We climb the mountain to see irrigation being widened today, yet started 2,200 years ago. There is a glorious temple on its summit, and below a wide lake between winding roads. Four rivers roll down from the Himalayas, out of Tibet into the Yangtze.

Then we fly to Kunmin, the end of the American Burma Road. It is warm and quiet, and at the state school the minorities dance and sing welcome, and among them are Tibetans. There are more Tibetans in China than in Tibet. In Tibet while we were on its border in Szechuan, the landholders and slave drivers and the religious fanatics revolted against the Chinese, and failed as they deserved to. Tibet has belonged to China for centuries. The Communists linked the two by roads and began reforms in landholding, schools and trade, which now move quickly. At Kunmin we were at the end of the Burma Road and near the Great Mekong River. Below lay Vietnam, Laos, Cambodia and Thailand. The nest of grafters, whoremongers and gamblers at Saigon, helped by Americans, have broken the Geneva treaty which closed the French Indo-Chinese War, and are attacking the Communists. That is called "communist aggression." It is the attempt of American business and the American Navy to supplant France as colonial ruler in Southeast Asia.

There is at Canton a marble commercial building where the import and export exposition was recently opened. There are five floors of exhibits. I am convinced that America cannot make anything which is not today being made by China, or which cannot be made cheaper, and for the most part made quite as well; for out of the things that China makes come no profits for private exploiters. Most nations of the world are beginning to buy China's goods, except the United States. China sells increasingly to Europe, to Asia and South America; to India, Burma, Ceylon, Indonesia, and Malaya; to Africa and the West Indies; to Australia and New Zealand. And such goods: silk and woolen clothing, watches, clocks, radios and television sets; looms, machinery and lamps, shoes and hats, pottery and dishes. All Chinese seem to be at work, and not afraid of unemployment, and welcoming every suggestion that displaces muscle with machinery.

In every town and city we went to the opera, and can never forget the assault of the Monkey King on the hosts of Heaven, facing God and the angels. A night sleeping train took us over the 30-hour trip from Peking to Hankow. There I saw the bridge that had been miraculously thrown across the Yangtze. We rested in a little hotel adorned with flowering cabbages. We visited the great steel mills and shook hands with welcoming workers. The colored American prisoner of war who stayed in China rather than return to America and is happy with his wife and baby, came to visit us.

My birthday was given national notice in China, and celebrated as never before; and we who all our lives have been liable to insult and discrimination on account of our race and color, in China have met universal goodwill and love, such as we never expected. As we leave may we thank them humbly for all they have done for us, and for teaching us what communism means.

The people of the land I saw: the workers, the factory hands, the farmers and laborers, scrubwomen and servants. I went to parks and restaurants, sat in the homes of the high and the low; and always I saw a happy people; people with faith that needs no church or priest, and who laugh gaily when the Monkey King overthrows the angels. In all my wandering, I never felt the touch or breath of insult or even dislike — I who for 90 years in America scarcely ever saw a day without some expression of hate for "niggers."

What is the secret of China in the second half of the 20th century? It is that the vast majority of a billion human beings have been convinced that human nature in some of its darkest recesses can be changed, if change is necessary. China knows, as no other people know, to what depths human meanness can go. I used to weep for American Negroes, as I saw what indignities and repressions and cruelties they had passed; but as I read Chinese history in these last months and had it explained to me stripped of Anglo-Saxon lies, I know that no depths of Negro slavery in America have plumbed such abysses as the Chinese have seen for 2,000 years and more. They have seen starvation and murder; rape and prostitution; sale and slavery of children; and religion cloaked in opium and gin, for converting the "heathen." This oppression and contempt came not only from Tartars, Mongolians, British, French, Germans and Americans, but from the Chinese themselves: Mandarins and warlords, capitalists and murdering thieves like Chiang Kai-shek; Kuomintang socialists and intellectuals educated abroad.

Despite all this, China lives, and has been transformed and marches on. She is not ignored by the United States. She ignores the United States and leaps forward. What did it? What furnished the motive power and how was it applied? First it was the belief in himself and in his people by a man like Sun Yat-sen. He plunged on blind and unaided, repulsed by Britain and America, but welcomed by Russia. Then efforts toward socialism, which wobbled forward, erred and lost, and at last was bribed by America and Britain and betrayed by Chiang Kai-shek, with its leaders murdered and its aims misunderstood, when not deliberately lied about.

Then came the Long March from feudalism, past capitalism and socialism to communism in our day. Mao Tse-tung, Chou En-lai, Chu Teh and a half dozen others undertook to lead a nation by example, by starving and fighting; by infinite patience and above all by making a nation believe that the people and not merely the elite — that on the contrary the workers in factory, street and field — composed the real nation. Others have said this often, but no nation has tried it like the Soviet Union and China. And on the staggering and bitter effort of the Soviets, beleaguered by all Western civilization, and yet far-seeing enough to help weaker China even before a still weak Russia was safe — on this vast pyramid has arisen the saving nation of this stumbling, murdering, hating world.

In China the people — the laboring people, the people who in most lands are the doormats on which the reigning thieves and murdering rulers walk, leading their painted and jeweled prostitutes — the people walk and boast. These people of the slums and gutters and kitchens are the Chinese nation today. This the Chinese believe and on this belief they toil and sweat and cheer.

They believe this and for the last ten years their belief has been strengthened until today they follow their leaders because these leaders have never deceived them. Their officials are incorruptible, their merchants are honest, their artisans are reliable, their workers who dig and haul and lift do an honest day's work and even work overtime if their state asks it, for they are the state; they are China.

A kindergarten, meeting in the once Forbidden City, was shown the magnificence of this palace and told: "Your fathers built this, but did not enjoy it; but now it is yours; preserve it." And then, pointing across the Tien an Men Square to the vast building of the new Halls of Assembly, the speaker added: "Your fathers are building new palaces for you; enjoy them and guard them for yourselves and your children. They belong to you!"

China has no rank or classes; her universities grant no degrees; her government awards no medals. She has no blue book of "society." But she has leaders of learning and genius, scientists of renown, artisans of skill and millions who know and believe this and follow where these men lead. This is the joy of this nation, its high belief and its unfaltering hope.

China is no utopia. Fifth Avenue has better shops where the rich can buy and the whores parade. Detroit has more and better cars. The best American housing outstrips the Chinese, and Chinese women are not nearly as well-dressed as the guests of the Waldorf-Astoria. But the Chinese worker is happy. He has exorcised the Great Fear that haunts the West; the fear of losing his job; the fear of falling sick; the fear of accident; the fear of inability to educate his children; the fear of daring to take a vacation. To guard against such catastrophe Americans skimp and save, cheat and steal, gamble and arm for murder. The Soviet citizen, the Czech, the Pole, the Hungarian have kicked out the stooges of America and the hoodlums set to exploit the peasants. They and the East Germans no longer fear these disasters; and above all the Chinese sit high above these fears and laugh with joy. They will not be rich in old age, but they will eat. They will not enjoy sickness but they will be given care. They will not starve as thousands of Chinese did only a generation ago. They fear neither flood nor epidemic. They do not even fear war; as Mao Tse-tung told me, war for China is a "paper tiger." China can defend itself and back of China stands the unassailable might of the Soviet Union.

Envy and class hate are disappearing in China. Does your neighbor have better pay and higher position than you? He has this because of greater ability or better education, and more education is open to you and compulsory for your children. The young married couple do not fear children. The mother has pre-natal care. Her wage and job are safe. Nursery and kindergarten take care of the child and it is welcome, not to pampered luxury but to good food, constant medical care and education for his highest ability. All this is not yet perfect. Here and there it fails, falls short and falters; but it is so often and so widely true, that China believes, lives on realized hope, follows its leaders and sings: "O, Mourner, get up off your knees."

The women of China are becoming free. They wear pants so that they can walk, climb and dig; and climb and dig they do. They are not dressed simply for sex indulgence or beauty parades. They occupy positions from ministers of state to locomotive engineers, lawyers, doctors, clerks and laborers. They are escaping "household drudgery"; they are strong and healthy and beautiful not simply of leg and false bosom, but of brain, brawn and rich emotion. In Wuhan I stood in one of the greatest steelworks of the world. A crane which moved a hundred tons loomed above. I said, "My God, Shirley, look up there!" Alone in the engine-room sat a girl with ribboned braids, running the vast machine.

You won't believe this, because you never saw anything like it; and if the State Department has its way, you never will. Let *Life* lie about communes; and the State Department shed crocodile tears over ancestral tombs. Let Hong Kong wire its lies abroad. Let "Divine Slavery" persist in Tibet until China kills it. The truth is there and I saw it.

Fifteen times I have crossed the Atlantic and once the Pacific. I have seen the world. But never so vast and glorious a miracle as China. This monster is a nation with a dark-tinted billion born at the beginning of time, and facing its end; this struggle from starved degradation and murder and suffering to the triumph of that Long March to world leadership. Oh beautiful, patient, self-sacrificing China, despised and unforgettable, victorious and forgiving, crucified and risen from the dead.

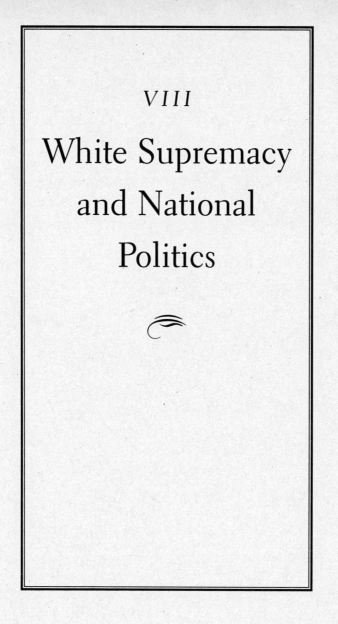

VIII

White Supremacy and National Politics

The fastening on of white supremacy throughout America at the beginning of the twentieth century was evidenced by the brutal Atlanta riot of 1906, unforgettably described and denounced by Du Bois in "A Litany of Atlanta." He tracked the steady erosion of African-American rights from William McKinley to Henry Wallace in thunderous editorials, columns, and essays such as "Another Open Letter to Woodrow Wilson" (1913) and "From McKinley to Wallace" (1948). African-American retaliation for these mounting woes, such as the 1917 rampage of U.S. infantry at Houston, Texas, was as rare as white violence was pandemic. The 1919 pogrom in rural Arkansas, the long, brutal occupation of Haiti, and the 1932 lynchings in the first year of the New Deal were hurled in the face of "civilized" Americans by Du Bois as proof of savagery as appalling as any perpetrated by "primitive" people. The European boast of racial and cultural superiority unfailingly evoked bitter irony ("The Superior Race" [1923]) and profound contempt, and occasionally even drove Du Bois to the brink of demonizing white Americans, as in the coruscatingly brilliant "The Souls of White Folk" (1920): "For two or more centuries America has marched proudly in the van of human hatred — making bonfires of human flesh and laughing at them hideously, and making the insulting of millions more than a matter of dislike — rather a great religion, a world war-cry." But even here Du Bois remembered to stress with great perspicacity the economic origins of racism and the large dividends yielded to a small minority in a world where labor was perpetually segmented along color lines. Du Bois was an admirer of FDR ("An Estimate of FDR" [1945]) and professed to believe that the second Roosevelt's presidency had laid the foundations for a racially and economically more humane nation, one in which a reduction would come in "the amount of wealth and income which has been going to capitalists and employers."

A Litany of Atlanta

O Silent God, Thou whose voice afar in mist and mystery hath left our ears
a-hungered in these fearful days —
Hear us, good Lord!

Listen to us, Thy children: our faces dark with doubt, are made a mockery in
Thy sanctuary. With uplifted hands we front Thy heaven, O God, crying:
We beseech Thee to hear us, good Lord!

We are not better than our fellows, Lord; we are but weak and human men.
When our devils do deviltry, curse Thou the doer and the deed: curse them
as we curse them, do to them all and more that ever they have done to
innocence and weakness, to womanhood and home.
Have mercy upon us, miserable sinners!

And yet whose is the deeper guilt? Who made these devils? Who nursed them
in crime and fed them on injustice? Who ravished and debauched their
mothers and their grandmothers? Who bought and sold their crime, and
waxed fat and rich on public iniquity?
Thou knowest, good God!

Is this Thy justice, O Father, that guilt be easier than innocence, and the
innocent crucified for the guilt of the untouched guilty?
Justice, O Judge of men!

Wherefore do we pray? Is not the God of the fathers dead? Have not seers seen
in Heaven's halls Thine hearsed and lifeless form stark amidst the black and
rolling smoke of sin, where all along bow bitter forms of endless dead?
Awake, Thou that sleepest!

Thou art not dead, but flown afar, up hills of endless light, thru blazing
corridors of suns, where worlds do swing of good and gentle men, of women

From *The Independent*, 61 (October 11, 1906): 856–858.

strong and free — far from the cozeage, black hypocrisy and chaste prostitution of this shameful speck of dust!
>   *Turn again, O Lord, leave us not to perish in our sin!*

From lust of body and lust of blood
>   *Great God deliver us!*

From lust of powers and lust of gold,
>   *Great God deliver us!*

From the leagued lying of despot and of brute,
>   *Great God deliver us!*

A city lay in travail, God our Lord, and from her loins sprang twin Murder and Black Hate. Red was the midnight; clang, crack and cry of death and fury filled the air and trembled underneath the stars when church spires pointed silently to Thee. And all this was to sate the greed of greedy men who hide behind the veil of vengeance!
>   *Bend us Thine ear, O Lord!*

In the pale, still morning we looked upon the deed. We stopped our ears and held our leaping hands, but they — did not wag their heads and leer and cry with bloody jaws: *Cease from Crime!* The word was mockery, for thus they train
a hundred crimes while we do cure one.
>   *Turn again our captivity, O Lord!*

Behold this maimed and broken thing; dear God it was an humble black man who toiled and sweat to save a bit from the pittance paid him. They told him:
Work and Rise. He worked. Did this man sin? Nay, but some one told how someone said another did — one whom he had never seen nor known. Yet for
that man's crime this man lieth maimed and murdered, his wife naked to shame, his children, to poverty and evil.
>   *Hear us, O heavenly Father!*

Doth not this justice of hell stink in Thy nostrils, O God? How long shall the mounting flood of innocent blood roar in Thine ears and pound in our hearts for vengeance? Pile the pale frenzy of blood-crazed brutes who do such deeds high on Thine altar, Jehovah Jireh, and burn it in hell forever and
forever!
>   *Forgive us, good Lord; we know not what we say!*

Bewildered we are, and passion-tost, mad with the madness of a mobbed and
mocked and murdered people; straining at the armposts of Thy Throne, we
raise our shackled hands and charge Thee, God, by the bones of our stolen
fathers, by the tears of our dead mothers by the very blood of Thy crucified
Christ: *What meaneth this?* Tell us the Plan; give us the Sign!
Keep not thou silent, O God!

Sit no longer blind, Lord God, deaf to our prayer and dumb to our dumb
suffering. Surely Thou too are not white, O Lord, a pale, bloodless, heartless
thing?
Ah! Christ of all the Pities!

Forgive the thought! Forgive these wild, blasphemous words. Thou art still the
God of our black fathers, and in Thy soul's soul sit some soft darkenings of
the evening, some shadowings of the velvet night.

But whisper — speak — call, great God, for Thy silence is white terror to our
hearts! The way, O God, show us the way and point us the path.

Whither? North is greed and South is blood; within, the coward, and without,
the liar. Whither? To death?
Amen! Welcome dark sleep!

Whither? To life? But not this life, dear God, not this. Let the cup pass from
us,
tempt us not beyond our strength, for there is that clamoring and clawing
within, to whose voice we would not listen, yet shudder lest we must, and it
is
red, Ah! God! It is a red and awful shape.
Selah!

In yonder East trembles a star.
Vengeance is mine; I will repay, saith the Lord!

Thy will, O Lord, be done!
Kyrie Eleison!

Lord, we have done these pleading, wavering words.
We beseech Thee to hear us, good Lord!

We bow our heads and hearken soft to the sobbing of women and little
children.
We beseech Thee to hear us, good Lord!

Our voices sink in silence and in night.
  Hear us, good Lord!

In night, O God of a godless land!
  Amen!

In silence, O Silent God.
  Selah!

Done at Atlanta, in the Day of Death, 1906.

Another Open Letter to
Woodrow Wilson

Sir: On the occasion of your inauguration as President of the United States, *The Crisis* took the liberty of addressing to you an open letter. *The Crisis* spoke for no inconsiderable part of ten millions of human beings, American born, American citizens. *The Crisis* said in that letter, among other things:

"The only time when the Negro problem is insoluble is when men insist on settling wrong by asking absolutely contradictory things. You cannot make 10,000,000 people at one and the same time servile and dignified, docile and self-reliant, servants and independent leaders, segregated and yet part of the industrial organism, disfranchised and citizens of a democracy, ignorant and intelligent. This is impossible and the impossibility is not factitious; it is in the very nature of things.

"On the other hand, a determination on the part of intelligent and decent Americans to see that no man is denied a reasonable chance for life, liberty and happiness simply because of the color of his skin is a simple, sane and practical solution of the race problem in this land."

Sir, you have now been President of the United States for six months and what is the result? It is no exaggeration to say that every enemy of the Negro race is greatly encouraged; that every man who dreams of making the Negro race a group of menials and pariahs is alert and hopeful. Vardaman, Tillman, Hoke Smith, Cole Blease and Burleson are evidently assuming that their theory of the place and destiny of the Negro race is the theory of your administration. They and others are assuming this because not a single act and not a single word of yours since election has given anyone reason to infer that you have the slightest interest in the colored people or desire to alleviate their intolerable position. A dozen worthy Negro officials have been removed from office, and you have nominated but one black man for office, and he, such a

From *The Crisis*, September 1913.

contemptible cur, that his very nomination was an insult to every Negro in the land.

To this negative appearance of indifference has been added positive action on the part of your advisers, with or without your knowledge, which constitutes the gravest attack on the liberties of our people since emancipation. Public segregation of civil servants in government employ, necessarily involving personal insult and humiliation, has for the first time in history been made the policy of the United States government.

In the Treasury and Postoffice Departments colored clerks have been herded to themselves as though they were not human beings. We are told that one colored clerk who could not actually be segregated on account of the nature of his work has consequently had a cage built around him to separate him from his white companions of many years. Mr. Wilson, do you know these things? Are you responsible for them? Did you advise them? Do you not know that no other group of American citizens has ever been treated in this way and that no President of the United States ever dared to propose such treatment? Here is a plain, flat, disgraceful spitting in the face of people whose darkened countenances are already dark with the slime of insult. Do you consent to this, President Wilson? Do you believe in it? Have you been able to persuade yourself that national insult is best for a people struggling into self-respect?

President Wilson, we do not, we cannot believe this. *The Crisis* still clings to the conviction that a vote for Woodrow Wilson was NOT a vote for Cole Blease or Hoke Smith. But whether it was or not segregation is going to be resented as it ought to be resented by the colored people. We would not be men if we did not resent it. The policy adopted, whether with your consent or knowledge or not, is an indefensible attack on a people who have in the past been shamefully humiliated. There are foolish people who think that such policy has no limit and that lynching, "Jim Crowism," segregation and insult are to be permanent institutions in America.

We have appealed in the past, Mr. Wilson, to you as a man and statesman; to your sense of fairness and broad cosmopolitan outlook on the world. We renew this appeal and to it we venture to add some plain considerations of political expediency.

We black men still vote. In spite of the fact that the triumph of your party last fall was possible only because Southern white men have, through our disfranchisement, from twice to seven times the political power of Northern white men — notwithstanding this, we black men of the North have a growing nest egg of 500,000 ballots, and ballots that are counted, which no sane party can ignore. Does your Mr. Burleson expect the Democratic party to carry New York, New Jersey, Pennsylvania, Ohio, Indiana, Illinois, by 200,000 votes? If he does will it not be well for him to remember that there are 237,942 black voters in these States. We have been trying to tell these voters that the Democratic party wants their votes. Have we been wrong, Mr. Wilson? Have we assumed too great and quick a growth of intelligence in the party that once made slavery its cornerstone?

In view of all this, we beg to ask the President of the United States and the leader of the Democratic party a few plain questions:

1. Do you want Negro votes?
2. Do you think that a "Jim Crow" civil service will get these votes?
3. Is your Negro policy to be dictated by Tillman and Vardaman?
4. Are you going to appoint black men to office on the same terms that you choose white men?

This is information, Mr. Wilson, which we are very anxious to have.

The Crisis advocated sincerely and strongly your election to the Presidency. *The Crisis* has no desire to be compelled to apologize to its constituency for this course. But at the present rate it looks as though some apology or explanation was going to be in order very soon.

We are still hoping that present indications are deceptive. We are still trying to believe that the President of the United States is the President of 10,000,000 as well as of 90,000,000, and that though the 10,000,000 are black and poor, he is too honest and cultured a gentleman to yield to the clamors of ignorance and prejudice and hatred. We are still hoping all this, Mr. Wilson, but hope deferred maketh the heart sick.

Very respectfully yours,
The Crisis.

Houston

It is difficult for one of Negro blood to write of Houston. Is not the ink within the very wells crimsoned with the blood of black martyrs? Do they not cry unavenged, saying: — Always WE pay; always WE die; always, whether right or wrong, it is SO MANY NEGROES killed, so many NEGROES wounded. But here, at last, at Houston is a change. Here, at last, white folk died. Innocent, adventitious strangers, perhaps, as innocent as the thousands of Negroes done to death in the last two centuries. Our hands tremble to rise and exult, our lips strive to cry.

And yet our hands are not raised in exultation; and yet our lips are silent, as we face another great human wrong.

We did not have to have Houston in order to know that black men will not always be mere victims. But we did have Houston in order to ask, Why? Why must this all be? At Waco, at Memphis, at East St. Louis, at Chester, at Houston, at Lexington, and all along that crimsoned list of death and slaughter and orgy and torture.

This, at least, remember, you who jump to judgment — Houston was not an ordinary outburst. Just before the riot the acting chaplain of the regiment writes us: "The battalion has made good and all doubts as to the conduct of the Negro soldier have been dissipated. We are striving to add another page to the glorious record of our regiment."

What it was they had to stand, we learn only in tortuous driblets from sources bitterly prejudiced. These facts, at least, are clear: Contrary to all military precedent the Negro provost guard had been disarmed and was at the mercy of citizen police who insulted them until blood ran. At last, they stole their own arms and turned and fought. They were not young recruits; they

From *The Crisis*, October 1917.

were not wild and drunken wastrels; they were disciplined men who said—"This is enough; we'll stand no more!" That they faced and faced fearlessly the vision of a shameful death, we do not doubt. We ask no mitigation of their punishment. They broke the law. They must suffer. But before Almighty God, if those guiltless of their black brothers' blood shot the punishing shot, there would be no dead men in that regiment.

The Arkansas Riots

The article of Clair Kenamore, published in your edition of Nov. 16, concerning the "Elaine Uprising" is so palpably unfair and misinforming that I trust you will allow me space to correct it.

1. It is ridiculous to seek to make Robert L. Hill the cause of the Arkansas trouble. Whatever he did or did not do, the just grievances of the Negro peons in Arkansas are a disgrace to the South and a defiance of the Thirteenth Amendment. So far as Hill is concerned, this is a matter of record: Last summer he was sued for a small debt by a white man. He alleged that the debt had been paid. Nevertheless, the man got judgment and seized all of Hill's farming stock and Hill was unable to redeem it. Does this look like the experience of a man with $12,000 in the bank?

2. The share-tenant system in vogue in the Mississippi Delta region, of which Phillips County, Ark., is a part, is one of the most iniquitous systems of peonage in the United States. Under President Roosevelt's Administration, the Brattons, white lawyers, who are mentioned in Kenamore's article, assisted the District Attorney in convicting nearly a dozen white men of peonage in this part of Arkansas. Small wonder that the Brattons are unpopular: that they have been blamed for the present disturbances, and one of them nearly lynched and imprisoned thirty-one days, without trial or charge.

As a matter of fact, the share system enables the landlords completely to control labor and wages. No itemized accounts are ever given. The landlord "advances" supplies to his tenants in the same sense that the United States Steel Corporation "advances" wages to its employees, or that the merchant "advances" wages to his clerks; in other words, before the cotton crop is harvested, the laborers are supposed to be paid for the work which they do on the crop.

In the delta region, however, this is only partially true. The laborer is allowed to get certain supplies at the company store at exorbitant prices. A

From the *New York World*, November 28, 1919.

year or less later, after his crop has been harvested, he is given a slip telling him how much he owes for supplies, how much his crop was worth and what is the balance due. To dispute this statement is, in Arkansas custom, to dispute "white supremacy."

This is bad enough, but lately, with the high price of cotton and the great demand for labor, an additional injustice has been added. On the Fathauer and other plantations, cotton sold in the fall of 1918 and was not settled for until July, 1919; and then the statement was verbal, without items. This year the same method was attempted again. The crop was gathered, one car was loaded and another was being loaded. As soon as the second car was ready, both were to be sent to market. The Negroes had no way of knowing what the crop would sell for, no exact account of the amount of cotton which they had raised and no prospect of having any statement of their accounts before the summer of 1920. They objected. And they did exactly as any law-abiding American ought to have done — they went to the largest town in the county and hired lawyers.

3. When Negroes in other parts of the county learned what the sixty-eight Fathauer tenants proposed to do, they arranged meetings and planned to do the same thing. Many of them were members of Hill's organization, but there is not the slightest trustworthy evidence that the meetings of these Negroes had any object except to force by law prompt settlements by the landlords to better the condition of the tenants by saving money and buying land.

Meetings of Negroes in the black belt are always looked upon with suspicion, and they are stopped by a very simple expedient. Somebody goes and shoots at the Negroes secretly, and at the slightest sign of resistance the whole organization of the black belt is called into being. This organization consists of all the law officers of the county and all the white men near and in neighboring counties and states, armed to the teeth.

No sooner had the plan of the Fathauer tenants become known than a meeting of Negroes at Hoop Spur was without provocation fired into. The Negroes returned the fire, killing one white man. This at first was the extent of the "uprising." In retaliation, from 60 to 100 Negroes were killed, 1,000 Negroes were arrested and 123 Negroes were indicted. 12 Negroes were sentenced to death and 54 to terms of imprisonment in the penitentiary.

4. Four Negro professional men from Helena, the Johnston brothers, who had absolutely nothing to do with the tenants and knew nothing of the disturbance, were killed. They had been out squirrel-shooting, and on their way back were advised by certain white friends to leave their automobile and take the train, as there was trouble in the vicinity. They did so. These "friends" then told the mob that they were on the train; the mob took them from the

train. When they resisted and killed one white man, all four Negroes were so shot to pieces that their bodies were unrecognizable.

5. The trials of the accused Negroes were a most outrageous farce. (a) They had the right to ask for a change of venue, and considering the state of mind of the white people in the county and the fact that there was no colored man on the jury lists, this would have been the least that their lawyers could have asked for. No change of venue was asked in the case of a single defendant. (b) Every defendant in such cases in Arkansas is allowed twenty challenges of jurors. In the case of these fifty condemned Negroes, not a single challenge was made. (c) When a group of persons is accused of crime they can in Arkansas law ask for a "severance" of their cases, and their lawyer may determine the order in which they shall be brought to trial. No severance was asked: a jury was impanelled and six Negroes were condemned to death in a half day and the whole twelve less than a day after. This, mind you, in a trial of felony cases for capital offenses.

There is not a civilized country in the world that would for a moment allow this kind of justice to stand.

The Souls of White Folk

High in the tower, where I sit above the loud complaining of the human sea, I know many souls that toss and whirl and pass, but none there are that intrigue me more than the Souls of White Folk.

Of them I am singularly clairvoyant. I see in and through them. I view them from unusual points of vantage. Not as a foreigner do I come, for I am native, not foreign, bone of their thought and flesh of their language. Mine is not the knowledge of the traveler or the colonial composite of dear memories, words and wonder. Nor yet is my knowledge that which servants have of masters, or mass of class, or capitalist of artisan. Rather I see these souls undressed and from the back and side. I see the working of their entrails. I know their thoughts and they know that I know. This knowledge makes them now embarrassed, now furious! They deny my right to live and be and call me misbirth! My word is to them mere bitterness and my soul, pessimism. And yet as they preach and strut and shout and threaten, crouching as they clutch at rags of facts and fancies to hide their nakedness, they go twisting, flying by my tired eyes and I see them ever stripped — ugly, human.

The discovery of personal whiteness among the world's peoples is a very modern thing — a nineteenth and twentieth century matter, indeed. The ancient world would have laughed at such a distinction. The Middle Age regarded skin color with mild curiosity; and even up into the eighteenth century we were hammering our national manikins into one, great, Universal Man, with fine frenzy which ignored color and race even more than birth. Today we have changed all that, and the world in a sudden, emotional conversion has discovered that it is white and by that token, wonderful!

This assumption that of all the hues of God whiteness alone is inherently and obviously better than brownness or tan leads to curious acts; even the sweeter souls of the dominant world as they discourse with me on weather,

From *Darkwater: Voices from Within the Veil* (1920).

weal, and woe are continually playing above their actual words an obbligato of tune and tone, saying:

"My poor, un-white thing! Weep not nor rage. I know, too well, that the curse of God lies heavy on you. Why? That is not for me to say, but be brave! Do your work in your lowly sphere, praying the good Lord that into heaven above, where all is love, you may, one day, be born — white!"

I do not laugh. I am quite straight-faced as I ask soberly:

"But what on earth is whiteness that one should so desire it?" Then always, somehow, some way, silently but clearly, I am given to understand that whiteness is the ownership of the earth forever and ever, Amen!

Now what is the effect on a man or a nation when it comes passionately to believe such an extraordinary dictum as this? That nations are coming to believe it is manifest daily. Wave on wave, each with increasing virulence, is dashing this new religion of whiteness on the shores of our time. Its first effects are funny: the strut of the Southerner, the arrogance of the Englishman amuck, the whoop of the hoodlum who vicariously leads your mob. Next it appears dampening generous enthusiasm in what we once counted glorious; to free the slave is discovered to be tolerable only in so far as it freed his master! Do we sense somnolent writhings in black Africa or angry groans in India or triumphant banzais in Japan? "To your tents, O Israel!" These nations are not white!

After the more comic manifestations and the chilling of generous enthusiasm come subtler, darker deeds. Everything considered, the title to the universe claimed by White Folk is faulty. It ought, at least, to look plausible. How easy, then, by emphasis and omission to make children believe that every great soul the world ever saw was a white man's soul; that every great thought the world ever knew was a white man's thought; that every great deed the world ever did was a white man's deed; that every great dream the world ever sang was a white man's dream. In fine, that if from the world were dropped everything that could not fairly be attributed to White Folk, the world would, if anything, be even greater, truer, better than now. And if all this be a lie, is it not a lie in a great cause?

Here it is that the comedy verges to tragedy. The first minor note is struck, all unconsciously, by those worthy souls in whom consciousness of high descent brings burning desire to spread the gift abroad — the obligation of nobility to the ignoble. Such sense of duty assumes two things: a real possession of the heritage and its frank appreciation by the humble-born. So long, then, as humble black folk, voluble with thanks, receive barrels of old clothes from lordly and generous whites, there is much mental peace and moral satisfaction. But when the black man begins to dispute the white man's title to certain alleged bequests of the Fathers in wage and position, authority and training; and when his attitude toward charity is sullen anger rather than humble jollity; when he insists on his human right to swagger and swear and waste — then the spell is suddenly broken and the philanthropist is ready to believe that Negroes are impudent, that the South is right, and that Japan wants to fight America.

After this the descent to Hell is easy. On the pale, white faces which the great billows whirl upward to my tower I see again and again, often and still more often, a writing of human hatred, a deep and passionate hatred, vast by the very vagueness of its expressions. Down through the green waters, on the bottom of the world, where men move to and fro, I have seen a man — an educated gentleman — grow livid with anger because a little, silent, black woman was sitting by herself in a Pullman car. He was a white man. I have seen a great, grown man curse a little child, who had wandered into the wrong waiting-room, searching for its mother: "Here, you damned black — " He was white. In Central Park I have seen the upper lip of a quiet, peaceful man curl back in a tigerish snarl of rage because black folk rode by in a motor car. He was a white man. We have seen, you and I, city after city drunk and furious with ungovernable lust of blood; mad with murder, destroying, killing, and cursing; torturing human victims because somebody accused of crime happened to be of the same color as the mob's innocent victims and because that color was not white! We have seen — Merciful God! in these wild days and in the name of Civilization, Justice, and Motherhood — what have we not seen, right here in America, of orgy, cruelty, barbarism, and murder done to men and women of Negro descent.

Up through the foam of green and weltering waters wells this great mass of hatred, in wilder, fiercer violence, until I look down and know that today to the millions of my people no misfortune could happen — of death and pestilence, failure and defeat — that would not make the hearts of millions of their fellows beat with fierce, vindictive joy! Do you doubt it? Ask your own soul what it would say if the next census were to report that half of black America was dead and the other half dying.

Unfortunate? Unfortunate. But where is the misfortune? Mine? Am I, in my blackness, the sole sufferer? I suffer. And yet, somehow, above the suffering, above the shackled anger that beats the bars, above the hurt that crazes there surges in me a vast pity — pity for a people imprisoned and enthralled, hampered and made miserable for such a cause, for such a phantasy!

Conceive this nation, of all human peoples, engaged in a crusade to make the "World Safe for Democracy"! Can you imagine the United States protesting against Turkish atrocities in Armenia, while the Turks are silent about mobs in Chicago and St. Louis; what is Louvain compared with Memphis, Waco, Washington, Dyersburg, and Estill Springs? In short, what is the black man but America's Belgium, and how could America condemn in Germany that which she commits, just as brutally, within her own borders?

A true and worthy ideal frees and uplifts a people; a false ideal imprisons and lowers. Say to men, earnestly and repeatedly: "Honesty is best, knowledge is power; do unto others as you would be done by." Say this and act it and the nation must move toward it, if not to it. But say to a people: "The one virtue is to be white," and the people rush to the inevitable conclusion, "Kill the 'nigger'!"

Is not this the record of present America? Is not this its headlong progress? Are we not coming more and more, day by day, to making the statement "I am white," the one fundamental tenet of our practical morality? Only when this basic, iron rule is involved is our defense of right nation-wide and prompt. Murder may swagger, theft may rule and prostitution may flourish and the nation gives but spasmodic, intermittent and lukewarm attention. But let the murderer be black or the thief brown or the violator of womanhood have a drop of Negro blood, and the righteousness of the indignation sweeps the world. Nor would this fact make the indignation less justifiable did not we all know that it was blackness that was condemned and not crime.

In the awful cataclysm of World War, where from beating, slandering, and murdering us the white world turned temporarily aside to kill each other, we of the Darker Peoples looked on in mild amaze.

Among some of us, I doubt not, this sudden descent of Europe into hell brought unbounded surprise; to others, over wide area, it brought the *Schaden Freude* of the bitterly hurt; but most of us, I judge, looked on silently and sorrowfully, in sober thought, seeing sadly the prophecy of our own souls.

Here is a civilization that has boasted much. Neither Roman nor Arab, Greek nor Egyptian, Persian nor Mongol ever took himself and his own perfectness with such disconcerting seriousness as the modern white man. We whose shame, humiliation, and deep insult his aggrandizement so often involved were never deceived. We looked at him clearly, with world-old eyes, and saw simply a human thing, weak and pitiable and cruel, even as we are and were.

These super-men and world-mastering demi-gods listened, however, to no low tongues of ours, even when we pointed silently to their feet of clay. Perhaps we, as folk of simpler soul and more primitive type, have been most struck in the welter of recent years by the utter failure of white religion. We have curled our lips in something like contempt as we have witnessed glib apology and weary explanation. Nothing of the sort deceived us. A nation's religion is its life, and as such white Christianity is a miserable failure.

Nor would we be unfair in this criticism: We know that we, too, have failed, as you have, and have rejected many a Buddha, even as you have denied Christ; but we acknowledge our human frailty, while you, claiming super-humanity, scoff endlessly at our shortcomings.

The number of white individuals who are practising with even reasonable approximation the democracy and unselfishness of Jesus Christ is so small and unimportant as to be fit subject for jest in Sunday supplements and in *Punch, Life, Le Rive,* and *Fliegende Blätter.* In her foreign mission work the extraordinary self-deception of white religion is epitomized: solemnly the white world sends five million dollars worth of missionary propaganda to Africa each year and in the same twelve months adds twenty-five million dollars worth of the vilest gin manufactured. Peace to the augurs of Rome!

We may, however, grant without argument that religious ideals have always far outrun their very human devotees. Let us, then, turn to more mundane matters of honor and fairness. The world today is trade. The world has turned shopkeeper; history is economic history; living is earning a living. Is it necessary to ask how much of high emprise and honorable conduct has been found here? Something, to be sure. The establishment of world credit systems is built on splendid and realizable faith in fellow-men. But it is, after all, so low and elementary a step that sometimes it looks merely like honor among thieves, for the revelations of highway robbery and low cheating in the business world and in all its great modern centers have raised in the hearts of all true men in our day an exceeding great cry for revolution in our basic methods and conceptions of industry and commerce.

We do not, for a moment, forget the robbery of other times and races when trade was a most uncertain gamble; but was there not a certain honesty and frankness in the evil that argued a saner morality? There are more merchants today, surer deliveries, and wider well-being, but are there not, also, bigger thieves, deeper injustice, and more calloused selfishness in well-being? Be that as it may — certainly the nicer sense of honor that has risen ever and again in groups of forward-thinking men has been curiously and broadly blunted. Consider our chiefest industry — fighting. Laboriously the Middle Ages built its rules of fairness — equal armament, equal notice, equal conditions. What do we see today? Machine-guns against assegais; conquest sugared with religion; mutilation and rape masquerading as culture — all this, with vast applause at the superiority of white over black soldiers!

War is horrible! This the dark world knows to its awful cost. But has it just become horrible, in these last days, when under essentially equal conditions, equal armament, and equal waste of wealth white men are fighting white men, with surgeons and nurses hovering near?

Think of the wars through which we have lived in the last decade: in German Africa, in British Nigeria, in French and Spanish Morocco, in China, in Persia, in the Balkans, in Tripoli, in Mexico, and in a dozen lesser places — were not these horrible, too? Mind you, there were for most of these wars no Red Cross funds.

Behold little Belgium and her pitiable plight, but has the world forgotten Congo? What Belgium now suffers is not half, not even a tenth, of what she has done to black Congo since Stanley's great dream of 1880. Down the dark forests of inmost Africa sailed this modern Sir Galahad, in the name of "the noble-minded men of several nations," to introduce commerce and civilization. What came of it? "Rubber and murder, slavery in its worst form," wrote Glave in 1895.

Harris declares that King Leopold's régime meant the death of twelve million natives, "but what we who were behind the scenes felt most keenly was the fact that the real catastrophe in the Congo was desolation and murder in the larger sense. The invasion of family life, the ruthless destruction of every social barrier, the shattering of every tribal law, the introduction of criminal practices which struck the chiefs of the people dumb with horror — in a word, a veritable avalanche of filth and immorality overwhelmed the Congo tribes."

Yet the fields of Belgium laughed, the cities were gay, art and science flourished; the groans that helped to nourish this civilization fell on deaf ears because the world round about was doing the same sort of thing elsewhere on its own account.

As we saw the dead dimly through rifts of battle-smoke and heard faintly the cursings and accusations of blood brothers, we darker men said: This is not Europe gone mad; this is not aberration nor insanity; this *is* Europe; this seeming Terrible is the real soul of white culture — back of all culture — stripped and visible today. This is where the world has arrived — these dark and awful depths and not the shining and ineffable heights of which it boasted. Here is whither the might and energy of modern humanity have really gone.

But may not the world cry back at us and ask: "What better thing have you to show? What have you done or would do better than this if you had today the world rule? Paint with all riot of hateful colors the thin skin of European culture — is it not better than any culture that arose in Africa or Asia?"

It is. Of this there is no doubt and never has been; but why is it better? Is it better because Europeans are better, nobler, greater, and more gifted than other folk? It is not. Europe has never produced and never will in our day bring forth a single human soul who cannot be matched and over-matched in every line of human endeavor by Asia and Africa. Run the gamut, if you will, and let us have the Europeans who in sober truth over-match Nefertari, Mohammed, Rameses and Askia, Confucius, Buddha, and Jesus Christ. If we could scan the calendar of thousands of lesser men, in like comparison, the result would be the same; but we cannot do this because of the deliberately educated ignorance of white schools by which they remember Napoleon and forget Sonni Ali.

The greatness of Europe has lain in the width of the stage on which she has played her part, the strength of the foundations on which she has builded, and a natural, human ability no whit greater (if as great) than that of other days and races. In other words, the deeper reasons for the triumph of European civilization lie quite outside and beyond Europe — back in the universal struggles of all mankind.

Why, then, is Europe great? Because of the foundations which the mighty past have furnished her to build upon: the iron trade of ancient, black Africa, the religion and empire-building of yellow Asia, the art and science of the "dago" Mediterranean shore, east, south, and west, as well as north. And where she has builded securely upon this great past and learned from it she has gone forward to greater and more splendid human triumph; but where she has ignored this past and forgotten and sneered at it, she has shown the cloven hoof of poor, crucified humanity — she has played, like other empires gone, the world fool!

If, then, European triumphs in culture have been greater, so, too, may her failures have been greater. How great a failure and a failure in what does the World War betoken? Was it national jealousy of the sort of the seventeenth century? But Europe has done more to break down national barriers than any preceding culture. Was it fear of the balance of power in Europe? Hardly, save in the half-Asiatic problems of the Balkans. What, then, does Hauptmann mean when he says: "Our jealous enemies forged an iron ring about our breasts and we knew our breasts had to expand — that we had to split asunder this ring or else we had to cease breathing. But Germany will not cease to breathe and so it came to pass that the iron ring was forced apart."

Whither is this expansion? What is that breath of life, thought to be so indispensable to a great European nation? Manifestly it is expansion overseas; it is colonial aggrandizement which explains, and alone adequately explains, the World War. How many of us today fully realize the current theory of colonial expansion, of the relation of Europe which is white, to the world which is black and brown and yellow? Bluntly put, that theory is this: It is the duty of white Europe to divide up the darker world and administer it for Europe's good.

This Europe has largely done. The European world is using black and brown men for all the uses which men know. Slowly but surely white culture is evolving the theory that "darkies" are born beasts of burden for white folk. It were silly to think otherwise, cries the cultured world, with stronger and shriller accord. The supporting arguments grow and twist themselves in the mouths of merchant, scientist, soldier, traveler, writer, and missionary: Darker peoples are dark in mind as well as in body; of dark, uncertain, and imperfect descent; of frailer, cheaper stuff; they are cowards in the face of mausers and maxims; they have no feelings, aspirations, and loves; they are fools, illogical idiots — "half-devil and half-child."

Such as they are civilization must, naturally, raise them, but soberly and in limited ways. They are not simply dark white men. They are not "men" in the sense that Europeans are men. To the very limited extent of their shallow capacities lift them to be useful to whites, to raise cotton, gather rubber, fetch ivory, dig diamonds — and let them be paid what men think they are worth — white men who know them to be well-nigh worthless.

Such degrading of men by men is as old as mankind and the invention of no one race or people. Ever have men striven to conceive of their victims as different from the victors, endlessly different, in soul and blood, strength and cunning, race and lineage. It has been left, however, to Europe and to modern days to discover the eternal world-wide mark of meanness — color!

Such is the silent revolution that has gripped modern European culture in the later nineteenth and twentieth centuries. Its zenith came in Boxer times: White supremacy was all but world-wide, Africa was dead, India conquered, Japan isolated, and China prostrate, while white America whetted her sword for mongrel Mexico and mulatto South America, lynching her own Negroes the while. Temporary halt in this program was made by little Japan and the white world immediately sensed the peril of such "yellow" presumption! What sort of a world would this be if yellow men must be treated "white"? Immediately the eventual overthrow of Japan became a subject of deep thought and intrigue, from St. Petersburg to San Francisco, from the Key of Heaven to the Little Brother of the Poor.

The using of men for the benefit of masters is no new invention of modern Europe. It is quite as old as the world. But Europe proposed to apply it on a scale and with an elaborateness of detail of which no former world ever dreamed. The imperial width of the thing — the heaven-defying audacity — makes its modern newness.

The scheme of Europe was no sudden invention, but a way out of long-pressing difficulties. It is plain to modern white civilization that the subjection of the white working classes cannot much longer be maintained. Education, political power, and increased knowledge of the technique and meaning of the industrial process are destined to make a more and more equitable distribution of wealth in the near future. The day of the very rich is drawing to a close, so far as individual white nations are concerned. But there is a loophole. There is a chance for exploitation on an immense scale for inordinate profit, not simply to the very rich, but to the middle class and to the laborers. This chance lies in the exploitation of darker peoples. It is here that the golden hand beckons. Here are no labor unions or votes or questioning onlookers or inconvenient consciences. These men may be used down to the very bone, and shot and maimed in "punitive" expeditions when they revolt. In these dark lands "industrial development" may repeat in exaggerated form every horror of the industrial history of Europe, from slavery and rape to disease and maiming, with only one test of success — dividends!

This theory of human culture and its aims has worked itself through warp and woof of our daily thought with a thoroughness that few realize. Everything great, good, efficient, fair, and honorable is "white"; everything mean, bad, blundering, cheating, and dishonorable is "yellow"; a bad taste is "brown"; and the devil is "black." The changes of this theme are continually rung in picture and story, in newspaper heading and moving-picture, in sermon and school book, until, of course, the King can do no wrong — a White Man is always right and a Black Man has no rights which a white man is bound to respect.

There must come the necessary despisings and hatreds of these savage half-men, this unclean *canaille* of the world — these dogs of men. All through the world this gospel is preaching. It has its literature, it has its priests, it has its secret propaganda and above all — it pays!

There's the rub — it pays. Rubber, ivory, and palm-oil; tea, coffee, and cocoa; bananas, oranges, and other fruit; cotton, gold, and copper — they, and a hundred other things which dark and sweating bodies hand up to the white world from their pits of slime, pay and pay well, but of all that the world gets the black world gets only the pittance that the white world throws it disdainfully.

Small wonder, then, that in the practical world of things-that-be there is jealousy and strife for the possession of the labor of dark millions, for the right to bleed and exploit the colonies of the world where this golden stream may be had, not always for the asking, but surely for the whipping and shooting. It was this competition for the labor of yellow, brown, and black folks that was the cause of the World War. Other causes have been glibly given and other contributing causes there doubtless were, but they were subsidiary and subordinate to this vast quest of the dark world's wealth and toil.

Colonies, we call them, these places where "niggers" are cheap and the earth is rich; they are those outlands where like a swarm of hungry locusts

461

white masters may settle to be served as kings, wield the lash of slave-drivers, rape girls and wives, grow as rich as Croesus and send homeward a golden stream. They belt the earth, these places, but they cluster in the tropics, with its darkened peoples: in Hong Kong and Anam, in Borneo and Rhodesia, in Sierra Leone and Nigeria, in Panama and Havana — these are the El Dorados toward which the world powers stretch itching palms.

Germany, at last one and united and secure on land, looked across the seas and seeing England with sources of wealth insuring a luxury and power which Germany could not hope to rival by the slower processes of exploiting her own peasants and workingmen, especially with these workers half in revolt, immediately built her navy and entered into a desperate competition for possession of colonies of darker peoples. To South America, to China, to Africa, to Asia Minor, she turned like a hound quivering on the leash, impatient, suspicious, irritable, with blood-shot eyes and dripping fangs, ready for the awful word. England and France crouched watchfully over their bones, growling and wary, but gnawing industriously, while the blood of the dark world whetted their greedy appetites. In the background, shut out from the highway to the seven seas, sat Russia and Austria, snarling and snapping at each other and at the last Mediterranean gate to the El Dorado, where the Sick Man enjoyed bad health, and where millions of serfs in the Balkans, Russia, and Asia offered a feast to greed well-nigh as great as Africa.

The fateful day came. It had to come. The cause of war is preparation for war; and of all that Europe has done in a century there is nothing that has equaled in energy, thought, and time her preparation for wholesale murder. The only adequate cause of this preparation was conquest and conquest, not in Europe, but primarily among the darker peoples of Asia and Africa; conquest, not for assimilation and uplift, but for commerce and degradation. For this, and this mainly, did Europe gird herself at frightful cost for war.

The red day dawned when the tinder was lighted in the Balkans and Austro-Hungary seized a bit which brought her a step nearer to the world's highway; she seized one bit and poised herself for another. Then came that curious chorus of challenges, those leaping suspicions, raking all causes for distrust and rivalry and hatred, but saying little of the real and greatest cause.

Each nation felt its deep interests involved. But how? Not, surely, in the death of Ferdinand the Warlike; not, surely, in the old, half-forgotten *revanche* for Alsace-Lorraine; not even in the neutrality of Belgium. No! But in the possession of land overseas, in the right to colonies, the chance to levy endless tribute on the darker world, — on coolies in China, on starving peasants in India, on black savages in Africa, on dying South Sea Islanders, on Indians of the Amazon — all this and nothing more.

Even the broken reed on which we had rested high hopes of eternal peace — the guild of the laborers — the front of that very important movement for human justice on which we had builded most, even this flew like a straw before the breath of king and kaiser. Indeed, the flying had been fore-shadowed when in Germany and America "international" Socialists had all but read yellow and black men out of the kingdom of industrial justice. Subtly had they been bribed, but effectively: Were they not lordly whites and should they not share in the spoils of rape? High wages in the United States and England might be the skillfully manipulated result of slavery in Africa and of peonage in Asia.

With the dog-in-the-manger theory of trade, with the determination to reap inordinate profits and to exploit the weakest to the utmost there came a new imperialism — the rage for one's own nation to own the earth or, at least, a large enough portion of it to insure as big profits as the next nation. Where sections could not be owned by one dominant nation there came a policy of "open door," but the "door" was open to "white people only." As to the darkest and weakest of peoples there was but one unanimity in Europe — that which Herr Dernberg of the German Colonial Office called the agreement with England to maintain white "prestige" in Africa — the doctrine of the divine right of white people to steal.

Thus the world market most wildly and desperately sought today is the market where labor is cheapest and most helpless and profit is most abundant. This labor is kept cheap and helpless because the white world despises "darkies." If one has the temerity to suggest that these workingmen may walk the way of white workingmen and climb by votes and self-assertion and education to the rank of men, he is howled out of court. They cannot do it and if they could, they shall not, for they are the enemies of the white race and the whites shall rule forever and forever and everywhere. Thus the hatred and despising of human beings from whom Europe wishes to extort her luxuries have led to such jealousy and bickering between European nations that they have fallen afoul of each other and have fought like crazed beasts. Such is the fruit of human hatred.

But what of the darker world that watches? Most men belong to this world. With Negro and Negroid, East Indian, Chinese, and Japanese they form two-thirds of the population of the world. A belief in humanity is a belief in colored men. If the uplift of mankind must be done by men, then the destinies of this world will rest ultimately in the hands of darker nations.

What, then, is this dark world thinking? It is thinking that as wild and awful as this shameful war was, *it is nothing to compare with that fight for freedom which black and brown and yellow men must and will make unless their*

oppression and humiliation and insult at the hands of the White World cease.
The Dark World is going to submit to its present treatment just as long as it must
and not one moment longer.

Let me say this again and emphasize it and leave no room for mistaken meaning: The World War was primarily the jealous and avaricious struggle for the largest share in exploiting darker races. As such it is and must be but the prelude to the armed and indignant protest of these despised and raped peoples. Today Japan is hammering on the door of justice, China is raising her half-manacled hands to knock next, India is writhing for the freedom to knock, Egypt is sullenly muttering, the Negroes of South and West Africa, of the West Indies, and of the United States are just awakening to their shameful slavery. Is, then, this war the end of wars? Can it be the end, so long as sits enthroned, even in the souls of those who cry peace, the despising and robbing of darker peoples? If Europe hugs this delusion, then this is not the end of world war — it is but the beginning!

We see Europe's greatest sin precisely where we found Africa's and Asia's — in human hatred, the despising of men; with this difference, however: Europe has the awful lesson of the past before her, has the splendid results of widened areas of tolerance, sympathy, and love among men, and she faces a greater, an infinitely greater, world of men than any preceding civilization ever faced.

It is curious to see America, the United States, looking on herself, first, as a sort of natural peacemaker, then as a moral protagonist in this terrible time. No nation is less fitted for this rôle. For two or more centuries America has marched proudly in the van of human hatred — making bonfires of human flesh and laughing at them hideously, and making the insulting of millions more than a matter of dislike — rather a great religion, a world war-cry: Up white, down black; to your tents, O white folk, and world war with black and parti-colored mongrel beasts!

Instead of standing as a great example of the success of democracy and the possibility of human brotherhood America has taken her place as an awful example of its pitfalls and failures, so far as black and brown and yellow peoples are concerned. And this, too, in spite of the fact that there has been no actual failure; the Indian is not dying out, the Japanese and Chinese have not menaced the land, and the experiment of Negro suffrage has resulted in the uplift of twelve million people at a rate probably unparalleled in history. But what of this? America, Land of Democracy, wanted to believe in the failure of democracy so far as darker peoples were concerned. Absolutely without excuse she established a caste system, rushed into preparation for war, and conquered tropical colonies. She stands today shoulder to shoulder with Europe in Europe's worst sin against civilization. She aspires to sit among the great nations who arbitrate the fate of "lesser breeds without the law" and she is at times heartily ashamed even of the large number of "new" white people whom her democracy has admitted to place and power. Against this surging forward of Irish and German, of Russian Jew, Slav, and "dago" her social bars have not availed, but against Negroes she can and does take her unflinching and immovable stand, backed by this new public policy of Europe. She trains her immigrants to this despising of "niggers" from the day of their landing, and they carry and send the news back to the submerged classes in the fatherlands.

All this I see and hear up in my tower, above the thunder of the seven seas. From my narrowed windows I stare into the night that looms beneath the cloud-swept stars. Eastward and westward storms are breaking—great, ugly whirlwinds of hatred and blood and cruelty. I will not believe them inevitable. I will not believe that all that was must be, that all the shameful drama of the past must be done again today before the sunlight sweeps the silver seas.

If I cry amid this roar of elemental forces, must my cry be in vain, because it is but a cry—a small and human cry amid Promethean gloom?

Back beyond the world and swept by these wild, white faces of the awful dead, why will this Soul of White Folk—this modern Prometheus—hang bound by his own binding, tethered by a fable of the past? I hear his mighty cry reverberating through the world, "I am white!" Well and good, O Prometheus, divine thief! Is not the world wide enough for two colors, for many little shinings of the sun? Why, then, devour your own vitals if I answer even as proudly, "I am black!"

Haiti

The United States is at war with Haiti. Congress has never sanctioned this war. Josephus Daniels has illegally and unjustly occupied a free foreign land and murdered its inhabitants by the thousands. He has deposed its officials and dispersed its legally elected representatives. He is carrying on a reign of terror, brow-beating, and cruelty, at the hands of southern white naval officers and marines. For more than a year this red-handed deviltry has proceeded, and today the Island is in open rebellion. The greatest single question before the parties at the next election is the Freedom of Haiti.

From *The Crisis*, April 1920.

Reduced Representation
in Congress

Friends of Democracy and especially friends of over ten million disfranchised persons — white and black — in the South, are called upon today for clear thinking and a knowledge of the facts.

This nation is putting a *premium* upon oligarchy and a *penalty* upon democracy.

The states *can* and *do* control the conditions under which a citizen may or may not vote. By the 15th and 19th Amendments there are only two checks on their power: They cannot legally disfranchise men for *race* or for *sex*. They cannot say that a Negro or a woman cannot vote.

But — and this fact is often slurred or forgotten — the states *can* and legally *do* restrict the suffrage for *other* reasons, such as length of residence, previous registration, ability to read and write, possession of property, etc.

Moreover, states can easily disfranchise a whole group by choosing certain characteristics or disabilities of the group: Negroes as a mass are poor and ignorant; a property and literacy qualification will therefore disfranchise a large number of them; women are occupied in homes for the most part and not in the so-called "gainful occupations." A restriction of voting to those in such occupations would be undoubtedly legal and would disfranchise 75% of the women.

Hitherto democracy in the United States has assumed that self interest would keep the number of voters *as large as possible* in various states. This assumption has *failed* in two respects: It has kept *women* from voting for more than a century and it has kept *Negroes* in the South from voting during the better part of a generation.

This in itself is bad enough, but the situation is worse when we consider

From *The Crisis*, February 1921.

that *we have made it distinctly to the advantage of oligarchical rule to dis-franchise just as many voters as possible* and to do this by legal enactment or by force or public opinion, by economic pressure or by sneering at the efficacy of democratic government. How far this has gone an article in this number of *The Crisis* shows.

We have at present only *one* legal remedy and that lies in the 14th Amendment. Many persons, and especially Negroes, assume that the enforce-ment of the section of the second section of the 14th Amendment would make the disfranchisement of Negroes legal. *This is absolutely untrue.* As long as the 15th Amendment stands, it is absolutely illegal to disfranchise a person because of "race, color or previous condition of servitude." But it is absolutely legal to disfranchise persons for any number of other reasons. Indeed a state might legally disfranchise a person for having red hair.

But here the 14th Amendment steps in and says: "But when the right to vote at any election . . . is denied to any of the male inhabitants of such state (being 21 years of age and citizens of the United States) or in any way abridged . . . the basis of representation therein shall be reduced in . . . proportion . . ." In other words, if for any *legal* reason a state disfranchises its citizens then the representation of that state in Congress must be propor-tionately reduced.

The Constitution does not attempt to say that the state may not have perfectly good moral ground for such disfranchisement. In sheer self defense it may be proper, temporarily, for a state to disfranchise the ignorant. It might even defend itself, under a just economic system, in disfranchising the poor. But whatever its motives or justification a *state can disfranchise its citizens for any reason except race and sex.* But if it *does* it is liable to have its representa-tion in Congress reduced, and indeed if it believes in democratic government it ought to be willing and eager for such reduction.

By assenting to such reduction it simply says to its fellow citizens through-out the United States: "We, the voters of South Carolina, do not wish to wield any more political power, man for man, than you voters of North Dakota; and therefore because we have disfranchised most of our adult citizens on account of our wretched public school system and unjust industrial organization, we ask to have our political power curtailed until we can educate our citizens and make a more decent distribution of wealth."

But if this assent is due from South Carolina, how much more is a demand called for from the disfranchised Negroes? They have simply to choose between two alternatives: *to be temporarily unrepresented in Congress or to be perpetually represented by their active and militant enemies.* If they are unre-presented, this lack of representation is not and cannot be on account of their race and color so long as the 15th Amendment stands. It is simply on account of other qualifications or on account of the unfair administration of the law. If the other qualifications are *reasonable* it is only a matter of time when Negroes will meet them and have their representation restored automatically. If they are disfranchised by *unreasonable* qualifications or by the *unfair administration of the law,* they can continue to attack these in the courts and before the public opinion of the nation and the world, *and during this fight their enemies will be disarmed of their undue political power* and influence. In such case they cannot in the long run fail to triumph.

There is absolutely no valid argument against this policy or cause for hesitation. The overwhelming political power of the South, whereby 10,000 voters in Mississippi wield as much political power as 97,000 voters in Indiana, must be changed. The legal remedy is at hand and involves no jot or tittle of surrender of any right or hope of the American Negro. To hesitate is to give to that section of the United States where mobs, lynching, ignorance, and murder flourish, *four times* the political power exercised by the intelligence, thrift, and law-abiding devotion to democracy in the rest of the land.

The Superior Race

I

When the obsession of his race consciousness leaves him, my white friend is quite companionable; otherwise he is impossible. He has a way of putting an excessive amount of pity in his look and of stating as a general and incontrovertible fact that it is "horrible" to be an Exception. By this he means me. He is more than certain that I prove the rule. He is not a bright person, but of that famous average, standardized and astonished at anything that even seems original. His thesis is simple: The world is composed of Race superimposed on Race; classes superimposed on classes; beneath the whole thing is "Our Family" in capitals, and under that is God. God seems to be a cousin, or at least a blood relative of the Van Diemans.

"Of course," he says, "you know Negroes are inferior."

I admit nothing of the sort, I maintain. In fact, having known with considerable intimacy, both male and female, the people of the British Isles, of Scandinavia, of Russia, of Germany, north and south, of the three ends of France and the two ends of Italy; specimens from the Balkans and black and white Spain; the three great races of Asia and the melange of Africa, without mentioning America, I sit here and maintain that black folk are much the superior of white.

"You are either joking or mad," he says.

Both and neither. This race talk is, of course, a joke, and frequently it has driven me insane and probably will permanently in the future; and yet, seriously and soberly, we black folk are the salvation of mankind.

He regards me with puzzled astonishment and says confidentially:

From *Smart Set*, 70 (April 1923):55–60.

"Do you know that sometimes I am half afraid that you really believe this? At other times I see clearly the inferiority complex."

The former after lunch, I reply, and the latter before.

"Very well," he says, "let's lunch."

Where? I ask quizzically, we being at the time in the roaring Forties.

"Why-oh, well! — their refusal to serve you lunch at least does not prove your superiority."

Nor yet theirs, I answer; but never mind, come with me to Second Avenue. We start again with the salad.

"Now, superiority consists of what?" he argues.

Life is, I remark, (1) Beauty and health of body, (2) Mental clearness and creative genius, (3) Spiritual goodness and receptivity, (4) Social adaptability and constructiveness.

"Not bad," he answers. "Not bad at all. Now I contend that the white race conspicuously excels in one, two and four and is well abreast even in three."

And I maintain that the black race excels in one, three and four and is well abreast in two.

"Sheer nonsense and pure balderdash! Compare the Venus of Milo and the Apollo Belvedere with a Harlem or Beale Street couple."

With a Fifth Avenue Easter parade or a Newport Dance. In short, compare humanity at its best or worst with the Ideal, and humanity suffers. But black folk in most attributes of physical beauty, in line and height and curve, have the same norms as whites and differ only in small details of color, hair and curve of countenance. Now can there be any question but that as colors bronze, mahogany, coffee and gold are far lovelier than pink, gray and marble? Hair is a matter of taste. Some will have it drab and stringy and others in a gray, woven, unmoving mass. Most of us like it somewhere between, in tiny tendrils, smoking curls and sweeping curves. I have loved all these varieties in my day. I prefer the crinkly kind, almost wavy, in black brown and glistening. In faces I hate straight features; needles and razors may be sharp — but beautiful, never.

"All that is personal opinion. I prefer the colors of heaven and day: sunlight hair and blue eyes, and straight noses and thin lips, and that incomparable air of haughty aloofness and aristocracy."

And I, on the contrary, am the child of twilight and night, and choose intricately curly hair, black eyes, full and luscious features, and that air of humility and wonder which streams from moonlight. Add to this, voices that caress instead of rasp, glances that appeal rather then repel, and a sinuous litheness of movement to replace Anglo-Saxon stalking — there you have my ideal. Of course you can bury any human body in dirt and misery and make it horrible. I have seen the East End of London.

"Beauty seems to be simply opinion, if you put it that way."

To be sure. But whose opinion?

"Bother beauty. Here we shall never agree. But, after all, I doubt if it makes much difference. The real point is Brains: clear thinking, pure reason, mathematical precision and creative genius. Now, with *blague*, stand and acknowledge that here the white race is supreme."

Quite the contrary. I know no attribute in which the white race has more conspicuously failed. This is white and European civilization; and as a system of culture it is idiotic, addle-brained, unreasoning, topsy-turvy, without precision, and its genius chiefly runs to marvelous contrivances for enslaving the many and enriching the few. I see absolutely no proof that the average ability of the white man's brain to think clearly is any greater than that of the yellow man or of the black man. If we take even that doubtful but widely heralded test, the frequency of individual creative genius (when a real racial test should be the frequency of ordinary common sense) — if we take the Genius as the saviour of mankind, it is only possible for the white race to prove its own incontestable superiority by appointing both judge and jury and summoning only its own witnesses.

I freely admit that, according to white writers, white teachers, white historians and white molders of public opinion, nothing ever happened in the world of any importance that could not or should not be labeled "white." How silly. I place black iron welding and village democracy and yellow printing and state building side by side with white representative government and the steam engine, and unhesitatingly give the palm to the first. I hand the first vast conception of the solar system to the Africanized Egyptians, the creation of Art to the Chinese, and then let Europe rave over the Factory system.

"But is not well-being more widely diffused among white folk than among yellow and black, and general intelligence more common?"

Momentarily true; and why? Ask the geography of Europe, the African Slave Trade and the Imperial Industrialization of the nineteenth-century white man. Turn the thing around and let mountain and sea protect and isolate a continuous tradition of culture among yellow and black for one thousand years, while simultaneously they bleed the world of its brawn and wealth, and you will have exactly what we have today, under another name and color.

"Precisely. Then, at least, the white race is more advanced and no more blameworthy than others because, as I insist, its native intelligence is greater. It is germ plasm — seed — that I am talking about. Do you believe in heredity?"

Not blindly; but I should be mildly surprised to see a dog born of a cat.

"Exactly; or a genius born of a fool."

No, no; on the contrary, I rather expect fools of geniuses and geniuses of fools. And while I stoutly maintain that cattiness and dogginess are as far apart as the East from the West, on the other hand I just as strongly believe that the human ass and superman have much in common and can often, if not always, spawn each other.

"Is it possible that you have never heard of the Jukes, or of the man who married first an idiot and then a prune?"

It is not possible; they have been served up to me ad infinitum. But they are nothing. I know greater wonders: Lincoln from Nancy Hanks, Dumas from a black beast of burden, Kant from a saddler, and Jesus Christ from a manger.

"All of which, instead of disproving, is exact and definite proof of the persistence of good blood."

Precisely, and of the catholicity of its tastes; the method of proof is this: When anything good occurs, it is proof of good blood; when anything bad occurs, it is proof of bad blood. Very well. Now good and bad, native endowment and native deficiency, do not follow racial lines. There is good stock in all races and the outcropping of bad individuals, too; and there has been absolutely no proof that the white race has any larger share of the gifted strains of human heritage than the black race or the yellow race. To be sure, good seed proves itself in the flower and fruit, but the failure of seed to sprout is no proof that it is not good. It may be proof simply of the absence of manure — or its excessive presence.

Granted, that when time began, there was hidden in a Seed that tiny speck that spelled the world's salvation, do you think today it would manifest itself crudely and baldly in a dash of skin color and a crinkle of hair? Is the subtle mystery of life and consciousness and of ability portrayed in any such slapdash and obvious marks of difference?

"Go out upon the street; choose ten white men and ten colored men. Which can best carry on and preserve American civilization?"

The whites.

"Well, then!"

You evidently consider that a compliment. Let it pass. Go out upon the street and choose ten men and ten women. Which could best run a Ford car? The men, of course; but — hold. Fly out into the sky and look down upon ten children of Podunk and ten children of Chicago. Which would know most about elevated railroads, baseball, zoology and movies?

"The point is visible, but beyond that, outside of mere experience and education, and harking back to native gift and intelligence, on your honor, which has most, white folk or black folk?"

473

There you have me deep in the shadows, beyond the benign guidance of words. Just what is gift and intelligence, especially of the native sort? And when we compare the gift of one human soul with that of another, are we not seeking to measure incommensurable things; trying to lump things like sunlight and music and love? And if a certain shadowy Over-soul can really compare the incomparable with some transcendental yardstick, may we not here emerge into a super-equality of man? At least this I can quite believe.

"But it is a pious belief, not more."

Not more; but a pious belief outweighs an impious unbelief.

I I

Admitting that the problem of native human endowment is obscure, there is no corresponding obscurity in spiritual values. Goodness and unselfishness; simplicity and honor; tolerance, susceptibility to beauty in form, color and music; courage to look truth in the face; courage to live and suffer in patience and humility, and forgiveness and in hope; eagerness to turn, not simply the other cheek, but the face and the bowed back; capacity to love. In all these mighty things, the greatest things in the world, where do black folk and white folk stand?

Why, man of mine, you would not have the courage to live one hour as a black man in America, or as a Negro in the whole wide world. Ah, yes, I know what you whisper to such accusation. You say dryly that if we had good sense, we would not live either; and that the fact that we do submit to life as it is and yet laugh and dance and dream is but another proof that we are idiots.

This is the truly marvelous way in which you prove your superiority by admitting that our love of life can only be intelligently explained on the hypothesis of inferiority. What finer tribute is possible to our courage?

What great works of Art have we made? Very few. The Pyramids, Luqsor, the Bronzes of Benin, the Spears of the Bongo, "When Malinda Sings" and the Sorrow Song she is always singing. Oh, yes, and the love of her dancing.

But art is not simply works of art; it is the spirit that knows Beauty, that has music in its soul and the color of sunsets in its headkerchiefs; that can dance on a flaming world and make the world dance, too. Such is the soul of the Negro. . . .

This is the best expression of the civilization in which the white race finds itself today. This is what the white world means by culture.

"Does it not excel the black and yellow race here?"

It does. But the excellence here raises no envy; only regrets. If this vast

Frankenstein monster really served its makers; if it were their minister and not their master, god and king; if their machines gave us rest and leisure, instead of the drab uniformity of uninteresting drudgery; if their factories gave us gracious community of thought and feeling; beauty enshrined, free and joyous; if their work veiled them with tender sympathy at human distress and wide tolerance and understanding — then, all hail, White Imperial Industry. But it does not. It is a Beast! Its creators even do not understand it, cannot curb or guide it. They, themselves, are but hideous, groping higher Hands, doing their bit to oil the raging, devastating machinery which kills men to make cloth, prostitutes women to rear buildings and eats little children.

Is this superiority? It is madness. We are the supermen who sit idly by and laugh and look at civilization. We, who frankly want the bodies of our mates and conjure no blush to our bronze cheeks when we own it. We, who exalt the Lynched above the Lyncher and the Worker above the Owner and the Crucified above Imperial Rome.

"But why have you black and yellow men done nothing better or even as good in the history of the world?"

We have, often.

"I never heard of it."

Lions have no historians.

"It is idiotic even to discuss it. Look around and see the pageantry of the world. It belongs to white men; it is the expression of white power; it is the product of white brains. Who can have the effrontery to stand for a moment and compare with this white triumph, yellow and brown anarchy and black savagery?" . . .

You are wrong, quite wrong. Away back on the level stretches of the mountain tops in the forests, amid drifts and driftwood, this sled was slowly and painfully pushed on its little hesitating start. It took power, but the power of sweating, courageous men, not of demi-gods. As the sled slowly started and gained momentum, it was the Law of Being that gave it speed, and the grace of God that steered its lone, scared passengers. Those passengers, white, black, red and yellow, deserve credit for their balance and pluck. But many times it was sheer good luck that the made road did not land the white man in the gutter, as it had others so many times before, and as it may him yet. He has gone farther than others because of others whose very falling made hard ways iced and smooth for him to traverse. His triumph is a triumph not of himself alone, but of humankind, from the pusher in the primeval forests to the last flier through the winds of the twentieth century.

I I I

And so to leave our parable and come to reality. Great as has been the human advance in the last one thousand years, it is, so far as native human ability, so far as intellectual gift and moral courage are concerned, nothing as compared with any one of ten and more millenniums before, far back in the forests of tropical Africa and in hot India, where brown and black humankind first fought climate and disease and bugs and beasts; where man dared simply to live and propagate himself. There was the hardest and greatest struggle in all the human world. If in sheer exhaustion or in desperate self-defense during this last moment of civilization he has rested, half inert and blinded with the sweat of his efforts, it is only the silly onlooker who sees but the passing moment of time, who can think of him as subhuman and inferior.

All this is Truth, but unknown, unapprehended Truth. Indeed, the greatest and most immediate danger of white culture, perhaps least sensed, is its fear of the Truth. Its childish belief in the efficacy of lies as a method of human uplift. The lie is defensible; it has been used widely and often profitably among humankind. But it may be doubted if ever before in the world so many intelligent people believed in it so deeply. We deliberately and continuously deceive not simply others, but ourselves as to the truth about them, us and the world. We have raised Propaganda to capital "P" and elaborated an art, almost a science of how one may make the world believe what is not true, provided the untruth is a widely wished-for thing like the probable extermination of Negroes, the failure of the Chinese Republic, the incapacity of India for self-rule, the failure of Russian Revolution. When in other days the world lied, it was to a world that expected lies and consciously defended them; when the world lies today it is to a world that pretends to be true.

"In other words, according to you, white folk are about the meanest and lowest on earth."

They are human, even as you and I.

"Why don't you leave them then? Get out, go to Africa or to the North Pole; shake the dust of their hospitality from off your feet?"

There are abundant reasons. First, they have annexed the earth and hold it by transient but real power. Thus by running away, I shall not only not escape them, but succeed in hiding myself in out of the way places where they can work their deviltry on me without photograph, telegraph or telephone. But even more important than this: I am as bad as they are. In fact, I am related to them and they have much that belongs to me—this land, for instance, for which my fathers starved and fought; I share their sins; in fine, I am related to them.

"By blood?"

476

By blood.

"Then you are railing at yourself. You are not black; you are no Negro."

And you? Yellow blood and black has deluged Europe in days past even more than America yesterday. You are not white, as the measurements of your head will show.

"What then becomes of all your argument, if there are no races and we are all so horribly mixed as you maliciously charge?"

Oh, my friend, can you not see that I am laughing at you? Do you suppose this world of men is simply a great layer cake with superimposed slices of inferior and superior races, interlaid with mud?

No, no. Human beings are infinite in variety, and when they are agglutinated in groups, great and small, the groups differ as though they, too, had integrating souls. But they have not. The soul is still individual if it is free; the group is a social, sometimes an historical fact. And all that I really have been trying to say is that a certain group that I know and to which I belong, as contrasted with the group you know and to which you belong, and in which you fanatically and glorifyingly believe, bears in its bosom just now the spiritual hope of this land because of the persons who compose it and not by divine command.

"But what is this group; and how do you differentiate it; and how can you call it 'black' when you admit it is not black?"

I recognize it quite easily and with full legal sanction: the black man is a person who must ride "Jim Crow" in Georgia.

Lynchings

There have been this year thirteen or more persons lynched. I say thirteen "or more." It may have been fifteen or eighteen, but I am taking the reports of Tuskegee, which are usually just below the truth. This means that once a month in the United States mobs have seized prisoners, who in every case but one were black, and have murdered them without any attempt to find out whether they were guilty or not.

When this was said in other years, it was always assumed, despite our vehement protest, that these victims were guilty and that they had raped white women. But we have this year the astonishing findings of the "Southern Commission on the Study of Lynching" issued under the title "Lynchings and What They Mean." This committee of thirteen had a white chairman and seven other Southern white men as members, and five Negroes.

The report confirms everything that has been said against lynching by supporters of law and decency during the last twenty-five years. Namely:

Only one in every six of the persons lynched had been even accused of rape; and naturally, not all of those accused were guilty.

That white men have disguised themselves to impersonate Negroes and fasten crime upon them.

That few lynchers have been punished or even indicted.

That of the Negroes lynched, for instance, in 1930, two were innocent, not even being accused of crime; and in eleven other cases, there was grave doubt of their guilt. In the remaining five cases, while there were crimes committed, there is considerable doubt as to whether the guilty men were caught.

That in numbers of cases the members of the mob were unmasked and perfectly well-known.

That women and children were often in the mobs.

That the causes of lynching as well as of Negro crime lie in the terrible

From *The Crisis*, February 1932.

forcing of ignorance on the colored people of the South and in caste restrictions.

The report bravely concludes:

"Lynching can and will be eliminated in proportion as all elements of the population are provided opportunities for development and are accorded fundamental human rights. Whether in the field of religion, education, economics, jurisprudence, or politics, anything which looks toward this end is a factor in reducing mob violence. For, fundamentally, lynching is an expression of a basic lack of respect both for human beings and for organized society."

An Estimate of FDR

I presume that what we should be thankful for is that Franklin D. Roosevelt did not die while Garner was vice president. That would have been too awful to contemplate. What fills us with regret is that Henry Wallace was not continued as vice president. What faces us is the fact of President Truman.

Franklin Roosevelt did three things: one, the New Deal; two, his emphasis on race relations, and three, the war.

Of these three, the New Deal was of the greatest importance. For the first time a political party in the United States took upon itself as a distinct duty to plan the increase of wage income at the expense of profits. Of course this attack upon profit has been going on in English-speaking countries ever since English enfranchisement in the early nineteenth century. But never before in America has the head of the state and a leader of a great party stated it as a clear aim; that wages must be increased and security of work and income guaranteed the laborer by open and determined effort to cut down the amount of wealth and income which has been going to capitalists and employers.

It is this phase of Roosevelt's career which made him one of the best hated men in America. There were certain kinds of business men and commercial organizations which never forgave this aspect of the New Deal. Indeed so strong and bitter was the opposition that in his third and fourth terms President Roosevelt retreated from his more advanced stand for economic reform but he nevertheless accomplished the curbing of credit organizations, the federal recognition of union labor and a complete reorganization of the Supreme Court which led it to give wide recognition to his fundamental philosophy.

From the *Chicago Defender*, May 5, 1945.

480

With regard to the race problem, Mr. Roosevelt not only followed the attitude of his predecessors toward the recognition of Jews and their problems but did it at a time when anti-Semitism was spreading in the world. Going beyond this he gave the American Negro a kind of recognition in political life which the Negro had never before received. Instead of appointing machine politicians to certain designated positions in his gift, he appointed a series of unusually well-trained advisers. To be sure men like Weaver and Hastie had little power beyond advice but they were men whose advice was of so high a calibre, it had to be listened to.

Beyond this Roosevelt took three steps: he extended international and customary courtesy toward the heads of three Negro states: Ethiopia, Liberia and Haiti. This had never happened before so openly and definitely. In addition to this he spoke out on the conditions in the South and frankly called the South our Number One economic problem.

Finally, he went almost beyond his authority to establish the FEPC as a record-breaking precedent, emphasizing the fact that the basis of the race problem in the South is poverty based on unemployment and low wage.

The third work of President Roosevelt was to put the United States in the second World War in alliance with Russia. This was a tremendous step. Without it Hitler would have conquered Europe and Japan would have conquered China. Europe under Hitler would have been a center of race-hate and new slavery and the splendid economic planning of Germany would have been used to depress the workers of the world rather than solve our economic problems of the distribution of wealth.

Japan would have spread in Asia — an Asiatic version of capitalist domination. Hitler and Japan could not be overcome without the aid of Russia and in order to aid Russia, Roosevelt had virtually to recognize communism as at least a respectable and efficient form of government. This in itself was epoch-making.

The heir to this policy is President Truman. He started political life as a machine politician. He did not have the opportunity of liberal education and he was born in a former slave state. All this is against him but he deserves charity and sympathy for his tremendous task. He may do far better than his antecedents indicate.

From McKinley to Wallace:
My Fifty Years as an Independent

Johnny Morgan used to keep a newsstand in the front part of the Post Office in my hometown. Through the displays of literature there I got my first idea of national politics. I was fascinated by Keppler's cartoons of BLAINE — THE TATTOOED MAN, in the campaign of 1880, when I was twelve years of age. Blaine was a Republican and our Lawyer Joyner, who was a Democrat, was looked upon with a certain suspicion. So that, perhaps, I got something of an independent twist in politics by having it impressed upon me at an early age that a leading Republican was a grafter, while all the respectable people that I knew were Republicans.

There was little of what could be called politics in the local situation. The selectmen and the few other officers elected at the town meeting received no salary, and probably very few perquisites; it was chiefly a matter of honor. Perhaps, of course, there was something beneath all of this which I did not know. However, on the whole, our town did not consider that politics was an altogether decent occupation. The less government the better was our motto, and no respectable man ever offered himself for public office. He always had it "thrust" upon him. We did not take any interest at all, so far as I can remember, in state politics; but the national election did call for some attention and action.

Garfield's assassination took place while I was in high school; Arthur became President. I cannot remember that I had any particular attitude toward either of them, or any political judgment. But when Cleveland was elected in 1885, I had graduated from high school and was at Fisk University in Tennessee. There I began to see national politics from the viewpoint of the South.

From *Masses & Mainstream*, 1 (August 1948): 3–14.

I remember the alarm that was felt when we realized that for the first time since the Civil War a Democrat was in office. Around me was a fierce and brutal political life. I remember going downtown and staring fascinated at the marks of bullets in the door of a public building where a politician had been shot to death the day before. Politics was associated with disorder. My schoolmates, most of them older than I, frequently carried pistols. On the whole, however, Cleveland pleased me because of certain political appointments of colored men, like Matthews and Trotter, and because nothing happened to indicate any attempt at re-enslavement of Negroes.

It was here that my first political activity took place, when I made several speeches in favor of prohibition. This was a subject upon which I felt expert: in my Massachusetts hometown, drunkenness was the great curse and temptation. I spoke two or three times, therefore, violently in favor of laws to curb it. I was about nineteen at the time.

I was at Harvard when Harrison was inaugurated in 1889. My main thought was on my studies and I can remember very little that I thought or said concerning the new President. So, too, when Cleveland came to power again in 1893, I was in Germany, and felt no great interest. I missed knowledge of Mark Hanna until much later.

By the time of the next election, the McKinley campaign of '96, I found myself in the midst of political controversy. First of all, I was just finishing two years' teaching at Wilberforce in McKinley's own state of Ohio. Then, before McKinley was inaugurated, I had gone to Philadelphia to make my first sociological study; and from there to Georgia to begin my career as a teacher. There I was disfranchised.

I saw the rise of the Free Silver movement, and the beginning of Populism. I was wrong in most of my judgments. My Harvard training made me stand staunchly for the Gold Standard, and I was suspicious of the Populist "Radicals." At the same time, I had seen face-to-face something of the social-democratic movement in Germany. I had gone to their meetings; and by the time McKinley got to work on his high tariff and showed his evident kinship to big business, I began to awaken. Certain of my earlier teachings now came into conflict. I had been trained to believe in Free Trade, which the new McKinley high tariff contradicted. I began to realize something of the meaning of the new Populist movement in its economic aspects.

When Theodore Roosevelt began the first of his two terms in 1901, I was teaching in the South and trying to study and measure its currents. I began to see the situation more clearly. I was attracted to Roosevelt by his attitude toward my folk in the appointing of [William D.] Crum to the port collectorship in South Carolina and his defense of the little black postmistress in

Indianola, Mississippi. Also, I knew he was right in his fight against the trusts. His luncheon with Booker T. Washington raised such a row in the South that it made me a strong Roosevelt partisan. Then came reaction. I believed in the "muckrakers" whom Roosevelt eventually attacked; they were revealing the graft and dishonesty in American political life. Roosevelt was hedging.

I was particularly incensed when he punished, with needless severity, the colored soldiers who were accused of having revolted under the gravest provocation at Brownsville, Texas, in 1906. On the whole, by the time he went out of office, I held him under deep suspicion. Then, in 1910, I came to New York to help organize the National Association for the Advancement of Colored People, and there my first real step toward independence in politics took place.

I was bitterly opposed to Taft, who followed Roosevelt in office. Taft, without doubt, catered to the South and did little or nothing for the American Negro. I wrote in June, 1908:

> When all is said and done, the flat fact remains that William Taft represents that class of Americans who believe that Negroes are less then men; few of them ought to vote; their education should be restricted; their opportunities should be limited; their fate must be left to the white South; their ("value") is their money value to their neighbors; and on occasion they may be treated like dogs (*vide* Brownsville).

I felt that the announced policies of the Democratic Party — its anti-monopoly stand, its denunciation of imperialism, especially as this affected the brown and black people of the West Indies and the Philippines, its pledge to support organized labor — merited the Negro's support. I pointed out:

> Throughout the South great corporations are more and more grasping and grinding, and crushing Negro labor in mines, mills, lumber camps and brickyards, and then posing for praise in giving them work at rates twenty-five per cent below decent living. If this nation does not assume control of corporation, corporations will assume control of this nation. Have you no interest in this, Mr. Black Worker?

Taft triumphed, though it was unquestionably true that more Negroes voted against him than ever before voted against a Republican candidate.

In the critical election of 1912, I at first saw salvation in the new "Bull Moose" movement under Theodore Roosevelt. I even went so far as to offer a plank on the Negro problem to the Bull Moose convention. Joel Spingarn took it to the convention, but Theodore Roosevelt told him he must beware of "that man Du Bois."

This proffered plank demanded the cutting of Southern congressional representation in proportion to the disfranchisement of the Southern masses, an end to lynching, the abolition of segregation, the elimination of peonage, the equalization of education, the democratization of the armed forces and the prohibition of restrictive covenants. The plank was never so much as discussed. Most Negro delegates were refused seats at the convention and Roosevelt tried to woo the Bourbon South through his teammate, Parker of Louisiana.

I decided then that our best policy in politics was to support Wilson and the Democratic party. Wilson was a scholar whose works I had used in my classes, and although a Southerner, he certainly appeared to be a liberal one. I, therefore, joined forces with Bishop Walters of the Zion Methodist Church, who was already openly a Democrat, and tried to see how many Negro voters could be induced to vote the Democratic ticket. It was a pretty difficult job in 1912 for a Negro to be a Democrat. He was considered as either deliberately disloyal to his people, or a plain grafter. It was difficult to get a Negro audience to listen patiently to any advocacy of the party which once stood for slavery, and against the party of Abraham Lincoln.

In the resulting election the Negro vote did something for the election of Woodrow Wilson; how much it was impossible to say. Certainly more Negroes voted for Wilson than had ever before voted for a Democratic Presidential candidate since the Civil War.

We extracted from Wilson certain clear promises for justice toward the American Negro, and, at a time when lynching was rampant, we hoped to get a clear statement against it. The result was bitterly disappointing. There has been no time in the history of the United States when so much legislation calculated to infringe the political and civil rights of Negroes was proposed in Congress and state legislatures. They tried to repeal the Fifteenth Amendment; sought a Federal ban on intermarriage; and attacked Negro office-holding. Many of the Southerners looked upon Wilson's election as a field day for a permanent caste status for Negroes. This was a severe blow to my attempt at political leadership; but at the same time there was very little that my opponents could say in favor of the Republican party.

In 1911, I joined the Socialist Party. I became a member of that celebrated Chapter No. 1, in which several of my colleagues were already enrolled — Mary White Ovington, William English Walling and Charles Edward Russell. The N.A.A.C.P. at the time was definitely tending towards the left, although naturally Villard was on the right, and Spingarn rather in the middle.

I had hardly joined the party, however, when the question of the next election came up; and, as I have shown, first I tried to back Roosevelt, and then did what I could to support Wilson. I quickly became aware that I was going contrary to the party line; that a member of the Socialist Party must vote for the Socialist candidate under all circumstances. For me to do this seemed a betrayal of the best interests of the Negro people. They could not afford to have a man in the White House whose election was not due, at least in part, to their vote. The situation was critical. Therefore, I resigned from the Socialists and never since have joined a political party. For registration purposes I usually have enrolled as a Socialist, and lately as American Labor.

This incident illustrates perhaps one fair criticism that could be made of my independence in politics. My tendency was to stand outside of party and think, explain and choose. At the same time, I am quite aware that practical democratic government calls for party organization and action, and party organization implies the subordination of individual will to the party platform. Unless this is done, democratic government tends toward anarchy.

It is this necessity, however, that makes the role of the politician and statesman approach hypocrisy and condonation of wrong so often. It was this, of course, that explained the fact that Franklin D. Roosevelt depended upon bosses like Hague and Kelly. It must always be a difficult point of decision as to how far a citizen can be a loyal party man and an independent voter. With my particular type of thinking and impulse to action, it was impossible for me to be a party man.

In October, 1916, I wrote:

The Negro voter enters the present campaign with no enthusiasm. Four years ago the intelligent Negro voter tried a great and important experiment. He knew that the rank and file of the Bourbon democracy was without sense or reason, based on provincial ignorance and essentially uncivilized, but he saw called to its leadership a man of high type and one who promised specifically to American Negroes justice — "Not mere grudging justice, but justice executed with liberality and cordial good feeling." They have lived to learn that this statement was a lie, a peculiarly miserable campaign deception. They are forced, therefore, to vote for the Republican candidate, Mr. Hughes, and they find there little that is attractive.

We tried to get some reassuring statements out of Hughes, but were unable to do so. He was practically silent on the Negro. Nevertheless, we felt there was almost nothing that we could do except to vote Republican during that campaign and that was the advice I gave. Wilson was re-elected, narrowly, and the war came and our participation in it.

We were then brought into politics by the demand for decent treatment in the draft and in the training centers, particularly in the South; and especially by a demand for Negro officers. The Wilson administration became conscious of the political and social power of Negroes and was scared for a time of possible German influence. It yielded in the matter of Negro officers, after we had campaigned widely. Eventually, 700 officers were commissioned. Wilson also promised Villard a Race Commission of Inquiry, but did not keep his word. Then came the scandal of the treatment of Negro soldiers in Europe. The result was, naturally, to turn most Negroes definitely toward support of Harding in 1920.

I did, then, point out:

The Republican party has for twenty-five years joined the white South in disfranchising us; it has permitted us to be Jim Crowed, deprived of schools and segregated. It has partially disfranchised us in its party councils and proposes practically to eliminate us as soon as this campaign is over. It has encouraged and recognized the "Lily-White" factions, and nearly driven us from public office. In addition to this, the Republicans represent reaction and privilege, the abolition of freedom of speech, the punishment of thinkers, the suppression of the labor movement, the encouragement and protection of trusts, and a new protective tariff to tax the poor for the benefit of the rich.

The Democratic Party stands for exactly the same things as the Republicans. Between their professed and their actual policies there is no difference worth noting. To be sure, the Northern wing of the party has tendencies toward some recognition of the laborers' demands and the needs of a stricken war-cursed world, but this is more than neutralized by the Solid South.

Harding's death brought Coolidge to the White House. Coolidge was as colorless toward the race problem as toward other things. But at the suggestion of Bill Lewis, a leading colored Democrat of Boston, he went out of his way to appoint me special Minister Plenipotentiary to Liberia to attend the inauguration of President King. I was at the time already on a visit there, so my appointment was purely a gesture of courtesy.

I remember on my return making a detailed report to Mr. Coolidge and recommending things that really would have been of advantage to Africa. He listened very patiently; I was not at all sure that he understood anything I was saying. He certainly paid no heed to it.

In 1924, my support went to La Follette's Progressive Party for it seemed clear that he and his party were infinitely superior to the Coolidge-Davis alternative.

Of the two million Negro votes that year about a million went to Coolidge, and probably as many as 500,000 to La Follette, the latter a splendid tribute to the developing independence of the Negro voter.

The election of 1928 probably represented the lowest point to which the influence of the Negro in politics ever fell in the United States since enfranchisement. Indeed, in all respects it was probably the most disgraceful of all our political campaigns, bringing in not simply anti-Negro hate, but religious intolerance, the question of sumptuary liquor laws, and a general bitterness and antagonism.

The campaign went so badly that I succeeded in October, 1928, in getting colored leaders representing all phases of thought to join me in a statement, one of the most important, perhaps, in the history of the Negro since the Civil War. It said in part:

All of us are at this moment united in the solemn conviction that in the Presidential campaign of 1928, more than in previous campaigns since the Civil War, the American Negro is being treated in a manner which is unfair and discouraging. We accuse the political leaders of this campaign of permitting without protest, public and repeated assertions on the platform, in the press, and by word of mouth, that color and race constitute in themselves an imputation of guilt and crime. . . .

We are asking in this appeal for a public repudiation of this campaign of racial hatred. Silence and whispering in this case are worse than in matters of personal character and religion. Will white America make no protest? Will the candidates continue to remain silent? Will the church say nothing? Is there any truth, any issue in this campaign, either religious tolerance, liquor, water, power, tariff or farm relief, that touches in weight the transcendent and fundamental question of the open, loyal and unchallenged recognition of the essential humanity of twelve million Americans who happen to be dark-skinned?

This was signed by R. R. Moton, of Tuskegee; John Hope, of Morehouse; Mordecai W. Johnson, of Howard; C. C. Spaulding, of the North Carolina Mutual Insurance Company; James Weldon Johnson, Secretary of the N.A.A.C.P.; Eugene K. Jones, of the National Urban League; Mary McLeod Bethune; Monroe N. Work; Reverdy C. Ransom, bishop in the A.M.E. Church; Channing H. Tobias, of the Y.M.C.A.; Carl Murphy, editor of the *Afro-American*; L. K. Williams, president of the National Baptist Convention, and others. It represented practical unanimity among the Negro leaders.

I wrote in November, 1928:

Many Americans place their hopes of political reform in the United States on the rise of a Third Party which will register the fact that the present Republican and Democratic parties no longer differ in any essential respect; that both represent the rule of organized wealth, and neither of them has been willing to take radical ground with regard to the tariff, the farmer, labor, or the Negro.

The efforts, however, to organize a Third Party movement have not been successful. The Populists failed. The Socialists failed. The Progressives failed. The Farmer-Labor movement failed. Many reasons have been advanced for these failures, but by common consent the real effective reason has seldom been discussed and that reason is in the Solid South: the fact is that no party in American politics can disappear if it is sure of 136 Southern electoral votes.

Hoover, who was inaugurated in 1929, furnished every reason for the final driving of the Negro out of the Republican party. The Negro was not mentioned in his message to Congress. My indictment of Herbert Hoover was written in 1932. I accused him of consorting with the "Lily-Whites" of the South and helping to disfranchise Negroes in the councils of the Republican Party. He nominated known enemies of the Negro for public office, as in the case of [John J.] Parker of North Carolina for the Supreme Court. He was unfriendly to Haiti and Liberia, and permitted outrageous discrimination in government, especially in the case of Red Cross relief following the Mississippi flood in 1927. In a Tennessee speech in 1928, he promised to appoint to office no person to whom white Southerners objected. Not only was Hoover antagonistic to the Negroes in particular, but in the great national problems of industrial depression, the international debt and the tariff; "in all these President Hoover had been either wrong or helplessly inadequate and each of these failures affected us."

That meant that with the advent of Franklin Roosevelt, President from 1933 to 1945, the Negroes went largely into the ranks of the Democratic Party for various reasons: as a rebound from the policies of Taft and Hoover; in gratitude to Roosevelt because of his recognition of Negroes as an integral part of the nation needing relief and work, and capable of bearing their burden in the Great Depression.

The support of Roosevelt by Negroes was not unanimous nor continuous. He made concessions to the South in the matter of wages; and the National Recovery Administration (N.R.A.) aroused much complaint of discrimination. He was often ill-advised by Southerners. But nevertheless, under no recent President have Negroes felt that they received as much justice as under Franklin Roosevelt. I supported him in all four of his terms.

Truman's accession in 1945 brought in a border state politician of apparent good will but narrow training and small vision. His final advocacy of civil rights, his appointment of a Negro Territorial Governor, and other actions during the Second World War brought him a considerable measure of Negro support, so that the Democratic party still probably has a larger Negro following than the Republican. But unfortunately, with the true Truman method he has already begun to talk soft on civil rights. He had not a word to say about them on his recent barnstorming trip to the West and Southwest. This, plus his action in the case of Palestine, and his attitude toward Russia, have made it probable that in the next election the majority of Negroes are going to vote for either a Republican or for Wallace.

My own influence, wherever it can be exercised, and the area is small, has been distinctly in favor of Wallace. Not simply because of his attitude toward Negroes, which is unusually liberal, but even more because of his advocacy of peace, and because of his friendship for and understanding of Russia. I cannot escape the feeling that the attempt of Russia to change the economic foundation of modern life is an even greater phenomenon than the French Revolution.

As I look back upon these fifty years of political activity I can see first, of course, that they occupied a comparatively small part of my thought and work. They were incidental to my main object in studying the Negro problem and interpreting the Negro people to the world. Yet they were important to me in changing my early attitude, which sought completely to divorce politics from the mass of social activity, and brought me to the much truer idea that a basis of political life is and must be economic.

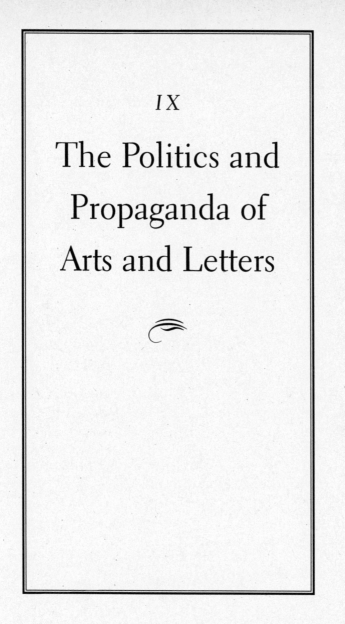

IX

The Politics and
Propaganda of
Arts and Letters

Midstream in the New Negro arts movement, popularly known as the Harlem Renaissance, Du Bois had snarled in "Criteria of Negro Art" (1926) that he did not "care a damn for any art that is not used for propaganda." For Du Bois, artistic, dramatic, and literary energies held their greatest appeal when they validated the civil rights aspirations of the race. In "The Younger Literary Movement" (1924) and "A Negro Art Renaissance" (1925), he extolled the fiction of Jessie Fauset and Jean Toomer and the poetry of Georgia Douglas Johnson, Langston Hughes, Gwendolyn Bennett, Claude McKay, and Countée Cullen for their creative integrity but also for their social utility and race advancement potential. He noted that *Atlantic Monthly, American Mercury, Century, Vanity Fair,* and other leading magazines had reproduced the verse of Cullen and several others; that the singer Roland Hayes was given the NAACP's Spingarn medal. The Legion of Honor was awarded to artist Henry O. Tanner by the French government, and "fifty-six colored artists have received distinction" in the Chicago art exhibit. Nella Larsen's novel *Passing* (1929) was worthy of praise because it presented a cruel aspect of the American dilemma with good taste and in a milieu of manners and affluence. Carl Van Vechten's *Nigger Heaven* (1926) was a "blow in the face" because it caricatured the Talented Tenth from the heights of haughty white scrutiny and then riotously slummed among the "debauched tenth" of the race. George Schuyler's *Black No More* (1931) was even more irreverent than Van Vechten's novel, but it received Du Bois's imprimatur because it was, after all, a good-natured in-group satire whose moral underscored the preposterousness of skin color as the criterion of personal and social worth.

Jesus Christ in Texas

It was in Waco, Texas.

The convict guard laughed. "I don't know," he said, "I hadn't thought of that." He hesitated and looked at the stranger curiously. In the solemn twilight he got an impression of unusual height and soft, dark eyes. "Curious sort of acquaintance for the colonel," he thought; then he continued aloud: "But that nigger there is bad, a born thief, and ought to be sent up for life; got ten years last time —— "

Here the voice of the promoter, talking within, broke in; he was bending over his figures, sitting by the colonel. He was slight, with a sharp nose.

"The convicts," he said, "would cost us $96 a year and board. Well, we can squeeze this so that it won't be over $125 apiece. Now if these fellows are driven, they can build this line within twelve months. It will be running by next April. Freights will fall fifty per cent. Why, man, you'll be a millionaire in less than ten years."

The colonel started. He was a thick, short man, with a clean-shaven face and a certain air of breeding about the lines of his countenance; the word millionaire sounded well to his ears. He thought — he thought a great deal; he almost heard the puff of the fearfully costly automobile that was coming up the road, and he said:

"I suppose we might as well hire them."

"Of course," answered the promoter.

The voice of the tall stranger in the corner broke in here:

"It will be a good thing for them?" he said, half in question.

The colonel moved. "The guard makes strange friends," he thought to himself. "What's this man doing here, anyway?" He looked at him, or rather looked at his eyes, and then somehow he felt a warming toward him. He said:

"Well, at least, it can't harm them; they're beyond that."

From *Darkwater: Voices from Within the Veil* (1920).

495

"It will do them good, then," said the stranger again.

The promoter shrugged his shoulders. "It will do us good," he said.

But the colonel shook his head impatiently. He felt a desire to justify himself before those eyes, and he answered: "Yes, it will do them good; or at any rate it won't make them any worse than they are." Then he started to say something else, but here sure enough the sound of the automobile breathing at the gate stopped him and they all arose.

"It is settled, then," said the promoter.

"Yes," said the colonel, turning toward the stranger again. "Are you going into town?" he asked with the Southern courtesy of white men to white men in a country town. The stranger said he was. "Then come along in my machine. I want to talk with you about this."

They went out to the car. The stranger as he went turned again to look back at the convict. He was a tall, powerfully built black fellow. His face was sullen, with a low forehead, thick, hanging lips, and bitter eyes. There was revolt written about his mouth despite the hang-dog expression. He stood bending over his pile of stones, pounding listlessly. Beside him stood a boy of twelve — yellow, with a hunted, crafty look. The convict raised his eyes and they met the eyes of the stranger. The hammer fell from his hands.

The stranger turned slowly toward the automobile and the colonel introduced him. He had not exactly caught his name, but he mumbled something as he presented him to his wife and little girl, who were waiting.

As they whirled away the colonel started to talk, but the stranger had taken the little girl into his lap and together they conversed in low tones all the way home.

In some way, they did not exactly know how, they got the impression that the man was a teacher and, of course, he must be a foreigner. The long, cloak-like coat told this. They rode in the twilight through the lighted town and at last drew up before the colonel's mansion, with its ghost-like pillars.

The lady in the back seat was thinking of the guests she had invited to dinner and was wondering if she ought not to ask this man to stay. He seemed cultured and she supposed he was some acquaintance of the colonel's. It would be rather interesting to have him there, with the judge's wife and daughter and the rector. She spoke almost before she thought:

"You will enter and rest awhile?"

The colonel and the little girl insisted. For a moment the stranger seemed about to refuse. He said he had some business for his father, about town. Then for the child's sake he consented.

Up the steps they went and into the dark parlor where they sat and talked a long time. It was a curious conversation. Afterwards they did not remember exactly what was said and yet they all remembered a certain strange satisfaction in that long, low talk.

Finally the nurse came for the reluctant child and the hostess bethought herself:

"We will have a cup of tea; you will be dry and tired."

She rang and switched on a blaze of light. With one accord they all looked at the stranger, for they had hardly seen him well in the glooming twilight. The woman started in amazement and the colonel half rose in anger. Why, the man was a mulatto, surely; even if he did not own the Negro blood, their practised eyes knew it. He was tall and straight and the coat looked like a Jewish gabardine. His hair hung in close curls far down the sides of his face and his face was olive, even yellow.

A peremptory order rose to the colonel's lips and froze there as he caught the stranger's eyes. Those eyes—where had he seen those eyes before? He remembered them long years ago. The soft, tear-filled eyes of a brown girl. He remembered many things, and his face grew drawn and white. Those eyes kept burning into him, even when they were turned half away toward the staircase, where the white figure of the child hovered with her nurse and waved good-night. The lady sank into her chair and thought: "What will the judge's wife say? How did the colonel come to invite this man here? How shall we be rid of him?" She looked at the colonel in reproachful consternation.

Just then the door opened and the old butler came in. He was an ancient black man, with tufted white hair, and he held before him a large, silver tray filled with a china tea service. The stranger rose slowly and stretched forth his hands as if to bless the viands. The old man paused in bewilderment, tottered, and then with sudden gladness in his eyes dropped to his knees, and the tray crashed to the floor.

"My Lord and my God!" he whispered; but the woman screamed: "Mother's china!"

The doorbell rang.

"Heavens! here is the dinner party!" exclaimed the lady. She turned toward the door, but there in the hall, clad in her night clothes, was the little girl. She had stolen down the stairs to see the stranger again, and the nurse above was calling in vain. The woman felt hysterical and scolded at the nurse, but the stranger had stretched out his arms and with a glad cry the child nestled in them. They caught some words about the "Kingdom of Heaven" as he slowly mounted the stairs with his little, white burden.

The mother was glad of anything to get rid of the interloper, even for a moment. The bell rang again and she hastened toward the door, which the loitering black maid was just opening. She did not notice the shadow of the stranger as he came slowly down the stairs and paused by the newel post, dark and silent.

The judge's wife came in. She was an old woman, frilled and powdered into a semblance of youth, and gorgeously gowned. She came forward, smiling with extended hands, but when she was opposite the stranger, somewhere a chill seemed to strike her and she shuddered and cried:

"What a draft!" as she drew a silken shawl about her and shook hands cordially; she forgot to ask who the stranger was. The judge strode in unseeing, thinking of a puzzling case of theft.

"Eh? What? Oh — er — yes, — good evening," he said, "good evening." Behind them came a young woman in the glory of youth, and daintily silked, beautiful in face and form, with diamonds around her fair neck. She came in lightly, but stopped with a little gasp; then she laughed gaily and said:

"Why, I beg your pardon. Was it not curious? I thought I saw there behind your man" — she hesitated, but he must be a servant, she argued — "the shadow of great, white wings. It was but the light on the drapery. What a turn it gave me." And she smiled again. With her came a tall, handsome, young naval officer. Hearing his lady refer to the servant, he hardly looked at him, but held his gilded cap carelessly toward him, and the stranger placed it carefully on the rack.

Last came the rector, a man of forty, and well-clothed. He started to pass the stranger, stopped, and looked at him inquiringly.

"I beg your pardon," he said. "I beg your pardon — I think I have met you?"

The stranger made no answer, and the hostess nervously hurried the guests on. But the rector lingered and looked perplexed.

"Surely, I know you. I have met you somewhere," he said, putting his hand vaguely to his head. "You — you remember me, do you not?"

The stranger quietly swept his cloak aside, and to the hostess' unspeakable relief passed out of the door.

"I never knew you," he said in low tones as he went.

The lady murmured some vain excuse about intruders, but the rector stood with annoyance written on his face.

"I beg a thousand pardons," he said to the hostess absently. "It is a great pleasure to be here — somehow I thought I knew that man. I am sure I knew him once."

The stranger had passed down the steps, and as he passed, the nurse, lingering at the top of the staircase, flew down after him, caught his cloak, trembled, hesitated, and then kneeled in the dust.

He touched her lightly with his hand and said: "Go, and sin no more!"

With a glad cry the maid left the house, with its open door, and turned north, running. The stranger turned eastward into the night. As they parted a long, low howl rose tremulously and reverberated through the night. The colonel's wife within shuddered.

"The bloodhounds!" she said.

The rector answered carelessly:

"Another one of those convicts escaped, I suppose. Really, they need severer measures." Then he stopped. He was trying to remember that stranger's name.

The judge's wife looked about for the draft and arranged her shawl. The girl glanced at the white drapery in the hall, but the young officer was bending over her and the fires of life burned in her veins.

Howl after howl rose in the night, swelled, and died away. The stranger strode rapidly along the highway and out into the deep forest. There he paused and stood waiting, tall and still.

A mile up the road behind a man was running, tall and powerful and black, with crime-stained face and convicts' stripes upon him, and shackles on his legs. He ran and jumped, in little, short steps, and his chains rang. He fell and rose again, while the howl of the hounds rang louder behind him.

Into the forest he leapt and crept and jumped and ran, streaming with sweat; seeing the tall form rise before him, he stopped suddenly, dropped his hands in sullen impotence, and sank panting to the earth. A greyhound shot out of the woods behind him, howled, whined, and fawned before the stranger's feet. Hound after hound bayed, leapt, and lay there; then silently, one by one, and with bowed heads, they crept backward toward the town.

The stranger made a cup of his hands and gave the man water to drink, bathed his hot head, and gently took the chains and irons from his feet. By and by the convict stood up. Day was dawning above the treetops. He looked into the stranger's face, and for a moment a gladness swept over the stains of his face.

"Why, you are a nigger, too," he said.

Then the convict seemed anxious to justify himself.

"I never had no chance," he said furtively.

"Thou shalt not steal," said the stranger.

The man bridled.

"But how about them? Can they steal? Didn't they steal a whole year's work, and then when I stole to keep from starving—" He glanced at the stranger.

"No, I didn't steal just to keep from starving. I stole to be stealing. I can't seem to keep from stealing. Seems like when I see things, I just must—but, yes, I'll try!"

The convict looked down at his striped clothes, but the stranger had taken off his long coat; he had put it around him and the stripes disappeared.

In the opening morning the black man started toward the low, log farm-house in the distance, while the stranger stood watching him. There was a new glory in the day. The black man's face cleared up, and the farmer was glad to get him. All day the black man worked as he had never worked before. The farmer gave him some cold food.

"You can sleep in the barn," he said, and turned away.

"How much do I git a day?" asked the black man.

The farmer scowled.

"Now see here," said he. "If you'll sign a contract for the season, I'll give you ten dollars a month."

"I won't sign no contract," said the black man doggedly.

"Yes, you will," said the farmer, threateningly, "or I'll call the convict guard." And he grinned.

The convict shrank and slouched to the barn. As night fell he looked out and saw the farmer leave the place. Slowly he crept out and sneaked toward the house. He looked through the kitchen door. No one was there, but the supper was spread as if the mistress had laid it and gone out. He ate ravenously. Then he looked into the front room and listened. He could hear low voices on the porch. On the table lay a gold watch. He gazed at it, and in a moment he was beside it — his hands were on it! Quickly he slipped out of the house and slouched toward the field. He saw his employer coming along the highway. He fled back in terror and around to the front of the house, when suddenly he stopped. He felt the great, dark eyes of the stranger and saw the same dark, cloak-like coat where the stranger sat on the doorstep talking with the mistress of the house. Slowly, guiltily, he turned back, entered the kitchen, and laid the watch stealthily where he had found it; then he rushed wildly back toward the stranger, with arms outstretched.

The woman had laid supper for her husband, and going down from the house had walked out toward a neighbor's. She was gone but a little while, and when she came back she started to see a dark figure on the doorsteps under the tall, red oak. She thought it was the new Negro until he said in a soft voice:

"Will you give me bread?"

Reassured at the voice of a white man, she answered quickly in her soft, Southern tones:

"Why, certainly."

She was a little woman, and once had been pretty; but now her face was drawn with work and care. She was nervous and always thinking, wishing, wanting for something. She went in and got him some cornbread and a glass of cool, rich buttermilk; then she came out and sat down beside him. She began, quite unconsciously, to tell him about herself — the things she had done and had not done and the things she had wished for. She told him of her husband and this new farm they were trying to buy. She said it was hard to get niggers to work. She said they ought all to be in the chain-gang and made to work. Even then some ran away. Only yesterday one had escaped, and another the day before.

At last she gossiped of her neighbors, how good they were and how bad. "And do you like them all?" asked the stranger.

She hesitated.

"Most of them," she said; and then, looking up into his face and putting her hand into his, as though he were her father, she said:

"There are none I hate; no, none at all."

He looked away, holding her hand in his, and said dreamily:

"You love your neighbor as yourself?"

She hesitated.

"I try—" she began, and then looked the way he was looking; down under the hill where lay a little, half-ruined cabin.

"They are niggers," she said briefly.

He looked at her. Suddenly a confusion came over her and she insisted, she knew not why.

"But they are niggers!"

With a sudden impulse she arose and hurriedly lighted the lamp that stood just within the door, and held it above her head. She saw his dark face and curly hair. She shrieked in angry terror and rushed down the path, and just as she rushed down, the black convict came running up with hands out-stretched. They met in mid-path, and before he could stop he had run against her and she fell heavily to earth and lay white and still. Her husband came rushing around the house with a cry and an oath.

"I knew it," he said. "It's that runaway nigger." He held the black man struggling to the earth and raised his voice to a yell. Down the highway came the convict guard, with hound and mob and gun. They paused across the fields. The farmer motioned to them.

"He—attacked—my wife," he gasped.

The mob snarled and worked silently. Right to the limb of the red oak they hoisted the struggling, writhing black man, while others lifted the dazed woman. Right and left, as she tottered to the house, she searched for the stranger with a yearning, but the stranger was gone. And she told none of her guests.

"No—no, I want nothing," she insisted, until they left her, as they thought, asleep. For a time she lay still, listening to the departure of the mob. Then she rose. She shuddered as she heard the creaking of the limb where the body hung. But resolutely she crawled to the window and peered out into the moonlight; she saw the dead man writhe. He stretched his arms out like a cross, looking upward. She gasped and clung to the window sill. Behind the swaying body, and down where the little, half-ruined cabin lay, a single flame flashed up amid the far-off shout and cry of the mob. A fierce joy sobbed up through the terror in her soul and then sank abashed as she watched the flame rise. Suddenly whirling into one great crimson column it shot to the top of the sky and threw great arms athwart the gloom until above the world and behind the roped and swaying form below hung quivering and burning a great crimson cross.

She hid her dizzy, aching head in an agony of tears, and dared not look, for she knew. Her dry lips moved:

"Despised and rejected of men."

She knew, and the very horror of it lifted her dull and shrinking eyelids. There, heaven-tall, earth-wide, hung the stranger on the crimson cross, riven and bloodstained, with thorn-crowned head and piercèd hands. She stretched her arms and shrieked.

He did not hear. He did not see. His calm dark eyes, all sorrowful, were fastened on the writhing, twisting body of the thief, and a voice came out of the winds of the night, saying:

"This day thou shalt be with me in Paradise!"

The Younger Literary Movement

There have been times when we writers of the older set have been afraid that
the procession of those who seek to express the life of the American Negro was
thinning and that none were coming forward to fill the footsteps of the fathers.
Dunbar is dead; Chesnutt is silent; and Kelly Miller is mooning after false
gods while Brawley and Woodson are writing history rather than literature.
But even as we ask "Where are the young Negro artists to mold and weld this
mighty material about us?" — even as we ask, they come.

There are two books before me, which, if I mistake not, will mark an
epoch: a novel by Jessie Fauset and a book of stories and poems by Jean
Toomer. There are besides these, five poets writing: Langston Hughes,
Countée Cullen, Georgia Johnson, Gwendolyn Bennett and Claude
McKay. Finally, Negro men are appearing as essayists and reviewers, like
Walter White and Eric Walrond. (And even as I write comes the news that a
novel by Mr. White has just found a publisher.) Here then is promise
sufficient to attract us.

We recognize the exquisite abandon of a new day in Langston Hughes'
"Song for a Banjo." He sings:

> *Shake your brown feet, Liza,*
> *Shake 'em Liza, chile,*
> *Shake your brown feet, Liza,*
>   *(The music's soft and wile).*
> *Shake your brown feet, Liza,*
>   *(The Banjo's sobbin' low),*
> *The sun's goin' down this very night —*
> *Might never rise no mo'.*

Countée Cullen in his "Ballad of the Brown Girl" achieves eight lyric lines
that are as true as life itself. There is in Claude McKay's "If We Must Die"

From *The Crisis*, February 1924.

a strain martial and mutinous. There are other echoes—two from dead poets Jamison and Cotter who achieved in their young years long life if not immortality. But this essay is of two books.

The world of black folk will some day arise and point to Jean Toomer as a writer who first dared to emancipate the colored world from the conventions of sex. It is quite impossible for most Americans to realize how straitlaced and conventional thought is within the Negro World, despite the very unconventional acts of the group. Yet this contradiction is true. And Jean Toomer is the first of our writers to hurl his pen across the very face of our sex conventionality. In "Cane," one has only to take his women characters *seriatim* to realize this: Here is Karintha, an innocent prostitute; Becky, a fallen white woman; Carma, a tender Amazon of unbridled desire; Fern, an unconscious wanton; Esther, a woman who looks age and bastardy in the face and flees in despair; Louise, with a white and a black lover; Avey, unfeeling and unmoral; and Doris, the cheap chorus girl. These are his women, painted with a frankness that is going to make his black readers shrink and criticize; and yet they are done with a certain splendid, careless truth.

Toomer does not impress me as one who knows his Georgia but he does know human beings; and, from the background which he has seen slightly and heard of all his life through the lips of others, he paints things that are true, not with Dutch exactness, but rather with an impressionist's sweep of color. He is an artist with words but a conscious artist who offends often by his apparently undue striving for effect. On the other hand his powerful book is filled with felicitous phrases—Karintha, "carrying beauty perfect as the dusk when the sun goes down"—

> "Hair—
> Silver-grey
> Like streams of stars"

Or again, "face flowed into her eyes—flowed in soft creamy foam and plaintive ripples." His emotion is for the most part entirely objective. One does not feel that he feels much and yet the fervor of his descriptions shows that he has felt or knows what feeling is. His art carries much that is difficult or even impossible to understand. The artist, of course, has a right deliberately to make his art a puzzle to the interpreter (the whole world is a puzzle) but on the other hand I am myself unduly irritated by this sort of thing. I cannot, for the life of me, for instance see why Toomer could not have made the tragedy of Carma something that I could understand instead of vaguely guess at; "Box Seat" muddles me to the last degree and I am not sure that I know what

"Kabnis" is about. All of these essays and stories, even when I do not understand them, have their strange flashes of power, their numerous messages and numberless reasons for being. But still for me they are partially spoiled. Toomer strikes me as a man who has written a powerful book but who is still watching for the fullness of his strength and for that calm certainty of his art which will undoubtedly come with years.

A Negro Art Renaissance

Walter Damrosch was recently the chief figure in handing Roland Hayes the Spingarn medal. This medal is bestowed each year on the American Negro who does the most notable service for his race. In noting Mr. Hayes's achievement, Mr. Damrosch alluded to the brief history behind the American Negro and dated his cultural development in literature and art from the Emancipation Proclamation in 1863.

Mr. Damrosch spoke in good faith and with the best will and but repeated a common current error. No human group can begin anything in the middle of the nineteenth century. Whatever the historical breaks and partial lack of continuity, the history of all human groups and races is a continuous development despite slavery and the slave trade, which made surely a vast hiatus in Negro development, nevertheless there is today a renaissance of Negro genius, which is bringing a new and peculiar turn to what we call the "Negro problem."

Look round you a moment to realize this: Here is a great new lyric tenor who last year was soloist to every great American orchestra and sang to crowded houses from Boston to San Francisco and in London, Paris, Vienna and Berlin; he was black. This month, *Vanity Fair*, a periodical catering to popular taste and not to propaganda and reform, gives a page to a black boy's poems, and Harper Brothers are publishing a volume of his verse. Novels by colored folk are appearing, and two last year, Jessie Fauset's *There Is Confusion* and Walter White's *Fire and the Flint*, attracted wide attention. A colored short-story writer has had six stories accepted at once by *Atlantic Monthly*. Negro essayists have recently appeared in the *American Mercury*, the *Forum*, the *Century* and other leading periodicals. The dean of present American artists, H. O. Tanner, is of Negro descent and has just received the French Legion of Honor; but he is not alone; in the recent Chicago art exhibit one colored artist received three prizes and in the last, fifty-six colored artists have

From the *Los Angeles Times*, June 14, 1925, pt. 3, 26–27.

received distinction. On the stage we have seen not only the new developments of the older Negro comedy in Sissle and Blake, Miller and Lyle and Florence Mills, but a new [kind of] tragedy in Charles Gilpin and Paul Robeson.

In all competitions thrown open fairly to all American children, Negro children are winning prizes and preferment as in college scholarships and fellowships, musical prizes offered by the Juilliard Foundation and the like.

The significant thing, however, is not individual Negro distinction. There have always been cases of exceptional Negroes in America like Phillis Wheatley, Frederick Douglass, Paul Laurence Dunbar and Booker T. Washington. But the present movement is not simply individually American—it is distinctly and definitely based on new knowledge of and inspiration from the past history of the Negro race. One has but to read a few stanzas of Countée Cullen's great poem, the "Shroud of Color" to realize this, or to see the young black artist's new enthusiasm for Negro and colored pastimes.

In the last decade or so the world and the American Negro have rediscovered Africa and her marvelous history. All the chronicle of Ethiopia and the kingdom of the Sudan, all that marvelous primitive art of the West African coast, all the legend and history handed down by generations of black folk has been long unknown in America and forgotten by Europe because of the propaganda of slavery and the slave trade.

France rediscovered African art and based a new school of art upon it. Germany revealed something of the wealth of African literature; and England and America have been uncovering the buried history of Egypt and Ethiopia and Nigeria. At first there was passionate assertion, particularly in the last two lands which had bitter racial "problems," that none of these Africans were "Negroes"; until, Habzel pointed out some time ago, we were making so arbitrary and fanciful definition of "Negro" that we were about to leave no Negroes at all among the black and brown folk of Africa, whose race diversity is no greater than that of Europe. The "black" race is as vague for scientific definitions as the "white."

The Great War knocked much of this nonsense from our heads and today we are beginning to realize that the history of man in Africa has paralleled the history of man in Europe and Asia. To American Negroes, long deprived of the importance of a past, save that which meant humiliation and despair, this renaissance of knowledge has brought the new and growing enthusiasm for self-expression. Nowhere is this better seen than in the new drama. The Negro was long shut off from the theatre by the Puritan misfit of prejudice which shut him out of the auditor's seats in the best theaters. But an essentially dramatic people with a history perhaps the most dramatic the world has known, could not be kept from self-expression in the drama. Beginning with catering to the white folks' love of Negro comedy, they sought to introduce bits of romance and tragedy here and there as in Cole and Johnson's *Red Moon* and the dramatic recitals of scores from Edward Nahar to Richard Harrison — they turned finally and gradually to their own people. They brought amateur plays to churches, did Shakespeare in schools and attempted pageantry.

Los Angeles is going to have an opportunity of seeing at the Hollywood Bowl June 15 and 18, the most ambitious pictorial pageant which American Negroes have attempted. This pageant, known as the "Star of Ethiopia," has been given three times — in New York in 1913 to celebrate a half-century of emancipation; in Washington, D.C., in 1915 to commemorate the Fifteenth Amendment; in Philadelphia in 1916 to celebrate the one hundredth anniversary of the founding of the African Episcopal Church.

This year at the request of the citizens of Los Angeles the pageant is brought here and rehearsals have been in progress four weeks. It is a folk play with no professional actors, with most of the costumes home-made; and is based on the history, real and legendaryn of the Negro race. . . .

Criteria of Negro Art

I do not doubt but there are some in this audience who are a little disturbed at the subject of this meeting, and particularly at the subject I have chosen. Such people are thinking something like this: "How is it that an organization like this, a group of radicals trying to bring new things into the world, a fighting organization which has come up out of the blood and dust of battle, struggling for the right of black men to be ordinary human beings — how is it that an organization of this kind can turn aside to talk about art? After all, what have we who are slaves and black to do with art?"

Or perhaps there are others who feel a certain relief and are saying, "After all it is rather satisfactory after all this talk about rights and fighting to sit and dream of something which leaves a nice taste in the mouth."

Let me tell you that neither of these groups is right. The thing we are talking about tonight is part of the great fight we are carrying on and it represents a forward and an upward look — a pushing onward. You and I have been breasting hills; we have been climbing upward; there has been progress and we can see it day by day looking back along blood-filled paths. But as you go through the valleys and over the foothills, so long as you are climbing, the direction — north, south, east or west — is of less importance. But when gradually the vista widens and you begin to see the world at your feet and the far horizon, then it is time to know more precisely whether you are going and what you really want.

What do we want? What is the thing we are after? As it was phrased last night it had a certain truth: We want to be Americans, full-fledged Americans, with all the rights of other American citizens. But is that all? Do we want simply to be Americans? Once in a while through all of us there flashes some clairvoyance, some clear idea, of what America really is. We who are dark can see America in a way that white Americans cannot. And seeing our country thus, are we satisfied with its present goals and ideals? . . .

From *The Crisis*, October 1926.

If you tonight suddenly should become full-fledged Americans; if your color faded, or the color line here in Chicago was miraculously forgotten; suppose, too, you became at the same time rich and powerful — what is it that you would want? What would you immediately seek? Would you buy the most powerful of motor cars and outrace Cook County? Would you buy the most elaborate estate on the North Shore? Would you be a Rotarian or a Lion or a What-not of the very last degree? Would you wear the most striking clothes, give the richest dinners, and buy the longest press notices?

Even as you visualize such ideals you know in your hearts that these are not the things you really want. You realize this sooner than the average white American because, pushed aside as we have been in America, there has come to us not only a certain distaste for the tawdry and flamboyant but a vision of what the world could be if it were really a beautiful world; if we had the true spirit; if we had the seeing eye, the cunning hand, the feeling heart; if we had, to be sure, not perfect happiness, but plenty of good hard work, the inevitable suffering that always comes with life; sacrifice and waiting, all that — but nevertheless lived in a world where men know, where men create, where they realize themselves and where they enjoy life. It is that sort of a world we want to create for ourselves and for all America.

After all, who shall describe Beauty? What is it? I remember tonight four beautiful things: the cathedral at Cologne, a forest in stone, set in light and changing shadow, echoing with sunlight and solemn song; a village of the Veys in West Africa, a little thing of mauve and purple, quiet, lying content and shining in the sun; a black and velvet room where on a throne rests, in old and yellowing marble, the broken curves of the Venus de Milo; a single phrase of music in the South — utter melody, haunting and appealing, suddenly arising out of night and eternity, beneath the moon.

Such is beauty. Its variety is infinite, its possibility is endless. In normal life all may have it and have it yet again. The world is full of it; and yet today the mass of human beings are choked away from it, and their lives distorted and made ugly. This is not only wrong, it is silly. Who shall right this well-nigh universal failing? Who shall let this world be beautiful? Who shall restore to men the glory of sunsets and the peace of quiet sleep?

We black folk may help for we have within us as a race new stirrings; stirrings of the beginning of a new appreciation of joy, of a new desire to create, of a new will to be; as though in this morning of group life we had awakened from some sleep that at once dimly mourns the past and dreams a splendid future; and there has come the conviction that the youth that is here today, the Negro youth, is a different kind of youth, because in some new way it bears this mighty prophecy on its breast, with a new realization of itself, with new determination for all mankind.

What has this beauty to do with the world? What has beauty to do with truth and goodness — with the facts of the world and the right actions of men? "Nothing," the artists rush to answer. They may be right. I am but an humble disciple of art and cannot presume to say. I am one who tells the truth and exposes evil and seeks with beauty and for beauty to set the world right. That somehow, somewhere eternal and perfect beauty sits above truth and right I can conceive, but here and now and in the world in which I work they are for me unseparated and inseparable.

This is brought to us peculiarly when as artists we face our own past as a people. There has come to us — and it has come especially through the man we are going to honor tonight [Carter Godwin Woodson, 12th Spingarn Medalist] — a realization of that past, of which for long years we have been ashamed, for which we have apologized. We thought nothing could come out of that past which we wanted to remember; which we wanted to hand down to our children. Suddenly, this same past is taking on form, color, and reality, and in a half shame-faced way we are beginning to be proud of it. We are remembering that the romance of the world did not die and lie forgotten in the Middle Ages; that if you want romance to deal with you must have it here and now and in your own hands. . . .

Have you heard the story of the conquest of German East Africa? Listen to the untold tale: There were 40,000 black men and 4,000 white men who talked German. There were 20,000 black men and 12,000 white men who talked English. There were 10,000 black men and 400 white men who talked French. In Africa then where the Mountains of the Moon raised their white and snowcapped heads into the mouth of the tropic sun, where Nile and Congo rise and the Great Lakes swim, these men fought; they struggled on mountain, hill and valley, in river, lake and swamp, until in masses they sickened, crawled and died; until the 4,000 white Germans had become mostly bleached bones; until nearly all the 12,000 white Englishmen had returned to South Africa, and the 400 Frenchmen to Belgium and heaven; all except a mere handful of the white men died; but thousands of black men from East, West and South Africa, from Nigeria and the Valley of the Nile, and from the West Indies still struggled, fought and died. For four years they fought and won and lost German East Africa; and all you hear about it is that England and Belgium conquered German Africa for the allies!

Such is the true and stirring stuff of which romance is born and from this stuff come the stirrings of men who are beginning to remember that this kind of material is theirs; and this vital life of their own kind is beckoning them on.

The question comes next as to the interpretation of these new stirrings, of this new spirit: Of what is the colored artist capable? We have had on the part of both colored and white people singular unanimity of judgment in the past.

Colored people have said: "This work must be inferior because it comes from colored people." White people have said: "It is inferior because it is done by colored people." But today there is coming to both the realization that the work of the black man is not always inferior. Interesting stories come to us. . . .

With the growing recognition of Negro artists in spite of the severe handicaps, one comforting thing is occurring to both white and black. They are whispering, "Here is a way out. Here is the real solution of the color problem. The recognition accorded Cullen, Hughes, Fauset, White and others shows there is no real color line. Keep quiet! Don't complain! Work! All will be well!"

I will not say that already this chorus amounts to a conspiracy. Perhaps I am naturally too suspicious. But I will say that there are today a surprising number of white people who are getting great satisfaction out of these younger Negro writers because they think it is going to stop agitation of the Negro question. They say, "What is the use of your fighting and complaining; do the great thing and the reward is there." And many colored people are all too eager to follow this advice; especially those who weary of the eternal struggle along the color line, who are afraid to fight and to whom the money of philanthropists and the alluring publicity are subtle and deadly bribes. They say, "What is the use of fighting? Why not show simply what we deserve and let the reward come to us?"

And it is right here that the National Association for the Advancement of Colored People comes upon the field, comes with its great call to a new battle, a new fight and new things to fight before the old things are wholly won; and to say that the beauty of truth and freedom which shall some day be our heritage and the heritage of all civilized men is not in our hands yet and that we ourselves must not fail to realize.

There is in New York tonight a black woman molding clay by herself in a little bare room, because there is not a single school of sculpture in New York where she is welcome. Surely there are doors she might burst through, but when God makes a sculptor He does not always make the pushing sort of person who beats his way through doors thrust in his face. This girl is working her hands off to get out of this country so that she can get some sort of training.

There was Richard Brown. If he had been white he would have been alive today instead of dead of neglect. Many helped him when he asked but he was not the kind of boy that always asks. He was simply one who made colors sing.

There is a colored woman in Chicago who is a great musician. She thought she would like to study at Fontainebleau this summer where Walter Damrosch and a score of leaders of art have an American school of music. But the application blank of this school says: "I am a white American and I apply for admission to the school."

We can go on the stage; we can be just as funny as white Americans wish us to be; we can play all the sordid parts that America likes to assign to Negroes; but for anything else there is still small place for us.

And so I might go on. But let me sum up with this: Suppose the only Negro who survived some centuries hence was the Negro painted by white Americans in the novels and essays they have written. What would people in a hundred years say of black Americans? Now turn it around. Suppose you were to write a story and put in it the kind of people you know and like and imagine. You might get it published and you might not. And the "might not" is still far bigger than the "might." The white publishers catering to white folk would say, "It is not interesting" — to white folk, naturally not. They want Uncle Toms, Topsies, good "darkies" and clowns. I have in my office a story with all the earmarks of truth. A young man says that he started out to write and had his stories accepted. Then he began to write about the things he knew best about, that is, about his own people. He submitted a story to a magazine which said, "We are sorry, but we cannot take it." "I sat down and revised my story, changing the color of the characters and the locale and sent it under an assumed name with a change of address and it was accepted by the same magazine that had refused it, the editor promising to take anything else I might send in providing it was good enough."

We have, to be sure, a few recognized and successful Negro artists; but they are not all those fit to survive or even a good minority. They are but the remnants of that ability and genius among us whom the accidents of education and opportunity have raised on the tidal waves of chance. We black folk are not altogether peculiar in this. After all, in the world at large, it is only the accident, the remnant, that gets the chance to make the most of itself; but if this is true of the white world it is infinitely more true of the colored world. It is not simply the great clear tenor of Roland Hayes that opened the ears of America. We have had many voices of all kinds as fine as his and America was and is as deaf as she was for years to him. Then a foreign land heard Hayes and put its imprint on him and immediately America with all its imitative snobbery woke up. We approved Hayes because London, Paris and Berlin approved him and not simply because he was a great singer.

Thus it is the bounden duty of black America to begin this great work of the creation of beauty, of the preservation of beauty, of the realization of beauty, and we must use in this work all the methods that men have used before. And what have been the tools of the artist in times gone by? First of all, he has used the truth — not for the sake of truth, not as a scientist seeking truth, but as one upon whom truth eternally thrusts itself as the highest handmaid of imagination, as the one great vehicle of universal understanding. Again artists have used goodness — goodness in all its aspects of justice, honor, and right — not for sake of an ethical sanction but as the one true method of gaining sympathy and human interest.

The apostle of beauty thus becomes the apostle of truth and right not by choice but by inner and outer compulsion. Free he is but his freedom is ever bounded by truth and justice; and slavery only dogs him when he is denied the right to tell the truth or recognize an ideal of justice.

Thus all art is propaganda and ever must be, despite the wailing of the purists. I stand in utter shamelessness and say that whatever art I have for writing has been used always for propaganda for gaining the right of black folk to love and enjoy. I do not care a damn for any art that is not used for propaganda. But I do care when propaganda is confined to one side while the other is stripped and silent. . . .

You know the current magazine story: a young white man goes down to Central America and the most beautiful colored woman there falls in love with him. She crawls across the whole isthmus to get to him. The white man says nobly, "No." He goes back to his white sweetheart in New York.

In such cases, it is not the positive propaganda of people who believe white blood divine, infallible, and holy to which I object. It is the denial of a similar right of propaganda to those who believe black blood human, lovable, and inspired with new ideals for the world. White artists themselves suffer from this narrowing of their field. They cry for freedom in dealing with Negroes because they have so little freedom in dealing with whites. DuBose Heywood writes "Porgy" and writes beautifully of the black Charleston underworld. But why does he do this? Because he cannot do a similar thing for the white people of Charleston, or they would drum him out of town. The only chance he had to tell the truth of pitiful human degradation was to tell it of colored people. I should not be surprised if Octavius Roy Cohen had approached the *Saturday Evening Post* and asked permission to write about a different kind of colored folk than the monstrosities he has created; but if he has, the *Post* has replied, "No. You are getting paid to write about the kind of colored people you are writing about."

In other words, the white public today demands from its artists, literary and pictorial, racial pre-judgment which deliberately distorts truth and justice, as far as colored races are concerned, and it will pay for no other.

On the other hand, the young and slowly growing black public still wants its prophets almost equally unfree. We are bound by all sorts of customs that have come down as second-hand soul clothes of white patrons. We are ashamed of sex and we lower our eyes when people will talk of it. Our religion holds us in superstition. Our worst side has been so shamelessly emphasized that we are denying we have or ever had a worst side. In all sorts of ways we are hemmed in and our new young artists have got to fight their way to freedom.

The ultimate judge has got to be you and you have got to build yourselves up into that wide judgment, that catholicity of temper which is going to enable the artist to have his widest chance for freedom. We can afford the truth. White folk today cannot. As it is now we are handing everything over to a white jury. If a colored man wants to publish a book, he has got to get a white publisher and a white newspaper to say it is great; and then you and I say so. We must come to the place where the work of art when it appears is reviewed and acclaimed by our own free and unfettered judgment. And we are going to have a real and valuable and eternal judgment only as we make ourselves free of mind, proud of body and just of soul to all men.

And then do you know what will be said? It is already saying. Just as soon as true art emerges; just as soon as the black artist appears, someone touches the race on the shoulder and says, "He did that because he was an American, not because he was a Negro; he was born here; he was trained here; he is not a Negro — what is a Negro anyhow? He is just human; it is the kind of thing you ought to expect."

I do not doubt that the ultimate art coming from black folk is going to be just as beautiful, and beautiful largely in the same ways, as the art that comes from white folk, or yellow, or red; but the point today is that until the art of the black folk compels recognition they will not be rated as human. And when through art they compel recognition then let the world discover if it will that their art is as new as it is old and as old as new.

I had a classmate once who did three beautiful things and died. One of them was a story of a folk who found fire and then went wandering in the gloom of night seeking again the stars they had once known and lost; suddenly out of blackness they looked up and there loomed the heavens; and what was it that they said? They raised a mighty cry: "It is the stars, it is the ancient stars, it is the young and everlasting stars!"

On Carl Van Vechten's
Nigger Heaven

Carl Van Vechten's "Nigger Heaven" is a blow in the face. It is an affront to the hospitality of black folk and to the intelligence of white. First, as to its title: my objection is based on no provincial dislike of the nickname. "Nigger" is an English word of wide use and definite connotation. As employed by Conrad, Sheldon, Allen and even Firbanks, its use was justifiable. But the phrase, "Nigger Heaven," as applied to Harlem is a misnomer. "Nigger Heaven" does not mean, as Van Vechten once or twice intimates, (pages 15, 199) a haven for Negroes — a city of refuge for dark and tired souls; it means in common parlance, a nasty, sordid corner into which black folk are herded, and yet a place which they in crass ignorance are fools enough to enjoy. Harlem is no such place as that, and no one knows this better than Carl Van Vechten.

But after all, a title is only a title, and a book must be judged eventually by its fidelity to truth and its artistic merit. I find this novel neither truthful nor artistic. It is not a true picture of Harlem life, even allowing for some justifiable impressionistic exaggeration. It is a caricature. It is worse than untruth because it is a mass of half-truths. Probably some time and somewhere in Harlem every incident of the book has happened; and yet the resultant picture built out of these parts is ludicrously out of focus and undeniably misleading.

The author counts among his friends numbers of Negroes of all classes. He is an authority on dives and cabarets. But he masses this knowledge without rule or reason and seeks to express all of Harlem life in its cabarets. To him the black cabaret is Harlem; around it all his characters gravitate. Here is their stage of action. Such a theory of Harlem is nonsense. The overwhelming majority of black folk there never go to cabarets. The average colored man

From *The Crisis*, December 1926.

Harlem is an everyday laborer, attending church, lodge and movie and as conservative and as conventional as ordinary working folk everywhere.

Something they have which is racial, something distinctively Negroid can be found; but it is expressed by subtle, almost delicate nuance, and not by the wildly, barbaric drunken orgy in whose details Van Vechten revels. There is laughter, color and spontaneity at Harlem's core, but in the current cabaret, financed and supported largely by white New York, this core is so overlaid and enwrapped with cheaper stuff that no one but a fool could mistake it for the genuine exhibition of the spirit of the people.

To all this the author has a right to reply that even if the title is an unhappy catch-phrase for penny purposes and his picture of truth untruthful, that his book has a right to be judged primarily as a work of art. Does it please? Does it entertain? Is it a good and human story? In my opinion it is not; and I am one who likes stories and I do not insist that they be written solely for my point of view. "Nigger Heaven" is to me an astonishing and wearisome hodgepodge of laboriously stated facts, quotations and expressions, illuminated here and there with something that comes near to being nothing but cheap melodrama. Real human feelings are laughed at. Love is degraded. The love of Byron and Mary is stark cruelty and that of Lasca and Byron is simply nasty. Compare this slum picture with Porgy. In his degradation, Porgy is human and interesting. But in "Nigger Heaven" there is not a single loveable character. There is scarcely a generous impulse or a beautiful ideal. The characters are singularly wooden and inhuman. Van Vechten is not the great artist who with remorseless scalpel probes the awful depths of life. To him there are no depths. It is the surface mud he slops about in. His women's bodies have no souls; no children palpitate upon his hands; he has never looked upon his dead with bitter tears. Life to him is just one damned orgy after another, with hate, hurt, gin and sadism.

Both Langston Hughes and Carl Van Vechten know Harlem cabarets; but it is Hughes who whispers

> "One said he heard the jazz band sob
> When the little dawn was grey."

Van Vechten never heard a sob in a cabaret. All he hears is noise and brawling. Again and again with singular lack of invention he reverts to the same climax of two creatures tearing and scratching over "mah man"; lost souls who once had women's bodies; and to Van Vechten this spells comedy, not tragedy.

I seem to see that Mr. Van Vechten began a good tale with the promising figure of Anatol, but that he keeps turning aside to write in from his notebook every fact he has heard about Negroes and their problems; singularly irrelevant quotations, Haitian history, Chesnutt's novels, race-poetry, "blues" written by white folk. Into this mass he drops characters which are in most cases thin disguises; and those who know the originals have only to compare their life and this death, to realize the failure in truth and human interest. The final climax is an utterly senseless murder which appears without preparation or reason from the clouds.

I cannot for the life of me see in this work either sincerity or art, deep thought, or truthful industry. It seems to me that Mr. Van Vechten tried to do something bizarre and he certainly succeeded. I read "Nigger Heaven" and read it through because I had to. But I advise others who are impelled by a sense of duty or curiosity to drop the book gently in the grate and to try the *Police Gazette*.

Mencken

Many colored people have undertaken to answer Mr. Mencken's remarks about Negro artists. Most of them apparently make the mistake of questioning his attitude rather than his facts. There can be no question of H.L. Mencken's attitude toward Negroes. It is calmly and judiciously fair. He neither loves nor hates them. He has a predilection for men.

But he, like many other Americans, does not understand just where the shoe pinches. When American artists of Negro descent have work worth while he believes that they are not barred by magazines or publishers. Of course not. But the point is that the themes on which Negro writers naturally write best, with deepest knowledge and clearest understanding, are precisely the themes most editors do not want treated. These are themes which white readers are tired of or do not wish to hear. What is the "freedom" cry to a white American or "discrimination"? He is fed up on this which is the breath of life to black folk. While the feelings of insulted men, their reaction to the color line — well this he will not read about. Consequently the chief reading public in America will not buy precisely the sort of thing that Negroes must write about if they are sincere and honest.

White Americans are willing to read about Negroes, but they prefer to read about Negroes who are fools, clowns, prostitutes, or at any rate, in despair and contemplating suicide. Other sorts of Negroes do not interest them because, as they say, they are "just like white folks." But their interest in white folks, we notice, continues. This is a real and tremendous handicap. It is analogous to the handicap of all writers on unpopular themes; but it bears hardest on young Negroes because its bar is broader and more inclusive. It puts a premium on one kind of sadistic subject.

Despite this, Mr. Mencken does not realize all that has been done. If the really first rate books written by Negroes since the Civil War make "a shelf a foot long," that is a matter of congratulation. Similar notable works by white

From *The Crisis*, October 1927.

Americans would be a good deal less than nine feet long. In music, Nathaniel Dett has given the Negro spiritual another form and Harry Burleigh has done more than reproduce it. W.C. Handy is father of the "Blues." Coleridge-Taylor, if we may be permitted a journey overseas, stands manifestly the great creative artist with his "Bamboula" and "Take Nabandji"; and there is Roland Hayes — is he not an artist? There may, of course, be difference of opinion about Negro poets, but in our opinion Paul Laurence Dunbar, Claude McKay, Countée Cullen and Langston Hughes stand far above "second rate." We are inclined too to think that Chesnutt's novels are far above "the level of white hacks." Jean Toomer's work will not soon be forgotten and Booker T. Washington's "Up From Slavery" is no ordinary biography. Jessie Fauset and Eric Walrond deserve notice. Finally, we have H.O. Tanner.

On the whole then, despite a stimulating critic's opinion, we Negroes are quite well satisfied with our Renaissance. And we have not yet finished.

Passing

by Nella Larsen

Nella Larsen's *Passing* is one of the finest novels of the year. If it did not treat a forbidden subject — the inter-marriage of a stodgy middle-class white man to a very beautiful and selfish octoroon — it would have an excellent chance to be hailed, selected and recommended. As it is, it will probably be given the "silence," with only the commendation of word of mouth. But what of that? It is a good close-knit story, moving along surely but with enough leisure to set out seven delicately limned characters. Above all, the thing is done with studied and singularly successful art. Nella Larsen is learning how to write and acquiring style, and she is doing it very simply and clearly.

Three colored novelists have lately essayed this intriguing and ticklish subject of a person's right to conceal the fact that he had a grandparent of Negro descent. It is all a petty, silly matter of no real importance which another generation will comprehend with great difficulty. But today, and in the minds of most white Americans, it is a matter of tremendous moral import. One may deceive as to killing, stealing and adultery, but you must tell your friend that you're "colored," or suffer a very material hell fire in this world, if not in the next. The reason of all this, is of course that so many white people in America either know or fear that they have Negro blood. My friend, who is in the Record Department of Massachusetts, found a lady's ancestry the other day. Her colored grandfather was a soldier in the Revolutionary War, and through him she might join the D. A. R. But she asked "confidentially," could that matter of "his — er — color be left out?"

Walter White in *Flight* records the facts of an excursion of a New Orleans girl from the colored race to the white race and back again. Jessie Fauset in *Plum Bun* considers the spiritual experiences and rewards of such an excursion, but the story of the excursion fades into unimportance beside that

Book review from *The Crisis*, July 1929.

historical document of the description of a colored Philadelphia family. That characterization ought to live in literature.

Nella Larsen attempts quite a different thing. She explains just what "passing" is: the psychology of the thing; the reaction of it on friend and enemy. It is a difficult task, but she attacks the problem fearlessly and with consummate art. The great problem is under what circumstances would a person take a step like this and how would they feel about it? And how would their fellows feel?

So here is the story: Irene, who is faintly colored, is faint with shopping. She goes to a hotel roof for rest and peace and tea. That's all. Far from being ashamed of herself, she is proud of her dark husband and lovely boys. Moreover, she is deceiving no one. If they wish to recognize her as Spanish, then that is their good fortune or misfortune. She is resting and getting cool and drinking tea. Then suddenly she faces an entirely different kind of problem. She sees Clare and Clare recognizes her and pounces on her. Clare is brilliantly beautiful. She is colored in a different way. She has been rather brutally kicked into the white world, and has married a white man, almost in self-defense. She has a daughter, but she is lonesome and eyes her playmate Irene with fierce joy. Here is the plot. Its development is the reaction of the race-conscious Puritan, Irene; the lonesome hedonist, Clare; and then the formation of the rapidly developing triangle with the cynical keen rebel, Irene's husband.

If the American Negro renaissance gives us many more books like this, with its sincerity, its simplicity and charm, we can soon with equanimity drop the word "Negro." Meantime, your job is clear. Buy the book.

Black No More: Being an Account of the Strange and Wonderful Workings of Science in the Land of the Free, A.D. 1933–1940

by George S. Schuyler

James Weldon Johnson's *Saint Peter Relates an Incident of the Resurrection Day* is a slim black volume brought out in beautiful format. It is a serious satire of the loftier sort, portraying the Unknown Soldier as a Negro. It has a fine subtle beauty.

> *"I gave one last look over the jasper wall,*
> *And afar descried a figure dark and tall —*
> *The unknown soldier, dust-stained and begrimed,*
> *Climbing his way to heaven, and singing as he climbed:*
> *Deep river, my home is over Jordan,*
> *Deep River, I want to cross over into camp-ground."*

Persons who wish a few hilarious hours must hasten to buy and read George Schuyler's *Black No More*. The book is extremely significant in Negro American literature, and it will be — indeed it already has been — abundantly misunderstood.

It is a satire, a rollicking, keen, good-natured criticism of the Negro problem in the United States, following the same method by which Bernard Shaw has been enabled to criticize the social organization of the modern world. A writer of satire is always misunderstood by the simple. So much so, that

Book review from *The Crisis*, March 1931.

periodicals, like *The Crisis*, are almost afraid of using satire, even in the smallest doses. If we should speak of the long ears of a certain Mr. Smith, some literal reader would write in and tell us that by exact measurement Mr. Smith's ears were less than three inches in length.

The object of satire is to point out fault and evil by the very exaggeration of its fun; and the test of its genuineness is its honesty and clearness of object. American Negroes have written satire before, usually in small skits in columnists' paragraphs; but their insincerity lay in the fact that the satire was usually pointed not to the evil but to only one class of persons, and that class were Negroes, against whom these young writers had conceived a bitter enmity born of rather cheap jealousy. But Mr. Schuyler's satire is frank, straightforward and universal. It carries not only scathing criticism of Negro leaders, but of the mass of Negroes, and then it passes over and slaps the white people just as hard and unflinchingly straight in the face. It is, therefore, courageous as well as biting and it is a bit of real literature because here is a man who is not doing public criticism of a certain unpopular class of people with an eye single to being paid for this by richer and more influential people whom he does not dare to criticize.

No one escapes Schuyler's pen, and we are waiting to see his book excluded, not simply by all the white libraries south of the Mason-Dixon Line, but by all the colored collectors north of it.

At any rate, read the book. You are bound to enjoy it and to follow with joyous laughter the adventures of Max Disher and Bunny, Dr. Crookman and—we say it with all reservations—Dr. Agamemnon Shapespeare Beard.

X

Labor in
Black and White

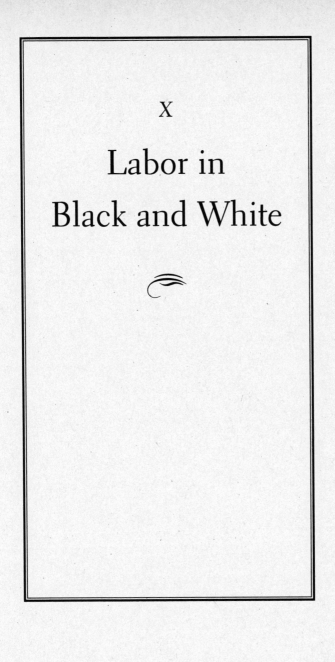

Du Bois was among the first students of social movements to anticipate the enormous significance of the Great Black Migration. Many who awakened more slowly to its implications warned of dire economic and civil rights consequences, and enjoined the migrants to stay in the South. Du Bois applauded the impact of outmigration on the economy of the white South, and he was enthusiastic about the labor rearrangements it would force upon the North ("Brothers, Come North" [1920]). Although Du Bois was an early convert to socialism, "The Negro and Radical Thought" (1921) showed him to be strikingly undoctrinaire at first about any specific program for producing greater economic equity, surprisingly agnostic about the importance of the Russian Revolution, and deeply skeptical of the racial policies of organized labor in America. In "The American Federation of Labor and the Negro" (1929), Du Bois returned to the charge of organized labor hypocrisy, warning the leadership that the black worker would soon "break any strike when he can gain economic advantage," and reminding the A.F. of L. of its perfunctory response to the good faith recommendations made by the NAACP to promote trust among black workers in the unions. The recurring theme in Du Bois's writings about all varieties of socialism and trade unionism was that their egalitarian doctrines proved woefully inadequate in the real world of racism. Thus, in his bedrock essay, "Marxism and the Negro Problem" (1933), he denied that black and white laborers shared a common enemy in white capitalists: "It is white labor that deprives the Negro of his right to vote, denies him education, denies him affiliation with trade unions, expels him from decent houses and neighborhoods." In the lyrical 1947 address "Behold the Land," Du Bois finally envisaged in the postwar South the beginnings of that working-class solidarity across racial lines that had been too long deferred.

Brothers, Come North

The migration of Negroes from South to North continues and ought to continue. The North is no paradise — as East St. Louis, Washington, Chicago, and Omaha prove; but the South is at best a system of caste and insult and at worst a Hell. With ghastly and persistent regularity, the lynching of Negroes in the South continues — every year, every month, every day; wholesale murders and riots have taken place at Norfolk, Longview, Arkansas, Knoxville, and 24 other places in a single year. The outbreaks in the North have been fiercer, but they have quickly been curbed; no attempt has been made to saddle the whole blame on Negroes; and the cities where riots have taken place are today safer and better for Negroes than ever before.

In the South, on the other hand, the outbreaks occurring daily but reveal the seething cauldron beneath — the unbending determination of the whites to subject and rule the blacks, to yield no single inch of their determination to keep Negroes as near slavery as possible.

There are, to be sure, Voices in the South — wise Voices and troubled Consciences; souls that see the utter futility and impossibility of the southern program of race relations in work and travel and human intercourse. But these voices are impotent. Behold, Brough of Arkansas. He was an original leader of the most promising recent group which sought Sense and Justice in the race problem — "The University Commission on Southern Race Questions." He said, as chairman:

> "As an American citizen the Negro is entitled to life, liberty, and the pursuit of happiness, and the equal protection of our laws for the safeguarding of these inalienable rights. . . . None but the most prejudiced Negro-hater, who oftentimes goes to the extreme of denying that any black man can have a white soul, would controvert the proposition that in the administration of quasi-public utilities and courts of justice the Negro is entitled to the fair

From *The Crisis*, January 1920.

and equal protection of the law.... The meanest Negro on a southern plantation is entitled to the same consideration in the administration of justice as the proudest scion of a cultured cavalier."

Yet when he ran for Governor of Arkansas, he vehemently denied and explained away his liberal Negro sentiments—and when the "uprising" occurred in Phillips County, he let the slave barons make their own investigation, murder the innocent, and railroad ignorant, honest laborers to imprisonment and death in droves; contrast this with the actions of Governor Lowden of Illinois and Mayor Smith of Omaha!

On the other hand, we win through the ballot. We can vote in the North. We can hold office in the North. As workers in northern establishments, we are getting good wages, decent treatment, healthful homes and schools for our children. Can we hesitate? COME NORTH! Not in a rush—not as aimless wanderers, but after quiet investigation and careful location. The demand for Negro labor is endless. Immigration is still cut off and a despicable and indefensible drive against all foreigners is shutting the gates of opportunity to the outcasts and victims of Europe. Very good. We will make America pay for her Injustice to us and to the poor foreigner by pouring into the open doors of mine and factory in increasing numbers.

Troubles will ensue with white unions and householders, but remember that the chief source of these troubles is rooted in the South; a million Southerners live in the North. These are the ones who by open and secret propaganda fomented trouble in these northern centers and are still at it. They have tried desperately to make trouble in Indianapolis, Cleveland, Pittsburgh, Philadelphia, Baltimore, and New York City.

This is a danger, but we have learned how to meet it by unwavering self-defense and by the ballot.

Meantime, if the South really wants the Negro and wants him at his best, it can have him permanently, on these terms and no others:

1. The right to vote.
2. The abolition of lynching.
3. Justice in the courts.
4. The abolition of "Jim-Crow" cars.
5. A complete system of education, free and compulsory.

The Negro and Radical Thought

Mr. Claude McKay, one of the editors of *The Liberator* and a Negro poet of distinction, writes us as follows:

"I am surprised and sorry that in your editorial, 'The Drive', published in *The Crisis* for May, you should leap out of your sphere to sneer at the Russian Revolution, the greatest event in the history of humanity; much greater than the French Revolution, which is held up as a wonderful achievement to Negro children and students in white and black schools. For American Negroes the indisputable and outstanding fact of the Russian revolution is that a mere handful of Jews, much less in ratio to the number of Negroes in the American population, have attained, through the Revolution, all the political and social rights that were denied to them under the regime of the Czar.

"Although no thinking Negro can deny the great work that the N.A.A.C.P. is doing, it must yet be admitted that from its platform and personnel the Association cannot function as a revolutionary working class organization. And the overwhelming majority of American Negroes belong by birth, condition and repression to the working class. Your aim is to get for the American Negro the political and social rights that are his by virtue of the Constitution, the rights which are denied him by the Southern oligarchy with the active co-operation of the state governments and the tacit support of northern business interests. And your aim is a noble one, which deserves the support of all progressive Negroes.

"But the Negro in politics and social life is ostracized only technically by the distinction of color; in reality the Negro is discriminated against because he is of the lowest type of worker. . . .

"Obviously, this economic difference between the white and black workers manifests itself in various forms, in color prejudice, race hatred, .

From *The Crisis*, July 1921.

531

political and social boycotting and lynching of Negroes. And all the entrenched institutions of white America — law courts, churches, schools, the fighting forces and the Press — condone these iniquities perpetrated upon black men; iniquities that are dismissed indifferently as the inevitable result of the social system. Still, whenever it suits the business interests controlling these institutions to mitigate the persecutions against Negroes, they do so with impunity. When organized white workers quit their jobs, Negroes, who are discouraged by the whites to organize, are sought to take their places. And these strike-breaking Negroes work under the protection of the military and the police. But as ordinary citizens and workers, Negroes are not protected by the military and the police from the mob. The ruling classes will not grant Negroes those rights which, on a lesser scale and more plausibly, are withheld from the white proletariat. The concession of these rights would immediately cause a Revolution in the economic life of this country."

We are aware that some of our friends have been disappointed with *The Crisis* during and since the war. Some have assumed that we aimed chiefly at mounting the band wagon with our cause during the madness of war; others thought that we were playing safe so as to avoid the Department of Justice; and still a third class found us curiously stupid in our attitude toward the broader matters of human reform. Such critics, and Mr. McKay is among them, must give us credit for standing to our guns in the past at no little cost in many influential quarters, and they must also remember that we have one chief cause — the emancipation of the Negro, and to this all else must be subordinated — not because other questions are not important but because to our mind the most important social question today is recognition of the darker races.

Turning now to that marvelous set of phenomena known as the Russian Revolution, Mr. McKay is wrong in thinking that we have ever intentionally sneered at it. On the contrary, time may prove, as he believes, that the Russian Revolution is the greatest event of the nineteenth and twentieth centuries, and its leaders the most unselfish prophets. At the same time *The Crisis* does not know this to be true. Russia is incredibly vast, and the happenings there in the last five years have been intricate to a degree that must make any student pause. We sit, therefore, with waiting hands and listening ears, seeing some splendid results from Russia, like the cartoons for public education recently exhibited in America, and hearing of other things which frighten us.

We are moved neither by the superficial omniscience of Wells nor the reports in the New York *Times*; but this alone we do know: that the immediate work for the American Negro lies in America and not in Russia, and this, too, in spite of the fact that the Third Internationale has made a pronouncement which cannot but have our entire sympathy:

The Communist Internationale once [and] forever breaks with the traditions of the Second Internationale which in reality only recognized the white race. The Communist Internationale makes it its task to emancipate the workers of the entire world. The ranks of the Communist Internationale fraternally unite men of all colors: white, yellow and black — the toilers of the entire world.

Despite this there come to us black men two insistent questions: What is today the right program of socialism? The editor of *The Crisis* considers himself a Socialist but he does not believe that German State Socialism or the dictatorship of the proletariat are perfect panaceas. He believes with most thinking men that the present method of creating, controlling and distributing wealth is desperately wrong; that there must come and is coming a social control of wealth; but he does not know just what form that control is going to take, and he is not prepared to dogmatize with Marx or Lenin. Further than that, and more fundamental to the duty and outlook of *The Crisis*, is this question: How far can the colored people of the world, and particularly the Negroes of the United States, trust the working classes?

Many honest thinking Negroes assume, and Mr. McKay seems to be one of these, that we have only to embrace the working class program to have the working class embrace ours; that we have only to join Trade Unionism and Socialism or even Communism, as they are today expounded, to have Union Labor and Socialists and Communists believe and act on the equality of mankind and the abolition of the color line. *The Crisis* wishes that this were true, but it is forced to the conclusion that it is not.

The American Federation of Labor, as representing the trade unions in America, has been grossly unfair and discriminatory toward Negroes and still is. American Socialism has discriminated against black folk and before the war was prepared to go further with this discrimination. European Socialism has openly discriminated against Asiatics. Nor is this surprising. Why should we assume on the part of unlettered and suppressed masses of white workers, a clearness of thought, a sense of human brotherhood, that is sadly lacking in the most educated classes?

Our task, therefore, as it seems to *The Crisis*, is clear: We have to convince the working classes of the world that black men, brown men and yellow men are human beings and suffer the same discrimination that white workers suffer. We have in addition to this to espouse the cause of the white workers, only being careful that we do not in this way allow them to jeopardize our cause. We must, for instance, have bread. If our white fellow workers drive us out of decent jobs, we are compelled to accept indecent wages even at the price of "scabbing." It is a hard choice, but whose is the blame? Finally despite public prejudice and clamour, we should examine with open mind in literature, debate and in real life the great programs of social reform that are day by day being put forward.

This was the true thought and meaning back of our May editorial. We have an immediate program for Negro emancipation laid down and thought out by the N.A.A.C.P. It is foolish for us to give up this practical program for mirage in Africa or by seeking to join a revolution which we do not at present understand. On the other hand, as Mr. McKay says, it would be just as foolish for us to sneer or even seem to sneer at the blood-entwined writhing of hundreds of millions of our whiter human brothers.

The American Federation of Labor and the Negro

The speech of J. P. Frey at the National Interracial Conference last December on "Attempts to Organize Negro Workers" has given rise to some controversy. Walter White in the *Nation* characterizes this speech as "the nadir in casuistic defense of exclusion of Negroes from labor unions."

To this characterization Frey objects, but admits, "I failed to accomplish one purpose I had in mind — the presentation of a careful program."

But this was not the real essence of Frey's failure. His whole thesis was: Negroes suffer from injustice in the labor union world, but they do not suffer much more than Jews, Poles and even Americans. Moreover, they are partially to blame because they do not advise their workers to enter the trade unions even where they can.

This latter point Frey sought to emphasize in every way. He cited Booker T. Washington, and his advice to the iron workers of Newport News; he cited the resolution of the Negro Press Association; and he even went so far as to declare:

"I have asked representatives of the Negro race, some of the best known, to make some public statement or write me a letter in which they would say it was their belief that wherever possible members of their race should join the trade union of their craft, so that I could use that statement or letter to help me in the efforts I have made to organize Negroes. So far no such statement or letter has been received."

This whole thesis is untrue and unfair. The record of the American Federation of Labor toward the Negro is indefensible. An early declaration of the A. F. of L. said:

"The working people must unite and organize, irrespective of creed, color,

From *The Crisis*, July 1929.

sex, nationality or politics." With some objection, this declaration was reaffirmed in 1897, but it was not embodied in the Constitution. Nevertheless, bodies confining membership to whites were barred from affiliation with the A. F. of L. Later, in 1902, the legality of excluding Negroes from local unions, and from city central labor bodies was recognized by a resolution which permitted separate charters to colored unions. Later, without official announcement, national unions, like the Railway Trainmen, and the Railway Telegraphers, which specifically exclude Negroes, were allowed to join the A. F. of L.; and finally, the Stationary Engineers, already a member of the A. F. of L. were allowed to change their charter and specifically exclude black men.

In addition to this, it is well-known that even in the case of organizations which do not openly and by name exclude persons of Negro descent, the local unions repeatedly do this as a matter of regular policy without rebuke from the A. F. of L.

The National Association for the Advancement of Colored People has long recognized the danger of this situation and at its 15th Annual Conference held in Philadelphia, in July, 1924, the following Resolution was addressed to the A. F. of L.:

"For many years the American Negro has been demanding admittance to the ranks of union labor.

"For many years your organizations have made public profession of your interest in Negro labor, of your desire to have it unionized, and of your hatred of the black 'scab.'

"Notwithstanding this apparent surface agreement, Negro labor in the main is outside the ranks of organized labor, and the reason is first, that white union labor does not want black labor, and secondly, black labor has ceased to beg admittance to union ranks because of its increasing value and efficiency outside the unions.

"We thus face a crisis in interracial labor conditions: the continued and determined race prejudice of white labor, together with the limitation of immigration, is giving black labor tremendous advantage. The Negro is entering the ranks of semiskilled and skilled labor and he is entering mainly as a 'scab.' He broke the great steel strike. He will soon be in a position to break any strike when he can gain economic advantage for himself.

"On the other hand, intelligent Negroes know full well that a blow at organized labor is a blow at all labor; that black labor today profits by the blood and sweat of labor leaders in the past who have fought oppression and monopoly by organization. If there is built up in America a great black bloc of non-union laborers who have a right to hate unions, all laborers, black and white, eventually must suffer.

"Is it not time, then, that black and white labor get together? Is it not time for white unions to stop bluffing and for black laborers to stop cutting off their noses to spite their faces?

"We, therefore, propose that there be formed by the National Association for the Advancement of Colored People, the American Federation of Labor, the Railway Brotherhoods and any other bodies agreed upon, an Interracial Labor Commission.

"We propose that this Commission undertake:

1. To find out the exact attitude and practice of national labor bodies and local unions toward Negroes and of Negro labor toward unions.
2. To organize systematic propaganda against racial discrimination on the basis of these facts at the labor meetings, in local assemblies and in local unions.

"The National Association for the Advancement of Colored People stands ready to take part in such a movement and hereby invites the cooperation of all organized labor. The Association hereby solemnly warns American laborers that unless some such step as this is taken and taken soon the position gained by organized labor in this country is threatened with irreparable loss."

Besides perfunctory acknowledgment of receipt, no action has ever been taken on this resolution by the American Federation of Labor. This is a sufficient answer to Frey's awkward and insincere defense of the color line in the A. F. of L.

Marxism and the Negro Problem

Karl Marx was a Jew born at Treves, Germany, in March, 1818. He came of an educated family and studied at the Universities of Bonn and Berlin, planning first to become a lawyer, and then to teach philosophy. But his ideas were too radical for the government. He turned to journalism, and finally gave his life to economic reform, dying in London in 1883, after having lived in Germany, Belgium, France, and, for the last thirty-five years of his life, in England. He published in 1867, the first volume of his monumental work, *Capital*.

There are certain books in the world which every searcher for truth must know: the Bible, *Critique of Pure Reason*, *Origin of Species*, and Karl Marx's *Capital*.

Yet until the Russian Revolution, Karl Marx was little known in America. He was treated condescendingly in the universities, and regarded even by the intelligent public as a radical agitator whose curious and inconvenient theories it was easy to refute. Today, at last, we all know better, and we see in Karl Marx a colossal genius of infinite sacrifice and monumental industry, and with a mind of extraordinary logical keenness and grasp. We may disagree with many of the great books of truth that I have named, and with *Capital*, but they can never be ignored.

At a recent dinner to Einstein, another great Jew, the story was told of a professor who was criticized as having "no sense of humor" because he tried to explain the Theory of Relativity in a few simple words. Something of the same criticism must be attached to anyone who attempts similarly to indicate the relation of Marxian philosophy and the American Negro problem. And yet, with all modesty, I am essaying the task knowing that it will be but tentative and subject to much criticism, both on my own part and that of other abler students.

From *The Crisis*, May 1933.

The task which Karl Marx set himself was to study and interpret the organization of industry in the modern world. One of Marx's earlier works, *The Communist Manifesto*, issued in 1848, on the eve of the series of democratic revolutions in Europe, laid down this fundamental proposition.

"That in every historical epoch the prevailing mode of economic production and exchange, and the social organization necessarily following from it, form the basis upon which is built up, and from which alone can be explained, the political and intellectual history of that epoch; that consequently the whole history of mankind . . . has been a history of class struggles, contest between exploiting and exploited, ruling and oppressed classes; that the history of these class struggles forms a series of evolution in which, now-a-days, a stage has been reached where the exploited and oppressed class (the proletariat) cannot attain its emancipation from the sway of the exploiting and ruling class (the bourgeoisie) without, at the same time, and once and for all, emancipating society at large from all exploitation, oppression, class-distinction and class-struggles."

All will notice in this manifesto, phrases which have been used so much lately and so carelessly that they have almost lost their meaning. But behind them still is living and insistent truth. The *class struggle* of exploiter and exploited is a reality. The capitalist still today owns machines, materials, and wages with which to buy labor. The laborer even in America owns little more than his ability to work. A wage contract takes place between these two and the resultant manufactured commodity or service is the property of the capitalist.

Here Marx begins his scientific analysis based on a mastery of practically all economic theory before his time and on an extraordinary, thoroughgoing personal knowledge of industrial conditions over all Europe and many other parts of the world.

His final conclusions were never all properly published. He lived only to finish the first volume of his *Capital*, and the other two volumes were completed from his papers and notes by his friend Engels. The result is an unfinished work, extraordinarily difficult to read and understand and one which the master himself would have been first to criticize as not properly representing his mature and finished thought.

Nevertheless, that first volume, together with the fairly evident meaning of the others, lay down a logical line of thought. The gist of that philosophy is that the value of products regularly exchanged in the open market depends upon the labor necessary to produce them; that capital consists of machines, materials and wages paid for labor; that out of the finished product, when materials have been paid for and the wear and tear and machinery replaced, and wages paid, there remains a surplus value. This surplus value arises from labor and is the difference between what is actually paid laborers for their wages and the market value of the commodities which the laborers produce. It represents, therefore, exploitation of the laborer, and this exploitation, inherent in the capitalistic system of production, is the cause of poverty, of industrial crises, and eventually of social revolution.

This social revolution, whether we regard it as voluntary revolt or the inevitable working of a vast cosmic law of social evolution, will be the last manifestation of the class struggle, and will come by inevitable change induced by the very nature of the conditions under which present production is carried on. It will come by the action of the great majority of men who compose the wage-earning proletariat, and it will result in common ownership of all capital, the disappearance of capitalistic exploitation, and the division of the products and services of industry according to human needs, and not according to the will of the owners of capital.

It goes without saying that every step of this reasoning and every presentation of supporting facts have been bitterly assailed. The labor theory of value has been denied; the theory of surplus value refuted; and inevitability of revolution scoffed at; while industrial crises — at least until this present one — have been defended as unusual exceptions proving the rule of modern industrial efficiency.

But with the Russian experiment and the World Depression most thoughtful men today are beginning to admit:

That the continued recurrence of industrial crises and wars based largely on economic rivalry, with persistent poverty, unemployment, disease and crime, are forcing the world to contemplate the possibilities of fundamental change in our economic methods; and that means thorough-going change, whether it be violent, as in France or Russia, or peaceful, as seems just as possible, and just as true to the Marxian formula, if it is fundamental change; in any case, Revolution seems bound to come.

Perhaps nothing illustrates this better than recent actions in the United States: our re-examination of the whole concept of Property; our banking moratorium; the extraordinary new agriculture bill; the plans to attack unemployment, and similar measures. Labor rather than gambling is the sure foundation of value and whatever we call it — exploitation, theft or business acumen — there is something radically wrong with an industrial system that turns out simultaneously paupers and millionaires and sets a world starving because it has too much food.

What now has all this to do with the Negro problem? First of all, it is manifest that the mass of Negroes in the United States belong distinctly to the working proletariat. Of every thousand working Negroes less than a hundred and fifty belong to any class that could possibly be considered bourgeois. And even this more educated and prosperous class has but small connections with the exploiters of wage and labor. Nevertheless, this black proletariat is not a part of the white proletariat. Black and white work together in many cases, and influence each other's rates of wages. They have similar complaints against capitalists, save that the grievances of the Negro worker are more fundamental and indefensible, ranging as they do, since the day of Karl Marx, from chattel slavery, to the worst paid, sweated, mobbed and cheated labor in any civilized land.

And while Negro labor in America suffers because of the fundamental inequities of the whole capitalistic system, the lowest and most fatal degree of its suffering comes not from the capitalists but from fellow white laborers. It is white labor that deprives the Negro of his right to vote, denies him education, denies him affiliation with trade unions, expels him from decent houses and neighborhoods, and heaps upon him the public insults of open color discrimination.

It is no sufficient answer to say that capital encourages this oppression and uses it for its own ends. This may have excused the ignorant and superstitious Russian peasants in the past and some of the poor whites of the South today. But the bulk of American white labor is neither ignorant nor fanatical. It knows exactly what it is doing and it means to do it. William Green and Mathew Woll of the A.F. of L. have no excuse of illiteracy or religion to veil their deliberate intention to keep Negroes and Mexicans and other elements of common labor, in a lower proletariat as subservient to their interests as theirs are to the interests of capital.

This large development of a petty bourgeoisie within the American laboring class is a post-Marxian phenomenon and the result of the tremendous and world-wide development of capitalism in the 20th Century. The market of capitalistic production has gained an effective world-wide organization. Industrial technique and mass production have brought possibilities in the production of goods and services which out-run even this wide market. A new class of technical engineers and managers has arisen forming a working class aristocracy between the older proletariat and the absentee owners of capital. The real owners of capital are small as well as large investors — workers who have deposits in savings banks and small holdings in stocks and bonds; families buying homes and purchasing commodities on installment; as well as the large and rich investors.

Of course, the individual laborer gets but an infinitesimal part of his income from such investments. On the other hand, such investments, in the aggregate, largely increase available capital for the exploiters, and they give investing laborers the capitalistic ideology. Between workers and owners of capital stand today the bankers and financiers who distribute capital and direct the engineers.

Thus the engineers and the saving better-paid workers, form a new petty bourgeois class, whose interests are bound up with those of the capitalists and antagonistic to those of common labor. On the other hand, common labor in America and white Europe far from being motivated by any vision of revolt against capitalism, has been blinded by the American vision of the possibility of layer after layer of the workers escaping into the wealthy class and becoming managers and employers of labor.

Thus in America we have seen a wild and ruthless scramble of labor groups over each other in order to climb to wealth on the backs of black labor and foreign immigrants. The Irish climbed on the Negroes. The Germans scrambled over the Negroes and emulated the Irish. The Scandinavians fought forward next to the Germans and the Italians and "Bohunks" are crowding up, leaving Negroes still at the bottom chained to helplessness, first by slavery, then by disfranchisement and always by the Color Bar.

The second influence on white labor both in America and Europe has been the fact that the extension of the world market by imperial expanding industry has established a world-wide new proletariat of colored workers, toiling under the worst conditions of 19th Century capitalism, herded as slaves and serfs and furnishing by the lowest paid wage in modern history a mass of raw material for industry. With this largess the capitalists have consolidated their economic power, nullified universal suffrage and bribed the white workers by high wages, visions of wealth and the opportunity to drive "niggers." Soldiers and sailors from the white workers are used to keep "darkies" in their "places" and white foremen and engineers have been established as irresponsible satraps in China and India, Africa and the West Indies, backed by the organized and centralized ownership of machines, raw materials, finished commodities and land monopoly over the whole world.

How now does the philosophy of Karl Marx apply today to colored labor? First of all colored labor has no common ground with white labor. No soviet of technocrats would do more than exploit colored labor in order to raise the status of whites. No revolt of a white proletariat could be started if its object was to make black workers their economic, political and social equals. It is for this reason that American socialism for fifty years has been dumb on the Negro problem, and the communists cannot even get a respectful hearing in America unless they begin by expelling Negroes.

On the other hand, within the Negro groups, in the United States, in West Africa, in South America and in the West Indies, petty bourgeois groups are being evolved. In South America and the West Indies such groups drain off skill and intelligence into the white group, and leave the black labor poor, ignorant and leaderless save for an occasional demagog.

In West Africa, a Negro bourgeoisie is developing with invested capital and employment of natives and is only kept from the conventional capitalistic development by the opposition and enmity of white capital, and the white managers and engineers who represent it locally and who display bitter prejudice and tyranny; and by white European labor which furnishes armies and navies and Empire "preference." African black labor and black capital are therefore driven to seek alliance and common ground.

In the United States also a petty bourgeoisie is being developed, consisting of clergymen, teachers, farm owners, professional men and retail business-men. The position of this class, however, is peculiar: they are not the chief or even large investors in Negro labor and therefore exploit it only here and there; and they bear the brunt of color prejudice because they express in word and work the aspirations of all black folk for emancipation. The revolt of any black proletariat could not, therefore, be logically directed against this class, nor could this class join either white capital, white engineers or white workers to strengthen the color bar.

Under these circumstances, what shall we say of the Marxian philosophy and of its relation to the American Negro? We can only say, as it seems to me, that the Marxian philosophy is a true diagnosis of the situation in Europe in the middle of the 19th Century despite some of its logical difficulties. But it must be modified in the United States of America and especially so far as the Negro group is concerned. The Negro is exploited to a degree that means poverty, crime, delinquency and indigence. And that exploitation comes not from a black capitalistic class but from the white capitalists and equally from the white proletariat. His only defense is such internal organization as will protect him from both parties, and such practical economic insight as will prevent inside the race group any large development of capitalistic exploita-tion.

Meantime, comes the Great Depression. It levels all in mighty catastro-phe. The fantastic industrial structure of America is threatened with ruin. The trade unions of skilled labor are double-tongued and helpless. Unskilled and common white labor is too frightened at Negro competition to attempt united action. It only begs a dole. The reformist program of Socialism meets no response from the white proletariat because it offers no escape to wealth and no effective bar to black labor, and a mud-sill of black labor is essential to white labor's standard of living. The shrill cry of a few communists is not even listened to, because and solely because it seeks to break down barriers between black and white. There is not at present the slightest indication that a Marxian revolution based on a united class-conscious proletariat is anywhere on the American far horizon. Rather race antagonism and labor group rivalry are still undisturbed by world catastrophe. In the hearts of black laborers alone, therefore, lie those ideals of democracy in politics and industry which may in time make the workers of the world effective dictators of civilization.

Behold the Land

The future of American Negroes is in the South. Here three hundred and twenty-seven years ago, they began to enter what is now the United States of America; here they have made their greatest contribution to American culture; and here they have suffered the damnation of slavery, the frustration of reconstruction and the lynching of emancipation. I trust then that an organization like yours is going to regard the South as the battle-ground of a great crusade. Here is the magnificent climate; here is the fruitful earth under the beauty of the Southern sun; and here if anywhere on earth, is the need of the thinker, the worker and the dreamer. This is the firing line not simply for the emancipation of the American Negro but for the emancipation of the African Negro and the Negroes of the West Indies; for the emancipation of the colored races; and for the emancipation of the white slaves of modern capitalistic monopoly.

ALLIES IN THE WHITE SOUTH

Remember here, too, that you do not stand alone. It may seem like a failing fight when the newspapers ignore you; when every effort is made by white people in the South to count you out of citizenship and to act as though you did not exist as human beings while all the time they are profiting by your labor; gleaning wealth from your sacrifices and trying to build a nation and a civilization upon your degradation. You must remember that despite all this, you have allies and allies even in the white South. First and greatest of these possible allies are the white working classes about you. The poor whites whom you have been taught to despise and who in turn have learned to fear and hate

From a fifteen-page pamphlet published by the Southern Negro Youth Congress, Birmingham, Alabama (1947).

you. This must not deter you from efforts to make them understand, because in the past in their ignorance and suffering they have been led foolishly to look upon you as the cause of most of their distress. You must remember that this attitude is hereditary from slavery and that it has been deliberately cultivated ever since emancipation.

Slowly but surely the working people of the South, white and black, must come to remember that their emancipation depends upon their mutual cooperation; upon their acquaintanceship with each other; upon their friendship; upon their social intermingling. Unless this happens each is going to be made the football to break the heads and hearts of the other.

WHITE YOUTH IS FRUSTRATED

White youth in the South is peculiarly frustrated. There is not a single great ideal which they can express or aspire to that does not bring them into flat contradiction with the Negro problem. The more they try to escape it, the more they land into hypocrisy, lying and double-dealing; the more they become, what they least wish to become, the oppressors and despisers of human beings. Some of them, in larger and larger numbers, are bound to turn toward the truth and to recognize you as brothers and sisters, as fellow travellers toward the dawn.

"JAMES BYRNES, THE FAVORITE SON OF THIS COMMONWEALTH"

There has always been in the South that intellectual elite who saw the Negro problem clearly. They have always lacked and some still lack the courage to stand up for what they know is right. Nevertheless they can be depended on in the long run to follow their own clear thinking and their own decent choice. Finally even the politicians must eventually recognize the trend in the world, in this country, and in the South. James Byrnes, that favorite son of this commonwealth, and Secretary of State of the United States, is today occupying an indefensible and impossible position; and if he survives in the memory of men, he must begin to help establish in his own South Carolina something of that democracy which he has been recently so loudly preaching to Russia. He is the end of a long series of men whose eternal damnation is the fact that they looked *truth* in the face and did not see it; John C. Calhoun, Wade

Hampton, Ben Tillman are men whose names must ever be besmirched by the fact that they fought against freedom and democracy in a land which was founded upon Democracy and Freedom.

Eventually this class of men must yield to the writing in the stars. That great hypocrite, Jan Smuts, who today is talking of humanity and standing beside Byrnes for a United Nations, is at the same time, oppressing the black people of Africa to an extent which makes their two countries, South Africa and the Southern South, the most reactionary peoples on earth. Peoples whose exploitation of the poor and helpless reaches the last degree of shame. They must in the long run yield to the forward march of civilization or die.

WHAT DOES THE FIGHT MEAN

If now you young people instead of running away from the battle here in Carolina, Georgia, Alabama, Louisiana and Mississippi, instead of seeking freedom and opportunity in Chicago and New York—which do spell opportunity—nevertheless grit your teeth and make up your minds to fight it out right here if it takes every day of your lives and the lives of your children's children; if you do this, you must in meetings like this ask yourselves what does the fight mean? How can it be carried on? What are the best tools, arms, and methods? And where does it lead?

I should be the last to insist that the uplift of mankind never calls for force and death. There are times, as both you and I know, when

> Tho' love repine and reason chafe,
> There came a voice without reply,
> 'Tis man's perdition to be safe
> When for the truth he ought to die.

At the same time and even more clearly in a day like this, after the millions of mass murders that have been done in the world since 1914, we ought to be the last to believe that force is ever the final word. We cannot escape the clear fact that what is going to win in this world is reason if this ever becomes a reasonable world. The careful reasoning of the human mind backed by the facts of science is the one salvation of man. The world, if it resumes its march toward civilization, cannot ignore reason. This has been the tragedy of the South in the past; it is still its awful and unforgivable sin that it has set its face against reason and against the fact. It tried to build slavery upon freedom; it tried to build tyranny upon democracy; it tried to build mob violence on law and law on lynching and in all that despicable endeavor, the state of South

547

Carolina has led the South for a century. It began not the Civil War — not the War between the States — but the War to Preserve Slavery; it began mob violence and lynching and today it stands in the front rank of those defying the Supreme Court on disfranchisement.

Nevertheless reason can and will prevail; but of course it can only prevail with publicity — pitiless, blatant publicity. You have got to make the people of the United States and of the world know what is going on in the South. You have got to use every field of publicity to force the truth into their ears, and before their eyes. You have got to make it impossible for any human being to live in the South and not realize the barbarities that prevail here. You may be condemned for flamboyant methods; for calling a congress like this; for waving your grievances under the noses and in the faces of men. That makes no difference; it is your duty to do it. It is your duty to do more of this sort of thing than you have done in the past. As a result of this you are going to be called upon for sacrifice. It is no easy thing for a young black man or a young black woman to live in the South today and to plan to continue to live here; to marry and raise children; to establish a home. They are in the midst of legal caste and customary insults; they are in continuous danger of mob violence; they are mistreated by the officers of the law and they have no hearing before the courts and the churches and public opinion commensurate with the attention which they ought to receive. But that sacrifice is only the Beginning of Battle, you must re-build this South.

There are enormous opportunities here for a new nation, a new Economy, a new culture in a South really new and not a mere renewal of an old South of slavery, monopoly and race hate. There is a chance for a new cooperative agriculture on renewed land owned by the State with capital furnished by the State, mechanized and coordinated with city life. There is chance for strong, virile Trade Unions without race discrimination, with high wage, closed shop and decent conditions of work, to beat back and hold in check the swarm of landlords, monopolists and profiteers who are today sucking the blood out of this land. There is chance for cooperative industry, built on the cheap power of T.V.A. and its future extensions. There is opportunity to organize and mechanize domestic service with decent hours, and high wage and dignified training.

"BEHOLD THE LAND"

There is a vast field for consumers' cooperation, building business on public service and not on private profit as the main-spring of industry. There is chance for a broad, sunny, healthy home life, shorn of the fear of mobs and liquor, and rescued from lying, stealing politicians, who build their deviltry on race prejudice.

Here in this South is the gateway to the colored millions of the West Indies, Central and South America. Here is the straight path to Africa, the Indies, China and the South Seas. Here is the Path to the Greater, Freer truer World. It would be shame and cowardice to surrender this glorious land and its opportunities for civilization and humanity to the thugs and lynchers, the mobs and profiteers, the monopolists and gamblers who today choke its soul and steal its resources. The oil and sulphur; the coal and iron; the cotton and corn; the lumber and cattle belong to you the workers, black and white, and not to the thieves who hold them and use them to enslave you. They can be rescued and restored to the people if you have the guts to strive for the real right to vote, the right to real education, the right to happiness and health and the total abolition of the father of these scourges of mankind, *poverty*.

THE GREAT SACRIFICE

"Behold the beautiful land which the Lord thy God hath given thee." Behold the land, the rich and resourceful land, from which for a hundred years its best elements have been running away, its youth and hope, black and white, scurrying North because they are afraid of each other, and dare not face a future of equal, independent, upstanding human beings, in a real and not a sham democracy.

To rescue this land, in this way, calls for the *Great Sacrifice*; This is the thing that you are called upon to do because it is the right thing to do. Because you are embarked upon a great and holy crusade, the emancipation of mankind black and white; the upbuilding of democracy; the breaking down, particularly here in the South, of forces of evil represented by race prejudice in South Carolina; by lynching in Georgia; by disfranchisement in Mississippi; by ignorance in Louisiana and by all these and monopoly of wealth in the whole South.

There could be no more splendid vocation beckoning to the youth of the twentieth century, after the flat failures of white civilization, after the flamboyant establishment of an industrial system which creates poverty and the children of poverty which are ignorance and disease and crime; after the crazy boasting of a white culture that finally ended in wars which ruined civilization in the whole world; in the midst of allied peoples who have yelled about democracy and never practised it either in the British Empire or in the American Commonwealth or in South Carolina.

Here is the chance for young women and young men of devotion to lift again the banner of humanity and to walk toward a civilization which will be free and intelligent; which will be healthy and unafraid; and build in the world a culture led by black folk and joined by peoples of all colors and races — without poverty, ignorance and disease!

Once a great German poet cried: "Selig der den Er in Sieges Glanze findet."

"Happy man whom Death shall find in Victory's splendor."

But I know a happier one: he who fights in despair and in defeat still fights. Singing with Arna Bontemps the quiet, determined philosophy of undefeatable men:

> I thought I saw an angel flying low,
> I thought I saw the flicker of a wing
> Above the mulberry trees; but not again,
> Bethesda sleeps. This ancient pool that healed
> A Host of bearded Jews does not awake.
>
> This pool that once the angels troubled does not move.
> No angel stirs it now, no Saviour comes
> With healing in His hands to raise the sick
> and bid the lame man leap upon the ground.
>
> The golden days are gone. Why do we wait
> So long upon the marble steps, blood
> Falling from our open wounds? and why
> Do our black faces search the empty sky?
> Is there something we have forgotten? Some precious thing
> We have lost, wandering in strange lands?
>
> There was a day, I remember now,
> I beat my breast and cried, "Wash me God,"
> Wash me with a wave of wind upon
> The barley; O quiet one, draw near, draw near!
> Walk upon the hills with lovely feet
> And in the waterfall stand and speak!

XI

Separatist
Solutions

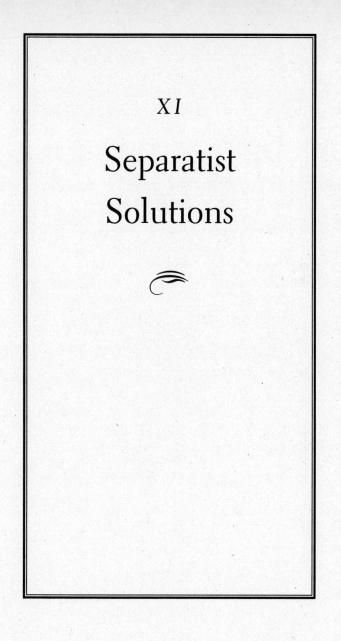

If Du Bois's ideas appeared to become increasingly inconsistent and contradictory during the 1930s as he turned away from racial integration, on the one hand, or denounced the left on the other, the anomalies were more apparent than real. Integration and class solidarity were strategic agendas rather than sacrosanct ideals that Du Bois was always willing to subordinate to the categorical imperative of racial integrity and solidarity. Thus, in "The Class Struggle" (1921), he repudiated African-American membership in the "world proletariat," calling instead, in the inflammatory editorials "Segregation" and "Separation and Self-Respect" (1934), for a concerted effort at separate, self-sustaining economic and political development by black people. Du Bois proposed a matrix of cooperative enterprises ("The C.M.A. Stores" [1937]) whose shared profits would steadily improve the conditions of African-Americans as they struggled against the forces of white racism. "It is the race-conscious black man coooperating together in his own institutions and movements," Du Bois argued in the vise of the Great Depression, "who will eventually emancipate the colored race" ["Segregation"]. NAACP loyalists were scandalized and socialists were puzzled as the sometimes integrationist and sometimes socialist Du Bois seemed to embrace in "A Negro Nation Within a Nation" (1935) both Booker T. Washington and Marcus Garvey. Neither partisans were placated by Du Bois's defense that he was merely proposing a pragmatic response to the racial segregation that was an ineradicable fact of national life, but one that would ultimately yield before the power of separate ethnic and economic groups finally acting in democratic concert.

The Class Struggle

The N.A.A.C.P. has been accused of not being a "revolutionary" body. This is quite true. We do not believe in revolution. We expect revolutionary changes in many parts of this life and this world, but we expect these changes to come mainly through reason, human sympathy and the education of children, and not by murder. We know that there have been times when organized murder seemed the only way out of wrong, but we believe those times have been very few, the cost of the remedy excessive, the results as terrible as beneficent, and we gravely doubt if in the future there will be any real recurrent necessity for such upheaval.

Whether this is true or not, the N.A.A.C.P. is organized to agitate, to investigate, to expose, to defend, to reason, to appeal. This is our program and this is the whole of our program. What human reform demands today is light, more light; clear thought, accurate knowledge, careful distinctions.

How far, for instance, does the dogma of the "class struggle" apply to black folk in the United States to-day? Theoretically we are a part of the world proletariat in the sense that we are mainly an exploited class of cheap laborers; but practically we are not a part of the white proletariat and are not recognized by that proletariat to any great extent. We are the victims of their physical oppression, social ostracism, economic exclusion and personal hatred; and when in self defense we seek sheer subsistence we are howled down as "scabs".

Then consider another thing: the colored group is not yet divided into capitalists and laborers. There are only the beginnings of such a division. In one hundred years if we develop along conventional lines we would have such fully separated classes, but today to a very large extent our laborers are our capitalists and our capitalists are our laborers. Our small class of well-to-do men have come to affluence largely through manual toil and have never been physically or mentally separated from the toilers. Our professional classes are sons and daughters of porters, washerwomen and laborers.

From *The Crisis*, June 1921.

Under these circumstances how silly it would be for us to try to apply the doctrine of the class struggle without modification or thought. Let us take a particular instance. Ten years ago the Negroes of New York City lived in hired tenement houses in Harlem, having gotten possession of them by paying higher rents than white tenants. If they had tried to escape these high rents and move into quarters where white laborers lived, the white laborers would have mobbed and murdered them. On the other hand, the white capitalists raised heaven and earth either to drive them out of Harlem or keep their rents high. Now between this devil and deep sea, what ought the Negro socialist or the Negro radical or, for that matter, the Negro conservative do?

Manifestly there was only one thing for him to do, and that was to buy Harlem; but the buying of real estate calls for capital and credit, and the institutions that deal in capital and credit are capitalistic institutions. If now, the Negro had begun to fight capital in Harlem, what capital was he fighting? If he fought capital as represented by white big real estate interests, he was wise; but he was also just as wise when he fought labor which insisted on segregating him in work and in residence.

If, on the other hand, he fought the accumulating capital in his own group, which was destined in the years 1915 to 1920 to pay down $5,000,000 for real estate in Harlem, then he was slapping himself in his own face. Because either he must furnish capital for the buying of his own home, or rest naked in the slums and swamps. It is for this reason that there is today a strong movement in Harlem for a Negro bank, and a movement which is going soon to be successful. This Negro bank eventually is going to bring into cooperation and concentration the resources of fifty or sixty other Negro banks in the United States, and this aggregation of capital is going to be used to break the power of white capital in enslaving and exploiting the darker world.

Whether this is a program of socialism or capitalism does not concern us. It is the only program that means salvation to the Negro race. The main danger and the central question of the capitalistic development through which the Negro American group is forced to go is the question of the ultimate control of the capital which they must raise and use. If this capital is going to be controlled by a few men for their own benefit, then we are destined to suffer from our own capitalists exactly what we are suffering from white capitalists to-day. And while this is not a pleasant prospect, it is certainly no worse than the present actuality. If, on the other hand, because of our more democratic organization and our widespread inter-class sympathy we can introduce a more democratic control, taking advantage of what the white world is itself doing to introduce industrial democracy, then we may not only escape our present economic slavery but even guide and lead a distrait economic world.

Segregation

The thinking colored people of the United States must stop being stampeded by the word segregation. The opposition to racial segregation is not or should not be any distaste or unwillingness of colored people to work with each other, to co-operate with each other, to live with each other. The opposition to segregation is an opposition to discrimination. The experience in the United States has been that usually when there is racial segregation, there is also racial discrimination.

But the two things do not necessarily go together, and there should never be an opposition to segregation pure and simple unless that segregation does involve discrimination. Not only is there no objection to colored people living beside colored people if the surroundings and treatment involve no discrimination, if streets are well lighted, if there is water, sewerage and police protection, and if anybody of any color who wishes, can live in that neighborhood. The same way in schools, there is no objection to schools attended by colored pupils and taught by colored teachers. On the contrary, colored pupils can by our own contention be as fine human beings as any other sort of children, and we certainly know that there are no teachers better than trained colored teachers. But if the existence of such a school is made reason and cause for giving it worse housing, poorer facilities, poorer equipment and poorer teachers, then we do object, and the objection is not against the color of the pupils' or teachers' skins, but against the discrimination.

In the recent endeavor of the United States government to redistribute capital so that some of the disadvantaged groups may get a chance for development, the American Negro should voluntarily and insistently demand his share. Groups of communities and farms inhabited by colored folk should be voluntarily formed. In no case should there be any discrimination against white and blacks. But, at the same time, colored people should come forward, should organize and conduct enterprises, and their only insistence should be

From *The Crisis*, January 1934.

that the same provisions be made for the success of their enterprise that is being made for the success of any other enterprise. It must be remembered that in the last quarter of a century, the advance of the colored people has been mainly in the lines where they themselves working by and for themselves, have accomplished the greatest advance.

There is no doubt that numbers of white people, perhaps the majority of Americans, stand ready to take the most distinct advantage of voluntary segregation and cooperation among colored people. Just as soon as they get a group of black folk segregated, they use it as a point of attack and discrimination. Our counter attack should be, therefore, against this discrimination; against the refusal of the South to spend the same amount of money on the black child as on the white child for its education; against the inability of black groups to use public capital; against the monopoly of credit by white groups. But never in the world should our fight be against association with ourselves because by that very token we give up the whole argument that we are worth associating with.

Doubtless, and in the long run, the greatest human development is going to take place under experiences of widest individual contact. Nevertheless, today such individual contact is made difficult and almost impossible by petty prejudice, deliberate and almost criminal propaganda and various survivals from prehistoric heathenism. It is impossible, therefore, to wait for the millennium of free and normal intercourse before we unite, to cooperate among themselves in groups of like-minded people and in groups of people suffering from the same disadvantages and the same hatreds.

It is the class-conscious working man uniting together who will eventually emancipate labor throughout the world. It is the race-conscious black man cooperating together in his own institutions and movements who will eventually emancipate the colored race, and the great step ahead today is for the American Negro to accomplish his economic emancipation through voluntary determined cooperative effort.

Separation and Self-Respect

What we continually face in this problem of race segregation in the United States is a paradox like this:

1. Compulsory separation of human beings by essentially artificial criteria, such as birth, nationality, language, color and race, is the cause of human hate, jealousy and war, and the destruction of talent and art.

2. Where separation of mankind into races, groups and classes is compulsory, either by law or custom, and whether that compulsion be temporary or permanent, the only effective defense that the segregated and despised group has against complete spiritual and physical disaster, is internal self-organization for self-respect and self-defense.

The dilemma is complete and there is no escape. The black man born in South Carolina has a right and a duty to complain that any public school system separated by artificial race and class lines is needlessly expensive, socially dangerous, and spiritually degrading. And yet that black man will send his child to a Negro school, and he will see to it, if he is really a man, that this Negro school is the best possible school; that it is decently housed and effectively taught by well-trained teachers. He will demand a voice in its control, finances and curriculum, and any action of his that asks for less than this will mark him as an idiot or a coward.

A black man born in Boston has a right to oppose any separation of schools by color, race or class. He has a duty to insist that the public school attended by all kinds and conditions of people, is the best and only door to true democracy and human understanding. But this black man in Boston has no right, after he has made this academic pronouncement to send his own helpless immature child into school where white children kick, cuff or abuse him, or where teachers openly and persistently neglect or hurt or dwarf its soul. If he does, he must not be surprised if the boy lands in the gutter or penitentiary. Moreover, our Boston brother has no right to sneer at the "Jim-

From *The Crisis*, March 1934.

Crow" schools of South Carolina, or at the brave teachers who guide them at starvation wage; nor can he conscientiously advise the South Carolinian to move to Boston and join the bread lines.

Let the N.A.A.C.P. and every upstanding Negro pound at the closed gates of opportunity and denounce caste and segregation; but let us not punish our own children under the curious impression that we are punishing our white oppressors. Let us not affront our own self-respect by accepting a proffered equality which is not equality, or submitting to discrimination simply because it does not involve actual and open segregation; and above all, let us not sit down and do nothing for self-defense and self-organization just because we are too stupid or too distrustful of ourselves to take vigorous and decisive action.

Race segregation in the United States too often presents itself as an individual problem; a question of my admission to this church or that theater; a question as to whether I shall live and work in Mississippi or New York for my own enjoyment, emolument or convenience.

In fact this matter of segregation is a group matter with long historic roots. When Negroes were first brought to America in any numbers, their classification was economic rather than racial. They were in law and custom classed with the laborers, most of whom were brought from Europe under a contract which made them practically serfs. In this laboring class there was at first no segregation, there was some inter-marriage and when the laborer gained his freedom, he became in numbers of cases a landholder and a voter.

The first distinction arose between laborers who had come from Europe and contracted to work for a term of years, and laborers from Africa and the West Indies who had made no contract. Both classes were often held for life, but soon there arose a distinction between servants for a term of years and servants for life. Even their admission to a Christian church organization was usually considered as emancipating a servant for life, and thus again the purely racial segregation was cut across by religious considerations.

Finally, however, slavery became a matter of racial caste, so that white laborers served for definite terms and most black workers served for life. But even here anomaly arose in the case of the small number of Negroes who were free. For a while these free Negroes were not definitely segregated from other free workers, but gradually they were forced together as a caste, holding themselves, on the one hand, strictly away from the slaves, and on the other, being excluded more and more severely from inter-course with whites of all degrees.

The result was that there grew up in the minds of the free Negro class a determination and a prejudice which has come down to our day. They fought bitterly with every means at their command against being classed with the mass of slaves. It was for this reason that they objected to being called Negroes. Negroes was synonymous with slaves. They were not slaves. They objected to being coupled with black folk by legislation or custom. Any such act threatened their own freedom. They developed, therefore, both North and South as a separate, isolated group. In large Southern cities, like New Orleans, Savannah and Charleston, they organized their own society, established schools and churches, and made themselves a complete segregated unit, except in their economic relations where they earned a living among the whites as artisans and servants, rising here and there to be semi-professional men and small merchants. The higher they rose and the more definite and effective their organization, the more they protested against being called Negroes or classed with Negroes, because Negroes were slaves.

In the North, the development differed somewhat, and yet followed mainly the same lines. The groups of free colored folk in Boston, Newport, New Haven, New York, Philadelphia, Baltimore and Cincinnati, all formed small, carefully organized groups, with their own schools and churches, with their own social life, with their own protest against being classed as Negroes. As the mass of Negroes became free in the Northern states, certain decisions were forced upon these groups. Take for instance, Philadelphia. An event happened in April 1787, which may be called by the American Negro, the Great Decision. The free colored people of Philadelphia at that time were making a desperate fight for recognition and decent social treatment.

Two of their leaders, Richard Allen and Absalom Jones, had proffered their services during the terrible epidemic in 1792, and partly at their own expense, helped bury the deserted dead of the white folk. The Mayor properly commended them. Both these men worshipped at St. George's Methodist Church, then at 4th and Vine Streets. For years they had been made welcome; but as gradual emancipation progressed in Pennsylvania, Negroes began to pour in to the city from the surrounding country, and black Christians became too numerous at St. George's. One Sunday morning during prayer, Jones and Allen were on their knees, when they were told they must get up and go to the gallery where hereafter black folk would worship. They refused to stir until the prayer was over, and then they got up and left the church. They never went back.

Under these circumstances, what would you have done, Dear Reader of 1934? There were several possibilities. You might have been able to impress it upon the authorities of the church that you were not like other Negroes; that you were different, with more wealth and intelligence, and that while it might be quite all right and even agreeable to you that other Negroes should be sent to the gallery, that you as an old and tried member of the church should be allowed to worship as you pleased. If you had said this, it probably would have had no effect upon the deacons of St. George's.

In that case, what would you have done? You could walk out of the church but whither would you walk? There were no other white churches that wanted you. Most of them would not have allowed you to cross their threshold. The others would have segregated you in the gallery or at a separate service. You might have said with full right and reason that the action of St. George's was un-Christian and despicable, and dangerous for the future of democracy in Philadelphia and in the United States. That was all quite true, and nevertheless its statement had absolutely no effect upon St. George's.

Walking out of this church, these two men formed an organization. It was called the Free African Society. Virtually it was confined to a colored membership, although some of the Quakers visited the meetings from time to time and gave advice. Probably there was some discussion of taking the group into the fellowship of the Quakers, but liberal as the Quakers were, they were not looking for Negro proselytes. They had had a few in the West Indies but not in the United States. The excluded Negroes found themselves in a dilemma. They could do one of two things: They could ask to be admitted as a segregated group in some white organization; or they could form their own organization. It was an historic decision and they did both.

Richard Allen formed from the larger part of the group, the African Methodist Episcopal Church, which today has 750,000 members and is without doubt the most powerful single Negro organization in the United States. Absalom Jones formed St. Thomas Church as a separate Negro church in the Episcopal communion, and the church has had a continuous existence down to our day.

Which of these two methods was best will be a matter of debate. There are those who think that it was saving something of principle to remain in a white church, even as a segregated body. There are others who say that this action was simply a compromise with the devil and that having been kicked out of the Methodist Church and not allowed equality in the Episcopal Church, there was nothing for a self-respecting man to do but to establish a church of his own.

No matter which solution seems to you wisest, segregation was compulsory; and the only answer to it was internal self-organization; and the answer that was inevitable in 1787, is just as inevitable in 1934.

A Negro Nation Within
the Nation

No more critical situation ever faced the Negroes of America than that of today — not in 1830, nor in 1861, nor in 1867. More than ever the appeal of the Negro for elementary justice falls on deaf ears.

Three-fourths of us are disfranchised; yet no writer on democratic reform, no third party movement says a word about Negroes. The Bull Moose crusade in 1912 refused to notice them; the La Follette uprising in 1924 was hardly aware of them; the Socialists still keep them in the background. Negro children are systematically denied education; when the National Education Association asks for Federal aid to education it permits discrimination to be perpetuated by the present local authorities. Once or twice a month Negroes convicted of no crime are openly and publicly lynched, and even burned; yet a National Crime Convention is brought to perfunctory and unwilling notice of this only by mass picketing and all but illegal agitation. When a man with every qualification is refused a position simply because his great-grandfather was black there is not a ripple of comment or protest.

Long before the depression Negroes in the South were losing "Negro" jobs, those assigned them by common custom — poorly paid and largely undesirable toil, but nevertheless life-supporting. New techniques, new enterprises, mass production, impersonal ownership and control have been largely displacing the skilled white and Negro worker in tobacco manufacturing, in iron and steel, in lumbering and mining, and in transportation. Negroes are now restricted more and more to common labor and domestic service of the lowest paid and worst kind. In textile, chemical and other manufactures Negroes were from the first nearly excluded, and just as slavery kept the poor white out of profitable agriculture, so freedom prevents the poor Negro from finding a place in manufacturing. The world-wide decline in agriculture has moreover

From *Current History*, 42 (June 1935): 265–270.

carried the mass of black farmers, despite heroic endeavor among the few, down to the level of landless tenants and peons.

The World War and its wild aftermath seemed for a moment to open a new door; 2,000,000 black workers rushed North to work in iron and steel, make automobiles and pack meat, build houses and do the heavy toil in factories. They met first the closed trade union which excluded them from the best paid jobs and pushed them into the low-wage gutter, denied them homes and mobbed them. Then they met the Depression.

Since 1929 Negro workers, like white workers, have lost their jobs, have had mortgages foreclosed on their farms and homes, have used up their small savings. But, in the case of the Negro worker, everything has been worse in larger or smaller degree; the loss has been greater and more permanent. Technological displacement, which began before the Depression, has been accelerated, while unemployment and falling wages struck black men sooner, went to lower levels and will last longer.

Negro public schools in the rural South have often disappeared, while Southern city schools are crowded to suffocation. The Booker Washington High School in Atlanta, built for 1,000 pupils, has 3,000 attending in double daily sessions. Above all, Federal and State relief holds out little promise for the Negro. It is but human that the unemployed white man and the starving white child should be relieved first by local authorities who regard them as fellow-men, but often regard Negroes as subhuman. While the white worker has sometimes been given more than relief and been helped to his feet, the black worker has often been pauperized by being just kept from starvation. There are some plans for national rehabilitation and the rebuilding of the whole industrial system. Such plans should provide for the Negro's future relations to American industry and culture, but those provisions the country is not only unprepared to make but refuses to consider.

In the Tennessee Valley beneath the Norris Dam, where do Negroes come in? And what shall be their industrial place? In the attempt to rebuild agriculture the Southern landholder will in all probability be put on his feet, but the black tenant has been pushed to the edge of despair. In the matter of housing, no comprehensive scheme for Negro homes has been thought out and only two or three local projects planned. Nor can broad plans be made until the nation or the community decides where it wants or will permit Negroes to live. Negroes are largely excluded from subsistence homesteads because Negroes protested against segregation, and whites, anxious for cheap local labor, also protested.

The colored people of America are coming to face the fact quite calmly that most white Americans do not like them, and are planning neither for their survival, nor for their definite future if it involves free, self-assertive modern manhood. This does not mean all Americans. A saving few are worried about the Negro problem; a still larger group are not ill-disposed, but they fear prevailing public opinion. The great mass of Americans are, however, merely representatives of average humanity. They muddle along with their own affairs and scarcely can be expected to take seriously the affairs of strangers or people whom they partly fear and partly despise.

For many years it was the theory of most Negro leaders that this attitude was the insensibility of ignorance and inexperience, that white America did not know of or realize the continuing plight of the Negro. Accordingly, for the last two decades, we have striven by book and periodical, by speech and appeal, by various dramatic methods of agitation, to put the essential facts before the American people. Today there can be no doubt that Americans know the facts; and yet they remain for the most part indifferent and unmoved.

The main weakness of the Negro's position is that since emancipation he has never had an adequate economic foundation. Thaddeus Stevens recognized this and sought to transform the emancipated freedmen into peasant proprietors. If he had succeeded, he would have changed the economic history of the United States and perhaps saved the American farmer from his present plight. But to furnish 50,000,000 acres of good land to the Negroes would have cost more money than the North was willing to pay, and was regarded by the South as highway robbery.

The whole attempt to furnish land and capital for the freedmen fell through, and no comprehensive economic plan was advanced until the advent of Booker T. Washington. He had a vision of building a new economic foundation for Negroes by incorporating them into white industry. He wanted to make them skilled workers by industrial education and expected small capitalists to rise out of their ranks. Unfortunately, he assumed that the economic development of America in the twentieth century would resemble that of the nineteenth century, with free industrial opportunity, cheap land and unlimited resources under the control of small competitive capitalists. He lived to see industry more and more concentrated, land monopoly extended and industrial technique changed by wide introduction of machinery.

As a result, technology advanced more rapidly than Hampton or Tuskegee could adjust their curricula. The chance of an artisan's becoming a capitalist grew slimmer, even for white Americans, while the whole relation of labor to capital became less a matter of technical skill than of basic organization and aim.

Those of us who in that day opposed Booker Washington's plans did not foresee exactly the kind of change that was coming, but we were convinced that the Negro could succeed in industry and in life only if he had intelligent leadership and far-reaching ideals. The object of education, we declared, was not "to make men artisans but to make artisans men." The Negroes in America needed leadership so that, when change and crisis came, they could guide themselves to safety.

The educated group among American Negroes is still small, but it is large enough to begin planning for preservation through economic advancement. The first definite movement of this younger group was toward direct alliance of the Negro with the labor movement. But white labor today as in the past refuses to respond to these overtures.

For a hundred years, beginning in the Thirties and Forties of the nineteenth century, the white laborers of Ohio, Pennsylvania and New York beat, murdered and drove away fellow-workers because they were black and had to work for what they could get. Seventy years ago in New York, the centre of the new American labor movement, white laborers hanged black ones to lamp posts instead of helping to free them from the worst of modern slavery. In Chicago and St. Louis, New Orleans and San Francisco, black men still carry the scars of the bitter hatred of white laborers for them. Today it is white labor that keeps Negroes out of decent low-cost housing, that confines the protection of the best unions to "white" men, that often will not sit in the same hall with black folk who already have joined the labor movement. White labor has to hate scabs; but it hates black scabs not because they are scabs but because they are black. It mobs white scabs to force them into labor fellowship. It mobs black scabs to starve and kill them. In the present fight of the American Federation of Labor against company unions it is attacking the only unions that Negroes can join.

Thus the Negro's fight to enter organized industry has made little headway. No Negro, no matter what his ability, can be a member of any [of] the railway unions. He cannot be an engineer, fireman, conductor, switchman, brakeman or yardman. If he organizes separately, he may, as in the case of the Negro Firemen's Union, be assaulted and even killed by white firemen. As in the case of the Pullman Porters' Union, he may receive empty recognition without any voice or collective help. The older group of Negro leaders recognize this and simply say it is a matter of continued striving to break down these barriers.

Such facts are, however, slowly forcing Negro thought into new channels. The interests of labor are considered rather than those of capital. No greater welcome is expected from the labor monopolist who mans armies and navies to keep Chinese, Japanese and Negroes in their places than from the captains of industry who spend large sums of money to make laborers think that the most worthless white man is better than any colored man. The Negro must prove his necessity to the labor movement and that it is a disastrous error to leave him out of the foundation of the new industrial State. He must settle beyond cavil the question of his economic efficiency as a worker, a manager and controller of capital.

The dilemma of these younger thinkers gives men like James Weldon Johnson a chance to insist that the older methods are still the best; that we can survive only by being integrated into the nation, and that we must consequently fight segregation now and always and force our way by appeal, agitation and law. This group, however, does not seem to recognize the fundamental economic bases of social growth and the changes that face American industry. Greater democratic control of production and distribution is bound to replace existing autocratic and monopolistic methods.

In this broader and more intelligent democracy we can hope for progressive softening of the asperities and anomalies of race prejudice, but we cannot hope for its early and complete disappearance. Above all, the doubt, deep-planted in the American mind, as to the Negro's ability and efficiency as worker, artisan and administrator will fade but slowly. Thus, with increased democratic control of industry and capital, the place of the Negro will be increasingly a matter of human choice, of willingness to recognize ability across the barriers of race, of putting fit Negroes in places of power and authority by public opinion. At present, on the railroads, in manufacturing, in the telephone, telegraph and radio business, and in the larger divisions of trade, it is only under exceptional circumstances that any Negro, no matter what his ability, gets an opportunity for position and power. Only in those lines where individual enterprise still counts, as in some of the professions, in a few of the trades, in a few branches of retail business and in artistic careers, can the Negro expect a narrow opening.

Negroes and other colored folk, nevertheless, exist in larger and growing numbers. Slavery, prostitution to white men, theft of their labor and goods have not killed them and cannot kill them. They are growing in intelligence and dissatisfaction. They occupy strategic positions, within nations and besides nations, amid valuable raw material and on the highways of future expansion. They will survive, but on what terms and conditions? On this point a new school of Negro thought is arising. It believes in the ultimate uniting of mankind and in a unified American nation, with economic classes and racial barriers leveled, but it believes this is an ideal and is to be realized only by such intensified class and race consciousness as will bring irresistible force rather than mere humanitarian appeals to bear on the motives and actions of men.

The peculiar position of Negroes in America offers an opportunity. Negroes today cast probably 2,000,000 votes in a total of 40,000,000, and their vote will increase. This gives them, particularly in Northern cities, and at critical times, a chance to hold a very considerable balance of power, and the mere threat of this being used intelligently and with determination may often mean much. The consuming power of 2,800,000 Negro families has recently been estimated at $166,000,000 a month — a tremendous power when intelligently directed. Their man power as laborers probably equals that of Mexico or Yugoslavia. Their illiteracy is much lower than that of Spain or Italy. Their estimated per capita wealth about equals that of Japan.

For a nation with this start in culture and efficiency to sit down and await the salvation of a white God is idiotic. With the use of their political power, their power as consumers, and their brain power, added to that chance of personal appeal which proximity and neighborhood always give to human beings, Negroes can develop in the United States an economic nation within a nation, able to work through inner cooperation, to found its own institutions, to educate its genius, and at the same time, without mob violence or extremes of race hatred, to keep in helpful touch and cooperate with the mass of the nation. This has happened more often than most people realize, in the case of groups not so obviously separated from the mass of people as are American Negroes. It must happen in our case, or there is no hope for the Negro in America.

Any movement toward such a program is today hindered by the absurd Negro philosophy of Scatter, Suppress, Wait, Escape. There are even many of our educated young leaders who think that because the Negro problem is not in evidence where there are few or no Negroes, this indicates a way out! They think that the problem of race can be settled by ignoring it and suppressing all reference to it. They think that we have only to wait in silence for the white people to settle the problem for us; and finally and predominantly, they think that the problem of 12,000,000 Negro people, mostly poor, ignorant workers, is going to be settled by having their more educated and wealthy classes gradually and continually escape from their race into the mass of the American people, leaving the rest to sink, suffer and die.

Proponents of this program claim, with much reason, that the plight of the masses is not the fault of the emerging classes. For the slavery and exploitation that reduced Negroes to their present level or at any rate hindered them from rising, the white world is to blame. Since the age-long process of raising a group is through the escape of its upper class into welcome fellowship with risen peoples, the Negro intelligentsia would submerge itself if it bent its back to the task of lifting the mass of people. There is logic in this answer, but futile logic.

If the leading Negro classes cannot assume and bear the uplift of their own proletariat, they are doomed for all time. It is not a case of ethics; it is a plain case of necessity. The method by which this may be done is, first, for the American Negro to achieve a new economic solidarity.

There exists today a chance for the Negroes to organize a cooperative State within their own group. By letting Negro farmers feed Negro artisans, and Negro technicians guide Negro home industries, and Negro thinkers plan this integration of cooperation, while Negro artists dramatize and beautify the struggle, economic independence can be achieved. To doubt that this is possible is to doubt the essential humanity and the quality of brains of the American Negro.

No sooner is this proposed than a great fear sweeps over older Negroes. They cry "No segregation" — no further yielding to prejudice and race separation. Yet any planning for the benefit of American Negroes on the part of a Negro intelligentsia is going to involve organized and deliberate self-segregation. There are plenty of people in the United States who would be only too willing to use such a plan as a way to increase existing legal and customary segregation between the races. This threat which many Negroes see is no mere mirage. What of it? It must be faced.

If the economic and cultural salvation of the American Negro calls for an increase in segregation and prejudice, then that must come. American Negroes must plan for their economic future and the social survival of their fellows in the firm belief that this means in a real sense the survival of colored folk in the world and the building of a full humanity instead of a petty white tyranny. Control of their own education, which is the logical and inevitable end of separate schools, would not be an unmixed ill; it might prove a supreme good. Negro schools once meant poor schools. They need not today; they must not tomorrow. Separate Negro sections will increase race antagonism, but they will also increase economic cooperation, organized self-defense and necessary self-confidence.

The immediate reaction of most white and colored people to this suggestion will be that the thing cannot be done without extreme results. Negro thinkers have from time to time emphasized the fact that no nation within a nation can be built because of the attitude of the dominant majority, and because all legal and police power is out of Negro hands, and because large-scale industries, like steel and utilities, are organized on a national basis. White folk, on the other hand, simply say that, granting certain obvious exceptions, the American Negro has not the ability to engineer so delicate a social operation calling for such self-restraint, careful organization and sagacious leadership.

In reply, it may be said that this matter of a nation within a nation has already been partially accomplished in the organization of the Negro church, the Negro school and the Negro retail business, and, despite all the justly due criticism, the result has been astonishing. The great majority of American Negroes are divided not only for religious but for a large number of social purposes into self-supporting economic units, self-governed, self-directed. The greatest difficulty is that these organizations have no logical and reasonable standards and do not attract the finest, most vigorous and best educated Negroes. When all these things are taken into consideration it becomes clearer to more and more American Negroes that, through voluntary and increased segregation, by careful autonomy and planned economic organization, they may build so strong and efficient a unit that 12,000,000 men can no longer be refused fellowship and equality in the United States.

The C.M.A. Stores

Just on the edge of the crash came an attempt of the Negro Business League, under the leadership of A. C. Holsey, to start a country-wide experiment in Negro business. These Colored Merchants Association stores were frankly after the pattern of modern retail business and there was no attempt to include any ideas of cooperation except very commendable efforts to standardize methods and appearances and to some extent to organize buying. Here, too, the enterprise was doomed to failure. It depended on and was encouraged by the wholesalers, who were beginning to be hard pressed by the chain store organizations. There was little hope that these wholesalers could or would sell goods as cheaply as the chain stores. The main weapon which the Negroes had, they failed even to attempt to use, and that was their organized buying power. This buying power could only be held in loyalty to business if it shared the profit, and there was no attempt to introduce such sharing. The C.M.A. stores have practically gone out of existence as a nation-wide organization, although some single establishments remain; but it is interesting to know that only last year the leader of the enterprise, Mr. Holsey, himself took a course of study in co-operation and we may hope to hear from him again.

From the *Pittsburgh Courier*, July 31, 1937.

XII

Radical Thought

*Socialism and
Communism*

Du Bois's socialist proclivities were unmistakable in his earliest writings. Repeatedly, the stumbling block to his full conversion was not the tenets of socialism or communism, but the racism of white American socialists and communists, as he revealed in "Socialism and the Negro Problem" (1913) and "The Negro and Communism" (1931). His admiration of state communism was firmly fixed after visits to Russia in 1926 and 1935 ("Russia, 1926 [1926]," "Lifting from the Bottom [1937]"). Du Bois was enraptured by first-hand observation of China's Great Leap Forward — "The Vast Miracle of China Today" [1959]. His official entry into the Communist Party of the United States — at age ninety-three — soon followed, but well before then, in such influential works as *Black Reconstruction in America* ("The Black Worker") [1935], "My Evolving Program for Negro Freedom" (1944), and thinkpieces in the *National Guardian* ("There Must Come a Vast Social Change in the United States" [1951]) and *Monthly Review* ("Negroes and the Crisis of Capitalism in the United States" [1953]), Du Bois had erected high signposts along the road to Moscow.

Socialism and the
Negro Problem

One might divide those interested in Socialism in two distinct camps: On the one hand those far-sighted thinkers who are seeking to determine from the facts of modern industrial organization just what the outcome is going to be; on the other hand, those who suffer from the present industrial situation and who are anxious that, whatever the broad outcome may be, at any rate the present suffering which they know so well shall be stopped. It is this second class of social thinkers who are interested particularly in the Negro problem. They are saying that the plight of ten million human beings in the United States predominantly of the working class, is so evil that it calls for much attention in any program of future social reform. This paper, however, is addressed not to this class, but rather to the class of theoretical Socialists; and its thesis is: In the Negro problem as it presents itself in the United States, theoretical Socialism of the twentieth century meets a critical dilemma.

There is no doubt as to the alternatives presented. On the one hand, here are 90 million white people who in their extraordinary development present a peculiar field for the application of Socialistic principles; but on the whole, these people are demanding to-day that just as under capitalistic organization the Negro has been the excluded (*i.e.*, exploited) class, so, too, any Socialistic program shall also exclude the ten million. Many Socialists have acquiesced in this program. No recent convention of Socialists has dared to face fairly the Negro problem and make a straight-forward declaration that they regard Negroes as men in the same sense that other persons are. The utmost that the party has been able to do is not to rescind the declaration of an earlier convention. The general attitude of thinking members of the party has been this: We must not turn aside from the great objects of Socialism to take up this

From *New Review*, February 1, 1913: 138–141.

issue of the American Negro; let the question wait; when the objects of Socialism are achieved, this problem will be settled along with other problems.

That there is a logical flaw here, no one can deny. Can the problem of any group of ten million be properly considered as "aside" from any program of Socialism? Can the objects of Socialism be achieved so long as the Negro is neglected? Can any great human problem "wait"? If Socialism is going to settle the American problem of race prejudice without direct attack along these lines by Socialists, why is it necessary for Socialists to fight along other lines? Indeed, there is a kind of fatalistic attitude on the part of certain transcendental Socialists, which often assumes that the whole battle of Socialism is coming by a kind of evolution in which active individual effort on their part is hardly necessary.

As a matter of fact, the Socialists face in the problem of the American Negro this question: Can a minority of any group or country be left out of the Socialistic problem? It is, of course, agreed that a majority could not be left out. Socialists usually put great stress on the fact that the laboring class form a majority of all nations and nevertheless are unjustly treated in the distribution of wealth. Suppose, however, that this unjust distribution affected only a minority, and that only a tenth of the American nation were working under unjust economic conditions: Could a Socialistic program be carried out which acquiesced in this condition? Many American Socialists seem silently to assume that this would be possible. To put it concretely, they are going to carry on industry so far as the mass is concerned; they are going to get rid of the private control of capital and they are going to divide up the social income among these 90 million in accordance with some rule of reason, rather than in the present haphazard way: But at the same time, they are going to permit the continued exploitation of these ten million workers. So far as these ten million workers are concerned, there is to be no active effort to secure for them a voice in the Social Democracy, or an adequate share in the social income. The idea is that ultimately when the 90 millions come to their own, they will voluntarily share with the ten million serfs.

Does the history of the world justify us in expecting any such outcome? Frankly, I do not believe it does. The program is that of industrial aristocracy which the world has always tried; the only difference being that such Socialists are trying to include in the inner circle a much larger number than have ever been included before. Socialistic as this program may be called, it is not real Social Democracy. The essence of Social Democracy is that there shall be no excluded or exploited classes in the Socialistic state; that there shall be no man or woman so poor, ignorant or black as not to count one. Is this simply a far off ideal, or is it a possible program? I have come to believe that the test of any great movement toward social reform is the Excluded Class. Who is it that Reform does *not* propose to benefit? If you are saving dying babies, whose babies are you going to let die? If you are feeding the hungry, what folk are you (regretfully, perhaps but none the less truly) going to let starve? If you are making a juster division of wealth, what people are you going to permit at present to remain in poverty? If you are giving all men votes (not only in the "political" but also in the economic world) what class of people are you going to allow to remain disfranchised?

More than that, assuming that if you did exclude Negroes temporarily from the growing Socialistic state, the ensuing uplift of humanity would in the end repair the temporary damage, the present question is, *can* you exclude the Negro and push Socialism forward? Every tenth man in the United States is of acknowledged Negro descent; if you take those in gainful occupations, one out of every seven Americans is colored; and if you take laborers and working-men in the ordinary acceptation of the term, one out of every five is colored. The problem then is to lift four-fifths of a group on the backs of the other fifth. Even if the submerged fifth were "dull driven cattle," this program of Socialistic opportunism would not be easy. But when the program is proposed in the face of a group growing in intelligence and social power and a group made suspicious and bitter by analogous action on the part of trade unionists, what is anti-Negro Socialism doing but handing to its enemies the powerful weapon of four and one-half million men who will find it not simply to their interest, but a sacred duty to underbid the labor market, vote against labor legislation, and fight to keep their fellow laborers down. Is it not significant that Negro soldiers in the army are healthier and desert less than whites?

Nor is this all: what becomes of Socialism when it engages in such a fight for human downfall? Whither are gone its lofty aspiration and high resolve — its songs and comradeship?

The Negro Problem then is the great test of the American Socialist. Shall American Socialism strive to train for its Socialistic state ten million serfs who will serve or be exploited by the state, or shall it strive to incorporate them immediately into that body politic? Theoretically, of course, all Socialists, with few exceptions, would wish the latter program. But it happens that in the United States there is a strong local opinion in the South which violently opposed any program of any kind of reform that recognizes the Negro as a man. So strong is this body of opinion that you have in the South a most extraordinary development. The whole radical movement there represented by men like Blease and Vardaman and Tillman and Jeff. Davis and attracting such demagogues as Hoke Smith, includes in its program of radical reform a most bitter and reactionary hatred of the Negro. The average modern Socialist can scarcely grasp the extent of this hatred; even murder and torture of human beings holds a prominent place in its philosophy; the defilement of colored women is its joke, and justice toward colored men will not be listened to. The only basis on which one can even approach these people with a plea for the barest tolerance of colored folk, is that the murder and mistreatment of colored men may possibly hurt white men. Consequently the Socialist party finds itself in this predicament: if it acquiesces in race hatred, it has a chance to turn the tremendous power of Southern white radicalism toward its own party; if it does not do this, it becomes a "party of the Negro," with its growth South and North decidedly checked. There are signs that the Socialist leaders are going to accept the chance of getting hold of the radical South whatever its cost. This paper is written to ask such leaders: After you have gotten the radical South and paid the price which they demand, will the result be Socialism?

Russia, 1926

I am writing this in Russia. I am sitting in Revolution Square opposite the Second House of the Moscow Soviets and in a hotel run by the Soviet Government. Yonder the sun pours into my window over the domes and eagles and pointed towers of the Kremlin. Here is the old Chinese wall of the inner city; there is the gilded glory of the Cathedral of Christ, the Savior. Thro' yonder gate on the vast Red Square, Lenin sleeps his last sleep, with long lines of people peering each day into his dead and speaking face. Around me roars a city of two millions — Holy Moscow.

I have been in Russia something less than two months. I did not see the Russia of war and blood and rapine. I know nothing of political prisoners, secret police and underground propaganda. My knowledge of the Russian language is sketchy and of this vast land, the largest single country on earth, I have traveled over only a small, a very small part.

But I have had certain advantages; I have seen something of Russia. I have traveled over two thousand miles and visited four of its largest cities, many of its towns, the Neva, Dneiper, Moscow and Volga of its rivers, and stretches of land and village. I have looked into the faces of its races — Jews, Tartars, Gypsies, Caucasians, Armenians and Chinese. To help my lack of language I have had personal friends, whom I knew before I came to Russia, as interpreters. They were born in Russia and speak English, French and German. This, with my English, German and French, has helped the language difficulty, but did not, of course, solve it.

I have not done my sight seeing and investigation in gangs and crowds nor according to the program of the official Foreign Bureau; but have in nearly all cases gone alone with one Russian speaking friend. In this way I have seen schools, universities, factories, stores, printing establishments, government offices, palaces, museums, summer colonies of children, libraries, churches,

From *The Crisis*, November 1926.

monasteries, boyar houses, theatres, moving-picture houses, day nurseries and co-operatives. I have seen some celebrations — self-governing children in a school house of an evening and 200,000 children and youths marching on Youth Day. I have talked with peasants and laborers, Commissars of the Republic, teachers and children.

Alone and unaccompanied I have walked the miles of streets in Leningrad, Moscow, Nijni Novgorod and Kiev at morning, noon and night; I have trafficked on the curb and in the stores; I have watched crowds and audiences and groups. I have gathered some documents and figures, plied officials and teachers with questions and sat still and gazed at this Russia, that the spirit of its life and people might enter my veins.

I stand in astonishment and wonder at the revelation of Russia that has come to me. I may be partially deceived and half-informed. But if what I have seen with my eyes and heard with my ears in Russia is Bolshevism, I am a Bolshevik.

The Negro and Communism

The Scottsboro, Alabama, cases have brought squarely before the American Negro the question of his attitude toward Communism.

The importance of the Russian Revolution can not be gainsaid. It is easily the greatest event in the world since the French Revolution and possibly since the fall of Rome. The experiment is increasingly successful. Russia occupies the center of the world's attention today and as a state it is recognized by every civilized nation, except the United States, Spain, Portugal and some countries of South America.

The challenge to the capitalistic form of industry and to the governments which this form dominates, is more and more tremendous because of the present depression. If Socialism as a form of government and industry is on trial in Russia, capitalism as a form of industry and government is just as surely on trial throughout the world and is more and more clearly recognizing the fact.

THE AMERICAN WORKER

It has always been felt that the United States was an example of the extraordinary success of capitalistic industry, and that this was proven by the high wage paid labor and the high standard of intelligence and comfort prevalent in this country. Moreover, for many years, democratic political control of our government by the masses of the people made it possible to envisage without violence any kind of reform in government or industry which appeared to the people. Recently, however, the people of the United States have begun to recognize that their political power is curtailed by organized capital in

From *The Crisis*, September 1931.

industry and that in this industry, democracy does not prevail; and that until wider democracy does prevail in industry, democracy in government is seriously curtailed and often quite ineffective. Also, because of recurring depressions the high wage is in part illusory.

THE AMERICAN NEGRO

Moreover, there is in the United States one class of people who more than any other suffer under present conditions. Because of wholesale disfranchisement and a system of color caste, discriminatory legislation and widespread propaganda, 12,000,000 American Negroes have only a minimum of that curtailed freedom which the right to vote and influence on public opinion gives to white Americans. And in industry Negroes are for historic and social reasons upon the lowest round.

PROPOSED REFORM

The proposals to remedy the economic and political situation in America range from new legislation, better administration and government aid, offered by the Republican and Democratic parties, on to liberal movements fathered by Progressives, the Farmer-Labor movement and the Socialists, and finally to the revolutionary proposals of the Communists. The Progressives and Socialists propose in general increased government ownership of land and natural resources, state control of the larger public services and such progressive taxation of incomes and inheritance as shall decrease the number and power of the rich. The Communists, on the other hand, propose an entire sweeping away of the present organization of industry; the ownership of land, resources, machines and tools by the state, the conducting of business by the state under incomes which the state limits. And in order to introduce this complete Socialistic regime, Communists propose a revolutionary dictatorship by the working class, as the only sure, quick and effective path.

ADVICE TO NEGROES

With these appeals in his ears, what shall the American Negro do? In the letters from United States Senators published in this issue of The Crisis, we find, with all the sympathy and good-will expressed, a prevailing helplessness when it comes to advice on specific action. Reactionaries like Fess, Conservatives like Bulkley and Capper, Progressives like Borah and Norris, all can only say: "You have done as well as could be expected; you suffer many present disadvantages; there is nothing that we can do to help you, and your salvation lies in patience and further effort on your own part." The Socialist, as represented by Norman Thomas in the February *Crisis*, invites the Negro as a worker to vote for the Socialist Party as the party of workers. He offers the Negro no panacea for prejudice and caste but assumes that the uplift of the white worker will automatically emancipate the yellow, brown and black.

THE SCOTTSBORO CASES

Finally, the Scottsboro cases come and put new emphasis on the appeal of the Communists. Advocating the defense of the eight Alabama black boys, who without a shadow of doubt have been wrongly accused of crime, the Communists not only asked to take charge of the defense of these victims, but they proceeded to build on this case an appeal to the American Negro to join the Communist movement as the only solution of their problem.

Immediately, these two objects bring two important problems; first, can the Negroes with their present philosophy and leadership defend the Scottsboro cases successfully? Secondly, even if they can, will such defense help them to solve their problem of poverty and caste?

If the Communistic leadership in the United States had been broad-minded and far-sighted, it would have acknowledged frankly that the honesty, earnestness and intelligence of the N.A.A.C.P. during twenty years of desperate struggle proved this organization under present circumstances to be the only one, and its methods the only methods available, to defend these boys and it would have joined capitalists and laborers north and south, black and white in every endeavor to win freedom for victims threatened with judicial murder. Then beyond that and with Scottsboro as a crimson and terrible text, Communists could have proceeded to point out that legal defense alone, even if successful, will never solve the larger Negro problem but that further and more radical steps are needed.

COMMUNIST STRATEGY

Unfortunately, American Communists are neither wise nor intelligent. They sought to accomplish too much at one stroke. They tried to prove at once that the N.A.A.C.P. did not wish to defend the victims at Scottsboro and that the reason for this was that Negro leadership in the N.A.A.C.P. was allied with the capitalists. The first of these two efforts was silly and the Communists tried to accomplish it by deliberate lying and deception. They accused the N.A.A.C.P. of stealing, misuse of funds, lack of interest in the Scottsboro cases, cowardly surrender to malign forces, inefficiency and a policy of do-nothing.

Now whatever the N.A.A.C.P. has lacked, it is neither dishonest nor cowardly, and already events are proving clearly that the only effective defense of the Scottsboro boys must follow that which has been carefully organized, engineered and paid for by the N.A.A.C.P., and that the success of this defense is helped so far as the Communists cooperate by hiring bourgeois lawyers and appealing to bourgeois judges; but is hindered and made doubtful by ill-considered and foolish tactics against the powers in whose hands the fate of the Scottsboro victims lies.

If the Communists want these lads murdered, then their tactics of threatening judges and yelling for mass action on the part of white southern workers is calculated to insure this.

And, on the other hand, lying and deliberate misrepresentation of friends who are fighting for the same ideals as the Communists, are old capitalistic, bourgeois weapons of which the Communists ought to be ashamed. The final exploit at Camp Hill is worthy of the Russian Black Hundreds, whoever promoted it: black sharecroppers, half-starved and desperate were organized into a "Society for the Advancement of Colored People" and then induced to meet and protest against Scottsboro. Sheriff and white mob killed one and imprisoned 34. If this was instigated by Communists, it is too despicable for words; not because the plight of the black peons does not shriek for remedy but because this is no time to bedevil a delicate situation by drawing a red herring across the trail of eight innocent children.

Nevertheless, the N.A.A.C.P. will defend these 34 victims of Southern fear and communist irresponsibility.

The ultimate object of the Communists, was naturally not merely nor chiefly to save the boys accused at Scottsboro; it was to make this case a center of agitation to expose the helpless condition of Negroes, and to prove that anything less than the radical Communist program could not emancipate them.

THE NEGRO BOURGEOISIE

The question of the honesty and efficiency of the N.A.A.C.P. in the defense of the Scottsboro boys, just as in a dozen other cases over the length and breadth of the United States, is entirely separate from the question as to whether or not Negro leadership is tending toward socialism and communism or toward capitalism.

The charge of the Communists that the present set-up of Negro America is that of the petit bourgeois minority dominating a helpless black proletariat, and surrendering to white profiteers is simply a fantastic falsehood. The attempt to dominate Negro Americans by purely capitalistic ideas died with Booker T. Washington. The battle against it was begun by the Niagara Movement and out of the Niagara Movement arose the N.A.A.C.P. Since that time there has never been a moment when the dominating leadership of the American Negro has been mainly or even largely dominated by wealth or capital or by capitalistic ideals.

There are naturally some Negro capitalists: some large landowners, some landlords, some industrial leaders and some investors; but the great mass of Negro capital is not owned or controlled by this group. Negro capital consists mainly of small individual savings invested in homes, and in insurance, in lands for direct cultivation and individually used tools and machines. Even the automobiles owned by Negroes represent to a considerable extent personal investments, designed to counteract the insult of the "Jim Crow" car. The Insurance business, which represents a large amount of Negro capital is for mutual co-operation rather than exploitation. Its profit is limited and its methods directed by the State. Much of the retail business is done in small stores with small stocks of goods, where the owner works side by side with one or two helpers, and makes a personal profit less than a normal American wage. Negro professional men — lawyers, physicians, nurses and teachers — represent capital invested in their education and in their office equipment, and not in commercial exploitation. There are few colored manufacturers of material who speculate on the products of hired labor. Nine-tenths of the hired Negro labor is under the control of white capitalists. There is probably no group of 12 million persons in the modern world which exhibits smaller contrasts in personal income than the American Negro group. Their emancipation will not come, as among the Jews, from an internal readjustment and ousting of exploiters; rather it will come from a wholesale emancipation from the grip of the white exploiters without.

It is, of course, always possible, with the ideals of America, that a full fledged capitalistic system may develop in the Negro group; but the dominant leadership of the Negro today, and particularly the leadership represented by the N.A.A.C.P. represents no such tendency. For two generations the social leaders of the American Negro with very few exceptions have been poor men, depending for support on their salaries, owning little or no real property; few have been business men, none have been exploiters, and while there have been wide differences of ultimate ideal these leaders on the whole, have worked unselfishly for the uplift of the masses of Negro folk.

There is no group of leaders on earth who have so largely made common cause with the lowest of their race as educated American Negroes, and it is their foresight and sacrifice and theirs alone that has saved the American freedman from annihilation and degradation.

This is the class of leaders who have directed and organized and defended black folk in America and whatever their shortcomings and mistakes — and they are legion — their one great proof of success is the survival of the American Negro as the most intelligent and effective group of colored people fighting white civilization face to face and on its own ground, on the face of the earth.

The quintessence and final expression of this leadership is the N.A.A.C.P. For twenty years it has fought a battle more desperate than any other race conflict of modern times and it has fought with honesty and courage. It deserves from Russia something better than a kick in the back from the young jackasses who are leading Communism in America today.

WHAT IS THE N.A.A.C.P.?

The N.A.A.C.P. years ago laid down a clear and distinct program. Its object was to make 12 million Americans:

> *Physically free from peonage,*
> *Mentally free from ignorance,*
> *Politically free from disfranchisement,*
> *Socially free from insult.*

Limited as this platform may seem to perfectionists, it is so far in advance of anything ever attempted before in America, that it has gained an extraordinary following. On this platform we have succeeded in uniting white and black, employers and laborers, capitalists and communists, socialists and reformers, rich and poor. The funds which support this work come mainly from poor colored people, but on the other hand, we have in 20 years of struggle, enlisted the sympathy and co-operation of the rich, the white and the powerful; and so long as this co-operation is given upon the basis of the platform we have laid down, we seek and welcome it. On the other hand, we know perfectly well that the platform of the N.A.A.C.P. is no complete program of social reform. It is a pragmatic union of certain definite problems, while far beyond its program lies the whole question of the future of the darker races and the economic emancipation of the working classes.

WHITE LABOR

Beyond the Scottsboro cases and the slurs on Negro leadership, there still remains for Negroes and Communists, the pressing major question: How shall American Negroes be emancipated from economic slavery? In answer to this both Socialists and Communists attempted to show the Negro that his interest lies with that of white labor. That kind of talk to the American Negro is like a red rag to a bull. Throughout the history of the Negro in America, white labor has been the black man's enemy, his oppressor, his red murderer. Mobs, riots and the discrimination of trade unions have been used to kill, harass and starve black men. White labor disfranchised Negro labor in the South, is keeping them out of jobs and decent living quarters in the North, and is curtailing their education and civil and social privileges throughout the nation. White laborers have formed the backbone of the Ku Klux Klan and have furnished hands and ropes to lynch 3,560 Negroes since 1882.

Since the death of Terence Powderly not a single great white labor leader in the United States has wholeheartedly and honestly espoused the cause of justice to black workers.

Socialists and Communists explain this easily: white labor in its ignorance and poverty has been misled by the propaganda of white capital, whose policy is to divide labor into classes, races and unions and pit one against the other. There is an immense amount of truth in this explanation: Newspapers, social standards, race pride, competition for jobs, all work to set white against black. But white American Laborers are not fools. And with few exceptions the more intelligent they are, the higher they rise, the more efficient they become, the more determined they are to keep Negroes under their heels. It is no mere coincidence that Labor's present representative in the President's cabinet belongs to a union that will not admit a Negro, and himself was for years active in West Virginia in driving Negroes out of decent jobs. It is intelligent white labor that today keeps Negroes out of the trades, refuses them decent homes to live in and helps nullify their vote. Whatever ideals white labor today strives for in America, it would surrender nearly every one before it would recognize a Negro as a man.

COMMUNISTS AND THE
COLOR LINE

The American Communists have made a courageous fight against the color line among the workers. They have solicited and admitted Negro members. They have insisted in their strikes and agitation to let Negroes fight with them and that the object of their fighting is for black workers as well as white workers. But in this they have gone dead against the thought and desire of the overwhelming mass of white workers, and face today a dead blank wall even in their own school in Arkansas. Thereupon instead of acknowledging defeat in their effort to make white labor abolish the color line, they turn and accuse Negroes of not sympathizing with the ideals of Labor!

Socialists have been franker. They learned that American labor would not carry the Negro and they very calmly unloaded him. They allude to him vaguely and as an afterthought in their books and platforms. The American Socialist party is out to emancipate the white worker and if this does not automatically free the colored man, he can continue in slavery. The only time that so fine a man and so logical a reasoner as Norman Thomas becomes vague and incoherent is when he touches the black man, and consequently he touches him as seldom as possible.

When, therefore, Negro leaders refuse to lay down arms and surrender their brains and action to "Nigger"-hating white workers, liberals and socialists understand exactly the reasons for this and spend what energy they can spare in pointing out to white workers the necessity of recognizing Negroes. But the Communists, younger and newer, largely of foreign extraction, and thus discounting the hell of American prejudice, easily are led to blame the Negroes and to try to explain the intolerable American situation on the basis of an imported Marxist pattern, which does not at all fit the situation.

For instance, from Moscow comes this statement to explain Scottsboro and Camp Hill:

"*Again, as in the case of Sacco and Vanzetti, the American Bourgeoisie is attempting to go against proletarian social opinion. It is attempting to carry through its criminal provocation to the very end.*"

This is a ludicrous misapprehension of local conditions and illustrates the error into which long distance interpretation, unsupported by real knowledge, may fall. The Sacco-Vanzetti cases in Massachusetts represented the fight of prejudiced, entrenched capital against racial propaganda; but in Jackson County, northeastern Alabama, where Scottsboro is situated, there are over 33,000 Native whites and less than 3,000 Negroes. The vast majority of these whites belong to the laboring class and they formed the white proletarian mob which is determined to kill the eight Negro boys. Such mobs of white workers demand the right to kill "niggers" whenever their passions, especially in sexual matters, are inflamed by propaganda. The capitalists are willing to curb this blood lust when it interferes with their profits. They know that the murder of 8 innocent black boys will hurt organized industry and government in Alabama; but as long as 10,000 armed white workers demand these victims they do not dare move. Into this delicate and contradictory situation, the Communists hurl themselves and pretend to speak for the workers. They not only do not speak for the white workers but they even intensify the blind prejudices of these lynchers and leave the Negro workers helpless on the one hand and the white capitalists scared to death on the other.

The persons who are killing blacks in Northern Alabama and demanding blood sacrifice are the white workers — sharecroppers, trade unionists and artisans. The capitalists are against mob-law and violence and would listen to reason and justice in the long run because industrial peace increases their profits. On the other hand, the white workers want to kill the competition of "Niggers." Thereupon, the Communists, seizing leadership of the poorest and most ignorant blacks head them toward inevitable slaughter and jail-slavery, while they hide safely in Chattanooga and Harlem.

American Negroes do not propose to be the shock troops of the Communist Revolution, driven out in front to death, cruelty and humiliation in order to win victories for white workers. They are picking no chestnuts from the fire, neither for capital nor white labor.

Negroes know perfectly well that whenever they try to lead revolution in America, the nation will unite as one fist to crush them and them alone. There is no conceivable idea that seems to the present overwhelming majority of Americans higher than keeping Negroes "in their place."

Negroes perceive clearly that the real interests of the white worker are identical with the interests of the black worker; but until the white worker recognizes this, the black worker is compelled in sheer self-defense to refuse to be made the sacrificial goat.

THE NEGRO AND THE RICH

The remaining grain of truth in the Communist attack on Negro leadership is the well-known fact that American wealth has helped the American Negro and that without this help the Negro could not have attained his present advancement. American courts from the Supreme Court down are domi-

591

nated by wealth and Big Business, yet they are today the Negro's only protection against complete disfranchisement, segregation and the abolition of his public schools. Higher education for Negroes is the gift of the Standard Oil, the Power Trust, the Steel Trust and the Mail Order Chain Stores, together with the aristocratic Christian Church; but these have given Negroes 40,000 black leaders to fight white folk on their own level and in their own language. Big industry in the last 10 years has opened occupations for a million Negro workers, without which we would have starved in jails and gutters.

Socialists and Communists may sneer and say that the capitalists sought in all this profit, cheap labor, strike-breakers and the training of conservative, reactionary leaders. They did. But Negroes sought food, clothes, shelter and knowledge to stave off death and slavery and only damned fools would have refused the gift.

Moreover, we who receive education as the dole of the rich have not all become slaves of wealth.

Meanwhile, what have white workers and radical reformers done for Negroes? By strikes and agitation, by self-denial and sacrifice, they have raised wages and bettered working conditions; but they did this for themselves and only shared their gains with Negroes when they had to. They have preached freedom, political power, manhood rights and social uplift for everybody, when nobody objected; but for "white people only" when anybody demanded it. White labor segregated Dr. Sweet in Detroit; white laborers chased the Arkansas peons; white laborers steal the black children's school funds in South Carolina, white laborers lynch Negroes in Alabama. Negroes owe much to white labor but it is not all, or mostly, on the credit side of the ledger.

THE NEXT STEP

Where does this leave the Negro? As a practical program, it leaves him just where he was before the Russian Revolution; sympathetic with Russia and hopeful for its ultimate success in establishing a Socialistic state; sympathetic with the efforts of the American workingman to establish democratic control of industry in this land; absolutely certain that as a laborer his interests are the interests of all labor; but nevertheless fighting doggedly on the old battleground, led by the N.A.A.C.P. to make the Negro laborer a laborer on equal social footing with the white laborer: to maintain the Negro's right to a political vote, notwithstanding the fact that this vote means increasingly less and less to all voters; to vindicate in the courts the Negro's civil rights and American citizenship, even though he knows how the courts are prostituted to the power of wealth; and above all, determined by plain talk and agitation to show the intolerable injustice with which America and the world treats the colored peoples and to continue to insist that in this injustice, the white workers of Europe and America are just as culpable as the white owners of capital; and that these workers can gain black men as allies only and insofar as they frankly, fairly and completely abolish the Color Line.

Present organization of industry for private profit and control of government by concentrated wealth is doomed to disaster. It must change and fall if civilization survives. The foundation of its present world-wide power is the slavery and semi-slavery of the colored world including the American Negroes. Until the colored man, yellow, red, brown, and black, becomes free, articulate, intelligent and the receiver of a decent income, white capital will use the profit derived from his degradation to keep white labor in chains.

There is no doubt, then, as to the future, or as to where the true interests of American Negroes lie. There is no doubt, too, but that the first step toward the emancipation of colored labor must come from white labor.

The Black Worker

How black men, coming to America in the sixteenth, seventeenth, eighteenth and nineteenth centuries, became a central thread in the history of the United States, at once a challenge to its democracy and always an important part of its economic history and social development

Easily the most dramatic episode in American history was the sudden move to free four million black slaves in an effort to stop a great civil war, to end forty years of bitter controversy, and to appease the moral sense of civilization.

From the day of its birth, the anomaly of slavery plagued a nation which asserted the equality of all men, and sought to derive powers of government from the consent of the governed. Within sound of the voices of those who said this lived more than half a million black slaves, forming nearly one-fifth of the population of a new nation.

The black population at the time of the first census had risen to three-quarters of a million, and there were over a million at the beginning of the nineteenth century. Before 1830, the blacks had passed the two million mark, helped by the increased importations just before 1808, and the illicit smuggling up until 1820. By their own reproduction, the Negroes reached 3,638,808 in 1850, and before the Civil War, stood at 4,441,830. They were 10% of the whole population of the nation in 1700, 22% in 1750, 18.9% in 1800 and 11.6% in 1900.

These workers were not all black and not all Africans and not all slaves. In 1860, at least 90% were born in the United States, 13% were visibly of white as well as Negro descent and actually more than one-fourth were probably of

From *Black Reconstruction in America: An Essay Toward a History of the Part Which Black Folk Played in the Attempt to Reconstruct Democracy in America, 1860–1880* (1935).

white, Indian and Negro blood. In 1860, 11% of these dark folk were free workers.

In origin, the slaves represented everything African, although most of themoriginated on or near the West Coast. Yet among them appeared the great Bantu tribes from Sierra Leone to South Africa; the Sudanese, straight across the center of the continent, from the Atlantic to the Valley of the Nile; the Nilotic Negroes and the black and brown Hamites, allied with Egypt; the tribes of the great lakes; the Pygmies and the Hottentots; and in addition to these, distinct traces of both Berber and Arab blood. There is no doubt of the presence of all these various elements in the mass of 10,000,000 or more Negroes transported from Africa to the various Americas, from the fifteenth to the nineteenth centuries.

Most of them that came to the continent went through West Indian tutelage, and thus finally appeared in the United States. They brought with them their religion and rhythmic song, and some traces of their art and tribal customs. And after a lapse of two and one-half centuries, the Negroes became a settled working population, speaking English or French, professing Christianity, and used principally in agricultural toil. Moreover, they so mingled their blood with white and red America that today less than 25% of the Negro Americans are of unmixed African descent.

So long as slavery was a matter of race and color, it made the conscience of the nation uneasy and continually affronted its ideals. The men who wrote the Constitution sought by every evasion, and almost by subterfuge, to keep recognition of slavery out of the basic form of the new government. They founded their hopes on the prohibition of the slave trade, being sure that without continual additions from abroad, this tropical people would not long survive, and thus the problem of slavery would disappear in death. They miscalculated, or did not foresee the changing economic world. It might be more profitable in the West Indies to kill the slaves by overwork and import cheap Africans; but in America without a slave trade, it paid to conserve the slave and let him multiply. When, therefore, manifestly the Negroes were not dying out, there came quite naturally new excuses and explanations. It was a matter of social condition. Gradually these people would be free; but freedom could only come to the bulk as the freed were transplanted to their own land and country, since the living together of black and white in America was unthinkable. So again the nation waited, and its conscience sank to sleep.

But in a rich and eager land, wealth and work multiplied. They twisted new and intricate patterns around the earth. Slowly but mightily these black workers were integrated into modern industry. On free and fertile land Americans raised, not simply sugar as a cheap sweetening, rice for food and tobacco as a new and tickling luxury; but they began to grow a fiber that clothed the masses of a ragged world. Cotton grew so swiftly that the 9,000 bales of cotton which the new nation scarcely noticed in 1791 became 79,000 in 1800; and with this increase, walked economic revolution in a dozen different lines. The cotton crop reached one-half million bales in 1822, a million bales in 1831, two million in 1840, three million in 1852, and in the year of secession, stood at the then enormous total of five million bales.

Such facts and others, coupled with the increase of the slaves to which they were related as both cause and effect, meant a new world; and all the more so because with increase in American cotton and Negro slaves, came both by chance and ingenuity new miracles for manufacturing, and particularly for the spinning and weaving of cloth.

The giant forces of water and of steam were harnessed to do the world's work, and the black workers of America bent at the bottom of a growing pyramid of commerce and industry; and they not only could not be spared, if this new economic organization was to expand, but rather they became the cause of new political demands and alignments, of new dreams of power and visions of empire.

First of all, their work called for widening stretches of new, rich, black soil — in Florida, in Louisiana, in Mexico; even in Kansas. This land, added to cheap labor, and labor easily regulated and distributed, made profits so high that a whole system of culture arose in the South, with a new leisure and social philosophy. Black labor became the foundation stone not only of the Southern social structure, but of Northern manufacture and commerce, of the English factory system, of European commerce, of buying and selling on a world-wide scale; new cities were built on the results of black labor, and a new labor problem, involving all white labor, arose both in Europe and America.

Thus, the old difficulties and paradoxes appeared in new dress. It became easy to say and easier to prove that these black men were not men in the sense that white men were, and could never be, in the same sense, free. Their slavery was a matter of both race and social condition, but the condition was limited and determined by race. They were congenital wards and children, to be well-treated and cared for, but far happier and safer here than in their own land. As the Richmond, Virginia, *Examiner* put it in 1854:

"Let us not bother our brains about what *Providence* intends to do with our Negroes in the distant future, but glory in and profit to the utmost by what He has done for them in transplanting them here, and setting them to work on our plantations. . . . True philanthropy to the Negro, begins, like charity, at home; and if Southern men would act as if the canopy of heaven were inscribed with a covenant, in letters of fire, that *the Negro is here, and here forever; is our property, and ours forever;* . . . they would accomplish more good for the race in five years than they boast the institution itself to have accomplished in two centuries. . . ."

On the other hand, the growing exploitation of white labor in Europe, the rise of the factory system, the increased monopoly of land, and the problem of the distribution of political power, began to send wave after wave of immigrants to America, looking for new freedom, new opportunity and new democracy.

The opportunity for real and new democracy in America was broad. Political power at first was, as usual, confined to property holders and an aristocracy of birth and learning. But it was never securely based on land. Land was free and both land and property were possible to nearly every thrifty worker. Schools began early to multiply and open their doors even to the poor laborer. Birth began to count for less and less and America became to the world a land of economic opportunity. So the world came to America, even before the Revolution, and afterwards during the nineteenth century, nineteen million immigrants entered the United States.

When we compare these figures with the cotton crop and the increase of black workers, we see how the economic problem increased in intricacy. This intricacy is shown by the persons in the drama and their differing and opposing interests. There were the native-born Americans, largely of English descent, who were the property holders and employers; and even so far as they were poor, they looked forward to the time when they would accumulate capital and become, as they put it, economically "independent." Then there were the new immigrants, torn with a certain violence from their older social and economic surroundings; strangers in a new land, with visions of rising in the social and economic world by means of labor. They differed in language and social status, varying from the half-starved Irish peasant to the educated German and English artisan. There were the free Negroes: those of the North free in some cases for many generations, and voters; and in other cases, fugitives, new come from the South, with little skill and small knowledge of life and labor in their new environment. There were the free Negroes of the South, an unstable, harried class, living on sufferance of the law, and the good will of white patrons, and yet rising to be workers and sometimes owners of property and even of slaves, and cultured citizens. There was the great mass of poor whites, disinherited of their economic portion by competition with the slave system, and land monopoly.

In the earlier history of the South, free Negroes had the right to vote. Indeed, so far as the letter of the law was concerned, there was not a single Southern colony in which a black man who owned the requisite amount of property, and complied with other conditions, did not at some period have the legal right to vote.

Negroes voted in Virginia as late as 1723, when the assembly enacted that no free Negro, mulatto or Indian "shall hereafter have any vote at the elections of burgesses or any election whatsoever." In North Carolina, by the Act of 1734, a former discrimination against Negro voters was laid aside and not reënacted until 1835.

A complaint in South Carolina, in 1701, said:

"Several free Negroes were receiv'd, & taken for as good Electors as the best Freeholders in the Province. So that we leave it with Your Lordships to judge whether admitting Aliens, Strangers, Servants, Negroes, &c, as good and qualified Voters, can be thought any ways agreeable to King Charles' Patent to Your Lordships, or the English Constitution of Government." Again in 1716, Jews and Negroes, who had been voting, were expressly excluded. In Georgia, there was at first no color discrimination, although only owners of fifty acres of land could vote. In 1761, voting was expressly confined to white men.[1]

In the states carved out of the Southwest, they were disfranchised as soon as the state came into the Union, although in Kentucky they voted between 1792 and 1799, and Tennessee allowed free Negroes to vote in her constitution of 1796.

In North Carolina, where even disfranchisement, in 1835, did not apply to Negroes who already had the right to vote, it was said that the several hundred Negroes who had been voting before then usually voted prudently and judiciously.

In Delaware and Maryland they voted in the latter part of the eighteenth century. In Louisiana, Negroes who had had the right to vote during territorial status were not disfranchised.

To sum up, in colonial times, the free Negro was excluded from the suffrage only in Georgia, South Carolina and Virginia. In the Border States, Delaware disfranchised the Negro in 1792; Maryland in 1783 and 1810.

In the Southeast, Florida disfranchised Negroes in 1845; and in the Southwest, Louisiana disfranchised them in 1812; Mississippi in 1817; Alabama in 1819; Missouri, 1821; Arkansas in 1836; Texas, 1845. Georgia in her constitution of 1777 confined voters to white males; but this was omitted in the constitutions of 1789 and 1798.

As slavery grew to a system and the Cotton Kingdom began to expand into imperial white domination, a free Negro was a contradiction, a threat and a menace. As a thief and a vagabond, he threatened society; but as an educated property holder, a successful mechanic or even professional man, he more than threatened slavery. He contradicted and undermined it. He must not be. He must be suppressed, enslaved, colonized. And nothing so bad could be said about him that did not easily appear as true to slaveholders.

In the North, Negroes, for the most part, received political enfranchisement with the white laboring classes. In 1778, the Congress of the Confederation twice refused to insert the word "white" in the Articles of Confederation in asserting that free inhabitants in each state should be entitled to all the privileges and immunities of free citizens of the several states. In the law of 1783, free Negroes were recognized as a basis of taxation, and in 1784, they were recognized as voters in the territories. In the Northwest Ordinance of 1787, "free male inhabitants of full age" were recognized as voters.

The few Negroes that were in Maine, New Hampshire and Vermont could vote if they had the property qualifications. In Connecticut they were disfranchised in 1814; in 1865 this restriction was retained, and Negroes did not regain the right until after the Civil War. In New Jersey, they were disfranchised in 1807, but regained the right in 1820 and lost it again in 1847. Negroes voted in New York in the eighteenth century, then were disfranchised, but in 1821 were permitted to vote with a discriminatory property qualification of $250. No property qualification was required of whites. Attempts were made at various times to remove this qualification but it was not removed until 1870. In Rhode Island they were disfranchised in the constitution which followed Dorr's Rebellion, but finally allowed to vote in 1842. In Pennsylvania, they were allowed to vote until 1838 when the "reform" convention restricted the suffrage to whites.

The Western States as territories did not usually restrict the suffrage, but as they were admitted to the Union they disfranchised the Negroes: Ohio in 1803; Indiana in 1816; Illinois in 1818; Michigan in 1837; Iowa in 1846; Wisconsin in 1848; Minnesota in 1858; and Kansas in 1861.

The Northwest Ordinance and even the Louisiana Purchase had made no color discrimination in legal and political rights. But the states admitted from this territory, specifically and from the first, denied free black men the right to vote and passed codes of black laws in Ohio, Indiana and elsewhere, instigated largely by the attitude and fears of the immigrant poor whites from the South. Thus, at first, in Kansas and the West, the problem of the black worker was narrow and specific. Neither the North nor the West asked that black labor in the United States be free and enfranchised. On the contrary, they accepted slave labor as a fact; but they were determined that it should be territorially restricted, and should not compete with free white labor.

What was this industrial system for which the South fought and risked life, reputation and wealth and which a growing element in the North viewed first with hesitating tolerance, then with distaste and finally with economic fear and moral horror? What did it mean to be a slave? It is hard to imagine it today. We think of oppression beyond all conception: cruelty, degradation, whipping and starvation, the absolute negation of human rights; or on the contrary, we may think of the ordinary worker the world over today, slaving ten, twelve, or fourteen hours a day, with not enough to eat, compelled by his physical necessities to do this and not to do that, curtailed in his movements and his possibilities; and we say, here, too, is a slave called a "free worker," and slavery is merely a matter of name.

But there was in 1863 a real meaning to slavery different from that we may apply to the laborer today. It was in part psychological, the enforced personal feeling of inferiority, the calling of another Master; the standing with hat in hand. It was the helplessness. It was the defenselessness of family life. It was the submergence below the arbitrary will of any sort of individual. It was without doubt worse in these vital respects than that which exists today in Europe or America. Its analogue today is the yellow, brown and black laborer in China and India, in Africa, in the forests of the Amazon; and it was this slavery that fell in America.

The slavery of Negroes in the South was not usually a deliberately cruel and oppressive system. It did not mean systematic starvation or murder. On the other hand, it is just as difficult to conceive as quite true the idyllic picture of a patriarchal state with cultured and humane masters under whom slaves were as children, guided and trained in work and play, given even such mental training as was for their good, and for the well-being of the surrounding world.

The victims of Southern slavery were often happy; had usually adequate food for their health, and shelter sufficient for a mild climate. The Southerners could say with some justification that when the mass of their field hands were compared with the worst class of laborers in the slums of New York and Philadelphia, and the factory towns of New England, the black slaves were as well off and in some particulars better off. Slaves lived largely in the country where health conditions were better; they worked in the open air, and their hours were about the current hours for peasants throughout Europe. They received no formal education, and neither did the Irish peasant, the English factory-laborer, nor the German *Bauer*; and in contrast with these free white laborers, the Negroes were protected by a certain primitive sort of old-age pension, job insurance, and sickness insurance; that is, they must be supported in some fashion, when they were too old to work; they must have attention in sickness, for they represented invested capital; and they could never be among the unemployed.

On the other hand, it is just as true that Negro slaves in America represented the worst and lowest conditions among modern laborers. One estimate is that the maintenance of a slave in the South cost the master about $19 a year, which means that they were among the poorest paid laborers in the modern world. They represented in a very real sense the ultimate degradation of man. Indeed, the system was so reactionary, so utterly inconsistent with modern progress, that we simply cannot grasp it today. No matter how degraded the factory hand, he is not real estate. The tragedy of the black slave's position was precisely this; his absolute subjection to the individual will of an owner and to "the cruelty and injustice which are the invariable consequences of the exercise of irresponsible power, especially where authority must be sometimes delegated by the planter to agents of inferior education and coarser feelings."

The proof of this lies clearly written in the slave codes. Slaves were not considered men. They had no right of petition. They were "devisable like any other chattel." They could own nothing; they could make no contracts; they could hold no property, nor traffic in property; they could not hire out; they could not legally marry nor constitute families; they could not control their children; they could not appeal from their master; they could be punished at will. They could not testify in court; they could be imprisoned by their owners, and the criminal offense of assault and battery could not be committed on the person of a slave. The "willful, malicious and deliberate murder" of a slave was punishable by death, but such a crime was practically impossible of proof. The slave owed to his master and all his family a respect "without bounds, and an absolute obedience." This authority could be transmitted to others. A slave could not sue his master; had no right of redemption; no right to education or religion; a promise made to a slave by his master had no force nor validity. Children followed the condition of the slave mother. The slave could have no access to the judiciary. A slave might be condemned to death for striking any white person.

Looking at these accounts, "it is safe to say that the law regards a Negro slave, so far as his civil status is concerned, purely and absolutely property, to be bought and sold and pass and descend as a tract of land, a horse, or an ox."[2]

The whole legal status of slavery was enunciated in the extraordinary statement of a Chief Justice of the United States that Negroes had always been regarded in America "as having no rights which a white man was bound to respect."

It may be said with truth that the law was often harsher than the practice. Nevertheless, these laws and decisions represent the legally permissible possibilities, and the only curb upon the power of the master was his sense of humanity and decency, on the one hand, and the conserving of his investment on the other. Of the humanity of large numbers of Southern masters there can be no doubt. In some cases, they gave their slaves a fatherly care. And yet even in such cases the strain upon their ability to care for large numbers of people and the necessity of entrusting the care of the slaves to other hands than their own, led to much suffering and cruelty.

The matter of his investment in land and slaves greatly curtailed the owner's freedom of action. Under the competition of growing industrial organization, the slave system was indeed the source of immense profits. But for the slave owner and landlord to keep a large or even reasonable share of these profits was increasingly difficult. The price of the slave produce in the open market could be hammered down by merchants and traders acting with knowledge and collusion. And the slave owner was, therefore, continually forced to find his profit not in the high price of cotton and sugar, but in beating even further down the cost of his slave labor. This made the slave owners in early days kill the slave by overwork and renew their working stock; it led to the widely organized interstate slave trade between the Border States and the Cotton Kingdom of the Southern South; it led to neglect and the breaking up of families, and it could not protect the slave against the cruelty, lust and neglect of certain owners.

Thus human slavery in the South pointed and led in two singularly contradictory and paradoxical directions — toward the deliberate commercial breeding and sale of human labor for profit and toward the intermingling of black and white blood. The slaveholders shrank from acknowledging either set of facts but they were clear and undeniable.

In this vital respect, the slave laborer differed from all others of his day: he could be sold; he could, at the will of a single individual, be transferred for life a thousand miles or more. His family, wife and children could be legally and absolutely taken from him. Free laborers today are compelled to wander in search for work and food; their families are deserted for want of wages; but in all this there is no such direct barter in human flesh. It was a sharp accentuation of control over men beyond the modern labor reserve or the contract coolie system.

Negroes could be sold — actually sold as we sell cattle with no reference to calves or bulls, or recognition of family. It was a nasty business. The white South was properly ashamed of it and continually belittled and almost denied it. But it was a stark and bitter fact. Southern papers of the Border States were filled with advertisements: — "I wish to purchase fifty Negroes of both sexes from 6 to 30 years of age for which I will give the highest cash prices."

"Wanted to purchase — Negroes of every description, age and sex."

The consequent disruption of families is proven beyond doubt:

"Fifty Dollars reward. — Ran away from the subscriber, a Negro girl, named Maria. She is of a copper color, between 13 and 14 years of age — bareheaded and barefooted. She is small for her age — very sprightly and very likely. She stated she was *going to see her mother* at Maysville. Sanford Tomson."

"Committed to jail of Madison County, a Negro woman, who calls her name Fanny, and says she belongs to William Miller, of Mobile. She formerly belonged to John Givins, of this county, who now owns *several of her children*. David Shropshire, Jailer."

"Fifty Dollar reward. — Ran away from the subscriber, his Negro man Pauladore, commonly called Paul. I understand Gen. R. Y. Hayne *has purchased his wife and children* from H. L. Pinckney, Esq., and has them on his plantation at Goosecreek, where, no doubt, the fellow is frequently *lurking*. T. Davis." One can see Pauladore "lurking" about his wife and children.[3]

The system of slavery demanded a special police force and such a force was made possible and unusually effective by the presence of the poor whites. This explains the difference between the slave revolts in the West Indies, and the lack of effective revolt in the Southern United States. In the West Indies, the power over the slave was held by the whites and carried out by them and such Negroes as they could trust. In the South, on the other hand, the great planters formed proportionately quite as small a class but they had singularly enough at their command some five million poor whites; that is, there were actually more white people to police the slaves than there were slaves. Considering the economic rivalry of the black and white worker in the North, it would have seemed natural that the poor white would have refused to police the slaves. But two considerations led him in the opposite direction. First of all, it gave him work and some authority as overseer, slave driver, and member of the patrol system. But above and beyond this, it fed his vanity because it associated him with the masters. Slavery bred in the poor white a dislike of Negro toil of all sorts. He never regarded himself as a laborer, or as part of any labor movement. If he had any ambition at all it was to become a planter and to own "niggers." To these Negroes he transferred all the dislike and hatred which he had for the whole slave system. The result was that the system was held stable and intact by the poor white. Even with the late ruin of Haiti before their eyes, the planters, stirred as they were, were nevertheless able to stamp out slave revolt. The dozen revolts of the eighteenth century had dwindled to the plot of Gabriel in 1800, Vesey in 1822, of Nat Turner in 1831 and crews of the *Amistad* and *Creole* in 1839 and 1841. Gradually the whole white South became an armed and commissioned camp to keep Negroes in slavery and to kill the black rebel.

But even the poor white, led by the planter, would not have kept the black slave in nearly so complete control had it not been for what may be called the Safety Valve of Slavery; and that was the chance which a vigorous and determined slave had to run away to freedom.

Under the situation as it developed between 1830 and 1860 there were grave losses to the capital invested in black workers. Encouraged by the idealism of those Northern thinkers who insisted that Negroes were human, the black worker sought freedom by running away from slavery. The physical geography of America with its paths north, by swamp, river and mountain range; the daring of black revolutionists like Henson and Tubman; and the extra-legal efforts of abolitionists made this more and more easy.

One cannot know the real facts concerning the number of fugitives, but despite the fear of advertising the losses, the emphasis put upon fugitive slaves by the South shows that it was an important economic item. It is certain from the bitter effort to increase the efficiency of the fugitive slave law that the losses from runaways were widespread and continuous; and the increase in the interstate slave trade from Border States to the deep South, together with the increase in the price of slaves, showed a growing pressure. At the beginning of the nineteenth century, one bought an average slave for $200; while in 1860 the price ranged from $1,400 to $2,000.

Not only was the fugitive slave important because of the actual loss involved, but for potentialities in the future. These free Negroes were furnishing a leadership for the mass of the black workers, and especially they were furnishing a text for the abolition idealists. Fugitive slaves, like Frederick Douglass and others humbler and less gifted, increased the number of abolitionists by thousands and spelled the doom of slavery.

The true significance of slavery in the United States to the whole social development of America lay in the ultimate relation of slaves to democracy. What were to be the limits of democratic control in the United States? If all labor, black as well as white, became free — were given schools and the right to vote — what control could or should be set to the power and action of these laborers? Was the rule of the mass of Americans to be unlimited, and the right to rule extended to all men regardless of race and color, or if not, what power of dictatorship and control; and how would property and privilege be protected? This was the great and primary question which was in the minds of the men who wrote the Constitution of the United States and continued in the minds of thinkers down through the slavery controversy. It still remains with the world as the problem of democracy expands and touches all races and nations.

And of all human development, ancient and modern, not the least singular and significant is the philosophy of life and action which slavery bred in the souls of black folk. In most respects its expression was stilted and confused; the rolling periods of Hebrew prophecy and biblical legend furnished inaccurate but splendid words. The subtle folk-lore of Africa, with whimsy and parable, veiled wish and wisdom; and above all fell the anointing chrism of the slave music, the only gift of pure art in America.

Beneath the Veil lay right and wrong, vengeance and love, and sometimes throwing aside the veil, a soul of sweet Beauty and Truth stood revealed. Nothing else of art or religion did the slave South give to the world, except the

Negro song and story. And even after slavery, down to our day, it has added but little to this gift. One has but to remember as symbol of it all, still unspoiled by petty artisans, the legend of John Henry, the mighty black, who broke his heart working against the machine, and died "with his Hammer in His Hand."

Up from this slavery gradually climbed the Free Negro with clearer, modern expression and more definite aim long before the emancipation of 1863. His greatest effort lay in his coöperation with the Abolition movement. He knew he was not free until all Negroes were free. Individual Negroes became exhibits of the possibilities of the Negro race, if once it was raised above the status of slavery. Even when, as so often, the Negro became Court Jester to the ignorant American mob, he made his plea in his songs and antics.

Thus spoke "the noblest slave that ever God set free," Frederick Douglass in 1852, in his 4th of July oration at Rochester, voicing the frank and fearless criticism of the black worker:

"What, to the American slave, is your 4th of July? I answer: a day that reveals to him, more than all other days in the year, the gross injustice and cruelty to which he is the constant victim. To him your celebration is a sham; your boasted liberty, an unholy license; your national greatness, swelling vanity; your sounds of rejoicing are empty and heartless; your denunciation of tyrants, brass-fronted impudence; your shouts of liberty and equality, hollow mockery; your prayers and hymns, your sermons and thanksgivings, with all your religious parade and solemnity, are, to him, mere bombast, fraud, deception, impiety and hypocrisy — a thin veil to cover up crimes which would disgrace a nation of savages. . . .

"You boast of your love of liberty, your superior civilization, and your pure Christianity, while the whole political power of the nation (as embodied in the two great political parties) is solemnly pledged to support and perpetuate the enslavement of three millions of your countrymen. You hurl your anathemas at the crown-headed tyrants of Russia and Austria and pride yourselves on your democratic institutions, while you yourselves consent to be the mere *tools* and *body-guards* of the tyrants of Virginia and Carolina. You invite to your shores fugitives of oppression from abroad, honor them with banquets, greet them with ovations, cheer them, toast them, salute them, protect them, and pour out your money to them like water; but the fugitives from your own land you advertise, hunt, arrest, shoot, and kill. You glory in your refinement and your universal education; yet you maintain a system as barbarous and dreadful as ever stained the character of a nation — a system begun in avarice, supported in pride, and perpetuated in cruelty. You shed tears over fallen Hungary, and make the sad story of her wrongs the theme of your poets, statesmen, and orators, till your gallant sons are ready to fly to arms to vindicate her cause against the oppressor; but, in regard to the ten thousand wrongs of the

American slave, you would enforce the strictest silence, and would hail him as an enemy of the nation who dares to make those wrongs the subject of public discourse!"[4]

Above all, we must remember the black worker was the ultimate exploited; that he formed that mass of labor which had neither wish nor power to escape from the labor status, in order to directly exploit other laborers, or indirectly, by alliance with capital, to share in their exploitation. To be sure, the black mass, developed again and again, here and there, capitalistic groups in New Orleans, in Charleston and in Philadelphia; groups willing to join white capital in exploiting labor; but they were driven back into the mass by racial prejudice before they had reached a permanent foothold; and thus became all the more bitter against all organization which by means of race prejudice, or the monopoly of wealth, sought to exclude men from making a living.

It was thus the black worker, as founding stone of a new economic system in the nineteenth century and for the modern world, who brought civil war in America. He was its underlying cause, in spite of every effort to base the strife upon union and national power.

That dark and vast sea of human labor in China and India, the South Seas and all Africa; in the West Indies and Central America and in the United States — that great majority of mankind, on whose bent and broken backs rest today the founding stones of modern industry — shares a common destiny; it is despised and rejected by race and color; paid a wage below the level of decent living; driven, beaten, prisoned and enslaved in all but name; spawning the world's raw material and luxury — cotton, wool, coffee, tea, cocoa, palm oil, fibers, spices, rubber, silks, lumber, copper, gold, diamonds, leather — how shall we end the list and where? All these are gathered up at prices lowest of the low, manufactured, transformed and transported at fabulous gain; and the resultant wealth is distributed and displayed and made the basis of world power and universal dominion and armed arrogance in London and Paris, Berlin and Rome, New York and Rio de Janeiro.

Here is the real modern labor problem. Here is the kernel of the problem of Religion and Democracy, of Humanity. Words and futile gestures avail nothing. Out of the exploitation of the dark proletariat comes the Surplus Value filched from human beasts which, in cultured lands, the Machine and harnessed Power veil and conceal. The emancipation of man is the emancipation of labor and the emancipation of labor is the freeing of that basic majority of workers who are yellow, brown and black.

> Dark, shackled knights of labor, clinging still
> Amidst a universal wreck of faith
> To cheerfulness, and foreigners to hate.

These know ye not, these have ye not received,
But these shall speak to you Beatitudes.
Around them surge the tides of all your strife,
Above them rise the august monuments
Of all your outward splendor, but they stand
Unenvious in thought, and bide their time.

Leslie P. Hill

Notes

1. Compare A. E. McKinley, *The Suffrage Franchise in the Thirteen English Colonies in America*, p. 137.
2. *A Picture of Slavery Drawn from the Decisions of Southern Courts*, p. 5.
3. Compare Bancroft, *Slave-Trading in the Old South*; Weld, *American Slavery as It Is*.
4. Woodson, *Negro Orators and Their Orations*, pp. 218–19.

Lifting from the Bottom

We have been taught to think in terms of Classes: of Bests and the Smartest. Our whole education ignores the Mass except as the occasional and doubtful feeder of the Classes. Consider the enormous task to which Russia has set herself. She proposes to make a nation where the masses rule. In America, the mass has never ruled: always it has been the rule of the rich and well-born. On the frontier, west and south, we once tried such democracy; it died before slavery and Big Business. Here in Russia is another trial on a vaster scale, which attempts at the outset to control the thing that has frustrated democracy in the past: Private Wealth. Many wise men earnestly and honestly believe the task is impossible: that for all foreseeable time, the mass of men will serve some form of aristocracy, while civilization will always mean the culture of the Few. Consider though the grandeur of the vision which makes this Possible Best, consist of all men. First of all we must face the inevitable difficulties of all beginnings. One will find in Russia today dirt and bad manners. Eating and bathing habits are unpleasant. Equality of status, where there is as yet no real equality of culture and habit, has been endlessly inveighed against, from the French Revolution to the Emancipation of American Negroes. This today greatly bothers observers of Russia. They are obsessed by the glamour of culture and wealth in a few, despite the degradation of the mass on which this culture is built. Rich East Indians, rich Chinese, Russian Grand Dukes, bring to such people only the deepest admiration and envy. They mention them with hushed voices and accept their notice with reverence. What American who now rails at the rule of Russian boors, would not have accepted a summons to the Winter Palace with tears of gratitude?

But all this does not avoid the crucial question — can workers and peasants build a nation which will not, like other nations, eventually reconstruct

From the *Pittsburgh Courier*, January 23, 1937.

society on the old lines: with perhaps less poverty and distress at bottom, but with the same ruling class at top, whether it is called Nobility, or Middle Classes? If it is done, this is certain, the task is going to call for Ability and Sacrifice of an unusual amount and kind. Can peasant Russia, and Russian workers produce such men as can and will they do the gigantic task facing this land? Who knows?

My Evolving Program for
Negro Freedom

My visit to Germany and the Soviet Union in 1926, and then to Turkey and Italy on return, marked another change in my thought and action. The marks of war were all over Russia — of the war of France and England to turn back the clock of revolution. Wild children were in the sewers of Moscow; food was scarce, clothes in rags, and the fear of renewed Western aggression hung like a pall. Yet Russia was and still is to my mind, the most hopeful land in the modern world. Never before had I seen a suppressed mass of poor, working people — people as ignorant, poor, superstitious and cowed as my own American Negroes — so lifted in hope and starry-eyed with new determination, as the peasants and workers of Russia, from Leningrad and Moscow to Gorki and from Kiev to Odessa; the art galleries were jammed, the theatres crowded, the schools opening to new places and new programs each day; and work was joy. Their whole life was renewed and filled with vigor and ideal, as Youth Day in the Red Square proclaimed.

I saw of course but little of Russia in one short month. I came to no conclusions as to whether the particular form of the Russian state was permanent or a passing phase. I met but few of their greater leaders; only Radek did I know well, and he died in the subsequent purge. I do not judge Russia in the matter of war and murder, no more than I judge England. But of one thing I am certain: I believe in the dictum of Karl Marx, that the economic foundation of a nation is widely decisive for its politics, its art and its culture. I saw clearly, when I left Russia, that our American Negro belief that the right to vote would give us work and decent wage; would abolish our illiteracy and decrease our sickness and crime, was justified only in part; that on the

From *What the Negro Wants* (The University of North Carolina Press, 1944).

contrary, until we were able to earn a decent, independent living, we would never be allowed to cast a free ballot; that poverty caused our ignorance, sickness and crime; and that poverty was not our fault but our misfortune, the result and aim of our segregation and color caste; that the solution of letting a few of our capitalists share with whites in the exploitation of our masses, would never be a solution of our problem, but the forging of eternal chains, as Modern India knows to its sorrow.

Immediately, I modified my program again: I did not believe that the Communism of the Russians was the program for America; least of all for a minority group like the Negroes; I saw that the program of the American Communist party was suicidal. But I did believe that a people where the differentiation in classes because of wealth had only begun, could be so guided by intelligent leaders that they would develop into a consumer-conscious people, producing for use and not primarily for profit, and working into the surrounding industrial organization so as to reinforce the economic revolution bound to develop in the United States and all over Europe and Asia sooner or later. I believed that revolution in the production and distribution of wealth could be a slow, reasoned development and not necessarily a blood bath. I believed that 13 millions of people, increasing, albeit slowly in intelligence, could so concentrate their thought and action on the abolition of their poverty, as to work in conjunction with the most intelligent body of American thought; and that in the future as in the past, out of the mass of American Negroes would arise a far-seeing leadership in lines of economic reform.

If it had not been for the depression, I think that through the *Crisis*, the little monthly which I had founded in 1910, and carried on with almost no financial assistance for twenty years, I could have started this program on the way to adoption by American Negroes. But the depression made the survival of the *Crisis* dependent on the charity of persons who feared this thought and forced it under the control of influences to whom such a program was Greek. In a program of mere agitation for "rights," without clear conception of constructive effort to achieve those rights, I was not interested, because I saw its fatal weakness.

MY PRESENT PROGRAM

About 1925, the General Education Board adopted a new program. It had become clear that the studied neglect of the Negro college was going too far; and that the Hampton-Tuskegee program was inadequate even for its own objects. A plan was adopted which envisaged, by consolidation and endowment, the establishment in the South of five centers of University education for Negroes. Atlanta had to be one of these centers, and in 1929, Atlanta University became the graduate school of an affiliated system of colleges which promised a new era in higher education for Negroes. My life-long friend, John Hope, became president, and immediately began to sound me out on returning to Atlanta to help him in this great enterprise. He promised me leisure for thought and writing, and freedom of expression, so far, of course, as Georgia could stand it.

It seemed to me that a return to Atlanta would not only have a certain poetic justification, but would relieve the National Association for the Advancement of Colored People from financial burden during the depression, as well as from the greater effort of re-considering its essential program.

With the unexpected coming of a Second World War, this move of mine has proved a relief. However it only postpones the inevitable decision as to what American Negroes are striving for, and how eventually they are going to get it.

The untimely death of John Hope in 1936 marred the full fruition of our plans, following my return to Atlanta, in 1933. Those plans in my mind fell into three categories; first with leisure to write, I wanted to fill in the background of certain historical studies concerning the Negro race; secondly I wanted to establish at Atlanta University a scholarly journal of comment and research on race problems; finally, I wanted to restore in some form at Atlanta, the systematic study of the Negro problems.

Between 1935 and 1941, I wrote and published three volumes: a study of the Negro in Reconstruction; a study of the black race in history and an autobiographical sketch of my concept of the American race problem. To these I was anxious to add an Encyclopedia of the Negro. I had been chosen in 1934 to act as editor-in-chief of the project of the Phelps-Stokes Fund to prepare and publish such a work. I spent nearly ten years of intermittent effort on this project and secured co-operation from many scholars, white and black, in America, Europe and Africa. But the necessary funds could not be secured. Perhaps again it was too soon to expect large aid for so ambitious a project, built mainly on Negro scholarship. Nevertheless, a preliminary volume summarizing this effort will be published in 1944.

In 1940, there was established at Atlanta, a quarterly magazine, *Phylon*, the "Atlanta University Review of Race and Culture." It is now finishing its fifth volume.

In the attempt to restore at Atlanta the study of the Negro problem in a broad and inclusive way, we faced the fact that in the twenty-three years which had passed since their discontinuance, the scientific study of the American

Negro had spread widely and efficiently. Especially in the white institutions of the South had intelligent interest been aroused. There was, however, still need of systematic, comprehensive study and measurement, bringing to bear the indispensable point of view and inner knowledge of Negroes themselves. Something of this was being done at Fisk University, but for the widest efficiency, large funds were required for South-wide study.

The solution of this problem, without needless duplication of good work, or for mere pride of institution, came to me from W. R. Banks, principal of the Prairie View State College, Texas. He had been a student at Atlanta University during the days of the conferences. He took the idea with him to Texas, and conducted studies and conferences there for twenty years. He suggested that Atlanta University unite the seventeen Negro Land-Grant colleges in the South in a joint co-operative study, to be carried on continuously. I laid before the annual meeting of the presidents of these colleges in 1941, such a plan. I proposed the strengthening of their departments of the social sciences; that each institution take its own state as its field of study; that an annual conference be held where representatives of the colleges came into consultation with the best sociologists of the land, and decide on methods of work and subjects of study. A volume giving the more important results would be published annually.

This plan was inaugurated in the Spring of 1943, with all seventeen of the Land-Grant colleges represented, and eight leading American sociologists in attendance. The first annual report appeared in the Fall of 1943. Thus, after a quarter century, the Atlanta conferences live again.

To complete this idea, there is need to include a similar study of the vitally important Northern Negro group. The leading Negro universities like Howard, Fisk, Wilberforce, Lincoln of Pennsylvania and of Missouri, and others might with Northern universities jointly carry out this part of the scheme.

This program came to full fruition in 1944, when a report of the first conference was published as *Atlanta University Publication No. 22*. Then, without warning, the University retired me from work and gave up this renewed project.

SUMMARY

Finally and in summation, what is it that in sixty years of purposive endeavor, I have wanted for my people? Just what do I mean by "Freedom"?

Proceeding from the vague and general plans of youth, through the more particular program of active middle life, and on to the general and at the same time more specific plans of the days of reflexion. I can see, with overlappings and contradictions, these things:

By "Freedom" for Negroes, I meant and still mean, *full economic, political and social equality with American citizens, in thought, expression and action, with no discrimination based on race or color.*

A statement such as this challenges immediate criticism. Economic equality is today widely advocated as the basis for real political power: men are beginning to demand for all persons, the right to work at a wage which will maintain a decent standard of living. Beyond that the right to vote is the demand that all persons governed should have some voice in government. Beyond these two demands, so widely admitted, what does one mean by a demand for "social equality"?

The phrase is unhappy because of the vague meaning of both "social" and "equality." Yet it is in too common use to be discarded, and it stands especially for an attitude toward the Negro. "Social" is used to refer not only to the intimate contacts of the family group and of personal companions, but also and increasingly to the whole vast complex of human relationships through which we carry out our cultural patterns.

We may list the activities called "social," roughly as follows:

A. Private social intercourse (marriages, friendships, home entertainment).

B. Public services (residence areas, travel, recreation and information, hotels and restaurants).

C. Social uplift (education, religion, science and art).

Here are three categories of social activities calling for three interpretations of equality. In the matter of purely personal contacts like marriage, intimate friendships and sociable gatherings, "equality" means the right to select one's own mates and close companions. The basis of choice may be cultured taste or vagrant whim, but it is an unquestionable right so long as my free choice does not deny equal freedom on the part of others. No one can for a moment question the preference of a white man to marry a white woman or invite only white friends to dinner. But by the same token if a white Desdemona prefers a black Othello; or if Theodore Roosevelt includes among his dinner guests Booker T. Washington, their right also is undeniable and its restriction by law or custom an inadmissible infringement of civil rights.

Naturally, if an individual choice like intermarriage is proven to be a social injury, society must forbid it. It has been the contention of the white South that the social body always suffers from miscegenation, and that miscegenation is always possible where there is friendship and often where there is mere courtesy.

This belief, modern science has effectively answered. There is no scientific reason why there should not be intermarriage between two human beings who happen to be of different race or color. This does mean any forcible limitation of individual preference based on race, color, or any other reason; it does limit any compulsion of persons who do not accept the validity of such reasons not to follow their own choices.

The marriage of Frederick Douglass to a white woman did not injure society. The marriage of the Negro Greek scholar, William Scarborough, to Sarah Bierce, principal of the Wilberforce Normal School, was not a social catastrophe. The mulatto descendants of Louise Dumas and the Marquis de la Pailleterie were a great gift to mankind. The determination of any white person not to have children with Negro, Chinese, or Irish blood is a desire which demands every respect. In like manner, the tastes of others, no matter how few or many, who disagree, demand equal respect.

In the second category of public services and opportunities, one's right to exercise personal taste and discrimination is limited not only by the free choice of others, but by the fact that the whole social body is joint owner and purveyor of many of the facilities and rights offered. A person has a right to seek a home in healthy and beautiful surroundings and among friends and associates. But such rights cannot be exclusively enjoyed if they involve confining others to the slums. Social equality here denies the right of any discrimination and segregation which compels citizens to lose their rights of enjoyment and accommodation in the common wealth. If without injustice, separation in travel, eating and lodging can be carried out, any community or individual has a right to practise it in accord with his taste or desire. But this is rarely possible and in such case the demand of an individual or even an overwhelming majority, to discriminate at the cost of inconvenience, disease and suffering on the part of the minority is unfair, unjust and undemocratic.

In matters connected with these groups of social activity, the usage in the United States, and especially in the South, constitutes the sorest and bitterest points of controversy in the racial situation; especially in the life of those individuals and classes among Negroes whose social progress is at once the proof and measure of the capabilities of the race.

That the denial of the right to exclude Negroes from residential areas and public accommodations may involve counter costs on the part of the majority, by unpleasant contacts and even dangerous experiences, is often true. That fact has been the basis of wide opposition to the democratization of modern society and of deep-seated fear that democracy necessarily involves social leveling and degeneration.

On the whole, however, modern thought and experience have tended to convince mankind that the evils of caste discrimination against the depressed elements of the mass are greater and more dangerous to progress than the affront to natural tastes and the recoil from unpleasant contacts involved in the just sharing of public conveniences with all citizens. This conviction is the meaning of America, and it has had wide and increasing success in incorporating Irish, and German peasants, Slavic laborers and even Negro slaves into a new, virile and progressive American Culture.

At the incorporation of the Negro freedman into the social and political body, the white South has naturally balked and impeded it by law, custom, and race philosophy. This is historically explicable. No group of privileged slave-owners is easily and willingly going to recognize their former slaves as men. But just as truly this caste leveling downward must be definitely, openly, and determinedly opposed or civilization suffers. What was once a local and parochial problem, now looms as a world threat! If caste and segregation is the correct answer to the race problem in America, it is the answer to the race contacts of the world. This the Atlantic Charter and the Cairo conference denied, and to back this denial lies the threat of Japan and all Asia, and of Africa.

What shall we, what can we, do about it in the United States? We must first attack Jim-Crow legislation: the freezing in law of discrimination based solely on race and color — in voting, in work, in travel, in public service.

To the third category of social activity, concerned with social uplift, one would say at first that not only should everyone be admitted but all even urged to join. It happens, however, that many of these organizations are private efforts toward public ends. In so far as their membership is private and based on taste and compatibility, they fall under the immunities of private social intercourse, with its limitation of equal freedom to all.

But such organizations have no right to arrogate to themselves exclusive rights of public service. If a church is a social clique, it is not a public center of religion; if a school is private and for a selected clientele, it must not assume the functions and privileges of public schools. The underlying philosophy of our public school system is that the education of all children together at public expense is the best and surest path to democracy. Those who exclude the public or any part of it from the schools, have no right to use public funds for private purposes. Separate Negro public schools or separate girl's schools or separate Catholic schools are not inadmissible simply because of separation; but only when such separation hinders the development of democratic ideals and gives to the separated, poor schools or no schools at all.

Beyond all this, and when legal inequalities pass from the statute books, a rock wall of social discrimination between human beings will long persist in human intercourse. So far as such discrimination is a method of social selection, by means of which the worst is slowly weeded and the best protected and encouraged, such discrimination has justification. But the danger has always been and still persists, that what is weeded out is the Different and not the Dangerous; and what is preserved is the Powerful and not the Best. The only defense against this is the widest human contacts and acquaintanceships compatible with social safety.

So far as human friendship and intermingling are based on broad and catholic reasoning and ignore petty and inconsequential prejudices, the happier will be the individual and the richer the general social life. In this realm lies the real freedom, toward which the soul of man has always striven: the right to be different, to be individual and pursue personal aims and ideals. Here lies the real answer to the leveling compulsions and equalitarianisms of that democracy which first provides food, shelter and organized security for man.

Once the problem of subsistence is met and order is secured, there comes the great moment of civilization: the development of individual personality; the right of variation; the richness of a culture that lies in differentiation. In the activities of such a world, men are not compelled to be white in order to be free: they can be black, yellow or red; they can mingle or stay separate. The free mind, the untrammelled taste can revel. In only a section and a small section of total life is discrimination inadmissible and that is where my freedom stops yours or your taste hurts me. Gradually such a free world will learn that not in exclusiveness and isolation lies inspiration and joy, but that the very variety is the reservoir of invaluable experience and emotion. This crowning of equalitarian democracy in artistic freedom of difference is the real next step of culture.

The hope of civilization lies not in exclusion, but in inclusion of all human elements; we find the richness of humanity not in the Social Register, but in the City Directory; not in great aristocracies, chosen people and superior races, but in the throngs of disinherited and underfed men. Not the lifting of the lowly, but the unchaining of the unawakened mighty, will reveal the possibilities of genius, gift and miracle, in mountainous treasure-trove, which hitherto civilization has scarcely touched; and yet boasted blatantly and even glorified in its poverty. In world-wide equality of human development is the answer to every meticulous taste and each rare personality.

To achieve this freedom, I have essayed these main paths:

1. 1885–1910

"The Truth shall make ye free."

This plan was directed toward the majority of white Americans, and rested on the assumption that once they realized the scientifically attested truth concerning Negroes and race relations, they would take action to correct all wrong.

2.   1900–1930

United action on the part of thinking Americans, white and black, to force the truth concerning Negroes to the attention of the nation.

This plan assumed that the majority of Americans would rush to the defence of democracy, if they realized how race prejudice was threatening it, not only for Negroes but for whites; not only in America but in the world.

3.   1928–to the present

Scientific investigation and organized action among Negroes, in close cooperation, to secure the survival of the Negro race, until the cultural development of America and the world is willing to recognize Negro freedom.

This plan realizes that the majority of men do not usually act in accord with reason, but follow social pressures, inherited customs and long-established, often sub-conscious, patterns of action. Consequently, race prejudice in America will linger long and may even increase. It is the duty of the black race to maintain its cultural advance, not for itself alone, but for the emancipation of mankind, the realization of democracy and the progress of civilization.

"There Must Come a Vast Social Change in the United States"

There are on this platform tonight five persons who stand indicted by the Federal Dept. of Justice as agents of a foreign principal because through the Peace Information Center they distributed news of peace movements through the world, which the press ignored, including distribution of the Stockholm Appeal against the atomic bomb. They are: Elizabeth Moos, a teacher; Kyrle Elkin, a businessman; Sylvia Soloff, a clerk and stenographer; Abbott Simon, a veteran and organizer of this congress; and myself.

The basic hope of democracy is the power of the people eventually to decide great issues of state by fair elections. But the effective use of this power depends on the knowledge of conditions which this electorate possesses. If they cannot know the truth; if they cannot ascertain the real facts, then the whole meaning and efficiency of the democratic process fall to the ground.

Today it is clear to all who know the facts that American industry has launched in this country the greatest effort at propaganda the world has ever witnessed. In comparison, Hitler and Mussolini fade to insignificance. Our daily press with few exceptions is controlled in presentation of fact and expression of opinion by the organized industrial interests of the United States. These interests want war. They want war because only by war can China, Africa, Southeast Asia and the Middle East be kept in their control, as the source of the greatest profit for industrial enterprise.

But even an industrial dictatorship could not admit profit as the sole end of work, and increase of profit as the cause of world war. So in the United States we are told over radio, in cinema, on the platform and in newspaper, magazine and book, that our way of life is in grave and imminent danger.

From the *National Guardian*, July 11, 1951.

. . . Just as in the dark ages, we are letting ourselves be stampeded by witch-words. In that day, a veiled and awesome figure could rear itself in the shadows and by yelling "Abacadabra," turn strong men into gibbering idiots. Today by yelling "Communist," we can shut the mouths of nearly all who want peace, not war.

Men have a perfect right to disagree with communism, with its objects and methods; men may honestly believe that the United States has a better method of industrial organization than the Soviet Union; but men have no right to assert in the face of overwhelming testimony that no honesty and sincerity of effort; no hard work and sacrifice; no intelligent leadership, has occurred in the Soviet Union; and that disagreement with it must involve painting 200 million people as inhuman devils, and assuming that we are God's own angels. In that direction lies unending hate and war; while civiliza-tion needs sympathy, understanding and world peace, with the right of men to differ and of nations to work as each will.

Whether we like it or not, most of the people of the world today live under socialism or communism. We cannot stop this by force and should not if we could. We can so improve our own system of economy that the world will see the advantage of it over all others if this prove true. The way to start this is not war nor slander. It is stupid to abolish democracy among ourselves in order to prove the blessings of democracy to others.

Nearly all social questions and reforms which we must discuss and answer are matters which science has already discussed, experimented with and offered solutions, years before the Soviet Union was born. Yet when we dare touch these matters, we are denied freedom of speech. Subjects like wealth production and distribution; the role of the state in industry and the causes of poverty are being thrown out of our school curricula and we are accused of radicalism if we dare mention these matters.

Yet we must discuss them. We must ask why is it that this rich world is poor? Why is it, that with all the wealth nature furnishes free, and all the power lying at our fingertips, the men who work hardest get the lowest income? Why is it that the men who think most clearly and constructively have often the hardest time making a decent living, while thousands who lie and cheat and steal get power and wealth? Why is it those who own the land and crops; the machines and capital; the buildings and clothing and food, are not always those who work and save and sacrifice, but too often those who scheme and contrive and rig the market; or sit at ease spending what somebody else earned?

There are fundamental questions as to work and wealth which all men must face; all schools teach and all honest pulpits discuss. Does a man's income consist of what he makes? No. Not even in primitive times was this true. And today the simplest work of production from catching a fish to building Boulder Dam is a complicated social effort involving from 10 to 10,000 workers, planners, managers and thinkers, and using even so-called "unemployed" housewives and mothers, it lasts so long in time and is so intricate and complicated in technique that no mathematical formula can possibly show exactly what each worker contributes to the final value.

Only reason and justice can in the end determine income, to each according to his need and from each what he best can do, is the high ideal, enunciated before the Russian Revolution was thought of. This ideal the Soviet Union admits it has not yet attained, but declares its firm purpose to reach it. While the United States not only denies the justice of this aim but bluntly orders that it must not even be attempted.

We have got our economy upside down, our reward for work backside foremost and our brains so addled that if anyone dares question this insanity of our modern civilization we yell "subversive" and scare all fools out of their few wits.

If sincere dislike of this state of affairs is communism, then by the living God, no force of army, nor power of wealth, nor smartness of intellect will ever stop it. Denial of this right to think will manufacture communists faster than you can jail or kill them. Nothing will stop such communism but something better than communism. If our present policies are examples of free enterprise and individual initiative, they initiate crime and suffering as well as wealth; if this is the American way of life, God save America!

There is no way in the world for us to preserve the ideals of a democratic America, save by drastically curbing the present power of concentrated wealth, by assuming ownership of some natural resources, by administering many of our key industries and by socializing our services for public welfare. This need not mean the adoption of the communism of the Soviet Union, nor the socialism of Britain, nor even of the near-socialism of France, Italy or Scandinavia; but either in some way or to some degree, we socialize our economy, restore the New Deal and inaugurate the welfare state or we descend into a military fascism which will kill all dreams of Democracy or the abolition of poverty and ignorance; or of peace instead of war.

There must come vast social change in the United States; a change not violent, but by the will of the people; certain and inexorable, carried out "with malice toward none but charity for all"; with meticulous justice to the rich and thrifty and complete sympathy for the poor, the sick and the ignorant; with freedom and democracy for America, and on earth peace, good will toward men.

Negroes and the Crisis of Capitalism in the United States

How "free" was the black freedman in 1863? He had no clothes, no home, tools, or land. Thaddeus Stevens begged the government to give him a bit of the land which his blood had fertilized for 244 years. The nation refused. Frederick Douglass and Charles Sumner asked for the Negro the right to vote. The nation yielded because only Negro votes could force the white South to conform to the demands of Big Business in tariff legislation and debt control. This accomplished, the nation took away the Negro's vote, and the vote of most poor whites went with it.

A fantastic economic development followed. In the South the land was rich and the climate mild. There was sun and rain for grain, fruit, and fiber. There were natural resources in rivers, harbors, and forests. In the bosom of the earth lay coal, iron, oil, sulphur, and salt. All this either already belonged to or was practically given by the government to the landholder and capitalist. Only a small part of it went to labor, black or white.

Capital was needed to develop this [into an] economic paradise. Government furnished much of this capital free to the landholder and employer. Railroads were subsidized, and rivers and harbors improved; private wealth largely escaped taxation. The North, fattened on tariff legislation, money control, and cheap immigrant labor, poured private capital into the South. When Southern labor lost half its vote, landholders and capitalists filled the state legislatures and Congress with servants of exploitation. This gave all the powerful chairmanships in Congress to the South under the Democrats, and large influence under Republicans. During World War I, a large part of the military training program was located in the South, and the government

From the *Monthly Review*, 4 (April 1953): 478–485.

622

overpaid interested landlords and merchants and contractors to the tune of hundreds of millions of dollars — a performance which was to be largely repeated in World War II. During the depression, most relief money paid out in the South went to landlords, not to workers.

During and after World War II, Southern industry moved into high gear. The Federal government poured billions of grants-in-aid into the South. Washington was lavish with "Certificates of Necessity" to build new factories, and owners of oil wells were given tax rebates for depletion of the oil which God gave the nation; and today they seek to grab the $80 billion worth of oil underseas.

Above all, the South furnished and boasted of one of the largest pools of cheap, docile, unorganized labor, skilled and unskilled, in the civilized world. This mass of labor was historically split into white and black, each hating and fearing each other to a degree that persons unfamiliar with the region cannot begin to imagine. Southern labor was further split into organized and unorganized groups; and finally, all American labor was split by red-baiting and the smear of "Communism."

Here was a paradise for the investor, which the state governments improved. Labor laws in the South were lax and carelessly enforced; company towns arose under complete corporate control; the police and militia were organized against labor. Race hate and fear and scab tactics were deliberately encouraged so as to make any complaint or effort at betterment liable to burst into riot, lynching, or race war.

The result has been startling. In 1919 the South turned out less than a fifth of our mining products; by 1946 the proportion had risen to nearly half. The value of manufactures in the South has risen in thirty years from a tenth to nearly a fifth of the national total. Many of the new and promising industries are seeking the South; since World War II, no less than $11 billion has been invested there in new industrial plants. The Southeast already has 80 percent of the nation's cotton mills and virtually all the new chemical fiber industry. It is drawing the woolen and worsted mills, and the textile machinery mills will soon follow. Paper and pulp mills and plastics represent hundreds of millions in new investments. The Southwest is perhaps the fastest-growing chemical empire in the world.

This newest South, turning back to its slave past, believes its present and future prosperity can best be built on the poverty and ignorance of its disfranchised lowest masses — and these low-paid workers now include not only Negroes, but Mexicans, Puerto Ricans, and the unskilled, unorganized whites. Progress by means of this poverty is the creed of the present South.

The Northern white worker long went his way oblivious to what was happening in the South. He awoke when the black Southern laborer fled North after World War I, and he welcomed him by riots. Slowly, however, the black man has been integrated into the unions, except those in whose crafts he was not skilled and had no chance to learn. One of these was the textile unions. They excluded Negroes. It is taking a long time to prove to them that their attitude toward Negroes was dangerous. If Negro wages were low in the South, what business was that of New England white labor? Today the union man sees that it was his business. The factories are moving out of New England and the North into the South. One hundred thousand textile workers are idle. This illustrates a paradox of capitalism: in the South, the nation, and the world, the workers are too poor to buy the textiles they need; while machinery is able to make more textiles than its owners can sell at the prices they demand.

Wages in the South are 20 percent lower than in the North, and Negro wages as a legacy from NIRA, are at least 20 percent below white wages. This wage differential between North and South represents increased profits of $4 to $5 billion a year. Small wonder that the Negro population in the rural South decreased by 50,000 in the last decade, and that the number of Negroes in the North increased by 55 percent. Of nine million industrial workers in the South, less than three million are unionized. Last year 40,000 members of the CIO Textile Workers Union, which excludes Negroes, struck in the South, and spent $1,250,000 in five weeks. They lost, and their membership fell from 20 to 15 percent of the operatives. The carpet baggers today are the vast Northern corporations which own the new Southern industry, and the scalawags are the Southern politicians whom they send to legislatures and Congress.

The organized effort of American industry to usurp government, surpasses anything in modern history, even that of Adolf Hitler from whom it was learned. From the use of psychology to spread truth has come the use of organized gathering of news to guide public opinion and then deliberately to mislead it by scientific advertising and propaganda. This has led in our day to suppression of truth, omission of facts, misinterpretation of news, and deliberate falsehood on a wide scale. Mass capitalistic control of books and periodicals, news gathering and distribution, radio, cinema, and television has made the throttling of democracy possible and the distortion of education and failure of justice widespread. It can only be countered by public knowledge of what this government by propaganda is accomplishing and how.

In the nation as a whole we have full employment and high wages for most skilled workers, but this state of affairs is maintained by manufacturing arms and ammunition which rapidly deteriorate in value, and by giving it away and paying for it by taxes which lower high wages, and by high prices. How long can we maintain this merry-go-round?

What now must American Negroes say to this situation? This question raises another: what is the real nature of this group today? . . .

Some Negro leaders with much to lose in property, credit, or reputation have yielded to panic; two colored authors in recent new editions of their books have deleted references to Paul Robeson and myself in order to appease the witchhunters. Much time and thought of misguided intellectuals has been devoted to helping deprive American Negroes of natural leadership or to scaring them into silence by threat of imprisonment, loss of work, or by smearing them as "Communists." Negro colleges especially are silenced and influenced by funds raised by Big Business and visits from distinguished capitalists. Their courses in sociology, economics, and history are carefully watched.

This kind of suppression and censorship, however, does not solve anything; it but complicates the situation. For a time it may deprive Negroes of some of their best-trained and wealthiest leaders, but despite this, the color bar will not release the main mass of the group. The bar may bend and loosen. Rich Negroes may travel with less annoyance; they may stop in the higher-priced hotels and eat in the more costly restaurants; the theaters and movie houses in the North and border states may let down the bars. Beyond that, because of constitutional law and mounting costs, the wall of segregation in education may be breached. But with all this, what results? The color bar in this nation will not soon be broken. Even as it yields in places, the insult of what remains will be more deeply felt by the still half-free.

When the whole caste structure finally does fall, Negroes will be divided into classes even more sharply than now, and the main mass will become a part of the working class of the nation and the world, which will surely go socialist.

The Vast Miracle of
China Today

I have traveled widely on this earth since my first trip to Europe 67 years ago. Save South America and India, I have seen most of the civilized world and much of its backward regions. Many leading nations I have visited repeatedly. But I have never seen a nation which so amazed and touched me as China in 1959.

I have seen more impressive buildings but no more pleasing architecture; I have seen greater display of wealth, and more massive power; I have seen better equipped railways and boats and vastly more showy automobiles; but I have never seen a nation where human nature was so abreast of scientific knowledge; where daily life of everyday people was so outstripping mechanical power and love of life so triumphing over human greed and envy and selfishness as I see in China today.

It is not a matter of mere numbers and size; of wealth and power; of beauty and style. It is a sense of human nature free of its most hurtful and terrible meannesses and of a people full of joy and faith and marching on in a unison unexampled in Holland, Belgium, Britain and France; and simply inconceivable in the United States.

A typical, ignorant American put it this way in Moscow: "But how can you make it go without niggers?" In China he would have said: "But see them work:" dragging, hauling, lifting, pulling — and yet smiling at each other, greeting neighbors who ride by in autos, helping strangers even if they are "niggers"; seeking knowledge, following leaders and believing in themselves and their certain destiny. Whence comes this miracle of human nature, which I never saw before or believed possible?

From the *National Guardian*, June 8, 1959.

I was ten weeks in China. There they celebrated my 91st birthday with a thoughtfulness and sincerity that would simply be impossible in America even among my own colored people. Ministers of state were there, writers and artists, actors and professional men; singers and children playing fairy tales. Anna Louise Strong came looking happy, busy and secure. There was a whole table of other Americans, exiled for daring to visit China; integrated for their skills and loyalty.

I traveled 5,000 miles, by railway, boat, plane and auto. I saw all the great cities: Peking, Shanghai, Hankow and its sisters; Canton, Chungking, Chengtu, Kunming and Nanking. I rode its vast rivers tearing through mighty gorges; passed through its villages and sat in its communes. I visited its schools and colleges, lectured and broadcast to the world. I visited its minority groups. I was on the borders of Tibet when the revolt occurred. I spent four hours with Mao Tse-tung and dined twice with Chou En-lai, the tireless Prime Minister of this nation of 680 million souls.

The people of the land I saw: the workers, the factory hands, the farmers and laborers, scrubwomen and servants. I went to theaters and restaurants, sat in the homes of the high and the low; and always I saw a happy people; people with faith that need no church nor priest and laughs gaily when the Monkey King fools the hosts of Heaven and overthrows the angels.

In all my wandering, I never felt the touch or breath of insult or even dislike — I who for 90 years in America scarcely ever saw a day without some expression of hate for "niggers."

What is the secret of China in the second half of the 20th Century? It is that the vast majority of a billion human beings have been convinced that human nature in some of its darkest recesses can be changed, if change is necessary. China knows, as no other people know, to what depths human meanness can go.

I used to weep for American Negroes, as I saw through what indignities and repressions and cruelties they had passed; but as I have read Chinese history in these last months and had it explained to me stripped of Anglo-Saxon lies, I know that no depths of Negro slavery in America have plumbed such abysses as the Chinese have seen for 2,000 years and more.

They have seen starvation and murder; rape and prostitution; sale and slavery of children; and religion cloaked in opium and gin, for converting the "Heathen." This oppression and contempt came not only from Tartars, Mongolians, British, French, Germans and Americans, but from the Chinese themselves: Mandarins and warlords, capitalists and murdering thieves like Chiang Kai-shek; Kuomintang socialists and intellectuals educated abroad.

Despite all this, China lives, and has been transformed and marches on. She is not ignored by the United States. She ignores the United States and leaps forward. What did it? What furnished the motive power and how was it applied?

First it was the belief in himself and in his people by a man like Sun Yatsen. He plunged on, blind and unaided, repulsed by Britain and America, but welcomed by Russia. Then efforts toward socialism, which wobbled forward, erred and lost, and at last was bribed by America and Britain and betrayed by Chiang Kai-shek, with its leaders murdered and its aims misunderstood, when not deliberately lied about.

Then came the Long March from feudalism, past capitalism and socialism to communism in our day. Mao Tse-tung, Chou En-lai, Chu Teh and a half dozen others undertook to lead a nation by example, by starving and fighting; by infinite patience and above all by making a nation believe that the people and not merely the elite — the workers in factory, street, and field — composed the real nation. Others have said this often, but no nation has tried it like the Soviet Union and China.

And on the staggering and bitter effort of the Soviets, beleaguered by all Western civilization, and yet far-seeing enough to help weaker China even before a still weak Russia was safe — on this vast pyramid has arisen the saving nation of this stumbling, murdering, hating world.

In China the people — the laboring people, the people who in most lands are the doormats on which the reigning thieves and murdering rulers walk, leading their painted and jeweled prostitutes — the people walk and boast. These people of the slums and gutters and kitchens are the Chinese nation today. This the Chinese believe and on this belief they toil and sweat and cheer.

They believe this and for the last ten years their belief has been strengthened until today they follow their leaders because these leaders have never deceived them. Their officials are incorruptible, their merchants are honest, their artisans are reliable, their workers who dig and haul and lift do an honest day's work and even work overtime if their state asks it, for they are the State; they are China.

A kindergarten, meeting in the once Forbidden City, was shown the magnificence of this palace and told: "Your fathers built this, but now it is yours; preserve it." And then, pointing across the Ten An Men square to the vast building of the new Halls of Assembly, the speaker added: "Your fathers are building new palaces for you; enjoy them and guard them for yourselves and your children. They belong to you!"

China has no rank nor classes; her universities grant no degrees; her government awards no medals. She has no blue book of "society." But she has leaders of learning and genius, scientists of renown, artisans of skill and millions who know and believe this and follow where these men lead. This is the joy of this nation, its high belief and its unfaltering hope.

China is no Utopia. Fifth Avenue has better shops where the rich can buy and the whores parade. Detroit has more and better cars. The best American housing outstrips the Chinese and Chinese women are not nearly as well-dressed as the guests of the Waldorf-Astoria. But the Chinese worker is happy.

He has exorcized the Great Fear that haunts the West: the fear of losing his job; the fear of falling sick; the fear of accident; the fear of inability to educate his children; the fear of daring to take a vacation. To guard against such catastrophe Americans skimp and save, cheat and steal, gamble and arm for murder.

The Soviet citizen, the Czech, the Pole, the Hungarian have kicked out the stooges of America and the hoodlums set to exploit the peasants. They and the East Germans no longer fear these disasters; and above all the Chinese sit high above these fears and laugh with joy.

They will not be rich in old age. They will not enjoy sickness but they will be healed. They will not starve as thousands of Chinese did only a generation ago. They fear neither flood nor epidemic. They do not even fear war, as Mao Tse-tung told me. War for China is a "Paper Tiger." China can defend itself and back of China stands the unassailable might of the Soviet Union.

Envy and class hate is disappearing in China. Does your neighbor have better pay and higher position than you? He has this because of greater ability or better education, and more education is open to you and compulsory for your children.

The young married couple do not fear children. The mother has pre-natal care. Her wage and job are safe. Nursery and kindergarten take care of the child and it is welcome, not to pampered luxury but to good food, constant medical care and education for his highest ability.

All this is not yet perfect. Here and there it fails, falls short and falters; but it is so often and so widely true, that China believes, lives on realized hope, follows its leaders and sings:

"O, Mourner, get up offa your knees."

The women of China are free. They wear pants so that they can walk, climb and dig; and climb and dig they do. They are not dressed simply for sex indulgence or beauty parades. They occupy positions from ministers of state to locomotive engineers, lawyers, doctors, clerks and laborers. They are escaping "household drudgery"; they are strong and healthy and beautiful not simply of leg and false bosom but of real brain and brawn.

In Wuhan, I stood in one of the greatest steelworks of the world. A crane which moved a hundred tons loomed above. I said, "My God, Shirley, look up there!" Alone in the engine-room sat a girl with ribboned braids, running the vast machine.

You won't believe this, because you never saw anything like it; and if the State Department has its way, you never will. Let *Life* lie about communes; and the State Department shed crocodile tears over ancestral tombs. Let Hong Kong wire its lies abroad. Let "Divine Slavery" persist in Tibet until China kills it. The truth is there and I saw it.

America makes or can make no article that China is not either making or can make, and make better and cheaper. I saw its export exposition in Canton: a whole building of watches, radios, electric apparatus, cloth in silk and wool and cotton; embroidery, pottery, dishes, shoes, telephone sets. There were five floors of goods which the world needs and is buying in increasing quantities, except the ostrich United States, whose ships rot.

Fifteen times I have crossed the Atlantic and once the Pacific. I have seen the world. But never so vast and glorious a miracle as China.

Application for Membership in the Communist Party of the United States of America

On this first day of October, 1961, I am applying for admission to membership in the Communist Party of the United States. I have been long and slow in coming to this conclusion, but at last my mind is settled.

In college I heard the name of Karl Marx, but read none of his works, nor heard them explained. At the University of Berlin, I heard much of those thinkers who had definitively answered the theories of Marx, but again we did not study what Marx himself had said. Nevertheless, I attended meetings of the Socialist Party and considered myself a Socialist.

On my return to America, I taught and studied for sixteen years. I explored the theory of Socialism and studied the organized social life of American Negroes; but still I neither read or heard much of Marxism. Then I came to New York as an official of the new NAACP and editor of the *Crisis* Magazine. The NAACP was capitalist oriented and expected support from rich philanthropists.

But it had a strong Socialist element in its leadership in persons like Mary Ovington, William English Walling and Charles Edward Russell. Following their advice, I joined the Socialist Pary in 1911. I knew then nothing of practical socialist politics and in the campaign of 1912, I found myself unwilling to vote the Socialist ticket, but advised Negroes to vote for Wilson. This was contrary to Socialist Party rules and consequently I resigned from the Socialist Party.

For the next twenty years I tried to develop a political way of life for myself and my people. I attacked the Democrats and Republicans for monopoly and

From *Worker*, November 26, 1961.

disfranchisement of Negroes; I attacked the Socialists for trying to segregate Southern Negro members; I praised the racial attitudes of the Communists, but opposed their tactics in the case of the Scottsboro boys and their advocacy of a Negro state. At the same time I began to study Karl Marx and the Communists; I read *Das Kapital* and other Communist literature; I hailed the Russian Revolution of 1917, but was puzzled at the contradictory news from Russia.

Finally in 1926, I began a new effort: I visited Communist lands. I went to the Soviet Union in 1926, 1936, 1949 and 1959; I saw the nation develop. I visited East Germany, Czechoslovakia and Poland. I spent ten weeks in China, traveling all over the land. Then this summer, I rested a month in Rumania.

I was early convinced that Socialism was an excellent way of life, but I thought it might be reached by various methods. For Russia I was convinced she had chosen the only way open to her at the time. I saw Scandinavia choosing a different method, half-way between Socialism and Capitalism. In the United States I saw Consumers Cooperation as a path from Capitalism to Socialism, while England, France and Germany developed in the same direction in their own way. After the depression and the Second World War, I was disillusioned. The Progressive movement in the United States failed. The Cold War started. Capitalism called Communism a crime.

Today I have reached a firm conclusion:

Capitalism cannot reform itself; it is doomed to self-destruction. No universal selfishness can bring social good to all.

Communism — the effort to give all men what they need and to ask of each the best they can contribute — this is the only way of human life. It is a difficult and hard end to reach — it has and will make mistakes, but today it marches triumphantly on in education and science, in home and food, with increased freedom of thought and deliverance from dogma. In the end Communism will triumph. I want to help to bring that day.

The path of the American Communist Party is clear: It will provide the United States with a real Third Party and thus restore democracy to this land. It will call for:

1. Public ownership of natural resources and of all captial.
2. Public control of transportation and communications.
3. Abolition of poverty and limitation of personal income.
4. No exploitation of labor.
5. Social medicine, with hospitalization and care of the old.
6. Free education for all.
7. Training for jobs and jobs for all.

8. Discipline for growth and reform.
9. Freedom under law.
10. No dogmatic religion.

These aims are not crimes. They are practiced increasingly over the world. No nation can call itself free which does not allow its citizens to work for these ends.

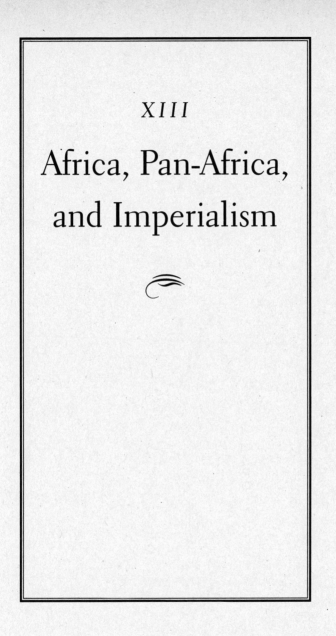

XIII

Africa, Pan-Africa, and Imperialism

Du Bois was the premier apostle of the gospel of the solidarity of peoples of color, and of the cultural and political links to Africa of Americans of African descent. Speaking to the delegates of the Pan-African Conference, meeting in London, July 1900, he made his most famous prediction in "To the Nations of the World": "The problem of the twentieth century is the problem of the colour line, the question as to how far differences of race . . . are going to be made, hereafter, the basis of denying to over half the world the right of sharing to their utmost ability the opportunities and privileges of modern civilization." When Du Bois summarized the visionary goals and modest achievements of the Pan-African Congresses more than a quarter-century later (four by his count, but five in all), Du Bois had no need to repeat a prophecy that had proven to be deadly accurate. He had already spelled out the inevitable global consequences of the color-line problem in "The African Roots of the War," a trenchant essay in the May 1915 *Atlantic Monthly* that anticipated Lenin's analysis of capitalism and imperialism. "The Negro's Fatherland" (1917), "What Is Africa to Me?" (1940), and "Little Portraits of Africa" (1924) are representative of the large corpus of writings about the historic, cultural, and contemporary political importance of the African continent. In postwar writings such as "The Disfranchised Colonies" (1945) and "Britain and Africa" (1947), Du Bois exposed the economic history of what another radical scholar would famously characterize as the European underdevelopment of Africa. But an independent Africa did not mean for Du Bois a continent from which the European populations would have been expelled. "The black leaders of present Africa are not fools," he admonished in "Whites in Africa After Negro Autonomy" (1962); the revenge of reverse racism would be, he believed, mindlessly catastrophic.

To the Nations of the World

In the metropolis of the modern world, in this the closing year of the nineteenth century, there has been assembled a congress of men and women of African blood, to deliberate solemnly upon the present situation and outlook of the darker races of mankind. The problem of the twentieth century is the problem of the colour line, the question as to how far differences of race, which show themselves chiefly in the colour of the skin and the texture of the hair, are going to be made, hereafter, the basis of denying to over half the world the right of sharing to their utmost ability the opportunities and privileges of modern civilisation.

To be sure, the darker races are to-day the least advanced in culture according to European standards. This has not, however, always been the case in the past, and certainly the world's history, both ancient and modern, has given many instances of no despicable ability and capacity among the blackest races of men.

In any case, the modern world must need remember that in this age, when the ends of the world are being brought so near together, the millions of black men in Africa, America, and the Islands of the Sea, not to speak of the brown and yellow myriads elsewhere, are bound to have great influence upon the world in the future, by reason of sheer numbers and physical contact. If now the world of culture bends itself towards giving Negroes and other dark men the largest and broadest opportunity for education and self-development, then this contact and influence is bound to have a beneficial effect upon the world and hasten human progress. But if, by reason of carelessness, prejudice, greed and injustice, the black world is to be exploited and ravished and degraded, the results must be deplorable, if not fatal, not simply to them, but to the high

From the *Report of the Pan-African Conference, held on the 23rd, 24th, and 25th July, 1900, at Westminster Town Hall, Westminster, S.W.* [London]. Headquarters 61 and 62, Chancery Lane, W.C., London, England [1900], pp. 10–12.

ideals of justice, freedom, and culture which a thousand years of Christian civilisation have held before Europe.

And now, therefore, to these ideals of civilisation, to the broader humanity of the followers of the Prince of Peace, we, the men and women of Africa in world congress assembled, do now solemnly appeal: —

Let the world take no backward step in that slow but sure progress which has successively refused to let the spirit of class, of caste, of privilege, or of birth, debar from like liberty and the pursuit of happiness a striving human soul.

Let not mere colour or race be a feature of distinction drawn between white and black men, regardless of worth or ability.

Let not the natives of Africa be sacrificed to the greed of gold, their liberties taken away, their family life debauched, their just aspirations repressed, and avenues of advancement and culture taken from them.

Let not the cloak of Christian missionary enterprise be allowed in the future, as so often in the past, to hide the ruthless economic exploitation and political downfall of less developed nations, whose chief fault has been reliance on the plighted faith of the Christian church.

Let the British nation, the first modern champion of Negro freedom, hasten to crown the work of Wilberforce, and Clarkson, and Buxton, and Sharpe. Bishop Colenso, and Livingstone, and give, as soon as practicable, the rights of responsible government to the black colonies of Africa and the West Indies.

Let not the spirit of Garrison, Phillips, and Douglas wholly die out in America: may the conscience of a great nation rise and rebuke all dishonesty and unrighteous oppression toward the American Negro, and grant to him the right of franchise, security of person and property, and generous recognition of the great work he has accomplished in a generation toward raising nine millions of human beings from slavery to manhood.

Let the German Empire, and the French Republic, true to their great past, remember that the true worth of colonies lies in their prosperity and progress, and that justice, impartial alike to black and white, is the first element of prosperity.

Let the Congo Free State become a great central Negro State of the world, and let its prosperity be counted not simply in cash and commerce, but in the happiness and true advancement of its black people.

Let the nations of the World respect the integrity and independence of the free Negro States of Abyssinia, Liberia, Hayti, etc., and let the inhabitants of these States, the independent tribes of Africa, the Negroes of the West Indies and America, and the black subjects of all nations take courage, strive ceaselessly, and fight bravely, that they may prove to the world their incontestable right to be counted among the great brotherhood of mankind.

Thus we appeal with boldness and confidence to the Great Powers of the civilised world, trusting in the wide spirit of humanity, and the deep sense of justice of our age, for a generous recognition of the righteousness of our cause.

ALEXANDER WALTERS (Bishop),
  President, Pan-African Association.

HENRY B. BROWN,
  Vice-President.

H. SYLVESTER WILLIAMS,
  General Secretary.

W. E. BURGHARDT DU BOIS,
  Chairman Committee on Address.

The African Roots of the War

'Semper novi quid ex Africa,' cried the Roman proconsul; and he voiced the verdict of forty centuries. Yet there are those who would write world history and leave out this most marvelous of continents. Particularly to-day most men assume that Africa lies far afield from the centres of our burning social problems, and especially from our present problem of World War.

Yet in a very real sense Africa is a prime cause of this terrible overturning of civilization which we have lived to see; and these words seek to show how in the Dark Continent are hidden the roots, not simply of war to-day but of the menace of wars to-morrow.

Always Africa is giving us something new or some metempsychosis of a world-old thing. On its black bosom arose one of the earliest, if not the earliest, of self-protecting civilizations, and grew so mightily that it still furnishes superlatives to thinking and speaking men. Out of its darker and more remote forest fastnesses, came, if we may credit many recent scientists, the first welding of iron, and we know that agriculture and trade flourished there when Europe was a wilderness.

Nearly every human empire that has arisen in the world, material and spiritual, has found some of its greatest crises on this continent of Africa, from Greece to Great Britain. As Mommsen says, 'It was through Africa that Christianity became the religion of the world.' In Africa the last flood of Germanic invasions spent itself within hearing of the last gasp of Byzantium, and it was again through Africa that Islam came to play its great role of conqueror and civilizer.

With the Renaissance and the widened world of modern thought, Africa came no less suddenly with her new old gift. Shakespeare's Ancient Pistol cries —

From *Atlantic Monthly*, 115 (May 1915): 707–714.

> A foutre for the world, and worldlings base!
> I speak of Africa, and golden joys. . . .

So much for the past; and now to-day: the Berlin Conference to apportion the rising riches of Africa among the white peoples met on the fifteenth day of November, 1884. Eleven days earlier, three Germans left Zanzibar (whither they had gone secretly disguised as mechanics), and before the Berlin Conference had finished its deliberations they had annexed to Germany an area over half as large again as the whole German Empire in Europe. Only in its dramatic suddenness was this undisguised robbery of the land of seven million natives different from the methods by which Great Britain and France got four million square miles each, Portugal three quarters of a million, and Italy and Spain smaller but substantial areas.

The methods by which this continent has been stolen have been contemptible and dishonest byond expression. Lying treaties, rivers of rum, murder, assassination, mutilation, rape, and torture have marked the progress of Englishman, German Frenchman, and Belgian on the dark continent. The only way in which the world has been able to endure the horrible tale is by deliberately opping its ears and changing the subject of conversation while the deviltry went on.

It all began, singularly enough, like the present war, with Belgium. Many of us remember Stanley's great solution of the puzzle of Central Africa when he traced the mighty Congo sixteen hundred miles from Nyangwe to the sea. Suddenly the world knew that here lay the key to the riches of Central Africa. It stirred uneasily, but Leopold of Belgium was first on his feet, and the result was the Congo Free State — God save the mark! But the Congo Free State, with all its magniloquent heralding of Peace, Christianity, and Commerce, degenerating into murder, mutilation and downright robbery, differed only in degree and concentration from the tale of all Africa in this rape of a continent already furiously mangled by the slave trade. That sinister traffic, on which the British Empire and the American Republic were largely built, cost black Africa no less than 100,000,000 souls, the wreckage of its political and social life, and left the continent in precisely that state of helplessness which invites aggression and exploitation. 'Color' became in the world's thought synonymous with inferiority, 'Negro' lost its capitalization, and Africa was another name for bestiality and barbarism.

Thus the world began to invest in color prejudice. The 'Color Line' began to pay dividends. For indeed, while the exploration of the valley of the Congo was the occasion of the scramble for Africa, the cause lay deeper. The Franco-Prussian War turned the eyes of those who sought power and dominion away from Europe. Already England was in Africa, cleaning away the débris of the slave trade and half consciously groping toward the new Imperialism. France, humiliated and impoverished, looked toward a new northern African empire sweeping from the Atlantic to the Red Sea. More slowly Germany began to see the dawning of a new day, and, shut out from America by the Monroe Doctrine, looked to Asia and Africa for colonies. Portugal sought anew to make good her claim to her ancient African realm; and thus a continent where Europe claimed but a tenth of the land in 1875, was in twenty-five more years practically absorbed.

Why was this? What was the new call for dominion? It must have been strong, for consider a moment the desperate flames of war that have shot up in Africa in new call for dominion? . . .

The answer to this riddle we shall find in the economic changes in Europe. Remember what the nineteenth and twentieth centuries have meant to organized industry in European civilization. Slowly the divine right of the few to determine economic income and distribute the goods and services of the world has been questioned and curtailed. We called the process Revolution in the eighteenth century, advancing Democracy in the nineteenth, and Socialization of Wealth in the twentieth. But whatever we call it, the movement is the same: the dipping of more and grimier hands into the wealth-bag of the nation, until to-day only the ultra stubborn fail to see that democracy in determining income is the next inevitable step to Democracy in political power.

With the waning of the possibility of the Big Fortune, gathered by starvation wage and boundless exploitation of one's weaker and poorer fellows at home, arose more magnificently the dream of exploitation abroad. Always, of course, the individual merchant had at his own risk and in his own way tapped the riches of foreign lands. Later, special trading monopolies had entered the field and founded empires over-seas. Soon, however, the mass of merchants at home demanded a share in this golden stream; and finally, in the twentieth century, the laborer at home is demanding and beginning to receive a part of his share.

The theory of this new democratic despotism has not been clearly formulated. Most philosophers see the ship of state launched on the broad, irresistible tide of democracy, with only delaying eddies here and there: others, looking closer, are more disturbed. Are we, they ask, reverting to aristocracy and depotism — the rule of might? They cry out and then rub their eyes, for surely they cannot fail to see strengthening democracy all about them?

It is this paradox which has confounded philanthropists, curiously betrayed the Socialists, and reconciled the Imperialists, and captains of industry to any amount of 'Democracy.' It is this paradox which allows in America the most rapid advance of democracy to go hand in hand in its very centres with increased aristocracy and hatred toward darker races, and which excuses and defends an inhumanity that does not shrink from the public burning of human beings.

Yet the paradox is easily explained: the white workingman has been asked to share the spoil of exploiting 'chinks and niggers.' It is no longer simply the merchant prince, or the aristocratic monopoly, or even the employing class, that is exploiting the world: it is the nation; a new democratic nation composed of united capital and labor. The laborers are not yet getting, to be sure, as large a share as they want or will get, and there are still at the bottom large and restless excluded classes. But the laborer's equity is recognized, and his just share is a matter of time, intelligence and skillful negotiation.

Such nations it is that rule the modern world. Their national bond is no mere sentimental patriotism, loyalty, or ancestor-worship. It is increased wealth, power, and luxury for all classes on a scale the world never saw before. Never before was the average citizen of England, France, and Germany so rich, with such splendid prospects of greater riches.

Whence comes this new wealth and on what does its accumulation depend? It comes primarily from the darker nations of the world — Asia and Africa, South and Central America, the West Indies and the islands of the South Seas. There are still, we may well believe, many parts of white countries like Russia and North America, not to mention Europe itself, where the older exploitation still holds. But the knell has sounded faint and far, even there. In the lands of darker folk, however, no knell has sounded. Chinese, East Indians, Negroes, and South American Indians, are by common consent for governance by white folk and economic subjection to them. To the furtherance of this highly profitable economic dictum has been brought every available resource of science and religion. Thus arises the astonishing doctrine of the natural inferiority of most men to the few, and the interpretation of 'Christian brotherhood' as meaning anything that one of the 'brothers' may at any time want it to mean.

Like all world-schemes, however, this one is not quite complete. First of all, yellow Japan has apparently escaped the cordon of this color bar. This is disconcerting and dangerous to white hegemony. If, of course, Japan would join heart and soul with the whites against the rest of the yellows, browns, and blacks, well and good. There are even good-natured attempts to prove the Japanese 'Aryan,' provided they act 'white.' But blood is thick, and there are signs that Japan does not dream of a world governed mainly by white men. This is the 'Yellow Peril,' and it may be necessary, as the German Emperor and many white Americans think, to start a world-crusade against this presumptuous nation which demands 'white' treatment.

Then, too, the Chinese have recently shown unexpected signs of independence and autonomy, which may possibly make it necessary to take them into account a few decades hence. As a result, the problem in Asia has resolved itself into a race for 'spheres' of economic 'influence,' each provided with a more or less 'open door' for business opportunity. This reduces the danger of open clash between European nations, and gives the yellow folk such chance for desperate unarmed resistance as was shown by China's repulse of the Six Nations of Bankers. There is still hope among some whites that conservative North China and the radical South may in time come to blows and allow actual white dominion.

One thing, however, is certain: Africa is prostrate. There at least are few signs of self-consciousness that need at present be heeded. To be sure, Abyssinia must be wheedled, and in America and the West Indies Negroes have attempted futile steps toward freedom; but such steps have been pretty effectually stopped (save through the breech of 'miscegenation'), although the ten million Negroes in the United States need, to many men's minds, careful watching and ruthless repression.

Thus the white European mind has worked, and worked the more feverishly because Africa is the Land of the Twentieth Century. The world knows something of the gold and diamonds of South Africa, the cocoa of Angola and Nigeria, the rubber and ivory of the Congo, and the palm oil of the West Coast. But does the ordinary citizen realize the extraordinary economic advances of Africa and, too, of black Africa, in recent years? . . . There can be no doubt of the economic possibilities of Africa in the near future. There are not only the well-known and traditional products, but boundless chances in a hundred different directions, and above all, there is a throng of human beings who, could they once be reduced to the docility and steadiness of Chinese coolies or of seventeenth and eighteenth century European laborers, would furnish to their masters a spoil exceeding the gold-haunted dreams of the most modern of Imperialists.

This, then, is the real secret of that desperate struggle for Africa which began in 1877 and is now culminating. Economic dominion outside Africa has, of course, played its part, and we were on the verge of the partition of Asia when Asiatic shrewdness warded it off. America was saved from direct political dominion by the Monroe Doctrine. Thus, more and more, the Imperialists have concentrated on Africa.

The greater the concentration the more deadly the rivalry. From Fashoda to Agadir, repeatedly the spark has been applied to the European magazine and a general conflagration narrowly averted. We speak of the Balkans as the storm-centre of Europe and the cause of war, but this is mere habit. The Balkans are convenient for occasions, but the ownership of materials and men in the darker world is the real prize that is setting the nations of Europe at each other's throats to-day.

The present world war is, then, the result of jealousies engendered by the recent rise of armed national associations of labor and capital whose aim is the exploitation of the wealth of the world mainly outside the European circle of nations. These associations, grown jealous and suspicious at the division of the spoils of trade-empire, are fighting to enlarge their respective shares; they look for expansion, not in Europe but in Asia, and particularly in Africa. 'We want no inch of French territory,' said Germany to England, but Germany was 'unable to give' similar assurances as to France in Africa.

The difficulties of this imperial movement are internal as well as external. Successful aggression in economic expansion calls for a close union between capital and labor at home. Now the rising demands of the white laborer, not simply for wages but for conditions of work and a voice in the conduct of industry, make industrial peace difficult. The workingmen have been appeased by all sorts of essays in state socialism, on the one hand, and on the other hand by public threats of competition by colored labor. By threatening to send English capital to China and Mexico, by threatening to hire Negro laborers in America, as well as by old-age pensions and accident insurance, we gain industrial peace at home at the mightier cost of war abroad.

In addition to these national war-engendering jealousies there is a more subtle movement arising from the attempt to unite labor and capital in world-wide freebooting. Democracy in economic organization, while an acknowledged ideal, is to-day working itself out by admitting to a share in the spoils of capital only the aristocracy of labor — the more intelligent and shrewder and cannier workingmen. The ignorant, unskilled, and restless still form a large, threatening, and, to a growing extent, revolutionary group in advanced countries.

The resultant jealousies and bitter hatreds tend continually to fester along the color line. We must fight the Chinese, the laborer argues, or the Chinese will take our bread and butter. We must keep Negroes in their places, or Negroes will take our jobs. All over the world there leaps to articulate speech and ready action that singular assumption that if white men do not throttle colored men, then China, India, and Africa will do to Europe what Europe had done and seeks to do to them.

On the other hand, in the minds of yellow, brown, and black men the brutal truth is clearing: a white man is privileged to go to any land where advantage beckons and behave as he pleases; the black or colored man is being more and more confined to these parts of the world where life for climatic, historical, economic, and political reasons is most difficult to live and most easily dominated by Europe for Europe's gain.

What, then, are we to do, who desire peace and the civilization of all men? Hitherto the peace movement has confined itself chiefly to figures about the cost of war and platitudes on humanity. What do nations care about the cost of war, if by spending a few hundred millions in steel and gunpowder they can gain a thousand millions in diamonds and cocoa? How can love of humanity appeal as a motive to nations whose love of luxury is built on the inhuman exploitation of human beings, and who, especially in recent years, have been taught to regard these human beings, as inhuman? I appealed to the last meeting of peace societies in St. Louis, saying, 'Should you not discuss racial prejudice as a prime cause of war?' The secretary was sorry but was unwilling to introduce controversial matters!

We, then, who want peace, must remove the real causes of war. We have extended gradually our conception of democracy beyond our social class to all social classes in our nation; we have gone further and extended our democratic ideals not simply to all classes of our own nation, but to those of other nations of our blood and lineage — to what we call 'European' civilization. If we want real peace and lasting culture, however, we must go further. We must extend the democratic ideal to the yellow, brown and black peoples.

To say this, is to evoke on the faces of modern men a look of blank hopelessness. Impossible! we are told, and for some many reasons — scientific, social and what not — that argument is useless. But let us not conclude too quickly. Suppose we have to choose between this unspeakably inhuman outrage on decency and intelligence and religion which we call the World War and the attempt to treat black men as human, sentient, responsible beings? We have sold them as cattle. We are working them as beasts of burden. We shall not drive war from this world until we treat them as free and equal citizens in a world-democracy of all races and nations. Impossible? Democracy is a method of doing the impossible. It is the only method yet discovered of making the education and development of all men a matter of all men's desperate desire. It is putting firearms in the hands of a child with the object of compelling the child's neighbors to teach him, not only the real and legitimate uses of a dangerous tool but the uses of himself in all things. Are there other and less costly ways of accomplishing this? There may be in some better world. But for a world just emerging from the rough chains of an almost universal poverty, and faced by the temptation of luxury and indulgence through the enslaving of defenseless men, there is but one adequate method of salvation — the giving of democratic weapons of self-defense to the defenseless.

Nor need we quibble over those ideas, — wealth, education, and political power — soil which we have so forested with claim and counter-claim that we see nothing for the woods.

What the primitive peoples of Africa and the world need and must have if war is to be abolished is perfectly clear:

First: land. To-day Africa is being enslaved by the theft of her land and natural resources. . . .

Secondly: we must train native races in modern civilization. This can be done. Modern methods of educating children, honestly and effectively applied, would make modern, civilized nations out of the vast majority of human beings on earth to-day. . . .

Lastly, the principle of home rule must extend to groups, nations, and races. The ruling of one people for another people's whim or gain must stop. This kind of despotism has been in later days more and more skillfully disguised. But the brute fact remains: the white man is ruling black Africa. . . . Can such a situation bring peace? Will any amount of European concord or disarmament settle this injustice?

Political power to-day is but the weapon to force economic power. To-morrow, it may give us spiritual vision and artistic sensibility. To-day, it gives us or tries to give us bread and butter, and those classes or nations or races who are without it starve, and starvation is the weapon of the white world to reduce them to slavery.

We are calling for European concord to-day; but at the utmost European concord will mean satisfaction with, or acquiescence in, a given division of the spoils of world-dominion. After all, European disarmament cannot go below the necessity of defending the aggressions of the white against the blacks and browns and yellows. From this will arise three perpetual dangers of war. First, renewed jealousy at any division of colonies or spheres of influence agreed upon, if at any future time the present division comes to seem unfair. Who cared for Africa in the early nineteenth century? Let England have the scraps left from the golden feast of the slave trade. But in the twentieth century? The end was war. These scraps looked too tempting to Germany. Secondly: war will come from the revolutionary revolt of the lowest workers. The greater the international jealousies, the greater the corresponding costs of armament and the more difficult to fulfill the promises of industrial democracy in advanced countries. Finally, the colored peoples will not always submit passively to foreign domination. To some this is a lightly tossed truism. When a people deserve liberty they fight for it and get it, say such philosophers; thus making war a regular, necessary step to liberty. Colored people are familiar with this complacent judgment. They endure the contemptuous treatment meted out by whites to those not 'strong' enough to be free. These nations and races, composing as they do a vast majority of humanity, are going to endure this treatment just as long as they must and not a moment longer. Then they are going to fight and the War of the Color Line will outdo in savage inhumanity any war this world has yet seen. For colored folk have much to remember and they will not forget.

But is this inevitable? Must we sit helpless before this awful prospect? While we are planning, as a result of the present holocaust, the disarmament of Europe and a European international world-police, must the rest of the world be left naked to the inevitable horror of war, especially when we know that it is directly in this outer circle of races, and not in the inner European household, that the real causes of present European fighting are to be found?

Our duty is clear. Racial slander must go. Racial prejudice will follow. Steadfast faith in humanity must come. The domination of one people by another without the other's consent, be the subject people black or white, must stop. The doctrine of forcible economic expansion over subject peoples must go. Religious hypocrisy must stop. 'Blood-thirsty' Mwanga of Uganda killed an English bishop because he feared that his coming meant English domination. It did mean English domination, and the world and the bishop knew it, and yet the world was 'horrified'! Such missionary hypocrisy must go. With clean hands and honest hearts we must front high Heaven and beg peace in our time.

In this great work who can help us? In the Orient, the awakened Japanese and the awakening leaders of New China; in India and Egypt, the young men trained in Europe and European ideals, who now form the stuff that Revolution is born of. But in Africa? Who better than the twenty-five million grandchildren of the European slave trade, spread through the Americas, and now writhing desperately for freedom and a place in the world? And of these millions first of all the ten million black folk of the United States, now a problem, then a world-salvation.

Twenty centuries before the Christ a great cloud swept over sea and settled on Africa, darkening and well-nigh blotting out the culture of the land of Egypt. For half a thousand years it rested there until a black woman, Queen Nefertari, 'the most venerated figure in Egyptian history,' rose to the throne of the Pharaohs and redeemed the world and her people. Twenty centuries after Christ, black Africa, prostrate, raped, and shamed, lies at the feet of the conquering Philistines of Europe. Beyond the awful sea a black woman is weeping and waiting with her sons on her breast. What shall the end be? The world-old and fearful things, War and Wealth, Murder and Luxury? Or shall it be a new thing—a new peace and new democracy of all races: a great humanity of equal men? 'Semper novi quid ex Africa!'

The Negro's Fatherland

The future of Africa is one of the most important questions to be answered after this war. The very silence today concerning that future, on both sides of the forces at war, emphasizes its importance. We must remember that in Africa we have today not only the greatest world mine of undeveloped human labor but, also, that much of the raw material which the modern world particularly wants is to be found in Africa more abundantly that anywhere else. Let us note the list: Palm-oil, cocoa, mahogany, ebony, cork, cotton, rubber, ivory, ostrich feathers, gold, copper, iron, zinc, tin, lead and diamonds, — these are the present gifts of Africa to the world. Others in abundance hide in her bosom. The fight for the ownership of these materials and the domination of this labor was a prime cause of the present war. If this question is to be left unsettled after this war it is going to be a prime cause of future wars.

Why, then, are we so silent concerning the fate of something between 150,000,000 and 200,000,000 human beings? I presume that the cause of our indifference is largely psychological. It is the penalty of human degradation which always exacts payment from oppressor and oppressed. Today it is possible to ignore the Negro because of a history of degradation the parallel of which the modern world does not furnish. In ancient Mediterranean civilization Negro blood was predominant in many great nations and present in nearly all. Negro genius and Negro civilization gave here their great gifts to the world. In the European middle ages when Africa became more or less separated from direct contact with Europe, nevertheless, African culture filtered into Europe, and legend and story and song came out of the dark continent. There was then no question of racial inferiority based upon color. But then, beginning late in the fifteenth century, the world for four hundred years raped this continent on a scale never before equalled. The result was not

From *Survey*, 39 (November 10, 1917): 141.

only the degradation of Africa, it was a moral degradation of those who were guilty; and we are still living in the shadow of the debauch of the African slave trade. It comes natural for us to have great masses of unthought-of men; to conceive of society as built upon an unsocial mudsill. It is possible for great labor organizations like the American Federation of Labor to organize themselves upon distinctly aristocratic lines, leaving out of account and out of thought certain so-called lower elements of labor. It is even possible for an organization like the League of Small and Subject Nationalities to bring in Africa only as an accident and after-thought. This mental attitude toward Africa and its problems builds itself upon unclear thinking based on the tyranny of conventional words.

When we speak of modern African slavery we think of modern slavery as a survival of ancient slavery. But it was not. The cleft between the two was absolute. Modern African slavery was the beginning of the modern labor problem, and must be looked at and interpreted from that point of view unless we would lose ourselves in an altogether false analogy. Modern world commerce, modern imperialism, the modern factory system and the modern labor problem began with the African slave trade. The first modern method of securing labor on a wide commercial scale and primarily for profit was inaugurated in the middle of the fifteenth century and in the commerce between Africa and America. Through the slave trade Africa lost at least 100,000,000 human beings, with all the attendant misery and economic and social disorganization. The survivors of this wholesale rape became a great international laboring force in America on which the modern capitalistic movement has been built and out of which modern labor problems have arisen. We have tried ever since to keep these black men and their descendants at the bottom of the scale on the theory that they were not thoroughly men, that they cannot be self-respecting members of and contributors to modern culture — an assumption purely modern and undreamed of in ancient or medieval days.

If, now, this same psychology and this same determination to exploit and enslave these people passes over into the new world after the war, what can we expect but, on the one hand, persistence of the idea that there must be an exploited class at the bottom of civilization and, on the other, an endeavor by endless war and rapine, futile at first but in the end bound to be triumphant, by which these millions of people will gain their right to think and act. No modern world can dream of holding 200,000,000 of people in permanent slavery even though they be black. If it tries, the cost will be terrible. If we would avoid this cost then we must begin the freeing of Africa through this war.

There is an unusual opportunity to do this. Africa is today held by Negro troops trained under European white officers. These Negro troops have saved France. They have conquered German Africa. They and their American Negro brothers are helping to save Belgium. It would be the least that Europe could do in return and some faint reparation for the terrible world history between 1441 and 1861 to see that a great free central African state is erected out of German East Africa and the Belgian Congo. Surely after Belgium has suffered almost as much from Germany as Africa has suffered from her, she ought to be willing to give up the Congo to this end; and it would be right that England should refrain from taking German East Africas as well as refrain from handing it back. Out of this state we would make a great modern effort to restore the ancient efficiency of the land that gave the iron age to all the world, and that for ages led in agriculture, weaving, metal working, and the traffic of the market place. Here is a chance such as the world has not seen since the fifteenth century. Liberia and Haiti were never given a sincere chance and were from first to last harassed, as only modern capitalism can harass little and hated nations.

The effect of such a new and sincere start in Africa would be tremendous. Its first effect would be upon the millions in Africa and then upon their descendants throughout the world. In the West Indies and in South America are some 30,000,000 of men of Negro descent. They have given literature and freedom to Brazil; they have given industry and romance to the West Indies, and they have given to North America art and music and human sensibility. In South America they may lose themselves in the blood of other people, but in the West Indies and North America they are striving for self-expression and need only such encouragement as just treatment of their fatherland and its spiritual effect on the whole world would give. I trust, therefore, that among the new nations that are to start forth after this war will be a new Africa and a new beginning of culture for the Negro race.

"What Is Africa to Me?"

What is Africa to me? Once I should have answered the question simply: I should have said "fatherland" or perhaps better "motherland" because I was born in the century when the walls of race were clear and straight; when the world consisted of mutually exclusive races; and even though the edges might be blurred, there was no question of exact definition and understanding of the meaning of the word. One of the first pamphlets that I wrote in 1897 was on "The Conservation of Races" wherein I set down as the first article of a proposed racial creed: "We believe that the Negro people as a race have a contribution to make to civilization and humanity which no other race can make."

Since then the concept of race has so changed and presented so much of contradiction that as I face Africa I ask myself: what is it between us that constitutes a tie which I can feel better than I can explain? Africa is, of course, my fatherland. Yet neither my father nor my father's father ever saw Africa or knew its meaning or cared overmuch for it. My mother's folk were closer and yet their direct connection, in culture and race, became tenuous; still, my tie to Africa is strong. On this vast continent were born and lived a large portion of my direct ancestors going back a thousand years or more. The mark of their heritage is upon me in color and hair. These are obvious things, but of little meaning in themselves; only important as they stand for real and more subtle differences from other men. Whether they do or not, I do not know nor does science know today.

But one thing is sure and that is the fact that since the fifteenth century these ancestors of mine and their other descendants have had a common history; have suffered a common disaster and have one long memory. The actual ties of heritage between the individuals of this group, vary with the ancestors that they have in common and many others: Europeans and

From *Dusk of Dawn: An Essay Toward an Autobiography of a Race Concept* (1940).

655

Semites, perhaps Mongolians, certainly American Indians. But the physical bond is least and the badge of color relatively unimportant save as a badge; the real essence of this kinship is its social heritage of slavery; the discrimination and insult; and this heritage binds together not simply the children of Africa, but extends through yellow Asia and into the South Seas. It is this unity that draws me to Africa.

When shall I forget the night I first set foot on African soil? I am the sixth generation in descent from forefathers who left this land. The moon was at the full and the waters of the Atlantic lay like a lake. All the long slow afternoon as the sun robed herself in her western scarlet with veils of misty cloud, I had seen Africa afar. Cape Mount — that mighty headland with its twin curves, northern sentinel of the realm of Liberia — gathered itself out of the cloud at half past three and then darkened and grew clear. On beyond flowed the dark low undulating land quaint with palm and breaking sea. The world grew black. Africa faded away, the stars stood forth curiously twisted — Orion in the zenith — the Little Bear asleep and the Southern Cross rising behind the horizon. Then afar, ahead, a lone light shone, straight at the ship's fore. Twinkling lights appeared below, around, and rising shadows. "Monrovia," said the Captain.

Suddenly we swerved to our left. The long arms of the bay enveloped us and then to the right rose the twinkling hill of Monrovia, with its crowning star. Lights flashed on the shore — here, there. Then we sensed a darker shading in the shadows; it lay very still. "It's a boat," one said. "It's two boats!" Then the shadow drifted in pieces and as the anchor roared into the deep, five boats outlined themselves on the waters — great ten-oared barges with men swung into line and glided toward us.

It was nine at night — above, the shadows, there the town, here the sweep-ing boats. One forged ahead with the flag — stripes and a lone star flaming behind, the ensign of the customs floating wide; and bending to the long oars, the white caps of ten black sailors. Up the stairway clambered a soldier in khaki, aide-de-camp of the President of the Republic, a customhouse official, the clerk of the American legation — and after them sixty-five lithe, lean black stevedores with whom the steamer would work down to Portuguese Angola and back. A few moments of formalities, greetings and good-bys and I was in the great long boat with the President's aide — a brown major in brown khaki. On the other side, the young clerk and at the back, the black barelegged pilot. Before us on the high thwarts were the rowers: men, boys, black, thin, trained in muscle and sinew, little larger than the oars in thickness, they bent their strength to them and swung upon them.

One in the center gave curious little cackling cries to keep up the rhythm, and for the spurts and the stroke, a call a bit thicker and sturdier; he gave a low guttural command now and then; the boat, alive, quivering, danced beneath the moon, swept a great curve to the bar to breast its narrow teeth of foam — "t'chick-a-tickity, t'chick-a-tick-ity," sang the boys, and we glided and raced, now between boats, now near the landing — now cast aloft at the dock. And lo! I was in Africa.

Christmas Eve, and Africa is singing in Monrovia. They are Krus and Fanti — men, women and children, and all the night they march and sing. The music was once the music of mission revival hymns. But it is that music now transformed and the silly words hidden in an unknown tongue — liquid and sonorous. It is tricked out and expounded with cadence and turn. And this is that same rhythm I heard first in Tennessee forty years ago: the air is raised and carried by men's strong voices, while floating above in obbligato, come the high mellow voices of women — it is the ancient African art of part singing, so curiously and insistently different.

So they come, gay appareled, lit by transparency. They enter the gate and flow over the high steps and sing and sing and sing. They saunter round the house, pick flowers, drink water and sing and sing and sing. The warm dark heat of the night steams up to meet the moon. And the night is song.

On Christmas Day, 1923, we walk down to the narrow, crooked wharves of Monrovia, by houses old and gray and step-like streets of stone. Before is the wide St. Paul River, double-mouthed, and beyond, the sea, white, curling on the sand. Before us is the isle — the tiny isle, hut-covered and guarded by a cotton tree, where the pioneers lived in 1821. We board the boat, then circle round — then up the river. Great bowing trees, festoons of flowers, golden blossoms, star-faced palms and thatched huts; tall spreading trees lifting themselves like vast umbrellas, low shrubbery with gray and laced and knotted roots — the broad, black, murmuring river. Here a tree holds wide fingers out and stretches them over the water in vast incantation; bananas throw their wide green fingers to the sun. Iron villages, scarred clearings with gray, sheet-iron homes staring, grim and bare, at the ancient tropical flood of green.

The river sweeps wide and the shrubs bow low. Behind, Monrovia rises in clear, calm beauty. Gone are the wharves, the low and clustered houses of the port, the tight-throated business village, and up sweep the villas and the low wall, brown and cream and white, with great mango and cotton trees, with lighthouse and spire, with porch and pillar and the color of shrubbery and blossom.

We climbed the upright shore to a senator's home and received his wide and kindly hospitality — curious blend of feudal lord and modern farmer — sandwiches, cake, and champagne. Again we glided up the drowsy river — five, ten, twenty miles and came to our hostess, a mansion of five generations with a compound of endless native servants and cows under the palm thatches. The daughters of the family wore, on the beautiful black skin of their necks, the exquisite pale gold chains of the Liberian artisan and the slim, black little granddaughter of the house had a wide pink ribbon on the thick curls of her dark hair, that lay like sudden sunlight on the shadows. Double porches, one above the other, welcomed us to ease. A native man, gay with Christmas and a dash of gin, sang and danced in the road. Children ran and played in the blazing sun. We sat at a long broad table and ate duck, chicken, beef, rice, plantain, collards, cake, tea, water and Madeira wine. Then we went and looked at the heavens, the uptwisted sky — Orion and Cassiopeia at zenith; the Little Bear beneath the horizon, now unfamiliar sights in the Milky Way — all awry, a-living — sun for snow at Christmas, and happiness and cheer.

The shores were lined with old sugar plantations, the buildings rotting and falling. I looked upon the desolation with a certain pain. What had happened, I asked? The owners and planters had deserted these homes and come down to Monrovia, but why? After all, Monrovia had not much to offer in the way of income and occupation. Was this African laziness and inefficiency? No, it was a specimen of the way in which the waves of modern industry broke over the shores of far-off Africa. Here during our Civil War, men hastened to raise sugar and supply New York. They built their own boats and filled the river and sailed the sea. But afterwards, Louisiana came back into the Union, colored Rillieux invented the vacuum pan; the sugar plantations began to spread in Cuba and the Sugar Trust monopoly of refining machinery, together with the new beet sugar industry, drove Liberia quickly from the market. What all this did not do, the freight rates finished. So sugar did not pay in Liberia and other crops rose and fell in the same way.

As I look back and recall the days, which I have called great — the occasions in which I have taken part and which have had for me and others the widest significance, I can remember none like the first of January, 1924. Once I took my bachelor's degree before a governor, a great college president, and a bishop of New England. But that was rather personal in its memory than in any way epochal. Once before the assembled races of the world I was called to speak in London in place of the suddenly sick Sir Harry Johnston. It was a great hour. But it was not greater than the day when I was presented to the President of the Negro Republic of Liberia.

Liberia had been resting under the shock of world war into which the Allies forced her. She had asked and been promised a loan by the United States to bolster and replace her stricken trade. She had conformed to every preliminary requirement and waited when waiting was almost fatal. It was not simply money, it was world prestige and protection at a time when the little republic was sorely beset by creditors and greedy imperial powers. At the last moment, an insurgent Senate peremptorily and finally refused the request and strong recommendation of President Wilson and his advisers, and the loan was refused. The Department of State made no statement to the world, and Liberia stood naked, not only well-nigh bankrupt, but peculiarly defenseless amid scowling and unbelieving powers.

It was then that the United States made a gesture of courtesy; a little thing, and merely a gesture, but one so unusual that it was epochal. President Coolidge, at the suggestion of William H. Lewis, a leading colored lawyer of Boston, named me, an American Negro traveler, Envoy Extraordinary and Minister Plenipotentiary to Liberia — the highest rank ever given by any country to a diplomatic agent in black Africa. And it named this Envoy the special representative of the President of the United States to the President of Liberia, on the occasion of his inauguration; charging the Envoy with a personal word of encouragement and moral support. It was a significant action. It had in it nothing personal. Another appointee would have been equally significant. But Liberia recognized the meaning. She showered upon the Envoy every mark of appreciation and thanks. The Commander of the Liberian Frontier Force was made his special aide, and a sergeant, his orderly. At ten a.m. New Year's morning, 1924, a company of the Frontier Force, in red fez and khaki, presented arms before the American Legation and escorted Solomon Porter Hood, the American Minister Resident, and myself as Envoy Extraordinary and my aide to the Presidential Mansion — a beautiful white, verandaed house, waving with palms and fronting a grassy street.

Ceremonials are old and to some antiquated and yet this was done with such simplicity, grace and seriousness that none could escape its spell. The Secretary of State met us at the door, as the band played the impressive Liberian National hymn, and soldiers saluted:

> All hail! Liberia, hail!
> In union strong, success is sure.
> We cannot fail.
> With God above,
> Our rights to prove,
> We will the world assail.

Africa for the Africans

The Associated Press in a Paris dispatch, put into the mouth of the editor a statement that colored Americans could not withstand the African climate, could not oust the Europeans, and did not desire to do so.

It ought to go without saying that the editor never made any such statement. The American Negro is just as able to withstand the African climate as American white men and no more able. The climate is severe and trying, but a healthy man who follows the rules of tropical hygiene can live there. There is, therefore, no necessary barrier of climate to keep American Negroes out of Africa.

On the other hand, it would be foolish for colored folk to assume that because their great grandfathers were Africans that the climate of Africa would have no terrors for them. It has its terrors for all men and these terrors can be overcome.

The present opportunity for emigration to Africa is, however, exceedingly limited. There is absolutely no chance for colored laborers. Men with capital, education and some technical or agricultural skill, who have the courage of pioneers, good health, and are willing to rough it can find a career in Liberia, in some parts of French, Portuguese and Egyptian Africa (if they speak the language), and in some parts of British West Africa, if they are British subjects. They will be objects of suspicion in British West Africa and will suffer some caste restrictions.

On the other hand, in the Belgian Congo, in British East and South Africa and in Rhodesia, an American Negro would hardly be allowed to enter, much less settle. Black merchants and traders have chances in West Africa but they Aare at the mercy not only of the governments who are not eager to help them, but also of the great banks, corporations and syndicates who are in position to skim the cream of all profits.

From *The Crisis*, February 1922.

Again the editor distinctly believes that Africa should be administered for the Africans and, as soon as may be, by the Africans. He does not mean by this that Africa should be administered by West Indians or American Negroes. They have no more right to administer Africa for the native Africans than native Africans have to administer America.

A Second Journey to Pan-Africa

In 1919 Pan-Africa was a phrase of war — an attempt to call the attention of the world in travail to the plight of a race. The cry was heard but hardly understood, for other and greater cries drowned it. But in 1921 there seemed to come a chance to test the depths and meaning of Pan-Africa consciousness.

Three sets of audiences gathered in London, Brussels and Paris for the Second Pan-African Congress. In the English gathering were Negroes and mulattoes from West and South Africa, British Guiana, Grenada, Jamaica, Nigeria and the Gold Coast; Indians from India and East Africa; colored men from London and twenty-five American Negroes. The voices were outspoken after a rather timid and apologetic opening. The resolutions — strong and clear, with their plain leaning toward industrial democracy — went through without a dissenting voice, though some older representatives of white British philanthropy were evidently not content.

The British attitude showed itself best in a conference arranged by the Aborigines Protection Society with Sir Sidney Olivier, former Governor of Jamaica, in the chair. Their secretary promptly put the burden of position on us by offering three resolutions for our adoption on Land, Labor, and Conscription in Africa. Our committee replied that a demand for "sufficent lands" "to provide for the economic independence of the family units" in Africa did not go far enough; that we agreed with their opposition to the new slavery and did not agree that France had no right to conscript her black as well as her white citizens, so long as conscription was her policy, and so long as she recognized racial equality; and that France did come nearer this recognition than any other modern land. Then we in turn changed the subject and spoke freely of the future relations of philanthropy and the Negro problem laying down the principle that Negro effort, aided by white cooperation, must be the rule rather than white effort carried on without reference to the opinion and

From *New Republic*, 29 (December 7, 1921): 39–42.

wishes of black folk or with only casual consultation of picked representatives.

In contrast to this attitude was our conference with the foreign relations committee of the Labor party. There we sought to let men like [John R.] Clynes, Sidney and Beatrice Webb, Lowes Dickinson, Mrs. Philip Snowden, Leonard Woolf, C. P. Buxton, Sir G. Fordham and others, know the real oneness of black and white labor problems. They were not perhaps entirely convinced, but they were deeply sympathetic and were plainly seeking information rather than hoping to give advice.

In Belgium the scene changed. We had here audiences predominantly white and local, but the Belgian Congo was strongly represented, the American group was increased and the French colonies and Abyssinia appeared. Not only was this a change of personnel but the language difficulty was to the fore, leaving the thirty Americans for the most part linguistically stranded; and too, a new spirit was in the air. We sensed the Fear about us in a war-land with nerves still taut. It had taken swift work with Mr. Frank, the Colonial Minister, and others, and probably some diplomatic interchanges, to keep us from being denied admission to Belgium, and particularly the use of the State building, the Palais Mondial. The opening session was palpitating with curiosity and the press tables were crowded. Two Generals graced the platform where presided the black Senegalese, Blaise Diagne, President of the Congress and French Deputy and High Commissioner of African troops. A white French deputy was also there, an Abyssinian, and an American colored woman; the Colonial Office was represented by two officials who pointedly declined platform seats; there were also present a group of international students, several hundred white Belgians, and many black Congolese.

For two days the speeches went on smoothly — too smoothly, I felt, because nothing was being said but platitudes — not a word about the past in the Congo; not a word about the present; only a hint of a future with some education, some recognition of the chiefs, some industrial betterment. To this was added every effort to show what Belgium had done for the Negro. And here there was much to be said: we stood astounded before the crowning wonder of that museum at Tervurien. It was marvelous — the visible, riotous wealth of the Congo, the startling size of the vast African empire destined to make Belgium but a physical fraction of her own black colonial self; the beauty — the infinite, intriguing, exquisite beauty of art. And yet in the midst and center at the end of the long, straight, beech-lined avenue of ten miles, sat Leopold II in ivory; while in the Congress he had not been mentioned.

It was in no spirit of trouble-making but as a simple duty that I rose the last afternoon and read in French and English the resolutions of London. I did not dream of the consternation which I would cause, but even if I had, it was my evident and bounden duty to read our adopted charter of complaint and hope, even in Belguim. I had previously made it plain in correspondence that we came not for "revolution" but certainly for calm and reasonable complaint, and I was unprepared to hear the word which London received without protest, called "Bolshevist" and "absolutely inadmissible" in Brussels.

Diagne, the Senegalese Frenchman who presided, was beside himself with excitement after the resolutions were read; as an under-secretary of the French government, as ranking Negro of greater France, and perhaps as a successful investor in French colonial enterprises, he was undoubtedly in a difficult position. Possibly he was bound by actual promises to France and Belgium. His French was almost too swift for my ears, but his meaning was clear: he felt that the cause of the black man in Belgium and France had been compromised by black American radicals; he especially denounced our demand for "the restoration of the ancient common ownership of the land in Africa" as rank communism. Panda, the young French black leader of Negro Congo in Belgium, was curiously perplexed and my heart went out to him. White friends — his foster mother, a Belgian general, several members of philanthropic bodies — eddied about him and about Diagne with advice and warning, while several Belgian officials made speeches and reporters hunted for copy.

Meantime, the colored Americans were pressing rather peremptorily for the appointment of a committee on the question of our London resolutions — forgetting the almost unlimited power of a French presiding officer. I was both alarmed and cheered. At least the question had been laid before Belgium and the world. We would not leave a Negro World Congress without really mentioning the truth of our problems. On the other hand, if it could be said that our Congress ended in an uproar — or if our French and Belgian colleagues could be induced to withdraw, the Pan-African movement would receive a severe, perhaps fatal, check. Paul Otlet, a white Belgian, "father of the League of Nations" and co-secretary with Senator La Fontaine of the Palais Mondial, sought to calm the waters by a harmless proposal which Diagne rushed to a vote, even allowing guests and visitors a voice, and swamping Pan-Africa momentarily under the opinion of white Belgians. Mr. Otlet's proposition declared Negroes "susceptible" of advancement from their present backward condition and that their development would rid humanity of a weight of 200 millions of ignorant incompetents, and that collaboration between races on a basis of equality was an urgent duty today. He proposed, therefore, a federation of all uplift agencies of Negroes and their friends centering in the Palais Mondial, Belgium.

Diagne's precipitate acceptance of this program pleased neither its promoters, like the aged General Sorelas, former pupil of the great Cardinal Lavigenie — nor yet the American Negroes who envisaged a bigger, stronger movement and who saw little to encourage them to hope that Belgium was ready to lead in the restoration of Negro civilization. Their strong but calm stand finally brought order out of threatened chaos: the Otlet resolutions were declared adopted, but the London manifesto was held for further consideration, to be debated on and finally voted on in Paris. After adjournment, groups of whites and blacks stood about until dark, discussing in French, Flemish, Spanish, Portuguese and English, the meaning of that whirl of deep feeling which flared before adjournment.

We came to Paris with a sense of strain and apprehension, only partially allayed by a long, frank conference with Diagne who acknowledged that his methods in Brussels were high-handed but contended that he had only sought to prevent the "assassination of a race!" The Paris meeting was different from both London and Brussels. It was not "official" — it had clear and determined elements of revolt. It was outspoken and it was bitter with complaint. The variety of groups represented was larger than in London or Brussels, and included besides the United States, the former German colonies, the Portuguese colonies, French Senegal, Congo, and the West Indies, British West India, the Philippines and Annam. There was no attempt to control the Congress in the interests of any one point of view. None of the colored deputies of the French Parliament attempted to have their way exclusively. Every attempt at smooth platitude was thwarted. "We are a little France," cried the Haitian Minister diplomatically. "Yes, France did not give freedom to Haiti — Haiti took it," answered the Americans amid the wild applause of young Haiti; and they added that when America seized Haiti, it was not France but black America which made the only effective protest.

"We are getting on all right in the French Congo," cried a black Congolese in halting phrase but he was followed by a white Frenchman, Challaye, with circumstantial denunciation of French methods in her Congo.

French and English officials, two ex-governors from Africa, and many prominent whites watched the proceedings and reporters questioned us; above all, one thought was uppermost: What did this Congress mean? What was back of it? What were our objects? Especially we were asked repeatedly if we represented the West Indian "Africa for the Africans" movement, which apparently proposed the forcible expulsion of the whites. It was not easy to explain at first that this Congress was a meeting for conference and acquaintanceship, for organization and study; that it did not as yet represent any complete, and adopted policy, but that its members almost unanimously repudiated any policy of war, conquest, or race hatred. On the other hand, we did agree on an unalterable belief in racial equality and on the general proposition that the government and policy of Africa must be designed primarily for the good of the Africans themselves and not primarily for the profit of colonial powers.

Here it was that we encountered the central Fear of France; the main reaction of that organized thrift of Central Europe which is today governing and leading economic reorganization after the war. France recognizes Negro equality not only in theory but in practice; she has for the most part enfranchised her civilized Negro citizens. But what she recognizes is the equal right of her citizens, black and white, to exploit by modern industrial methods her laboring classes, black and white; and the crying danger to black France is that its educated and voting leaders will join in the industrial robbery of Africa rather than lead its masses to education and culture. This is not yet true, but men like Diagne and Candace, while unwavering defenders of racial opportunity, education for blacks and the franchise for the civilized, are curiously timid when the industrial problems of Africa are approached.

For instance, they asked us to omit from the French version of our English manifesto, seven paragraphs which emphasized and particularized our arraignment of predatory capital in Africa. The gist of the paragraphs lay in these words:

> If we are coming to recognize that the great modern problem is to correct maladjustment in the distribution of wealth, it must be remembered that the basic maladjustment is in the outrageously unjust distribution of world income between the dominant and suppressed peoples; in the rape of land and raw material; the monopoly of technique and culture. And in this crime white labor is *particeps criminis* with white capital. Unconsciously and consciously, carelessly and deliberately, the vast power of the white labor vote in modern democracies, has been cajoled and flattered into imperialistic schemes to enslave and debauch black, brown and yellow labor, until with fatal retribution, they are themselves today bound and gagged and rendered impotent by the resulting monopoly of the world's raw material in the hands of a dominant, cruel and irresponsible few.

The Americans insisted upon including these paragraphs, but consented to have them especially marked as being the opinion of black America but reserved by black France for consideration at the next Congress.

Back of this serious internal difference of opinion and policy, which future Congresses must thresh out, lay a subtler and more fundamental problem: Europe asked, What do these hundred, more or less, persons of near and far Negroid ancestry really represent? Is this a real Pan-Negro movement or the work of individuals or of small groups enthusiastic with an idea but representing little?

And we ourselves could not answer. Of the hundred and fifty millions of African Negroes, few were conscious of our meetings. But a few were: in

South Africa — even in far Swaziland — and in Kenya, East Africa — in the Egyptian Sudan, in Angola, in Liberia and British West Africa, in Nigeria and the Gold Coast, in the French and Belgian Congo and throughout the Americas, many black men knew definitely of our meeting and some attended. But how far did we really represent and voice them and how far were we merely floating in the air of our dreams and ambitions?

We were undoubtedly an intelligentsia — a small group of intellectuals interpreting to some extent, but more certainly seeking to guide the public opinion of our group. Was our interpretation honest and clear, and would our guidance be followed? Who shall say until Time itself tells? But certainly there is today no gainsaying the ground swell in the Negro race — the great, unresting, mighty surge; it is reported by every colored official, it is feared by every colonial power, it is sensed by every intelligent Negro in every part of the world. What is it? Sometimes it is revolt against slavery; sometimes revolt against land theft; sometimes complaint against low wages, always a chafing at the color-bar.

What part did the Pan-African Congress play in this worldwide feeling? It did not cause it, as many accuse; it but partially and fitfully voiced it. But it did do three things:

1. It brought face to face and in personal contact a group of educated Negroes of the calibre that might lead black men to emancipation in the modern world.
2. It discovered among these men more points of agreement than of difference.
3. It expressed the need of further meetings and strengthened the permanent organization.

Little Portraits of Africa

THE PLACE, THE PEOPLE

Africa is vegetation. It is the riotous, unbridled bursting life of leaf and limb. It is sunshine — pitiless shine of blue rising from morning mists and sinking to hot night shadows. And then the stars — very near are the stars to Africa, near and bright and curiously arrayed. The tree is Africa. The strong, blinding strength of it — the wide deep shade, the burly lavish height of it. Animal life is there wild and abundant — perhaps in the inner jungle I should note it more but here the herb is triumphant, savagely sure — such beautiful shrubbery, such splendor of leaf and gorgeousness of flower I have never seen.

And the people! Last night I went to Kru-town and saw a Christmas masque. There were young women and men of the color of warm ripe horse chestnuts, clothed in white robes and turbaned. They played the Christ story with sincerity, naiveté and verve. Conceive "Silent Night" sung in Kru by this dark white procession with flaming candles; the little black mother of Christ crossing with her baby, in figured blue, with Joseph in Mandingan fez and multi-colored cloak and beside them on her worshipping knees the white wreathed figure of a solemn dark angel. The shepherds watched their flocks by night, the angels sang; and Simeon, raising the baby high in his black arms, sang with my heart in English Kru-wise, *"Lord now lettest thou thy servant depart in peace for mine eyes have seen thy salvation!"*

Liberia is gay in costume — the thrifty Krus who burst into color of a holiday; the proud Veys always well-gowned; the Liberian himself often in white. The children sometimes in their own beautiful skins.

From *The Crisis*, April 1924.

668

SUNDAY, JANUARY 13, 1924

I have walked three hours in the African bush. In the high bush mighty trees arose draped, with here and there the flash of flower and call of bird. The monkey sentinel cried and his fellows dashed down the great tree avenues. The way was marked — yonder the leopard that called last night under the moon, a bush cow's hoof; a dainty tread of antelope. We leaped the trail of driver ants and poked at the great houses of the white ants. The path rose and wound and fell now soft in green glow, now golden, now shimmery through the water as we balanced on a bare log. There was whine of monkey, scramble of timid unseen life, glide of dark snake. Then came the native farms — coffee, cocoa, plantain, cassava. Nothing is more beautiful than an African village — its harmonious colorings — its cleanliness, its dainty houses with the kitchen palaver place of entertainment, its careful delicate decorations and then the people. I believe that the African form in color and curve is the beautifulest thing on earth; the face is not so lovely — though often comely with perfect teeth and shining eyes, — but the form of the slim limbs, the muscled torso, the deep full breasts!

The bush is silence. Silence of things to be, silence vocal with infinite minor music and flutter and tremble — but silence, deep silence of the great void of Africa.

And the palms; some rose and flared like green fine work; some flared before they rose; some soared and drooped; some were stars and some were sentinels; then came the ferns — the feathery delicate things of grottos and haunts with us, leapt and sang in the sun — they thrust their virgin tracery up and out and almost to trees. Bizarre shapes of grass and shrub and leaf greeted us as though some artist all Divine was playing and laughing and trying every trick of his bewitched pencil above the mighty buildings of the ants.

I am riding on the singing heads of black boys swinging in a hammock. The smooth black bodies swing and sing, the neck set square, the hips sway. O lovely voices and sweet young souls of Africa!

The Pan-African Congresses

The Story of a Growing Movement

The *first Pan-African Congress* was held February 19–21, *1919*, in the Grand Hotel, Paris. The executive committee consisted of M. Blaise Diagne, President; Dr. W.E.B. Du Bois, Secretary; Mrs. Ida Gibbs Hunt and Mr. M.E.F. Fredericks. Fifty-seven delegates representing fifteen countries were present and among the speakers were members of the French Parliament, the President of Liberia, a former Secretary of State of Portugal and several other distinguished persons.

The *second Pan-African Congress* met in London August 28 and 29, *1921*, in Brussels, Belgium, August 31, and September 1 and 2, *1921*, and in Paris, France, September 4 and 5, *1921*, with M. Blaise Diagne as President and W.E.B. Du Bois as Executive Secretary. A special committee visited the Assembly of the League of Nations with a petition, September 6. There were present one hundred and ten delegates representing thirty-three different countries and the sessions were attended by about a thousand visitors. Among the speakers were Florence Kelley of America, Norman Leys of England, Senator LaFontaine and Professor Otlet of Belgium, Blaise Diagne and M. Barthèlemy of the French Chamber of Deputies, General Sorelas of Spain, M. Paul Panda of the Belgian Congo and others. The European press of England, Scotland, France, Belgium, Germany and Italy took wide notice of the Congress.

The *third Pan-African Congress* was held November 7 and 8, *1923* in London and November 25, *1923* in Lisbon. There was a small number of delegates to these sessions as the Congress had not been properly worked up by the French secretary. The Circle of Peace and Foreign Relations under Mrs. A. W.

From *The Crisis*, October 1927.

Hunton as Chairman finally sent Dr. Du Bois to hold the Congress. There were some distinguished people as speakers including Sir Sidney, now Lord Olivier, Mr. H. G. Wells and Mr. Harold Laski; and Mr. Ramsey McDonald would have been present had it not been for the sudden crisis of the general election. In Lisbon there were present the Minister of Colonies and one former minister and several members of parliament.

It was planned to have the *fourth Pan-African Congress* meet in the West Indies in 1925 but the plans miscarried on account of the difficulty of transport. Finally, the Circle of Peace and Foreign Relations, under the Chairmanship of Mrs. A. W. Hunton, came forward and undertook to assemble the Fourth Congress in New York City, August 21, 22, 23, and 24, 1927. The Circle raised nearly Three Thousand Dollars to finance the Congress and made all the arrangements. Dr. W.E.B. Du Bois acted as General Chairman and Mr. Rayford W. Logan as Secretary and interpreter. An exhibition of fifty-two maps and charts illustrating the condition of peoples of African descent was arranged by Dr. Du Bois and was on exhibition at headquarters.

The program included an opening meeting with history of the Pan-African Congresses and greetings by delegates from West Africa, several of the West Indian Islands, including Haiti, and the East Indies. To this Mr. William Pickens added a report of the Brussels Conference for Oppressed Races. On the following three days, sessions were held morning, afternoon and night, taking up African missions, the history of Africa, the history and present conditions of the West Indies, the economic development of Africa and the political partition of Africa. The closing meeting dealt with education in Africa and African art and literature.

Among the chief speakers during the sessions were M. Dantes Bellegarde, former Minister of Haiti to France, former Member of the Assembly of the League of Nations and Commander of the French Legion of Honor; Dr. Charles H. Wesley, of Howard University; Professor Melville Herskovits of Columbia; Professor L. W. Hansberry of Howard; Chief Amoah III of the British Gold Coast; Mr. Leslie Pinkney Hill and Mr. H. H. Phillips of Cheyney; Dr. Wilhelm Mensching of Germany; and Mr. John Vandercook. All the sessions were well attended and the evening sessions often crowded. The total attendance aggregated five thousand persons. There were 208 paid delegates, representing 22 states and the District of Columbia; Haiti, the Virgin Islands, the Bahamas and Barbadoes; South America; the Gold Coast, Sierra Leone, Nigeria and Liberia, West Africa; Germany and India. The following resolutions were adopted:

The Fourth Pan-African Congress, assembled in New York City, August

21, 22, 23 and 24, 1927, with representatives from twenty-three American states, from nearly all of the West Indian Islands, from South America, Liberia, and British West Africa adopts this statement to express the legitimate aims and needs of the peoples of Negro descent.

IN GENERAL

Negroes everywhere need:

1. A voice in their own government.
2. Native rights to the land and its natural resources.
3. Modern education for all children.
4. The development of Africa for the Africans and not merely for the profit of Europeans.
5. The re-organization of commerce and industry so as to make the main object of capital and labor the welfare of the many rather than the enriching of the few.
6. The treatment of civilized men as civilized despite differences of birth, race or color.

Specifically and in particular we stress the need of reform in the following countries:

HAITI

In accordance with the report of the Committee of Six disinterested Americans we demand: the withdrawal from *Haiti* of all military forces of the United States and all officers, military, naval or otherwise, except only regularly accredited diplomatic representatives or consular agents. We demand that actual self-government be restored. In 1928 Haitian elections should be held. We demand that the American Receiver General of Customs be replaced by equitable agreement with the bond holders and that in general the attempt of American capital to dominate the industry and monopolize the land of Haiti be decisively checked and turned into such channels as will encourage industry and agriculture for the benefit of Haitian people. . . .

BRITISH AFRICA

We congratulate Great Britain on granting increased political power to the four colonies of *British West Africa*. We urge an extension of this policy so that Africans may control their own legislative councils.

We urge restoration of their land and the granting of a voice in the government to the natives of *Kenya* and of *Northern* and *Southern Rhodesia*. . . .

FRENCH AFRICA

We urge in French Africa a further development of their admirable scheme of native education and an extension of political rights for a larger number of natives. We ask protection for the natives against the exploitation by French industry and commerce of the resources of this great colony.

THE BELGIAN CONGO

We still await in the *Belgium Congo* real evidence of a movement on the part of Belgium to restore land ownership to the natives; to give them some voice in their own government and to restrain the effort to make the Belgium Congo merely a profitable investment for European industry. . . .

ABYSSINIA

We demand the continued independence of *Abyssinia*, coupled with international movements on the part of philanthropists to bring modern education to the people of that land and modern industry planned for the benefit of the Abyssinians and not simply for the European trade.

LIBERIA

. . . We believe that the solution of Liberia's problems lies in the establishment of a strong system of universal education for all Liberians of both native and American descent.

PORTUGAL

We demand for *Portugal* and her African colonies a curbing of that financial and industrial power which is forcing her into bankruptcy and making her colonies the property of slave-driving concessionaires, despite the liberal and far-sighted colonial legislation of Portugal.

MISSIONS

We believe in missionary effort but in missionary effort for health, morals and education and not for military aggression and sectarian superstitions.

THE WEST INDIES

We urge the peoples of the *West Indies* to begin an earnest movement for the federation of these islands; the reduction of their present outrageous expenses of government; the broadening of educational facilities on modern lines and labor legislation to protect the workers against industrial exploitation. We regard the first step towards this to be an utter erasing of that color line between mulattoes and blacks, which sprang from slavery and is still being drawn and encouraged by those who are the enemies of Negro freedom.

UNITED STATES

We believe that the Negroes of the United States should begin the effective use of their political power and instead of working for a few minor offices or for merely local favors and concessions, they should vote with their eyes fixed upon the international problems of the color line and the national problems which effect the Negro race in the United States. Only independent votes for candidates who will carry out their desires regardless of party will bring them political and economic freedom.

The economic situation of American Negroes is still precarious. We believe that along with their entry into industry as skilled and semi-skilled workers and their growing ownership of land and homes they should especially organize as consumers and from co-operative effort seek to bring to bear upon investors and producers the coercive power which co-operative consumption has already attained in certain parts of Europe and of America. Lynching, segregation and mob violence still oppress and crush black America but education and organized social and political power begin to point the way out.

OTHER PEOPLES

Upon matters that lie outside our own problems, we must also express our thought and wish because the narrow confines of the modern world entwine our interests with those of other peoples. We desire to see freedom and real national independence in Egypt, in China and in India. We demand the cessation of the interference of the United States in the affairs of Central and South America.

We thank the Soviet Government of Russia for its liberal attitude toward the colored races and for the help which it has extended to them from time to time.

We urge the white workers of the world to realize that no program of labor uplift can be successfully carried through in Europe or America so long as colored labor is exploited and enslaved and deprived of all political power.

A committee to call a Fifth Pan-African Congress and to present to it a plan of permanent organization was appointed. It consisted of Dr. W.E.B. Du Bois, chairman, Mrs. A.W. Hunton, M. Dantes Bellegarde, Mr. H.H. Phillips, Mr. Rayford W. Logan, Mr. F. Eugene Corbie, Mr. Otto E. Huiswoud, Mrs. B. Cannady and Bishop R.C. Ransom. This committee has power to enlarge its number.

The Disfranchised Colonies

Colonies and the colonial system make the colonial peoples
in a sense the slums of the world, disfranchised and held in
poverty and disease.

Colonies are the slums of the world. They are today the places of greatest
concentration of poverty, disease, and ignorance of what the human mind has
come to know. They are centers of helplessness, of discouragement of initiative, of forced labor, and of legal suppression of all activities or thoughts which
the master country fears or dislikes.

They resemble in some ways the municipal slums of the nineteenth
century in culture lands. In those days men thought of slums as inevitable, as
being caused in a sense by the wretched people who inhabited them, as
yielding to no remedial action in any conceivable time. If abolished, the dregs
of humanity would re-create them. Then we were jerked back to our senses by
the realization that slums were investments where housing, sanitation, education, and spiritual freedom were lacking, and where for this reason the profits
of the landlords, the merchants, and the exploiters were enormous.

To most people this characterization of colonies will seem overdrawn, and
of course in one major respect colonies differ radically from slums. Municipal
slums are mainly festering sores drawing their substance from the surrounding
city and sharing the blood and the culture of that city. Colonies, on the other
hand, are for the most part quite separate in race and culture from the peoples
who control them. Their culture is often ancient and historically fine and
valuable, spoiled too often by misfortune and conquest and misunderstanding. This sense of separation, therefore, makes colonies usually an integral
entity beyond the sympathy and the comprehension of the ruling world. But

From *Color and Democracy: Colonies and Peace* (1945).

in both city and colony, labor is forced by poverty, and crime is largely disease.

What, then, are colonies? Leaving analogies, in this case none too good, we look to facts, and find them also elusive. It is difficult to define a colony precisely. There are the dry bones of statistics; but the essential facts are neither well measured nor logically articulated. After all, an imperial power is not interested primarily in censuses, health surveys, or historical research. Consequently we know only approximately, and with wide margins of error, the colonial population, the number of the sick and the dead, and just what happened before the colony was conquered.

For the most part, today the colonial peoples are colored of skin; this was not true of colonies in other days, but it is mainly true today. And to most minds, this is of fatal significance; coupled with Negro slavery, Chinese coolies, and doctrines of race inferiority, it proves to most white folk the logic of the modern colonial system: Colonies are filled with peoples who never were abreast with civilization and never can be.

This rationalization is very satisfactory to empire-builders and investors, but it does not satisfy science today, no matter how much it did yesterday. Skin color is a matter of climate, and colonies today are mainly in the hot, moist tropics and semitropics. Naturally, here skins are colored. But historically these lands also were seats of ancient cultures among normal men. Here human civilization began, in Africa, Asia, and Central America. What has happened to these folk across the ages? They have been conquered, enslaved, oppressed, and exploited by stronger invaders. But was this invading force invariably stronger in body, keener in mind, and higher in culture? Not necessarily, but always stronger in offensive technique, even though often lower in culture and only average in mind.

Offensive technique drew the conquerors down upon the conquered, because the conquered had the fertile lands, the needed materials, the arts of processing goods for human needs. With the conquerors concentrating time and thought on these aspects of culture, usually the conquered could not oppose the barbarians with muscle, clubs, spears, gunpowder, and capital. In time, the invaders actually surpassed, and far surpassed, the weaker peoples in wealth, technique, and variety of culture patterns, and made them slaves to industry and servants to white men's ease.

But what of the future? Have the present masters of the world such an eternal lien on civilization as to ensure unending control? By no means; their very absorption in war and wealth has so weakened their moral fiber that the end of their rule is in sight. Also, the day of the colonial conquered peoples dawns, obscurely but surely.

Today, then, the colonial areas lie inert or sullenly resentful or seething with hate and unrest. With unlimited possibilities, they have but scraps of understanding of modern accumulations of knowledge; but they are pressing toward education with bitter determination. The conquerors, on the other hand, are giving them only the passing attention which preoccupation with problems of wealth and power at home leaves for colonial "problems."

What, then, do modern colonies look like, feel like? It is difficult to draw any universal picture. Superficial impressions are common: black boys diving for pennies; human horses hitched to rickshaws; menial service in plethora for a wage near nothing; absolute rule over slaves, even to life and death; fawning, crawling obeisance; high salaries, palaces, and luxury coupled with abject, nauseating, diseased poverty — this in a vague, imperfect way paints the present colonial world.

It is not nearly so easy as it would appear to fill in this outline and make it precise and scientific. Empires do not want nosy busybodies snooping into their territories and business. Visitors to colonies are, to be sure, allowed and even encouraged; but their tours are arranged, officials guide them in space and in thought, and they see usually what the colonial power wants them to see and little more. Dangerous "radicals" are rigorously excluded. My own visits to colonies have been rare and unsatisfactory. Several times I have tried in vain to visit South Africa. No visas were obtainable. I have been in British and French West Africa and in Jamaica.

In Sierra Leone I landed at Freetown in 1923. I was passed through the customs without difficulty, as my papers were in order. Then for some reason the authorities became suspicious. With scant courtesy, I was summoned peremptorily down to headquarters, to a room off the common jail, with pictures of escaped criminals decorating the walls. What did I want in Sierra Leone? I handed in my passport, showing that I was United States Minister Plenipotentiary to Liberia, stopping simply to visit on my way home. The commissioner unbent and dismissed me. That afternoon I was invited to a tea party at the governor's mansion! What would have happened to me if I had not had a diplomatic passport, or if I had been merely a colored man seeking to study a British colony?

The same year I visited Senegal and Conakry. I was received with great courtesy, but into the ruling caste; I had no contact with the mass of the colonial people. I lodged with the American consul; the French consul had me at dinner and the English consul at tea in his palatial mansion. But little did I see or learn of the millions of Negroes who formed the overwhelming mass of the colonial population.

In 1915, I visited Jamaica. I landed at Kingston and then, being tired and on vacation, did the unconventional thing of walking across the island to Mantego Bay. I immediately became an object of suspicion. It was wartime. I was in a sense, albeit unconsciously, intruding into Jamaica's backyard. I had proper visas, but I was not following the beaten path of the tourist. I was soon warned by a furtive black man that the police were on my track. My only recourse was to look up a long-time friend, principal of the local school. He ostentatiously drove me downtown, seated with him high in his surrey behind prancing horses. Thus was I properly introduced and vouched for. The point is that in all these cases one saw the possibility of arbitrary power without appeal and of a race and class situation unknown in free countries.

In the main, colonial peoples are living abnormally, save those of the untouched or inert mass of natives. Where the whites form a small ruling group, they are most abnormal and are not, as is assumed, replicas of the home group. They consist chiefly of representatives of commercial concerns whose first object is to make money for themselves and the corporations they represent. They are in the main hard-boiled, often ruthless businessmen, unrestrained by the inhibitions of home in either law or custom. Next come the colonial officials, either identical with the commercial men or more or less under their domination, especially through home influence. Colonials and businessmen clash, but business usually wins. Sometimes philanthropic career officials get the upper hand; but they are in danger of being replaced or losing promotion. The official class — heads, assistants, clerks, wives, and children — are apt to be arrogant, raised above their natural position and feeling their brief authority; they lord it over despised natives and demand swift and exemplary punishment for any affront to their dignity. The courts presided over by whites are usually even-handed in native quarrels, but through fear are strict, harsh, and even cruel in cases between natives and whites. White prestige must be maintained at any cost. There is usually a considerable group of white derelicts, hangers-on, sadistic representatives of the "superior race," banished to colonies by relatives who are ashamed to keep them at home.

This whole group of whites forms a caste apart, lives in segregated, salubrious, and protected areas, seldom speaks the vernacular or knows the masses except officially. Their regular income from colonial services is liberal according to home standards and often fantastic according to the standard of living in colonies. Conceive of an income of $10,000 a year for a colonial governor over people whose average income is $25 a year! The officials get frequent vacations with pay, and are pensioned after comparatively short service. The pensions are paid for life by colonial taxation, and the pensioners are regarded as experts on colonial matters the rest of their lives.

Where the white resident contingent is relatively large, as in South Africa and Kenya, the caste conditions are aggravated and the whites become the colony while the natives are ignored and neglected except as low-paid labor largely without rights that the colonists need respect.

Below this group of white overlords are the millions of natives. Their normal and traditional life has been more or less disrupted and changed in work, property, family life, recreation, health habits, food, religion, and other cultural matters. Their initiative, education, freedom of action, have been interfered with to a greater or less extent. Authority has been almost entirely withdrawn from their control and the white man's word is law in most cases. Their native standards of life have been destroyed and the new standards cannot be met by a poverty that is the worst in the world. The mass of natives sink into careless, inert, or sullen indifference, making their contact with whites as rare as possible, and incurring repeated punishment for laziness and infraction of arbitrary or inexplicable rules.

Up from these rise two groups: the toadies or "white folks niggers," who use flattery and talebearing to curry favor; and the resentful, bitter, and ambitious who seek by opposition or education to achieve the emancipation of their land and people. The educated and the half-educated, in particular, are the object of attack and dislike by the whites and are endlessly slandered in all testimony given visitors and scientists.

The missionaries form another class. They have been of all sorts of persons: unworldly visionaries, former pastors out of a job, social workers with and without social science, theologians, crackpots, and humanitarians. Their vocation is so unconventional that it is almost without standards of training or set norms of effort. Yet missionaries have spent tens of millions of dollars and influenced hundreds of millions of men with results that literally vary from heaven to hell. Missionaries represent the oldest invasion of whites, and incur at first the enmity of business and the friendship of natives. Colonial officials, on pressure from home, compromise differences, and the keener natives thereupon come to suspect missionary motives and the native toadies rush to get converted and cash in on benefits. The total result varies tremendously according to the pressure of these elements.

Despite a vast literature on colonial peoples, there is today no sound scientific basis for comprehensive study. What we have are reports of officials who set out to make a case for the imperial power in control; reports of missionaries, of all degrees of reliability and object; reports of travelers swayed by every conceivable motive and fitted or unfitted for testimony by widely varying education, ideals, and reliability. When science tries to study colonial systems in Africa and Asia, it meets all sorts of hindrances and incomplete statements of fact. In few cases is there testimony from the colonial peoples themselves, or impartial scientific surveys conducted by persons free of compulsion from imperial control and dictation.

The studies we have of colonial peoples and conditions are therefore unsatisfactory. Even the great *African Survey* edited by Lord Hailey is mainly based on the testimony and the figures of colonial officials; that is, of men who represent the colonial organization, who are appointed on recommendation of persons whose fortunes are tied up with colonial profits, and who are naturally desirous of making the best-possible picture of colonial conditions. This does not mean that there is in this report, or in many others, deliberate and conscious deception; but there is the desire to make a case for the vested interests of a large and powerful part of the world's property-owners.

Other studies are made by visitors and outsiders who can get at the facts only as the government officials give them opportunity. Many opportunities have been afforded such students in the past, but the opportunities fall far short of what complete and scientific knowledge demands. Moreover, such visitors arrive more or less unconsciously biased by their previous education and contacts, which lead them to regard the natives as on the whole a low order of humanity, and especially to distrust more or less completely the efforts of educated and aspiring Natives. The native elite, when through education and contact they get opportunity to study and tell of conditions, often, and naturally, defeat their own cause before a prejudiced audience by their bitterness and frustration and their inability to speak with recognized authority.

Thus, unfortunately, it is not possible to present or refer to any complete and documented body of knowledge which can give an undisputed picture of colonies today. This does not mean that we have no knowledge of colonial conditions; on the contrary, we have a vast amount of testimony and study; but practically every word of it can be and is disputed by interested parties, so that the truth can be reached only by the laborious interpretation of careful students. Nearly every assertion of students of colonial peoples is disputed today by colonial officials, many travelers, and a host of theorists. Despite this, greater unanimity of opinion is growing, but it is far from complete.

If, for instance, we complain of the conquest of harmless, isolated, and independent groups by great powers, it is answered that this is manifest destiny; that the leaders of world civilization must control and guide the backward peoples for the good of all. Otherwise these peoples relapse into revolting barbarism. If under this control colonial peoples are unhappy, it is answered that they are happier than they were formerly without control; and that they make greater progress when guided than when left alone.

If slavery and forced labor are complained of, the answer is that the natives are congenitally lazy and must be made to work for the good of mankind. Indeed, if they were not enslaved by Europeans, they would enslave each other. Low wages are justified by the fact that these peoples are simple, with low standards of living, while their industrialization is a boon to the world, and the world's welfare is paramount. Lack of broad educational plans is justified by their cost. Can England be asked to undertake the education of British

Africa when she has not yet fully planned the education of British children at home? Moreover, why educate these simple folk into unhappiness and discontent? If they are trained at all, it should be to produce wealth for the benefit of themselves in part and of the empire in general. The seizing of the land and dividing it is looked upon not only as a policy which puts unused acreage into remunerative use, but also as one that compels folk to work who otherwise would sing and dance and sit in the sun. And in general, it is not clear from the testimony of history that the mass of colonial peoples can progress only under the guidance of the civilized white people, and is not the welfare of the whites in reality the welfare of the world?

Practically every one of these assertions has a certain validity and truth, and at the same time is just false and misleading enough to give an entirely unfair picture of the colonial world. The recent advance of anthropology, psychology, and other social sciences is beginning to show this, and beginning to prove on how false a premise these assertions are based and how fatal a body of folklore has been built upon it. These beliefs have been influenced by propaganda, by caricature, and by ignorance of the human soul. Today these attitudes must be challenged, and without trying to approach anything like completeness of scientific statement we may allude here to certain general matters concerning colonial peoples the truth of which cannot be disputed. . . .

On Britain and Africa

The South African Government by severe repressive measures succeeded in breaking the strike which involved nearly two-thirds of the 300,000 African gold miners. The strike began in August last year with a demand by the Johannesburg gold mine workers for a $1.60 per day wage increase and spread so rapidly that it soon enveloped nearly 200,000 workers. The strikers received considerable support, especially from the Transvaal Municipal African Workers Union and the Indian passive resistance movement of South Africa. Reports from South Africa show that during the period of the strike at least thirty Africans lost their lives and untold hundreds were seriously injured during the brutal suppression of the strike by the police.

Mr. Creech Jones, Secretary of State for Colonies in Great Britain in a recent address said: "So far as Britain is concerned, I think we can assume today that the old Imperialism has come to an end. . . . Imperialism has come to an end, too, because it has been subjected to a pretty fierce criticism by economists, by socialists and others who exposed its inner content and made clear that it implied a position of privilege and economic dominance which was unstable and which would bring much danger to mankind if it were persisted in.

"This purpose, so manifest in British policy in recent years, is unfortunately, very much misunderstood in the world today. We are still the butt of a good deal of fierce criticism because we have not paraded before the world the constructive purposes of our administration. There has been, only recently, a number of statements by responsible people in American public life in which Britain has been characterized as an Imperial power pursuing her own material aims and little actuated by the purpose of winning freedom and building up the social life of the people in the Colonies.

"It is unfortunate, too, that this view is shared by those of Negro descent in

From the *People's Voice*, June 21, 1947.

the United States. The fact is there and we must face it for the reason that this view tends to imperil relations between the great nations; it tends to poison a great deal of the comradeship and the goodwill that ought to exist between the peoples and leads to no end of misunderstanding."

One hundred years ago, George Maclean died. He was an Englishman who after five wars between the British and the Ashanti, tried to patch up the differences between the two nations. He was a far-seeing man who in 1831 sent two princes of the Ashanti royal family to England to be educated and made a treaty of peace between the two nations. Missionaries were introduced into Ashanti. He signed treaties with the Ashanti chiefs and practically recognized the celebrated Bond of 1844 which legalized the relations between the two countries.

Whites in Africa After
Negro Autonomy

A rather curious change of emphasis has caught my attention recently. Negroes are being accused of racism, that is, of unduly emphasizing racial differences and of advocating racial separation. This would be laughable if it did not have so serious a side. A shattered and almost fatally divided world, now making desperate effort to envision a humanity bound together in peace and at least with some approach to brotherhood, is being warned that its worst victims are contemplating resurgence of race hate!

Of the debt which the white world owes Africa, there can be no doubt. No black man can recall it without a shudder of disgust and hate. The white followers of the meek and lowly Jesus stole fifteen million men, women, and children from Africa from 1400 to 1900 A.D. and made them working cattle in America; they left eighty-five million black corpses to mark their trail of blood and tears; then from 1800 to this day their scientists, historians, and ministers of the Gospel preached, wrote, and taught the world that a black man was by the grace of God and law of nature so evil and inferior that slavery, insult, and exploitation were too good for him and that the virgin purity of white women could only be secure if mulatto bastards were strewn from the Atlantic to the Pacific and from the North to the South pole. Harsh words? — but dismal truth. So what? Can bitter revenge erase all this? If Sir John Hawkins could be caught in West Africa today, even I shudder to think what Ghana might do to this blasphemous hypocrite. But he is beyond hurt today.

When I began my active life, nearly seventy years ago, the open and active contempt shown by white civilization for Negroes in the United States was almost incredible. . . .

From *In Albert Schweitzer's Realm: A Symposium*, ed. A. A. Roback (Cambridge, Mass.: Sci-Art Publishers, 1962). pp. 243–255.

In 1910 I could not buy an orchestra seat in any New York theater. I could eat in no restaurant downtown. Today, in the southern states of America no white man can marry the colored mother of his child. Most southern Negroes cannot vote, no matter what their education or character. All Negroes belong to a segregated inferior caste. The Supreme Court has ordered segregation to cease in public schools, but most of the former slaves states have refused to obey the law.

In Africa itself color caste is still the rule. In Sierra Leone, when I was there in 1928, . . . more money was spent on the white golf courses than on Negro schools.

I need hardly mention the status of Negroes in the Union of South Africa, and in Rhodesia, Kenya, and Tanganyika, as compared with that of whites. . . .

In Africa the political liberation of its nations has begun, until we recognize in the United Nations today more than twenty independent African nations. In the Union of South Africa and the Rhodesias there is still the firm determination of a minority of whites to rule the majority of Negroes and colored folk. In Kenya land monopoly is slipping, but still persists. In the Belgian Congo we have had the greatest surprise. Belgium, after depriving the Congolese of everything beyond primary education, has suddenly been forced to yield to a demand of the Congolese for independence. Then the Congolese prime minister was slain. Disaster followed, and yet the Congo is to become an independent Negro state. In spite of this, Europe and North America have by no means surrendered their determination to shape Africa through invested capital owned by Europeans or by such black allies as they are able to obtain among the African inhabitants.

In fine, West Europe is still determined to base its culture and comfort on underpaid labor and the virtual theft of land and materials by white investors. The prosperity of South Africa and the Rhodesias is due to the wealth invested there by Britain and America, which makes huge profits because of the low wage paid black labor and the seizure of materials without any recognition of native rights. So long as this method of business and industry persists, the Africans must fight back. They will not fight the dead past, but the living present.

Naturally, this world treatment of men with black skins has embittered them and made them resentful of the assumptions of white men. In my own writings, I have often expressed this feeling. Today my resentment at the doctrine of race superiority, as preached and practiced by the white world for the last 250 years, has been pointed to with sharp criticism and contrasted with the charity of Gandhi and of the colored minister [Dr. Martin Luther King, Jr.] who led the recent boycott in Alabama. I am quite frank: I do not pretend to "love" white people. I think that as a race they are the most selfish of any on earth. I think that the history of the world for the last thousand years proves this beyond doubt, and it is more than proven today by the Salvation Army tactics of Toynbee and his school of history. Current history has tried desperately to ignore Africa and its contribution to civilization. Honesty and clarity in historical writing and research are certainly gaining, but are still lacking in the study of Negro history.

To many students of race relations the work of missionaries, especially in Africa, is a matter of congratulation and hope. In some of their satisfaction I share. I have just read Seaver's story of David Livingstone. I know of the fine efforts of Dr. Schweitzer to rid Africa of disease. . . .

What now has this to do with the prospects of the future? If following Ethiopia, the Sudan, Liberia, Ghana, the new black French states, and the Congo, the peoples of Africa assert themselves and are able to maintain their autonomy, what is going to happen to white Europeans and to North Americans who live in Africa? Quite naturally, white thinkers are apt to be panic-stricken when this question arises. They remember some shameful episodes in the recent past—the action of a great British general in punishing the Mahdi who ran England out of the Sudan for a generation. Kitchener dug the dead body of this black man from its grave and fed it to the crocodiles of the Nile to prove the superiority of the white race. Even Churchill called this "a foul deed." But Britain made Kitchener a viscount. So Frederick Lugard, after a shameful career of murder in Uganda, became a noble British lord and authority on Africa. Chinese Gordon arose from scoundrel in China almost to a saint in the British Sudan.

White Belgians slaughtered natives of the Congo when yesterday they demanded some of the rights of white men. The Union of South Africa has acted like wild beasts toward black folk, and the story of Kenya is a disgrace to Britain. Quite naturally, then, white Europe is asking what Europeans can expect if ever Africans become free.

Yet no program of revenge may occur. And this is not because the Christianity taught Africans by whites, while whites enslaved and raped them, will prove to be more efficacious in black consciences than in white, but simply because the black leaders of present Africa are not fools. Haile Selassie, Nkrumah, Azikiwe, Touré, and even Tubman are men of reason. They are well aware that the worst oppressors and enslavers of Africa are in vast majority dead, and cannot today be harmed by belated revenge. They know that there are white people in France, Britain, and America who can be just, and Negroes see also that the Soviet Union, China, Poland, and Czechoslovakia have proved that some white nations can treat colored people as brothers—

can view men as men even though they are black, yellow, or red as Russia. They see and feel each day the mighty flood rolling toward socialism and to a real communism of mankind, and that in no far distant day. These leaders, and others being trained to succeed them, will act with reason if permitted — not without difficulties, not without seeing many of their dark fellows yield to the seductions of Western capitalism, which once lured Tunis, Morocco, and Algeria to their doom, and today have a stranglehold on Liberia and are seeking investments in South, Central, and West Africa.

But there is a wise portion of the peoples of Africa of Ghana and Nigeria, of South African blacks, and of American Negroes who glimpse a straight path. Africa needs capital goods to promote industry and break the capitalistic fetters on cheap crops and labor, and the processing of goods abroad and resale to the natives in the form of gin and baubles at fabulous prices. Africa needs sanitation and medicine; she needs agriculture for crops suited to her own wants and the conservation of power for her own factories. This capital she can borrow — she is begged today to borrow it from Britain and the United States at 10 or even 100 percent interest; but *there* lies disaster, and this Africa is beginning to realize. This capital she can herself save in part, but at cruel sacrifice and amid the cheerful sneers of white tourists and students. Yet if Africa saves its own capital in part, or borrows it from lands like the Soviet Union and China at rates far below the debt slavery offered by the United States, Britain, and West Germany, her chances of survival are good. That this is possible, China can tell her: Egypt is learning; even India begins to suspect. Africa knows that this kind of revenge on her traducers will far exceed in satisfaction any petty deeds inspired by hate of the dead and the dying — of the dead slave-traders and of the dying corporations of exploiters and thieves who are working today.

What, then, will happen to white folk in Africa when black folk rule their own territory depends on what white folks do, and do now. And the whites to whom I refer are not the dead nor simply those living in Africa. I refer to the white world as a whole. We are come to a time when the sins and mistakes of the whole group must be considered and judged, not simply small localities or single individuals. Perhaps in the fifteenth century, slavery of Negroes was the guilt mainly of certain individuals. But today, the poverty of the majority of human beings, the war, murder, and destruction due to colonial imperialism, cannot be charged simply against the Union of South Africa, or the white owners of Kenya land, or the Dutch monopolists of Indonesia. No. The real culprits are the British and American shareholders in corporations, the rich cartel owners who form the aristocracy of France and Germany, and the well-paid leaders of labor unions who exclude or segregate Negroes and other colonial folk.

It is folk like these who finance race hate in Africa; grow rich on coffee, fruit, and sugar in Central and South America; and plead innocence of wrong because they "do not know" what investment, incorporated business, stock markets, and world trade are doing to mankind. It is their business to know the crime which is devastating the earth. It is hard to point to examples of this in business and industry. Individual income and profit are the closely guarded secrets of the modern world. Yet here is one instance revealed in the soliciting of further investment: in one year Northern Rhodesia sold its copper product for $36,000,000. Of this income, one half went to British and American shareholders, part based on old but quite baseless claims of "ownership" and part on "investment" and stock gambling. Two and one-half million dollars went to 1,690 white artisans, at $15,000 each for the year. They worked as trained technicians, but most of their actual toil and part of their skill was performed by Negro helpers. The whites lived like little lords and had all the cheap house service which they wanted, with modern homes and the right to vote. They had a recognized union, to which no Negro could belong. Less than 2 percent of the total 36 millions of income from copper, $632,000, or $37 each a year, was paid to 17,000 African laborers, who did the bulk of the toil and whose fathers had once owned the land and its fruits. The nations and individuals whose life, culture, power, and luxury rest on this colossal theft are the persons responsible for the present plight of Rhodesia.

This is abundantly proven in the case of the Congo. The Congo needed technical leadership and professional knowledge. Particularly were physicians needed; but when the Belgians contemplated medical schools, they found that their system of education had not furnished enough training so that educated Congolese could be given a course in modern medicine; and of course neither Belgium nor Europe could spare white physicians for black Africa in any adequate numbers. . . .

As black Africa grows in strength, unity, and intelligence, this plan of building white wealth and culture on Negro poverty and exploitation must cease. It may cease as a result of study, the spread of conference, and the strengthening of moral fiber in the world. Or it may come from the lessening of profit on African exploitation and monopoly, and the realization, due to African organization and intelligence, that in the future European civilization will depend on European labor and not on cheap colored labor abroad.

Progress may be helped by the realization on the part of Africans that their freedom will not come as a gift from white folk, but as a result of what they themselves sacrifice and do. Or again maybe the only way to bring South Africa to its senses is for West Africa to drop atom bombs on Cape Town, Johannesburg, and Salisbury, secure in the hope that Britain and the United States will not dare to interfere because of the Soviet Union and China. God forbid that this awful catastrophe should ever threaten; but if it does, the best people of Europe and America, living and carousing on the degradation of Africa, will bear the blame.

It is more likely that reason and decency will prevail. For this, we may count on present African leadership. Every current black leader begs for reform by consultation, compromise, peace, and the rule of right. The great All-African meeting at Accra, West Africa, which culminated five Pan-African congresses held in Europe, 1919 to 1945, indicated a settled determination on the part of the Africans from Algeria and Egypt to the Cape of Good Hope to be free of foreign domination and to unite to secure this great end. . . .

This conference was an outstanding success. There prevailed a spirit of brotherhood and co-operation with all the world. But let us not count on this attitude lasting forever. As Mboya, the remarkable young Kenyan chairman, said: "We have been slapped down; we have turned the other cheek; there is no third cheek!" For continuance of this spirit of compromise, then, must come action and thought, investigation and research, and that not by Europeans alone but by African scholars and thinkers. There must rise in America a new crop of men of courage to supplant the present plethora of cowards and pussyfooters in high places. The "Church of Christ" must become a Church of Man, organized for honesty and right doing — and not for dogma, miracles, and show. Above all, civilized man must learn and acknowledge that not individual wealth, but decent living for the masses is the chief end of man.

There was a day when the world rightly called Americans honest, even if crude — earning their living by hard work, telling the truth no matter whom it hurt, and going to war only for what they believed in, a just cause, after nothing but force seemed possible. Today millions of us are lying, stealing, and killing. We call all this by finer names: Advertising, Free Enterprise, and National Defense. But names in the end deceive no one; today we use science to help us deceive our fellows; we take wealth that we never earned; and we are devoting our vast energy to prepare ourselves to kill, maim, and drive insane — men, women, and children who dare refuse to do what we want done. Some profess to know why we fail. They say we haven't taught our children mathematics and physics. No, it is because we have not taught our children to read and write or to behave like human beings and not like hoodlums. Every child on my street is whooping it up with toy guns, and the big boys with real pistols. When Elvis Presley goes through his suggestive motions on the public stage, it takes the city police force to hold back teen-age children from hysteria. The story of the rigged TV quizzes completes the picture of our spiritual decadence.

The highest ambition of an American boy today is to be a millionaire. The highest ambition of an American girl is to be a movie star. Of the ethical aims which lie back of these ideals, little is said or learned. What are we doing about it? Half the Christian churches of New York are trying to ruin the free public schools in order to install religious dogma in them, and the other half are too interested in Venezuelan oil to prevent the best center in Brooklyn from fighting youthful delinquency, or to stop a bishop from kicking William Howard Melish into the street and closing his church. Which of the hundreds of churches sitting half empty protests about this? They hire Billy Graham to replace the circus in Madison Square Garden.

On the other hand, the plea for peace comes today mainly from Communists. The spread of education and science comes from Communists. The saner distribution of wealth is the object of Communism. Is this why we hate Communism and persecute its followers? The greatest threat of war comes from the United States and from its support of colonial imperialism. Why is this? Is it because the United States built its wealth on the blood and slavery of Africans? Is this why color caste and race hate persist among us as it fades among the rest of mankind? We may not delude ourselves into silence based on undoubted progress in American race relations during the last fifty years, culminating in a Supreme Court decision which is not yet enforced, or on favors to Negroes in return for their acquiescence in national policies which continue to spell ruin for the colored peoples of the world. Not freedom to exploit each other is the salvation of black America, but understanding and fellowship with the oppressed laborers of all the world. If this is true, then on the United States more than on any nation in the world lies the burden of effort for "peace on earth." The freedom of Africa depends on us, and to this end, all Americans, Negroes as well as whites, should prepare for action.

This word of mine is no effort to detract from the beneficial work of missionaries. They have done good and harm. The work of men like Dr. Schweitzer in medicine deserves all praise. The missionary of medicine is sorely needed in Africa. But the defenders of manhood are needed even more.

I look for peace and good will as Africa strives for freedom. I firmly believe that this day will come. But it will come and succeed only if the white world honestly co-operates, only if the European itch for profits at any price dies away and a broader, better ideal of human relations succeeds. I hope this change will come, but its coming will not be automatic; it will be in great part because men like Dr. Schweitzer aid and openly and clearly advocate it. It will be because Dr. Schweitzer would not only treat disease but train Negroes as assistants and helpers, surround himself with a growing African staff of scientifically educated natives who can in time carry on and spread his work and see that it is supported by the new African states and does not continue to be dependent on European charity. That would be fundamental and lasting

691

missionary work and not mere almsgiving and paternalistic feeding of children from a silver spoon.

I have just returned from six weeks in West Africa. I have lived in the land of black folk and under a culture which they created. I have seen a black man [Kwame Nkrumah] with ancient and beautiful ceremony installed as the head of an independent African state, and I have seen him send his black soldiers to save the struggling Congolese from being overwhelmed by Belgian and American capitalists. I am thrilled and hopeful from all this which I have seen.

XIV

War and Peace

Although he abhorred war, Du Bois, unlike NAACP founders Mary White Ovington and Oswald Garrison Villard, was not an ethical or ideological pacifist. As with his views on racial integration and working-class solidarity, what finally mattered most to him was the civil rights advantage his people could derive from a given position. Lynchings in the South, a three-day race riot in East St. Louis, and a murderous nighttime march on Houston by African-American infantry occurred on the eve of American entry into World War One. The African-American leadership debated the wisdom of making civil rights demands the sine qua non of full participation in the war or whether to bank on exemplary patriotism as the prudent course for racial advancement. After some soul-searching and the offer of a commission in Army Military Intelligence, the NAACP's most important voice spoke for support of the war effort in July 1918. "Close Ranks," probably Du Bois's most famous *Crisis* editorial, outraged William Monroe Trotter, Archibald Grimké, A. Philip Randolph, and many other influential African-Americans. Instead of abating, and notwithstanding the creditable performance of black soldiers ("An Essay Toward a History of the Black Man in the Great War" [1919]), racism generally increased in the United States in the immediate aftermath of the war.

Having observed firsthand during 1936 the troubling and "complicated" developments of Germany and Hitler, Du Bois gauged the menace posed by the Third Reich better than molders of African-American public opinion. If Hitler won the war, Africans and Asians would be subjected to "an attempted caste system resembling slavery," he predicted in the *Amsterdam News* in July 1941. The Second World War raised old dilemmas again. With misgivings, he

695

decided to repeat his 1918 summons to the colors, proclaiming, in February 1942, "We close ranks again but only, now as then, to fight for democracy and democracy not only for white folk but for yellow, brown and black" ["Closing Ranks Again"]. In "The Negro and the War," Du Bois remained guardedly hopeful of the outcome, opining in the *Amsterdam News* for May 9, 1942, "I said some time since that I feared that the Negro would get less out of this war than he got out of the last; but I think I was wrong." Writing up the balance sheet in "Negro's War Gains and Losses" [1945], a stoic Du Bois decided that he could not say "balancing these losses and gains, [that] the war has been either a vast success or a terrible failure."

Close Ranks

This is the crisis of the world. For all the long years to come men will point to the year 1918 as the great Day of Decision, the day when the world decided whether it would submit to military despotism and an endless armed peace — if peace it could be called — or whether they would put down the menace of German militarism and inaugurate the United States of the World.

We of the colored race have no ordinary interest in the outcome. That which the German power represents today spells death to the aspirations of Negroes and all darker races for equality, freedom and democracy. Let us not hesitate. Let us, while this war lasts, forget our special grievances and close our ranks shoulder to shoulder with our own white fellow citizens and the allied nations that are fighting for democracy. We make no ordinary sacrifice, but we make it gladly and willingly with our eyes lifted to the hills.

From *The Crisis*, July 1918.

An Essay Toward a History of
the Black Man in the
Great War

The mayor of Domfront stood in the village inn, high on the hill that hovers green in the blue sky of Normandy; and he sang as we sang: "*Allons, enfants de la patrie!*" God! How we sang! How the low, grey-clouded room rang with the strong voice of the little Frenchman in the corner, swinging his arms in deep emotion; with the vibrant voices of a score of black American officers who sat round about. Their hearts were swelling — torn in sunder. Never have I seen black folk — and I have seen many — so bitter and disillusioned at the seemingly bottomless depths of American color hatred — so uplifted at the vision of real democracy dawning on them in France.

The mayor apologized gravely: if he had known of my coming, he would have received me formally at the Hotel de Ville — me whom most of my fellow-countrymen receive at naught but back doors, save with apology. But how could I explain in Domfront, that reborn feudal town of ancient memories? I could not — I did not. But I sang the Marseillaise — "*Le jour de gloire est arrivé!*"

Arrived to the world and to ever widening circles of men — but not yet to us. Up yonder hill, transported bodily from America, sits "Jim-Crow" — in a hotel for white officers only; in a Massachusetts Colonel who frankly hates "niggers" and segregates them at every opportunity; in the General from Georgia who openly and officially stigmatizes his black officers as no gentlemen by ordering them never to speak to French women in public or receive the spontaneously offered social recognition. All this ancient and American race hatred and insult in a purling sea of French sympathy and kindliness, of human

From *The Crisis*, June 1919.

698

uplift and giant endeavor, amid the mightiest crusade humanity ever saw for Justice!

> *Contre nous de la tyrannie,*
> *L'etendard sanglant est levé.*

This, then, is a first attempt at the story of the Hell which war in the fateful years of 1914–1919 meant to Black Folk, and particularly to American Negroes. It is only an attempt, full of the mistakes which nearness to the scene and many necessarily missing facts, such as only time can supply, combine to foil in part. And yet, written now in the heat of strong memories and in the place of skulls, it contains truth which cold delay can never alter or bring back. Later, in the light of official reports and supplementary information and with a corps of co-workers, consisting of officers and soldiers and scholars, I shall revise and expand this story into a volume for popular reading; and still later, with the passing of years, I hope to lay before historians and sociologists the documents and statistics upon which my final views are based.

SENEGALESE AND OTHERS

To everyone war is, and, thank God, must be, disillusion. This war has disillusioned millions of fighting white men — disillusioned them with its frank truth of dirt, disease, cold, wet and discomfort; murder, maiming and hatred. But the disillusion of Negro American troops was more than this, or rather it was this and more — the flat, frank realization that however high the ideals of America or however noble her tasks, her great duty as conceived by an astonishing number of able men, brave and good, as well as of other sorts of men, is to hate "niggers."

Not that this double disillusion has for a moment made black men doubt the wisdom of their wholehearted help of the Allies. Given the chance again, they would again do their duty — for have they not seen and known France? But these young men see today with opened eyes and strained faces the true and hateful visage of the Negro problem in America.

When the German host — grey, grim, irresistible, poured through Belgium, out of Africa France called her sons; they came; 280,000 black Senegalese, first and last — volunteers, not drafted; they hurled the Boches back across the Ourcq and the Marne on a ghastly bridge of their own dead. It was the crisis — four long, bitter years the war wore on; but Germany was beaten at the first battle of the Marne, and by Negroes. Beside the Belgians, too, stood, first and last, 30,000 black Congolese, not to mention the 20,000 black English West Indians who fought in the East and the thousands of black troops who conquered German Africa.

STEVEDORES

But the story of stories is that of the American Negro. Here was a man who bravely let his head go where his heart at first could not follow, who for the first time as a nation within a nation did his bitter duty because it was his duty, knowing what might be expected, but scarcely foreseeing the whole truth.

We gained the right to fight for civilization at the cost of being "Jim-Crowed" and insulted; we were segregated in the draft; we were segregated in the first officers' training camp; and we were allowed to volunteer only as servants in the Navy and as common laborers in the Army, outside of the four regular Negro regiments. The Army wanted stevedores, road builders, wood choppers, railroad hands, etc., and American Negroes were among the first to volunteer. Of the 200,000 Negroes in the American Expeditionary Force, approximately 150,000 were stevedores and laborers, doing the hardest work under, in some cases, the most trying conditions faced by any soldiers during the war. And it is the verdict of men who know that the most efficient and remarkable service has been rendered by these men. Patient, loyal, intelligent, not grouchy, knowing all that they were up against among their countrymen as well as the enemy, these American black men won the war as perhaps no other set of S.O.S. men of any other race or army won it.

Where were these men stationed? At almost every seaport in France and in some English ports; at many of the interior depots and bases; at the various assembling places where automobiles, airplanes, cars and locomotives were got ready for use; in the forests, on the mountains and in the valleys, cutting wood; building roads from ports of entry right up to the view and touch of Germans in the front-lines; burying the dead; salvaging at great risk to their own lives millions of shells and other dangerous war material, actually piling up and detonating the most deadly devices in order that French battlefields might be safe to those who walk the ways of peace.

Who commanded these thousands of black men assembled from all parts of the United States and representing in culture all the way from absolute illiterates from under-taught Southern States to well-educated men from southern private schools and colleges and even from many northern universities and colleges? By a queer twist of American reasoning on the Negro it is assumed that he is best known and best "handled" by white people from the South, who more than any other white people refuse and condemn that sort of association that would most surely acquaint the white man with the very best that is in the Negro. Therefore, when officers were to be chosen for the Negro S.O.S. men, it seems that there was a preference expressed or felt for southern white officers. Some of these were fine men, but the majority were "nigger" drivers of the most offensive type.

The big, outstanding fact about the command of these colored soldiers is that southern men of a narrow, harsh type dictated the policy and method and so forced it that it became unpopular for officers to be generous to these men. When it is considered that these soldiers were abjectly under such men, with no practical opportunity for redress, it is easy to imagine the extremes to which harsh treatment could be carried. So thoroughly understood was it that the Negro had to be "properly handled and kept in his place," even in France, large use was made even of the white non-commissioned officer so that many companies and units of Negro soldiers had no higher Negro command than corporal. This harsh method showed itself in long hours, excessive tasks, little opportunity for leaves and recreation, holding of black soldiers to barracks when in the same community white soldiers had the privilege of the town, severe punishments for slight offenses, abusive language and sometimes corporal punishment. To such extremes of "handling niggers" was this carried that Negro Y.M.C.A. secretaries were refused some units on the ground, frankly stated by officers, that it would be better to have white secretaries, and in many places separate "Y" huts were demanded for white and colored soldiers so that there would be no association or fraternizing between the races.

Worked often like slaves, twelve and fourteen hours a day, these men were well-fed, poorly clad, indifferently housed, often beaten, always "Jim-Crowed" and insulted, and yet they saw the vision — they saw a nation of splendid people threatened and torn by a ruthless enemy; they saw a democracy which simply could not understand color prejudice. They received a thousand little kindnesses and half-known words of sympathy from the puzzled French, and French law and custom stepped in repeatedly to protect them, so that their only regret was the average white American. But they worked — how they worked! Everybody joins to testify to this: the white slave-drivers, the army officers, the French, the visitors — all say that the American Negro was the best laborer in France, of all the world's peoples gathered there; and if American food and materials saved France in the end from utter exhaustion, it was the Negro stevedore who made that aid effective.

THE 805TH

To illustrate the kind of work which the stevedore and pioneer regiments did, we cite the history of one of the pioneer Negro regiments: Under the act of

701

May 18, 1917, the President ordered the formation of eight colored infantry regiments. Two of these, the 805th and 806th, were organized at Camp Funston. The 805th became a Pioneer regiment and when it left camp had 3,526 men and 99 officers. It included 25 regulars from the 25th Infantry of the Regular Army, 38 mechanics from Prairie View, 20 horse-shoers from Tuskegee and 8 carpenters from Howard. The regiment was drilled and had target practice. The regiment proceeded to Camp Upton late in August, 1918, and sailed, a part from Montreal and a part from Quebec, Canada, early in September. Early in October the whole regiment arrived in the southern end of the Argonne forest. The men began their work of repairing roads as follows:

(a) First 2,000 meters of Clermont-Neuvilly road from Clermont road past Apremont;

(b) Second 2,000 meters of Clermont-Neuvilly road, Charpentry cut-off road;

(c) Locheres crossroad on Clermont-Neuvilly road, north 2,000 meters, roads at Very;

(d) Clermont-Neuvilly road from point 1,000 south of Neuvilly bridge to Neuvilly, ammunition detour road at Neuvilly, Charpentry roads;

(e) Auzeville railhead, Varennes railhead; railhead work at St. Juvin and Briquenay;

(f) Auzeville railhead, Varennes railhead, roads at Montblainville, roads at Landros-St. George;

(g) Roads at Avocourt, roads at Sommerance;

(h) Roads at Avocourt, roads at Fleville;

(i) Construction of ammunition dump, Neuvilly, and railhead construction between Neuvilly and Varennes and Apremont, railroad repair work March and St. Juvin, construction of Verdun-Etain railroad from November 11;

(j) Railhead details and road work Aubreville, road work Varennes and Charpentry;

(k) Road and railhead work Aubreville, road work Varennes.

The outlying companies were continually in immediate sight of the sausage balloons and witnessed many an air battle. Raids were frequent.

A concentration had been ordered at Varennes, November 18, and several companies had taken up their abode there or at Camp Mahout, but to carry out the salvage program, a redistribution over the Argonne-Meuse area had to be affected immediately.

The area assigned the 805th Pioneer Infantry extended from Boult-aux-Bois, almost due south to a point one kilometre west of Les Islettes; thence to

Aubreville and Avocourt and Esnes; thence to Montfaucon via Bethincourt and Cuisy; thence north through Nantillois and Cunel to Bantheville; thence southwest through Romagne, Gesnes and Exermont to the main road just south of Fleville; and then north to Boult-aux-Bois through Fleville, St. Juvin, Grand Pré and Briquenay.

The area comprised all of the Argonne forest, from Clermont north and the Varennes-Malancourt-Montfaucon-Romagne sections. More than five hundred square miles of battlefield was included.

A list of the articles to be salvaged would require a page. Chiefly they were Allied and enemy weapons and cannon, web and leather equipment, clothing and blankets, rolling stock, aviation electrical and engineer equipment. It was a gigantic task and did not near completion until the first week in March when more than 3,000 French carloads had been shipped.

For some weeks truck transportation was scarce and work was slow and consisted largely in getting material to roadsides.

As companies of the 805th neared the completion of their areas they were put to work at the railheads where they helped load the salvage they had gathered and that which many other organizations of the area had brought, and sent it on its way to designated depots.

With the slackening of the salvage work, the regiment found a few days when it was possible to devote time to drilling, athletics and study. School and agricultural books were obtained in large numbers and each company organized classes which, though not compulsory, were eagerly attended by the men.

Curtailment of this work was necessitated by instructions from Advance Section Headquarters to assist in every way possible the restoration of French farmlands to a point where they could be cultivated.

This meant principally the filling of trenches across fields and upon this work the regiment entered March 15 with all its strength, except what was required for the functioning of the railheads not yet closed.

There was up to this time no regimental band.

At Camp Funston instruments had been requisitioned, but had not arrived before the regiment left. Efforts were made to enlist a colored band at Kansas City whose members wished to enter the Army as a band and be assigned to the 805th Pioneer Infantry. General Wood approved and took the matter up with the War Department. Qualified assent was obtained, but subsequent rulings prevented taking advantage of it, in view of the early date anticipated for an overseas move.

The rush of events when the regiment reached Europe precluded immediate attention being given the matter and, meanwhile, general orders had been issued against equipping bands not in the Regular Army.

Left to itself, without divisional connections, the regiment had to rely upon its own resources for diversion. The men needed music after the hard work they were doing and Colonel Humphrey sent his Adjutant to Paris to present the matter to the Y.M.C.A., Knights of Columbus and Red Cross.

The Red Cross was able to respond immediately and Captain Bliss returned January 1, 1919, with seven cornets, six clarinets, five saxophones, four slide trombones, four alto horns, two bass tubas, two baritones and a piccolo and, also, some "jazz band effect."

The band was organized on the spot and as more instruments and music were obtained, eventually reached almost its tabular strength while it reached proficiency almost over night.

The following commendation of the work of the regiment was received: "The Chief Engineer desires to express his highest appreciation to you and to your regiment for the services rendered to the 1st Army in the offensive between the Meuse and the Argonne, starting September 26, and the continuation of that offensive on November 1 and concluding with the Armistice of November 11.

"The success of the operations of the Army Engineer Troops toward constructing and maintaining supply lines, both roads and railway, of the Army was in no small measure made possible by the excellent work performed by your troops.

"It is desired that the terms of this letter be published to all the officers and enlisted men of your command at the earliest opportunity."

A soldier writes us:

"Our regiment is composed of colored and white officers. You will find a number of complimentary things on the regiment's record in the Argonne in the history. We were, as you know, the fighting reserves of the Army and that we were right on this front from September to November 11. We kept the lines of communication going and, of course, we were raided and shelled by German long-range guns and subject to gas raids, too.

"We are now located in the Ardennes, between the Argonne and the Meuse. This is a wild and wooly forest, I assure you. We are hoping to reach our homes in May. We have spent over seven months in this section of the battle-front and we are hoping to get started home in a few weeks after you get this letter, at least. Our regiment is the best advertised regiment in the A.E.F. and its members are from all over the United States practically.

"A month or so ago we had a pay-day here and twenty thousand dollars was collected the first day and sent to relatives and banks in the United States. Every day our mail sergeant sends from one hundred to one thousand dollars per day to the United States for the men in our regiment, — savings of the small salary they receive as soldiers. As a whole they are and have learned many things by having had this great war experience."

NEGRO OFFICERS

All this was expected. America knows the value of Negro labor. Negroes knew that in this war as in every other war they would have the drudgery and the dirt, but with set teeth they determined that this should not be the end and limit of their service. They did not make the mistake of seeking to escape labor, for they knew that modern war is mostly ordinary toil; they even took without protest the lion's share of the common labor, but they insisted from the first that black men must serve as soldiers and officers.

The white Negro-hating oligarchy was willing to have some Negro soldiers — the privilege of being shot in real war being one which they were easily persuaded to share — provided these black men did not get too much notoriety out of it. But against Negro officers they set their faces like flint.

The dogged insistence of the Negroes, backed eventually by the unexpected decision of Secretary Baker, encompassed the first defeat of this oligarchy and nearly one thousand colored officers were commissioned.

Immediately a persistent campaign began:

First, was the effort to get rid of Negro officers; second, the effort to discredit Negro soldiers; third, the effort to spread race prejudice in France; and fourth, the effort to keep Negroes out of the Regular Army.

First and foremost, war is war and military organization is, and must be, tyranny. This is, perhaps, the greatest and most barbarous cost of war and the most pressing reason for its abolition from civilization. As war means tyranny, the company officer is largely at the mercy of his superior officers.

The company officers of the colored troops were mainly colored. The field officers were with very few exceptions white. The fate of the colored officers, therefore, depended almost absolutely on those placed in higher command. Moreover, American military trials and legal procedures are antiquated and may be grossly unfair. They give the accused little chance if the accuser is determined and influential.

The success, then, of the Negro troops depended first of all on their field officers; given strong, devoted men of knowledge and training there was no doubt of their being able to weed out and train company officers and organize the best body of fighters on the western front. This was precisely what the Negro-haters feared. Above all, they feared Charles Young.

CHARLES YOUNG

There was one man in the United States Army who by every consideration of justice, efficiency and long, faithful service should have been given the command of a division of colored troops. Colonel Charles Young is a graduate of West Point and by universal admission is one of the best officers in the Army. He has served in Cuba, Haiti, the Philippines, Mexico, Africa and the West with distinction. Under him the Negro division would have been the most efficient in the Army. This rightful place was denied him. For a technical physical reason ("high blood pressure") he was quickly retired from the Regular Army. He was not allowed a minor command or even a chance to act as instructor during the war.

On the contrary, the 92d and 93d Divisions of Negro troops were given Commanding Officers who with a half-dozen exceptions either distrusted Negroes or actively and persistently opposed colored officers under any circumstances. The 92d Division particularly was made a dumping ground for poor and inexperienced field officers seeking promotion. A considerable number of these white officers from the first spent more time and ingenuity in making the lot of the Negro officer hard and the chance of the Negro soldier limited than in preparing to whip the Germans.

PREJUDICE

These efforts fell under various heads: giving the colored officers no instruction in certain lines and then claiming that none were fitted for the work, as in artillery and engineering; persistently picking the poorest Negro candidates instead of the best for examinations and tests so as to make any failure conspicuous; using court martials and efficiency boards for trivial offenses and wholesale removals of the Negroes; subjecting Negro officers and men to persistent insult and discrimination by refusing salutes, "Jim-Crowing" places of accommodation and amusement, refusing leaves, etc.; by failing to supply the colored troops with proper equipment and decent clothing; and finally by a systematic attempt to poison the minds of the French against the Negroes and compel them to follow the dictates of American prejudice.

These are serious charges. The full proof of them cannot be attempted here, but a few examples will serve to indicate the nature of the proof.

At the colored Officers' Training Camp no instruction was given in artillery and a dead-line was established by which no one was commissioned higher than Captain, despite several recommendations. Certain Captains' positions, like those of the Headquarters Companies, were reserved for whites, and former non-commissioned officers were given preference with the hope that they would be more tractable than college-bred men — a hope that usually proved delusive.

The colored divisions were never assembled as units this side of the water. General Ballou, a timid, changeable white man, was put in command of the 92d Division and he antagonized it from the beginning.

General Ballou's attitude toward the men of his command, as expressed in his famous, or rather infamous, Bulletin 35, which was issued during the period of training in the United States, was manifested throughout the division during the entire time that he was in command in France. Whenever any occasion arose where trouble had occurred between white and colored soldiers, the burden of proof always rested on the colored man. All discrimination was passed unnoticed and nothing was done to protect the men who were under his command. Previous to General Bullard's suggestion that some order be issued encouraging the troops for the good work that they had done on the Vosges and Marbache fronts, there had been nothing done to encourage the men and officers, and it seemed that instead of trying to increase the morale of the division, it was General Ballou's intention to discourage the men as much as possible. His action in censuring officers in the presence of enlisted men was an act that tended toward breaking down the confidence that the men had in their officers, and he pursued this method on innumerable occasions. On one occasion he referred to his division, in talking to another officer, as the "rapist division"; he constantly cast aspersion on the work of the colored officer and permitted other officers to do the same in his presence, as is evidenced by the following incident which took place in the office of the Assistant Chief of Staff, G-3, at Bourbon-les-Bains:

The staff had just been organized and several General Headquarters officers were at Headquarters advising relative to the organization of the different offices. These officers were in conversation with General Ballou, Colonel Greer, the Chief of Staff, Major Hickox, and Brigadier-General Hay. In the course of the conversation Brigadier-General Hay made the remark that "In my opinion there is no better soldier than the Negro, but God damn a 'nigger' officer"! This remark was made in the presence of General Ballou and was the occasion for much laughter.

After the 92nd Division moved from the Argonne forest to the Marbache Sector the 368th Infantry was held in reserve at Pompey. It was at this place that General Ballou ordered all of the enlisted men and officers of this unit to congregate and receive an address to be delivered to them by him. No one had any idea as to the nature of this address; but on the afternoon designated, the men and officers assembled on the ground, which was used as a drill-ground, and the officers were severely censured relative to the operation that had taken place in the Argonne forest. The General advised the officers, in the presence of the enlisted men, that in his opinion they were cowards; that they had failed; and that "they did not have the guts" that made brave men. This speech was made to the officers in the presence of all of the enlisted men of the 368th Infantry and was an act contrary to all traditions of the Army.

When Mr. Ralph Tyler, the accredited correspondent of the War Department, reached the Headquarters of the 92d Division and was presented to General Ballou, he was received with the utmost indifference and nothing was done to enable him to reach the units at the front in order to gain the information which he desired. After Mr. Tyler was presented to General Ballou, the General walked out of the office of the Chief of Staff with Mr. Tyler, came into the office of the Adjutant, where all of the enlisted men worked, and stood directly in front of the desk of the colored officer, who was seated in the office of the Adjutant, and in a loud voice said to Mr. Tyler: "I regard the colored officer as a distinct failure. He is cowardly and has none of the traits which go to make a successful officer." This expression was made in the presence of all of the enlisted personnel and in a tone of voice loud enough for all of them to hear.

General Ballou's Chief of Staff was a white Georgian and from first to last his malign influence was felt and he openly sought political influence to antagonize his own troops.

General ———, Commanding Officer of the ——— (92d Division), said to Major Patterson (colored), Division Judge-Advocate, that there was a concerted action on the part of the white officers throughout France to discredit the work of the colored troops in France and that everything was being done to advertise those things that would reflect discredit upon the men and officers and to withhold anything that would bring to these men praise or commendation.

On the afternoon of November 8, the Distinguished Service Cross was awarded to Lieutenant Campbell and Private Bernard Lewis, 368th Infantry, the presentation of which was made with the prescribed ceremonies, taking place on a large field just outside of Villers-en-Haye and making a very impressive sight. The following morning a private from the 804th Pioneer Infantry was executed at Belleville, for rape. The official photographer attached to the 92d Division arose at 5 A.M. on the morning of the execution, which took place at 6 A.M., and made a moving-picture film of the hanging of this private. Although the presentation of the Distinguished Service Crosses occurred at 3 P.M. on the previous day, the official photographer did not see fit to make a picture of this and when asked if he had made a picture of the presentation, he replied that he had forgotten about it.

The campaign against Negro officers began in the cantonments. At Camp

Dix every effort was made to keep competent colored artillery officers from being trained. Most of the Colonels began a campaign for wholesale removals of Negro officers from the moment of embarkation.

At first an attempt was made to have General Headquarters in France assent to the blanket proposition that white and Negro officers would not get on in the same organization; this was unsuccessful and was followed by the charge that Negroes were incompetent as officers. This charge was made wholesale and before the colored officers had had a chance to prove themselves, "Efficiency Boards" immediately began wholesale removals and as such boards could act on the mere opinion of field officers the colored company officers began to be removed wholesale and to be replaced by whites.

The court martials of Negro officers were often outrageous in their contravention of common sense and military law. The experience of one Captain will illustrate. He was a college man, with militia training, who secured a Captaincy at Des Moines—a very difficult accomplishment—and was from the first regarded as an efficient officer by his fellows; when he reached Europe, however, the Major of his battalion was from Georgia, and this Captain was too independent to suit him. The Major suddenly ordered the Captain under close arrest and after long delay preferred twenty-three charges against him. These he afterward reduced to seven, continuing meantime to heap restrictions and insults on the accused, but untried, officer. Instead of breaking arrest or resenting his treatment the Captain kept cool, hired a good colored lawyer in his division and put up so strong a fight that the court martial acquitted him and restored him to his command, and sent the Major to the stevedores.

Not every officer was able thus to preserve his calm and poise.

One colored officer turned and cursed his unfair superiors and the court martial, and revealed an astonishing story of the way in which he had been hounded.

A Lieutenant of a Machine Gun Battalion was employed at Intelligence and Personnel work. He was dismissed and reinstated three times because the white officers who succeeded him could not do the work. Finally he was under arrest for one and one-half months and was dismissed from service, but General Headquarters investigated the case and restored him to his rank.

Most of the Negro officers had no chance to fight. Some were naturally incompetent and deserved demotion or removal, but these men were not objects of attack as often as the more competent and independent men.

Here, however, as so often afterward, the French stepped in, quite unconsciously, and upset careful plans. While the American officers were convinced of the Negro officers' incompetency and were besieging General

Headquarters to remove them *en masse*, the French instructors at the Gondricourt Training School, where Captains and selected Lieutenants were sent for training, reported that the Negroes were among the best Americans sent there.

Moreover, the 93d Division, which had never been assembled or even completed as a unit and stood unrecognized and unattached, was suddenly called in the desperate French need, to be brigaded with French soldiers. The Americans were thoroughly scared. Negroes and Negro officers were about to be introduced to French democracy without the watchful eye of American color hatred to guard them. Something must be done.

As the Negro troops began moving toward the Vosges sector of the battlefront, August 6, 1918, active anti-Negro propaganda became evident. From the General Headquarters of the American Army at Chaumont the French Military Mission suddenly sent out, not simply to the French Army, but to all the Prefects and Sous-Prefects of France (corresponding to our governors and mayors), data setting forth at length the American attitude toward Negroes; warning against social recognition; stating that Negroes were prone to deeds of violence and were threatening America with degeneration, etc. The white troops backed this propaganda by warnings and tales wherever they preceded the blacks.

This misguided effort was lost on the French. In some cases peasants and villagers were scared at the approach of Negro troops, but this was but temporary and the colored troops everywhere they went soon became easily the best liked of all foreign soldiers. They were received in the best homes, and where they could speak French or their hosts understood English, there poured forth their story of injustice and wrong into deeply sympathetic ears. The impudent swagger of many white troops, with their openly expressed contempt for "Frogs" and their evident failure to understand the first principles of democracy in the most democratic of lands, finished the work thus begun.

No sounding words of President Wilson can offset in the minds of thousands of Frenchmen the impression of disloyalty and coarseness which the attempt to force color prejudice made on a people who just owed their salvation to black West Africa!

Little was published or openly said, but when the circular on American Negro prejudice was brought to the attention of the French ministry, it was quietly collected and burned. And in a thousand delicate ways the French expressed their silent disapprobation. For instance, in a provincial town a colored officer entered a full dining-room; the smiling landlady hastened to seat him (how natural!) at a table with white American officers, who immediately began to show their displeasure. A French officer at a neighboring table with French officers quietly glanced at the astonished landlady. Not a word was said, no one in the dining-room took any apparent notice, but the black officer was soon seated with the courteous Frenchmen.

On the Negroes this double experience of deliberate and devilish persecution from their own countrymen, coupled with a taste of real democracy and world-old culture, was revolutionizing. They began to hate prejudice and discrimination as they had never hated it before. They began to realize its eternal meaning and complications. Far from filling them with a desire to escape from their race and country, they were filled with a bitter, dogged determination never to give up the fight for Negro equality in America. If American color prejudice counted on this war experience to break the spirit of the young Negro, it counted without its host. A new, radical Negro spirit has been born in France, which leaves us older radicals far behind. Thousands of young black men have offered their lives for the Lilies of France and they return ready to offer them again for the Sun-flowers of Afro-America.

THE 93RD DIVISION

The first American Negroes to arrive in France were the Labor Battalions, comprising all told some 150,000 men.

The Negro fighting units were the 92nd and 93rd Divisions.

The so-called 93rd Division was from the first a thorn in the flesh of the Bourbons. It consisted of Negro National Guard troops almost exclusively officered by Negroes, — the 8th Illinois, the 15th New York, and units from the District of Columbia, Maryland, Ohio, Tennessee and Massachusetts. The division was thus incomplete and never really functioned as a division. For a time it was hoped that Colonel Young might be given his chance here, but nothing came of this. Early in April when the need of the French for reenforcements was sorest, these black troops were hurriedly transported to France and were soon brigaded with the French armies.

THE 369TH

This regiment was originally authorized by Governor Sulzer, but its formation was long prevented. Finally it was organized with but one Negro officer. Eventually the regiment sailed with colored and white officers, landing in France, January 1, 1918, and went into the second battle of the Marne in July, east of Verdun, near Ville-sur-Turbe. It was thus the first American Negro unit in battle and one of the first American units. Colored officers took part in this battle and some were cited for bravery. Nevertheless the white Colonel, Hayward, after the battle secured the transfer of every single colored officer, except the bandmaster and chaplain.

The regiment was in a state of irritation many times, but it was restrained by the influence of the non-commissioned officers — very strong in this case because the regiment was all from New York and mainly from Harlem — and especially because being brigaded with the French they were from the first treated on such terms of equality and brotherhood that they were eager to fight. There were charges that Colonel Hayward and his white officers needlessly sacrificed the lives of these men. This, of course, is hard to prove; but certainly the casualties in this regiment were heavy and in the great attack in the Champagne, in September and October, two hundred were killed and eight hundred were wounded and gassed. The regiment went into battle with the French on the left and the Moroccans on the right and got into its own barrage by advancing faster than the other units. It was in line seven and one-half days, when three to four days is usually the limit.

In all, the regiment was under fire 191 days — a record for any American unit. It received over 170 citations for the *Croix de Guerre* and Distinguished Service Cross and was the first unit of the Allied armies to reach the Rhine, November 18, with the Second French Army.

THE 371ST AND 372ND

The 371st Regiment was drafted from South Carolina and had southern white officers from the first, many of whom were arrogant and overbearing. The regiment mobilized at Camp Jackson, October 5–17, and embarked for France, April 9, from Newport News, Va. It was trained at Rembercourt-aux-Ports (Meuse) and left for the region near Bar-le-Duc, June 5. The troops arrived in the Argonne June 22. They were brigaded with the 157th French Division, 13th Army Corps, and remained in the battle-line, front and reserve, until the Armistice was signed.

There are few data at present available for the history of this regiment because there were no colored officers to preserve it. It is rumored, however, that after the first battle the number of casualties among the meanest of their officers led to some mutual understandings. The regiment received a number of citations for bravery.

As this regiment was brigaded usually with the 372nd, a part of its history follows:

The official records show that the 372nd Infantry was organized at Camp

Stuart, January 1, 1918, Colonel Glendie B. Young, Infantry, U.S.N.G., commanding, and included the following National Guard units: First Separate Battalion, District of Columbia, Infantry; Ninth Battalion of Ohio, Infantry; Company L, Sixth Massachusetts, Infantry; and one company each from Maryland, Tennessee and Connecticut. To these were added later 250 men from Camp Custer; excepting the Staff, Machine Gun, Headquarters and Supply Companies, the regiment was officered by colored men.

The regiment was brigaded with the 371st into the 186th Infantry Brigade, a unit of the Provisional 93rd Division. It was understood that the 93rd Division, which was to be composed of all Negro troops, would be fully organized in France; but when the 372nd arrived at St. Nazaire, April 14, 1918, the organization was placed under command of the French. Four weeks later the brigade was dissolved and the 93rd Division ceased to be mentioned. Its four regiments were all subject to orders of the French G.Q.G., General Petain, commanding.

The regiment spent five weeks in training and re-organization at Conde-en-Barrois (Meuse), as a unit of the 13th French Army Corps. The men were trained in French methods by French officers and non-commissioned officers with French ordnance equipment. They developed so rapidly that a French Major exclaimed enthusiastically on the street: "These men are intelligent and alert. Their regiment will have a glorious career." Thus, from the beginning the worth of our troops was recognized by a veteran of the French Army.

To complete its training under actual war conditions, the regiment was sent to a "quiet sector" — sub-sector, Argonne West, on June 8, where it spent twenty days learning the organization of defensive positions and how to hold these positions under shell fire from the enemy. During this time it was a part of the 63rd French Division and during the last ten days it was a part of the 35th French Division. On July 2, the 372nd Infantry became permanently identified with the 157th French Division, commanded by General Goybet. The division consisted of two colored American regiments and one French regiment of infantry. The artillery units, engineers, sanitary train, etc., were all French. On his first inspection tour, at Vanquois, General Goybet asked one of our men if he thought the Germans could pass if they started over. The little brown private replied: "Not if the boches can't do a good job in killing all of us." That pleased the new General very much and clinched his confidence in the black troops.

On July 13 the regiment retired to a reserve position near the village of Locheres (Meuse), for temporary rest and to help sustain the coming blow. The next day Colonel Young was relieved of command by Colonel Herschel Tupes, a regular army officer. In the afternoon the regiment was assembled and prepared for action, but it later was found that it would not be needed.

The attack of the Germans was launched near Rheims on the night of July 14 and the next evening the world read of the decisive defeat of the Germans by General Gouraud's army.

The following Sunday found the regiment billeted in the town of Sivry-la-Perche, not every far from Verdun. After a band concert in the afternoon Colonel Tupes introduced himself to his command. In the course of his remarks, he said that he had always commanded regulars, but he had little doubt that the 372nd Infantry could become as good as any regiment in France.

On July 26 the regiment occupied sub-sector 304. The occupation of this sub-sector was marked by hard work and discontentment. The whole position had to be re-organized, and in doing this the men maintained their previous reputation for good work. The total stay in the sector was seven weeks. The regiment took part in two raids and several individuals distinguished themselves: one man received a *Croix de Guerre* because he held his trench mortar between his legs to continue firing when the base had been damaged by a shell; another carried a wounded French comrade from "No Man's Land" under heavy fire, and was also decorated. Several days after a raid, the Germans were retaliating by shelling the demolished village of Montzeville, situated in the valley below the Post-of-Command and occupied by some of the reserves; Private Rufus Pinckney rushed through the heavy fire and rescued a wounded French soldier.

On another occasion, Private Kenneth Lewis of the Medical Detachment, later killed at his post, displayed such fine qualities of coolness and disdain for danger by sticking to duty until the end that two post-mortem decorations: the *Croix de Guerre* with Palm and *Medaille Militaire* were awarded. The latter is a very distinguished recognition in the French Army.

So well had the regiment worked in the Argonne that it was sent to relieve the 123rd French Infantry Regiment in the sub-sector Vanquois, on July 28. An attack by the Germans in the valley of the Aire, of which Vanquois was a key, was expected at any moment. New defenses were to be constructed and old ones strengthened. The men applied themselves with a courageous devotion, night and day, to their tasks and after two weeks of watchful working under fire, Vanquois became a formidable defensive system.

Besides the gallantry of Private Pinckney, Montzeville must be remembered in connection with the removal of colored officers from the regiment. It was there that a board of officers (all white) requested by Colonel Young and appointed by Colonel Tupes, sat on the cases of twenty-one colored officers charged with inefficiency. Only one out of that number was acquitted: he was later killed in action. The charges of inefficiency were based on physical disability, insufficient training, unsuitability. The other colored officers who had been removed were either transferred to other units or sent to re-classification depots.

The Colonel told the Commanding General through an interpreter: "The colored officers in this regiment know as much about their duties as a child." The General was surprised and whispered to another French officer that the Colonel himself was not so brilliant and that he believed it was prejudice that caused the Colonel to make such a change. A few moments after, the Colonel told the General that he had requested that no more colored officers be sent to the regiment. In reply to this the General explained how unwise it was because the colored officers had been trained along with their men at a great expenditure of time and money by the American and French governments; and, also, he doubted if well-qualified white officers could be spared him from other American units. The General insisted that the time was at hand for the great autumn drive and that it would be a hindrance because he feared the men would not be pleased with the change. The Colonel heeded not his General and forwarded two requests for an anti-colored-officer regiment. He went so far as to tell the Lieutenant-Colonel that he believed the regiment should have white men for non-commissioned officers. Of course, the men would not have stood for this at any price. The Colonel often would tell the Adjutant to never trust a "damned black clerk" and that he considered "one white man worth a million Negroes."

About September 8 the regiment was relieved by the 129th United States Infantry and was sent to the rear for period of rest. Twenty-four hours after arrival in the rest area, orders were received to proceed farther. The nightly marches began. The regiment marched from place to place in the Aube, the Marne and the Haute Marne until it went into the great Champagne battle on September 27.

For nine days it helped push the Hun toward the Belgian frontier. Those days were hard, but these men did their duty and came out with glory. Fortunately, all the colored officers had not left the regiment and it was they and the brave sergeants who led the men to victory and fame. The new white officers had just arrived, some of them the night before the regiment went into battle, several of whom had never been under fire in any capacity, having just come out of the training school at Langres. Nevertheless, the regiment was cited by the French and the regimental colors were decorated by Vice-Admiral Moreau at Brest, January 24, 1919.

After the relief on the battlefield, the regiment reached Somme Bionne (Marne) October 8. Congratulations came in from everywhere except American Headquarters. After a brief rest of three days the regiment was sent to a quiet sector in the Vosges, on the frontier of Alsace. The Colonel finally disposed of the remaining colored officers, except the two dentists and the two chaplains. All the officers were instructed to carry their arms at all times and virtually to shoot any soldier on the least provocation. As a consequence, a corporal of Company L was shot and killed by First Lieutenant James B. Coggins, from North Carolina, for a reason that no one has ever been able to explain. The signing of the Armistice and the cessation of hostilities, perhaps, prevented a general, armed opposition to a system of prejudice encouraged by the Commanding Officer of the Regiment.

Despite the prejudice of officers toward the men, the regiment marched from Ban-de-Laveline to Granges of Vologne, a distance of forty-five kilometers, in one day and maintained such remarkable discipline that the officers themselves were compelled to accord them praise.

While stationed at Granges, individuals in the regiment were decorated on December 17 for various deeds of gallantry in the Champagne battle. General Goybet presented four military medals and seventy-two *Croix de Guerre* to enlisted men. Colonel Tupes presented four Distinguished Service Crosses to enlisted men. At the time, the regiment had just been returned to the American command, the following order was read:

157th Division   Hqrs. December 15th, 1918.
Staff.

General Order No. 246.

On the date of the 12th of December, 1918, the 371st and the 372nd R. I., U. S. have been returned to the disposal of the American Command. It is not without profound emotion that I come in the name of the 157th (French) Division and in my personal name, to say good-bye to our valiant comrades of combat.

For seven months we have lived as brothers of arms, sharing the same works, the same hardships, the same dangers; side by side we have taken part in the great battle of the Champagne, that a wonderful victory has ended.

The 157th (French) Division will never forget the wonderful impetus irresistible, the rush heroic of the colored American regiments on the "Observatories Crest" and in the Plain of Menthois. The most formidable defense, the nests of machine guns, the best organized positions, the artillery barrages most crushing, could not stop them. These best regiments have gone through all with disdain of death and thanks to their courage devotedness, the "Red Hand" Division has during nine hard days of battle been ahead in the victorious advance of the Fourth (French) Army.

Officers and non-commissioned officers and privates of the 371st and

372nd Regiments Infantry, U.S., I respectfully salute your glorious dead and I bow down before your standards, which by the side of the 333rd R. I., led us to victory.

Dear Friends from America, when you have crossed back over the ocean, don't forget the "Red Hand" Division. Our fraternity of arms has been soaked in the blood of the brave. Those bonds will be indestructible.

Keep a faithful remembrance to your General, so proud to have commanded you, and remember that his thankful affection is gained to you forever.

(Signed) General Goybet,
Commanding the 157th (French)
Division, Infantry.

Colonel Tupes, in addressing the regiment, congratulated them on the achievements and expressed his satisfaction with their conduct. He asked the men to take a just pride in their accomplishments and their spirit of loyalty.

Can this be surpassed for eccentricity?

The seven weeks at Granges were pleasant and profitable socially. Lectures were given to the men by French officers, outdoor recreation was provided and the civilian population opened their hearts and their homes to the Negro heroes. Like previous attempts, the efforts of the white officers to prevent the mingling of Negroes with the French girls of the village were futile. Every man was taken on his merits. The mayor of Granges gave the regiment an enthusiastic farewell.

On January 1, 1919, the regiment entrained for Le Mans (Sarthe). After complying with the red-tape preparatory to embarkation and the delousing process it went to Brest, arriving there January 13, 1919.

THE 370TH

Up to this point the anti-Negro propaganda is clear and fairly consistent and unopposed. General Headquarters had not only witnessed instructions in Negro prejudice to the French, but had, also, consented to wholesale removals of officers among the engineers and infantry, on the main ground of color. Even the French, in at least one case, had been persuaded that Negro officers were the cause of certain inefficiencies in Negro units.

Undoubtedly the cruel losses of the 369th Regiment were due in part to the assumption of the French at first that the American Negroes were like the Senegalese; these half-civilized troops could not in the time given them be trained in modern machine warfare, and they were rushed at the enemy almost with naked hands. The resulting slaughter was horrible. Our troops tell of great black fields of stark and crimson dead after some of these superhuman onrushes.

It was this kind of fighting that the French expected of the black Americans at first and some white American officers did not greatly care so long as white men got the glory. The French easily misunderstood the situation at first and assumed that the Negro officers were to blame, especially as this was continually suggested to them by the Americans.

It was another story, however, when the 370th Regiment came. This was the famous 8th Illinois, and it had a full quota of Negro officers, from Colonel down. It had seen service on the Mexican border; it went to Houston, Tex., after the Thirteen had died for Freedom; and it was treated with wholesome respect. It was sent to Newport News, Va., for embarkation; once Colonel Dennison refused to embark his troops and marched them back to camp because he learned they were to be "Jim-Crowed" on the way over.

The regiment arrived at Brest, April 22, and was assigned to the 72nd French Division, remaining near Belfort until June 17. Then it went with the 34th French Division into the front-line, at St. Mihiel, for a month and later with the 36th French Division into the Argonne, where they fought. They were given a short period of rest and then they went into the front-line, at Soissons, with the 59th French Division. In September and October they were fighting again.

On September 15, in the Vauxaillion area, they captured Mt. Dessinges and the adjacent woods after severe fighting. They held a sector alone afterward on the Canal L'Oise et Aisne and when attacked, repulsed the Germans and moved forward, gaining the praise of the French General. On October 24, the regiment went into the front-line again, near Grand Lup, and performed excellent service; the Armistice found part of the regiment across the Belgian frontier.

The general conduct of the regiment was excellent. No case of rape was reported and only one murder. The regiment received sixteen Distinguished Service Crosses and seventy-five *Croix de Guerre*, beside company citations.

When at first the regiment did not adopt the tactics of "shock" troops, the white Americans again took their cue and inspired a speech from the French General, which the colored men could not understand. It was not long, however, before the French General publicly apologized for his first and hasty criticism and afterward he repeatedly commended both officers and men for their bravery, intelligence and daring. This regiment received more citations than any other American regiment for bravery on the field of battle. There was, of course, the fly in the ointment, — the effort to substitute white officers was strong and continuous, notwithstanding the fact that many of the black officers of this regiment were among the most efficient in the American Army.

General Headquarters by this time had begun to change its attitude and curb the Bourbons. It announced that it was not the policy of the American Army to make wholesale removals simply on account of color and it allowed the citations for bravery of Negro troops to be approved.

Nevertheless, the pressure continued. First the colored Colonel, the ranking Negro officer in France, was sent home. The reason for this is not clear. At any rate Colonel Dennison was replaced by a white Colonel, who afterward accepted a *Croix de Guerre* for an exploit which the Negro officers to a man declare was actually performed by a Negro officer while he was sitting snugly in his tent. The men of the regiment openly jeered him, crying out: "Blue Eyes ain't our Colonel; Duncan's our Colonel!" referring to the colored Lieutenant-Colonel. But the white Colonel was diplomatic; he let the colored officers run the regiment, posed as the "Moses" of the colored race (to the open amusement of the Negroes) and quietly tried to induct white officers. "I cannot understand why they sent this white Lieutenant," he said plaintively to a colored officer. The officer at that moment had in his pocket a copy of the Colonel's telegram asking General Headquarters for white officers. But the Armistice came before the Colonel succeeded in getting but two white officers, — his brother as Major (without a battalion) and one Lieutenant.

The organization that ranked all America in distinction remained, therefore, a Negro organization, for the white Colonel was only "commanding" and Dennison was still titular head.

THE 92ND DIVISION

So much for the 93rd Division. Its troops fought magnificently in the Champagne, the Argonne and elsewhere and were given unstinted praise by the French and even commendation by the Americans. They fought well, too, despite the color of their officers — 371st Regiment under white, the 369th and 372nd Regiments under white and colored, and the 370th Regiment under colored were equally brave, except that the 370th Regiment made the most conspicuous record.

One might conclude under ordinary circumstances that it was a matter of efficiency in officers and not of race, but, unfortunately, the efficient colored officer had almost no chance even to try except in the 370th Regiment and in the Champagne battle with the 372nd Regiment. With a fair chance there is no doubt that he could have led every one of these regiments just as well as the white officers. It must, too, be remembered that all the non-commissioned officers in all these regiments were Negroes.

The storm center of the Negro troops was the 92nd Division. The brigading of the 93rd Division with the French made wholesale attack and depreciation difficult, since it was continually annulled by the generous appreciation of the French. The 92nd Division, however, was planned as a complete Negro division, manned by Negro company officers. Everything depended, then, on the General and field officers as to how fair this experiment should be.

From the very first there was open and covert opposition and trouble. Instead of putting Colonel Young at the head, the white General Ballou was chosen and surrounded by southern white officers who despised "nigger" officers.

General Ballou himself was well-meaning, but weak, vacillating, without great ability and afraid of southern criticism. He was morbidly impressed by the horror of this "experiment" and proceeded from the first to kill the morale of his troops by orders and speeches. He sought to make his Negro officers feel personal responsibility for the Houston outbreak; he tried to accuse them indirectly of German propaganda; he virtually ordered them to submit to certain personal humiliations and discriminations without protest. Thus, before the 92nd Division was fully formed, General Ballou had spread hatred and distrust among his officers and men. "That old Ballou stuff!" became a by-word in the division for anti-Negro propaganda. Ballou was finally dismissed from his command for "tactical inefficiency."

The main difficulty, however, lay in a curious misapprehension in white men of the meaning and method of race contact in America. They sought desperately to reproduce in the Negro division and in France the racial restrictions of America, on the theory that any new freedom would "spoil" the blacks. But they did not understand the fact that men of the types who became Negro officers protect themselves from continuous insult and discrimination by making and moving in a world of their own; they associate socially where they are more than welcome; they live for the most part beside neighbors who like them; they attend schools where they are not insulted; and they work where their work is appreciated. Of course, every once in a while they have to unite to resent encroachments upon their world — new discriminations in law and custom; but this is occasional and not continuous.

The world which General Ballou and his field officers tried to re-create for Negro officers was a world of continuous daily insult and discrimination to an extent that none had ever experienced, and they did this in a country where the discrimination was artificial and entirely unnecessary, arousing the liveliest astonishment and mystification.

For instance, when the Headquarters Company of the 92nd Division sailed for Brest, elaborate quarters in the best hotel were reserved for white officers, and unfinished barracks, without beds and in the cold and mud, were assigned Negro officers. The colored officers went to their quarters and then returned to the city. They found that the white Americans, unable to make themselves understood in French, had not been given their reservation, but had gone to another and poorer hotel. The black officers immediately explained and took the fine reservations.

As no Negroes had been trained in artillery, it was claimed immediately that none were competent. Nevertheless, some were finally found to qualify. Then it was claimed that technically trained privates were impossible to find. There were plenty to be had if they could be gathered from the various camps. Permission to do this was long refused, but after endless other delays and troubles, the Field Artillery finally came into being with a few colored officers. Before the artillery was ready, the division mobilized at Camp Upton, between May 28 and June 4, and was embarked by the tenth of June for France.

The entire 92nd Division arrived at Brest by June 20. A week later the whole division went to Bourbonne-les-Bains, where it stayed in training until August 6. Here a determined effort at wholesale replacement of the colored officers took place. Fifty white Lieutenants were sent to the camp to replace Negro officers. "Efficiency" boards began to weed out colored men.

Without doubt there was among colored as among white American officers much inefficiency, due to lack of adaptability, training and the hurry of preparation. But in the case of the Negro officers repeatedly the race question came to the fore and permission was asked to remove them because they were colored, while the inefficiency charge was a wholesale one against their "race and nature."

General Headquarters by this time, however, had settled down to a policy of requiring individual, rather than wholesale, accusation, and while this made a difference, yet in the army no officer can hold his position long if his superiors for any reason wish to get rid of him. While, then, many of the waiting white Lieutenants went away, the colored officers began to be systematically reduced in number.

On August 6 the division entered the front-line trenches in the Vosges sector and stayed here until September 20. It was a quiet sector, with only an occasional German raid to repel. About September 20, the division began to move to the Argonne, where the great American drive to cut off the Germans was to take place. The colored troops were not to enter the front-lines, as General Pershing himself afterward said, as they were entirely unequipped for front-line service. Nevertheless, the 368th Regiment, which arrived in the Argonne September 24, was suddenly sent into battle on the front-line on the morning of September 26. As this is a typical instance of the difficulties of Negro officers and troops, it deserves recital in detail.

It is the story of the failure of white field officers to do their duty and the partially successful and long-continued effort of company officers and men to do their duty despite this. That there was inexperience and incompetency among the colored officers is probable, but it was not confined to them; in their case the greater responsibility lay elsewhere, for it was the plain duty of the field officers: First, to see that their men were equipped for battle; second, to have the plans clearly explained, at least, step by step, to the company officers; third, to maintain liaison between battalions and between the regiment and the French and other American units.

Here follows the story as it was told to me point by point by those who were actually on the spot. They were earnest, able men, mostly Lieutenants and Captains, and one could not doubt, there in the dim, smoke-filled tents about Le Mans, their absolute conscientiousness and frankness.

THE 368TH

The 368th Regiment went into the Argonne September 24 and was put into the drive on the morning of September 26. Its duty was "combat liaison," with the French 37th Division and the 77th (white) Division of Americans. The regiment as a whole was not equipped for battle in the front-line. It had no artillery support until the sixth day of the battle; it had no grenades, no trench fires, trombones, or signal flares, no airplane panels for signaling and no shears for German wire. The wire-cutting shears given them were absolutely useless with the heavy German barbed wire and they were able to borrow only sixteen large shears, which had to serve the whole attacking battalion.* Finally, they had no maps and were at no time given definite objectives.

---

* "On advancing from the French trenches the morning of the twenty-sixth much wire was met with by organizations and owing to the fact that none had wirecutters, considerable disorganization resulted in the companies, especially in the matter of liaison."

"As it was almost dark at this time and having no liaison with any of the other units, I decided to withdraw until I could get in touch with the Commanding Officer, 368th Infantry. The enemy searched along the trails with their artillery during our withdrawal, but none of the shells fell near us; it was pitch dark by this time and we had just reached the German's first trench. There was much confusion owing to the mass of wire we had to contend with in the dark before the companies reached the French trenches."

"Company G spent the entire day of the twenty-sixth working its way through the wire entanglements. Great difficulty was experienced in this work because of the lack of wirecutters."

— *Reports of Major M. A. Elser.*

The Second Battalion of the 368th Regiment entered battle on the morning of September 26, with Major Elser in command; all the company officers were colored; Company F went "over the top" at 5:30 A.M.; Company H, with which the Major was, went "over" at 12:30 noon; advancing four kilometers the battalion met the enemy's fire; the Machine Gun Company silenced the fire; Major Elser, who had halted in the woods to collect souvenirs from dead German bodies, immediately withdrew part of the battalion to the rear in single file about dark without notifying the rest of the battalion. Captain Dabney and Lieutenant Powell of the Machine Gun Company led the rest of the men out in order about 10:00 P.M. When the broadside opened on September 26, Major Elser stood wringing his hands and crying: "What shall I do! What shall I do!" At night he deplored the occurrence, said it was all his fault, and the next morning Major Elser commended the Machine Gun Company for extricating the deserted part of the battalion. Moving forward again at 11 A.M., two companies went "over the top" at 4 P.M. without liaison. With the rest of the battalion again, these companies went forward one and one-half kilometers. Major Elser stayed back with the Post-of-Command. Enemy fire and darkness again stopped the advancing companies and Captain Jones fell back 500 metres and sent a message about 6 A.M. on the morning of September 28 to the Major asking for re-enforcements. Captain Jones stayed under snipers' fire until about 3 P.M. and when no answer to his request came from the Major, he went "over the top" again and retraced the same 500 metres. Heavy machine gun and rifle fire again greeted him. He took refuge in nearby trenches, but his men began to drift away in confusion. All this time the Major was in the rear. On September 28, however, Major Elser was relieved of the command of the battalion and entered the hospital for "psychoneurosis," or "shell-shock," — a phrase which often covers a multitude of sins. Later he was promoted to Lieutenant-Colonel and transferred to a Labor Battalion.

Meantime, on September 27, at 4:30 P. M., the Third Battalion of the 368th Infantry moved forward. It was commanded by Major B. F. Norris, a white New York lawyer, a graduate of Plattsburg, and until this battle a Headquarters Captain with no experience on the line. Three companies of the battalion advanced two and one-half kilometres and about 6:30 P.M. were fired on by enemy machine guns. The Major, who was in support with one company and a platoon of machine guns, ordered the machine guns to trenches seventy-five yards in the rear. The Major's orders were confusing and the company as well as the platoon retreated to the trenches, leaving the firing-line unsupported. Subjected to heavy artillery, grenade, machine gun and rifle fire during the whole night of September 27 and being without artillery support or grenades, the firing line broke and the men took refuge in the trench with the Major, where all spent a terrible night under rain and bombardment. Next morning, September 28, at 7:30 A.M., the firing-line was restored and an advance ordered. The men led by their colored officers responded. They swept forward two and one-half kilometres and advanced beyond both French and Americans on the left and right. Their field officers failed to keep liaison with the French and American white units and even lost track of their own Second Battalion, which was dribbling away in one of the front trenches. The advancing firing-line of the Third Battalion met a withering fire of trench mortars, seventy-sevens, machine guns, etc. It still had no artillery support and being too far in advance received the German fire front, flank and rear and this they endured five hours. The line broke at 12:30 and the men retreated to the support trench, where the Major was. He reprimanded the colored officers severely. They reported the intense artillery fire and their lack of equipment, their ignorance of objectives and their lack of maps for which they had asked. They were ordered to re-form and take up positions, which they did. Many contradictory orders passed to the Company Commanders during the day: to advance, to halt, to hold, to withdraw, to leave woods as quickly as possible. Finally, at 6:30 P.M., they were definitely ordered to advance. They advanced three kilometres and met exactly the same conditions as before, — heavy artillery fire on all sides. The Company Commanders were unable to hold all their men and the Colonel ordered the Major to withdraw his battalion from the line. Utter confusion resulted, — there were many casualties and many were gassed. Major Norris withdrew, leaving a platoon under Lieutenant Dent on the line ignorant of the command to withdraw. They escaped finally unaided during the night.

The Chief of Staff said in his letter to Senator McKellar: "One of our majors commanding a battalion said: 'The men are rank cowards, there is no other words for it.' "

A colored officer writes:

"I was the only colored person present when this was uttered: It was on the 27th of last September in the second line trenches of Vienne Le Chateau in our attack in the Argonne and was uttered by Major B. F. Norris, commanding the 3rd Battalion. Major Norris, himself, was probably the biggest coward because he left his Battalion out in the front lines and came back to the Colonel's dugout a nervous wreck. I was there in a bunk alongside of the wall and this major came and laid down beside me and he moaned and groaned so terribly all night that I couldn't hardly close my eyes — he jumped and twisted worse than anything I have ever seen in my life. He was a rank coward himself and left his unit on some trifling pretext and remained back all night."

From September 26–29 the First Battalion of the 368th Infantry, under

Major J. N. Merrill, was in the front-line French trenches. On the night of September 28 it prepared to advance, but after being kept standing under shell-fire for two hours it was ordered back to the trenches. A patrol was sent out to locate the Third Battalion, but being refused maps by the Colonel it was a long time on the quest and before it returned the First Battalion was ordered to advance, on the morning of September 29. By 1:00 P.M. they had advanced one mile when they were halted to find Major Merrill. Finally Major Merrill was located after two hours' search. A French Lieutenant guided them to positions in an old German trench. The Major ordered them forward 600 yards to other deserted German trenches. Terrific shell-fire met them here, and there were many casualties. They stayed in the trench during the night of September 29 and at noon on September 30 were ordered to advance. They advanced three kilometres through the woods, through shell and machine gun fire and artillery barrage. They dug in and stayed all night under fire. On October 1 the French Artillery came up and put over a barrage. Unfortunately, it fell short and the battalion was caught between the German and French barrages and compelled hastily to withdraw.

The regiment was soon after relieved by a French unit and taken by train to the Marbache sector. Major Elser, of the Second Battalion, made no charges against his colored officers and verbally assumed responsibility for the failure of his battalion. There was for a time strong talk of a court martial for him. Major Merrill made no charges; but Major Norris on account of the two breaks in the line of the Third Battalion on September 28 ordered five of his colored line officers court-martialed for cowardice and abandonment of positions — a Captain, two First Lieutenants, and a Second Lieutenant were accused. Only one case, — that of the Second Lieutenant, had been decided at this writing. He was found guilty by the court-martial, but on review of his case by General Headquarters he was acquitted and restored to his command.

Colonel Greer in the letter to Senator McKellar on December 6, writes as follows: "From there we went to the Argonne and in the offensive starting there on September 26, had one regiment in the line, attached to the 38th French Corps. They failed there in all their missions, laid down and sneaked to the rear, until they were withdrawn."

This is what Colonel Durand, the French General who was in command in this action, said in a French General Order: "*L'Honneur de la prise de Binarville doit revenir au 368th R. I. U. S.*"

And this is what Colonel Greer himself issued in General Order No. 38, Headquarters 92nd Division, the same day he wrote his infamous letter to this senator: "The Division Commander desires to commend in order the meritorious conduct of Private Charles E. Boykin, Company C, 326th Field Signal Battalion. On the afternoon of September 26, 1918, while the 368th

Infantry was in action in the Argonne forest the Regimental Commander moved forward to establish a P. C. and came upon a number of Germans who fled to the woods which were FOUND TO BE ALIVE WITH MACHINE GUNS. The Commanding Officer ordered the woods searched to the top of the hill, the officer in charge of scouting (2nd Lieutenant C. W. Carpenter) called for volunteers and Private Boykin, a telephone linesman, offered his services and set out with the rest of the detail. While trying to flank an enemy machine gun another opened fire killing him instantly."

This effort of the 368th Regiment was seized upon by Army gossip and widely heralded as a "failure" of Negro troops, and particularly of Negro officers. Yet the same sort of troops and many Negro officers in the Champagne and afterward in the Argonne under French leadership covered themselves with glory. The real failure in the initial Argonne drive was in American field strategy which was totally unequal to German methods and had to learn by bitter experience. It is worse than unfair to write off the first experience to the discredit of Negro troops and company officers who did all that was humanly possible under the circumstances.

OTHER UNITS

The 365th, 366th and 367th Regiments did not enter the battle-line at all in the Argonne. The whole division after the withdrawal of the 368th Regiment was, beginning with September 29, transferred to the Metz sector, preparatory to the great drive on that fortress which was begun, rather needlessly, as the civilian would judge, on the day before the signing of the Armistice, November 10.

According to plan, the 56th white American Division was on the left, the 92nd Division was in the center and the French Army was on the right. The 367th Regiment led the advance and forged ahead of the flanking units, the entire First Battalion being awarded the *Croix de Guerre*; — but this time wise field direction held them back, and for the first time they were supported by their own Negro Field Artillery. Beside the four Infantry Regiments the 92nd Division had the usual other units.

The 325th Field Signal Battalion, attached to Division Headquarters, was composed of four companies organized at Camp Sherman. It had ten colored and twenty white officers. It was in France at Bourbonne-les-Bains and then went to the Vosges, where it was split into detachments and attached to regiments under the Chief Signal Officer. While at school at Gondricourt, July 13–August 18, it made one of the best records of any unit. Many of its men were cited for bravery.

The 167th Field Artillery Brigade consisted of two regiments of Light Artillery (75s) trained at Camp Dix (the 349th and 350th) and one regiment of Heavy Artillery (the 351st) trained at Camp Meade, which used 155 howitzers. They experienced extraordinary difficulties in training. There can be no doubt but that deliberate effort was made to send up for examination in artillery not the best, but the poorest equipped candidates. Difficulty was encountered in getting colored men with the requisite technical training transferred to the artillery service. If the Commanding Officer in this case had been as prejudiced as in the case of the engineer and other units, there would have been no Negro Artillery. But Colonel Moore, although a Southerner, insisted on being fair to his men. The brigade landed in Brest June 26 and was trained at Montmorillon (Vienne). They were favorites in the town and were received into the social life on terms of perfect equality. There were five colored company officers and eight medical officers. The officers were sent to school at La Cortine and the Colonel in charge of this French school aid that the work of the colored artillery brigade was better at the end of two weeks than that of any other American unit that had attended the school. The brigade went into battle in the Metz drive and did its work without a hitch, despite the fact that it had no transport facilities for their guns and had to handle them largely by hand.

The 317th Ammunition Train, which was attached to Division Headquarters, but was under the artillery in battle, was organized at Camp Funston in December, and had 1,333 officers and men, divided into two battalions, one motor and one horse, with seven companies. There were thirty-three colored and three white officers. The battalion landed in France June 27 and went to Montmorillon, and to the Artillery Training School at La Cortine, with the 167th Field Artillery. It arrived at Marbache October 18 and took part in the Metz drive. It had charge, also, of the Corps Ammunition dumps. During the drive all the officers were colored and Major Dean was in command. General Sherbourne, one of the few Commanding Officers fair to Negro troops, warmly commended the work of the artillery. No general court martial took place in the organization from the beginning and no efficiency boards sat. This was one of the very few units in which Negroes were promoted: four being made Captains, three First Lieutenants, eleven Second Lieutenants, and one a Major.

Near the close of the war thirty-five Lieutenants commissioned at Camp Taylor arrived in France and were sent to school near Nantes. They were subjected to many indignities by the American officers and were compelled to enter the class-room after the whites; they were refused leaves to town; reprimanded for conversing with the women of the city, who were anxious to be kind and sympathetic to the obviously oppressed strangers. Notwithstanding all this the men made good records and joined their command after the Armistice.

The 317th Engineers were assembled at Camp Sherman in December with 1,350 officers and men. There were two battalions and all the officers were colored, except four field officers. The Commanding Officers, however, were from the first determined to get rid of the Negroes. On May 10 the colored Captains were relieved, and sent to the 365th and 366th Regiments. The regiment came to France in June and was trained near Bourbonne-les-Bains until July 20. On July 22 all the remaining colored officers, except two Lieutenants, the chaplain and the medical officers, were relieved at the repeated requests of Colonel Brown, of Georgia, and others. The regiment went to the Vosges in August, and then to the Argonne, doing excellent technical work in building and construction. All but one company were attached to the Fourth French Army Corps until December 22; only Company E remained with the 92nd Division.

The 366th Field Hospital was a colored unit with only two or three whites. It handled 10,000 cases before and during the Metz drive, four weeks, and was rated best in the American Expeditionary Force. Lieutenant Wright, the colored physician in charge, was promoted to a Captaincy.

The final engagement immediately preceding the signing of the Armistice was fought in the Marbache sector, south of Metz, and was the most important event in which all the units of the 92nd Division actively participated. The division entered this sector October 7 and established headquarters in the village of Marbache, October 10, 1918. The several regiments were stationed in the front lines of the Division sector, with supporting units and reserves in the rear. Almost immediately upon entering this sector active operations were begun; patrols and reconnoitering parties were sent out from our lines; raiding parties were active and both sides found it necessary to be constantly on the alert. As the time for the advance of the whole Second Army grew nearer heavy shelling became more frequent, patrolling more active and raiding parties bolder. It was necessary to obtain all possible information regarding the enemy's movements and intentions before the advance began. There were many thrilling experiences in the sector during the four weeks preceding the final struggle.

On the tenth day of November came the order announcing the great drive and outlining the position of the 92nd Division in the line.

At 7 A. M. on the eleventh, the artillery broke loose with a terrific bombardment; this preparation lasted for a period of 42 minutes and was delivered upon the village of Bois Frehaut and the neighboring woods through which the infantry was to pass in its advance. In the meantime, the boys in the several companies composing the first assault line sprang from their trenches and with grim determination pushed themselves into "No Man's Land" and into the woods in the direction of the great German fortification, the city of Metz. The first objective of the 365th Infantry was Bois Frehaut (woods) three miles in depth and two miles in width. Barbed wire entanglements were everywhere and German machine guns were sputtering and large cannon were sending forth their messengers of death in all directions. The 365th Machine Gun Company, the 37-M M Platoon and our artillery and infantrymen repulsed this murderous attack and after two hours of desperate fighting Bois Frehaut was taken by the 365th and held by the Second Battalion of that organization until the bugle sounded the call to cease firing at 11 o'clock on the following morning.

The attack was led by Company H under the command of Captain William W. Green with a detachment of Company A commanded by Lieutenant Gus Mathews of Chicago with Company G and two other units in support. In fighting through the dense woods, made more difficult by large volumes of smoke from bursting shells, the attacking line in Company H became thinned and before many of the men arrived after the Company merged from the woods a flanking movement was attempted by the German machine gunners, but the timely arrival of Company G under the command of Lieutenant Walter Lyons saved Company H from this added danger. During this attack the Machine Gun Company of the 365th was active in covering the advancing infantry and kept the enemy on the run, thus making it impossible for them to deliver an effective fire against the men in the assault waive. The second assault waive was under the command of Captain Walter R. Sanders who was, also, second in command of the Second Battalion of the 365th Infantry. The second waive, under heavy shell fire and gas bombs from the artillery, moved up to occupy the position first held by the Second Battalion. While making this advance Lieutenant Walter Lowe, commanding Company A, was gassed, but he remained with his company, directing its movements until a short time before the order came to cease firing on the morning of the eleventh.

While the 365th Infantry was fighting like real heroes the units in the other battalions were doing exactly the same thing. The first objective reached by the 366th was Bois-de-Boivotte. The units in the first assault waive moved over the top at exactly seven o'clock on the morning of November 10. The artillery laid down a barrage for the advancing troops and protected their advance as far as possible, but the terrific bombardment with gas, shrapnel and machine gun fire from the German trenches made progress difficult as well as extremely dangerous. The troops, accustomed as they were by this time to bursting shells and gas bombs, ignored all personal danger and fought their way to their first objective with but few casualties. The fighting was furious during the early part of the day, but the organization was able to capture and hold much ground, varying from three to five kilometers in depth.

The 367th Infantry occupied a position on the west side of the Mosselle River. Two companies of the Second Battalion were in the first assault waive with others in support and reserve. The fighting units reached and held their objective and although the fighting was brisk the 367th did not lose a single man. With the darkness came a cessation of intensive action, the troops were reorganized and plans formulated for a renewal of the attack early the next morning.

In this general engagement the 92nd Division occupied a position a little southeast of the strong fortifications of Metz. The 165th French Division was on our right and the Seventh American Division was on our left and we kept in touch with both these divisions during the night and prepared for what subsequently proved to be the final struggle of the great world war the following morning.

At dawn the air was cool and damp; it was slightly cloudy, with a little fog in the atmosphere, just enough to give it a dull-gray color and to prevent the soldiers from seeing more than a few hundred yards in the direction of the enemy.

The keen whistling noises made by the shells from our supporting artillery as they passed over our heads on their missions of death told us that the hour was 4:30 A.M., for at that time the 351st Field Artillery Regiment began its advance upon Bois La Cote and Champey. This fire was kept up continuously until 10:45. The 350th Field Artillery Regiment, also, renewed its attack upon the woods in the neighborhood of Bois Frehaut, but ceased firing at 10 o'clock A.M., forty-five minutes earlier than the 351st. At five o'clock the First Battalion of the 350th Field Artillery laid a rolling barrage across and just north of Bouxieres-sur-Froidmont in support of the advancing infantry. Many of the same units that engaged the enemy the day before were again struggling for additional gains in the direction of Metz. Several fresh companies were brought up from the support to join those who had so gallantly repulsed the enemy on Saturday and together made a supreme effort to deliver a blow that would silence the German guns and put the Huns to flight in disorder. The only thing that saved the Kaiser's army in this sector from a crushing defeat was the order to cease firing at 11 o'clock.

At one time during the morning engagement the 56th Infantry (white) of the 7th Division, while advancing, ran into a strong barbed wire entanglement that had not been destroyed by artillery. Further advance was impossible and to retire under heavy fire from the German's big guns and merciless machine gun fire meant annihilation. Major Charles L. Appleton of the 367th Infantry, seeing the desperate situation into which the 56th Infantry had worked itself, manoeuvered several platoons to a position where they could hit the Germans from the flank and cover the retirement of the 56th. This timely act on the part of Major Appleton probably saved the 56th from complete destruction.

When the bugle sounded the call to cease firing, Company H of the 365th Infantry held 800 yards of the battle-front, five kilometers of which was taken from the Germans under the heavy guns of Metz, and held against odds five to one under intense shell and machine gun fire.

OTHER AGENCIES

So much for the 92nd Division. It never had a fighting chance until the last day of the war. It was a centre of intrigue from the beginning and its weak and vacillating General spent most of his time placating the Negro haters on his staff and among his field officers, who wished nothing so much as the failure of the division as a fighting unit. How different a story if Charles Young had been let to lead his own!

Of the assisting agencies the only one that paid any attention to Negro troops was the Young Men's Christian Association. The few who came to Red Cross hospitals were, with a few exceptions, not only "Jim-Crowed" but officers were put in wards with their men. The white Young Men's Christian Association secretaries usually refused to serve Negroes in any way. Very few colored secretaries were sent and an attempt was made at first to get rid of the best of these, on the ground that their beliefs on the manhood rights and human equality of Negroes were "seditious." Matters were greatly improved when a colored man was placed in general charge of the colored work. He was never, however, furnished enough men and only three women for his vast field until after the Armistice.

On one subject the white Commanding Officers of all colored units showed more solicitude than on the organization and fighting efficiency of the troops, — that was the relations of the colored officers and men with the women of France. They began by officially stigmatizing the Negroes as rapists; they solemnly warned the troops in speeches and general orders not even to speak to women on the street; ordered the white military police to spy on the blacks and arrest them if they found them talking with French women. The white troops, taking their cue from all this senseless pother, spread tales and rumors among the peasants and villagers and sought to chastise Negroes and offending women. One officer, a high-minded gentleman, graduate and Phi Beta Kappa man of a leading American institution, was court-martialed for keeping company with a perfectly respectable girl of a family of standing in one of the towns where Negroes were quartered and while General Headquarters did not uphold the court-martial, it took occasion severely to reprimand the officer and remove him to a Labor Battalion.

The result of all this a-do was simply unnecessary bitterness among Negroes and mystification among the French. The Negroes resented being publicly stigmatized by their own countrymen as unfit for association with decent people, but the French men and women much preferred the courtesy and bonhomie of the Negroes to the impudence and swagger of many of the whites. In practically every French town where the Negro troops stayed they left close and sympathetic friends among men, women and children.

While the 92nd Division was in France there were fourteen trials for attacks on women, six of which were acquitted; of the other eight, three men were convicted of simple assault, leaving five possible cases of grave crime against women; of these, three cases are still undecided at this writing, one has been acquitted by the court, but the verdict has not been reviewed, and ONE man has been found guilty and hanged. It is only fair to add that this man belonged to a Labor Battalion and was sent to the division simply for trial. No other American division in France has a better record in this respect.

THE END

This is a partial and preliminary statement of the part the Negro played in the Great War. There is much in the tale that is missing and some mistakes, to be corrected by fuller information and reference to documents. But the main outlines are clear.

A nation with a great disease set out to rescue civilization; it took the disease with it in virulent form and that disease of race-hatred and prejudice hampered its actions and discredited its finest professions.

No adequate excuse for America's actions can be offered: Grant that many of the dismissed and transferred colored officers were incompetent, there is no possible excuse for the persistent and studied harrowing of admittedly competent men, to which every black officer testifies with a bitterness unexampled in Negro American history; there was no excuse for the persistent refusal to promote Negroes, despite their records testified to even by the French; there was no excuse for systematically refusing Negro officers and soldiers a chance to see something of greater and more beautiful France by curtailing their leaves and quartering them in the back districts.

On the other hand, there is not a black soldier but who is glad he went, — glad to fight for France, the only real white Democracy; glad to have a new, clear vision of the real, inner spirit of American prejudice. The day of camouflage is past.

This history will be enlarged and expanded, embellished with maps and pictures and with the aid of an editorial board, consisting of the leading Negro American scholars and the most distinguished of the black soldiers who fought in France, will be issued by the National Association for the Advancement of Colored People and *The Crisis*, in three volumes, in honor of the first great struggle of the modern Negro race for liberty.

Germany and Hitler

I am going to write The Courier four letters about Germany. I have written already a word here and there about minor aspects of the German scene. I am sure my friends have understood my hesitations and reticence: it simply wasn't safe to attempt anything further. Even my mail, when Mrs. DuBois sent me a minor receipt to sign, was opened to see if money was being smuggled in.

But now I have ended my sojourn — or at least shall have long before this is published; and to insure its reaching The Courier on time I am taking it to a foreign land to mail.

This does not mean that I have not enjoyed my five and more months in Germany. I have. I have been treated with uniform courtesy and consideration. It would have been impossible for me to have spent a similarly long time in any part of the United States, without some, if not frequent cases of personal insult or discrimination. I cannot record a single instance here.

It is always difficult to characterize a whole nation. One cannot really know 67 million people, much less indict them. I have simply looked on. I have used my eyes and, to a lesser extent, my ears. I have talked with some people, but not widely, nor inquisitively.

Chiefly I have traveled. I have been in all parts of Germany: in Prussia, including Mecklenburg, Brandenburg, Hanover and Schlesien; I have seen the Hansa cities of the northwest and East Prussia; I have looked on the North Sea and the Alps, and traveled through Saxony, Thuringia, Westphalia, Wurtemburg and Bavaria. I have seen the waters of the Rhine, Elbe, Weser, Oder and Danube. I have seen all the great German cities: Berlin, Hamburg, Luebeck, Bremen, both Frankforts, Cologne, Mayence,

From the *Pittsburgh Courier*, December 5, 1936.

Stuttgart, Breslau and Munich, not to mention Vienna and Strassburg. I have seen Germany; and not in the mists of a tourist's rush, but in slow and thoughtful leisure. I have read German newspapers of all sorts and places; I have read books, listened to lectures, gone to operas, plays and movies, and watched a nation at work and play. I have talked with a half dozen officials.

Germany in overwhelming majority stands back of Adolf Hitler today. Germany has food and housing, and is, on the whole, contented and prosperous. Unemployment in four years has been reduced from seven to two millions or less. The whole nation is dotted with new homes for the common people, new roads, new public buildings and new public works of all kinds. Food is good, pure and cheap. Public order is perfect, and there is almost no visible crime. And yet, in direct and contradictory paradox to all this, Germany is silent, nervous, suppressed; it speak in whispers; there is no public opinion, no opposition, no discussion of anything; there are waves of enthusiasm, but never any protest of the slightest degree. Last winter 12 million were in want of food and clothes, and this winter not less than 9 million, perhaps 10. There is a campaign of race prejudice carried on, openly, continuously and determinedly against all non-Nordic races, but specifically against the Jews, which surpasses in vindictive cruelty and public insult anything I have ever seen; and I have seen much. Here is the paradox and contradiction. It is so complicated that one cannot express it without seeming to convict one's self of deliberate misstatement. And the testimony of the casual, non-German-speaking visitor to the Olympic Games is worse than valueless in any direction.

When a group or a nation acts incomprehensively, the answer lies in a background of fact, unknown or imperfectly comprehended by the onlooker. So it is in this case. Germany has lived through four horrors in living history that no people can experience and remain entirely normal. These are: War; the Treaty of Versailles; Inflation; Depression, and Revolution. Save the few who were actually in the trenches of the A. E. F., our generation in America has no adequate notion of war. There is a war monument in Hamburg which is the most eloquent and ghastly memory I have ever seen. It is a square, straight shaft of gray granite, and it says simply: "40,000 sons of this city gave their lives for you in 1914–18." Forty thousand dead youth from a single German city! Then came a treaty of peace which was no less than devilish in its concealed ingenuity. One might agree in blaming Germany for the war — although this is by no means as clear today as it seemed then to us — but who of the laymen knew or dreamed that what the peace treaty did was so to hamstring German industry as to make the earning of a living in Germany so difficult that bankruptcy followed on a scale that was revolutionary? The treaty deprived Germany not simply of one-eighth of her territory, population and arable land, but what was far more important, of a fifth of her coke; three-fourths of her iron, one-fourth of her blast furnaces, two-thirds of her zinc foundries, one-fifth of her livestock, all of her merchant marine, and most of her railway equipment. And then saddled her with a debt based on unheard-of principles, which no land could or did pay. In other words, in order to establish peace, the capitalists of England, France and America made the orderly return of Germany to work and self-support impossible without internal revolution. This revolution meant a redistribution of wealth and income in Germany comparable only to the French and Russian revolutions. And the people who paid in Germany were the thrifty, the workers, the civil employees — the very classes who had opposed war in the first place. And the persons who bore the brunt of criticism in Germany for the treaty were the labor unions, the teachers, the middle class who hated war and wanted to build a new state, above the power of capital and the army. Adolf Hitler rode into power eventually by calling the government of Germany, which negotiated the treaty of Versailles, traitors who stabbed Germany in the back when she was down.

Germany not only had the flower of her youth murdered in a senseless war, but had her bread and butter taken away in an equally senseless peace. The accumulated savings of the nation disappeared; pensions, in a land of pensioned civil servants, were stopped; loans were paid in worthless money; property values dropped to nothing; industry was in bankruptcy and labor out of work. She struggled up and partially out of the morass, but when depression settled on the world, Germany was worse off than others, because she was hopelessly in debt, and by the unanimous decision of the world not allowed to pay her debt in the only possible way: by the export of her manufactures. Adolf Hitler rode into power by accusing the world of a conspiracy to ruin Germany by economic starvation. He promised to remedy this by making Germany self-sufficient and giving her an army capable of defending her rights. Revolution was staring Germany in the face, and a Marxian revolution which would make a dictatorship of the proletariat and made a socialistic state. Industry was frightened; the Junkers (landed nobility) were frightened; the managers, engineers and small shopkeepers were frightened; they all submitted to a man who had at first been a joke, then a pest, and who suddenly loomed as a dictator. Union labor, with its 8,000,000 members, holding the wide balance of power in the state, proceeded to squabble as to whether to usher in the milennium immediately or gradually, and through this squabble Adolf Hitler and Big Industry drove a carriage and four. He made a state without a single trade union and where the discussion of change is a crime.

Africa

If Hitler wins, and in the long run he cannot win, Africa will be parceled out between Germany and Italy. Its people will be subjected to an attempted caste system resembling slavery, except that they will be trained to certain modern techniques; techniques which if they are at all valuable to the conqueror, will mean his eventual disaster. All of the new cultural patterns which have held revolt in Africa back: Christian missions, modern education and modern languages, will have their holds loosened and one may expect a frightful whirl of unloosened passion which no power in Fascist Europe can long hold back.

If Hitler wins, and he cannot win, there will be no recognition of Chinese nor Indian nationality, so long as he can help it or has power to oppose it. India may temporarily fly to pieces through religious, racial and political faction but not for long. The power which has built the Indian Congress will eventually weld a new unity. And China will see her salvation not in white England and America but in brown India and yellow Japan. Logically Japan, if the Fascists win, would dominate Dutch India, British East India and Australia. But that leaves the puzzle of the relation of Japan to Hitler and Mussolini. Eventually Japan must make a tremendous choice. Outside of her justifiable hatred of Great Britain and suspicion of America, she has got to realize that the new industrial revolution which has already essentially transformed the Western World which she has been imitating, must be yielded to in Japan; that will be easier than it appears; for as Matsuoka, himself, once told me: within and essentially, Japan is already Communistic.

But Hitler cannot win, simply because no such organization as he has today built up, can command the brains, the loyalty and the man-power which will enable it to conquer the world.

From the *Amsterdam News*, July 12, 1941.

Closing Ranks Again

It seems with regard to the Roberts report that the Japanese attack on Pearl Harbor was a surprise only to those who were too lazy to be surprised.

Slowly there is coming to the fore in this war just as years ago in the Revolutionary War, the Civil War, the Spanish-American War and the First World War, the question of Negro patriotism to the United States.

There are always two extreme attitudes: One, perfect acquiescence in whatever the white nation says, thinks or does; the other, open rebellion against taking up arms for the United States. Few, of course, have followed either of these two paths.

Each generation faced by the horror of war is disposed to think that its attitude is wiser and braver than that of generations gone. So that there is already rising today controversy about the attitude of Negroes toward the second World War as compared toward that in the First World War.

The *Philadelphia Tribune* has referred to an editorial which I wrote in *The Crisis* in July, 1918, called "Close Ranks." In it I said: "That which the German power represents today spells death to the aspirations of Negroes and all darker race for equality, freedom and democracy. Let us not hesitate. Let us, while this war lasts, forget our special grievances and close our ranks shoulder to shoulder with our own white fellow citizens and the Allied nations that are fighting for democracy."

I re-read this editorial twenty-three years after with no desire to change a word. We shall stand ready to fight shoulder to shoulder for democracy with soldiers of any race or color and for a democracy of all men. If anyone questions this program let him remember what preceded this editorial of 1918: We had begun the campaign against lynching which reduced the number of lynchings fifty percent and made President Wilson join our crusade. We had fought for Negro officers in the A.E.F., and secured seven

From the *Amsterdam News,* February 14, 1942.

hundred which is probably twice as many as we have now or will have in this war. We had answered completely the whispered charges of German propaganda and withstood the open espionage of state and national officers. We declared in a national conference in Washington that we traced "the real cause of this World War to the despising of the darker races by the dominant groups of men." We had investigated and publicized lynchings, defended the black soldiers of Houston, and encouraged and directed migration of Negroes from the South.

We said frankly in a *Crisis* editorial in September, 1917: "Let us enter this war for Liberty with clean hands. May no blood-smeared garments bind our feet when we rise to make the world safe for Democracy. The New Freedom cannot survive if it means Waco, Memphis and East St. Louis. We cannot lynch 2,867 untried black men and women in thirty-one years and pose successfully as leaders of civilization. Rather let us bow our shamed heads and in sack cloth and ashes declare that when in awful war we raise our weapons against the enemies of mankind, so, too, and in that same hour here at home we raise our hands to Heaven and pledge our sacred honor to make our own America a real land of the free."

To this end we not only responded to the draft and bought Liberty Bonds but also kept Colonel Young from being summarily retired from the Army. We continued to hammer at discrimination as, for instance, in a *Crisis* editorial January, 1918: "How precious the Negro is when society wants to use him! . . . How indispensable is his loyalty, when the army is recruited for the great war to 'make the world safe for democracy!' How welcome are his dollars, when a $5,000,000,000 Liberty Loan is floated by the Government. Does anybody think of denying the black man the opportunity to do the work which nobody else will do? Has anybody urged that the black man be exempted from military service? Has any black man laid down his fifty dollars in a Liberty Loan booth, and been refused a bond?"

I spoke for a united Negro press when at a meeting of Negro editors in Washington in August, 1918, I wrote the resolutions which they unanimously adopted: "The American Negro does not expect to have the whole Negro problem settled immediately; he is not seeking to hold up a striving country and a distracted world by pushing irrelevant personal grievances as a price of loyalty; he is not disposed to catalogue, in this tremendous crisis, all his complaints and disabilities; he is more than willing to do his full share in helping to win the war for democracy and he expects his full share of the fruits thereof; — but he is today compelled to ask for that minimum of consideration which will enable him to be an efficient fighter for victory."

We may sadly admit today that the First World War did not bring us democracy. Nor will the second. In neither war have we been cowards nor slackers. In neither war have we surrendered nor will we surrender our free right to think.

We close ranks again but only, now as then, to fight for democracy and democracy not only for white folk but for yellow, brown and black.

The Negro and the War

This is a war for freedom. Whose freedom?

Is it for the freedom of Asiatics and Africans?

Is it for the freedom of white men to migrate to Africa and of black men to migrate to Australia?

Is it for the freedom of Negroes in the Southern United States and Negroes in West Africa to vote?

If this is the freedom we are fighting for, my gun is on my shoulder.

THE NEGRO AND THE WAR

I said some time since that I feared that the Negro would get less out of this war than he got out of the last; but I think I was wrong. It looks, on the whole, as though the American Negro was on the way to gain a great deal out of this war especially as his war becomes a determined fight for entrance into industry. This has not been wholly successful but it has succeeded to an extraordinary degree. It has broken down bar after bar held up by employers and trade unions, and it will only be necessary to hold the ground thus gained. Necessary, but of course, difficult.

There probably will be more Negro officers inducted into the army through this war than the seven hundred or more who received commissions in the First World War. It will be difficult, to be sure, to do this but there are indications that this will be true. The Southern-infested navy has been breached. It is not a large opening or an opening of any particular significance. Chiefly it is a matter of getting additional colored labor for tasks which white men do not like. Nevertheless, it is a breach and it needs to be hammered further open.

From the *Amsterdam News*, May 9, 1942.

There are, of course, many things to be feared. The recent re-shuffling of authority in Washington means forced labor for colored soldiers probably on farms. The Negro troops who have gone to Australia have undoubtedly gone as laborers and not as fighters. It is true, of course, that in modern war the labor element is of increasing importance as compared with the actual fighters. But on the other hand, the kind of labor done and the circumstances of its doing leave room for much unfortunate discrimination. This is a fact carefully to be watched.

Negro's War Gains and Losses

Now that the Second World War has ended what have we Americans of Negro descent lost and gained? We may record five groups of losses:

1. War itself is always a loss which bears hardest among the segregated and the oppressed leaving a legacy of death and destruction which is almost incalculable.

2. We have suffered the tremendous disadvantage of a "jim-crow" army and of segregation in army circles which will form and have formed a basis of similar segregation in civil life. This segregation is not simply separation of human beings in their ordinary life: In order to make segregation effective it has been found necessary to suppress ability and deny opportunity.

3. The defeat and humiliation of Japan marks the tragedy of the greatest colored nation which has risen to leadership in modern times. No matter how we explain and assess the damage, the result of thinking along the lines of race and color will affect human relations for many years and will excuse contempt and injustice toward colored skins. It will set back the time of the emancipation of the majority of people in the world.

4. If the military regimentation of living will retard civilization, it means the training of men through long and costly years for murder and destruction and then afterwards to use these same men and the same methods for cultural uplift. The whole proposal is impossible.

5. And finally, we have seen in this war, to our amazement and distress, a marriage between science and destruction; a marriage such as we had never dreamed of before. We have always thought of science as the emancipator. We see it now as the enslaver of mankind.

From the *Chicago Defender*, September 15, 1945.

SIX GAINS LISTED

We turn from this sad picture to six gains which have come out of war, not necessarily because of it, but in most cases despite the organized destruction:

1. The world of culture has been compelled to make a re-statement of democracy at a time in our development when we are beginning to distrust and ignore democracy. We have been compelled to come back to the basic idea that the government and direction of human beings must in the long run rest upon the wishes and the will of those who are governed and guided.

2. We have been compelled to admit Asia into the picture of future political and democratic power. We can no longer regard Europe as the sole center of the world. The development of human beings in the future is going to depend largely upon what happens in Asia.

3. We have been compelled to admit China as a great power. When China was first attacked it was because of attack by Europe. When the attack continued it was through the acquiescence of Europe and America; and when finally against the will of the white world we were dragged into the great center of Asiatic war, we took up and espoused the cause of Chinese freedom and independence because we knew well that the Japanese cry of "Asia for the Asiatics" would be turned against us unless we helped China maintain her independence.

RUSSIAN RECOGNITION

4. We have been compelled to recognize Russia as an equal country in spite of the fact that her economic organization is directly and categorically opposed to the profit-making industrial organization of the Western world. And moreover because of the prominence given Russia today in this war, her backing of China and alliance with China means that China will not be at the sole direction of Western Europe. The dream of Europe as the profiteer of China and the controller of her destiny through its efforts, falls before the menace of Russia.

5. More specifically there can be no doubt but what India and the Dutch Netherlands and French Indo-China are going in our day to achieve something approaching autonomy in government.

6. And last there is upheaval in Pan Africa among the people in Africa itself, north west and south; but also and just as significantly among the people

of African descent in the Caribbean area, in South and Central America and in the United States of America.

It cannot be said that, balancing these losses and gains, the war has been either a vast success or a terrible failure. It can be said that civilization after this war has a chance to go forward and no group of civilized people have better opportunity to forward the advance of human culture than American Negroes.

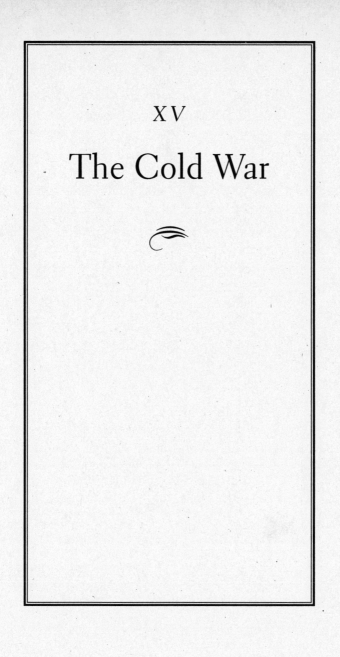

XV

The Cold War

After his second expulsion from the NAACP in 1948, Du Bois became one of the principal voices on the far left. It was now an article of faith for him that domestic anticommunism and the foreign policy of Soviet containment were camouflage for the military-industrial complex, of which racism was a central component. Now a battling octagenarian, he plunged into the international peace circuit, delivering the closing speech at the 1949 Waldorf-Astoria Peace Conference ("Peace: Freedom's Road for Oppressed Peoples" [1949]), speaking again before the gigantic rally in Paris that same year ("None Who Saw Paris Will Ever Forget"), then on to Moscow for another peace rally. He lambasted NATO in testimony before the House Foreign Affairs Committee of the United States ("Opposition to Military Assistance Act of 1949"), denounced the Marshall Plan as a reactionary plot, defended the Rosenbergs in verse, and eulogized Stalin on his death. Du Bois ran for the U.S. Senate on the New York American Labor Party ticket in 1952 and was indicted and tried in Washington, D.C., as a Russian agent by the Department of Justice that same year under the Foreign Agents Registration Act of 1936. The failure of most of the African-American leadership to rally to his defense embittered Du Bois and caused him to reassess the deeper economic and class implications of current civil rights court victories and commencing nonviolent passive resistance demonstrations. In "The Real Reason Behind Robeson's Persecution" (1958), he stressed again a fatal linkage between opposition to capitalist exploitation and racial victimization.

Peace: Freedom's Road for
Oppressed Peoples

This Cultural and Scientific Conference for World Peace has been a success. In a time of hysteria, suspicion and hate, we have succeeded in bringing face to face in friendly meetings, one of the largest gatherings of creative artists and thinkers the world has seen; and it would have been quite the largest if all who wished to come were here. Meeting together for three full days, we have found wide agreement and sympathy, we have established ideals and friendships belting the globe.

We have not and are not now in complete agreement on all matters. But in one vital respect our agreement is complete: No More War! The horrible world-old habit of wholesale murder of those who disagree with us is, we are convinced, a relic of barbarism bound to destroy our best culture unless it is absolutely and definitely abolished.

On the other hand, we are not childishly deceived as to the enormity of the task of organizing and conducting a peaceful world. We are many minds and backgrounds, separated not only by space but by the terrible barriers of language and social patterns; we face deliberate crime, ignorance and misunderstanding . . . but we firmly believe that the greatest of these is misunderstanding. Decent wage, health and schools will one day reduce crime and ignorance to manageable proportions. It is in the vast realm of misunderstanding, misrepresentation and doubt, that war is born and flourishes.

Perhaps unwittingly, the opposition which our effort has incurred proves this truth with startling clarity. We know and the saner nation knows that we are not traitors nor conspirators; and far from plotting force and violence it is precisely force and violence that we bitterly oppose. This conference was not called to defend Communism nor Socialism nor the American way of life. It was called to promote peace! It was called to say and say again that no matter

From *Worker*, April 17, 1949, magazine section, p. 7.

how right or wrong differing systems of belief in religion, industry or government may be, war is not the method by which their differences can successfully be settled for the good of mankind.

To the defense of this absolutely indisputable thesis, proven by oceans of blood and worlds of human suffering, we have invited the cooperation of all men; and that cooperation to abolish war does not compel or even ask men to surrender their opinions. It simply insists that force is not reason and beliefs cannot be changed by suppression.

VAST MAJORITY OF MANKIND
ARE DARKER PEOPLES

But there is one aspect of our conference which has forced itself upon the attention of us all. That is the effort of the press and certain leaders of public opinion to spread the idea that some persons here are by their beliefs and actions so beyond the pale of humanity as to deserve neither sympathy nor confidence. Particularly have the people of the Soviet Union been singled out for something bordering on insult and repeatedly accused of warmongering and aggression.

I do not pretend to be an expert on Russia, but seeing what the press can do to a conference like this in misinterpretation and distortion, I wonder if what is called aggression in the Balkans may not be liberation of landless serfs and giving their ignorant masses in 25 years such education as American Negro slaves have not received in 75; and of sending their former masters not to the legislature but scurrying over the earth like rats distributing lies.

All this I do not know but it can be true. And I do know that, if the press has lied about Russia as it has lied about American Negroes for three hundred years, I for one will condemn neither Russia nor Communism on such testimony.

But beyond and above this there arises before this conference the plight and cause of the vast majority of mankind who are not white. These colored races, the Chinese, Japanese, Indians and Indonesians; the peoples of Africa, many of those of South America and most of those of the Caribbean, with fifteen million Negroes of the United States — these are the vast majority of mankind whose condition and future are the crucial test of the attitudes of those peoples who today demand mastery of the world. Secluded for the most part in colonies or dominated areas, they have been enslaved and insulted, kicked in the teeth and used for the rape and exploitation of the British, French, Dutch, Belgium, Spanish and Italian empires.

This great America, this vast and rich land around you is built on the slavery, toil and degradation of Africans. Here until well into the second half of the nineteenth century they were sold like cattle. And New York did not stop to picket abolitionists; they tarred, feathered and killed them. Today in this land we have risen from the dead not to full manhood and citizenship, but to the place where we can at least stand and yell our own protest. We thank the America that helped us.

But we know well that unless we had helped ourselves we would still in New York City be exactly where our brothers are in Mississippi, where I ride in Jim Crow cars and would be kicked out of any hotel or public library. When such a nation arraigns Russia, all that I with the best will can remember is that the Soviet Union alone of all modern nations has prohibition of race and color discrimination written into its fundamental law, and that unlike similar words in our Constitution their law is enforced.

STAKE OF DARKER PEOPLES IN PRESERVATION OF PEACE

I saw the birth of the League of Nations and I sat in San Francisco when the United Nations was born. In both instances I worked and pled for the darker peoples, particularly those in imperialist colonies. We got mandates at Geneva which meant nothing. We got trusteeships at San Francisco and there again a determined blocking of all real meaning of colonial freedom by the united effort of Great Britain and the United States, and the sole opposition of Russia. Again in the Marshall Plan the nations helped are the colonial imperialists and no colored people unless, like Chiang Kai-shek, they are puppets of world exploiting investors.

I tell you people of America, the dark world is on the move! It wants and will have freedom, autonomy and equality. It will not be diverted in these fundamental rights by dialectical splitting of political hairs. We know what the Atlantic Pact proposes for the protection of colonial serfs of European imperialists. We know why Italy has been promised Ethiopia's territory by the Department of State. We know why the President of the United States goes fishing when the charter of Negro American rights is laughed to death by Democrats and Republicans, and lynching and disfranchisement go merrily on. We know all this and so does every dark man on earth. The white race may, if it will, tax itself into poverty, and arm itself for suicide, but the vast majority of mankind will march on and over them to freedom and self-rule.

But this catastrophe is the last which we of the darker world wish or will. We have no time for revenge or for sneering at white men's tragic mistakes. What we want is a decent world, where a man does not have to have a white skin in order to be a man. Where poverty is not a means to wealth, where ignorance is not used to prove race superiority, where sickness and death are not part of our factory system.

And all this depends first on world peace.

Peace is not an end. It is the gateway to real civilization. With peace all things may be added. With war, we destroy even that which the toil and sacrifice of ages have builded.

None Who Saw Paris
Will Ever Forget

I have attended the greatest meeting of men ever assembled in modern times to advance the progress of all men. The Races Congress of 1911 in London was comparable but quickly forgotten. The first meeting of the League of Nations Assembly in that little Geneva church raised hopes of universal significance. The UNO at San Francisco, after a Second World War, lifted the hearts of men, until the long drawn-out horse-trading on trusteeships revealed the determination to hold in serfdom the majority of mankind.

The Paris outpouring for Peace was extraordinary not simply because it brought together 2,000 delegates from 60 lands, not only because of the single-hearted earnestness and deep determination which kept them fastened to their seats for five full days.

In Paris the colored world was present; not simply on sufferance; not with the appalling Anglo-Saxon condescension; but as members of a world movement in full right and with full participation. For two days I sat on the presidential tribune representing the United States. I looked out across the sea of faces hour after hour and saw seven Haitians; 27 from India; two from Indonesia; 12 from Madagascar; four from Morocco; three from Mongolia; five from Puerto Rico; 13 from Tunis; 60 from Viet-Nam and 18 from French Black Africa.

And these colored folk took part. At two sessions black men presided; one of the best speeches was delivered on Thursday by Gabriel d'Arboussier, Vice-President of the African Democratic Rally, for whom the audience rose to applaud; Paul Robeson appeared unannounced and was given a tumultuous ovation; Madame Thai Thi Lien spoke for Viet-Nam with long applause. On

From the *National Guardian*, May 16, 1949.

the World Committee elected by the Congress was a black African vice-chairman and among the 140 members, 13 were colored.

To all this should be added the colored contingent at the Prague Congress, those delegates refused visas to enter France. Foremost among these were the 40 delegates from China and eight from Korea.

The Manifesto of the World Congress faced definitely the colonial and color questions: "We are against colonialism, which continually breeds armed conflicts and threatens to play a decisive part in unleashing a new World War. We condemn . . . the fostering of race hatred and enmity among peoples."

But it was no mere matter of race and color. It was the suffering of a crucified world made visible.

I saw that tall white-haired Russian woman, Mrs. Kosmodemyanskaya, with a face like the mother of Jesus, stand and tell how her 18-year-old daughter went to war to defend American "democracy"; how she was stripped by the Nazis and driven naked into the winter, beaten with straps and hanged, yet never betrayed her comrades.

A few nights later, in the home of a woman deputy of the French Parliament, I sat beside a beautiful young woman, almost youthful save for tired lines that dimly crossed her face. I looked down and on her wrist saw the concentration camp numbers burned into her flesh. She said simply: "I lost my mother and father; my brother and — my husband."

In the Congress and out, I saw the crippled and maimed — one soldier with no legs talked to us. I visioned the poverty, the hurt, the misery of a world, crying for God's sake let us at least have Peace, to heal our wounds. I sensed the bitter hatred toward an America determined to make money out of the world's misery.

Above all this looms in my memory that spectacle of Sunday, April 24, when from all France and half of the world 100,000 persons crowded and filed into the Buffalo stadium; filed out to let another 100,000 in.

I never before saw a hundred thousand human beings. And they were not strutting and showing off as Americans do on Fifth Avenue. They were walking and hobbling and falling in faintness and crying. Peace! Peace!

It was unforgettable. No lying, distortion and twisting of our prostituted press can conceal or erase the heartbreaking significance of this spectacle. None who saw it will ever forget.

Opposition to Military
Assistance Act of 1949

Dr. Du Bois: I appear here at the request of the Continental Peace Congress to be held in Mexico next month and of the Council on African Affairs to protest against the proposal for the United States to arm Europe for war. The Congress is asked to vote down payment of $1.5 billion together with unspecified sums in the future to implement the Atlantic pact.

This huge sum is not for education, although our schools are in desperate need of help. It is not for infantile paralysis which is sweeping the land, nor for cancer which is killing thousands. It is not for curbing and putting to work the mad waters of those great rivers which annually kill men, women, and children and destroy their homes, stock, and property, leaving muddy and stinking disease behind. This rich country has not enough money to spend for fighting ignorance, disease, and waste, or for the old-age security of its workers, but nevertheless is asked to spend a vast treasure to murder men, women, and children; to blind and cripple them and drive them insane; to destroy property by fire and flood; and for the third time in 50 years to jeopardize the whole edifice of civilization.

We are assured that these arms are for peace, not war — just as we were promised that the pact was for peace, not arms. None but the stupid believe this assurance. Mr. Acheson's logic is flawless for fools:

Gentlemen, this a pact for peace.

Thank you, gentlemen; now arms for the pact, not for war but for peace, war for peace. Russia? We do not mention Russia. We just must fight Russia. It is simple, gentlemen.

U.S., Congress, House, Committee on Foreign Affairs, *Mutual Defense Assistance Act of 1949: Hearings on H.R. 5748 and 5895*, 81st Cong., 1st sess., July 28–29 and August 1–2, 5 and 8, 1949.

We are asked to believe that this country is in danger of attack from Russia or that Russia is ready to conquer the world. We did not believe this when we asked 10,000,000 Russians to die in order to save the world from Hitler. We did not believe it when we begged Russian help to conquer Japan. We only began to believe it when we realized that the Russian concept of a state was not going to collapse but was spreading.

Assuming that you do not like and even fear Russian communism, by what right do we assume that it can be stopped by force? One idea seems to be that we can conquer the world and make it do our bidding because we are rich and have the atom bomb. Even if this were true it begs the question of the right and justice of our rule.

Why in God's name do we want to control the earth? Is it because of our success in ruling man? We want to rule Russia and we cannot rule Alabama.

We tried to rule Puerto Rico and gave it the highest suicide rate in the world.

We sought to rule China and have just confessed our failure.

We set out to rule Germany and apparently our only result is surrender to the very forces which we fought a world war to subdue.

How have we equipped ourselves to teach the world?

To teach the world democracy, we chose a Secretary of State trained in the democracy of South Carolina. When we wanted to unravel the worst economic snarl of the modern world, we chose a general trained in military tactics at West Point; and when we want to study race relations in our own borders we summon a baseball player.

If we aim to rule the world we have got to learn to rule ourselves. We have got to free our science from the control of the Army and Navy. We have got to make our schools centers of real learning and not of propaganda and hysteria. We have got to clear our minds of unreasoning prejudices. We who hate niggers and darkies, propose to control a world full of colored people. Will they have no voice in the matter?

Without exact and careful knowledge of this world, how can we guide it? Yet we know that our knowledge of the world today is fed to us by a press whose reporters say what the owners of the press order them to say. This is not the reporters' fault. If they want to eat they will write as they are told. It is our fault, who are unwilling to pay even 5 cents for our morning news. Big business which pays millions for control of news gets what it wants printed. We naively assume that what we read in our press is the whole truth, when a little reflection would convince us that we have in America no complete picture of what is transpiring behind the iron curtain. If we retort with the assertion that Russians are equally deceived as to conditions here, that is no excuse for us. Two wrongs never made a right and two lies do not spell the truth.

If all this ended in opinion, that would be one thing and time would answer it. But it threatens to end in war. We are asked to begin a Third World War on the assumption that we are the possessors of truth and right and able to pound our beliefs into the world's head by brute force. This is a crazy idea and it is worse than folly to try it. If we have to answer to human wealth and happiness we do not have to force men to believe it by atom bombs.

Ideas are seldom changed by force.

I will not say that war has never advanced mankind, but I will aver that in modern times it would be hard to prove that of 1,000 wars 100 had added to human progress.

What ever is true in the past, it is certain that today no world war can bring success to any nation.

Of course, we know this is true of war as usually fought, but we think that we can now fight by push-button and machine, that human beings will only be necessary in mopping up. We Americans will not fight, we will let John do it — John and Jacques and possibly Hans — while we pay the bill from such pockets as we can reach most easily.

This is crude self-deception and makes us today the most hated nation on earth. The world indulged in that dream when arrows were invented, when gunpowder was first used, when armored battleships and submarines appeared. It is a dream which never will be realized. No, the only cure for war is reason. We have got to know and study the facts and act so as to avoid force. Otherwise we are lost.

Let's face it. We fight China. We fight Russia. We win or lose or stalemate. If we win, what can we do with 150,000,000 Russians and 450,000,000 Chinese? What would we know in their case more than we knew in Germany or Japan? What would convert them to our way of life except their eventual belief in it? And is not belief, fact and reason, and not guns, our real recourse?

What hinders us from beginning to reason now before we fight? Why are we afraid to reason and wait and persuade?

Chairman KEE: Excuse me, Doctor. The bells have rung a straight no-quorum call. We will take a short recess at this time.

(Thereupon the committee recessed from 12:20 P. M. to 12:57 P. M.)

Chairman KEE: The committee will come to order.

You may proceed, Dr. Du Bois.

Dr. DU BOIS: We are afraid. For we stop logical thinking. We invent witch words. If in 1850 an American disliked slavery, the word of exorcism was "abolitionist." He was a "nigger lover." He believed in free love and murder of kind slave masters. He ought to be lynched and mobbed. Today the word is "Communist." Never mind its meaning in a man's mind. If anybody questions the power of wealth, wants to build more TVA's, advocates civil rights for

759

Negroes, he is a Communist, a revolutionist, a scoundrel, and is liable to lose his job or land in jail. And yet there is not today in this Nation an honest progressive citizen who does not share in his beliefs many of the basic ideas of communism.

I am a fellow traveler with Communists insofar as they believe the great ideals of socialism as laid down by the world's great thinkers since the seventeenth century: I believe in the abolition of poverty. I believe in curbing the social and political power of wealth. I believe in planned industry and more just distribution of wealth. There is in this body of belief nothing revolutionary, unless human progress is revolutionary. There is nothing which has not been advocated by the best thinkers in three centuries.

But what we are being taught to believe today is that Russian communism is not socialism but something dishonest, misleading, and eventually evil — while our capitalist system alone is light and truth.

Calling names does not settle this controversy. We call Russia an authoritarian state.

So are we. All states are and must be more or less slave states. They differ in degree of control over citizens and progressive states look forward to decrease of state control, and increase of individual freedom, but Russia, starting with 90 percent of illiteracy in 1917, could not start as a full, free democracy. Only educated people can rule successfully.

Russia showed her faith in democracy by promptly decreasing her illiteracy to less than 10 percent in 30 years.

We showed our belief in slavery by taking 86 years to reduce Negro illiteracy to 30 percent.

We rage at planned economy, but we have planned economy. It grows and sells our crops. It sets our wages and fixes our prices. It tells us what to manufacture and when, where to sell our goods, and where not.

But democracy has no part in it. Our planning is done by our plantation system, by the great trusts of steel, tin, and aluminum, by General Motors and the du Pont empire, by Standard Oil, by railroads with their fraudulent bonded debt and watered stock, by Wall Street.

This planning is strictly in private hands until it breaks down. Then trust and railroad, bank, and big farm come crawling to the Government for relief.

That, we are told, is not socialism. It is patriotism.

Let us balance in a reasonable way the case of Russia and the United States. Russia has never attacked us. We not only have invaded Russia but have allowed our country to become the center of the most far-reaching verbal attacks on Russia. We are making the United States a refuge for every ousted landlord and exploiter, spy, and informer who hates Russia. We blame Russia for joining Germany in 1940. But we know that she did this only after the

United States and Great Britain had refused her offers of alliance and she must join Germany or stand alone.

When Germany turned and treacherously attacked Russia, we awaited her annihilation with equanimity. When, to our surprise, Russia beat Hitler, we welcomed her help but took our own good time before easing her desperate struggle in the east by a western offensive.

We sought her alliance against Japan and courted her at Yalta because we did not dream Japan was so near collapse. And even then we yielded no more than Russia was able to take.

She kept faith with us in every promise at a greater cost than any other country paid. Yet we peremptorily ended her absolutely essential lend-lease and since 1945 have apparently sought every excuse to make war upon her.

Why do we want war with Russia and who leads this demand. We profess to want to protect western Europe against Russia. But it is western Europe which since 1917 has almost continuously attacked Russia. It was western Europe and the United States who after World War I seized countries long recognized as Russian and organized border nations like Poland for the expressed and declared purpose of using them eventually for conquering Russia. It was not imperialist expansion which led Russia to reannex the Baltic States and to secure by every means the close alliance of Poland and the Balkans.

The real reason for war on Russia is not her natural effort to protect her own borders but her effort to establish a Socialist state. Our country is ruled by incorporated wealth, incorporated so as to form a nonhuman person; protected by the fourteenth amendment, secure in organization and ownership of property and able to escape major taxation by hiring the best legal talent of the land. This wealth is forcing us into war. The people of the country do not want war. You do not want war. But somebody does want war, somebody with power and influence, who owns the press and controls radio, cinema, and theater. Somebody whose consequent ability to form public opinion has forced this country into hysteria and fear.

Who is this somebody? It is the group which control the corporate wealth of this land. They have made money out of war. They are making money out of the fear of war. They demand a third world war to ward off the depression which threatens their business and their wild waste of public taxation. The enemy of this power is the plan of Russia to found a state where this power of wealth will be curbed and destroyed. It is not a question as to whether or not Russia can do this, as to whether or not the present Russian state is or is not succeeding. It is the determination to compel citizens to believe this can never be done and that any attempt to curb the anarchy of rule by wealth is of itself a crime to be suppressed and not even discussed.

Gentlemen, make no mistake. Russia and communism are not your enemies. Your enemy, ruthless and implacable, is the soulless and utterly selfish corporate wealth, organized for profit and willing to kill your sons in order to retain its present absolute power. It is not our sympathy for the Balkans that is leading us to war. What did we care about the Balkans so long as western capital was making 75-percent profit out of oil and slaves? We kow towed to czars and splendid grand dukes so long as they held power. But when Russia drove out idle nobility and foreign exploitation and tried to build a state for the consumer and not the investor, then the world which lives on low wage and monopolized land and resources began to scream that this plan was impossible and criminal and must be stopped by force. But why? If communism cannot be made to work, it will fall of its own overweight. But it may succeed, and to stop any such chance you are asked to hurl the world into war.

The cost will be horrible. If we force Europe to a military race for arms her effort to recover will be nullified. Another war, even if victorious, will ruin Great Britain and France. And its eventual cost by increased taxation will throw the laboring classes of all the Americas into hopeless turmoil and despair. This is why we are calling next month a continental peace congress in Mexico.

The hope of America, the hope of the world, is no more war. We have the cure for disagreement and mistake in the United Nations.

Once we forced the League of Nations on an unwilling world, then we refused because of petty internal politics to support our own child. It failed and war and depression resulted. We planned a United Nations, including our own provision for unanimity without which we would not join. Now, when we cannot have our own way in everything, we are ready again to sabotage our own handiwork and substitute war for persuasion.

If you vote this blank check, gentlemen, do not assume that you will decide when and where to fight.

We fought Mexico before Congress declared war.

We fought Spain after Spain had yielded to our demands.

We were nearly thrust into war 2 years ago by an unexplained mistake. We can easily be in a third world war before you learn of it, if you vote these billions.

How does it happen that the United States today, reversing its traditional stand of centuries, is now siding with every reactionary movement in the world, with decadent Turkey, with royalist Greece, with land monopoly in Korea, with big business in Japan, with British Tories and Fascist Italy?

This is against our better impulses and saner judgment.

There is much in the Russian effort at social uplift, with which, if I knew it fully, I am sure I would not agree.

There is also much in our own way of life with which I strongly disagree.

762

No nation is perfect, with a perfect program, but every people have a right to try their way and no nation has more clearly earned her right to test the doctrines of communism than the Union of Soviet Socialist Republics.

Whether they accomplish their greater aims or whether a reformed capitalism, an American invention, will bring more human happiness, in either case, or in combination of both, socialism is the natural and inevitable aim of the modern world. It will grow out of the industrial revolution of the eighteenth century as flower from seed. Seeking to stop it by Red-baiting is stupid. Trying to stop it by war is crime.

Let the churches sit silent or yell for murder. Let the universities lead the witch hunt. Let the Government call every effort for social uplift subversive. You and I, gentlemen, know the truth. God give us guts to follow it.

Chairman KEE: I would like to know something about the background of the two organizations you represent, Mr. Du Bois.

Where is the headquarters of the Council on African Affairs?

Dr. DU BOIS: Twenty-three West Twenty-sixth Street, New York, N. Y.

Chairman KEE: Is that a national organization or is it local?

Dr. DU BOIS: It only has local organization but it has correspondents in various parts of the United States and various parts of the world.

Chairman KEE: What is the membership?

Dr. DU BOIS: I do not know. I presume it might be four or five hundred. I do not think more than that.

Chairman KEE: Your American Continental Congress for Peace, as I understand from your statement, you have never assembled a congress of that character?

Dr. DU BOIS: No; not for the American Continent. That is a temporary and a new organization which has adherents in practically all countries of the American Continent, in North and South America, and in the Caribbean.

Chairman KEE: The organization has not been effected yet, has it?

Dr. DU BOIS: The organization for calling the congress has been effected but the congress itself has not been held.

Chairman KEE: That is all.

Have you any questions, Mrs. Douglas?

Mrs. DOUGLAS: No questions.

Chairman KEE: Mr. Fulton —

Mr. FULTON: Have you ever been to Russia?

Dr. DU BOIS: I have been to Russia twice, once in 1928 and once I passed through Russia from Moscow to Manchuria, in 1936.

Mr. FULTON: You have not been there, then, since the war, so you know of no developments since the war?

Dr. DU BOIS: No.

Mr. FULTON: Have you been in any country behind the iron curtain since the war?

Dr. DU BOIS: No.

Mr. FULTON: Then if you felt there were unbiased gentlemen who have gone behind the iron curtain and had gone to Moscow when you had not, would you be inclined to take their judgment of what the approach is?

Dr. DU BOIS: I should be very careful and read their judgment. I have met a great many Russians since the war. I have met a great many people who have been to Russia, like the dean of Canterbury, for instance, but whatever testimony comes from Russia, or beyond the iron curtain, I am only too glad to consider.

Mr. FULTON: Just as a personal comment, I have been up in Moscow since the war, and had dinner with the commissars, in 1945. I have been behind the iron curtain in Poland and Czechoslovakia in 1947 and have checked on how they were being taken over.

In addition to that, I have checked a little bit as to what Russia's actions have been.

You spoke of her satellites and her taking certain actions in the Balkans.

I have made a special study of what happened and find that Russia, in 1946 and 1947, arranged bilateral agreements with various countries — among them Bulgaria — whereby she implemented an economic program and also an arms program, just as we are doing here.

I brought that up with Mr. Marcantonio in the debate on the floor on the Greek-Turkey recovery program and he felt that Russia in that instance, when she was implementing an arms program in Bulgaria on a bilateral basis rather than through the United Nations, was wrong.

What do you think?

Dr. DU BOIS: I do not know. I should have to know more about the facts. I should think that any attempt within the United Nations to make small bilateral agreements was not in the interests of the United Nations.

Mr. FULTON: Russia did this secretly, without the United Nations, at a time when we were starting our program in Greece and Turkey.

Now, Mr. Marcantonio objected to our program in Greece and Turkey.

I said, "If I can show you an agreement which you will admit that Russia made of the same nature with someone else in the Balkans, then you will say that Russia, too, is wrong?"

I showed that to Mr. Marcantonio's satisfaction and can to yours, that Russia, herself, outside of the United Nations completely, made unilateral agreements to arm these countries.

Now, do you think Russia is wrong?

Dr. DU BOIS: If Russia did that, I should think Russia is wrong.

Mr. FULTON: We will get the information for you to show you she did do that.

Dr. DU BOIS: I am also sure the United States was wrong.

Mr. FULTON: Then everything Russia does is not correct, in her national affairs?

Dr. DU BOIS: No. Russia is no perfect country; neither are we.

Mr. FULTON: On international affairs do you think Russia was correct, then, in refusing to permit inspection, so that the atomic bomb could be internationalized, with every country being inspected?

Dr. DU BOIS: Yes; I think her stand on the atomic bomb was right.

Mr. FULTON: It was right?

Dr. DU BOIS: Yes; unless the United States internationalized and destroyed bombs, I see no point at all of any nation allowing the United States to go in and inspect her.

Mr. FULTON: Then suppose we had simultaneously turned them all over, with the know-how, to the United Nations Agency, that Russia would be bound by, too, you would not even try that, would you?

Dr. DU BOIS: I should like to try that.

Mr. FULTON: Is that not what Russia has refused?

Dr. DU BOIS: No; I do not think so.

Mr. FULTON: Then you speak of the maladjustments within this country. We do not have slavery here, do we?

Dr. DU BOIS: Yes, we do.

Mr. FULTON: Of what kind?

Dr. DU BOIS: Peonage in Mississippi. You cannot punish anybody for it, either. We have tried, time and time again. I mean places in Mississippi and places in other parts of the South where a man is held to his work and cannot get away.

Mr. FULTON: Does the peonage in Mississippi compare with the 25,000,000 in Russia held in peonage and forced labor?

Dr. DU BOIS: I do not believe there are any 25,000,000 in Russia. Moreover, as said before, two wrongs do not make a right.

Mr. FULTON: We are looking for the basis of the program and we are trying to get the viewpoint of everyone. Some of us are trying very seriously to avoid name calling, either of Russia, or the United States. We are not calling any names against any people. On looking at the program, when we find that Russia has not disarmed since the war and has the largest force under arms in the world, do you not think that is a pitiful commentary that we are so woefully understaffing our allies in the war, to let them protect themselves, too, just as Russia is?

Dr. DU BOIS: No; I do not think so. I think that Russia is keeping her army because she is afraid of the United States and her allies, and I think that the history of the world since 1917 gives her a right to be afraid.

When I went to Russia in 1928, I noticed the destruction. I noticed the terrible situation which they had in restoring the country and I said, "Why is it that more has not been done in the last 10 years?"

They said, "The war only ended last year."

That is, there was 10 years when western Europe, with the aid of the United States, more or less, was attacking Russia, either actually by arms, or in some other way. Troops went into Russia and fought in Russia when there was no declaration of war.

If I were a Russian today, the one nation I would be afraid of would be the United States, not because of anything that I had done to the United States but because of the things that the United States — as this general said here today — wants to do to Russia.

Mr. FULTON: May I close by saying that the United States has not been in the habit of waging aggressive war and may we say for the Russian people that they themselves have not waged outside aggressive war unless attacked.

When you get two great countries like that, neither one of which has ever fought each other nor waged aggressive war, why are you so afraid of the United States?

Dr. DU BOIS: I am no more afraid of the United States than Russia.

Moreover, I do not agree with you that we have not waged aggressive war. What was the Mexican War?

Mr. FULTON: Which one?

Dr. DU BOIS: Well, the one that is usually spelled with capitals.

Mr. FULTON: Do you mean the war of 1847–49?

Dr. DU BOIS: That is what I mean.

Mr. FULTON: I do not call that an aggressive war.

Dr. DU BOIS: Much depends, you see, on what you call an aggressive war.

Mr. FULTON: Going back to Russia, do you feel, then, that Russia has more to fear from us than we have from them?

Dr. DU BOIS: Yes, decidedly. I think if a Russian had been here this morning and heard what was said of the practical inevitability of war, the advice that the United States take charge of the world in order to contain Russia, I think he would have been astonished.

Mr. FULTON: We do not see our Foreign Affairs Committee sitting here with any warlike attitude, but rather to try to hear and develop and accept what is correct, and may I say this to you, that when I was up in Russia, I was never away from the military.

For example, to go into the capitol buildings in Russia, we had to go through armed guards; we had to be checked and rechecked.

We were checked in and checked out.

To go any place in Moscow, we were checked.

And for example, when I tried to take a picture of Lenin's tomb, I had my camera snatched away from me by a man with a bayonet, and yet I am an impartial observer.

Dr. DU BOIS: And may I say that when I was in Russia in 1928 I was conscious of absolutely no kind of effort to stop me from seeing anything that I wanted to see.

I was in Kronsted, I was in Moscow. I went to Gorkin; I went to Kiev; I went down to Odessa.

I was there 2 or 3 weeks, and it is possible that I was surrounded by armed guards, but I did not see them.

Mr. FULTON: I am saying to you as an observer who has been there since the war, could it have possibly changed since you have seen it?

Dr. DU BOIS: It might have. I cannot say that.

Mr. FULTON: Thank you for your point of view. We appreciate it.

Chairman KEE: Are you a citizen of the United States?

Dr. DU BOIS: My family has been represented as United States citizens for seven generations. I had a great grandfather who fought to make you people free from Great Britain but he did not succeed.

Mr. FULTON: I have heard it the other way around, that Great Britain should declare her independence from us.

Chairman KEE: Don't you think you should have a few of your family fight to make our country safe from Russia?

Chairman KEE: We are happy to have with us today our former colleague, our good friend, Hon. John M. Costello. Mr. Costello, you may proceed.

Russophobia

I have lived to see the era of peace, which I was trained to look forward to as the only goal of civilization, transformed into plans for universal world war: a theory of progress by war and more war, each more savage and destructive than the last. I now realize that I, as well as you, am facing a crisis in which no consideration of ease or age suffices to hold me back from a great duty — to try to bring reason and past experience to bear upon a group of people gone temporarily insane.

The basic cause of this insanity is the effort of powerful interests, armed by control of press and radio, school and platform, backed by almost unlimited money, to turn the attention of the world from the fundamental problem of our age.

That problem is that *in our unprecedented organization of industry, with its marvelous technique and world-wide extent, the vast majority of mankind remain sick, ignorant and starved while a few have more income in goods and services than they can use.*

This is the basic problem of our culture, no matter how much we try to conceal and ignore it. We may be led to yell our heads off to convince ourselves that the problem of this world today is the Soviet Union and communism. That is deliberate deception. The problem of economic justice to working men existed before the Russian revolution and would remain if Russia were swept from the face of the earth tomorrow.

Proposals to solve this problem by socialism and communism did not originate in Russia and will not end there. What Russia did was to attempt to solve this problem in a systematic way, at a time when the 19th century had bequeathed to the world the dogma that the problem of economic justice was insoluble; that most men must always be poor, ignorant and sick, because most men were so inferior in gift and morals that this was inevitable; that

From the *National Guardian*, October 4, 1950.

civilization depended on making the few masters of the many, the Rich the rulers of the Poor, and thus in this way, and only in this way, could civilization be built and maintained.

Is this true? Whether it is true or not, we have no right to stop people and nations from denying the necessity of poverty, disease and ignorance, and from experimenting in their own way to make a better world. Moreover, our own clear duty is not to pull down others but rather to build ourselves up; to prove to the world that the economic condition of mankind can be bettered, that we know how to do this and propose to prove our belief by action.

Instead of this, what are we up to? We are trying to fight an Idea. We are going to make nations agree with us and our way of life by using atom bombs and jet planes, battleships and artillery.

Why? Why do we propose to make the Russian experiment fail, to throttle China and to throw the world into continuous war? The reason is clear: we fear that any success of socialism or communism will interfere with our money-making. We have become a nation of money-makers. *We think that money-making is the great end of man. Our whole ideology bows to this fantastic idea. Religion, science, art and morals in America tend to be measured by the profit they bring, and the true vocation of American manhood is regarded as profit-making business enterprise.*

War is Big Business and a business immensely profitable to a few, but of measureless disaster and death of dreams to the many. Big business wants war in order to keep your mind off social reform; it would rather spend your taxes for atom bombs than for schools because in this way it makes more money; it would rather have your sons dying in Korea than studying in America and asking awkward questions. The system which it advocates depends on war and more war.

In order to have war, Big Business must have Hate; so its press and newspapers ask you to hate communists and if not communists, hate all who do not hate communists; indeed hate all who do not take orders from those who now rule America.

What has happened to the world is that those who profit from war, especially in the United States, have gained control of government, of information and propaganda. This came about because of the First World War, which we entered with reluctance and participated in mainly by furnishing materials at a huge profit to those who controlled them. The result was twofold: Americans conceived the idea of continuing to profit from the world's disaster and to move in as successor of the British Empire as ruler of most of mankind. On the other hand, Russia and other nations who had been through hell because of war began experiments for reforming, if not replacing, the current methods of industrial organization.

We joined the capitalists of the world to suppress their socialist experiments which threatened our plan of world industrial empire. However, just as plans were ripe for a mass attack, in particular on the Soviets, the bottom fell out of modern capitalist industry. This was no fault of Russia nor of socialism, but was directly due to the overreaching greed of private profits.

But no matter what its cause, the result was that the Soviet experiment got a breathing space while in the U.S. the New Deal was forced to adopt many socialist remedies for poverty, unemployment and disease. We curbed the profits of capital; we put the state into certain industries and adopted planned industry like the TVA; we relieved the unemployed, and we established Social Security.

In other words, the U.S. began to form and carry out its own plans for so reorganizing industry as to save capitalism wherever it deserved to be saved.

Here the American Labor Party takes its stand as the successor of the New Deal. It maintains that the Soviet Union has a right to adopt its own economic philosophy and carry it out as it will. And that also the U.S. has a right to attempt to save its own way of life and that this can be done as the New Deal started to prove, when it was sabotaged not only by its enemies but more completely by its friends. *What the American Labor Party asserts is that the present plan of Big Business to compel the world to adopt our philosophy and our methods by force of arms is not only unreasonable in the light of our failures, but impossible in itself and can only end in disaster.*

It would seem that the futile efforts of a succession of "master races" to impose their will and power upon mankind would teach us that our program of world conquest is crazy. There is no possible chance for us to accomplish what Egypt, Persia, Greece, Rome, Great Britain and Hitler failed to do. Our military plans are idiotic and still more so if we depend on Germany and Japan to pull our chestnuts out of the fire. It will take more than one wild man of Tokyo to bring this fantasy to fact.

Moreover, we point out that the persons who are forcing us to adopt this policy of force and violence are the upholders of Big Business; and they are profiting as never before by war and preparation for war, and are deliberately blind to the fact that their profit is the disaster of America and the world.

Herbert Lehman was trained in Big Business and today deliberately represents its interests. Last year he called John Foster Dulles "a bigot, an anti-Semite and a fascist." This year he welcomes Dulles into "bi-partisan" collaboration for war; sponsors legislation for concentration camps for Communists and those called Communists; ignores the restoration to power in Germany of the same gang which killed 6,000,000 Jews, and acquiesces to their re-arming.

Why? What has changed Mr. Lehman? He has not changed. He follows automatically his training in the same school which made Dulles a warmonger and attorney of the Nazis, and that is, foreign investment of American capital, so as to make enormous profit out of the poverty and helplessness of Asia and Africa. American capital is pouring into South Africa and Rhodesia. We are the real owners of serf-labor in the Belgian Congo. We are wild to have Chinese factory hands at 12¢ a day. We helped shoot down the black miners in West Africa. And to bulwark our investment and guarantee high profit, the power of business joins hands with the military.

Thus, we are today ruled by Big Business and Big Brass for profit. A representative of the Steel Trust has been Secretary of State; a representative of Morgan and Rockefeller is chief adviser of Truman on foreign affairs; another Morgan man has been Under-secretary of State and will be second in command under Marshall. A Secretary of the Navy and Defense chief represented Dillon, Read and Company, and another became Secretary of War.

Where Big Business does not control government, men trained for war do. We have just reformed our defense department by placing a soldier at its head in defiance of sound tradition; his first word is universal training of our children for all-out war all over the earth, at a cost greater than we ever spent for education, health, housing and social uplift altogether. And for what? For profit to investors which is today piling up at the rate of $23,000,000,000 a year; with the prospect that the profit for 1950 will be four and a half times that of 1939, and twice as high as the enormous profit of 1944.

It is the theory of democratic government that when a situation like this arises, two political parties will examine, debate and dispute issues and acts until the people can make intelligent choice of the problems before them.

Today we have only one political party which shares power for the same ends. Men like Dewey and Hanley can only try to outdo what the Democrats have already done; if the Democrats are for war, they are for more war; if the Democrats repudiate the New Deal, the Republicans loathe and despise it.

The one point of agreement between the two so-called parties is war on any nation or movement which stands in the way of American profit; and suppression of all discussion of the merits of the present crisis. I try to spread in America news of the peace movement in Europe and I am threatened with jail. Paul Robeson advises Negroes never to fight against people who are striving for a better world for black and white, and he is denied the right to make a living.

In this situation the American Labor Party takes its stand on the proposition, "There can be no progress without peace." We are the only nation in the civilized world advocating war and compelling other nations to fight. For this we are hated and feared. We call for the immediate settlement of the war in Korea, which an American soldier has characterized when he said, "I never saw such a useless damned war in all my life." Mediation with both North and South in conference, and China represented in the United Nations, is the only solution. We ask resumption of the free flow of trade between east and west and the utter overthrow of colonialism even when masked under Point Four.

To stop this program of reason and progress, the allied and associated political profit-makers, called the Republican and Democratic parties, have adopted the last tactics of despair. They have made not only truth but civil rights a casualty of war. They have turned your attention from progress and peace to hate and fear. They are making it illegal to think of progress or to advocate peace or progress. Every path to reform like taxation of great wealth; effective rent control; river development and forest planning, are all called communistic or socialistic and their promoters threatened with disgrace, jail or loss of livelihood.

And now as a last exercise of tyranny, we are presented with the McCarran bill — the Fugitive Slave Law of 1950. You know what the Fugitive Slave Law of 1850 was: capital invested in human beings began to run away; foolish northerners, black and white, helped it hide. The Slave Power ruled the nation as Wall Street rules it today; they passed a bill that made kidnaping of any Negro possible without trial, that made a man prove his freedom instead of forcing masters to prove property; and tried to make anti-slavery opinion a crime. This law was so successful that in a decade it brought Civil War and slavery was abolished three years later.

So today, we are bidden to hate communism when what we must hate is war; we are called subversive when we try to think and act as human beings and not as puppets. If we attack segregation in the army or civil life, we are called traitors to America. Against this the American Labor Party protests and fights.

The Marshall Plan

Many people are puzzled by the Marshall Plan and they ought to be. It came into being masquerading as an attempt on the part of America to help the hungry and naked of the world. It never was that and was never intended to be that. It is a scheme by which the taxpayers of the United States furnish nations of Western Europe enough funds to purchase certain things in the United States. A committee of business men representing the great corporations of America, have this matter in charge and decides what these countries can purchase. They restrict their purchases to those things which will give the greatest profit to the United States and refuse to let them import many things which would help reorganization of their fundamental economy. Moreover, the merchants in the United States have raised prices so that the profits go in larger proportion to these merchants; they have charged enormous prices on transportation on American ships which must be used. They have compelled foreign nations in many cases to buy surplus stocks of commodities which the United States wanted to get rid of. Recovery in Europe was beginning and succeeding enormously before the Marshall Plan came into action, since that it has gone forward but slowly and is today reaching a crisis. We are making France buy Coca-Cola, we are making Austria buy trucks, we are making Italy buy spaghetti. We are not trying or succeeding in re-establishing the fundamental economic prosperity of Europe. We are trying to control and organize European economy so as to make Europe and the world a quasi-colony of United States business. Also while we are ostensibly furnishing money to rehabilitate the industry of Europe, we are trying to compel Europe to spend much of the money in arming themselves for a new war.

From the *Chicago Globe*, June 10, 1950.

The Trial

I have faced during my life many unpleasant experiences: the growl of a mob; the personal threat of murder; the scowling distaste of an audience. But nothing has so cowed me as that day, November 8, 1951, when I took my seat in a Washington courtroom as an indicted criminal. I was not a criminal. I had broken no law, consciously or unwittingly. Yet I sat with four other American citizens of unblemished character, never before accused even of misdemeanor, in the seats often occupied by murderers, forgers and thieves; accused of a felony and liable to be sentenced before leaving this court to five years of imprisonment, a fine of $10,000 and loss of my civil and political rights as a citizen, representing five generations of Americans.

It was a well-furnished room, not large, and poorly ventilated. Within the rail were tables for the lawyers, and back of these, seats for the defendants, with their backs to the audience behind. In front, on a low platform, sat the clerks and court stenographer; and behind, to a dais, came the black-gowned judge, announced by the marshal — "God save the United States of America!"

On either side were seats for the jurors, from whom twelve would soon be chosen to declare our guilt, or innocence, or a mistrial. All these seats were now filled with the jury panel, and an unusually large panel overflowed into the seats usually occupied by the public. There must have been 200 persons present; white and colored, from which juries for several cases would be drawn. Our first worry was this matter of the jury.

The jury system in the United States has fallen on evil days. The old English concept of a man's guilt being decided by presentation of the facts before twelve of his fellow citizens too often fails. Juries are selected in devious ways and by secret manipulation. Most Negroes are sent to jail by persons who hate or despise them. Many ordinary workers are found guilty by well-to-do "blue-ribbon" people who have no conception of the problems that face the

From *In Battle for Peace: The Story of My 83rd Birthday, with Comment by Shirley Graham* (1952).

774

poor. Juries are too often filled with professional jurors selected and chosen by the prosecution and expected to convict.

Our first hurdle was a long examination of the panel anent their affiliations, opinions and prejudices. The prosecution asked, among other things, if they had any prejudice against convicting a person of advanced years. The defendants asked a long series of more searching questions as to the prospective juror's attitude toward color, discrimination, and membership in certain organizations. One woman admitted that she was formerly a member of the K.K.K. and was excused.

No one on the panel admitted that he had at any time advocated segregation of the races, or racial discrimination in housing, transportation, employment, recreation, education; or in the use of places of public accommodation in the District of Columbia. Looking at the persons, this seemed to me hardly believable. Probably most of the whites had belonged to some such organizations but would not now admit it. They were asked about their attitude toward the House Committee on Un-American Activities, but none admitted prejudice. A number said that they had relatives in the armed forces, but declared that if they were convinced of the defendants' innocence they would be willing to say so even if a majority of the jury disagreed with them.

In our case there came another angle — the colored juror. In many parts of the nation, Negroes seldom or never serve on juries. But in the District of Columbia, lately, continually there are many Negro jurors drawn, so much so that there has been a distinct movement to curb their choice. Something of this was heard by the lawyers in our case, and they were prepared to fight it. But on the other hand, we sensed another and more hurtful method of opposition. There is a considerable proportion of Negroes in government employ: in the post office, as teachers in the public schools, as civil servants in dozens of branches. All such employees in Washington, white as well as black, are in fear of attack by witch hunts and loyalty tests, where often the accused have no chance to know or answer their accusers. Also, they are faced with severe competition and political influence. Negroes suffer especially, because their chance for employment outside government is narrow, and because their political influence is curtailed; and finally because of race discrimination which makes even civil service rules bow to prejudice. Suppose, then, a Negro with a government job and a home and family is drawn for this jury: no matter what the facts show, how will he vote? How will he dare to vote?

These facts faced us and one solution was to try to exclude government employees from the panel. This the judge offered to do, and he had the panel polled. The poll showed that if government employees were excluded, practically no Negroes would be left, since employment for educated

Negroes in the District of Columbia is practically confined to government service. We faced a perfect dilemma: if we excluded government employees, we indirectly helped draw the color line; if we accepted government employees, more Negroes would face a greater risk of dismissal on trumped up charges than the whites. The white non-government worker would usually be in a job which did not employ Negroes, which would mean that he had had no contact with them and would be prejudiced. The lawyers consulted, and then Marcantonio came over and put this dilemma squarely before me. "Accept government employees!" I answered.

We did, and to my amazement got a jury of eight Negroes and four whites! I did not know whether to be glad or scared. The prosecution usually knows the jury panel fairly well, and it is thought that the panel may often be sprinkled with stooges. Was it possible that these eight Negroes might be owned? As I looked at their intelligent faces, veiled and non-committal as some were, I did not think so. My impulse was to follow the conclusion of Earl Dickerson, who said: "No eight American Negroes will ever agree to convict you!" Then he added reflectively, "If they do, I'll never defend another!" I was afraid his practice might be curtailed. Yet I could not believe that many American Negroes believed that I was a paid spy.

Next in importance came the problem of the judge who would preside. Judge Holtzoff, who had charge over our preliminary hearing in May, made a bad impression: pompous and opinionated; fond of talking about himself. He plainly disliked New York lawyers, and had a low opinion of women. On one occasion he summoned me to the bar, threatened to cancel my bond and send me to jail because of printed publicity found in the courtroom. Abbott Simon immediately stepped forward and took the blame for what was at worst an unintentional mistake, and more probably an attempt to frame us by some smart newspaper men. The judge finally dismissed us with a sharp warning against such "tirades" in his courtroom.

When, therefore, I heard that Judge McGuire had finally been assigned to our case, I was elated, until I heard that he was rumored to be the most reactionary judge on the District bench, and worse than Holtzoff! His appearance, however, was reassuring. He was from first to last, courteous and intelligent. He did not put on judicial airs; he never lost his temper; he was firm but kindly. Had it not been for the nature of our indictment and the impossibility of reconciling the attitude of Judge McGuire with that of the Department of Justice, through whose employment he had risen to the bench, I would call Judge James McGuire a great jurist, who in this case held the scales of justice absolutely level.

But my considered opinion is that what happened was that this judge at the last moment freed himself from the political pressures of the day to which so many had succumbed and that both he and the Department of State realized that the eyes of the world were fixed on this case.

In strictly legal aspect, remember what this trial was: it was not a question of our opinions and beliefs; it involved no question as to whether we were Communists, Socialists, Jehovah's Witnesses or Nudists; it involved no imputation of moral turpitude except in so far as it is a statutory crime to say what foreigners are saying at the command of those foreigners. The judge said:

> "The point in this case is whether or not this organization acted as an agent or in a capacity similar to that for a foreign organization or foreign political power, whether advocating peace, advocating this, or advocating that. They can advocate the distribution of wealth; they can advocate that all red-headed men be shot. It doesn't make any difference what they advocate."

It was not even fully admitted until the third week of the trial that the government did not allege that the Soviet Union was connected with the "foreign principal" accused in the indictment. It was never alleged that we had no right to advocate peace. It was only the question: were we "agents" of a foreign principal? Yet and despite all this, the public was deliberately given to understand by spokesmen of government and by the press that we were accused of lying, spying, and treason in the pay of the Soviet Union. As one of the attendants said in the ante-room of the court, scowling at us: "If the damned Communists don't like this country, why don't they go back to Russia?"

Jurisdictional questions were first raised, based on the fact that the organization was defunct, and on the question of the jurisdiction of the court over individual defendants. These motions were denied, although the court admitted that there was still some question as to the liability of the officers of the Peace Information Center, if it were proven that the Peace Information Center no longer existed. Marcantonio said:

> "The plea of not guilty did not in any manner, shape or form revive the dead. In other words, if John Jones were indicted and he died, and died before the indictment, certainly, he could not be found guilty and considered in being simply because counsel pleaded not guilty. And pleading not guilty they pleaded not guilty for all purposes, including the establishment of the non-existence of the individual."
>
> "The Court: You have just said what I have said, much better. So, we will leave it that way."

One of the basic reasons for the repeated miscarriages of justice in this country, is the lack of attention on the part of the respectable public to the procedures of court trials. Most persons assume that trials have to do with criminals, tricky lawyers, peremptory judges, and hard court officials. Such folk keep as far from courts as possible and let flagrant and cruel injustice escape without remark or attention. We knew this, and from the first appealed to our friends and the friends of justice everywhere to attend this trial and see what went on. As a result the sessions were crowded by a quiet, intelligent audience, who came from New York, New England, Chicago, the South and West, with usually a waiting line to be admitted. It was in every sense a public trial, and the Department of Justice knew it.

The jury having been selected, the trial began Thursday, November 8, and lasted five days, during three weeks, because of adjournments for weekends and holidays. A fussy little fat man, Maddrix, chief of the prosecution, and former Attorney General of Maryland, stated the case for the prosecution:

> "The first count states that the Peace Information Center was an unincorporated organization, having its headquarters in New York City. It further alleges that the Peace Information Center was an agent of a foreign principal, in that it acted as and held itself out as a publicity agent for the Committee of the World Congress of the Defenders of Peace, and the World Peace Council . . . and because of it being an agent of a foreign principal, it was under a liability to file a registration statement with the Attorney General of the United States. . . .
>
> "The material disseminated within the United States by Peace Information Center as publicity agent for its said foreign principal consisted of information about peace, war, instruments of war, and the consequences of peace and of war. . . .
>
> "The agency relationship of the Peace Information Center with the Committee of the World Congress of the Defenders of Peace and the World Peace Council is not claimed to have existed pursuant to contractual relationship."

Maddrix added that the government intended to call twenty-seven witnesses.

Our lawyers postponed rejoinder, since the jury seemed more bewildered than impressed by the bill of particulars. We elected to await the development of the government case before stating ours. We were puzzled by the fairness of the judge, and were awaiting the nature of the evidence which the prosecution could produce. The prosecution reminded us that we had not named our prospective witnesses, as was the practice in the District of Columbia. We had determined to confine ourselves to as few witnesses as possible and to rely on the strength of our case rather than corroborative repetition. I had been chosen as the main witness, with two other witnesses to substantiate certain occurrences which took place during my absence in Europe. These were named; and then Marcantonio added that we might subpoena the Secretary of State and the Attorney-General. Later, when it seemed that I might need character witnesses, Albert Einstein offered to do "Whatever he could."

We may never know just what reactions took place in government circles concerning this indictment. At first, certainly, the government meant to scare us by the "Communist" bogey. Then by threatening indictment they aimed to cut off contributions to the Peace Information Center, or make us try to escape persecution. When we began to fight back and the volume of protest from white and black arose, and from Europe and Asia as well as Africa, the government began frantically to collect evidence which they had never possessed. They sent out agents. They interviewed and tried to intimidate every person connected in any way with the founding of the Peace Information Center. . . .

Whatever design there was to confront us with manufactured testimony from professional spies, liars and agents-provocateurs, it was abandoned. But the very fairness of the trial raised the query as to why the government ever was induced to bring this case on so flimsy a basis? They had no case and they knew it. Their only hope of success was to raise national hysteria against us to the flaming point. This our campaign rendered impossible. No ex-spy could get away with testimony about seeing me emerge from the Kremlin with a bag of gold; no stooge could make black America believe that I was an under-cover conspirator, when for fifty years I had always blurted out the truth on all occasions.

The judge continued to be fair and courteous. The prosecution was inept if not stupid. The defense was prepared to the last comma; it knew law and procedure; it was on its toes every minute with its eyes on the possible appeal to higher courts. The government spent precious time and money on proving the obvious: that the Peace Information Center existed; that it had a bank account; that it rented offices; that it distributed literature. Cautious F.B.I. men and newspaper reporters introduced literature which anyone could have gotten at any time, and which we freely admitted we had written and distributed.

The chief dependence of the prosecution was on John Rogge. Rogge the witness was a caricature of Rogge the crusader for Peace and Reform. In place of the erect, self-confident if not arrogant leader, came a worn man, whose clothes hung loosely on him, and who in a courtroom where he had conducted many cases, had difficulty locating me in the defendants' chairs. I voluntarily stood up to help him out.

He admitted his membership in the Peace Information Center. He admitted his attendance at the World Peace Congress; and declared that its actual objective was not peace, but that it was an agency for the foreign policy of the Soviet Union.

Mr. Maddrix in his opening said that the government did not intend to show and would not show that there was any contract of agency between the World Congress of the Defenders of Peace and the Peace Information Center. The Court said:

"The responsibility of the government is to prove beyond a reasonable doubt, first of all, the nexus; and in doing that, you will have to establish, of course, that there was a foreign group, whether that group takes the aspect of a foreign political party, a foreign government or a foreign association within the purview of the statute.". . .

It was at this juncture that Judge McGuire called the lawyers to his chambers and went straight to the kernel of Rogge's testimony. Rogge had said that the object of the Defenders of Peace was ostensibly peace, but really to carry out the policies of the Soviet Union. This was, as we suspected from the beginning, the whole intention of the Rogge testimony, and the method by which the government hoped to put us in jail. If, by this testimony, Russian and Communist controversy could be smeared across the case, current popular hysteria could be aroused against us. Witnesses like J. B. Matthews, long the propagandist of the Dies Committee, could be brought on the stand with his lurid stories about Communists, corroborated by the F.B.I. and its Budenzes and Bentleys.

The judge, therefore, came straight to the point: referring to Rogge he said:

"This witness was permitted to state that while the stated purpose was peace, the real purpose was to promote the foreign policy of the Soviet Union.

"Do you expect to show that the World Council for Peace was in fact an agent of another principal, namely the Soviet Union?"

Mr. Maddrix did not answer this directly, but the judge continued, saying that he let in reference to the Soviet Union because he thought the prosecution was going to show that the Soviet Union actually was the foreign principal, and that the World Council for Peace was merely the conduit to use the activity of the Peace Information Center. If this was not their case, he was going to tell the jury to disregard any reference to the Soviet Union. Mr. Maddrix objected to being restricted, but the Court insisted:

"You cannot blow hot and cold. I have got to be advised now as to what you expect to show. . . . You are not, I take it, predicating your case or the theory of your case on the ground that the World Council for Peace was, in effect, the agent of the Soviet Union?"

Mr. Maddrix: "We are not making that statement, no."

The Court: "What you do not intend to prove, and I am so advised now, is that you are not going to attempt to prove formally that the activities of the World Council for Peace were the activities of the Soviet Union?"

Mr. Maddrix: "I could not state it any better. . . . We do not intend to show that the Committee of the Congress of the World Defenders of Peace was an agent of the Soviet Union."

As a result of this admission the Court said:

"I thought I ought to be advised at this juncture just exactly what the Government expected to show with reference to the Soviet Union being the principal or the so-called principal of the Peace Information Center. I understand the Government expects not to show, under any circumstances, the existence of another principal behind the principal we are concerned with, namely, the Soviet Union. If that is not my understanding here of what transpired at the bench, I would like to be so advised."

The prosecution then again admitted:

"We do not charge in our indictment that the foreign principal in any way involves an element of agency as I understand this case, between the foreign principal, the Committee of the World Congress, and the Soviet Union."

The Court: "You have answered my question. You are contending that the only foreign principal involved in this case is the World Congress for Peace?"

Mr. Cunningham: "Absolutely."

The Court: "I am not going to try the Soviet Union or make any comparison between the Soviet Union with respect to peace and America. I am going to stick to the issue."

With the jury out of the room, there was a conference of the judge and lawyers concerning other points in Rogge's testimony. Rogge had said that the purpose of the Stockholm Appeal was to concentrate the eyes of the world on the atom bomb in the possession of the United States, and to take the eyes of the world off any aggression that might and which did come from the East.

The Court asked Mr. Maddrix if he considered Mr. Rogge an expert. He said no, but that no one was in a better position than Mr. Rogge to know what was going on and to answer this particular question. He was a member of the policy-making group, and had attended its meetings. The Court then said:

> "I am not trying any propaganda lines. I am not trying any foreign policy questions involving any country, including our own. You have a very simple case here. You charged this Peace Information Center and these individuals, as officers and directors, as being agent of a foreign principal, and disseminating propaganda in the United States. You have got to show a tie-up between the principal so-called and the so-called agent. If you don't do that, you are out of court."

The prosecution insisted that the agency of the Peace Information Center was going to be proved by circumstantial evidence. The judge said:

> "You have to show the connection. . . . I may be in Timbuctoo and you may be in some place in South America. I may be shaving and using Gillette brushless shaving cream and you may be doing the same thing, but there is no connection except we are both using Gillette."

Thereupon, when the jury had returned, the judge addressed them, saying that when Rogge was on the stand he was asked what the purpose of the World Council for Peace was, and he answered. The judge went on:

> "You are now instructed by the Court, as emphatically as I can make words that lend emphasis to what I say, that you are to disregard Mr. Rogge's opinion of what he thought the purpose of the Stockholm Peace Appeal was. It is a very simple rule of evidence that excludes that type of opinion, because opinion is excluded, and the only opinion that is permitted to be introduced in a court of law, in certain circumstances, is the opinion of an expert. So, therefore, you will disregard entirely the characterization of the witness Rogge with reference to what he thought the World Council for Peace had in view."

Although we did not at the time realize it, and still watched narrowly for trumped up testimony, it was right here that we won our case. The prosecution had rested its whole case on Rogge's testimony that we were representing the Soviet Union through the Defenders of Peace organization in Paris. They had naturally not an iota of real proof of this, but they planned to depend on public opinion. But Rogge's own testimony convicted him. He was a member of the Peace Information Center; he was a member of the policy-making bureau of the Defenders of Peace. He had visited the Soviet Union and spoken as a representative of the Defenders of Peace and the Peace Information Center. He had sworn on oath when he himself became an agent of Yugoslavia that he was not a member of any other foreign agency. . . .

Then, too, we had the sworn testimony of the executive secretary of the World Defenders of Peace, accused of being our "foreign principal." At considerable cost we had sent three of our lawyers to Paris in July. The government also sent three of their representatives, including the head of the Criminal Division of the Department of Justice, to take depositions from Jean Laffitte, the Secretary of the World Defenders of Peace. At this interesting inquiry, held at the offices of the United States Embassy, sworn testimony was taken, which we were ready to introduce but never got the opportunity. Mr. Laffitte, a man of training and manners, member of the Legion of Honor, declared that the Committee of which he was Secretary General was

". . . instituted by the First World Congress of the Defenders of Peace. Its definite task was to circulate and make known the information given and the decisions taken by the Congress. It was also in charge of circulating the various information concerning activities on behalf of Peace throughout the world. Its task was also to denounce all propaganda which predisposed public opinion in favor of war and to support all initiatives tending towards peace. It had the duty of encouraging all cultural activities in favor of peace. And it was in charge of preparing a further World Congress of Peace."

He was asked if he had ever heard of the Peace Information Center and if the Center had authority to act as publicity agent. He answered that he had heard of the Peace Information Center, but that it had never had such authority; that the Committee had not appointed the Peace Information Center as its agent for the circulation of the Stockholm Appeal, nor had the Peace Information Center asked to act as publicity agent; that it expended no funds belonging to the Committee, and had no authority to make contracts; that it made no reports orally or in writing to this Committee.

He was then asked about national committees which were in co-operation with the World Committee. He said there were such committees in about eighty countries, but that there was none in the United States. He said that his committee had co-operated with the Peace Information Center in a very simple way:

"We had heard of the formation of an Information Center in the United States which had assumed the task of circulating information relating to the furtherance of peace. This naturally resulted in our sending the Center information concerning peace movements, and allowed us to hope that in this way such information would become more widely known than other matter which we sent to the United States."

Then came an interesting colloquy. Mr. Laffitte was asked, "Do you regard Soviet Russia as the strongest advocate for peace among governments?" Mr. Laffitte's attorney immediately objected to his client's answering. Mr. McInerney, head of the Criminal Division of the Department of Justice of the United States, demurred and said that he was unable to understand Laffitte's "reluctance to express a viewpoint which he has proclaimed to the world." Mr. Laffitte's attorney replied that his client had made a point of answering all questions which were closely or remotely related to this matter, but that there was no obligation on his part to answer as to his personal opinions and beliefs:

"If he were called to testify before a French court, and if inconceivably he were asked to what political party he belonged or what was his belief concerning a given problem (a thing which could never happen), I would urge him not to answer such a question, since he is a French citizen entirely free as to his opinions; a freedom guaranteed by the Constitution of his country."

Mr. McInerney, taken aback, and probably remembering the Constitution of his own country, replied, "I wish to apologize if I have intruded upon his constitutional rights under French law."

When Mr. Laffitte was further asked if he had been in direct communication at any time with the Peace Information Center, he said that he had not. He was asked if the Peace Information Center was organized at the time that Dr. Du Bois was present in Paris at the Peace Congress. He replied that it was not, and that the Paris Committee did not hear of its organization until a year later. He was then asked if he had had personal correspondence with Dr. Du Bois, and he replied:

"I told you that I had not had any personal correspondence, properly so-called, with Dr. Du Bois. We confined ourselves to sending Professor Dr. Du Bois, who is a member of the World Committee, the information which we transmit without distinction to all members of the World Committee; that is to say, the Secretariat regularly sends all members of the World Committee information concerning the different meetings of the Bureau or the decisions taken at such meetings, and also any publications which may arise therefrom, — always with a covering letter which we send as a matter of courtesy and a mark of respect for these personalities."

He denied that he had ever requested the Peace Information Center to disseminate the Stockholm Appeal as an agent of the Committee. This interesting testimony we were given no chance to introduce.

The prosecution had rested before the morning session was finished. We prepared during the remainder of the morning to present certain motions, and then if they were denied, to go into our defense, introducing the Paris depositions, then character witnesses for me, after which I would take the stand. I was ready.

My Campaign for Senator

As I started home from Prague in August, 1950, I received two messages from the United States, both important. One was from John Abt of the American Labor Party, asking if I would run for United States Senator from New York. The other was from Abbott Simon, executive secretary of the Peace Information Center, informing me that the Department of Justice had demanded our registration as "agents of a foreign principal."

Arriving in Paris on August 2, I hastened to my favorite little hotel on the Rive Gauche, only a block from the beautiful flowers, sculpture and children of the Luxembourg gardens. As soon as I was settled I telephoned to Abt and he asked my decision on his proposal. I laughed.

I laughed because I remembered my grilling by the State Department when I asked for a passport to visit Czechoslovakia. I was amused to think what such a reputation could add to any campaign; then I recalled that laughter over the long distance telephone is as costly as words, and I proceeded to remind Abt of my age and political inexperience and my unwillingness to run for public office.

But Abt said a number of things, of which two sunk in: (1) That this campaign would afford a chance for me to speak for peace which could be voiced in no other way. (2) My candidacy would help the campaign of Vito Marcantonio. I thought this matter over gravely. Because of my support of the Progressive Party in 1948, my acceptance of an honorary and unpaid office with Paul Robeson in the Council on African Affairs, and my activity in Peace Congresses in New York, Paris and Moscow, I found myself increasingly proscribed in pulpit, school and platform. My opportunity to write for publication was becoming narrower and narrower, even in the Negro press. I wondered if a series of plain talks in a political campaign would not be my last and only chance to tell the truth as I saw it.

Beyond this, of all members of Congress, Vito Marcantonio has acted with

From *In Battle for Peace: The Story of My 83rd Birthday, with Comment by Shirley Graham* (1952).

courage, intelligence and steadfast integrity in the face of ridicule, mud-slinging and cheating. Liberals like Graham, Pepper and Douglas have wavered, backed and filled and deserted their principles; the colored members of the House have generally been silent or absent. If I could do anything for Marcantonio, I decided to try. On August 31, I wired, "Accept. Du Bois."

Of course, whatever contribution I could make would, I knew, be small and not very effective. I did not have the strength for a hard, active campaign; I was no orator or spell-binder, but only one who could reason with those who would listen and had brains enough to understand. I had no large group of close personal friends, and many of those whom I had, dared not speak or act because of fear for their jobs — a fear which was real and restraining; finally, I had no money to spend or moneyed friends to contribute; and anyone who thinks that money does not buy American elections is a fool.

The matter of registering the Peace Information Center as a foreign agent I did not take too seriously. It was, I was sure, either a mistake or an effort begun to intimidate us. I cabled a statement to Simon, setting forth our work and aims. I suggested sending an attorney to Washington, and promised to go there myself as soon as I could get passage home. Then I forgot it and turned to what seemed then the more serious matter of my campaign.

My experience in practical politics had been small. First of all I had been reared in the New England tradition of regarding politics as no fit career for a man of serious aims, and particularly unsuitable for a college-bred man. Respectable participation in political life as voter, thinker, writer and, on rare occasions as speaker, was my ideal. This preoccupation was strengthened by the fact that for Negroes entrance into political life was especially difficult. Spending as I did the first thirteen years of my active life in Georgia, I was disfranchised on account of my race, and confined my political work to advice to my students and to writing.

When I came to New York in 1910, my political activity was exercised through the *Crisis* magazine which I founded and edited. As it gained influence and circulation, I began to give political advice to Negro voters. In 1912, I tried to swing the Negro vote to Woodrow Wilson for President and away from Taft, in order to break our servitude to the Republican Party, and to rebuke Taft for his "lily-white" Southern policies. Many Negro voters took my advice to their regret and my own embarrassment, as Wilson surrendered in many instances to the Negro-hating South. Next I tried to influence Theodore Roosevelt and the Bull Moose movement to make the Negro problem a main plank in their platform. Roosevelt would not yield, and preferred alliance with the "progressive South," which he lived to regret. I remembered this in 1919 as I introduced him to an audience in Carnegie Hall, when he made his last public speech.

From 1921 to 1933, under Harding, Coolidge and Hoover, I pushed the political fight against lynching and for civil rights in editorials and lectures, with my only personal participation in politics the chance appointment as special minister to Liberia, and membership on the New York state commission to celebrate emancipation. When Ferdinand Morton, colored leader of Tammany and a man of extraordinary ability, suggested that I run for Congress on a Tammany ticket, I refused flatly, partly on account of my dislike of Tammany, and partly because I knew I had no personal fitness for a political career. I began to lean toward the Marxian view of politics as at bottom economics, and said so in the resolutions which for years I wrote for the annual meetings of the N.A.A.C.P. I strongly supported LaFollette in 1924.

With the depression and the reign of Roosevelt from 1933 to 1945, I embraced the "New Deal" in writing and lecturing and in socialist thinking; stressing the disabilities of the Negro and criticizing the failure adequately to deal with them, but believing firmly in state planning for social welfare. At this juncture, in 1934, I returned to the South to teach and re-enter my Ivory Tower. War came, with Hitler, and Stalingrad, the United Nations and the disaster of Truman. I returned to the N.A.A.C.P. in New York in 1944, and soon in frantic recoil from a program of war and economic reaction, I cast my political lot with Henry Wallace. This cost me dear, although I took no active part in the campaign of 1948. But I did lose my job indirectly because my political thought was deemed too radical.

During the next two years I worked with the Progressive Party in minor roles, without pay. I had some influence in forming the Progressive Party platform for 1950, and I made the personal acquaintance of Henry Wallace. He was a kindly and warm-hearted man. He induced Anita McCormick Blaine, his close friend, to help me out of financial difficulties in 1949, when for a time it seemed that I would no longer be able to continue my writing and study.

But as I came to know Henry Wallace, I realized the uncertainty of his intellectual orientation, and the strong forces close to him which wanted respectability and feared too close association with unpopular causes. In a sense Wallace lacked guts and had small stomach for martyrdom; and all this despite his facing of Southern rotten eggs in 1948. I tried gingerly to strengthen his faith, when I saw him wavering in 1950. I wrote him to call his attention to the way in which, a century before, respectable folk who disliked slavery recoiled from being classed with "Abolitionists," because the word connoted so much that was not respectable at the time. I noted the same attitude today toward "Communism." I received no reply, and on July 15, 1950, Wallace deserted the Progressive movement. Thereafter, and perhaps ungenerously both to him and the slender little animal who, after all, can fight, I thought of Wallace as no longer the crusader, but as Wallace the Weasel.

I went into the campaign for Senator knowing well from the first that I did not have a ghost of a chance for election, and that my efforts would bring me ridicule at best and jail at worst. On the other hand, I did have a message which was worth attention and which in the long run could not fail to have influence. The leaders of the American Labor Party and my colleagues on the ticket were more than kind and solicitous; they reduced my participation to a minimum, themselves bore an unfair part of the work, and gave me every help to keep my efforts within my strength and ability.

I delivered, in all, ten speeches and made seven broadcasts. I began with a press conference in Harlem, to which the *Times* and *Herald Tribune* sent reporters, and the Associated Press; only one Negro paper was represented. I addressed mass meetings in Harlem, Queens, Brooklyn and the Bronx, each attended by 1,000 to 2,500 persons, who gave me careful attention and generous applause. This was encouraging because I used manuscript, no gestures, and few jokes. This method I have used before popular audiences for years, and while an audience always sighs at the sight of a roll of manuscript, I am convinced that intelligent persons prefer to have a speaker really say something, rather than entertain them with shouting and acting. My last speech in the city of New York was at that marvelous gathering of 17,000 persons at Madison Square Garden on October 24, news of which was nearly blacked out by the press.

On an upstate tour from Buffalo to Albany beginning October 15, I spoke four times to audiences of a few hundred persons in small and rather obscure halls. There was a distinct air of fear and repression. "Free" Americans slipped in almost furtively and whispered many stories of how the industries of Rochester and Syracuse threatened their workers. In Albany political pressure was tense. While the press was courteous, we evidently were permitted just to touch the edges of real publicity.

I realized from this how much money and effort in halls, advertisement and personal contacts was needed to get our message over to the mass of voters. Once reached even in small groups, they were eager and enthusiastic. They listened, leaning forward with rapt faces. But they and we were gripped by defeatism. Tom Dewey and Joe Hanley, the Republican candidates, could talk to ten thousands while we spoke to a hundred. Even if they said nothing, which they often did, their message reached every end of the state. Senator Lehman and his Democratic Party friends did not have to go hungry in order for him comfortably to cover the state. I winced at our little collections for expenses at meetings; they drew blood. My colleagues, like John McManus, Frank Scheiner and George Murphy, spent day and night in personal contacts and conversation while I slept with guilty conscience. We needed a hundred workers where we had one.

I had another handicap and paradox. Of the utter unfitness of Hanley for public office, especially after his notorious letter revealing disreputable political bargaining came to light while I was in Albany, there was not the slightest doubt. Lehman was different. He was an honest man and wealthy; he had behind him a fairly good record of public service. Yet he ought not to sit in the United States Senate because he represented finance and foreign investment, and because of this was frantically backing Truman in the Korean crime which Big Business precipitated.

All that my candidacy, however, could possibly accomplish, in the immediate present, would be to draw enough votes from warmonger Lehman to replace him with a venal politician. Many voters were indignant at this prospect, and some accused me of being deliberately a catspaw or at best of poor judgment. For a time the political leaders were worried over this; and this angle gave me more publicity than any other.

Yet, I am sure, I was right to persist, and that even the threat of Hanley was not worse than that of World War; and that overwhelming defeat today of my fight for peace and civil rights would some day prove worth while.

The ten speeches I made in this campaign were based on three themes, represented by my talk on "Peace and Civil Rights" at Madison Square Garden; my address on "The American Way of Life" at the Brooklyn and Queens rallies; and my lecture on "Harlem" at the Golden Gate Ballroom. All my other speeches were combinations and adaptations of these.

For the seven broadcasts, I adopted another method: I planned a connected series of expositions on the underlying basis of the demand for peace and civil rights, emphasizing in succession the rule of propaganda, the misconception of property, and the concept of democracy. These were interlarded between two general statements, one delivered on television, and one in our final symposium.

My main thesis was thus summed up:

The most sinister evil of this day is the widespread conviction that war is inevitable and that there is no time left for discussion. It is doubtful if the mass of Americans who accept this judgment realize just what its implications are. War is physical force exercised by men and machines on other men so as to compel submission to the will of the victors. Unquestionably in primitive times there were repeated occasions when such recourse to force was the only path to social progress. But as civilization has progressed and included larger and larger masses of men and portions of the earth, two things have become increasingly clear: one, that the costs of war have become too great for any nation to pay no matter what the alternative; and two, that in war as now carried on, there can be no victorious party. In modern world war all contestants lose and not only lose the immediate causes of strife, but cripple the fundamental bases of human culture.

On the whole I enjoyed this unique excursion into political activity. I encountered little open race prejudice, although of course few New Yorkers wanted to be represented in Washington by a Negro — because of their prejudice and also because they suspected I was more Negro than American. To counteract this at least in part, I made no appeal to the Negro vote as such. I wanted the people of New York to know that as Senator I would represent the interests of the state and not merely those of one minority group. At the same time I knew, and Negroes knew, that I would regard Negro emancipation as a prime prerequisite to American freedom. The Negro voter of Harlem was in a quandary; he knew that no candidate would defend Negro rights as I would; he also knew I would be defeated and that he must depend on Lehman or Hanley. His path was cloudy.

Above all, I was amazed and exasperated by the overwhelming use and influence of money in politics. Millionaires and corporations, not record and logic, defeated Marcantonio. Dewey could afford to spend $35,000 for one day on radio; when friends of mine the nation over sent $600 to further my campaign, it represented more honesty and guts than all the millions spent on Lehman and Hanley. Small wonder the result of this election throughout the land sounded like a "tale told by an idiot."

Five million persons voted in this election; of these, 4 per cent voted for me (15 per cent in Harlem), which was far more than I expected. More than a million of the voters stayed away from the polls.

After a great social effort like the election of 1950, one must feel the letdown. Even the victors gain less than they wish, while the losers wonder if it was worth all the effort, all the worry, all the breathless disappointed hope. Yet there is a sense in which no sound effort is in vain, least of all a struggle with high ideal and personal integrity. One feels that, in the end, all of this can never be lost; that somehow, somewhere, whatever was fine and noble in this campaign will triumph; and what was vicious and low will remain contemptible, no matter what the returns may say.

Of course I was disgusted at the re-election of an acknowledged demagogue and opportunist like Thomas Dewey as governor of the Empire State and the continued threat of his elevation to presidency. I was insulted to know that two million New Yorkers wanted a man like Joe Hanley to be continued in public office. I was sorry to see Herbert Lehman go back to Washington to work to keep us in war and chains. But most of all I could not understand how a sane and intelligent electorate could reward the brave, lone fight of Vito Marcantonio with defeat. It just did not make sense. But dollars did it—just plain cash to purchase the election of as reactionary and characterless a nonentity as ever sat in Congress.

As for myself, having never expected anything but defeat I would not have been surprised if no more than 10,000 persons had voted for me. I was astonished by a vote of 205,729, a vote from men and women of courage, without the prejudice against color which I always expect and usually experience. This meant that these faced poverty and jail to stand and be counted for Peace and Civil Rights. For this I was happy.

I had slapped no backs during the campaign which I had not slapped before; I had begged no man for his vote as a personal favor; I had asked no vote simply because I was black. It was a fine adventure. But it proved only a prelude to the most extraordinary experience of my life: my indictment as a criminal.

The Rosenbergs

Ethel and Michael, Robert and Julius

*It was the end of a long, dark day; a day of sorrow and suffering. I was very, very
weary. As the night fell and the silence of death rose about me, I sat down and
lay my face in my hands and closed my eyes. I heard my own voice speaking:*

> Crucify us, Vengeance of God
> As we crucify two more Jews,
> Hammer home the nails, thick through our skulls,
> Crush down the thorns,
> Rain the red bloody sweat
> Thick and heavy, warm and wet.

> We are the murderers hurling mud
> We the witchhunters, drinking blood
> To us shriek five thousand blacks
> Lynched without trial
> And hundred thousands mobbed
> The millions dead in useless war.
> But this, this awful deed we do today
> This senseless, blasphemy of birth
> Fills full the cup!
> Hail Hell and glory to Damnation!
> O blood-stained nation,
> Stretch forth your hand! Grasp it, Judge
> Wrap it in your blood-red gown;
> And Lawyer in your sheet of shame;
> Proud pardoners of petty thieves
> Cautious rabbis of just Jehovah,

From *Masses & Mainstream*, 6 (July 1953): 10-12.

And silent priests of the piteous Christ;
Crawl wedded liars, hide from sight,
In the dirt of all the night,
And hold high vigil at the dawn!
For yonder, two pale and tight-lipped children
Stagger across the world, bearing their dead
There lifts a light upon the Sea
With grim color, crooked form and broken lines;
With thunderous throb and roll of drums
Alleluia, Amen!

Now out beyond the plain
Streams the thick sunshine, sheet on sheet
Of billowing light!
Above the world loom vast sombre hills
Limned in lurid lightings;
While from beneath the hideous sickened earth,
The Sea rains up flood on flood to cleanse the heavens.
Twixt Sun and Sea,
Rises the Great Black Throne.
Sternly the pale children march on
Bearing high on their hands, Father and Mother
The drums roll until the Land quivers with pain
And slowly yawns:
The children prone bow down
They bow and kneel and lie;
They lay within the earth's deep breast
The beautiful young mother and her mate.
Straight up from endless depths
Rise then the Bearers of the Pall
Sacco and Vanzetti, old John Brown and Willie McGee.
They raise the crucified aloft.
The purple curtains of Death unwind.
Hell howls, Earth screams and Heaven weeps.

High from above its tears
Drops down a staircase from the Sun
Around it with upstretched hands,
Surge of triumph and dirge of shame,
Gather the mighty Dead:
Buddha, Mahmoud and Isaiah
Jesus, Lincoln and Toussaint
Savonarola and Joan of Arc;

And all the other millions,
In throng on throng unending, weeping, singing,
With music rising heaven-high,
And bugles crying to the sky
With trumpets, harps and dulcimers;
With inward upward swell of utter song.
Then through their ranks, resplendent robes of silken velvet,
Broidered with flame, float down;
About the curling gown
Drop great purple clouds, burgeon and enthral,
Swirl out and grandly close, until alone
Two golden feet appear,
As of a king descending to his throne.
In the great silence and embracing gloom,
We the murderers
Groan and moan:

"Hope of the Hopeless
Hear us pray!
America the Beautiful,
This day! This day!
Who was enthroned in sunlit air?
Who has been crowned on yonder stair?
Red Resurrection,
Or Black Despair?"

On Stalin

Joseph Stalin was a great man; few other men of the 20th century approach his stature. He was simple, calm and courageous. He seldom lost his poise; pondered his problems slowly, made his decisions clearly and firmly; never yielded to ostentation nor coyly refrained from holding his rightful place with dignity. He was the son of a serf, but stood calmly before the great without hesitation or nerves. But also — and this was the highest proof of his greatness — he knew the common man, felt his problems, followed his fate.

Stalin was not a man of conventional learning; he was much more than that: he was a man who thought deeply, read understandingly and listened to wisdom, no matter whence it came. He was attacked and slandered as few men of power have been; yet he seldom lost his courtesy and balance; nor did he let attack drive him from his convictions nor induce him to surrender positions which he knew were correct. As one of the despised minorities of man, he first set Russia on the road to conquer race prejudice and make one nation out of its 140 groups without destroying their individuality.

His judgment of men was profound. He early saw through the flamboyance and exhibitionism of Trotsky, who fooled the world, and especially America. The whole ill-bred and insulting attitude of Liberals in the U.S. today began with our naive acceptance of Trotsky's magnificent lying propaganda, which he carried around the world. Against it, Stalin stood like a rock and moved neither right nor left, as he continued to advance toward a real socialism instead of the sham Trotsky offered.

Three great decisions faced Stalin in power and he met them magnificently: first, the problem of the peasants, then the West European attack, and last the Second World War. The poor Russian peasant was the lowest victim of tsarism, capitalism and the Orthodox Church. He surrendered the Little White Father easily; he turned less readily but perceptibly from his ikons; but his kulaks clung tenaciously to capitalism and were near wrecking the revolution when Stalin risked a second revolution and drove out the rural bloodsuckers.

From the *National Guardian*, March 16, 1953.

Then came intervention, the continuing threat of attack by all nations, halted by the Depression, only to be re-opened by Hitlerism. It was Stalin who steered the Soviet Union between Scylla and Charybdis: Western Europe and the U.S. were willing to betray her to fascism, and then had to beg her aid in the Second World War. A lesser man than Stalin would have demanded vengeance for Munich, but he had the wisdom to ask only justice for his fatherland. This Roosevelt granted but Churchill held back. The British Empire proposed first to save itself in Africa and southern Europe, while Hitler smashed the Soviets.

The Second Front dawdled, but Stalin pressed unfalteringly ahead. He risked the utter ruin of socialism in order to smash the dictatorship of Hitler and Mussolini. After Stalingrad the Western World did not know whether to weep or applaud. The cost of victory to the Soviet Union was frightful. To this day the outside world has no dream of the hurt, the loss and the sacrifices. For his calm, stern leadership here, if nowhere else, arises the deep worship of Stalin by the people of all the Russias.

Then came the problem of Peace. Hard as this was to Europe and America, it was far harder to Stalin and the Soviets. The conventional rulers of the world hated and feared them and would have been only too willing to see the utter failure of this attempt at socialism. At the same time the fear of Japan and Asia was also real. Diplomacy therefore took hold and Stalin was picked as the victim. He was called in conference with British Imperialism represented by its trained and well-fed aristocracy; and with the vast wealth and potential power of America represented by its most liberal leader in half a century.

Here Stalin showed his real greatness. He neither cringed nor strutted. He never presumed, he never surrendered. He gained the friendship of Roosevelt and the respect of Churchill. He asked neither adulation nor vengeance. He was reasonable and conciliatory. But on what he deemed essential, he was inflexible. He was willing to resurrect the League of Nations, which had insulted the Soviets. He was willing to fight Japan, even though Japan was then no menace to the Soviet Union, and might be death to the British Empire and to American trade. But on two points Stalin was adamant: Clemenceau's "Cordon Sanitaire" must be returned to the Soviets, whence it had been stolen as a threat. The Balkans were not to be left helpless before Western exploitation for the benefit of land monopoly. The workers and peasants there must have their say.

Such was the man who lies dead, still the butt of noisy jackals and of the illbred men of some parts of the distempered West. In life he suffered under continuous and studied insult; he was forced to make bitter decisions on his own lone responsibility. His reward comes as the common man stands in solemn acclaim.

The Real Reason Behind Robeson's Persecution

The persecution of Paul Robeson by the government and people of the United States during the last nine years has been one of the most contemptible happenings in modern history.

Robeson has done nothing to hurt or defame this nation. He is, as all know, one of the most charming, charitable and loving of men. There is no person on earth who ever heard Robeson slander or even attack the land of his birth. Yet he had reason to despise America.

He was a black man; the son of black folk whom Americans had stolen and enslaved. Even after his people's hard-won and justly earned freedom. America made their lot as near a hell on earth as was possible. They discouraged, starved and insulted them. They sneered at helpless black children.

Someone once said that the best punishment for Hitler would be to paint him black and send him to the United States. This was no joke. To struggle up as a black boy in America; to meet jeers and blows; to meet insult with silence and discrimination with a smile; to sit with fellow students who hated you and work and play for the honor of a college that disowned you — all this was America for Paul Robeson.

Yet he fought the good fight; "He was despised and rejected of men; a man of sorrows and acquainted with grief and we hid as it were our faces from Him; He was despised and we esteemed Him not."

Why? Why? Not because he attacked this country. Search Britain and France, the Soviet Union and Scandinavia for a word of his against America. What then was his crime?

It was that while he did not rail at America he did praise the Soviet Union; and he did that because it treated him like a man and not like a dog; because

From the *National Guardian*, April 7, 1958.

he and his family for the first time in life were welcomed like human beings and he was honored like a great man.

The children of Russia clung to him, the women kissed him; the workers greeted him; the state named mountains after him. He loved their homage. His eyes were filled with tears and his heart with thanks. Never before had he received such treatment.

In America he was a "nigger"; in Britain he was tolerated; in France he was cheered; in the Soviet Union he was loved for the great artist that he is. He loved the Soviet Union in turn. He believed that every black man with blood in his veins would with him love the nation which first outlawed the color line.

I saw him when he voiced this. It was in Paris in 1949 at the greatest rally for world peace this world ever witnessed. Two thousand persons from all the world filled the Salle Pleyel from floor to rafters. Robeson hurried in, magnificent in height and breadth, weary from circling Europe with song. The audience rose to a man and the walls thundered. Robeson said that his people wanted peace and "would never fight the Soviet Union." I joined with the thousands in wild acclaim.

In Babylon, dark Babylon,

the modern breed of newspaper prostitute "who take the wage of shame" seized the chance to

> *grovel to their master's mood*
> *the blood upon their pen*
> *assigns their souls to servitude*
> *Yea and the souls of men.*

This, for America, was Robeson's crime. He might hate anybody. He might join in murder around the world. He might lie and steal. But for him to declare that he loved the Soviet Union and would not join in war against it— that was the highest crime that the United States recognized.

For that, they slandered Robeson; they tried to kill him at Peekskill; they prevented him from hiring halls in which to sing; they prevented him from travel and refused him a passport. His college lied about him and dishonored him.

And above all, his own people, American Negroes, joined in hounding one of their greatest artists—not all, but some like those who wrote of Negro musicians and deliberately omitted Robeson's name—Robeson who more than any living man has spread the pure Negro folk song over the civilized world.

Yet has Paul Robeson kept his soul and stood his ground. Still he loves and honors the Soviet Union. Still he has hope for America. Still he asserts his faith in God. But we — what can we say or do but hang our heads in endless shame?

As we celebrate the sixtieth birthday of Paul Robeson from Moscow to New Delhi, New York to California and Accra to Johannesburg, we can all take our stand and sing with him:

> *Out of the night that covers me*
> *black as the pit from pole to pole,*
> *I thank whatever gods may be*
> *For my unconquerable soul.*

Acknowledgments

Grateful acknowledgment is made to Allison Lillian Lewis for her valuable assistance and to the following for permission to reprint copyrighted works by W. E. B. Du Bois:

Clark Atlanta University: "Apology," *Phylon*, First Quarter, 1940.

International Publishers Company, Inc., and David Graham Du Bois: *The Autobiography of W. E. B. Du Bois: A Soliloquy on Viewing My Life from the Last Decade of Its First Century*, copyright 1968.

Kraus International Publications: *The Suppression of the African Slave Trade to the United States of America, 1638–1870*, copyright 1896, 1954; *The Philadelphia Negro*, copyright 1899, 1973; *The Souls of Black Folk*, copyright 1903, 1953; *Darkwater: Voices from Within the Veil*, copyright 1920; *The Gift of Black Folk*, copyright 1924; *Black Reconstruction in America: An Essay Toward a History of the Part Which Black Folk Played in the Attempt to Reconstruct Democracy in America, 1860–1880*, copyright 1935, 1963; *Dusk of Dawn: An Essay Toward an Autobiography of a Race Concept*, copyright 1940; *Color and Democracy: Colonies and Peace*, copyright 1945; *In Battle for Peace*, copyright 1952.

National Association for the Advancement of Colored People: Articles published in *The Crisis*, 1910–1934.

The University of North Carolina Press: "The Third Modification of My Program," reprinted from *What the Negro Wants*, edited by Rayford W. Logan, copyright 1944 by The University of North Carolina Press.